MW00608726

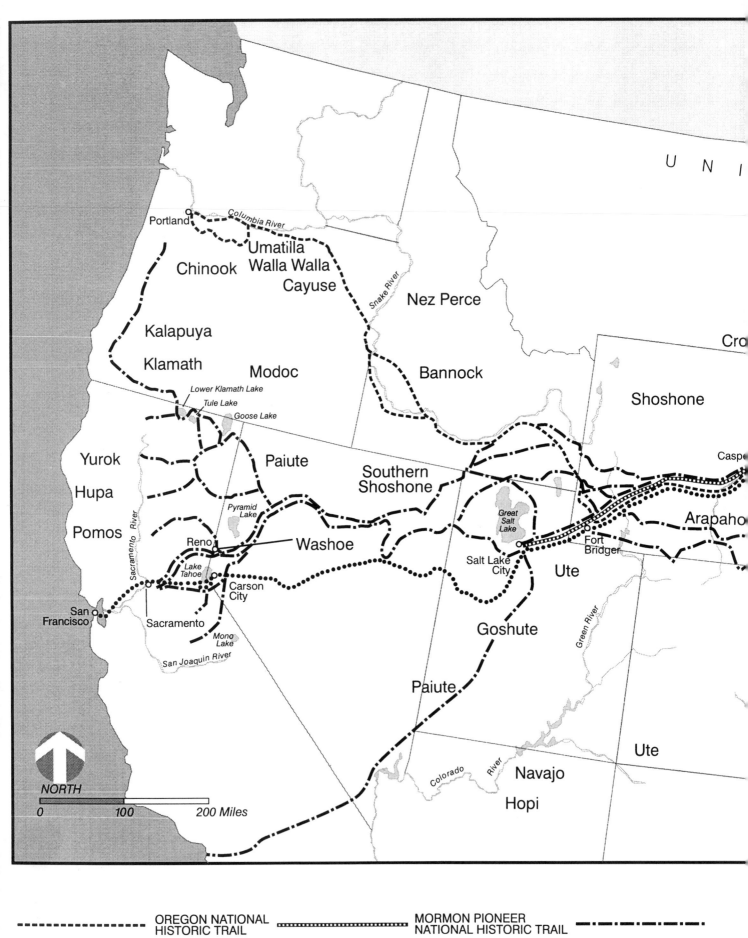

NORTH

0   100   200 Miles

- - - - - - - OREGON NATIONAL
HISTORIC TRAIL

·········· MORMON PIONEER
NATIONAL HISTORIC TRAIL

-··-··-·· CALIFORNIA NATIONAL
HISTORIC TRAIL

•••••••••• PONY EXPRESS
NATIONAL HISTORIC TRAIL

Tribes Encountered Along the Trails, 1840s, 1850s

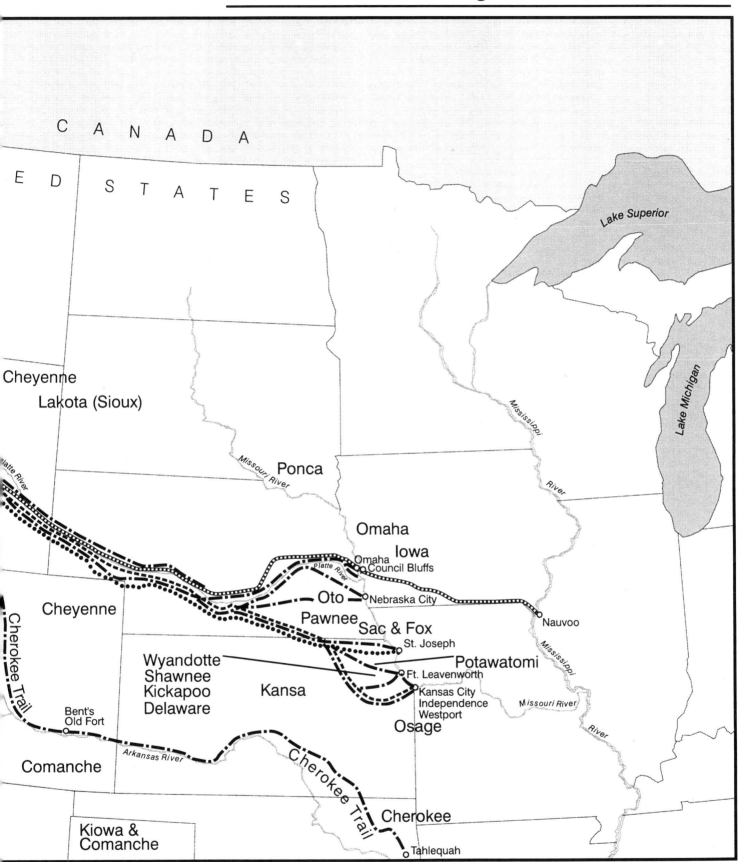

Cover and Map by Permission From:
Long Distance Trails Office
National Park Service

ᏣᎳᎩ, ᎤᏪᏘ ᏍᎤᏅᏔ, ᎤᏃᏈᏏᎤᎥ

CHEROKEE TRAIL DIARIES

Volume I – 1849 A New Route to the California Gold Fields
Volume II – 1850 Another New Route to the California Gold Fields

ᏣᎳᎩ, ᎤᏪᏘ ᏚᎪᏛᎢ, ᎤᏃᎮᏓ

CHEROKEE TRAIL DIARIES

Volume I – 1849 A New Route to the California Gold Fields
Volume II – 1850 Another New Route to the California Gold Fields

Patricia K. A. Fletcher
Dr. Jack Earl Fletcher
Lee Whiteley

DEDICATION

There was never a question about who to dedicate this work to. Loyd Glasier's "Let's talk a little history" greeted us each time we met. His encouragement was not only in urging us on over fifteen years, but also in turning up unexpected sources for us to investigate. His example of spending unending personal time in research over many years has resulted in historical preservation of records, buildings, and historical sites in the Cherry Creek Valley south of Denver. Loyd does what all historians should aspire to--accurate, thorough research, including extensive field work, willingly shared with all.

Loyd Glasier, core sampling 1872 Sarah Stone cabin, 1/2 mile east of the Cherokee Trail.

DEDICATION

When the authors became members of the Oregon-California Trails
Association in 1994, Merrill Mattes was a dedicated public servant
of long years and a strong proponent and charter member of the
Oregon-California Trails Association. During his federal career,
he was an avid supporter of both trail research and trail
preservation. Merrill spoke often of his wish to have research
done substantiating use of the long distance trails in Colorado.
He was primarily concerned with the California Trail around
Julesburg. However, his relationship with the Cherokee Trail began
when he examined it before the Cherry Creek Dam was constructed in
the late 1940s, and ended with Merrill's last field trip on
September 30, 1995, on the Cherokee Trail.

Merrill Mattes on Cherokee trail with Margaret Long in 1948
Credit: Denver District, U. S. Army Corps of Engineers.

TABLE OF CONTENTS

ILLUSTRATIONS

Photos

SKETCHES-William Quesenbury

MAPS by Lee Whiteley

Vol.I

Vol. II

GENERAL LAND OFFICE MAPS

Appendix A. Twenty-nine maps, route of the Cherokee Trail
                        with campsites by Lee Whiteley.

Preface

The net result of the combined efforts of novelists, historians, and the media has been to create the highly romanticized trail that is still not well understood in terms of the people who travelled this trail and the location of the actual route of this road taken by Cherokees travelling west from Oklahoma to California in 1850.

Dudley Gardner of Wyoming wrote the above referring to Louis L'Amour romanticizing the Trail in his novel *The Cherokee Trail*, and the 1960s television series entitled "Cherokee Trail" that drew national attention to it.

Cherokee Trail writings have punctuated western history for decades with fragments found in diaries, letters, surveyor notes, newspaper articles, journal articles, government reports, and even chapters in books. Not all of these literary trail fragments pertained to the years 1849 and 1850. What they did show was a long, continued use of the trail by large numbers of emigrants, gold seekers and livestock drovers. For nearly a century questions about the Cherokee Trail routes and emigrants have remained unanswered, sparking numerous written comments and speculation.

Local historians, primarily in Colorado and Wyoming, located bits and pieces of information, some based on facts, others based on interviews and reminiscences. The factual information, such as Government Land Office maps and survey notes, as well as actual swales and ruts, validated the trail's physical being but were too few and far between. Secondary sources, including interviews and reminiscences of oldtimers, confused the researchers, and set the trail in a helter-skelter fashion upon the landscape.

As a western history writer noted in 1922: "When local jealousies and individual claims, often sincere but usually based on utter lack of necessary information, have passed away, then the field will have been considerably cleared for more authentic work, and for more reliable records covering the frontier west."

We were not the only ones to note research problems associated with the Cherokee Trail. Dudley Gardner wrote:

As an alternate emigrant road, the Cherokee Trail that passes through extreme southern Wyoming provides numerous problems to the historian. First, there is a paucity of written documentation concerning the Cherokee Trail in this area. Secondly, secondary sources have tended to

muddy the waters....Conflicting reports [and] numerous conjectures...
compound this problem.

There was no known diary or journal from the 1849 Lewis
Evans-captained Cherokee and white company. The route they took
was unknown except for general directions given in letters and
cited by Ralph Bieber, Grant Foreman, LeRoy Hafen, and others.

Our fifteen years of research has resulted in this definitive
work of the Cherokee Trails. The trails' location, including campsites, and the emigrants that pioneered them has been identified.

A review of the secondary sources revealed they were based on
a scant few primary sources. Our search then, was to locate and
acquire access to new primary materials.

Literature search of previous published primary sources.

We first made an extensive search of the literature. This
turned up several notable publications that collectively provided
considerable data. The earliest, in 1934, was that of Muriel
Wright. Wright, like Louis L'Amour, had been a member of the WPA
history writing team in Oklahoma where both of them were privy to
material on the Cherokee Trail. Wright's significant contribution
was locating and editing Cherokee *John Lowry Brown's [1850] Diary
from the Cherokee Nation to the Gold Fields of California.* Brown's
names, and references to the three ox trains, proved to be
extremely valuable to us. The daily entries are brief and supply
little route information. This led Wright to "fit" John L. Brown's
1850 route onto the more northerly 1849 Evans/Cherokee route, and
over Bridger Pass. The long-time erroneous Bridger Pass inclusion
in the Cherokee Trail descriptions through Wyoming masked, for
nearly 150 years, the identification of the 1850 Edmonson/Cherokee
(Southern) Trail.

Grant Foreman, Oklahoma State Historian, compiled, edited
and published in 1939 *Marcy & the Gold Seekers The Journal of
Captain R.B. Marcy, with an account of the Gold Rush over the
Southern Route.* Foreman began writing about the trail in 1925, and
except for the erroneous inclusion of Bridger's Pass, the route
laid down by Foreman loosely follows the 1849 Evans/Cherokee wagon

trail. Foreman's description also confirmed there was an "1850
route" of "The Cherokee Trail." This route was correct as far as
the North Platte River but gave little detail:

> they left the Evans-Cherokee route and proceeding to the left of it
> crossed the Laramie River, arrived July 3 at the North Fork of the
> Platte River, near the [Colorado] Wyoming line.

Foreman's *Marcy* provided us with individual and emigrant company
names and newspaper sources.

Francile Oakley produced the first Arkansas work in 1947.
Especially valuable to us are the 1849 Arkansas members' names,
and additional newspaper sources. She erroneously placed the
Cherokee Trail route to Fort Laramie and South Pass, probably
because letters written from Pueblo anticipated that route.

In Colorado, State Historian LeRoy Hafen, beginning in 1925,
wrote a book and numerous articles on Cherokee and on the Trail.
Hafen never accumulated enough factual material to establish the
trail correctly, but provided us with much of Colorado's early
background.

Denver medical doctor Margaret Long's was the most ambitious
attempt to locate segments of, and trace the Cherokee Trail. A
western writer, Dr. Long produced numerous books. The most notable
were her three volume Trail series: *The Smokey Hill Trail*, 1947,
which included the Cherokee Trail; *The Santa Fe Trail*, and *The
Oregon Trail*. At the time she was writing, Dr. Long was the
leading authority on the Cherokee Trail. With the construction of
the Cherry Creek Dam east of Denver in the late 1940s, she worked
with young Merrill Mattes of the National Park Service in
identifying the ruts of the Cherokee/Smoky Hill Trail for the U.S.
Army Corps of Engineers.(see Dedication and photograph) Dr. Long
erred in placing the trail over the Arkansas/Platte River divide
too near the Rocky Mountain front range, rather than upon her
"Jimmy Camp Trail." The location was, in part, based on oral
interviews of those oldtimers who had heard of the trail, or
believed they had been on the trail.

Through the years many local historians working with "their"
segment of the trail produced reliable and noteworthy information

and many maps. Wyoming researchers not already noted were L.C.
Bishop, Paul C. Henderson, Dr. Grace Hebard, and Kleber Hadsell.

A greatly underused resource found invaluable on the
documentation of parties traveling across the plains up until 1854
is Louise Barry's *The Beginning of the West,* published in 1972.

Priscilla McArthur's *Arkansas in the Gold Rush*, 1986, brought
two new sources to light on the 1850 emigration. The William M.
Quesenbury and James T. Mitchell diaries, from which she quoted,
are significant primary sources that we added to our documentation
of the Cherokee Trail. McArthur's is an outstanding publication,
not to be overlooked by trail historians.

Pursuit of primary literature sources.

The known primary resource, until McArthur, was one 1850
diary. Therefore lack of knowledge of the 1850 trail's location,
who took the trail, and how long it was used, caused the
outstanding researchers of the past to relegate the Cherokee Trail
to a minor status. For all practical purposes, it dropped out of
the literature.

Acquisition of photocopies of the original William M.
Quesenbury and James T. Mitchell 1850 diaries provided us with the
first unedited 1850 primary material. A trip to the Gilcrease
Institute provided an unedited account of John Lowery Brown's 1850
diary. The three diaries provided a literary track over the 1850
Edmonson/Cherokee (Southern) Trail. We found it very useful to
work from unedited copies of original manuscripts. Therefore we
have printed the primary sources en toto to avoid the pitfalls of
extrapolation, inference, and conjecture.

Until early 1994 there was no known diary or journal from the
1849 Lewis Evans-captained Cherokee/white company. The route they
took was unknown. General descriptions in letters were excerpted
and cited by Ralph Bieber, Grant Foreman, LeRoy Hafen, and others.

A chance bit of information in *Flashback*, publication of the
Washington County, Arkansas, Historical Society, led us to query
the Old Greer County Museum of Mangum, Oklahoma. Records search by
an alert curator, Zoe Livingston-Burt, resulted in the location of

the 1849 diary of James Sawyer Crawford. Mr. Ben Lockerd carefully
photocopied the original for our use. Though somewhat faded, Most
of the diary is legible because it was written in a clear hand.

We were also able to find original letters in Special
Collections at the University of Arkansas Library, Fayetteville.
Written by 1849 company member John Rankin Pyeatt, the letters
were in chronological and geographical order. They are descriptive
throughout, naming persons of the company and describing events in
detail. Crawford's diary, enriched with the Pyeatt's letters,
provide a paper trail of the 1849 Evans/Cherokee Trail.

In January 1998, Mr. Paul Hershey of San Francisco contacted
us with information about Calvin H. Holmes, a member of the 1849
Evans/Cherokee train. A photocopy of Holmes' partial diary,
acquired from the Pioneer Society of California, enabled us to add
information about the company leaving Arkansas, and company
members' use of the Lassen Trail during the early 1849 snows.

The *Cherokee Advocate* provided us with progress reports along
both 1849 and 1850 emigrant routes. Letters home disclosed company
splits, routes, traffic, Indians, stock losses, and deaths.

Government Reports in the form of military reports,
surveyor's notes, journals, and letters pertaining to the army,
Indians, trading licenses, annuities, treaties, etc., supplied
additional information and background.

For even more obscure literature several trips were taken
over the years; the routes approximating the trails. The purpose
was to visit and search every county courthouse, library,
historical and genealogical society, as well as each state
historical society. Information always surfaced, especially in
Arkansas and Oklahoma. We had been researching for over nine years
when assistance became necessary for research and continuing work
on maps of the trail, including relationship to route, miles
traveled, and campsites. Further study of the GLO maps and
locating missing ones was crucial.

Another researcher with interest and time was necessary. Lee
Whiteley welcomed the chance to join in the research and produce
the maps. His wife Jane, an elementary school teacher, supported
his decision. The combined effort took another six years

researching literature and maps, and taking more auto trips over the entire trail, this time concentrating on early maps, especially those from the Government Land Offices (GLO).

After narrowing the focus to 1849 and 1850, the writing of the manuscript started in 1994. Documentation leaves no doubt as to the correctness of the trails, and the identity of those who took them. The outcome we think is a concise, factual, and hopefully an enlightening account of pioneering two new trails to the California gold rush. The adage the farther back one goes in history the dimmer it gets does not always apply to western trail history. This book could not have been written a decade ago. It was the recent finding of the diaries that made it possible.

ACKNOWLEDGMENTS

Interestingly, the large and noted institutions were less able to help than the local or regional. In an effort not to miss anything, our research trail has taken us into the large and small facilities along the trails themselves from Oklahoma, Missouri, and Arkansas, to California. When trail and general historical sources ran dry, we began to include the genealogical societies. Without them, a curiosity about the persons who made up these emigrant trains would have been left unsatisfied. From and through them came an amazing amount of information, which we then corroborated with official records.

The following primary sources will be found printed in accompanying sections:

VOL. I - 1849
Diaries:

James Sawyer Crawford. Credit: Lockerd Family of Arkansas and Oklahoma.

Calvin H. Holmes. Credit: The California Society of Pioneers, San Francisco.

Diary Excerpts:

GOLD RUSH by J. Goldsborough Bruff Copyright (c) 1944 by Columbia University Press. Reprinted with permission of the publisher.

Letters, in whole or in part, aside from those appearing in newspapers: Crawford Family members. Credit: Lockerd Family of Arkansas and Oklahoma. Hiram Davis, Edward Freyschlag. Credit: *Flashback*, Washington County Historical Society Journal, Fayetteville, Arkansas. John Rankin Pyeatt. Credit: Special Collections, University of Arkansas Libraries, Fayetteville.

VOL. II - 1850

Diaries:

John Lowery Brown. Credit: The collection of the Thomas Gilcrease Institute of American History and Art, Tulsa, Oklahoma.

Muriel Wright, ed. "The Journal of John Lowery Brown, of the Cherokee Nation En Route to California in 1850" *The Chronicles of Oklahoma,* vol 12 (June 1934) Oklahoma Historical Society.

James T. Mitchell. Credit: Mrs. Frank Wait and Arkansas Territorial Restoration Commission, Little Rock, Arkansas.

William M. Quesenbury. Credit: Special Collections Library, Duke University, Durham, North Carolina.

Sketches:

William M. Quesenbury Sketches 1850. Credit: *Omaha World Herald* Quesenbury Sketchbook, Omaha, Nebraska.

Letters, in whole or in part, aside from those in newspapers: Barbara Hildebrand Longknife. Credit: Stand Watie Letters, Western History Collection, University of Oklahoma Libraries, Norman.

The following sources of information for this research and this book are alphabetically listed within the respective states. Having been so long in our quest, we hope no person or place will be omitted from our list. If so, accept our apologies.

Arizona. Arizona State University Library, Tempe; Mesa Public Library, Mesa; Arizona Western College, Yuma.

Arkansas. Arkansas Territorial Restoration, Little Rock. William Worthen, Executive Director; and Swannee Bennett, MSS Curator for permission to use material from Priscilla McArthur *Arkansas in the Gold Rush* Copyrighted by the Arkansas Territorial Restoration Foundation, Inc. and published by August House, Inc., Little Rock, 1986; Carolyn Reno, Shiloh Museum, Springdale; Robert F. Richardson, Little Rock; Gaye Bland, Jan Harcourt, Rogers Historical Museum, Rogers; Maggie Smith, Siloam Springs Writers,

Siloam Springs; Ethel Simpson, University of Arkansas at Fayetteville, Special Collections Library for microfilm of Van Buren and Fort Smith, Arkansas newspapers, and information about William Quesenbury; B.O. Roop, for extensive information about Washington County sources, and editor Thomas E. Jordon, for permission to quote from *Flashback*, Washington County Historical Society Journal, Fayetteville.

California. Bert Ashton, Trails West, California, for a copy of T.H. Jefferson's *Map* and *Accompaniment*; Bancroft Library, University of California, Berkeley; Arthur E. Broaddus, Ukiah for information on 1853 emigrants; Joyce L. Crawford, Tuolumne, for sharing information on Andrew A. Crawford, 1849, and the Cherokee townsite in Tuolumne; Elizabeth Fischer, San Diego, for sharing information on Clement Vann McNair's life in California; Herbert Garcia, California Society of Pioneers, San Francisco; Paul Hershey, San Francisco, for help in acquiring Holmes material from California Society of Pioneers; Richard K. Grover, La Verne, for sharing information on Pyeatt, McCollochs, McKee, Hodges and Inks families; Tom Hunt, Oregon-California Trails Association, California Chapter, for information and discussions on the Lassen Trail; Huntington Library, San Marino; Dian Schwanz, Orange; Irene D. Wilson, San Diego, for information on Lewis Evans; Edith Winchester, Clovis, for information on Edmiston family members and William Crawford, brother of diarist James Sawyer Crawford.

Colorado. Arvada Historical Society, Arvada, and Lois C. Lindstrom for efforts to preserve Ralston Park, site of 1850 Cherokee gold find; Clarice Crowle, Cherry Creek Valley Historical Society, Aurora, for sharing knowledge of the valley; Connye Crump, Lafayette, descendant of town founders of El Dorado, Kansas, for information from Stewart journals; Denver Public Library, Western History Department; Louise Erb, Littleton, for sharing knowledge of southern Wyoming trails; Suzanne D. Fellows and Rhonda Lewis, U. S. Department of the Interior, Fish and Wildlife Service, Denver and Maybell, for information on Brown's Park; Peggy A. Ford, Division of Museums, City of Greeley; Richard & Mary Ann Gehling, Colorado Springs, for sharing expertise of the Pueblo-to-Colorado Springs area, including Jimmy Camp; Johanna

Harden, Archivist, Douglas County Public Library District, Local History Collection, Castle Rock, for sharing trail maps and photos of the Arkansas/Platte Divide region; Leroy Vance Hester, for ideas and continual support; Clyde Jones, Chairman, Douglas County Historical Preservation Board, Castle Rock, for help in Douglas County; Betty Larsen, Gladys Ellerman, Virginia Dale Community Club, Livermore; Jack Linkul, Russellville Historical Society, Franktown, for help in the Russellville area; Parker Area Historical Society, Inc., Parker; Martin H. Schloo, Fort Collins, for sharing his unpublished manuscript on the Cherokee-Overland Trails, Ft. Collins to the Wyoming state border, including Virginia Dale; Glenn R. Scott, Lakewood, for sharing vast knowledge of Colorado trails and USGS trail map series; South Platte Valley Historical Society, Ft. Lupton, Esther V. McCrumb, Executive Director; Wayne Sundberg, Fort Collins, for help in Fort Collins; Jim and Ruth Ann Steele for preserving the 1858 Fagan's grave area; John and Mary Welty for preserving the Point of Rocks area on the Arkansas River/Platte River Divide.

Connecticut. Ralph and Marjorie L. Crump, Trumbull, for information on El Dorado, Kansas and the Stewart journals; George A. Miles, Curator, Beinecke Rare Book and Manuscript Library, Yale University, New Haven.

Hawaii. James O. Sanders, Kailua, for help on Barbara Longknife.

Idaho. Kathleen Durfee, City of Rocks National Reserve, Almo, for help with Cassia Creek and Raft River, and indigenous snakes; Idaho State University Library, Pocatello.

Illinois. Newberry Library, Chicago.

Kansas. Bob Burgess, Director, Butler County Historical Society, El Dorado; Janet Cline, Dodge City, for arranging Black Pool field trip; John Dick, Santa Fe Trail Association, Goessel, for continuing to search for Cherokee Trail ruts and references; Lynn Perkins, Howard, for Elk County information; Lynn Peterson, McPherson, for Survey maps noting Cherokee Trail near McPherson; Shirley Ade, Director, McPherson Museum and Arts Foundation, McPherson; Kansas State Historical Society, Topeka, for permission to quote from Louise Barry's *The Beginning of the West, Annals of the Kansas Gateway to the American West 1540-1854*; Bob Knecht,

Assistant Curator, Manuscripts Department, Kansas State Historical Society, Topeka; Cheryl Collins, Archivist, Jean Dallas, Director, Riley County Historical Society and Museum, Manhattan; County Clerk, Chautauqua County, Sedan, for original survey notes and maps; Lucille Wise, Santa Fe Trail Center, Larned.

Mississippi. Frances Combs, Starkville, for information on Wiley Cosby, George Washington Lewis, Philander Powell, Van Hoose, and Mankins families.

Missouri. Kathy Conway, Oregon-California Trails Association Headquarters, Independence; Michele Hansford, Powers Museum, Carthage; John Mark Lambertson, Merrell Mattes Library, National Frontier Trails Center, Independence, for access to unpublished manuscripts; Lois Daniel, Independence, for assistance with the manuscript; Elaine McNabney, Kansas City; Lynn Morrow, Director, Local Records Preservation Program, State of Missouri, Office of Secretary of State, Jefferson City; Debra Nichols, Excelsior Springs, for information on Ben Simon and the Delaware Tribe.

Montana. Dave Walter, Research Historian, Montana Historical Society, Helena, for information on Ben Simon and Nathaniel Pryor.

Nebraska.R. Eli Paul, Nebraska State Historical Society, Lincoln, for assistance in obtaining permission to use Quesenbury sketches.

Nevada. Bob Pearce and Paul Sawyer, Elko, who led us to the Northeastern Nevada Museum and County Clerk's office at the Courthouse. University of Nevada Library and Washoe County Library, Reno.

North Carolina. William R. Erwin Jr., Special Collections Library, Duke University, Durham, for a copy of the original William Quesenbury diary, which helped clarify previous editing.

Oklahoma. John R. Crittenden, Westville, for information on Nelson R.N. Harlin; Evelyn Harrell, Big Cabin; Gerald Hurt, Colcord, for the title of our book written in the Cherokee syllabary; Sarah Irwin, Archivist, Thomas Gilcrease Museum, Tulsa, who shared examination of the John Lowery Brown journal with us; Zoe Livingstone-Burt, Curator, Old Greer County Museum, Mangum, for invaluable help in tracking down the James Sawyer Crawford Diary; Margaret L. McCoy, Archivist, Cherokee National Historical Society, Tahlequah; Joan Singleton, Librarian, Bartlesville Public

Library & History Museum, Bartlesville; Pearl Rogers Skitt, Welling, for information on Rueben Rogers and Miles Cunningham; June H. Smith, Spavinaw, for information on Taylor and Martin families; Delores T. Sumner, Special Collections, Northeastern University Library, Tahlequah; Virgil Talbot, Talbot Library and Museum, Colcord, publishes Talbot Library & Museum *Genealogy* as well as *Goingsnake Messenger*. To him we owe special thanks for multiple insertions in his publications which proved fruitful, for help in locating 1850 emigrants, and location of places mentioned in diaries; University of Oklahoma Press for permission to quote from Grant Foreman, *Marcy & the Gold Seekers; The Journal of Captain R.B. Marcy, with an account of the Gold Rush over the Southern Route*, 1939 and 1966; William Welge, Director, Archives & Manuscripts Division, Oklahoma Historical Society, Oklahoma City; C. W. West, Friends of Thomas-Foreman Home, Muskogee County Historical Society, Muskogee, for access to Foreman materials.

Oregon. Susan Badger-Doyle, Pendleton, for helpful suggestions on the manuscript.

Texas. Bill Henderson, Ft. Worth, for information on Joseph and Andrew Colville; Marilyn Hicks, Dallas, for information on wagonmaker Peter Van Winkle; Col. Richard McTaggart, Menard, for information on Russell brothers (Green, Oliver, and Levi) in Colorado; James A. Muncey, Jr., Fredericksburg, for information on James Stephen Muncey; Kelli Pickard, Director, Red River Museum, Sherman, for efforts to find Malinda Armstrong materials.

Utah. Will Bagley, Salt Lake City, for information on Ben Simon and Mormons; Robert Hoshide, Salt Lake City, for information on James Pierce, Lorenzo Dow Stephens diary, and for Archaeology of the Hastings Cutoff; Roy D. Tea, Salt Lake City, for help in mapping the Hastings Cutoff, and coordinating Crawford diary with the T. H. Jefferson map; Dr. David J. Whittaker, Curator of Western and Mormon Manuscripts, Brigham Young University, Provo, for information on Ellen Hundley.

Washington. Roseanne Anderson, Spokane, for information on James Bailey; Gunnar and Frances Fagerlund, for directing us to the Mary Ann Weston Maughan journal, and for many helpful suggestions offered after their reading of the manuscript; University of

Washington Suzzallo/Allen Library, Special Collections; U. S. Government National Archives, Seattle; Washington State Library, Olympia; Washington State Historical Society, Tacoma, for permission to excerpt from *John McLoughlin's Business Correspondence 1847-48*.

Wyoming. John and Judy Andrikopoulos, Encampment; Mike Brown, U. S. Forest Service, Rock Springs; Linda N. Byers, Director, Fort Bridger State Museum; Mark Dunning, Foreman, Big Creek Ranch, Encampment; Mike and Joyce Evans, Saratoga; A. Dudley Gardner for information on 1850 route in "Historical Overview and Evaluation of the Cherokee Trail" December 21, 1981; and "Historical Assessment of the Cherokee Trail and Bryan to Brown's Park Road..." February 1994, Rock Springs: Wyoming Archaeological Services, Western Wyoming College; Marna M. Grubb, City Clerk, City of Green River, and Board Member, Wyoming Historical Society, for assisting in identification of Green River sites in Quesenbury's sketches, and for recent photos included with the Green River Historic Preservation Commission's brochure "Nature's Art Shop"; Green River Historic Preservation Commission members James W. June (now decesased), Ruth Lauritzen, Bob Edwards, Bill Thompson. and Marna Grubb; Frank Hadsell and father Kleber Hadsell's map and research on Carbon County trails; Daniel L. Kinnaman for information on the Overland trail in Carbon, Sweetwater, and Albany Counties; Roderick D. Laird, Saratoga, for sharing knowledge of the Encampment-Saratoga area, and for arranging field trips; Ruth Lauritzen, Director, Sweetwater Historical Society, Green River; Mae Mattila and Vera Oldman, Grand Encampment Museum, for taking us on the 1986 field trip to the North Platte crossing, and for maintaining research collections in their facility that include the Cherokee Trail; Ray Ring, for help with the trail near Rawlins; Saratoga Historical and Cultural Association, Sonja Collamer, President; Susan M. Simpson, Albany County Public Library, Laramie; Russ Tanner and Terry del Bene, Bureau of Land Management, Rock Springs; University of Wyoming Western History Research Center, Laramie, for access to L.C. Bishop and Paul Henderson collections; Wyoming Archives, Museums, and Historical Department, Cheyenne.

Introduction

The name "Cherokee Trail" was the longest and most used, but certainly not the first for this trail. Evans Route, Arkansas Route, Middle Route, Main Wagon Route, Fayetteville-California Route, and Dry Route were all early names attached to the Trail or segments of it, and justifiably so. Now, 150 years later, all that remains is the name Cherokee.

The Cherokee Trail is the longest branch of the California National Historic Trail, approximately 1,300 miles. Originating in Arkansas, Missouri, and Oklahoma, the routes converge at either the Grand (Neosho) or the Verdigris River. Starting north through Oklahoma, the trail crosses two-thirds of Kansas and Wyoming east to west, and Colorado south to north. This transcontinental trail ties the historic Santa Fe Trail to the Oregon-California Trail, providing an avenue to the West and Northwest from the South and Southeast. Through this corridor poured gold seekers to California in '49, to Colorado in '58, to Idaho in '60, and to Montana in '62. Cattle drives went west to California over the Cherokee Trails beginning in 1851, continuing for a decade. From Oregon they went east to Wyoming until the last two decades of the 1800s.

However emigration was the primary use of the trail. Starting in 1849, and continuing until the turn of the twentieth century, emigrants trekked over parts of the Cherokee Trails to every western state. The emigrants and the paths of their travels have remained an obscurity. The uncovering of several diaries this decade has helped find both the emigrants and their routes.

The Cherokee Trails are divided into eastern and western segments. The eastern segment begins in northwest Arkansas (mainly Fayetteville), southwest Missouri, and the Cherokee Nation (mainly Tahlequah). These three combine to travel northwest joining the Santa Fe Trail east of McPherson, Kansas.

The name Cherokee, in connection with the trail, first appeared in print on a map, near the junction with the Santa Fe Trail. There at Running Turkey Creek, Charley Fuller established a ranch in 1855. The following year, 1856, the 6th Principal

Meridian was surveyed in Kansas, and the Cherokee Trail labeled at its crossing. In 1858, the name was noted at the crossing of Walnut River by one of the Stewarts, a founding family of El Dorado, Kansas. "A man came here to inquire the road to White Water. He came about 55 miles on the 'Cherokee Trail.'" Again in 1859, Stewart noted: "he was buried about 20 miles from here on the 'Cherokee Road.'"

The western segment of the Cherokee Trail begins at Bent's Old Fort and ends at Fort Bridger. Through Colorado and Wyoming there are two routes: a northern route, blazed by the 1849 Evans/Cherokee wagon company; and a southern route, pioneered by the 1850 Edmonson/Cherokee wagon company. On the western segment, the name Cherokee Trail or Route was first written in 1858. Two military men traveled over the 1849 Evans/Cherokee route that year. Lt. Francis T. Bryan in his third march, this one to build the military road over Bridger Pass that summer, called it the "Cherokee Road" in Wyoming. Capt. Randolph B. Marcy traveling over the trail with military supplies for General Johnston's troops in Utah, recorded "Cherokee Trail." The following year, 1859, Marcy noted the "Cherokee Trail" along the Colorado Front Range on a map in his guide *The Prairie Traveler, a Handbook for Overland Expeditions*. Two of his Itineraries note the trail in Wyoming.

The next notable mention of the trail's location and importance can be traced to W. J. Ghent in 1929. In his book *The Road to Oregon* he noted "So far as known Captain Evan's party of California emigrants were the first to travel continuously the route from Latham, Colorado [confluence of the Cache la Poudre with the South Platte River] to Fort Bridger. From this circumstance the whole route from Pueblo past future Denver and on to Fort Bridger was known for many years as the Cherokee Trail."

The name attained common usage during the gold rush era of the several western states. Many guidebooks and diaries to the Pikes Peak and later the Idaho and Montana gold rushes mention traveling the Cherokee Trail. The name usage peaked during the Civil War when Indian activity increased along the more northerly Oregon-California Trail. In 1862, the Overland Stage Company moved from that trail south to the Cherokee Trail. With new cutoffs, newly-dug springs, and a route over Bridger Pass, the Cherokee/Overland Trail name, after several years, was shortened to the Overland Trail.

Our aim was and is to have the Cherokee Trail recognized as a branch of the California National Historic Trail, to receive national historic trail status, and take its rightful place as an important trail of western migration. To this end our research for the last fifteen years has been to document the location and the years of emigrant use of the Cherokee Trails. Our documentation of "Significant Sites and Segments" of the trail was accepted by the National Park Service Long Distance Trails Office in 1997-98 for inclusion in the Comprehensive Management Plan of the California National Historic Trail. A recent ruling in Washington, D.C. stated it will not be included.

What began in the early 1980s out of curiosity about a road named Cherokee Trail near Denver, Colorado, led first two authors and then a third through nine states to document these Cherokee Trails. The authors feel very privileged to have filled in one of the blank pages of Western trail history with this work on the Cherokee Trails.

Ꮳ Ꮃ Ᏹ, Ꭴ ᏗᎵ ᏍᏓᏗᎢ, ᎤᏃᏱᏆᏳᎾ

CHEROKEE TRAIL DIARIES

Vol. I 1849—A New Route to the California Gold Fields

Chapter 1. BACKGROUND OF THE CHEROKEE

To address the question of who took the Cherokee Trails to California, it is necessary to understand some history of the Cherokee people and Nation. Available sources concentrate on 1) the 1838-1839 infamous Trail of Tears, account of the "Removal" of the eastern Cherokee to Indian Territory in the west, and 2) the 1861-1865 Civil War, during which Cherokee fought on both sides, often against each other. This work focuses on the Cherokee between those events--1838 to 1862.

By 1849, the last of the Cherokee who had been removed to Indian Territory had been there for eleven years--many longer. They were solidly divided into three political groups: Old Settlers; 1835 Treaty party; and followers of Chief John Ross.

In order to understand those times, it is necessary to go further back in Cherokee history. A concise statement of the Cherokee people and their history was given in Tahlequah by Cherokee Judge Elijah Hicks in spring of 1851.[1] He began his discourse with the year 1740 when Cherokee

> occupied the slopes of the Alleganies...better known [as] the Blue Ridge Va., in the hunter or first stages of society....habitations were ...covered with animal skins....They subsisted...easily...on the chase...with the partial aids of agriculture, their original occupation.

Hicks described the Cherokee contacts: "The European race...extended [their] settlements [which] produced collisions and bloody wars....although ...Cherokees...boldly maintained [their lands] they had to retire south and west to the Tennessee, Coosa and Chatahoochy rivers."

Through this hostile 1770s atmosphere William Bartram, noted American botanist, traveled from Savannah to the Tennessee (or Cherokee) River.[2] Bartram was a keen observer and recorded many

---

[1]"on the occasion of laying the corner stone for the buiding of a college for teaching the higher branches of education." *Cherokee Advocate* 1 April 1851 p 2, col 4-5. Tahlequah, the capital of Cherokee Nation then and now, in present Oklahoma.

[2]William Bartram, *Travels through North & South Carolina, Georgia, East & West Florida, The Cherokee Country, The Extensive Territories of the Muscolgulges, or Creek Confederacy, and the Country of the Chactaws; containing An Account of the Soil and Natural Productions of those Regions, together with*

details of Cherokee life, including dress, demeanor, and agriculture. He listed forty-three Cherokee towns inhabited at the time, most on the Tennessee River.

Plantings by individuals, he wrote, were within the primary settlements. Plantation-type common ground was separate from the settlement, where planting and harvesting were done by the entire group. Out of the common-ground harvest came each family's share, and some for the common good, such as supplies for journeys, food for travelers, and a surplus in event of crop failures. Bartram called this "a public treasury."

British traders were among the Cherokee since at least 1725 and they encouraged intermarriage, because they felt it would keep the trade.[3] In these marriages, Cherokee women took the names of their husbands. Thus began the lineage of European names which survive today among the Cherokee.[4] During the American Revolutionary War, the British had accepted the aid of Cherokee warriors.

The Cherokee had two reasons for helping the British. They wanted to keep the trade. And they feared that the colonists, if successful, would expand into the Cherokee lands. They were right. The diminishing of Cherokee titles to lands accelerated immediately following the Revolution.

Twenty-four-year-old Louis-Philippe, future King of France,

Observations on the Manners of the Indians. (Philadelphia: Printed by James & Johnson 1791).

[3]Emmet Starr cites the following information about one trader, who was not necessarily the first: "Ludovic Grant, who was said to have been a Scotchman, in a statement recorded on page 301 of the Charlestown, South Carolina probate court in the book of '1754-1758' in a sworn statement of January 12, 1756, says 'It is about thirty years since I went into the Cherokee Country where I have resided ever since...I speak their language.' He married a full blood Cherokee woman of the Long Hair clan. He was among the Cherokees at the same time that Christian Priber and James Adair was [sic] in the nation. Grant's half breed daughter married William Emory, an Englishman." Emmet Starr, *History of the Cherokee Indians and Their Legends and Folk Lore* reprinted as *Old Cherokee Families* "Old Families and Their Genealogy," with A Comprehensive Index by J. J. Hill (Norman, Okla: Univ. of Oklahoma Foundation 1968) p 466.

[4]For instance, Rim Fawling, Ezekial Buffington, Robert Due, John Rogers and Richard Fields were Englishmen; John Stuart was a British Captain, called Bushyhead by Cherokee. The Bushyhead name survives. Peter Hildebrand was German. Anthony Foreman, John Adair and William Shorey were Scots; Ludovic Grant was said to be Scot. John Bowles was the son of a Scotch trader. John Gunter was Welch. Starr...*Cherokee*...pp 466, 467, 472, 474.

traveled America in 1796-97, after the American Revolution.[5] He noted the condition of the Cherokee: "Some tell me that the Cherokees were so depleted by the last war that they would have trouble raising 500 warriors."

Louis-Philippe described their political system:

the Cherokees have a governing council, this council being composed of chiefs. In this nation the number of chiefs is not fixed. The council sees to its own successors and usually chooses them from the same families....This council can make war and peace, conclude treaties, and pass laws. As there is no written language...laws are not imperishable but...are enforced with great rigor until they are forgotten.[6]

The Frenchman noted that many Cherokee owned slaves: "which they buy and sell as...in Virginia and Carolina."

Regarding Cherokee families, Louis noted:

Among the Cherokees...the family is reckoned around women rather than around men....They claim that only motherhood is sure.[7] In consequence, the children of white men and Indian women are Indians like the others [though] The Americans call them *half breeds*.[8]

The Cherokee had a friend in Thomas Jefferson. His notes and letters commonly refer to Cherokee and often describe the hospitality at Monticello. Jefferson remembered a Cherokee in a letter to John Adams in 1812:

I knew much of the great Ontassette, the warrior and orator of the Cherokees. He was always the guest of my father on his journeys to and from Williamsburg. I was in his camp when he made his great farewell oration to his people the evening before he departed for England....His sounding voice, distinct articulaton, animated action, and the solemn silence of his people...filled me with awe and veneration, although I did not understand a word he uttered.[9]

---

[5]Louis-Philippe, King of France, 1830-1848, *Diary of My Travels in America*, Stephen Becker trans. (N.Y.: Delacorte Press 1977) pp 65-99.

[6]Ibid. p 73. Louis-Philippe gave theft as an example. "For the first offense, flogging, and for the second, the ears cut off. This law has already been applied....those...punished are...scorned by the others."

[7]Noted in another publication: "Every mother knows who are her children, but fathers have not such knowledge." Cephas Washburn, Letter 9, "Reminiscences of Blanket" *Cherokees "West" 1794 to 1839* (Claremore, Okla: Emmet Starr 1910) pp 94-95.

[8]Louis-Philippe...*Diary*...p 77.

[9]Francis Hirst, *Life and Letters of Thomas Jefferson* p 16 cited in Fred Eastman *Men of Power* (N.Y.: Abingdon-Cokesbury Press 1938) vol 1, pp 12-13.

CHEROKEE WEST

The Cherokee treaty of Hopewell, South Carolina in 1785 provided that, in addition to both sides restoring all prisoners, the Cherokee in effect took an oath of allegiance to the United States and "no other sovereign."[10] U.S. citizens would be excluded from settling on "new" Cherokee lands, and would be punished by the federal government if they trespassed. American traders only would be allowed. The hatchet "shall be forever buried [with] peace...and friendship...universal." Every succeeding treaty diminished Cherokee lands.

Cherokee began moving west in small groups after the American Revolution. Some were residing in the New Madrid area of Missouri in 1811, when the earthquake changed the course of the Mississippi River. The group petitioned for permission to move farther west. Under Chief Bowl, some moved to Spanish Territory in Texas.

Cherokee who had been in Arkansas since at least 1818, were referred to as "Western Cherokees" or "Old Settlers."[11] Tallantusky, elected chief in 1818, visited the Eastern Cherokee where he met an officer of the American Board of Foreign Missions. Subsequently, Tallantusky invited Cephas Washburn (and family) to organize a mission for Western Cherokee. Established in the spring of 1820 opposite Dardanelle, Arkansas, it was known as Dwight Mission.[12]

Thomas Nuttall, in his natural history journey up the Arkansas River in 1819, noted the character of Western Cherokee

---

[10]Cherokee negotiated their first treaty with South Carolina in 1721, "ceding land for promised protection and perpetual friendship." Donald E. Worcester, ed. *Forked Tongues and Broken Treaties*. Arthur H. DeRosier, Jr. "The Cherokee Indians: Disaster Through Negotiation" (Caldwell, Idaho: The Caxton Printers, Ltd. 1975) pp 37-38. Cherokee Treaties were made with the U.S. Government in 1785 at Hopewell; 1791 on Holston River; 1794 at Philadelphia; 1798, 1804 and 1805 at Tellico; 1806 at Washington; 1807, 1814, 1816 at Washington; 1816 at Chickasaw Council House; 1817 at Cherokee Agency; 1819 at Washington; 1828 at Washington; 1833 at Fort Gibson; 1835 at Camp Holmes; 1835 at New Echota; 1835, supplementary; 1846 at Washington; 1865 at Fort Smith; 1866 at Washington and 1868. "Western Band" 1828 at Washington; 1833. Charles J. Kappler, "Treaties" *Laws and Treaties* vol 2 (Washington: 1904.)

[11]Signers of the "Treaty with the Cherokee, 1846" were members of the 1)"regularly constituted authorities of the Cherokee Nation;" the 2)"Treaty Party;" and 3)"Western Cherokees," or "Old Settlers." Kappler...*laws*...p 561.

[12]Reuben Gold Thwaites, ed. "Nuttall's Journal" *Early Western Travels* (Cleveland, Ohio: The Arthur H. Clark Co. 1907) vol 13 1818-1820, pp 181-82 n.

settlements and their inhabitants.[13] He first saw groups of
Cherokee a few miles west of the Petit Jean River (Yell County).
Upriver he noted cabins and fertile farms

> of the Cherokees, this being the land allotted to them by congress, in
> exchange for others in the Mississippi Territory, where the principal
> part of the nation still remain....The number who have now emigrated
> hither are about 1500....their farms...were well fenced and stocked with
> cattle....some of them [have] property to the amount of many thousands
> of dollars, have houses handsomely and conveniently furnished, and their
> tables spread with our dainties and luxuries.[14]

On meeting chief Walter Webber, a Cherokee trader living near
the hills of the Dardanelle, Nuttall wrote:

> [he] lives in ease and affluence, possessing a decently furnished and
> well provided house, several negro slaves, a large, well cleared...well
> fenced farm....himself and his nephew read, write, and speak English.[15]

Stephen H. Long, a year later, also noted the prosperity of a
Cherokee settler, and:

> one of his slaves...interpreted the Cherokee language....They are almost
> exclusively agriculturists, raising large crops of corn, and cotton
> enough for clothing their families, which they manufacture in their own
> houses.[16]

Long wrote that Cherokee learned cotton culture many years before
from former Indian Agent: "governor Blount of North Carolina...who
advised them to manufacture it into clothing."[17]

Nuttall saw Cherokee upriver as far as Mulberry Creek "the
Cherokee line of demarkation."[18] Some of these lands along the
"Arkansa" river had been occupied by Osage Indians.

In 1800 Pierre Chouteau, extending his area of control over

---

[13]Thomas Nuttall, English born, with interests of Botany and Ornithology,
traveled extensively in the U.S., penetrating westward through Arkansas
territory in 1819. His publication *A Journey of Travels into the Arkansas
Territory during the Year 1819* was later duplicated by Thwaites. Details of
Nuttall's life are in *Appleton's Cyclopaedia of American Biography* (N.Y.: D.
Appleton and Company 1888) vol 4, p 547.

[14]Ibid. pp 172-74.

[15]Ibid. p 181.

[16]Edwin James, comp. *Account of An Expedition from Pittsburgh to the Rocky
Mountains...1819 and '20.* (Philadelphia: H. C. Carey and I. Lea 1823) vol 2,
pp 267-68.

[17]Ibid. p 271.

[18]Nuttall...*Journal*...p 195 and n. The final boundary between Indian Territory
and Arkansas was changed in 1828, resulting in white settlers moving some
miles east.

the fur trade, had induced some 3,000 members of an Osage band,
known as "La Chaniers," to move from Missouri to the mouth of the
Verdigris River, an area known as Three Rivers.[19]

In 1819, Nuttall noted the Osage objection to the Cherokee
emigrants:

> The arrival of the Cherokees in this country did not fail...to excite
> the jealousy of the Osages, within whose former territory they had now
> taken up their residence. Major Lovely, the first agent...to reside
> among the Cherokees of the Arkansa...held a council with the Osages at
> the falls of the Verdigris.[20]

Nor were the Osage the only occupants along the Arkansas
River. Several families of whites had settled near Mulberry Creek
beginning in 1814.[21] Members of some of these families--Pyeatts,
Marrs, Carnahans, and Edmistons--would help blaze the Cherokee
Trail to California in 1849. When these white families were
forced, by the establishment of the Indian boundary in 1828, to
leave their homes they migrated west and were among the first to
settle in the Cane Hill area of Washington County, Arkansas.[22]

CHEROKEE EAST

With the turn of the century, several significant changes
altered the lives of Cherokee. In the early 1800s, missionaries
were sent to work among the various tribes of Native Americans.[23]
The missionaries and Cherokee too, knew that if the Bible was to
become part of Cherokee life, it had to be available to them in
printed form, and they had to learn to read it.

The Cherokee syllabary developed by Sequoyah, was presented
to tribal leaders in 1821 and quickly came into general use by the

---

[19] Wayne Morris "Auguste Pierre Chouteau, Merchant Prince at the Three Forks of
the Arkansas" *The Chronicles of Oklahoma* vol 48, no 2 (Summer 1970) pp 156-57.
The Arkansas, Verdigris and Grand (Neosho) Rivers converge near present Fort
Gibson, Oklahoma.
[20] Ibid. p 191.
[21] Mulberry Creek empties into the Arkansas River south of the present town of
Mulberry (Franklin County), Arkansas.
[22] *History of Washington County, Arkansas* (Fayetteville, Ark:...1989 Edition)
Also Washington County Historical Society Bulletin Series "The Pyeatt
Genealogy." A year before (1827), Sheriff Lewis Evans (future captain of the
1849 emigrant company to California establishing the Cherokee Trail) took the
first Territorial Census in Washington County, Arkansas.
[23] William E. Strong *The Story of the American Board* (Boston: The Pilgrim Press
1910) p 36.

entire Cherokee nation.[24] A printing press adapted to use the syllabary produced the first Cherokee newspaper.[25] The *Cherokee Phoenix'* was established in 1828 in the Cherokee capital of New Echota (Georgia). Elijah Hicks, later orator and Judge, was the first editor.

The Cherokee sent some of their young men to missionary boarding schools in Cornwall, Connecticut and to other New England locations. By 1827 the Cherokee in the east had adopted a written constitution on the United States model. In 1851 Judge Hicks, alluding to the importance of the syllabary, said the "acquisition of letters so far back" made it possible for the Cherokee to have a government of written laws that defined the rights of the widespread population.[26]

The use of English became more common among them. In 1835 George W. Featherstonhaugh, English geologist, traveled through Cherokee country (Alabama, Tennessee and Georgia). At Gunter's Landing, (Alabama) he visited a family. What he learned encapsulated the significant changes.

> [The woman] asked me civilly, and in good English, to sit down... They said there were a great many Indians within two miles of the place, but that the whites had got possession of the country, and they all expected to be driven out of it...For the sake of tranquillity, they had not only in various treaties with the United States surrendered, as the Creeks had before done, important portions of their territory to the state of Georgia, but had, upon the urgent recommendation of the whites ...successfully entered upon [plantation] agriculture, and universally adopted the Christian religion. A remarkable man,[Sequoyah]...had invented alphabetical characters to express every separate sound in their language, and books of prayers, psalms and hymns, with the gospels, had been printed...in the familiar knowledge of which the whole Cherokee nation had been instructed...and [they] were most exemplary in the performance of their religious duties.[27]

---

[24]Sequoyah is a Cherokee family name. The developer of the syllabary was also called George Guess or George Gist.

[25]Non-Cherokee John F. Wheeler, later editor of the *Ft. Smith Herald*, "was the first man [to] set Cherokee type" according to his son Will Watie Wheeler Sr., in D.C. Gideon's *Indian Territory: Descriptive Biographical and Genealogical ...with a general history of the territory* (N.Y. and Chicago: The Lewis Publishing Company 1901) p 451.

[26]*Cherokee Advocate* 1 April 1851.

[27]George W. Featherstonhaugh *A Canoe Voyage Up The Minnay Sotor: with an account of the Lead and Copper Deposits in Wisconsin; of the Gold Region in the Cherokee Country; and Sketches of Popular Manners.* Reprint Ed. (St. Paul, Minn: Minnesota Historical Society 1970) vol 2, pp 198-243.

Featherstonhaugh, referring to America's first gold rush of 1829, noted that the Cherokee wrongly assumed other Christians would behave as they themselves did.

> The discovery...of several alluvial deposits of native gold in the Cherokee lands had removed the last moral restraint from the people of Georgia, who entered, without leave or license, upon the best possessions of the Indians.[28]

Featherstonhaugh visited the missionaries and met many leading Cherokee.[29] He was privileged to attend the Cherokee Council meeting at Red Clay (Tennessee) in August 1835. While there, Featherstonhaugh was told by Cherokee interpreter Stephen Foreman that Rev. John Schermerhorn had been appointed commissioner to negotiate the Removal treaty with the Cherokee.

> On coming amongst the Cherokees, instead of dealing fairly with them, and making an arrangement with the Council that could be sanctioned by a majority of the nation, he [Schermerhorn] corrupted a few individuals to consent to emigrate, and deliver up the Cherokee territory; and reported it to the Government as if it had been a solemn contract entered into with the whole nation.[30]

Federal government agent John Mason Jr. delivered the 1835 message in a pouring rain. The Cherokee listened intently for some indication that they would be allowed to keep their own land.[31] But it was clear that the United States government was "determined to enforce the treaty which the minority (later known as the "Treaty Party") had made with the Government..."[32]

This treaty was responsible for the forced Removal of the Eastern Cherokee to the West, over what would later be called the Cherokee Trail of Tears. It also resulted in the permanent

---

[28]Featherstonhaugh...*Voyage*...p 201. Census and Valuation records at that time reveal that in Georgia alone, Cherokee property values were $776,384.14. Douglas C. Wilms "Cherokee Indian Land Use in Georgia, 1800-1838" Dissertation, University of Georgia, Athens, Georgia 1973.

[29]Daniel S. Buttrick at the Moravian Mission at Brainerd (Tennessee) and Evan Jones at Red Clay (Tennessee). John Ross (long-time elected chief of the Cherokee) and Lewis Ross, Rev. Jesse Bushyhead, John A. Bell, David McNair, William (or Elijah?) Hicks.

[30]Featherstonhaugh...*Voyage*...p 240.

[31]The Eastern Cherokee owned considerable gold-bearing lands. One estimate, just prior to their Removal in 1838, was 7,200,000 acres in the several states. James Manford Carselowey "Cherokee Pioneers." (Adair, Okla: Published by Author 1961). In the Removal Treaty, these eastern Cherokee lands were "purchased" for $5,000.000.

[32]Featherstonhaugh...*Voyage*...p 244.

division of the Eastern Cherokee into 1) Treaty signers and families; and 2) the majority, headed by Chief John Ross.

In an attempt to keep their Georgia lands, the Eastern Cherokee sued the State of Georgia, a suit which went to the United States Supreme Court. Chief Justice John Marshall delivered the court's opinion that the lands had been assured to the Cherokee by the United States, and that they had surrendered their lands in treaty after treaty, each one guaranteed to be the last.[33]

The Court said that Cherokee had once been numerous and independent, and the Cherokee Nation was "capable of managing its own affairs and governing itself" but now had only enough land left as was "deemed necessary to their comfortable subsistence." The high court ruled in favor of the Cherokee, but President Andrew Jackson chose to ignore the Court ruling.

Removal was a certainty, which was widely reported in the newspapers.[34] General Winfield Scott reminded the Cherokee that President Andrew Jackson himself sent Scott to "cause you, in obedience to the Treaty of 1835, to join...your people who are already established in prosperity on the other side of the Mississippi." Scott reminded them they had already been given two years to remove themselves and had not done it. He promised that: "The full moon of May is already on the wane, and before another shall have passed away, every Cherokee man, woman, and child...must be in motion."

Scott called them "My Friends!" and stated that both he and the Cherokee had to obey the President. His troops were already in many places which were to be abandoned. Thousands more troops were coming, which would render escape hopeless. "Obey them when they tell you that you can remain no longer in this country."

Following that, Scott appealed to the "Chiefs, head-men and warriors!," telling them that if they fought, blood would be spilled, and war impossible to prevent. He appealed: "spare

---

[33]Wilcomb E. Washburn, ed. *The Indian and the White Man* AD2 Documents in American Civilization Series (Garden City, N.Y.: Anchor Books, Doubleday & Company Inc. 1964) Document 31 pp 118-22.

[34]*Helena* (Arkansas) *Spy* 11 June 1838, vol 1, no 9, p 2 col 6.

me...the horror of witnessing the destruction of the Cherokees."

A letter to the editor dated June 11, 1838, reported from New Echota (Cherokee capital) stated that nine military companies under General Floyd had already crossed the Oostenaula river, camping near the Coosawattee settlement. His campaign of "great importance" was conducted with "much skill and management...it requiring much of both to prevent escape, and successful resistance."

Over two thousand Cherokee had been rounded up from different places, and only one warrior was reported killed by troops. The article went on to praise General Floyd, a superior officer, who "manages every thing with skill and ease."[35]

The 1835 official Eastern Cherokee census had shown there were 16,542 Cherokee, with 1,592 negro slaves.[36] The final Removal was on. Most Cherokee would depart in Fall of 1838.

Many Cherokee went west voluntarily, captained by their own Cherokee leaders. The Treaty Party, those who had signed the 1835 Removal treaty with the U.S. government, numbered between 600 and 700, and traveled in a separate detachment under John Bell in 1838.[37]

Chief John Ross and brother Lewis administered the "Removal" of approximately 12,000 people.[38] Each group of approximately 1,000 persons, their detachment leaders, and time of traverse are shown below.[39] An additional three detachments traveled by river.

---

[35]*Helena* (Arkansas)*Spy* 25 June 1838, vol 1, no 11, p 2 col 5 and p 3 col 1.
[36]Sen. Doc. 120, 25 cong. 2 sess.
[37]Trail of Tears National Historic Trail Management Plan (Alabama, Arkansas, Georgia, Illinois, Kentucky, Missouri, North Carolina, Oklahoma, Tennessee). U.S. National Park Service Sept. 1992.
[38]Ibid.
[39]Peter Hildebrand's detachment was 1,766. In addition there was a "Roll of Cherokees who will remove themselves. 23 May to 1 October 1838." Later the federal government would reimburse those who chose to take care of themselves. Examples: John Ridge, 36 in his party for which $720 was paid for Removal and $1,199.88 for Subsistence; and Charles Timberlake, 14 persons, paid $233.31 for Subsistence.

Cherokee Captains of Removal		
	Left	Arrived
Hair Conrad	28 August 1838	17 January 1839
Situwakee	7 September 1838	17 January 1839
George Hicks	7 September 1838	14 March 1839
Elijah Hicks	9 September 1838	4 January 1839
James Brown	10 September 1838	5 March 1839
Choowalooka	14 September 1838	1 March 1839
Moses Daniel	20 September 1838	2 March 1839
Richard Taylor	20 September 1838	24 March 1839
Capt. Old Field	24 September 1838	23 February 1839
Rev. Jesse Bushyhead	5 October 1838	23 February 1839
Peter Hildebrand	23 October 1838	25 March 1839
John Drew	5 December 1838	18 March 1839

The remaining Eastern Cherokee faced forced removal. A few turned back, hid in the mountains, and were allowed to remain in North Carolina, where their descendants live today. The rest of the Cherokee trod the Trail of Tears to Indian Territory.

In Elijah Hicks' detachment, the first to arrive in Indian Territory in present Oklahoma, 54 of 858 died enroute. The other detachments, leaving later, arriving later, and at the mercy of the elements for a longer period of time probably had more deaths.

Twelve years later now Cherokee Judge Elijah Hicks wrote:

our race have retreated a thousand miles...from their stately mountains...leaving their noble rivers behind, and hastening as it were with the sun...until we have come here, and trust here we shall finally stand to perform the grand work of our national education.[40]

In their western Indian Territory home, eastern Cherokee fostered institutions of civilization on the frontier: schools and academies, courts and courthouses, newspapers, businesses, professions, skills and methods of successful farming.

Now there were three distinct groups of Cherokee in Indian

---

[40]*Cherokee Advocate* 1 April 1851.

Territory: the Western Cherokee, the Treaty Party (those who had signed the 1835 Treaty without full consent of the tribe), and the Eastern Cherokee under Chief John Ross. By 1839 there had been assassinations of some of the signers of the 1835 treaty. There was discontent and animosity between the newly-arrived Eastern Cherokee and the "Old Settlers" (Western Cherokee) who already had a system of self-government including their own chiefs.[41]

A long political struggle took place over what the rightful government should be. Western Cherokee chief John Brown invited the newcomers: "We joyfully welcome you to our country," told them the Eastern Cherokee could come and go, select land, had full voting rights, could run for office in "both houses of our legislature," but until after elections they were expected to "be subject to our government and laws."[42]

The Eastern Cherokee were unwilling to give up their system. A series of meetings took place over an extended period among the Cherokee groups, between the military commanders and some of the Cherokee, between the U.S. government at Washington D.C. and some of the Cherokee, and between the Indian Agent and Cherokee. Meanwhile the federal government held off payments for Removal, subsistence, and annuities until the question of rightful government should be settled. Though a kind of representative government was in place, assassinations, burning of property, and ambushes among the Cherokee groups continued well into 1846.

Aside from the political problems, the majority of Cherokee were having a hard time just making a living after Removal. To investigate the massive fraud in the contracts and beneficiaries connected with Removal, the U.S. War Department sent Maj. Ethan Allen Hitchcock into Indian Territory. Arriving in late 1841, he traveled extensively gathering information.[43]

Hitchcock saw that those who had wealth in the East still had

---

[41]Chiefs John Brown, John Rogers and John Looney. William G. McLoughlin *After the Trail of Tears: The Cherokees' Struggle for Sovereignty, 1839-1880* (Chapel Hill, N.C.: The Univ. of North Carolina Press 1993) p 10.

[42]Ibid. p 12.

[43]Grant Foreman, ed. *A Traveler in Indian Territory: The Journal of Ethan Allen Hitchcock, late Major-General in the United States Army* (Cedar Rapids, Iowa: The Torch Press 1930).

their wealth. But the majority of Eastern Cherokee, especially those who had held out the longest, had little, and less after they arrived.

They were hampered additionally by drought in 1841 and 1842. The spectre of starvation was avoided because the old system of sharing prevailed. Those who had crops shared their harvests.

CHEROKEE LOOK WEST

The turmoil in Indian Territory caused many Cherokee to continue looking west for better circumstances. By 1839, Old Settler (Western) Chief John Brown, his family, and some friends were so discouraged they left for Mexico. Other Old Settlers and Treaty Party members joined Brown later.

Cherokee trader Jesse Chisholm "headed an expedition to California...bearing a passport issued at Fort Gibson September 23, 1839, by General Matthew Arbuckle."[44]

In 1843 non-Cherokee John Henry Brown, with Capt. Dan Coody's company of Cherokee fur traders, went cross country to California via Fort Bridger and Fort Hall.[45] They entered "by the Humboldt and Truckee route, spending the winter at what was later Johnson's rancho...returning [to Cherokee Nation] in...'44."[46]

On this return trip east, they met the Stephens-Townsend-Murphy party, imparting information about California to them. "Capt. Dan Cody [Coody], while at Sutter's Fort had made minute inquiries about [California]"[47] Subsequently, members of the Stephens party opened "the [wagon] trail up the Truckee River and over Donner Pass...until 1849, the primary avenue for overland travel into and out of California."[48]

In 1845 a group of fifty-four Cherokee and whites went deep

[44]Grant Foreman *Marcy & the Gold Seekers: The Journal of Captain R.B. Marcy, with an account of the Gold Rush over the Southern Route* (Norman, Okla.: Univ. of Oklahoma Press 1939) p 4.

[45]John Henry Brown *Early Days of San Francisco California* (Oakland, Calif.: Biobooks 1949) pp 1-9.

[46]Hubert Howe Bancroft (the works of) *History of California* "Pioneer Register and Index" vol 19, pp 732-33.

[47]Brown...*San Francisco*...p 5.

[48]Louise Barry *The Beginning of the West: Annals of the Kansas Gateway to the American West 1540-1854* (Topeka, Kans.: Kansas State Historical Society 1972) p 511.

into Texas looking for a place to emigrate. Among them were some
who would trek to California in 1849 and 1850. A diary of the
journey was kept by non-Cherokee William Minor Quesenbury.[49]
Immediately following the burial of a Cherokee named Reese,
Quesenbury testified to the discontent under the all-powerful
Chief Ross:

> Mr. Reese was believed and respected by all, so much so that his word
> was law when persuasion and argument from others had failed...He was the
> most ardent lover of liberty and has often declared...that he would
> rather die over here than remain a subject under [Chief John] Ross'
> government at home.[50]

Most of the Cherokee party returned to Indian Territory early
in 1846, perhaps undecided about a permanent move because a war
with Mexico was imminent, or hopeful that the bloody Cherokee
years were over. But: "Between November 1845 and August 1846,
there were thirty-three violent deaths in the nation."[51]

In 1846, coincidentally the year the War with Mexico began,
the three groups: the "Treaty Party;" the Western Cherokee "Old
Settlers;" and the Eastern Cherokee, signed a treatywhich was
intended to finally solve their differences.[52] All compromised. As
a result, the monies from Removal began to be received; conditions
improved.

Tahlequah was becoming a permanent town, with brick
courthouse buildings and businesses. A Masonic Temple was built in
1849. Non-Cherokee P. Mellowhorn wrote:

> Tahlequah is a quiet and orderly place....four stores, one saddler's
> shop, a tailor's shop, three black-smiths' shops, a shoe-maker's shop,
> and three taverns....This is a superior farming and stock raising
> country....They raise Durham Cows, Berkshire Hogs, and Merino
> Sheep...and sell beef-cattle, corn, potatoes, butter, chickens, eggs,
> &c...manufacture cloth, both cotton and woollen, and very superior
> coverlets...
>   It is gratifying...to see nearly every body going to church on
> Sabbath mornings....As to preachers...We have the learned and eloquent

---

[49]Quesenbury also kept a diary of his 1850 California trip. See vol. 2.

[50]Pat Donat, ed. "Bill Cush's Trek to Texas-Part 2" *Flashback* vol 32, no 2,
(May 1982) p 16.

[51]"the bloodiest years of the factional dispute." McLoughlin...*Trail of
Tears*....pp 48-49.

[52]Geo. Minot, ed. *U.S. Statutes at Large and Treaties of the U.S.A. 1 December
1845 to 3 March 1851.* "Treaty with the Cherokees" (Boston: Little, Brown & Co.
1854) vol 9.

students of Andover [Massachusetts], and some specimens of the cane-
break orators of the frontiers....

You must know something about the [Cherokee] Temperance Societies,
Bible Societies, and Missionary Societies.[53]

The military men stationed at Fort Gibson saw signs of
wealth. A dragoon wrote: "[nearby lives a] Cherokee, named Rodger,
who has grown immensely rich....he owns a large tract of land [and]
so many head of cattle that he cannot count them."[54]

An 1851 census of Cherokee who were in the Removal revealed
the success of many individuals.[55] But among the Cherokee groups,
animosities over Removal would last at least through the Civil
War, when Cherokee fought on both sides.

With the lack of harmony among the various groups in Indian
Territory, it is not difficult to understand why many of the
Cherokee, in 1849, would heed the siren call of California. The
Eastern Cherokee were well aware of the value of gold. An article
in the *Fort Smith Herald* acknowledged the Cherokee experience with
gold mining:

> There are a great many Cherokees who came from Georgia, that understand
> gold-mining as well as any of the whites, having washed the precious
> metal out of the sands in the Old Nation in 1830-31. They are, also,
> well acquainted with what is termed the 'gold blossom,' which is found
> upon the surface of the ground where the metal lies beneath.[56]

California offered opportunity for all, far away from their
troubles.

---

[53] *Fort Smith Herald* 18 July 1849, vol 2, no 38, p 2.

[54] James Hildreth *Dragoon Campaigns to the Rocky Mountains: being a History of
the Enlistment, Organization, and first Campaigns of the Regiment of United
States Dragoons; together with incidents of a soldier's life, and sketches of
scenery and Indian Character* (N.Y.: Wiley & Long 1836) p 96.

[55] "emigrant Cherokees" owned 65 blacksmith shops, 14 gristmills, 10 sawmills,
2 tanyards, and 5 saltworks; as well as 5,770 horses, 28,705 cattle, 35,832
hogs, and 233 mules. The entire Cherokee nation's population was 17,000-
18,000, with 1,844 black slaves and 64 free blacks. The nation had 27 schools
and 38 Protestant churches or "regular preaching stations." McLoughlin...*Trail
of Tears*...p 81.

[56] *Fort Smith Herald* 6 June 1849, vol 2, no 42, p 2.

Chapter 2. GOLD FEVER

And shall We Cherokee not take advantage of the Times and be found trying to get to this Glorious Country? It is Free to All to take up their beds and walk; And if we mistake not...There will be A goodly number of Enterprising Spirits leave for California.

--James S. Vann

News of the California gold rush reached Arkansas in the October 6, 1848, *Arkansas Intelligencer*.[57] Many Arkansas newspapers carried articles on the gold finds in California throughout the late fall and early winter 1848. It was not until January 8, 1849, that the newspaper of the Cherokee Nation, the *Cherokee Advocate,* carried an article giving credence to the California reports.[58]

CALIFORNIA GOLD

We have received through the New Orleans papers...such accounts from California, as leave little doubt, that the stories of the mineral wealth of the country, however exaggerate, are founded in fact....a report derived from an officer of the Army, bearer of despatches... gives the following;--'The News which these Gentlemen bring...fully confirms all the accounts....The whole valley of Sacramento may be said to be one vast deposit of gold, the metal lying in more or less abundance, from the crags of the Sierra Nevada to the embouchures of that river, and its many tributaries. People were completely engrossed in collecting it, to the abandonment of almost every other occupation...

Many persons have collected in one day, of the finest grade gold, from three to eight hundred dollars, and for many days...averaged from 75 to $150....when a man with his pan or basket does not easily gather 30 to 40 dollars in a day he moves to another place....we may safely set down an ounce of pure Gold, or $16 per day to the man. Suppose there are 4000 persons at work, they will add to the aggregate wealth of the Territory about 4000 ounces, or $60,000 a day....'

A Letter in the National Intelligencer...contains the following eloquent language in relation to the yellow metal: 'The Shores are paved with it, and the Mountains swell in its Golden Girdle. It sparkles in the Sands of the Valley; It glitters in the Coronet of the Steep Cliffs...'I use strong terms but who can speak in whispers when an Earthquake rocks?

---

[57]Francile B. Oakley "Arkansas' Golden Army of '49" *Arkansas Historical Quarterly* vol 6, no 1 (Spring 1947) pp 1-85 M.A. Thesis, University of Arkansas.

[58]Cherokee Nation (People) as opposed to Cherokee Territory or Lands which are now in Oklahoma. The *Cherokee Advocate* was first published in 1844 in Tahlequah, Indian Territory, (Oklahoma); Suspended publication from September 28, 1853 to April 1870; was published again from January 1875 to March 4, 1876. Each edition was printed in both Cherokee and English.

Gold Fever had struck. Throughout the Cherokee Nation talk was that the neighboring communities of Fort Smith, Van Buren, and even nearby Fayetteville were forming California companies. Within the week some Cherokee decided to form a company. This intent appeared in the next *Advocate*.

FOR CALIFORNIA

There is a company forming in Tahlequah, Cherokee Nation, for California--with the design of joining the company now forming in Fort Smith, which company will leave the first of April. The regulations or the necessary equipments required by said company of each emigrants, 'are a good rifle gun plenty of ammunition, rations for the journey, consisting of 180 lbs of Flour, 100 lbs of Bacon,' to be transported in wagons drawn by horses, mules or oxen.

All young men in the Nation who may wish to try their fortunes in the Gold Regions of California, have now the opportunity. Any persons wishing further information with regard to the 'tramp,' can obtain it by applying to the undersigned, Tahlequah, C. Nation.

JAS. S. VANN[59]
DANL. M. GUNTER[60]

The January 22 edition of the Cherokee newspaper further fueled the rage for California with an article, "Information for California Emigrants," written by Edwin Bryant, who flatly declared that the only route to take was that from Independence or St. Joseph, Missouri to Fort Laramie, South Pass, Fort Hall, and the Humboldt Sink.[61]

Let no emigrant, carrying his family with him, deviate from it, or imagine to himself that he can find a better road. This road is the best that has yet been discovered.

The Bryant article was derived from *The Arkansas Democrat*, but James Vann, editor of the *Cherokee Advocate*, couldn't resist interjecting into Bryant's report his own bracketed information about the regional favorite route, the southern route from Fort Smith to Santa Fe.

[Emigrants should be at Fort Smith, Ark's on the 1st of April, as an expedition will start from that place at that date. The grass on the prairies over which the road lies will then be up sufficiently high to

---

[59]Notice of Vann's appointment as editor of the *Cherokee Advocate* (following the retirement of Wm. P. Ross) appeared in the *Fort Smith Herald* 29 November 1848.

[60]*Cherokee Advocate* 15 January 1849.

[61]Bryant was considered a reliable source of information. *Cherokee Advocate* 22 January 1849. Bryant compiled his information in *What I Saw In California in 1846 and 1847* (London: Richard Bently, 1849.)

afford fine grazing. All caravans by this route can, if they choose, get
a start of *forty days* of those who take the Independence route.][62]

In his book Josiah Gregg, famous Santa Fe trader, had noted
early grass on the southern route five years earlier.[63] Newspaper
reports made much of the fact that the military had used this
southern route: "Lt. [Abraham] Buford having recently passed over
it."[64]

Some of the Cherokee began to seriously consider forming a
company of their own. Editor Vann wrote:

It has been suggested to us...that there ought to be an Independent
Company formed in the [Cherokee] Nation. The suggestion may be a very
good one, as there will be some who desire to go that will not be able
to obtain waggons to transport their necessary provisions, and will be
compeled to pack. We have been authorized to say that there will be a
Public Meeting at the Court House in Tah-Quah[65] on Saturday, the 3rd of
Februry[sic], to take into consideration the expediency of forming an
independent company; and also to come to some definite conclusion, what
shall be the necessary equipment, amount of provision, requisite for the
journey and the best manner of transporting the same.
    All persons in the Nation and parts of Companies formed, are
especially invited to attend.[66]

In early February a non-Cherokee company was also forming,
which would later be joined by the Cherokee and take a new route.

A Company is now being formed at Fayetteville, Arkansas, consisting of
Vigorous, Enterprising and Substantial citizens of Washington and
adjoining counties with the intention of paying a visit to the gold
mines of California and securing a portion of the rich deposits of that
region. The Company will start from Fayetteville about the first of
April and will pursue the most advantageous route. A Committee has been

[62]*Cherokee Advocate* 15 January 1849.
[63]"the borders of Arkansas, where the pasturage springs up nearly a month
earlier." Josiah Gregg *Commerce of the Prairies: or the Journal of a Santa Fe
Trader, During Eight Expeditions Across The Great Western Prairies, and a
Residence of Nearly Nine Years in Northern Mexico.* (N.Y.: Henry G. Langley
1844) In two volumes. Reprint (Ann Arbor, Mich.: Univ. Microfilms, Inc. 1966)
vol 2, p 10.
[64]Foreman...*Marcy*...pp 7-8; *Santa Fe Republican* 12 September 1848 p 1; and
Niles Weekly Register 74, p 252. In 1848 the War Department ordered Capt.
Abraham Buford to explore a new route to Santa Fe, following the Arkansas
River to the Cimarron River and up that river; then crossing the North Fork of
the Canadian River striking the Santa Fe Trail near the Middle Cimarron
Spring, traveling on that trail to Santa Fe. Buford left Fort Gibson in mid-
July 1848, arrived in Santa Fe on September 9, 1848. He returned in June 1849
via the newly-pioneered Cherokee Trail from Turkey Creek near present
McPherson, Kansas to Fort Gibson, declaring it a vastly superior route to his
more southerly 1848 route.
[65]TAH-QUAH is Tahlequah, Capital of the Cherokee Nation then and now.
[66]*Cherokee Advocate* 22 January 1849.

appointed to collect all the facts that can be procured in relation to the several routes.[67]

The group selected the name The Fayetteville Gold Mining Company, with Dr. W. R. Cunningham as Corresponding Secretary. The "most advantageous route" was not yet identified.

By April one hundred and thirteen persons had registered as members of the Fayetteville Gold Mining Company, and fifty wagons were expected to be in the expedition, the Fayetteville Company planned to rendezvous on the Grand Saline by April 21, where the company expected to be joined by the Cherokees.[68]

The Cherokee Nation organizational meeting was also held in February, after which future Cherokee emigrants knew what the requirements would be.

Tahlequah Feb. 3RD, 1849.
such citizens of the Cherokee Nation as contemplated going to California, met this day in the Court House....a committee of five were appointed...to draft a Preamble, and resolutions....after a short absence, [they] presented the following...

WHEREAS, the intelligence which has reached us of the California gold mines, is corraborated by official reports, which render it certain that there is sufficient for all who wish to avail themselves of the opportunety of improving their fortunes,
---And whereas it is imperatively necessary that persons going should form themselves into a company, and remain united through the journey, in order to repel attacks, to afford mutal succor [sic], and ensure success of the enterprise, therefor, we a portion of the Cherokee People, designing to avail ourselves of the inducements held out for betering our condition by emigrating thither, and wishing to organize ourselves into a company to proceed in such manner as shall ensure our safety, our comfort, and success, do resolve,

1st. That it would be neither safe, nor expedient, to proceed with less than 100 able bodied efficient men, well armed with a rifle gun, a butcher knife, and sufficient ammunition to last through the journey, say, not less than 3 lbs of powder, and 9 lbs of lead.

Resolved 2nd, That each man shall furnish provisions sufficient to support him during the journey, not less than 100 lbs. of bacon, 200 lbs. of flour, 25 lbs salt and 2 lbs soap.

Resolved 3rd, That each waggon shall not be drawn by less than one yoke of cattle or mules to each ration, that each waggon be furnished with six gallons of tar, and not less than one axe one handsaw, one drawingknife and one set of necessary augers and chisels.

Resolved 4th, That no waggons carry more than 20 cwt., and small ones less in proportion, which is to be determined by a committee...

---

[67]Oakley..."Army"...p 31; Priscilla McArthur *Arkansas in the Gold Rush* (Little Rock, Ark.: August House, Inc. for the Arkansas Territorial Restoration Foundation Inc. 1986) p 237 citing *Arkansas State Democrat* of 9 February, and *Fort Smith Herald* of 21 February 1849.
[68]Oakley..."Army"...p 32 quoting the *Arkansas Intelligencer* of 7 April 1849.

Resolved 5th, That the company rendezvous by the 1st day of April at Richard Drews, on the south side of Arkansas River, where all necessary officers are to be elected...

Resolved 6th, That the Secretary tender an invitation to those in the neighboring States and in the Nation, who wish to go California, to join the company.[69]

The *Advocate* editor extended an invitation to Arkansans and Missourians, along with a good reason to go with the Cherokee.

This company will leave the first of April, if the grass will justify a company starting so early, if not, just as soon as possible.

All persons or parts of Companies forming at the following places, Fayetteville and Bentonville Ark., Sarcoxie, Cowskin Prairie, Springfield Mo., are cordially invited to join with us.

There is one very great advantage in going with the Cherokee company. The Cherokees are on the most friendly terms will all the Indian tribes of the Prairie--consequently there will be no danger of attacks from our red brethren.[70]

That "intelligence" was reinforced by Cherokee Senora Hicks, "our fellow citizen [who] has returned from the 'Prairies,' having made a very profitable trip, bringing in some thirty mules and quite a large lot of *peltries*."[71] Hicks was subsequently consulted as an authority on companies traveling overland:

He [Senora Hicks] says the Cherokee can pass across the prairies with perfect safety from the molestation of the Indians on the prairies, as they are on most friendly terms with the Cherokee; but (he) says the Comanche harbor the most hostile feelings towards the citizens of the United States. This we feel our duty to tell our neighbors, that they may prepare themselves to encounter difficulties with the Comanche should they fall in with them. Any persons along the line or in the neighboring states who may wish to avoid any difficulty with the Indians by joining the Cherokee company, are invited to do so.[72]

Senora Hicks and his brother Charles subsequently joined Cherokee Dr. Jeter Lynch Thompson's company to travel not over the southern prairies Senora said were so safe, but via the conventional California route along the Platte River.[73]

---

[69]*Cherokee Advocate* 12 February 1849.

[70]Ibid. p 2 col 1.

[71]*Cherokee Advocate* 22 January 1849.

[72] McArthur...*Arkansas*...p 21.

[73]They lost eight or nine members, mostly Cherokee, to cholera. Amazingly, Hicks was in California early enough in the 1849 season to be with the parties under Maj. Daniel Rucker rescuing late-arriving emigrants along the blizzard-ridden Lassen Trail. Hicks was noted by J. Goldsborough Bruff, Georgia Willis Read and Ruth Gaines, ed. *Gold Rush: The Journals, Drawings and other Papers of J. Goldsborough Bruff* (N.Y.: Columbia Univ. Press, 1944) 2 vols. Bruff used a "Cherokee Guide" [book?] for the Applegate/Lassen Cutoff.

Concerns about getting through safely were no doubt based on the late 1848 reports that came in from the country over which the southern route would take emigrants toward California.

"Late From the Plains" in the *St. Louis Reveille* in February:

> Col. Gilpin writes, that a large body of Indians and renegade Mexicans are collecting upon the Canadian [River], for the purpose of general marauding in the Spring. They have several thousand animals and oxen, stolen in the trail last summer--The Camanches, Kiowas, Apaches, and Pawnees, are floating about in large parties.
> A party of Toas[Taos] and Apaches, a few weeks ago, killed three teamsters and burned their wagons.[74]

Other advantages of traveling with the Cherokee were:

> The Cherokee company will travel more expediciously than any California company that will leave the western frontier--not being incumbered by a large party.
> The company will follow the route marked out by Lieut. Buford, from Ft. Gibson to Santa Fe. He made a very good road, Cuting down the banks of ravines, and in many places they are bridged. All letters...will receive...immediate attention.[75]

In 1849 many emigrating parties went out of their way to consult with Josiah Gregg, retired and living in Van Buren, who documented the early years on the western prairies while active in the Santa Fe trade.[76] Gregg recorded in great detail every aspect of travel for frontier survival, from the proper packing of mules or wagons to equipment and provisioning. The influence of his information on what to take and how much--wagons, teams, livestock, firearms, powder, shot; how to divide the company; assignments of responsibility; and how to proceed--is evident in the formation of the 1849 and 1850 Arkansas emigrating parties.

It is certain that future company captain Lewis Evans in making plans consulted with Josiah Gregg. Evans' namesake hometown Evansville was not a great distance from Van Buren, the shipping and receiving point for commerce and travelers of the time, and documentation was found that Evans registered at Van Buren hotels

---

[74]*Cherokee Advocate* 20 March 1848.

[75]*Cherokee Advocate* 12 February 1849.

[76]Gregg's book was in its second edition in 1845, according to the *Arkansas Intelligencer*, Van Buren, 18 October 1845 vol 4, no 36, p 2. Gregg's first trip to Santa Fe was made in 1831. In the Preface to his book he stated: "During the whole of the above periods [1831-1839] I crossed the Prairies eight different times."

prior to his 1849 departure. Most of the information available to Evans favored departure from Fort Smith or Van Buren. And according to Cherokee editor James Vann, the Cherokee were planning to travel a southern route from Fort Gibson to Santa Fe.

Why this southern route was not taken, and when the decision was made by the combined Cherokee and white companies to travel a totally different and uncharted way, is not recorded in any known letter or diary. Certainly the recent experiences of Indian conflicts must have been a factor in choosing an alternate route.

The combined company, made up of people from Cherokee Nation, plus both whites and Cherokee from Arkansas, Missouri, and Tennessee became known as the Evans/Cherokee company. They pioneered a route through Kansas and Oklahoma that was traveled until 1862, during the Civil War. The Evans/Cherokee trail was continuously used through Colorado and Wyoming before, during, and after the Colorado Pikes Peak gold rush beginning 1858, the Idaho and Montana gold rushes of the 1860s, for stock drives westbound and eastbound into the 1880s, and by emigrants to the turn of the century.

Chapter 3. RENDEZVOUS AT THE GRAND SALINE

We received a Flag from the Ladies of Fayetteville, on the day of our Rendevous, which was ixcepted with a grate dell of enthusiasm

--James Sawyer Crawford

THE GRAND SALINE

On April 21, 1849, the company from Fayetteville rendezvoused at the "Sulphur Spring," at the Grand Saline, Cherokee Nation, a very important and long used crossing on the Grand (Neosho) River. The Grand Saline, near the confluence of Saline Creek and the Grand (Neosho) River, was historically important as a source of salt. By 1833, salt was being produced under private ownership "boiled down" for sale throughout Western Arkansas, Southwest Missouri and the Indian Territories. In 1841 Major Hitchcock saw

[the] great (Grand) Saline...so much spoken of....There is made...about 15 bushels of salt a day and three times that quantity...can be made...owned by Captain Rodgers [John Rogers who] rents it for $1,000 for six months.[77]

The Cherokee Nation, under Cherokee law of 1843, bought the several saltworks. The officials of the Nation granted leases for these lucrative businesses.[78] In 1849, Lewis Ross, brother of Chief John Ross, was the operator of the saltworks. He also owned a store at this Grand Saline on the east side of the Grand (Neosho) River.[79] This was the place where 1849 and 1850 California emigrating companies planned to rendezvous. The Grand Saline became such an important meeting place during the gold rush that it was granted a U.S. post office in June 1849. Lewis' son Robert D. Ross was appointed postmaster.[80]

---

[77]Hitchcock...*Traveler*...pp 87, 89. "these springs [were] owned at one time by A.P. Chouteau and later by Sam Houston." Foreman...*Marcy*...n 53

[78]*Cherokee Advocate* 18 June 1849. "AN ACT in reference to Salines." An earlier law "An Act Relative to Salines" had been passed by the Western Cherokee on December 6, 1833 identifying the Nation as owner, spelling out terms of lease. Washburn...*Cherokees "West"*...pp 117-18.

[79]In 1850 diarist Quesenbury wrote he was camped "down below Lewis Ross' store." Diarist Mitchell: "we got to the Grand Salt works and intended crosing Grand river." See William M. Quesenbury's and James Mitchell's April 11, 1850 entries.

[80]Robert Daniel Ross is listed as a son of Lewis Ross by Starr...*Cherokee*... pp 410, 411 and by George Morrison Bell, Sr. *Genealogy of "Old & New Cherokee Indian Families"* (Bartlesville, Ok: Publ. by G.M. Bell Sr. 1972) p 365. Bell

In April 1849 parties had been arriving for days at Lewis Ross' establishment, from many geographic areas. Members of many of these groups were close friends or extended families, usually from the same general settlement area, and often referred to in letters as the "connection."

Evansville, Arkansas, residents included trader Lewis Evans and son Albert G. Evans, and Leonard and Gus A. Shuler, tanners.

They were joined by John Rankin Pyeatt and his group from Cane Hill, where they had lived since the late 1820s. The Pyeatt group included John's son Andrew, and his brother Henry Porter Pyeatt, and his nephews James and John Carnahan and James Pierce.[81] Also from Cane Hill were Jacob Myers, Samuel and Dr. James L. McCullock, George McKey, James Carter, John Carter, George McClure, Kidrick and Thomas Crumley, James, Hugh and William Morrow, Alexander Buchanan Crawford, William Crawford, J. M. Matthews, J. P. Kellum, James Ingram, and Robert Williamson.

Wiley Cosby was related to George Nathan Lewis and Peter Mankins, who were related to John Van Hoose, from Middle Fork of White River. Nathan Tharp was Hoose's son-in-law, as was James Dickinson. It is likely Nathan Lewis, John Lewis, and Jacob Stricklin were also with this group.

Some of those in the original Fayetteville Emigrating Company were letter writer Hiram Davis, John J. and Oscar Bean, Benjamin and John Sanders, James L. Cartwright, John R. Cline, George C. North, H.J. McRoy, Joseph Chew, William Mallet, Dr. W.R. Cunningham, Fred P. Sime (Simms), and Edward Freyschlag, and his brothers Christian and Henry and sisters Barbara and Herminia Freyschlag. The Freyschlags represented culture and education traveling to the West.[82]

---

wrote that Lewis built his family a large brick home at Saline, Oklahoma which the Cherokee Nation bought in 1870 and converted to use for the Cherokee Orphans, p 555.

[81]James Pearce (Pierce) was living in Park City, Utah in 1902. He responded with a reminiscence when an article stated forty-niners had died on the Hastings Cutoff. *Salt Lake Tribune* "The Find on the Desert" Sunday 11 May 1902, p 31, col 4-7. Pierce reported that when they left home they were "well armed and equipped, every man had a saddle horse, a rifle and pistol, and our wagons were well loaded with supplies and tools."

[82]At least three Freyschlags taught at Sophia Sawyer's Fayetteville Female Seminary in 1847-1849. "a Gentleman (Drawing)...sister...A.[Hermina]

Washington County residents Isaac and Caroline Hale were the only married couple in the company. Caroline and the Freyschlag girls were the only women. Also in the company from Washington County were Enos Slover, James Blake, Rev. William (Horse) Wilson, William Goddard, John Ingram, John Powers, Wyatt F. Woodruff, Isaac Murphy, E. H. Avald (Evard), James and William Irvin (Irwin), diarist James Sawyer Crawford and cousin Andrew Alexander Crawford, John M. Wham, Robert Epperson, Thomas and son Aaron Tyner, William and Hiram Shores, Thomas Maxwell, John Newman, B. Whitley, Boly and John Hand, and Thomas Creamer. Brothers James and Matthew A. Divin were brothers-in-law of John Thompson Edmonson and A. E. Edmonson (Edmiston). All were there.

Benton County, in the northwest corner of Arkansas sent residents James M. Hage (Hoge) and William Hoge, father and son, James and Andrew Colwell (Colville), James Garvin, James A. Thomas, Calvin Hall Holmes and brother Henderson Phineas Holmes, J. W. Hastings, Cuthbert Stokes, and George Callahan.

From Huntsville, Madison County, Arkansas, east of Washington County, came Allen and Joseph Waits (Waite, White), and C.B. and George Sanders. Others from Madison County were T.J. Kimbrel, Hiram and son John A. Sumner (Summers), and James McKenney.

From Tennessee came David C. Jackson and Bur Blackburn.

Cherokee Nation citizens who joined included Martin Matthew Schrimpsher, Walt J. B. Smith, Oliver Wack Lipe (a white married to Cherokee Catherine Gunter), James S. Vann, R. L. Coleman, Daniel M. Gunter, J. C. McMaster, brothers George W. and Richard N. Keys, Josiah N. Rattlingourd, N.R.N. Harlin, Joseph H. Sturdevant, Robert Williams, William P. McKey, and white schoolteacher Sam Potter. The Cherokee traveled with relatives too. Daniel McCoy Gunter's uncle was Martin Matthew Scrimpsher, who was elected Commissary of the 1849 combined company. Oliver Wack Lipe was also an uncle of Daniel Gunter. Walter Smith was a first cousin of Scrimpsher's wife. Joseph A. Sturdivant was

---

Freyschlag (Music, Piano)...sister B.[Barbara] Freyschlag (French)." *Fort Smith Herald* 6 September 1848, vol 2, no 5, p 3. Brother Herman was reported to be Dancing Master. They commissioned Peter Marsalis Van Winkle in Washington County to build a spring wagon for them. Van Winkle was one of three wagon builders listed in the 1850 Census of Washington County, Arkansas.

married to Arie Beck.[83] No doubt many more in the 1849 company were
related. The Cherokee also took five unnamed slaves with them.[84]
The combined company will be referred to throughout this work as
the Evans/Cherokee Company.[85]

At the outset, home residence did not seem important, but as
time went on, the men in the company formed into groups, labeling
the members as "we from..." and "those from..." especially when
describing undesirable behavior.

While many of the company members were assembling on April 21
at The Grand Saline, Calvin H. Holmes had left home in Benton
County the day before.

> April 20, 1849   I left my Father's dwelling for the long and tedious
> trip to California.
> We traveled 25 miles and making our way westward through by way of
> the Grand Saline in the Cherokee Na. It was on Friday and on Saturday we
> traveled 20 miles. Saturday [Sunday?] 20 miles   to the Rondivous on
> Monday 6 miles.[86]

A Cherokee member of the party wrote on April 29 from the
"Grand Pririe On the Cherokee Perpetual Outlet."[87]

> The company met according to notification on the 21st, but did no
> business until the 23rd...[April 22 was Sunday]. The company are
> officered by very excellent men, though the Cherokees did not parti-
> cipate in the choice of the same--they not having arrived at the
> rendezvous until Monday. Lewis Evans of Evansville was elected Captain.
> Thomas Tyner of Washington co., 1st Lieut., P. Mankin 2nd do., Jas. S.
> Vann [Cherokee] Secretary, Martin Scrimpsher [Cherokee] Commissary.[88]

---

[83]Arie Beck's brothers John and Jeffrey went to California in 1850 on the
Cherokee Trail, and were among those who found gold in Ralston Creek in
Colorado, returning there in 1858. Arie's first cousin Nannie Buffington,
married Thomas Fox Taylor, captain of the 1850 Cherokee company from the Cache
la Poudre River in Colorado to California.

[84]*Cherokee Advocate* 7 May 1849 p 2. There is no further mention of the slaves
in any known diary or letter.

[85] Ibid. Called the "Washington County Gold Mining Company" it listed the
company members.

[86]"Calvin Hall Holmes Diary," California Society of Pioneers, San Francisco.
Brought to our attention by Paul Hershey.

[87]"the government sold them [Cherokee] a strip of land, 25 miles wide and 50
miles long, lying between the State of Missouri and the Osage Reservation, for
$500,000, to be deducted from the $5,000,000 which the government owed the
Cherokee Indians for their Georgia lands. This strip of land, which now
comprises Cherokee and Crawford counties [Kansas], was then known as the
Cherokee Neutral Lands." Nathaniel Thompson Allison *History of Cherokee
County, Kansas and Representative Citizens.* (Chicago: Biographical Publishing
Company 1904) pp 27-29.

[88]*Cherokee Advocate* 7 May 1849 signed "OO-CHA-LOO-TA." Grant Foreman and

No record exists of the method of selection of officers, which must have been difficult for a company so diverse. Josiah Gregg, experienced Santa Fe trader, explained the process:

> we...held a 'grand council,' at which the respective claims of the different 'aspirants to office' were considered, leaders selected, and a system of government agreed upon,--as is the...custom....One would have supposed that electioneering and 'party spirit' would [not be important] ...but so it was. Even in our little community we had our 'office-seekers' and their 'political adherents,' as earnest and as devoted as any...politicians....After a great deal of bickering and wordy warfare...all...found it expedient to decline, and a gentleman...was unanimously proclaimed 'Captain of the Caravan.'...the captain is expected to direct the order of travel during the day, and to designate the camping-ground at night; with many other functions.[89]

Much later on the emigrant trail, in times of dissension, it became clear that not all Washington County Emigrating Company members had been pleased with these elections.

The Cherokee approved the elected officers, and the rules and regulations, but maintained a separate division. Oo-Cha-Loo-Ta:

> The Cherokee portion of the company are thrown into a Division together, and that hereditary disposition of clanishness, derived from their ancestry is distinctly shown now.
> They are determined to "stick together" through weal or woe.

Non-Cherokee diarist Crawford was pleased with his election:

> I have benn appointed to the honorable office of Waggon master of the 2nd division of the Company; the Company is laid off into 4 Divisions; And I have all the Cherokees in my division, they are all verry Smart men.[90]

Non-Cherokee diarist Holmes reported:

> our officers was elected as follows in this order: Lewis Eavins Cap Thomas Lyon [Tyner] 1st Lou   Peter Mankins 2nd Lou   Joseph Waits 1st Sarg   George Worth[North] 2nd Sarg   S B M [Squire Marrs] 3rd Sarg   Js Crawford 1st____ [division wagon master]   Jno Clinn [Cline] 2nd____   Js McCullock 3rd____   Henry Fryschlag 4th__.[91]

---

others have attempted to identify this person without success. There is a Cherokee family named "Oolootsa", whose first member is given as Oo-loo-tsa, of the Holly clan, by Starr...*Cherokee*...p 366. In-laws of the Oolootsa extended family who were also members of the "Washington County Emigrating Company" were Oliver Wack Lipe and Martin Matthew Scrimsher; a direct descendant was Joseph Sturdivant of the company.

[89]Gregg...*Commerce*...pp 44-45.

[90]Crawford letter to his wife from Grand Prairie, Cherokee Nation, April 29, 1849.

[91]Holmes diary entry.

The Company organization was based upon four divisions of ten wagons each, and two or more messes (usually four men who cooked and ate together) per wagon, much like the military. More than a few had served in the recent Mexican War and were accustomed to the necessity of such structure.[92] McArthur stated: "The articles of association were modeled after a military-type organization."[93]

Gregg outlined the process of election:

> The [group leaders] are first notified by 'proclamation' to furnish a list of their men and wagons. The latter are generally apportioned into four 'divisions,' particularly when the company is large....To each of these divisions, a 'lieutenant' was appointed, whose duty it was to inspect every ravine and creek on the route, select the best crossings, and superintend...the 'forming' of each encampment....There is nothing so much dreaded by inexperienced travellers as the ordeal of guard duty...no one has the smallest chance of evading [it]...The usual number of watches is eight...the captain usually appoints eight 'sergeants of the guard,' each ...takes an equal portion of men under his command.[94]

James Vann, newly elected Secretary of the combined company of 1849 goldseekers, had recently given up the editorship of the *Cherokee Advocate*. His departure was noted on April 30:

> Mr. Jas. S. Vann, the former Editor of this paper took his leave...for the Gold regions in california. We understand that on the 24th or 25th inst., the company that rendezvoused at Grand River, set out for the far west with about forty waggons in company and the rise of [more than] one hundred persons...
>
> Our fellow citizens and friends have been droping off for California, for some eight or ten days--the last of them from about this section started on last Monday [April 23] casting long and wistful looks upon the land of their homes and nativity.
>
> They all have the prayers and good wishes of their friends and relations for their peace and prosperity, hoping that a kind and beneficient Deity will preserve them from the pestilence that walketh in darkness.

Many of the Cherokee and whites were deeply religious. Concern for the bodies and souls of those leaving the frontier was manifested in several different ways by those who remained behind.

Reverend H. C. Thweatt on March 18 in Washington, Arkansas, delivered a sermon that was printed on the front page of the newspaper.

---

[92]James Sawyer Crawford, 1849 diarist, was a Captain, 2nd Battalion, 32nd Department, Washington County Militia, State of Arkansas, as early as 1842.
[93]McArthur...*Arkansas*...pp 41-42.
[94]Gregg...*Commerce*...pp 45-47.

Bannered across the top in large letters was:

"A Motto, selected from Psalm XiX, verse 127,
"I love thy commandments above gold, yea,
above fine gold."[95]

The intent of this lengthy sermon, printed verbatim, was obvious--
to keep the good citizens of northwest Arkansas from straying away
from their religious upbringing while on the emigrating trail and
after arrival in California.

This deep concern for the moral life of the travelers was
also expressed in a letter from W. D. Crawford to his emigrant
brother James Sawyer Crawford and cousin Andrew Alexander Crawford
some time after they left Arkansas:

> Recollect, Gold is corrupting, but "if riches increase set not your
> heart on them." The eye of God is upon you--let religion be the first
> and great concern of your life, keep constantly in view your
> accountability to God and the day of final retribution, let not the Gold
> of Ophir, Californa...allure you from the path of piety.[96]

Cumberland Presbyterian Churches, which many of the Cane Hill
and Evansville emigrants helped to establish, prayed for them.

> In April, 1849, special concern was expressed for the Washington County
> Emigrating Company, which must have been composed of persons who were
> moving farther west:[97]
> Whereas on the prayers of this Presbytery being earnestly solicited
> by bro. John Pollard in behalf of the...Company therefore, Resolved that
> this Presbytery will ask the Divine blessing upon all the Members during
> their absence, and that the Divine protection be thrown around Them, To
> preserve them from the danger to which they May be exposed and especialy
> from the Snares and temptation of the great adversary of human
> happiness.[98]

Diarist Crawford recorded it as the Washington County
Emigrating Company, though the *Cherokee Advocate* called the
company The Washington County Gold Mining Company.[99] Members were
listed and recorded after the Company crossed the Verdigris River,

---

[95]*Washington Telegraph*, Washington, Arkansas 4 April 1849, vol 9, no 14.
.[96]W. D. Crawford letter to A.A. and James Crawford from "State of Arkansas
County of Washington, 25th, July A.D. 1849.
[97]There apparently were no records in the Presbytery stating that these were
goldseekers. The Presbyterians of the time surely knew, but refrained from
stating it in records.
[98]Thomas H. Campbell, ed. *Arkansas Cumberland Presbyterians* (Memphis: Arkansas
Synod of the Cumberland Presbyterian Church 1985) pp 63-64.
[99]*Cherokee Advocate* 7 May 1849 listed company members.

five days after the election on the Grand (Neosho) River. Letters
were written home on April 29 noting the final count of everything
in the train. Crawford wrote:

> we have in our company 128 [written over 128 is 129] persons 40 waggons
> 304 oxen 41 mules 65 Horses and 31 Cows, making in all the Stock 441
> head.[100]

Diarist Holmes added the total net worth:

> Embarked in this train 128 souls 3 of those women 2 Boys and 4 Nigroes
> 304 Oxen 31 Cows 65 Horses 41 Mules 20 [40] Waggon and Suposed to be
> worth including what cash is in Company Twenty Thousand dollars.[101]

Letter writer Pyeatt remarked: "our Company has 40 wagons, and 123
men able to bair armes, 3 weman, 2 boys and one old man."[102]

If the numbers of emigrants are correct, there are two names
missing from the *Cherokee Advocate* list. One is Williamson. An A.
Williamson from Fayetteville was already on a journey. He indicated in a letter written later from the junction of the new
Evans/Cherokee Trail and the Santa Fe Trail:

> I left Fayetteville, Ark., on the 1st of April, and am acquainted with
> many of Mr. Evans' company, and am right glad to perceive that they
> succeeded so well in traversing a new and hitherto unthought of route
> from the confines of their state. It is my wish to overtake them before
> they enter the Mountain gorges.[103]

If or when he joined the Evans/Cherokee Company is unknown, but it
is clear that he was not one of the original 129 members.

Another possible member was James Bailey.[104] Though not on the
original list, family research concluded that:

> James Bailey came to California for the first time in 1849 with a wagon
> train which left Fayetteville, Arkansas, on April 20, 1849 with Captain
> Lewis Evans in charge....They arrived in California in October, 1849.
> James Bailey went to Placerville [the family appears in the] 1850
> census...Madison County, Arkansas, near Huntsville.[105]

---

[100]Crawford letter, Grand Prairie, April 29, 1849.

[101]Holmes' original flurry of writing stopped, resuming only when his portion
of the wagon train turned off at Lassen Meadows on the "Cherokee Cutoff"
(Applegate and Lassen Trails). Calvin arrived in California on November 8,
1849 having been caught by the snows in the Sierra Nevada.

[102]John Rankin Pyeatt letter to wife Elizabeth from "Indian territory Aprile
the 28 1849."

[103]*Daily Missouri Republican* 4 July 1849.

[104]There is a James Blake on the original roster.

[105]Information supplied by Roseanne Anderson of Spokane, Washington.

The 1850 census of Washington County, Arkansas shows that many of the wives listed their departed husbands and sons as being home.

Of the forty wagons of the combined company, one of the largest belonged to John Rankin Pyeatt. Pyeatt was a blacksmith who carried in his large wagon all of the tools and necessary equipment to perform "smithing," which he did at Fort Mann, Pueblo, Green River, Fort Bridger and Salt Lake.

One of Pyeatt's wagons was outfitted with what Sawyer called a "roadomiter," used to calculate mileage. No company diarist or letterwriter bothered to describe this machine. Perhaps it was like one described by another 1849 traveler, William Thomas:

> It is simple in its construction consisting of three small cogwheels-attached to the back part of the waggon bed so that the hub of the waggon wheel operates upon the first coggwheel, and that upon the second and so on loosing motion until the last wheel passes once round whilst the waggon turns often enough round to make a mile-it is easily constructed and measures as accurately as could be done by a [surveyor's] chain.[106]

In subsequent years and on later maps, the segments of this Evans/Cherokee trail bore several different names--none of which were used by the company of travelers in 1849. In Kansas, Colorado and Wyoming, "Cherokee Trail" appeared on early maps. In Kansas, "Cherokee Trail," "Ft. Smith to California" and "Fayetteville, Arkansas to California" were also recorded on maps. In Wyoming, "Cherokee Trail," "Cherokee Road," "Evans Trace" and "Evans Road" were recorded, beginning with Stansbury, Gunnison, and Carrington in 1850. In Colorado, "Cherokee Trail" first appeared in 1858.

---

[106]Unpublished diary of Dr. Wm. Thomas 1849. Merrill Mattes Library, National Trails Center, Independence, Missouri.

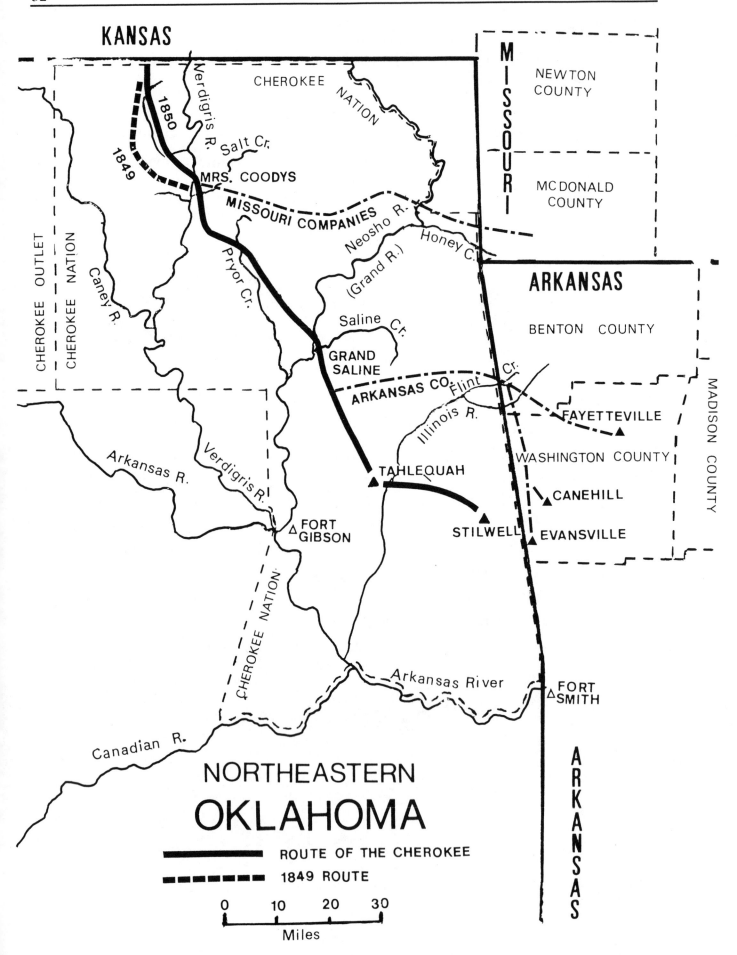

KANSAS

MISSOURI

NEWTON COUNTY

MCDONALD COUNTY

CHEROKEE NATION

1850

1849

Verdigris R.

Salt Cr.

MRS. COODYS

MISSOURI COMPANIES

Neosho R.

(Grand R.)

Honey C.

ARKANSAS

BENTON COUNTY

CHEROKEE OUTLET

CHEROKEE NATION

Caney R.

Pryor Cr.

Saline Cr.

GRAND SALINE

ARKANSAS CO.

Flint Cr.

Illinois R.

FAYETTEVILLE

WASHINGTON COUNTY

MADISON COUNTY

Arkansas R.

Verdigris R.

TAHLEQUAH

CANEHILL

△ FORT GIBSON

STILWELL

EVANSVILLE

CHEROKEE NATION

Arkansas River

FORT △ SMITH

Canadian R.

ARKANSAS

NORTHEASTERN
OKLAHOMA

――――― ROUTE OF THE CHEROKEE

- - - - 1849 ROUTE

0   10   20   30

Miles

Chapter 4: GRAND SALINE, Cherokee Nation, TO TURKEY CREEK, Junction of THE SANTA FE TRAIL

> Emigrating parties leaving Arkansas...would do well to follow this trail of Captain Evans'. It is a good and plain way to the old Santa Fe trace.
>
> --Captain Abraham Buford

The James Sawyer Crawford diary and letters are published here for the first time.[107] The diary begins:

> "Memos___ _____ ____[illegible] of the distance
> from Fayetteville Arkansas to
> California as traveled by the
> Washington County Emmigrating Company
> From Fayetteville to Rendezvous 6 miles
> west of Grand Island on Grand river."

> **"April 21 [1849, Saturday]   85 [miles from home]"**

Crawford began keeping days and dates, naming camps and campsites. The names reflected events, conditions, and observations or, as in Utah, were copied from a specific map. Crawford's recorded daily mileages, according to modern maps, are accurate throughout this journey from Arkansas to California. Mileages could well have come from measurements by Pyeatt's "Roadomiter." In the text Crawford's notations are in bold print, followed by a line giving the present location. Crawford:

> **"Tuesday 24 [April]   Prior's Creek[108]   15 [miles]"**
> [north of present Pryor, Mayes Co., Oklahoma]

Nathaniel Pryor, for whom the creek was named, was a member of the Lewis and Clark "Corps of Discovery" in 1804-6.[109] He was subsequently made an agent for the Osage Indians.

Crawford wrote: "John Whams waggon over set on Priors Creek...no injury."[110]

---

[107]James Sawyer Crawford's brother William and cousin Andrew Alexander Crawford were also on the journey.

[108]Approximately 18 miles east of Claremore. "[Nathaniel] Pryor died...in 1831 and was buried on the place where we moved." Statement of George W. Mayes. Harold Keith, *Chronicles of Oklahoma* vol 24 (October 24, 1991} pp 40-54.

[109]In Montana, a Pryor(s) creek, also named for Nathaniel Pryor, enters the Yellowstone River below the Clarks Fork near Huntley. Nearby Pryor Mountains, Pryor Cave, and the town of Pryor are all named for him. Personal communication with Dave Walter, Montana Historical Society, Helena.

[110]Crawford letter, Grand Prairie, April 29, 1849. Wham would get news that

Oo-Cha-Loo-Ta reported from the Grand Prairie:

The company left the rendezvous [The Grand Saline] on the 24th. The
first days travel was (owing to the heavy fall of rain a few days
previous,) very difficult.
    The company had quite a foretaste of what they will have to encounter
and overcome before they arrive at the auriferous mountains of the
"Sawyer Navada." Boging down, and prising out of waggons, was the
business of the first day. Since, we have traveled and gotten along with
less miring down, making short drives--which we did to enable a wagon to
join the caravan which did not arrive at the rendezvous in time to leave
with the company.[111]

Crawford:

"wednesday 25 [April]   Corall   5 [miles]"
[southwest of Adair, Mayes Co., Oklahoma]

They found it necessary to corral the wagons and animals at night.
Josiah Gregg described this system for "corraling" and camping at
night:

Upon encamping the wagons are formed into a 'hollow square'(each
division to a side), constituting at once an enclosure (or corral) for
the animals when needed, and a fortification against the Indians. Not to
embarrass this cattle-pen, the camp fires are all lighted outside of the
wagons.[112]

Crawford wrote home: "we have but little difficulty...as yet
except that we are Some times troubled in finding our oxen."[113] The
problem of oxen running off during the night plagued the company
for much of the journey to California.

The company traveled northwest. Crawford:

"thursday 26 [April]   Divide   15 [miles]"
[Pryor Creek/Verdigris River divide northwest of
Chelsea, Rogers Co., Oklahoma]

In his first letter home, John Rankin Pyeatt's strong
opinions emerged. He was a pious, hard-working, strong-willed man,
whose character did not change. Not on the trail or afterward. He
and most of the company considered they were on a dangerous
journey, which meant they must be vigilant and unwavering.

Pyeatt often mentioned details not found in other accounts,

---

his infant son could almost stand alone as of July 3, 1849.
[111]*Cherokee Advocate* 7 May 1849.
[112]Gregg ...*Commerce*...p 43.
[113]Crawford Letter, Grand Prairie, April 29, 1849.

which makes his observations all the more important. Obviously he
kept a daily record of some kind: his geographic order is too
precise for recollection alone. Not wanting to waste even the
smallest of spaces, Pyeatt wrote, mostly phonetically, from one
edge of the paper to the other, mostly without punctuation or room
between sentences. The text is presented exactly as he wrote, with
only the occasional clarification in brackets. Pyeatt:

> Dier companion...we have lost A.B. Crawford's mair. we lost hir the
> second nite after we laf the rendiveus   she is stolen no dout by the
> cherikees   we will rite to [Lewis] Ross at the grand Salien to git hir
> if he can and rite to James Crawford and he can go and get her if he
> chuses.[114]...James Carnahan mair got away from him [this] nite   run
> back som twelve miles to our camp the night befor whar some of our
> company met hir and cot hir just before James and Porter voetook
> [overtook] hir and brot hir back which took them till night to overtak
> the company again.[115]

Crawford:

"Friday 27 [April]   Verdigris   10 [miles]"
[west of New Alluwe, Nowata Co., Oklahoma]

Crawford wrote in his Sunday letter, "we got to the Virdigree
[River] last night, and it took us all this day [Saturday] till
late this evening to dig down the Banks and cross over."[116] Pyeatt
wrote of the task, "we had a good [d]eal of work to do on the
bankes of the Virdigre, all so on some of the bra[n]ches in the
parairy."[117]

Evidence from the Crawford diary and the two 1850 diaries
(Quesenbury and Mitchell) indicates the Evans/Cherokee Company
traveled northwest from Pryor, not straight west to Claremore as
indicated by Foreman.[118]

---

[114]James Crawford, cousin of diarist James Sawyer Crawford, stayed behind in
Arkansas. This James Crawford was a distiller and resident in Cane Hill.
"Survey notes" *Flashback*, Washington County Historical Society (February 1975)
p 5 map; and (May 1975) p 21.

[115]Pyeatt letter, Indian territory, April 28, 1849. This is the first of ten
Pyeatt letters.

[116]Crawford letter, Grand Prairie, April 29, 1849.

[117]Pyeatt letter, Indian Territory, April 28, 1849. In the 1850 census of
Washington County, Arkansas, (he was absent) he was recorded as 44 years old,
the father of four: Andrew-17 (who went on the trip with him and died on the
return sea journey); Catherine-10; Henry-8; and Marget-2. Wife Elizabeth-41.

[118]Grant Foreman wrote about this segment of trail "Their route[so] far...was
substantially that traveled by the Osages...to Chouteau's Trading Post at the
mouth of the Verdigris River....At the edge of the present Claremore, Rogers

Crawford:

"Saturday 28 [April]   Red-bud Creek[119]   6 [miles]"
[northeast of Watova, Nowata Co., Oklahoma]

Pyeatt's letter:

Indian Territory Aprile the 28 1849
we...will remain hear till monday morning....we have now got into hier
and drier paiary and forom the best information we can get will
contineue to the montains.

Crawford wrote, describing the grand prairie:

It will bee two weeks tuesday since we left home & we have not eatin but
one ham and two thirds of one midling of our Beacon...Eprosons;[120]
...Their has not been any game killed on our rout yet Except Some
Turkeys, (and one Wolf By Samuel Latty.)...
We are in a world of Prairie; you may See here as far as your eyes
will let you look. We have incamped in a butifull part of the Prairie.
...the Prairies are verry good and dry....Our Sleeping is first rate,
our bed is plenty Soft.

Crawford: "our teem gits on as well as or better than any
other." Pyeatt: "aur teams stand it very will yet most of them
mend [strengthen]."

Crawford described their meeting with the Osages:

The Osages tell us that we will have to fight the Pawnies, and
Camanchees before we git Through the mountain, But I think it is
uncertain; we may have to fight them, But I hardly think So....
the osage Indians are comeing to our camp every night, they are quite
filthy, but verry sivil; they made a big dance last night for the
amusement of our company. I know you would laugh to See them dance and
hear them Sing; I think they could have been heard Sing[ing] last night
3 miles; but I could not note the tune.

Pyeatt too described the Osages:

the boys was very much diverted last night [by] a company of Ocages that
camped cloast to us last night and had a dance   that tickeled them
very much.

Crawford: "this is Saturday after Sundown; If I live I will
write Some more in the morning." Sunday, April 29, obviously still

County, Oklahoma, in the Cherokee Nation, was the [trading post] home of
Elijah Hicks, a prominent Cherokee....Hick's home...was a noted stopping place
and landmark for the California emigrants. Hicks is buried here." Foreman...
Marcy...p 69.

[119]A tree, Eastern Redbud (*Cercis canadensis* L.) which is "typical of
bottomlands and stream borders;" maps show the company is near the western
limit of the tree's range. Richard J. Preston *North American Trees* (Ames,
Iowa: The Iowa State College Press 1948) p 273. When diarist William
Quesenbury copied these campsites in 1850 he wrote "Red-_buck_ Creek."

[120]Robert Epperson was a "mess" mate of Crawford's.

alive, he wrote, as the Company lay by: "This is sunday morning, and we are yet well and harty."

Pyeatt described the health of his group with more detail:

James Carnahan has had the dieree and was very sick a day or two but has got well and A B Crawford had the bowel complaint and has got well...som others of the compeny have had it...but all have got well... the boys ar all in fine sperits   S B Mars is giting along very well he is harty and mending   he thinks he will stan the [trip] very well.

Crawford lamented, missing his wife's skills:

I have worn one hole in my Pants; and I must git Some Buck Skin and Patch them...John Wham and Thompson Edmiston are gone Back to the River this morning for an ox that they left there last night ...Some of our oxen has not been Seen this morning; Their appears to bee a good deel of grumbling in camps this morning; Some wants to go on, and others wants to not travil on the Sabbath: I am one of the last number.

This was the first of many disagreements about how to spend Sunday on the trail. Virtually every company on every trail had to face this issue sooner or later.

The Company even had Sunday visitors on the prairie-- Cherokee, and from nearby. Crawford wrote "This day we have been visited by the widow Coody[121] and six of her girles."

Crawford wrote on about a prairie phenomenon--wind:

The wind has risen so high to day that we cannot Keep our tint[122] up and I have to Write in our Waggon, and it shakes so bad that I can hardly write. Tell Rachel[123] that Andrew[124] is well and would be glad to write to her but the wind blows so hard that it is almost imposible to Write ...he intends to take good care of himself and Bring Some gold from California.

---

[121]Coody is an important name in Cherokee history. A place which would be used by the 1850 emigration was the crossing of the Verdigris River at "Coody's Bluff," east of present Nowata, Oklahoma. Starr's *Old Cherokee Families* shows only one Coody, Daniel Ross Coody, had 6 girls possibly living in 1849; Alice, Mary, Sarah, Martha, Margaret and Letitia. Daniel Coody's sister Flora married Gen. Daniel Henry Rucker. An uncle was Chief John Ross. Lewis Ross, an uncle, leased the saltworks at the Grand Saline. Another uncle by marriage was Elijah Hicks; and yet another uncle was Jonathan Mulkey, forty-niner.
Starr...*Cherokee*...pp 410, 413.
[122]Gregg...*Commerce*...p 62. "Tents are so rare...In time of rain the traveller resorts to his wagon, which affords a far more secure shelter than a tent; for if the latter is not beaten down by the storms which so often accompany rain upon the prairies, the ground underneath is at least apt to be flooded."
[123]Andrew Alexander Crawford's wife, Rachel Tinnin Crawford.
[124]Andrew Alexander Crawford, James Sawyer Crawford's cousin.

Crawford closed his letter on a rather sad and lonesome note:

I have nothing to write of importance...I do not think that it is likely that I will have a chance to write to you soon again...
    P.S. When I think of you and the Children, I want to see you all so bad that there is no since in it. Kiss Emily and Wilson[125] once a week for me. tell them all if god Spares us all that we will see each other once more...may god Bless you and protect you all: so farewell.
                                                    James S.Crawford.

Pyeatt's closings were always softer than his usual remarks:

nothing more at presant but remain your affactionate companion till deth
                John R Pyeatt[126]

Written across the front of Crawford's envelope was: "By the Politeness of Samuel Latty." Though he did not make the trip in 1849, Samuel and relatives Jack and A. Latta all made the trip in 1850. Latta saw to the delivery of all three of the Company letters: one to Harriet Crawford in Washington County, one to Elizabeth Pyeatt in Boonsboro, and one to the *Cherokee Advocate,* which printed the first general information on the whereabouts of the company in the newspaper on May 7, 1849.

                            Grand Pririe, *On the Cherokee "Perpetual Outlet,"*
                                                    April 29th,1849.

MR. EDITOR:
    For the gratification of those citizens of your country who have friends in this company, on their way to the land of "Gold" I have snatched a few moments from *camp* duties to announce the safe progress for ninty miles from Tahlequah...
    We are all together now--and from the appearance of the face of the country, and from reports we have had since we arrived here, of our contemplated route, the "yellow fever" *with some* of the company having broken out afresh, and the glittering fortunes which they are determined to accumulate, are, even now snuffed upon the western Prairies.--The Laws which regulate, and by which the company are governed are few, but good--though susceptable of improvement...
    Although they [Cherokee] have left their country for a few months, nevertheless the fire of patriotic love burns with continued intensity of fervour for the future wellfare, progress and onward destiny of their country.
                                                    OO-CHA-LOO-TA

Crawford's diary entries continued as the company moved away from their camp six miles west of the Verdigris River crossing. After crossing the river, the company followed along the divide or

---

[125]Two of James Sawyer Crawford's children.
[126]Pyeatt letter, April 28, 1849.

highlands in a northwesterly direction between the (Big) Caney
River on the west and waters of the Verdigris River on the east.

On this trail from Oklahoma through Kansas to the Santa Fe
Trail, all travel was on the ridges between waterways where
possible. In addition, this company had been warned they would
have to face Comanches and Pawnees before they reached the Rocky
Mountains. Traveling the ridges gave them the ability to see long
distances, a defense strategy perhaps born of Cherokee experience.
Finding wood, water, and grass for camping off the ridges was the
responsibility of the company leadership.

Finally the Company was able to make the planned twenty miles
per day. These miles were north across the rolling hills of
Oklahoma. Crawford:

> **"Monday 30 [April 1849]   7th Camp   20 [miles]"**
> [Mormon Creek,[127] west of Delaware, Nowata Co., Oklahoma]

> **"May Tuesday 1   8 Camp   20 [miles]"**
> [south of Wann, Nowata Co., Oklahoma]

On May 2, 1849, the Company crossed the boundary line between
the present states of Oklahoma and Kansas. Crawford:

> **"Wednesday 2 [May]   Pond Camp   20 [miles]"**
> [near Tyro, Montgomery Co., Kansas]

> **"thursday 3 [May]   Fish Camp   20 [miles]"**
> [possibly Otter Creek, east of Sedan,
> Chautauqua Co., Kansas]

The campsite name suggests that the Company members were
successful in catching fish--or at least in seeing them. During
the next short mileage day, the Company passed over several
creeks, some intermittent, which are tributaries of North Caney
Creek. Crawford:

> **"friday 4 [May]   Rabbit Camp[128]   7 [miles]"**
> [NE of Sedan, Chautauqua Co., Kansas]

---

[127] In 1853 a party of Mormons from Texas wintered on this creek.

[128] Most likely Eastern Cottontail *Sylvilagus floridanus* Ralph S. Palmer *The Mammal Guide Mammals of North America north of Mexico* (Garden City, N.Y.: Doubleday & Company Inc. 1954) p 279. William Caire, Jack D. Tyler, Bryan P. Glass, Michael A. Mares *Mammals of Oklahoma* (Norman, Okla.: Univ. of Oklahoma Press 1989 "[it] is the most common cottontail in Oklahoma." p 163 and has occurred in some northern counties p 164.

The first surveyors of Chautauqua County, Kansas, recorded
wagon roads and cattle trails on and crossing section lines
throughout the county. In general, these recorded trails all ran
southeast to northwest in four areas of the county. The line
approximating the Evans/Cherokee Trail is best recorded near the
north county line on both sides of South Salt Creek.[129]

Crawford:

"saturday 5 [May]   Elm Branch   12 [miles]"
[SE of Moline, Elk Co., Kansas]

The Company stopped on Sunday, May 6. Crawford wrote only:

"Perseverance"

Was this a commentary on strain within the company, or the topic
of a Sunday sermon? At least one minister was in the traveling
group--Reverend William (Horse) Wilson, who gave the blessing on
the company's departure from the Grand Saline.

On Monday they were off again toward the northwest. Crawford:

"Monday 7 [May]   Spring Creek   12 [miles]"
[Mound Creek, NW of Moline, Elk Co., Kansas]

Being the first wagon company through on this route
guaranteed the Evans/Cherokee company excellent grass, something
they had counted on finding.

> This country was formerly known among the overland travelers to Oregon
> and California as the "Tall Grass." The blade is coarse and rough at its
> edges, like the grass of Illinois. It ordinarily attains the height of
> three feet, toward the close of summer...but when the land is moist, it
> grows more luxuriant...said to become 'tall enough to hide from view
> horse and rider.'[130]

Crawford:

"Tuesday 8 [May]   Arkansas Creek   20 [miles]"
[west of Beaumont, Butler Co., Kansas]

_____

[129]Original surveys and notes, Clerk's Office, Chautauqua County Courthouse,
Sedan, Kansas. The surveyors also made notes on the terrain, and in the parts
of the county where these wagon roads and cattle trails were marked,
descriptions include "Gently rolling; land gently undulating; land rolling;
rolling prairie." The absence of notation in the southeast part of the county
can be laid to the surveys not being completed until 1878 in that area.
Resurveys were mandated by the movement of the boundary line of the ODR (Osage
Diminished Reserves) further south, which also changed the southern boundary
of both Chautauqua County and the state of Kansas.
[130]John C. Van Tramp, *Life in the West Prairie and Rocky Mountain Adventures*
(Columbus, Ohio: Segner & Condit 1867) p 623.

The Company members recognized they were camped on a tributary of the Arkansas River, today's Hickory Creek.

Crawford:

"May Wednesday 9   Cottonwood fork Arkansas 20 [miles]"
[present El Dorado, Butler Co., Kansas]

This is the Walnut River. An 1881 history of Butler County described the river. "[it] rises in the SE part of Chase County and runs a little west of south...into the Arkansas River. It is about two hundred miles in length."[131] Another early writer noted fire as the reason for the absence of trees (and hence wood) in this area which is now treed: "[if] The annual, Autumnal, devastating fires [are] stopped, the indigenous forest growth will immediately come forth."[132]

The 1849 campsite was at the traditional Osage crossing of the Walnut, just south of the town of El Dorado.[133] In 1857 a company of settlers led by Samuel Charles Stewart chose a townsite based on the Cherokee Trail crossing at the Walnut River. Calling it the Cherokee Trail, Augusta Stewart recorded traffic throughout the 1850s and 1860s.[134]

From this camp to the next camp, the 1849 Evans/Cherokee Company track was the same as the Osage trail.

> in the westward wandering [Osages] wore a well defined trail across Butler County....It was used extensively and prior to 1821 [opening of the Santa Fe Trail] it was the route from St. Louis to the Rockies.[135]

Crawford:

"thursday 10 [May]   Wild Cat Creek   20 [miles]"
[near present Potwin, Butler Co., Kansas]

---

[131]C.H. Kurtz, "Butler County Its Settlement, Development, Resources & Wealth" *Southern Kansas Gazette* 6 January 1881 pp 26-27. "Walnut River... abundance of good timber....The supply of timber...on the Walnut River...Walnut, Sycamore, Oak, Hackberry, Cottonwood. If the fires were kept out of the area...timber would increase rapidly. Of the wild fruits there are plums, grapes, gooseberries, etc. in abundance..."

[132]Van Tramp...*Prairie*...p 279.

[133]According to a volunteer at the Butler County Museum, that crossing was approximately two miles south and west of the present El Dorado and was worn into rock.

[134]Journals of Augusta Stewart. Private.

[135]Jessie Perry Stratford & Lawrence P. Klintworth, *The Kingdom of Butler 1857-1970: A History of Butler County, Kansas* (El Dorado, Kans.: Butler County Historical Society 1970) pp 8, 9.

The present Whitewater River is fordable only at this spot, which Kansans would later call the "ford on the old California Trail,"[136] or the "California Crossing in Plum Grove Township"[137]

"The Whitewater rises in the NW part of [Butler] county and flows southeasterly until its junction with the Walnut River."[138]

The 1849 Company's first encounter with the buffalo droppings indicated the sometime presence of the animals, even though they were not immediately seen. <u>Crawford</u>:

"friday 11 [May]   Bois de Vache[139]   **18 [miles]"**
[Emma Creek east of present Walton, Harvey Co., Kansas]

O.W. Lipe, with the Cherokee, wrote a letter home:

we make use of Buffalo chips....we were obbliged to use such fuel two nights before we reach the Santa Fe road.[140]

The use of the chips for fuel was noted in commercial, civilian, and military journals on all prairie trails where wood was not available. For example, in the valley of the Platte River (then also known as the Nebraska River) in 1845, with the Stephen Kearny Expedition to the South Pass, Lieutenant J. Henry Carleton wrote:

Not a stick of wood can be seen within miles of us, and for the first time our fires are built and suppers cooked with *bois de vache*, or "buffalo chips," as the soldiers call this species of fuel. We find it in great quantities...and a dozen men with horse-blankets soon collect a sufficient quantity for the use of a company for the night.[141]

Carleton went on, explaining the process of use:

The men dig holes in the earth a foot deep...the same in width, and four or five feet long, with another little hole entering it near the bottom to let in a draught. A little dry grass is then placed in it and set on fire, when the pit is filled full of chips that soon get to burning with a slight flame, and uniform heat like peat. Camp kettles... are then set on top--while tin plates with thin cakes upon them are placed around....

---

[136]Vol P. Mooney, *History of Butler County* (Lawrence, Kans.: Standard Publ. Co. 1916) p 187.

[137]Not to be confused with modern Wildcat Branch of the Whitewater, a more westerly stream.

[138]Kurtz "...Butler..." p 27.

[139]Location: 38°09.22N latitude, 97°12.95W longitude.

[140]O.W. Lipe letter to the *Cherokee Advocate* from "Grand Pararie May 27th, 1849" in *Cherokee Advocate* 30 July 1849.

[141]Lieutenant J. Henry Carleton *The Prairie Logbooks* "A Dragoon Campaign to the Rocky Mountains in 1845" Chapter 7, p 209.

There is nothing unpleasant in having fires made, or a meal cooked with such a material;--and the odour arising from it while burning, is far from being disagreeable.[142]

Diarist William Quesenbury in 1850 wrote: "Found piles of buffalo chips that Evans' Company had gathered last year.[143]

Crawford:

"Saturday 12 [May]   Wolf Camp[144]   20 [miles]"
[one mile south of present Goessel, near
the Marion/McPherson Cos. line]

Six miles south of Goessel, in Marion County, Kansas, a monument commemorates the proximity of the Cherokee Trail.

The Evans/Cherokee Company passed through the northeast corner of Harvey County and the southwest corner of Marion County. In this area the trail was noted on later survey maps as the "Fort Smith, Arkansas, to California Road."[145]

Crawford:

**"Sunday 13 [May]   Little Turkey Creek forks of the road
15 [miles]"**
[Running Turkey Creek, and junction with the Santa Fe Trail,
8 miles east of McPherson, McPherson Co., Kansas]

The Evans/Cherokee Company had just completed the first-ever wagon traverse of the road, from Arkansas through Indian Territory and future Kansas to McPherson. At least one surveyor noted the "Cherokee Trail" in Sections 1, 2, and 12, R1W, T21S, Meridian Township, McPherson County.[146]

The road also survived in the memories of some Kansans. In 1893, in an address before the Kansas State Historical Society, J. R. Mead gave a verbal accounting of the wagon road:

What is known as the "old California trail" passed through Fayetteville, Ark., thence across the corner of the Indian territory, entering Kansas...[in] Chautauqua county; thence northwest between the Caney rivers across the corner of Elk [county], entering Butler [county] near its southeast corner, reaching the Walnut [River] at the Osage crossing

---

[142]Ibid. p 210.
[143]See Quesenbury diary entry of May 15, 1850.
[144]Since no further information is given, this could be either *Canis lupus* Linnaeus (Gray Wolf) or *Canis latrans* Say (Prairie Wolf/Coyote). Both ranged on the plains. Caire et al...*Mammals*...pp 278-81.
[145]Sondra Van Meter, Marion County Historical Society *Marion County, Kansas Past and Present* (Hillsboro, Kans.: M.B. Publishing House 1972) p 21.
[146]Maps--Linn Peterson, McPherson, Kansas.

near El Dorado; thence northwest to the Whitewater crossing below Plum Grove, and pursuing the same course to the old Santa Fe trail at Turkey creek, in McPherson county. This trail bore evidence of heavy wagon travel in former times. The writer passed over it in 1863. It was then abandoned.[147]

The Cherokee Trail in Kansas was closed in 1861 during the Civil War.[148] Another author noted:

In the days of the California emigration a road, long visible after it ceased to be used, was that coming from Fayetteville, Ark., northwestward, and joining the Santa Fe trail at Turkey creek, in McPherson county.[149]

A trail identified as "California Trail from Fayetteville, Ark." appears on a map in Kansas Historical Collections.[150] By 1855 there would be business activity and a post office near the junction of the Cherokee and Santa Fe trails.[151]

There had been no report home from the 1849 Evans/Cherokee Company since receipt of the letters written on April 29. However, the *Cherokee Advocate,* in the absence of fact, on May 14 reported a rumor about possible attack of the Company by hostile Indians:

The Osages and Camanches are going to join together to intercept, attack, and rob the Fayetteville mining company that lately rendezvous'd at the Grand Saline, and are now on their way to California....Mr. Charles Coody[152] of Saline District, has gone on to overtake the Company to give them information of the intentions of said Indians.

The company was just beginning to travel along the Santa Fe Trail. No correspondence mentions that Mr. Coody overtook them. Two weeks later, on May 28, the *Advocate* reported again:

---

[147]Hon. J. R. Mead, Wichita "Trails in Southern Kansas." Annual Meeting Notes, January 17, 1893, pp 90-91.

[148]Mooney...*Butler*...p 69. A local volunteer militia group in November 1861 saw "large train of [stolen] government wagons...from the West and headed toward Arkansas on the Old California Trail....all intercourse in that direction was prohibited at the time....we...overhauled them [captured and] escorted them to Fort Lincoln."

[149]Noble L. Prentis, *History of Kansas* (Winfield, Kans.: E.P. Greer 1899) p 30.

[150]Transactions of the Kansas State Historical Society 1905-06. Kansas Historical Collections, vol 9, 1905-06. An Explanation of the "Map Showing Indian Villages, Early Missions and Routes of Travel" is on pp 565-78.

[151]Raymond L. Flory, *Historical Atlas of McPherson County* (McPherson, Kans.: McPherson County Historical Society 1983) p 10. A site monument commemorates the 1855 Fuller's Ranch, and the Santa Fe Trail.

[152]There were several Charles Coodys: one was married to Nellie Riley; his son was the husband of Susan Fields; and his grand-nephews (3), one of whom was married to Laura Wilson. Starr...*Cherokees*...pp 323, 432, 433, 438.

We have no very late news from the parties that left here for California. Rumor states that the small company that left from Ft. Gibson has been killed off by the prairie Indians-but we do not believe the report.

A month later, still having heard nothing from the Evans/ Cherokee emigrants themselves, the *Advocate* reported again:

We have had no...information...from the Fayetteville Mining Company; only that a part of their oxen, some sixteen or eighteen head, have returned to Verdigris River, in the neighborhood of Mr. E.[lijah] Hicks. ...Some of our people express uneasiness concerning the company, from the belief that they would not have lost so many cattle, without some difficulty with the prairie Indians. Some again, suppose that they may have been searching for gold on the route, or may have found some, and through their eagerness to obtain the precious stuff, have neglected their cattle.[153]

The perception among both white and Cherokee relatives was that, at the least, the emigrants were not paying attention; at the worst, they were dead.

Finally, on July 3, diarist Crawford's brother, E. M., wrote a letter from Washington County, Arkansas addressed to James at "Sutters Fort Californy."

theree of your Steers has come back, about theree weeks ago..they had an old yoke on them....Ther is a rumor going, that there is about 30 yoke of oxen on the Verdigree belonging to your Company..but I dont beleve it The Supposition is by a great many, that you are diging gold at the big bend of Arkansas river.[154]

Three weeks later, relative W. D. Crawford wrote the diarist:

Remember that houses and lands, wives and children, Widows and orphans, and all the untold joys of domestic happiness, have been forsaken for the prospect of the filthy lucre of California....your other Steers came with an old yoke on the black one and one of the red ones....I shall advise that they be sold and the proseeds divided between your two widows.[155]

Arriving at the junction of their new wagon road and the Santa Fe Trail, the company devised a post office, wrapping news of their arrival and accomplishment in pasteboard and oilcloth, then placing it firmly under the only large rock they could find.

---

[153]*Cherokee Advocate* 25 June 1849. Elijah Hicks' lived near present Claremore.
[154]Around Great Bend, Kansas. Parties led by a Colonel Black, left from the Cherokee Nation and northwest Arkansas in July, August and September of 1849, and for the next few years, to hunt gold along the Arkansas River--much closer to home than California.
[155]W. D. Crawford letter to A.A. and James S. Crawford Sutters Fort, California from Boonsboro, Arkansas, July 25, 1849.

we obtained a large stone and planted it in the fork of the road, and
one of our cunning workmen cut these letters upon it: "To Fayetteville,
Ark., 300 miles--Capt. Evans' Cal.' Com'y, May 12, 1849," to apprise the
prairie traveler of a new road....The company crossed the Neosho [Grand]
at the Grand Saline, Cherokee nation, and proceeded up between the two
Verdigris [Verdigris and tributary Caney Rivers], almost a due northwest
course, until it struck the great road from Independence to Santa Fe;
the estimated distance being about 300 miles. No wagon had ever traveled
this route before, and it was considered impracticable by some; but a
better wagon road than we have made, I will venture to say, cannot be
found west of the Mississippi river. The travel was on the *divide*...
which we found to be exclusively of high, dry, rolling prairie slopes,
offering no obstacles whatever to any number of wagons. The course leads
over the head waters of the two streams named, and Neosho or Grand
river, which afford abundant water, timber and grass, at intervals of
five and fifteen miles. Even at this early season (May 12th, 1849) we
have had plenty of excellent grass, and our stock are improving every
day....We had thought of continuing our route and course, and strike the
Oregon road at the forks of the Platte, but find the grass will not
justify it, consequently we go directly to Bent's Fort.[156]

The letter, written by Company member Hiram Davis was carried by
traders to the *Daily Missouri Republican*, where it appeared on
July 4, after which it was printed in the *Cherokee Advocate* on
July 30.

Those following behind the Evans/Cherokee Company on the
Santa Fe Trail were noted in the P. B. Marple letter written May
25, which was found with the Davis letter under the rock at the
junction of the trails:

Capt. Bogue, numbering about twenty wagons, all of which were from
Greene county, Mo. Two other companies are here[157]...made up of
emigrants from different parts....Our intention was to take the South
Pass route, but owing to the immensity of numbers going, our conclusion
was that a large proportion would probably fail on the way for want of
grass....To the fear of perishing in the mountains, was added the
apprehension of the cholera, which pursued the emigrants from different
points on the Missouri to the Kansas river....the [companies] have
united and are all well, and getting on finely[158]

A. Williamson wrote his letter on June 1. It was also placed

---

[156]Josiah Gregg's "Map of 1844 of the Indian Territory in Northern Texas and
New Mexico" shows the route to Bent's Fort. It also records Gregg's southern
route in 1839 on the north side of the Canadian River from Van Buren to Santa
Fe. Gregg...*Commerce*...vol 2, following p 222.

[157]"One from Callaway county, Mo., numbering fifteen wagons, commanded by
Capt. Berry. The other...the writer is connected[to]."

[158]"the South Carolina company, the Johnson county, Missouri, company, and the
Greenville, Illinois, company...and also a company from Orleans county, New
York."

under the rock.

> Last night i staid at Cottonwood, and counted an hundred and eighty-
> seven vehicles of various descriptions, all destined for the *various
> gold regions*.
>
> From the best information [b]efore me...the number of teams in
> advance will reach seven hundred. Several trains have left the Oregon
> route after crossing the Kansas, and intersected this [Santa Fe] road
> this side of Council Grove."[159]

As the Evans/Cherokee Company joined the Santa Fe Trail, there had been no serious incidents other than the oxen running for home. Despite cholera being a fearful menace on the other western trails, and chasing the companies at locations further east on the Santa Fe route, there was no major sickness in the Evans/Cherokee Company. They were at the head of the migration on the Santa Fe route, and remained in the lead as they proceeded west along the Santa Fe Trail toward Bent's Fort and Pueblo in present Colorado.

---

[159]"Capt. Rodger's company from Howard co., Capt. Jackson's from Hannibal, Capt. Kirker's *miscellaneous*, and Capt. Allen, from Henry county, are all encamped in close proximity to-night -- besides a company of *packers*, and some three or four more, all in hailing distance."

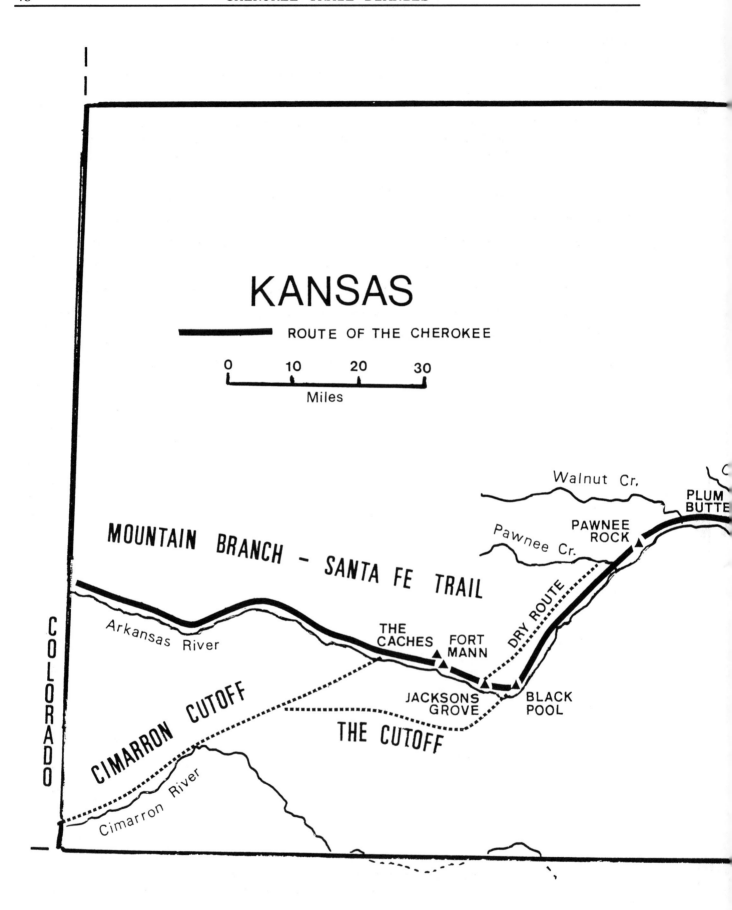

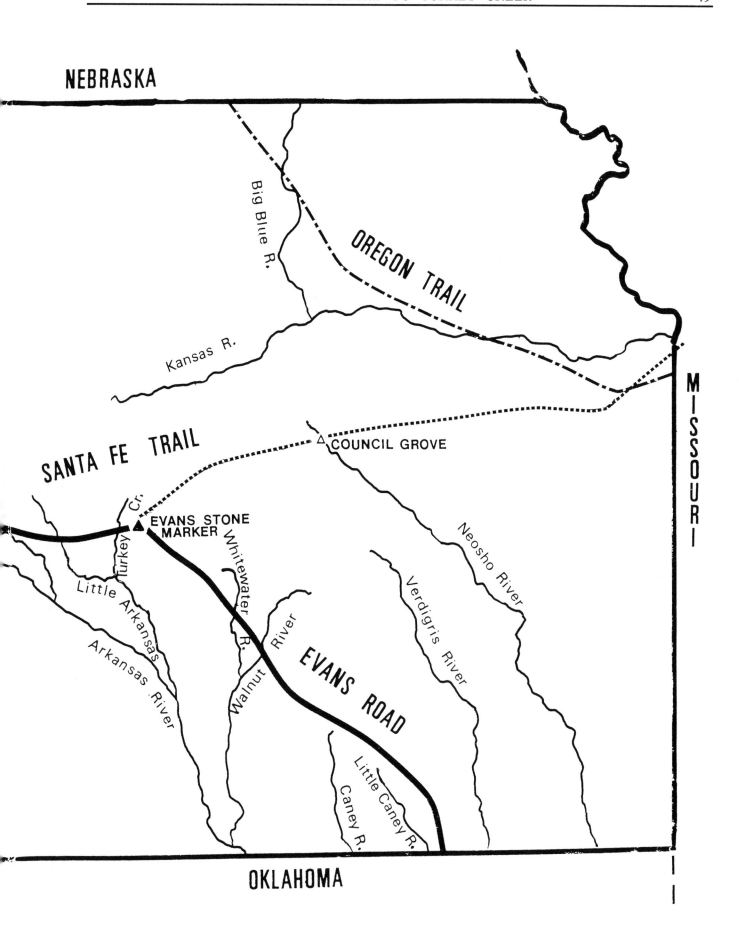

Chapter 5. TURKEY CREEK TO PUEBLO

The Santa Fe Trail to Bent's Old Fort and beyond

We are now on a Great Highway

--Oliver Wack Lipe

Company member O.W. Lipe wrote a letter to the *Cherokee Advocate* explaining their progress from home, and then noted their first company decision about which route to take:[160]

> A question arose at that point [Turkey Creek Junction with the Santa Fe Trail] what rout to pursue, whether we should continue our north west course to intersect the oregon road at the southe, fork of the platt or take the Santa Fe road to Fort Bent, the latter route carried so we are now on a great highway and can travel 20 miles per day with eas.[161]

The "great highway" had been used for commercial and military gransportation between points on the Missouri River and Santa Fe and Chihuahua, Mexico since at least 1821.[162] Thousands of people and animals traveled the Santa Fe Trail prior to 1849.[163]

The Evans/Cherokee Company left their newly-blazed trail and proceeded west on the "Highway." Crawford:

"Monday 14 [May]   Big Turkey Creek   10 [miles]"
[Running Turkey Creek, SE of McPherson, McPherson Co., Kansas]

Lipe described the Company's continuing problem with oxen, noting the loss of fifteen head on the first day.

Crawford:

"tuesday 15 [May]   Little Arkansas [River] 15 [miles]"
[7 miles SE of Little River, Rice Co., Kansas]

---

[160]Oliver Wack Lipe was born in New York in 1814. He married Cherokee Catherine Gunter Vaught in 1839; her sister Elizabeth was the wife of Martin Matthew Scrimsher, commissary of this 1849 company. Lipe's son DeWitt Clinton Lipe married Victoria Susan Hicks, sister of Senora and Charles Renatus Hicks, forty-niners in the cholera-ravaged company of Dr. Jeter Lynch Thompson. O. W. Lipe became Commissary in Stand Watie's Confederate Cherokee Regiment in the Civil War.

[161]*Cherokee Advocate* 30 July 1849. Letter written May 27, two days before the company reached Fort Mann (Dodge City).

[162]"The major eastern commercial terminus of the Santa Fe Trail was St. Louis, but commodities were shipped up the Missouri River before being transferred to wagons for the trip to Santa Fe. The earliest wagon trains left from Franklin, Missouri....By the early 1830s, however, most...began at Independence." Santa Fe National Historic Trail [Missouri, Kansas, Oklahoma, Colorado, New Mexico] Comprehensive Management and Use Plan.

[163]Barry...*West*...p 97.

Lipe described meeting an unidentified Missouri party:

[May 15] At little Arkansas [river] we over took a wagon with four
persons from the northern part of Missouri....they considered they had
arrived at hostile ground and were waiting for company. They are now
with us, and our caravan now numbers 41 wagons and 134 persons, we have
not seen and [sic] Indian, since we saw the osages at the verdigris.

More and more cattle were running off, despite the vigilance
of the traveling company.

on the Little Arkansas 45 more [stock] ran off,[164] which has detained
now 5 days, of the cattle only 21 head have been found, 8 men are still
in pursuit...the train delays [I] have no idea that they will find any
of the oxen....As a general cause for the cattle running of[f]...the
immense number of carcases of cattle which have died on this road, which
seem to have died last winter;[165] waggons and irons of every discription
are strewd all along the road, tons of iron could be picked up, it
seems...the waggons are first left and afterwards burned for fuel by
others passing and the iron remains.[166]

One explanation for the dead cattle might be that November
and December 1848 had been cruelly cold. Lt. Edward Beale, acting
as courier to Santa Fe during that time, reported the terrible
weather. Freighters lost great numbers of cattle on the Santa Fe
Trail in 1848. Therefore, "the immense number of carcases" were
there frightening the Evans/Cherokee cattle.

The eight forty-niners sent after the cattle included Dr. W.
R. Cunningham, David C. Jackson, Herman Freyschlag, and five other
men.[167] Lipe continued about the Cherokee oxen:

among the oxen lost [Martin Matthew] Schrimsher has one yoke of steers
he got of [Lorenzo] Delano[168] and his mate Geo. Key[169] lost one yoke
amuly and his mate, they started towards home and probably will reach
home if they are not stopted.[170]

During the six days of chasing cattle, diarist Crawford made

---

[164]Starting the trip with 304 oxen, forty-five lost would represent 15% of the
total. Recovering twenty-one would be significant.

[165]James M. White had experienced severe storms in November. Barry...West...p
786; Lt. Edward F. Beale described cruel and bitter cold, snowing, freezing
Ibid. p 787; government contractor Smith, Brown & Co., in December were losing
great numbers of cattle, 1600 by one account Ibid. pp 790-91.

[166]Lipe letter, May 27, 1849. *Cherokee Advocate* 30 July 1849.

[167]Foreman...*Marcy*...p 74.

[168]Merchant in Tahlequah, Indian Territory.

[169]George Washington Keys and brother Richard R. Keys were Cherokee. George
was a messmate of Scrimsher.

[170]Lipe letter May 27, 1849. See Chapter 4 for reports of 30 oxen returning to
the Verdigris River in Indian Territory.

no entries. When the company moved, <u>Crawford's</u> diary continued:

"Monday 21 [May]   Big Cow Creek   15 [miles]"
[4 miles SE of Chase, Rice Co., Kansas]

Apparently none of these forty-niners had ever been on the Santa
Fe Road. Crawford's use of this creek name probably came from
Gregg's information, including his map of 1844.

Unfortunately, the Evans/Cherokee Company members'
descriptions of the Santa Fe Road were scant. Therefore comments
of other travelers are occasionally included here.

George Ruxton, going east in 1847, saw the buffalo here:

Between Pawnee Fork and Cow Creek...they [buffalo] literally formed the
whole scenery, and nothing but dense masses...was to be seen in every
direction, covering valley and bluff, and...blocking up the trail[171]

Hiram Davis of the Evans/Cherokee Company later wrote:

For 2 weeks we travelled through the buffaloe ranges....we saw...
100,000. I killed a fine bull myself which satisfied my curiosity and I
would kill no more[172]

An 1848 map showed both Big Cow Creek and Camp Osage.[173] <u>Crawford</u>:

**"tuesday 22 [May]   Osage Camp bank of Arkansas[174]
22 [miles]"**
[on Walnut Creek, 3 miles east of Great Bend, Barton Co., Kansas]

In 1847 Ruxton remarked this was the most dangerous area on
the trail. Many ambushes occurred in former years. <u>Crawford</u>:

"wednesday 23 [May]   Little Ash Creek   25 [miles]"
[2 miles SE of Pawnee Rock, Pawnee Co., Kansas]

"thursday 24 [May] Pawnee fork Ark.   10 [miles]"
[Larned, Pawnee Co., Kansas]

The initial military fortification built here in 1859 was called
"Camp on Pawnee Fork."[175]

---

[171]George Frederick Ruxton *Wild Life in the Rocky Mountains* (N.Y.: The
MacMillan Company 1924) p 260.

[172]This Hiram Davis letter, written to his wife between June 18-22, 1849 from
Pueblo was published for the first time, with others, in *Flashback*, vol 9, no
1, (May 1959) Washington County Historical Society, Fayetteville, Arkansas.

[173]Frederick Wislizenus' "Map of a tour from Independence to Santa Fe" was
published in 1848. Barry...*West*...p 811.

[174]The Osage made annual buffalo hunting trips west, burning the prairie to
aid in the hunt. Washington Irving wrote a good account in *A Tour on the
Prairies* (London: John Murray 1835).

[175]National Park Service "Fort Larned" publication. Nearby is the Santa Fe
Trail Center at Larned, Kansas.

Leaving camp the Company traveled the "Wet Route" along the Arkansas River. Crawford:

"Saturday 26 [May] Elk Camp bank of Arkansas 22 [miles]"
[on Coon Creek near Kinsley, Edwards Co., Kansas;
"Wet Route" of the Santa Fe Trail]

May 27 was a Sunday; once again the Evans/Cherokee Company stopped for the Sabbath. Lipe described the incident which gave the camp its name: "Geo. Keys Caught a young Elk, as we arrived at this encampment and will probably let it go to-morrow morning."

Company member Davis later wrote "I have seen animals that I never saw before...the Elk, Antelope, Badger, Hare, Prairie Dog and Squirrel, and many others."[176]

Lipe used Sundays for letter writing. Here he recounted:

we are on the bank of the Arkansas 389 miles from home in the midst of the Buffalo, the Arkansas has asingular appearance, south [smooth?] prairie on each side without any timber or brush and with banks from two to four feet high, we make use of Buffalo chips for fuel, we were obbliged to use such fuel...several nights

Lipe and other Cherokee had another buffalo experience:

Any amount of Buffalo calfs could be caught--Daniel Gunter caught two when we first got to them kept them tied all night and let them go in the morning....The first day we got among Buffalo, schrimsher and I went and killed a large bull--I believe all have killed buffalo now but potter.[177]

In light of the many accidents and diseases which could befall emigrants, it was important to report on health matters. Lipe wanted to assure his family of his good health, some expertise he had acquired, and the value of the milk cows:

I have been extremely lucky I have had no accidents....I could have been purfectly happy could my dear family be with me, I am now in perfect health, perfectly well of the fall off my horse and a sore mouth with which I was afflicted for a few days, I never had a better appetite than I have now and above all let me inform you that I am a great cook, beat the company Baking Biscuits   our cattle have done finely and the cows give a good quantity of milk. I find cows very useful on the road and

---

[176]Davis letter, Pueblo, June 18-22, 1849.

[177]S.O. Potter was a white schoolteacher in the Cherokee Nation. Reported to be from Maine, Potter wrote a letter from California on February 14, 1851 stating he would go "home to Lowell, Massachusetts" before returning to the Cherokee Nation. *Cherokee Advocate* 15 April 1851, p 2. The town of Cherokee, Butte County, California, commemorates Potter for bringing the first Cherokee miners in 1849.

very little trouble, I think it would be difficult to leave them behind as they will follow. I have taken off the yoke and confine them together by a pole and strops.[178]

The Company moved on Monday, camping near the southernmost bend of the river. The next day they arrived at Fort Mann.[179]

Crawford:

"Monday 28 [May]   Island Camp Ark.   22 [miles]"
[NE of Ford, Ford Co., Kansas]

"tuesday 29 [May]   Fort Mann   25 [miles]"
[2 miles west of Dodge City, Ford Co., Kansas]

Fort Mann had been built in April 1847 by Daniel P. Mann and a party of forty civilian teamsters. The quartermaster at Santa Fe, Capt. W. M. D. McKissack, wrote of the necessity for the facility:

> Owing to the great number of wagons abandoned on the plains, I made arrangements to erect Wheelwright, Smith, & Store houses near the crossing of the Arkansas.[180]

The geographic determinant that is important here is the 100th meridian of west longitude. The Santa Fe traders, civilians, and government parties reported that at or near this point in their journeys west, the wooden wagon wheels and spokes had seriously shrunk due to the dryness of the atmosphere. One time-honored method of correcting the condition was to soak the wheels in water until the former size was attained. Another method employed on the plains was to cut the iron tire down to fit the new, shrunken size of the wheels. That took a blacksmith. Hence the importance of having "Wheelwright and Smith" facilities for travelers.

Fort Mann proved difficult to keep in operation. Ruxton passed by this fort in May 1847, while it was open:

> we passed a little log fort, built by the government employes, for the purpose of erecting here a forge to repair the commissariat wagons on their way to Santa Fe. We found the fort beleagured by the Pawnees, who killed [and] had carried off all their stock of mules and oxen.[181]

---

[178]*Cherokee Advocate* 30 July 1849.
[179]The Santa Fe caravans ordinarily used the "Dry Route," which left the Arkansas River south of Larned, Kansas and rejoined the river near present Fort Dodge, Kansas.
[180]Barry...*West*...p 669.
[181]Ruxton...*Wild Life*...pp 248-49.

During 1848 Lt. Col. William Gilpin had used Fort Mann as a base
camp during the Mexican War.[182]

What the forty-niners saw was a "fort" that had been
abandoned the year before their arrival, in 1848.

> On reaching Fort Mann...the 1849 Evans party...saw there some 50
> government wagons.[183]

Foreman described Fort Mann and the three days spent there.

> May 29 they [Evans/Cherokee Company] arrived at Fort Mann near "the
> Caches." When this adobe fort[184] was abandoned the year before, the
> government left behind about fifty wagons seen by the emigrants in a
> much damaged condition.[185]

Five weeks later, on July 3, 1849, another company passed by Fort
Mann and found; "The Fort is all in ruins, having been torn down
by Indians, and [used] by the emigrants for fuel."[186]

> At this [1849] camp...wrote one of the emigrants
>   "we thought it prudent to wait...therefore as our wagons, and a few
> of our tricks want repairing, we hoisted the forge and have been very
> busy for the last three days. Some of the boys are very homesick, but,
> poor fellows, they ought to have thought before acting. We have all
> enjoyed good health except old man Evard, who came near dying, but since
> has got pretty stout."[187]

The Evans/Cherokee company had at least one blacksmith with all
his equipage along--John Rankin Pyeatt.

Crawford made no entries whatever between May 30 and early
June. Possibly he was one of the men out chasing stock on the
prairies. Between that and the wagon repairs, there was much work
to do. His diary continues as they moved again. During the day's
travel the Company and trail moved away from the Arkansas River,
coming back to meet it at the Cimarron Cutoff.

---

[182]With Missouri volunteers, Gilpin went hunting Comanches south and downriver
on the Arkansas. At the conclusion of the campaigns, in mid-August, Gilpin was
on his way east, his battalion following. Barry...*West*...pp 766-67, 771.
[183]Ibid. p 854.
[184]Adobe was used for chimneys and breastworks, but the four houses (later
eight buildings) in the 60 foot square were log, had walls 20 feet high, and
large wooden gates one ft. thick. Ibid. p 670.
[185]Foreman...*Marcy*...p 75 quoting from *Arkansas Intelligencer* 28 July 1849.
[186]Barry...*West*...p 859. Joseph Simmons, nephew of ex-Missouri Governor John
C. Edwards was diarist.
[187]Foreman...*Marcy*...p 75 quoting from *Arkansas Intelligencer* 28 July 1849.

Crawford:

"June. Saturday 2   Camp Joy   22 [miles]"
[at Ingalls, Gray Co., Kansas]

This camp is located near the Cimarron Cutoff, which crosses the Arkansas River and proceeds southwesterly toward Santa Fe.[188]

From this point westward, the 1849 Evans/Cherokee wagon company traveled "the upper Arkansas, or mountain route--a longer, but better-watered, and therefore safer route, [to Santa Fe] by way of 'Bent's Fort'"[189] The next day they met the first persons encountered since overtaking four Missourians on the Little Arkansas. Crawford:

"Monday 4 [June]   Terapin[190] Camp   20 [miles]"
[two miles SE of Garden City, Finney Co., Kansas]

Lipe was able to send his first letter (written while at Fort Mann) east with Rocky Mountain traders. Hurriedly he added:

                                        June 4th 1849.
An opportunity now offers to send my letter[191] we are now 480 miles from home nothing has occurred of much importance   the bearer of this is a Trader going to Independence....we are 40 miles west of Ft. man.

The traders were William Guerrier and Seth Ward, who at the beginning of his career was the bookkeeper at Fort Davy Crockett in Brown's Hole, Colorado, in 1838.[192] Ward was experienced enough in the mountains to give the Evans/Cherokee Company information they sought about the routes further west from Pueblo. Ward could also have suggested guides to employ at Pueblo.[193]

---

[188]Gregory M. Franzwa *The Santa Fe Trail Revisited* (St. Louis, Mo: The Patrice Press, 1989) p 123. Located and Determined by the Kansas State Historical Society, Topeka, Kans. 1913. In Kenyon Riddle, comp., "Route of the Old Santa Fe Trail" *Records & Maps of the Old Santa Fe Trail* (Raton, N.Mex: *Raton Daily Range* 1948).

[189]Barry...*West*...p 277 The "Mountain Branch" of the Santa Fe Trail was opened in September 1834 by an eastbound train of Bent, St. Vrain and Company.

[190]Terrapin "any of various edible North American turtles living in fresh or brackish water." *Webster's Dictionary*. In this part of Kansas, they could have been either one of the two Box Turtles, or the Spiny soft-shell.

[191]*Cherokee Advocate* 30 July 1849. Lipe's letter of June 4 was added to his written on May 27.

[192]Both Kit Carson and Dick Owens had been employed as hunters at Fort Davy Crockett in the winter of 1837. Seth Ward departed from Independence July 12, 1838 as a hired hand of Lancaster P. Lupton. Barry...*West*...p 352. Seth would later become Sutler at Fort Laramie, which would make him very well to do.

[193]Both Kit Carson and Dick Owens were living in the Pueblo-to-Taos area.

Company members who had been out looking for oxen returned before Lipe finished his second short letter.[194] They brought news that other emigrant companies were behind them.

the men who were in pursuit of lost oxen have returned without any. The whole number lost is 48, the cattle were making their way to the Creek Nation. Three companies of Californias are on this road in our rear from green[195] and dade counties and Independence [Missouri]. We are all in good health and have had no sickness in the company.

The Santa Fe traders were in the habit of chronicling their journeys both directions, handing reports to newspapers on both ends--in Independence and/or St. Louis, and in Santa Fe. Everything and everyone they saw was usually reported in these newspaper dispatches.

In the July 30, 1849, *Cherokee Advocate*, along with the Lipe letters, were other reports:

ARRIVAL FROM SANTA FE

The Cherokee and Mississippi[196] companies, 38 strong, arrived in Santa Fe on the 3d June, and reported a company of 152 men, about four or five days in their rear...

The Santa Fe Republican says:

"There is a scarcity of water and grass about 200 miles from this place..."

By information received from the most reliable sources, there can be no doubt but that the route taken by Capt. Bradford [Abraham Buford], 1st Dragoons, in the summer of 1848, is by far the most direct and most practicable route from Fort Gibson to this point [Santa Fe]...[197]

Lt. Pleasanton, 2d Dragoons, Aid de Camp to Gen. Persifer P. Smith, with an escort of ten men from company H 2d Dragoons, left Santa Fe on

---

[194]Traders in general did not have as many problems as emigrating parties. They traveled slowly, with heavy wagons and large mule or ox team trains; they were more well-organized, usually heavily-armed and vigilant, habits born of many years of experience.

[195]Captain Bogue commanded the Greene County, Missouri, party "which had pioneered(?) the Ft. Scott-Council Grove trail." Barry also suggests that part of this company may have joined the (Cherokee) Jeter Lynch Thompson/Judge Tully party for the Oregon/California Trail. Barry...*West*...p 832. Unknown to the Evans/Cherokee company, Bogue and company turned off to Santa Fe on the Cimarron Cutoff. Ibid. p 855.

[196]The Cherokee and Mississippi Company traveled via the North Fork of the Canadian, Little River and Choteau's old trading house, to Santa Fe. They split at Santa Fe and several members joined ranks with Lieutenant Pleasanton until they reached Pueblo where they joined the Evans/Cherokee packer company.

[197]Following Buford's southern route, troops composed of fifty members of the 5th Infantry, and 28 men from Company F 1st Dragoons, under command of Captain Marcy, 5th Infantry, and an officer of the Topographical Engineers, were to escort the route from Fort Smith to Santa Fe. Foreman...*Marcy*...p 152.

the 9th [June] for California, via the South Pass.[198] Brv't Capt.
Buford, 1st Dragoons, with the mail, was to leave [Santa Fe] for the
United States on the 5th June.[199]

Both Buford and Pleasanton are important to the story of the
Cherokee Trail. Buford traveled from the Santa Fe Trail southeast
to Fort Gibson over the new trail blazed by the Evans/Cherokee
Company. His passage verified its existence, and he stated it was
much better than the southern route over which he had traveled to
Santa Fe. Lieutenant Pleasanton traveled with the "packer"
contingent of the Evans/Cherokee Company from Pueblo, Colorado
north, to California.

The recorded frequency of meetings between the 1849 emigrant
companies and the Santa Fe and/or Rocky Mountain traders, were
evidence of the heavy traffic on the Santa Fe Trail. Usually there
was a steady stream of traffic on the Santa Fe Trail, from one or
both directions, so it is ironic that no one except Guerrier and
Ward recorded meeting the Evans/Cherokee Company on the trail in
1849. There were no reports from traders, military companies,
freight contractors or mail parties from May 12 to the end of
May.[200]

On this trip traders Seth Ward and William Guerrier were
returning from their first expedition on the upper Arkansas with
6,000 buffalo robes.[201] They reported to the newspaper:

From the California Emigrants on the Santa Fe Route.
Correspondence of the Republican.
                                        Westport, June 25th, 1849.
Messrs. Ward & Guerrier's train from the Platte and Arkansas rivers,
left the Pueblo, on the Arkansas river, on the 9th May, and Bent's Fort
on the 26th of the same month.
    June 4th, above the Santa Fe Crossing,[202] met Capt. Evans' company,
from Fayetteville, Arkansas[203]--41 wagons, 132 men, all well. This

---

[198]Lieutenant Pleasanton, instead of going via South Pass, joined the
Evans/Cherokee packers under guide Dick Owens.
[199]*Cherokee Advocate* 30 July 1849.
[200]Trader William Curtis Skinner arrived at Independence on May 12. Barry...
West...p 850. James J. Webb departed from Council Grove for Santa Fe toward
the end of May. Ibid. p 866.
[201]Seth Edmund Ward and William Le Guerrier, trading partners, were licensed
by Indian Agent Thomas Fitzpatrick in 1849 to trade in the Upper Platte and
Arkansas Agency. Barry...*West*...p 765.
[202]Fifteen miles upriver (west) Ibid. p 855.
[203]The Evans/Cherokee Company was still maintaining the lead position, on the

company spoke of a determination of following the Arkansa river and crossing the mountains towards its head, to the Great Salt Lake, than which a more impracticable route could not have been selected.[204] Their ultimate determination, however, so far as I learned, was to send a party of twenty-five men ahead to the placer at the Sangare de Cristo, near Taos,[205] and await their return at the Pueblo, about seventy miles above Bent's Fort, when they would be able to determine as to proceeding.[206]

Ward and Guerrier also reported the number and sizes of companies that were following the Evans/Cherokee Company. The next company, which Lipe had mentioned in his letter home, was fifteen miles behind the Evans/Cherokee company. From June 4 to June 24, during the eastward traverse, "W. A. T." of the Ward and Guerrier train recorded all the groups met headed for Santa Fe and/or California. Several companies followed the Evans/Cherokee Company to Pueblo:

> *June 5th,* met at the [Cimarron] Crossing, Springfield, Mo. company[207] of 24 wagons, for California.
> *June 7th,* above Mann's Fort [west of Dodge City, Kansas] met Capt. [L.C.] Bostick's company[208] of 22 wagons; and at Mann's Fort, met Capt. Berry's company[209] of Calloway Pioneers; 15 wagons, 53 men.
> *June 8th,* passed Linn, Brunswick and Livingston companies, Capt. Barber[210]--27 wagons 90 men--above Jackson's Grove, bound for Taos gold mines. In the afternoon, met the Marion company, Capt. Galley[211] 44

Santa Fe Trail, in the race to California.

[204]Lewis Evans must have believed he could take his wagons west to the headwaters of the Arkansas River, a route traveled by John C. Fremont in 1845.

[205]Gregg...*Commerce*...p 123. "Placeres of gold have also been discovered [at] Taos [and] at a point called Sangre de Cristo....among the snow mountains of that region...a very rich placer has been discovered....it has been very little worked."

[206]*Missouri Republican* 30 June 1849. The *Daily Missouri Republican* printed this letter on 4 July 1849.

[207]Captain Bogue's company from Springfield and Greene County, Mo. were the first of the forty-niners to take the Cimarron route to Santa Fe. On June 13 at the Upper Cimarron Springs they were met by Captain Buford, U.S. Army. Barry...*West*...p 855.

[208]Bostick's company was organized at Council Grove intent on the South Pass route, but found it too crowded. Ibid. pp 855-56.

[209]In November 1849, Captain Berry's company was reported on the Gila Route (New Mexico and Arizona) reduced to three wagons with some of the company afoot. Ibid. p 856.

[210]Barber reached Pueblo June 23 and went on to Greenhorn where the party split, to follow different trails. Ibid. p 550. George W. Withers (from Salt Lake City in August) wrote that his "Sullivan County and California Mining Assn." left Independence, Mo. about May 14, with wagons and ox teams; and at Council Grove joined the Linn, Chariton, and Saline county men under "Captain Barke"[sic].

[211]Neither Capt. Rodger's nor Jackson's trains were mentioned by "W. A. T."

wagons, 120 men-via Santa Fe to California. Capt. Tuttle,[212] with 50
men, and pack animals took the Cut Off, leaving the Arkansas river.

June 9th, met three conjointed companies under pilotage of James
Kirker.[213] Their object is to examine the Taos mines, and if not
satisfied, to leave Santa Fe, in September, for California.

June 11th, nooned near the South Carolina, Illinois and Mormon
companies, from Johnson and Henry counties,[214] near Coon Creek. Met Mr.
Webb and others, bound to Santa Fe; and above Pawnee Fork, a party for
California, and traders for Santa Fe; some Germans in company.

June 12th, in the afternoon, met a train for California, via Santa
Fe, composed principally of Germans and Hungarians.[215]

June 13th, passed Mr. Ross' company for Santa Fe.

June 14th, near Plumb Bute, met Capt. Carr's[216] company.

June 15th, met Mr. Harley's train for Santa Fe. Arriving at Little
Arkansas, met U.S. Infantry, with Capt. St. Vrain[217] and Mr. Jones
traveling in company...

June 16th, met four companies of traders to Santa Fe and Chihuahua.

June 19th, passed ex-Governor Edwards'[of Missouri] and major Hart's
companies for California.

June 21st, near Diamond Spring passed F. McManus and others, for
Chihuahua. Same day, passed Judge Brown's train in camp. Buteris, with
three wagons, passed Council Grove, for Rio Abajo, New Mexico.

---

but were mentioned in A. Williamson's letter of June 1 addressed from "In
Camp, near Turkey Creek." Whether Capt. Jackson's train from Hannibal, Marion
County was connected with Capt. Galley's (Gully's) Marion County company is
not clear. If so there was a separation at the Cimarron crossing with Galley's
(Gully's) company going to California by way of Tucson and the Gila Route.
Jackson's train proceeded to the Upper Arkansas arriving there on June 15;
then proceeded to the Taos Mines. Ibid. p 856.

[212]Captain Tuttle, probably Caleb S. Tuttle, may have joined the Ithaca
company on May 15 just west of Independence. The Ithaca company was captained
by Charles V. Stuart. This letter writer inexplicably referred to it as
Captain Tuttle's company. The Ithaca and California Mining Company arrived in
Pueblo on June 27. Ibid. p 857.

[213]James Kirker was a mountaineer and pilot for the three Illinois companies
that jointly consisted of over 150 men, fifteen mule drawn wagons, and twenty-
nine ox drawn wagons. The Kirker-piloted train traveled up the Arkansas River
to Pueblo and south to Greenhorn. From there a detachment of fifty men
explored for gold on the "Sangre de Cristo Creek." The company divided at
Greenhorn and took various routes to California. Ibid. p 857. Also see Ross
Calvin, ed. *Lt. Emory Reports* (Albuquerque, N.Mex.: Univ. of New Mexico Press
1951; Paperback 1968), p 116.

[214]"United under Captain Lightner, of the Missouri train." Barry...*West*...
p 859.

[215]"An all-Wisconsin train." Ibid.

[216]Captain Croghan Ker's Company K, 2nd Dragoons, was the party of James
Collier, newly-appointed Collector for the port of San Francisco. Ibid. p 869.
Collier would leave from Santa Fe twice for California; first via the Spanish
Trail on August 15, returning to Santa Fe, then leaving September 15 via the
Gila River.

[217]Ceran St. Vrain was a partner of the Bents at Bent's Fort and Fort St.
Vrain. Ceran had arrived in Independence March 27 carrying the mail from Santa
Fe. Ibid. p 803. Marcellin St. Vrain, operator of the now abandoned Fort St.
Vrain on the South Platte, had arrived in Independence from the Santa Fe Trail
by May 12. Ibid. p 850.

June 23d, passed Lightner & McGoffin's[218] trains in camp at 110 Creek; met Domingo's wagons, for Mexico, at Willow Spring.

June 24th, passed Armijo's wagons for Rio Abajo. Arrived at Westport.

All symptoms of cholera appeared to have left the emigrants, as we met them...some burials...between Westport and Council Grove. All... wished us to say they were in good health. We received from the different trains nearly three hundred letters, which were mailed to-day at this place [Westport].

Your obd't serv't,   W.A.T.[219]

Additional information about the Santa Fe Trail travelers was supplied by the eastbound Capt. Abraham Buford, who left Santa Fe on June 6.

From the *Van Buren Intelligencer,* July 14th...

June 6th, 1849.--Left Santa Fe for the States, in company with Mr. Haywood, Mail Contractor [and] Chihuahua merchants [met] a California emigrant, who, after seeing Santa Fe, remarked, "that he had seen the elephant's tail, and had no wish to see anything more of the animal."

June 6th and 7th.--Met between Santa Fe and San Miguel some six or seven hundred California emigrants, from Ft. Smith and Van Buren, Ark...[220]

June 8th.--Was joined by an escort of ten men from Taos, Co. I, 1st Dragoons, at Barkley's Fort, on the Rio Moro.

June 9th.--Left Barkley's Fort on the old trace from Santa Fe to Independence.

June 13th.--Met a party of California emigrants[221] at the upper Cimarone Spring, the most advanced of those embarking from Independence--all well...

The Evans/Cherokee Company was ahead at Bent's Old Fort on June 13 and therefore not seen by Captain Buford. Between June 13 and 19, Buford, his men, and the mail reached the Arkansas River and traveled east along it. Buford collected mail from westbound parties to take back to the East.

June 19th.--Met at Jackson's Grove,[222] on the Arkansas river, Capt. Kerr's company of the 2d, Dragoons; Col. Collier, Collector of San Francisco, and party; Brevet Majors Stein [Enoch Steen] and [William N.] Grier, 1st Dragoons, and Jerry Folger, Sutler of New Mexico, in company--all well, and moving ahead rapidly...

James Collier had been appointed collector for the Port of San Francisco and was on his way to assume the post. Buford also

---

[218]Both Lightner and James Magoffin were well-established traders to Santa Fe and Mexico.

[219]*Missouri Republican* 30 June 1849. *Daily Missouri Republican* 4 July 1849.

[220]Including J. N. A. Carter and A. M. Wilson's Cherokee and Mississippi Company which took Buford's route to Santa Fe then went via the Gila route, to arrive in Sacramento by September 18, a trip of 4 months and 12 days.

[221]Captain Bogue's company. Barry...*West*...p 855.

[222]Jackson's Grove and Island was between today's Ford, Kansas and Dodge City.

helped an emigrant, and saw the Indians that the Evans/Cherokee Company did not see.

June 20th.--Found on the road a lost California emigrant, who said he had been out some five or six days without anything to eat; that he went off the road to shoot an antelope, and got lost from his party. Gave him some provisions, and started him on to join his party...about forty miles ahead of him. Passed the camps of some 3,000-4,000 Indians of the various tribes that inhabit the Prairies.--They were all very friendly, and were awaiting the arrival of Fitzpatrick, General Indian Agent, with whom they were to have a big talk...[223]

June 21.--Met at the Pawnee Fork[224] of the Arkansas river the 3d Infantry and 3d Artillery, Col. Alexander...Col. Calhoun, Indian Agent for New Mexico, and party, and Major Howe, 2d Dragoons...all well and no cholera, but had had a few fatal cases a short time previous...

Eastbound Lieutenant Buford turned south on the newly-made Evans/Cherokee trail to Fort Gibson, which he had left in September 1848. For his outbound trip he traveled the southern route on the Canadian River to Santa Fe (the route most Evans/Cherokee Company members had anticipated traveling.) Buford:

June 23.--Arrived at Turkey Creek on the trace, and considering the mail near enough the settlements to be entirely out of danger, took eight men of the escort...and followed the trail made by Capt. Evans' company of California emigrants, down between the Verdigris and Arkansas rivers; crossed the Verdigris at Big Island, and then followed down the divide between the Verdigris and Grand [Neosho] river, and arrived at Fort Gibson on the 27th instant, making the trip from Santa Fe to Fort Gibson, (with wagons) in twenty-five days. Emigrating parties leaving Arkansas, from the neighborhood of Fayetteville, would do well to follow this trail of Captain Evans'. It is a good and plain way to the old Santa Fe trace from Independence; from Big Island on the Verdigris river, to Turkey creek, where this trail strikes the trace, is about 175 miles...Emigrating parties leaving Fort Smith and Van Buren, Ark., should not, on any account whatever, go by the way of Santa Fe, because the route by the south side of the Canadian river strikes the mountains of New Mexico some 150 or 200 miles south of Santa Fe...Again, there is no grass worth speaking about within 60 miles of Santa Fe.[225]

On June 23, as Buford was turning south onto Evans trace, the Evans/Cherokee Company packers and the wagon company were traveling on the second day of their journey north from Pueblo.

The *Fort Smith Herald* reported on Buford's return via the

---

[223]Thomas Fitzpatrick had traveled east with William Bent, arriving in Westport, Missouri on May 1. Fitzpatrick went on to St. Louis, where he was noted arriving May 8.
[224]near Larned, Kansas.
[225]*Southern Shield* Helena, Arkansas 28 July 1849 p 3.

Evans/Cherokee new trace from Turkey Creek to Cherokee Nation. The first report:

> Lt. B.[uford] is 25 days from [Santa Fe], coming a great part of the distance on the Independence route, with the U.S. mail, and then turning his course came into Fort Gibson with eight men only....He met several companies on the road.[226]

In the next edition there was more information:

> Mr. Joseph Merrill...came in with Lt. Buford. They came along the Independence road to the trace made by Capt. L. Evans' company from Washington county and the Cherokee Nation. The trace strikes at a point on the Independence road where they have set up a stone, upon which is written: "300 miles from Fayetteville." [227]

The Evans/Cherokee Company continued west after meeting the Ward and Guerrier trading party on the upper Arkansas River on June 4. During the latter part of the day, they passed over a portion of the trail known today as "Charlie's Ruts."[228] Crawford:

"tuesday 5 [June]   Lower Chalybeate[229] wells   23 [miles]"
     [halfway between Deerfield and Lakin, Kearny Co., Kansas]
Having passed the Upper Crossings, or turnoffs, of the Cimarron Route to Santa Fe, the company began traveling on the upper Arkansas, or mountain route of the Santa Fe Trail.[230] Crawford:

"wednesday 6 [June] Upper Chalybeate wells   20 [miles]"
          [Kendall, Hamilton Co., Kansas]
First Lt. William Hemsley Emory, traveling west with Kearny's Army of the West, had described the area in 1846: "the hills along the river are vertical, as if the river had cut a passage through them."[231]

---

[226]*Fort Smith Herald* 4 July 1849 vol 2, no 46, p 2, col 2.
[227]*Fort Smith Herald* 11 July 1849 vol 2, no 47, p 2, col 2.
[228]Dale Bentrup donated the ruts to the Finney County Historical Society.
[229]Chalybeate (Ka-lib-e-at). Impregnated with iron. A mineral spring. Frank E. Wright *New Websterian Dictionary Illustrated*. 1912. Company members were familiar with the springs in Arkansas. The *Fort Smith Herald* 16 February 1848, vol 1, no 33, p 2 described "A Chalebyate Spring," which relieved intermittent fever, dropsy, dyspepsia, paralysis, chronic rheumatism, gout, debility of the digestive organs, etc. when used.
[230]Barry...*West*...p 277 (1834).
[231]Calvin...*Emory*...p 28. Emory's job was to explore and describe the trek to Mexico and California.

The change in scenery was not noted by <u>Crawford</u>:

"thursday 7 [June]   Sand hill Camp[232]   **20 [miles]"**
[six miles east of Coolidge, Hamilton Co., Kansas]

Emory described the soil: "The soil of the plains is a granitic sand...supporting a scanty vegetation."[233]

Crawford recorded the first incidence of hail. Given the frequency of hailstorms on the high plains, it is supposed that a significant one took place either this day, or during the night at the camp. <u>Crawford</u>:

"friday 8 [June]   Hail Camp   21 1/2 [miles]"
[approximately six miles west of Holly, Prowers Co., Colorado]

"Saturday 9 [June]   Camp Decision   18 [miles]"
[at mouth of Big Sandy Creek, Prowers Co., Colorado]

A decision at the intersection of Big Sandy Creek and the Arkansas River may well have been whether to make a cutoff northwest. A cursory look at a Colorado map shows that Fort St. Vrain appears to be on a direct northwest line from Big Sandy. From Fremont's maps, they probably thought it was possible. Traders Ward and Guerrier had probably made it clear to the company that taking wagons to Salt Lake via the headwaters of the Arkansas River was out of the question.

Emory described the conditions of the area the 1849 emigrants traveled through:

> Near the dry mouth of the Big Sandy creek, the Yucca Angustifolia, palmillo of the Spaniards, or soap plant, first made its appearance, and marked a new change in the soil and vegetation of the prairies.[234]

They reached Big Timbers the next day. <u>Crawford</u>:

"Monday 11 [June]   Camp Fitzpatric   20 1/2 [miles]"
[NW of Prowers, Bent Co., Colorado]

The campsite was named for Thomas Fitzpatrick, Indian agent. For the 1849 Company, as for many other weary travelers, this Big Timbers area was an oasis--the first trees sighted for many miles. In 1839 Matthew C. Field, correspondent for the *New Orleans*

---

[232]Sand Hill Camp of 1849 is near the noted "Pretty Encampment" site of 1847. Barry...*West*...p 688.
[233]Calvin...*Emory*...p 29.
[234]Ibid.

Picayune, made a trip to present New Mexico over the Santa Fe Trail. Among his reports in 1840 was one describing Big Timber:

> For weeks we have been reveling in anticipation...of this delightful place known to the old traders as Big Timbers. When exhausted beneath the blazing heat of the prairies, the older travellers would tell us of...the ancient trees, the cool stream, the gushing spring....
>
> A thick forest of venerable trees sheltered us from the heat, and beneath them...a stream yet cool from the mountain snow. From the bank a spring gushed....Vast sunflower beds spread far and near.... we drank and bathed, and...dropt beneath the trees and slept...[235]

Emory in 1846 wrote about its importance:

> About 35 miles before reaching Bent's Fort is found what is called the "big timber." [which] is a thinly scattered growth of large cotton-woods not more than three-quarters of a mile wide, and three or four miles long. It is here the Cheyennes, Arapahoes, and the Kioways sometimes winter, to avail themselves of the scanty supply of wood for fuel, and to let their animals browse on the twigs and bark of the cotton-wood. The buffaloes are sometimes driven by the severity of the winter, which is here intense for the latitude, to the same place to feed upon the cotton-wood....Mr. Bent thinks of moving his establishment...To this point, which has been indicated to the government as a suitable one for a military post....
>
> In addition to the grasses and cotton-wood mentioned, we find in the bottoms wild plum, wild cherry, willow, summer grape, cat-tail, scouring rush...Mexican poppy, and other.[236]

Fitzpatrick was not on the plains in June of 1849. But in October and November 1848 he had been at Big Timbers meeting with large numbers of Apache, Comanche, Kiowa and Arapahoe.[237] Companies traveling behind the 1849 Evans/Cherokee Company saw large numbers of Indians. Gathering numbers were seen on June 10 near Fort Mann on the Arkansas River. Still further east, Captain Buford saw 3,000 to 4,000 on June 20, one day's travel west of Pawnee Fork. The Indians were gathering to meet Thomas Fitzpatrick, who was to arrive from the East.[238]The Evans/Cherokee Company reportedly saw none of these Indians. Cherokee Daniel M. Gunter wrote that they

---

[235]Matthew W. Field, "Sketches of Big Timber, Bent's Fort and Milk Fort in 1839" *Colorado Magazine* vol 14, no 3, (May 1937) pp 102-03. Colorado State Historical Society. The sketch "Big Timber" appeared in the *New Orleans Picayune* 11 October 1840.

[236]Calvin...*Emory*...pp 29-30.

[237]Santa Fe Trader J. M. White estimated 600 lodges. John C. Fremont, westbound on his disastrous trip through the Rockies in November, estimated 6,000 Indians were met in three of four days. Barry...*West*...pp 781-82.

[238]Fitzpatrick apparently did not return until fall, when he married half-Arapahoe Margaret Poisal, daughter of trader John Poisal.

"saw but four Indians after leaving the Osages, until [we] got to Bents Fort."[239]

Their next camp was at an equally important place. <u>Crawford</u>:

"tuesday 12 [June]   Picketware Camp   20 [miles]"
[Purgatoire River,[240] 2 miles east of Las Animas,
Bent Co., Colorado]

In 1847 Ruxton camped here while traveling east:

opposite the mouth of...the Pickatwaire of the mountaineers...the stream itself widens out into sandy shallows, dotted with small islands covered with brush. At this camp we were joined by six or seven of Fremont's men, who had accompanied Kit Carson from California.[241]

The 1849 company reached Bent's Old Fort. <u>Crawford</u>:

"wednesday 13 [June]   Fort Bent   11 [miles]"
[Bent's Old Fort between La Junta and Las Animas,
Otero Co., Colorado]

Never a military post, the fort was the center of a successful trading empire. The first Bent brother, Charles, was trading on the upper Arkansas in 1829.[242] Charles Bent was elected Captain of the 1829 commercial group, perhaps the first to use oxen from the Arkansas River to Santa Fe.[243] For several years after, he led trading caravans to Santa Fe by the Cimarron Cutoff route. The first of Bent's trading licenses that included "Fort William, on

---

[239]*Cherokee Advocate* Monday 6 August 1849. The Osages were seen near the Verdigris in late April; Bent's Fort was reached on June 13.

[240]Rio de Las Animas Perdidas en Purgatorio, the Purgatory River, was named for "a rebellious force of Spanish soldiers who broke off from an official expedition [to the Raton Basin 1593-94] pushed off into the plains." Robert A. Murray *A History of the Raton Basin* BLM Cultural Resources Series no 6, p 13, Denver. Referenced from Jack D. Forbes *Apache, Navaho and Spaniard.* (Norman, Okla: Univ. of Oklahoma Press 1960) pp 74-76. "The rebels, traveling without priests, have given rise to the name for one of the [Arkansas] tributaries.... It is variously spelled, pronounced and translated." (In the Catholic Church belief, Purgatory is a place in afterlife for temporary residence until sins are absolved.)

[241]Ruxton...*Wild Life*...p 235. Carson himself had been ordered back to California by Kearny; Fitzpatrick continued east with Carson's dispatches.

[242]LeRoy R. Hafen "When Was Bent's Fort Built?"*Colorado Magazine* v 31 (1954) pp 105-19.

[243]The Arkansas River was the boundary between the United S. and Mexico. Before departing from the Arkansas River toward Santa Fe, Bent requested that military escort commander Bennet Riley lend him a yoke of oxen, to test their usefulness. They performed so well that many future Santa Fe Trail trader trains used oxen. Otis E. Young *The First Military Escort on the Santa Fe Trail 1829: From the Journal and Reports of Major Bennet Riley and Lieutenant Philip St. George Cooke.* (Glendale, Calif: Arthur H. Clark Co. 1952).

the north side of the Arkansas about 40 miles east of the Rocky Mts." was issued in 1834.[244]

Since neither the diarist nor letter writers in 1849 elaborated on Bent's Fort as they camped there, descriptions written by others who visited between 1834 and 1849 are included. Field was there in 1839, hosted and entertained by Robert Bent. Coming off the flat, sandy, sparsely vegetated and somewhat dull plains, he described the place:

> Round towers, pierced for cannon, command the sweep all around the building, the walls are not less than fifteen feet high....there are the storerooms, the extensive wagon houses, in which to keep the enormous heavy wagons used twice a year to bring merchandise from the States, and to carry back the skins of the buffalo and the beaver....the great wall encloses numerous separations for domestic cattle, poultry, creatures of the prairie, caught and tamed, blacksmith and carpenter shops.[245]

Another 1839 traveler came south from the South Platte River:

> It [Bent's Fort] lies on the left [north] bank of the Arkansas, close by the river, and is the finest and largest fort which we have seen on this journey. The outer wall is built of imperfectly burnt brick; on two sides arise two little towers with loop holes. In the ample court yard were many barn-yard fowl....they have cattle, sheep and goats, and three buffalo calves, that peacefully graze with the rest of the herd. At the time they had no superfluity of horses....a band of Indians...had driven away a hundred head.[246]

Kearny's March to South Pass placed his command at Bent's Fort on July 29, 1845. Heading homeward, he was there only long enough to load the government provisions "which had been sent out there some two years before." Lt. William B. Franklin compared Bent's to other western forts:

> On our approach...the national flag was displayed, and we received a

---

[244]An eleven-wagon eastbound train of Bent, St. Vrain & Company traveled from Santa Fe via Taos, and included the Fort William, or Bent's Fort trading post. This route became known as the "Mountain Route" to Santa Fe. Barry...*West*...p 257. Hafen..."Bent's Fort..." p 117. Hafen's research indicated 1833-34 as date for building Bent's Old Fort on the Arkansas; also cited in Barry...*West* ...pp 256-57. For a further discussion of possible construction dates, see David Lavender *Bent's Fort* (Lincoln, Nebr: Univ. of Nebraska Reprint 1978) Chapter 7 Endnote no 12, p 414. It was first published in 1954, the same year as Hafen's article.

[245]Hafen..."Sketches"...p 104. The sketch "Fort William" was in the *Picayune* 12 July 1840. In John E. Sunder, ed. *Matt Field on the Santa Fe Trail* (Norman, Okla: Univ. of Oklahoma Press 1995 Paperback) pp 142-46; also in the "Journal" written in poetry Ibid. pp 44-46.

[246]Wislizenus...*Journey*...p 141.

salute of two guns from their little field piece. We found the two
Messrs St. Vrain & George Bent ready to welcome us....

    This is a larger and more commodious fort than any we have yet seen.
It is built like the others of unburnt brick, but they had many of the
comforts and a few of the luxuries of civilized life about them. Some of
us took dinner at the Fort, and discovered that people can live as well
in the Mountains as they can in the States.[247]

In 1847, Ruxton described Bent's Fort as including rooms
"inhabited by the people engaged in the Indian trade."[248]

    War with Mexico began with the president's proclamation on
May 13, 1846. Stephen Watts Kearny and his Army of the West, en
route to Santa Fe via Raton Pass, traveled to Bent's Fort on the
Arkansas. He arrived July 28, one day less than a year after they
had been there in 1845. Although the company was at the fort for
only four days, the impact of the large numbers of men and animals
was noted by a small party which included Francis Parkman.

    It seemed as if a swarm of locusts had invaded the country. The grass
for miles around was cropped close by the horses of General Kearney's
soldiery....we found that not only had the horses eaten up the grass,
but their owners had made way with the stores of the little trading
post; so that we had great difficulty in procuring the few articles
which we required for our homeward journey....

    [Mr. Holt] invited us to dinner, where to our admiration, we found
a table laid with a white cloth, with castors[249] in the middle, and
chairs placed around it.[250]

Two months after the 1849 emigrants passed by, on August 20 or 21,
this "old" Fort Bent was destroyed by the owners, who blew up the
inside.[251]

    The Evans/Cherokee forty-niners headed west along the
Arkansas River from Bent's Fort toward Pueblo.

----

[247]Frank N. Schubert, ed. *March to South Pass: Lieutenant William B.
Franklin's Journal of the Kearny Expedition of 1845.* Engineer Historical
Studies No. 1 Historical Division, Office of Administrative Services, Office
of the Chief of Engineers. (Washington, D.C.: U.S. Gov't Printing Office 1979)
p 29.
[248]Ruxton...*Wild Life*...p 234.
[249]castor (a) A small bottle, pot, or shaker for holding a condiment. (b) A
stand for a set of condiment containers. *The American Heritage Dictionary*,
Standard Ed.
[250]Francis Parkman *The Oregon Trail* (N.Y.: Grosset & Dunlap 1927) pp 264-65.
[251]Barry...*West*...p 883 cites the "*Missouri Republican,* St. Louis 2 October
1849 (which printed a letter...giving an account of just-arrived travelers who
had heard the loud report [explosion] and who, a day or two later, came to the
still-smoking ruins.)." In 1850 Bents were "mobile" on the Santa Fe Trail. In
1853 Bents would establish another at Big Timbers 40 miles downstream from the
old on the Arkansas River, the "new" Bent's Fort.

Crawford:

   "thursday 14 [June]   Long Cane Camp   19 [miles]"
        [NE of Rocky Ford, Otero Co., Colorado][252]

   "friday 15 [June]   Camp No 42   16 [miles]"
       [NE of present Fowler, Otero Co., Colorado opposite
                   the mouth of Apishapa River]

   "Saturday 16 [June]   Camp No 43   18 [miles]"
        [immediately East of Boone, Pueblo Co., Colorado]

Nearby this camp, Haynes Creek joins the Arkansas River; on the
south side the Huerfano River runs into the Arkansas. After
stopping on Sunday, June 17, for which he made no notations,
Crawford must have been relieved to write:

       "Monday 18 [June]   Pueblo   20 [miles]"
     (confluence of Fountain Creek and the Arkansas River,
                   Pueblo Co., Colorado]

The Evans/Cherokee Company arrived at the second major junction on
their journey to California. At the first, Running Turkey Creek
and the Santa Fe Road, there had been discussions and voting as to
the best route to proceed. Pueblo could be expected to produce
spirited conversations about various options which presented
themselves. It was that and more.

        Almost from the beginning, there had been a basic difference
of opinion in the company about how Sunday should be observed.
There were a significant number who thought it sinful to perform
any kind of work on the Sabbath. Others, for practical rather than
religious reasons, knew the value of letting the animals rest
where grass and water were plentiful. Still others wanted to
travel every day. This difference as well as discontent with the

---

[252]Stephen H. Long, in 1820, camped in this area on July 21-23, three and a
half miles north and a little west of the town of Rocky Ford "making
astronomical observations and arranging the packs." George J. Goodman and
Cheryl A. Lawson *Retracing Major Stephen H. Long's 1820 Expedition: The
Itinerary and Botany* (Norman, Okla: Univ. of Oklahoma Press 1995) pp 68-69.
Among the plants noted here by botanist Dr. Edwin James are some milkweeds pp
130-31; green antelope horn pp 132-33; cactus p 141; Rocky Mountain Bee Plant
p 146; perhaps Greasewood pp 156-57; Willow Baccharis pp 160-61; Horseweed p
163; Nuttall's and Plains Sunflowers pp 167-68; Big Bluestem grass pp 201-02;
Barnyard Grass p 205; Blue Wild Rye pp 205-06; Squirreltail and Indian Grass p
209; Ten-Petal Mentzelia p 243; Shaggy Portulaca pp 278-79; Plains
Cottonwood."July 22...the point on which we are encamped is sparingly covered
with a growth of cottonwood intermixed with the Populus tremuloides [Quaking
Aspen] and some willows." pp 299-300.

slow pace of oxen travel caused splitting in the 1849 company,
first at Pueblo, and later at several other places on the road
ahead to California. By this time in their journey, smaller groups
of friends and relatives in the company had banded ever tighter
together.

Pyeatt wrote his second private letter to his wife two days
after they arrived at Pueblo.

> Pueblo, Arkansas River. 20th June 1849
> Dier Companion, thru the blessing of god I a gain have the opertunity to
> rite to you   we arived hear day before yesterday in good helth and our
> teams in good order   we have had a pleasant trip so fa[r] much more so
> than I antsapated [anticipated]   we heve had no bad luck since I rote
> to you last   we have traveled from 100 to 120 miles a week for
> sometime past and our teams a mending all the time.[253]

Circumstances dictated that the company would remain at Pueblo for
a few days. Pyeatt:

> we ar hear repairing some of the wagons that the dry weather has srunk
> up so the tire had to be cut and welded....since we came hear I have bin
> so buzy working on the wagons and showing [shoeing] horses.[254]

Hiram Davis was the writer of the very public letter which
had been folded, wrapped in oil cloth, and left at the base of the
"Arkansas Monument" at the junction of the Santa Fe Trail and the
Evans/Cherokee Trail at Running Turkey Creek. His second letter
was a private letter to his wife:

> we have been here several days repairing our wagons and resting our
> teams....You will see from the map[255] that we are on the Arkansas River
> 75 miles above Ft. Bent....I expect we have come the best route that
> could have been selected.[256]

Pueblo, later the county seat of Pueblo County, importantly
located at the junction of Fountain Creek and the Arkansas River,
has been reportedly occupied at intervals for over 160 years by
Spaniards, trappers, Indian traders, and Mexicans.[257] In 1842
traders and trappers constructed an adobe fort, Fort Pueblo.[258]

---

[253]Pyeatt letter to wife Elizabeth from Pueblo June 20, 1849.
[254]Among other things Pyeatt was a blacksmith. His was a large wagon, brought
to accommodate the forge and heavy equipment he used.
[255]Judge Hiram Davis' map has not been found.
[256]Davis letter, Pueblo, June 18-22, 1849.
[257]*Redbook* "Colorado Place Names" Colorado Writers Project, p 152. Material
derived from *Colorado Magazine. Also* from *The Trail* vol 15, no 11, p 16.
[258]LeRoy R. Hafen & Frank M. Young "The Mormon Settlement at Pueblo, Colorado
During the Mexican War" *The Colorado Magazine* vol 9, (July 4, 1932) pp 121-36,

Francis Parkman described it on August 20, 1846, three years before the arrival of the California forty-niners:

> closely nestled in the midst of wide cornfields and green meadows... rose the low mud walls of the Pueblo....It was a wretched species of fort...nothing more than a large square enclosure, surrounded by a wall of mud, miserably cracked and dilapidated. The slender pickets that surmounted it were half broken down....the gate dangled on its wooden hinges so loosely that to open or shut it seemed likely to fling it down altogether [we were shown] to...a small mud room, very neatly finished ...and garnished with a crucifix, a looking-glass, a picture of the Virgin, and a rusty horse-pistol....three or four Spanish girls...were baking cakes at a mud fireplace in the corner.[259]

Fremont arrived from the north and wrote: "a number of mountaineers, who had married Spanish women in...Taos, had collected together and occupied themselves in farming."[260] Richard Kern, one of Fremont's men in the disastrous Fourth Expedition, described Pueblo in November 1848 as a "miserable looking place, the inside resembling a menagerie--a compound of Spaniards, Horses, mules, dogs, chickens and bad stench."[261]

Evans/Cherokee Company member Davis departed from his gentlemanly norm when he wrote:

> No persons live here but about 10 men and as many women, the most abandoned set of thieves, Mexicans, Indians, halfbreeds that ever disgraced any spot of earth, and as <u>lousy</u> as rabbits.[262]

The Pueblo's other traditional function had been storage depot for "Taos lightning."[263]

---

p 181. The Pueblo was occupied most of the time from 1842 until Christmas Day 1854, when the inhabitants, including some Cherokee, were massacred by Ute Indians.

[259] Parkman...*Oregon Trail*...pp 259-61.

[260] D. Jackson & M. L. S. Spence. *Expeditions of John Charles Fremont 1838-44* (Urbana, Ill.: Univ. of Illinois Press 1970) p 445.

[261] LeRoy R. Hafen and Ann W. Hafen, eds. "Diaries and other Accounts by Members of the Expedition" C. Diary of Richard Kern 1848-1849." *Fremont's Fourth Expedition: A Documentary Account of the Disaster of 1848-1849 With Diaries, Letters, and Reports by Participants in the Tragedy.* Far West and The Rockies Historical Series 1820-1875 (Glendale, Calif: The Arthur H. Clark Co. 1960) vol 11, no 3, p 118.

[262] Davis letter, Pueblo, June 18-22, 1849.

[263] Ralph C. Taylor *Colorado South of The Border* (Denver, Colo: Sage Books 1963). Distilled spirits were manufactured principally by Simeon Turley at Taos, outside the jurisdiction of the United States government, which forbade transportation and sales. The Dragoons always searched the trader wagons they came across. From 1842 onward Charles Autobees, Charles Metcalf and others bought alcohol from Turley in Taos, using Pueblo as a storage depot, then traveling to Fort Lancaster (Lupton) on the So. Platte and other trader camps.

In 1848 war with Mexico was over, and there was a
"depression" in the Indian trade, due perhaps to the federal
government giving merchandise to the Indians. The Pueblo/Greenhorn
traders were ready and eager to do business with the forty-niners.
The emigrants, including the Evans/Cherokee Company members,
approached the residents of Greenhorn to find some experienced man
to guide them from Pueblo onward to Salt Lake, or perhaps even to
California.

Cherokee Daniel Gunter wrote home June 22 about the locals:

> some *trapers* told [us] that it was impossible...to cross the mountains
> with...wagons, which caused thirty men to dispose of their wagons and
> what provision they could not carry, to some trappers, at a place by the
> name of Green Horn, twenty five miles south of Pueblo--Some of them
> disposed of their wagons at a great sacrifice, one wagon selling as low
> as five dollars....one offered...one mule, and seven packsaddles for [a]
> wagon and team....These men (trappers) say it is impossible for wagons
> to cross the mountains, so they can sell their mules at a very high
> price, and get their [emigrants'] wagons and provision, that they could
> not take[,] for nothing...[264]

In their defense, some experienced plains residents seemed
genuinely concerned for the inexperienced emigrants, anticipating
"much suffering and innumerable deaths from starvation among the
emigrants in the mountains and in California....the emigrants will
not be counseled by experienced persons."[265] The Greenhorn
settlement of the time was 28 miles southwest of Pueblo on
Greenhorn Creek, east of the Wet Mountains, in the Spanish Vigil &
St. Vrain Land Grant of 1843-44.[266]

On their return, they loaded the traded furs at Pueblo to take to St. Louis.
Turley called Pueblo "Robert Fisher's fort on the Arkansas" in 1843, where
Turley had a "branch store." By 1844, government agents realized where the
liquor was coming from. Metcalf was caught in 1843 at Fort John (Fort Laramie)
resulting in his moving further south to Fort Lancaster (Fort Lupton), where
the trade continued. Simeon Turkey was killed along with Governor Charles Bent
in the Taos uprising of 1847.

[264]Daniel Gunter letter to his brother, Pueblo, June 22. *Cherokee Advocate*
Monday 6 August 1849.

[265]*Cherokee Advocate* 22 October 1849.

[266]Murray...*Raton*...pp 15-16. from *Comanches, The Destruction of a People* by
T.R. Ferhenbach.(N.Y.: Knopf 1974) pp 221-26. The circumstance of its naming
is: "New Mexico Governor Juan Bautista de Anza set out [in the] fall of 1779
[with a] force of 600. [they] destroyed the (Comanche) encampment and then
laid an ambush on what we now call Greenhorn Creek for the returning war
party....de Anza inflicted numerous casualties on the Comanche force. Among
the dead was the principal chief, Cuerno Verde so called because of the green-
painted buffalo horns of his headdress."

Ruxton described Greenhorn in the dead of winter 1846-47:

crossed on to the Cuernaverde or Greenhorn Creek. On a bluff. [I saw]
two or three Indian lodges and one adobe hovel....a mountaineer...
galloped up to us...(and him an American)....We found here two or three
hunters, French Canadians, with their Assinniboin and Sioux squaws, who
have made the Greenhorn their head-quarters; and game being abundant and
the rich soil of the valley affording them...Indian corn, they lead a
tolerably easy life.

Ruxton explained the decline in beaver prices and the use of
silk in men's hats as the reason the trappers had changed their
lives, now being sedentary, and out of employment.[267] Their choices
of residence were "the fruitful valleys" of the Rockies.[268]

Some of them attempted to conduct a little business. Mountain
man Charles Kinney kept "sundries" at John Brown's store in
Greenhorn in 1847.[269] In 1847 or 1848, Marcelino Baca moved to
Greenhorn where he raised cattle, corn, wheat, beans, and
watermelons for trade to Indians.[270]

Several of these men were at Greenhorn and Pueblo in 1849
when the emigration for California came through.[271] Some ex-
trappers from the vicinity were themselves on the way to
California by the time the emigration came through in 1849.[272]

There had been other residents of the Pueblo area--Mormons.
General Kearny sent a detachment of all men from the Mormon
Battalion who were sick and disabled, men with wives, and outfits

[267]Ruxton...*Wild Life*...p 146.
[268]Ibid. pp 115-16.
[269]Janet LeCompte "Charles Kinney" in Hafen...*Mountain Men* ...vol. 4, pp 169-
73. The summer of 1848 Bill New, Ben Ryder, Calvin Jones and some Mexicans
lived at Greenhorn.
[270]Janet LeCompte "Archibald Charles Metcalf." Hafen...*Mountain Men*...
Archibald Charles Metcalf, John Brown, William New and Marcelino Baca. Also
Janet LeCompte "Marcelino Baca" in the same series. In 1844 Baca moved to
nearby Hardscrabble with George Simpson and others. His daughter Elena was
born there in 1846. In 1852 the Utes destroyed his Greenhorn farm. He moved
back to Pueblo and built a house across the Fountain River. Baca was killed in
the Civil War in 1862.
[271]Charles Kinney, Dick Owens, Delawares Jim Dickey and Jim Swanock, Archibald
Metcalf, Joe Dennis, Half-Cheyenne Tesson, Marcelino Baca and Friend Montoya,
and probably John Poisal. Janet LeCompte *Pueblo, Hardscrabble, Greenhorn*, ^
(Norman, Okla.: Univ. of Oklahoma Press 1978) p 222. Traders Seth Ward and
William Guerrier were listed, though they met the Evans/Cherokee Company June
4 on the Santa Fe Trail on their way to the states with their first furs.
[272]John Brown, former store proprietor at Greenhorn, with Alexis Godey,
Valentine Herring, James W. Waters and Lancaster P. Lupton, former owner of
Fort Lancaster, (Fort Lupton) on the South Platte, who took his family.

with teams of given out or broken down animals to Pueblo for the
winter of 1846-47. "Here they put up houses for winter constructed
of cottonwood logs...joined together in the form of a stockade."[273]
Mormon John Steele recorded his family's journey from Santa Fe to
Pueblo.[274] Other Mormons came from Fort Laramie to winter; John Z.
Brown kept a diary.[275] Parkman saw "the white wagons of the Mormons
drawn up among the trees. Axes were sounding, trees falling, and
log huts rising along the edge of the woods and upon the adjoining
meadow."[276] In Spring of 1847 the Mormons left Pueblo for Salt
Lake, via Fort Laramie.

At least one Mormon stayed behind. Evans/Cherokee Company
member Davis wrote:

> Among them [Pueblo residents] is quite a good looking <u>white</u> woman and
> Mormon, that married among them when her people passed here on their way
> to the Salt Lake. Her situation must be intolerable, as she has a babe
> but 2 months old, and is willing to leave it and her man and go with us
> to her people, but no person will consent to take her.[277]

Davis did not say why they refused. Perhaps there was
apprehension of Mormon reaction in Salt Lake. Or perhaps the three
women in the Evans/Cherokee company had something to say about it.
While the company wagons were being repaired, the routes and
methods of travel being selected, the guides being procured, and
letters being written, this four-day respite from traveling

---

[273]Wanda Wood, ed."John W. Hess with the Mormon Battalion," *Utah Historical
Quarterly* vol 4, (April 1931), pp 47-55.
[274]'Catherine Steele' "Women and Children of the Mormon Battalion," Kate B.
Carter, ed. *Our Pioneer Heritage* vol. 1, (Salt Lake City: Daughters of Utah
Pioneers 1958) p 507. "On the morning of the 18th of October, 1846, we
commenced our journey for Bent's Fort [from Santa Fe]. We had 87 men, 20 women
and many children and our destination was Pueblo on the Arkansas River....We
built 18 or 20 houses, a blacksmith shop and a large corral. Later we also
built a meetinghouse. From November until May many companies joined us....On
May 24th [1847] the captain...brought word to us to leave Pueblo."
[275]John Z. Brown, *Autobiography of Pioneer John Brown* (Salt Lake City: Private
1941) Chapter 6, "The Mississippi Company" p 70. Also Hafen & Young "The
Mormon...Pueblo, Colorado..." pp 121-36. Describing their journey from Fort
Laramie to Pueblo, he wrote: "We crossed the South Fork [Platte River] the
27th of July, a few miles below St. Vrains Fort....We reached Pueblo on the
7th of August. We found some six or eight mountaineers in the fort with their
families....We counseled the brethren to prepare for winter to build them some
cabins in the form of a fort. The mountaineers said they would let them have
their supplies, corn for their labor."
[276]Parkman...*Oregon*...pp 262-63.
[277]Davis letter, Pueblo, June 18-22, 1849.

produced some bursts of energy. Feelings held in check on the
trail were expressed during the stopover. Company member Davis
wrote:

> Some members of our Company it is true have given us some trouble, and
> among the foremost of them I may give to you the names of Dock [Dr.
> William R.] Cunningham, [Fred P.] Sims, [George C.] North and John Bean.
> In the distribution of the offices they were overlooked[278] and from this
> it is thought has proceeded their discontent. I could tell you many
> laughable and characteristic anecdotes of them but not the time. The
> frowns and scorn of the whole Company have directed against them, and
> their present humiliation is punishment enough for their worst enemy.

Davis also noted quarrels among Company members:

> [Isaac] Murphy and [Old Man] Avard[279] and Jim Irvin [Irwin] have had
> some stiff quarrels that came well nigh ending in blows....as yet we
> have had but one fight in camps, that was between Judge [James M.] Hoge
> and a trifling little Irishman named Gavin [James Garvin] that came out
> in old Jo Colville's wagon. The difficulty originated about some
> leather. As they are both exceedingly unpopular in the Company, it
> excited but little attention. Gavin struck Hoge a time or two in the
> face with a shoe hammer and battered up right badly. He [Hoge] succeeded
> in getting Gavin in the fire and burnt out the seat of his pants. The
> affair on the whole was exceedingly laughable and ludicrous, as there
> was no serious injury inflicted on either.

Davis mentioned other questionable behavior:

> Speaking of Hoge, he is true to nothing but his old and vicious
> instincts. He is forever wheedling around the English woman I told you
> of, Mrs. [Caroline] Hail,[280] and there are many gross and scandalous
> reports in Camps about them, which I forbear to put on paper. You may
> hope nothing good from that man.[281]

During their four-day stay at Pueblo, the Evans/Cherokee
Company leaders learned that traders Ward & Guerrier had given
them the correct information two weeks earlier. The company could
not go through by their originally intended route, via the
headwaters of the Arkansas River. Member Davis confirmed the
information.

---

[278] In the formation of the Fayetteville Gold Mining Company, predecessor to
the Washington County Emigrating company, Cunningham was the "Secretary and
agent for..." Also in Ralph P. Beiber, ed. *Southern Trails to California in
1849.* (Glendale, Calif.: The Arthur H. Clark Company, 1937) p 331. Taken from
Van Buren Intelligencer and *Fort Smith Herald* 21 February 1849. Also
MacArthur...*Arkansas*...p 20.
[279] Avard, or Evard, had been quite ill during the Santa Fe Trail traverse.
[280] One of only three women in the train. The other two were sisters Hermina
and Barbara Freyschlag.
[281] Davis letter, Pueblo, June 18-22, 1849.

It is true we have found it impracticable to go directly out at the head of the Arkansas River and over to the Great Salt Lake[282] as we had anticipated, and will be compelled to turn to the north via of Ft. Larrimie and the South Pass, which will make our road some 500 miles further...[283]

Pyeatt wrote about the route north from Pueblo:

We will start...for the South Pass by the way of St. Vrain's Fort to intersect the Independence Road near the South Pass[284] finding that there is a good rout throu that way and that we couldn't git through the mountain strait to the Salt Lake hear.[285]

Tumbledown Pueblo, place of decision, was a hub of activity. A split, common to many trains, was developing within the company. Approximately thirty men decided, on the advice of the local mountain men, to sell their wagons and stores and "pack." Pyeatt gave more detail in his letter:

som sell, or rather give away thear load and wagons and pack therew, nearly the same way that the wagons will go,[286] withe th exception of som 200 or 300 miles, on which they will gain som 79 or 100 miles they have becom afraid about the grass being eat up on I[n]dependence rout   they think we will fall in behind the large trains that are on that rout and thos Idiveduels that live hear taking advantage of the times hav told them that the grass is very scarce any how throug that way and that we can not git throug this season with our oxen   they do this to get our wagons and teams and loades for a pony or two   but thears ar other Individeals that we have seen that now [know] they rout as well and perhaps bette then they [the naysayers] do that say that grass is plenty and that we can git therew this season...those Indviduels that live hear have axcomplished thea [their] endes by discurageing our men...all our Cane Hill friends[287] ar a going to pack but us[288] and the Carnahan boys [nephews James and John] Mars [Squire Brooks, relative] and [nephew James] Pierce.[289]

---

[282]A route taken by Fremont between June 16 and June 29, 1844 returning from California.

[283]Davis letter, Pueblo, June 18-22, 1849.

[284]A route approximating that taken by Fremont July 23 to August 7, 1843.

[285]Pyeatt letter, Pueblo, June 20-22, 1849.

[286]The exact route of the 1849 packers is documented in Chapter 6 " Pueblo to Salt Lake--Packer Route." The pack company arrived in Salt Lake July 24, some three weeks ahead of the Evans/Cherokee wagon group.

[287]There were twenty-five men in the Cane Hill list.

[288]Probably "us" means John Rankin Pyeatt and son Andrew, and John's older brother Henry Porter Pyeatt. Of the three, only John lived to see Arkansas again.

[289]Pyeatt letter, Pueblo, June 20-22, 1849. At least 17 Cane Hill men traveled all the way to California together in wagons.

Davis was very concerned about the packers:

The balance of the Company...have exchanged their wagons and teams for
mules and ponys and will go through on packs. I entertain serious fears
for their safety--they have 1200 miles to pack from this place to
California and in the band (30 in number) not one man of experience can
be found.

It is composed of such men as [Isaac] Murphy, old Jo Colville and
Andy [Jo's son], Jim Cartwright and Geo. Callahan, Dr.[Samuel]
McCulloch, many of them good men but they know nothing of packing,
hunting or the hardships of a mountain life. Many of them have
indifferent ponys and being ignorant of the method of packing, which
here is followed by Mexicans and others as a scientific profesion, they
may ruin their [horses'] backs and break them down by overpacking and
forced marches and be compelled to leave them without the possibility of
getting others. You may easily imagine the situation when left afoot in
a mountainous, savage country and have to depend on their guns entirely
for something to eat. Poor Murphy I fear for him, his ponys are trifling
and poor, but no persuasion can prevent him from going. He is urged to
this perhaps from the fact that he gets along badly with his mess.[290]

Cherokee Gunter finished his letter to his brother with news
about the packers and their hiring of an experienced guide.

The packing part of the company, including the former Editor of the
Advocate [James Vann], and...other Cherokees, employ a guide, by the
name of Owens,[291] a man that was once in Fremonts company, they pay him
seven dollars per day and he is to take them to the "diggins" in 60
days.[292]

The wagon company tried to get a guide too. Pyeatt:

Since I comence this letter thear has a man come into our camp that is
well acquainted with all the cuntry bttwee hear and the Sault Lake and
he sayes that he can ride it in 15 day it being only about 5 or six
hundred miles and wean [we can] git threw very easy with vey little work
and will have plenty of wood water and grass   this man[293] we will hire
for a pilot if we can but he has a famly and property that he sayes that
he can not leave on acount of the Youtaws [Ute][294] indians they being at
war with the whites and Spanyard and will steal his property he is
afraid if he leaves   this man has bin recomended to us as knowing more

---

[290]Davis letter, Pueblo, June 18-22, 1849.

[291]The famous mountain man Dick Owens was a good friend of Kit Carson. Both
had been employed several times by Fremont. Owens must have fulfilled his
contract with the Packers. He was listed in the 1850 Yolo County, California
Census (House no. 145 in Cash Creek Twp.) as Richard Owens 39-year-old
Mountaineer born in Ohio. None of the eight persons in the house was from the
Evans/Cherokee Company.

[292]Cherokee Advocate 1 August 1849.

[293]This is a good description of Dick Owens. However, there were several
others living in the Greenhorn, Colorado to Taos, New Mexico, area who might
also have fit the description.

[294]In this part of the Rocky Mountains, the Utes inhabited the front range,
the foothills, and in some parts of the year, the western edge of the plains.

about the cuntry then any man in this country but at the same time we
was toald that we could not git him...and we did not go to see him
had we wint to see him before our men had let thear wagons and teams
g[o] I think they woul not have let them go but it was to late before he
came to camp   I am in hopes that we can git him yet by paying him well
thow he has not said sow.[295]

If this anticipated guide was Dick Owens, the packers
succeeded where the wagon group did not.

Gunter wrote of obtaining another guide for the wagons:

The balance of the company, including 9 [90] men and thirty wagons, are
going to attempt to cross with their wagons, and had employed a guide,
part Osage,[296] to take them by the Salt Lake. They will endeavor to go
the mormon route [Pueblo to Fort Laramie]. The Salt Lake from Pueblo is
four hundred miles, but the way they were going, about six [hundred].[297]

Based on the above letter, previous researchers and writers
have concluded that the Evans/Cherokee wagon company had a
professional guide. However, the guide, for whatever reason, was
never hired.

Davis commented confidently:

Our Company is now reduced to 29 wagons and 91 men....So much for our
Company, and as to getting through to California this season, I don't
entertain a doubt....Some think if we go by the South Pass [we] will not
be able to find pasturage for our stock as they suppose the grass has
been consumed by the immense multitude of stock that has preceded us
from Independence and other points on the Missouri. This is all that can
possibly prevent us from getting through in good time with our teams and
wagons. If it should be true, however, that the grass is not
sufficiently abundant on the road to subsist our teams, we have horses
and mules enough to abandon our wagons and teams. Perhaps we can get
something for them from the Mormons and pack through a way that wagons
cannot travel, and have abundant grass at all times for our stock.[298]
This is a private understanding between myself, Evans and about a dozen
more good and true men that are the fine salt of this Company.[299]

A third group broke away from the original Evans/Cherokee
Company--the turnbackers--who would turn their wagons east from
Pueblo toward home, Cherokee Nation and Arkansas.

---

[295]Pyeatt letter, Pueblo, June 20-22, 1849.
[296]Barry...*West*...p 854 erroneously noted the guide was hired.
[297]*Cherokee Advocate* 6 August 1849.
[298]Davis was perhaps thinking about the Fort St. Vrain to Fort Bridger route
through southern Wyoming, the route which was taken by their thirty-man pack
party as well as others in 1849, but which would be "built" for wagon travel
in 1850 by the first of the four Cherokee/white California emigrant trains.
[299]Davis letter, Pueblo, June 18-22, 1849.

Davis cautioned his wife about turnbacker tales:

> Mr. John Ingram and several more, amounting in all perhaps to a dozen of
> our company, have concluded to return home, and he has promised me to
> deliver you this letter in person, and tell you a thousand things that
> will interest you about me, the company, and about the country we have
> traversed....You must not believe all he says, or all that you may hear
> about our company and the supposed impracticability of getting to
> California this season--these I understand are the reasons he and those
> who return with him give for retracing their footsteps homewards.[300]

Pyeatt, in his direct and pungent way, wrote his wife:

> a good many of our company get discuraged and will som turn back...[and]
> no dout will tell monstis [monstrous] taeles [tales] to justify
> themselves in goin back.[301]

Some previous researchers have claimed the four company
"turnbacker" wagons never made it home, that the men were
murdered. This conclusions may stem from the following letter
which Cherokee Joseph Sturdivant wrote to his family from
"Sacramento City" dated November 20, 1849:

> I have sent you a trunk and buffalo rug from Pueblo, by Mr. [Thomas]
> Tiner...but have since learned that they were all killed by the
> Indians.[302]

On July 4 the turnbacker wagons were east of the Cimarron
Crossing (or Cutoff) near Ingalls, Kansas. Diarist Joseph R.
Simmons (nephew of Missouri ex-Gov. John C. Edwards) noted meeting
four wagons of "Capt. Evans'" company of Californians, returning
from Taos and going back home to Arkansas.[303] Simmons also noted
they "carried our letters to Fayettevile, Ark."[304]

Evans/Cherokee Company member Hiram Davis' letter was also
delivered to Mrs. Davis in Fayetteville, Arkansas, carried by
turnbacker John Ingram.

---

[300] Ibid.

[301] Pyeatt Letter, Pueblo, June 20-22, 1849.

[302] *Cherokee Advocate* 11 March 1850, p 2 col 1.

[303] Simmons should have recorded that the Evans wagons were going back from
Pueblo rather than Taos. Traveling time of the turnbacker party from Pueblo
east to the Verdigris River matches the outbound time of the entire company.
Time could not allow for the additional miles from Pueblo (where we know the
four wagons were on June 22) to Taos (and return) on the Mountain Branch of
the Santa Fe Trail.

[304] Joseph R. Simmons "Across the Plains from Missouri to California 1849-1850"
MS 1259, Western Historical Manuscripts Collection of the University of
Missouri-Columbia; and Barry...*West*...p 860 citing *Kansas Historical
Quarterly*.

A third item disputing the "turnbacker" deaths appeared in the *Cherokee Advocate* in a heading above Gunter's letter:

> A short extract, from a letter written by Mr. Daniel M. Gunter, one of Capt. Evans' Company of Fayetteville Arks:
> Four wagons belonging to Capt. Evans' Washington Co. company, returned crossed the river here [Cherokee Nation] on Friday [August 3, 1849]. They turned back from the base of the Rocky mountains, on the 22nd June, and arrived here in thirty-five days. I received a letter from my brother, dated Pueblo, June 22nd.[305]

At Pueblo it was possible for emigrants to choose between very different trails going distinctly different directions toward California. The route south offered two choices; the Taos/Spanish Trail pack-only route, or the more southerly and more widely used Santa Fe/Gila River wagon route. The known wagon route north went to Fort St. Vrain and Fort Laramie over the old Trappers or Divide Trail.[306] At Fort St. Vrain it was also possible to pack west via the route to Brown's Hole (old Fort Davy Crockett) and Green River.

Lt. Alfred Pleasanton, aide to General Persifer Smith, was under orders to proceed from Santa Fe to the Pacific Coast (California).[307] McArthur wrote that Pleasanton & Company took the Old Spanish Trail.[308] The correct company was Colonel Collier's, who was appointed collector at the port of San Francisco.[309] A newspaper report indicates Collier tried to take the Spanish Trail first, leaving Santa Fe on August 15.[310] Another Collier departure date from Santa Fe, September 15, was also reported.[311] A.W. Whipple's Journal noted Collier arrived at the Yuma crossing of the Colorado River on October 15.[312] The next day John Woodhouse

---

[305]*Cherokee Advocate* 6 August 1849.

[306]Lee Whiteley "The Trappers Trail: 'The Road to Fort Laramie's Back Door'" *Overland Journal* vol 16, no 4, (Winter 1998-99) pp 2-16.

[307]Oakley..."Army"...p 46 citing *Arkansas State Democrat* 24 August 1849; *Memphis Appeal* 14 August 1849.

[308]MacArthur...*Arkansas*...p 79 citing *Southern Shield* 21 July 1849 and 22 December 1849, p 2, col 2.

[309]Foreman...*Marcy*...p 291; Barry...*West*...p 869.

[310]*Fort Smith Herald* 3 October 1849, vol 3, no 6, p 2. Leopold Loenthal to Captain John Rogers.

[311]*Fort Smith Herald* 10 October 1849, vol 3, no 7, p 2. "Very Late from Santa Fe."

[312]John Woodhouse Audubon *Audubon's Western Journal 1849-1850* (Tucson, Ariz: The Univ. of Arizona Press 1984) Photographic Reproduction of first edition of

Audubon encountered Collier at Yuma, and noted "the collector from San Francisco treated us with great courtesy."[313]

Some of the Helena, Arkansas Company members accompanied Lt. Pleasanton north. A company member wrote June 2 from Santa Fe:

> We are going to pack from this place. Twenty of us are going through from Taos with a Lieutenant who has been ordered to California as an aid to Gen. Smith. We expect to go north of [not "on"] the Old Spanish Trail, and will make the trip in 40 or 45 days.[314]

Lieutenant Pleasanton departed Santa Fe with a detachment of ten dragoons, proceeding northward by way of Taos. At the Arkansas River crossing (Pueblo) he met the Evans/Cherokee Company.[315] Foreman stated that Pleasanton proceeded to California via South Pass, perhaps based on the following:[316]

> Lt. Pleasanton, 2d Dragoons, Aid de Camp to Gen. Persifer P. Smith, with an escort of ten men from company H 2d Dragoons, left Santa Fe on the 9th for California, via the South Pass.[317]

Evans/Cherokee Company member Davis described meeting the Helena, Arkansas newcomers from Santa Fe:

> On our arrival here we fell in with a company of some 40 men from about Helena [Ark.] who came via Ft. Smith to Santa Fe[318] where they abandoned their wagons and procured pack mules and are going through on our route. They give sad and distressing accounts of the danger and suffering those on the southern route will have to encounter. They represent it as impossible for ox teams ever to make a trip over these dry sandy plains. Hence those having ox teams on that road, and they compose a very large majority, cannot possibly get through.[319]

Pyeatt also noted why the Helena men came to Pueblo:

> ...[area guides] som of them ar on the rot[road] now piliting a company throug forom Santifee [Santa Fe]...they [Helena Company] come by the way of Fort Smith...left fort Smith the firs of aprile with mule teams...and thear [Santa Fe] lef thear wagons for they could not git throug that way with thear wagons and could not git hear with them easy and ths being the best way even from Santifee...they alls say that there are thousands

1906 published by Arthur H. Clark Co., Cleveland, Ohio, note p 164.

[313]Ibid. pp 164-65. Son of John James Audubon, noted painter of birds.

[314]*Fort Smith Herald* 8 August 1849, vol 2, no 51, p 2.

[315]Oakley..."Army"...p 47 citing *New Orleans Weekly Delta* 16 July 1849; *Memphis Appeal 14* August 1849.

[316]Foreman...*Marcy*...p 285. Foreman's assertion is untrue. Instead, Pleasanton went with Dick Owens and the Evans/Cherokee pack company.

[317]*Cherokee Advocate* 30 July 1849, "Arrival from Santa Fe."

[318]The Helena, Arkansas Company was under the Captaincy of H.P. Dorsey.

[319]Davis letter, Pueblo, June 18-22, 1849.

at Santifee with ox teams and cant git any furder for they can't by[buy]
mules...[which]...sell from one to two hundred dollars apiece...[320]

By the time the Evans/Cherokee Company had reached Pueblo on
June 18, their lead on the trail to California had dwindled down
to a slim two to four days. Additional California-bound emigrants
followed into Pueblo, then decided how and which way to travel
further.[321] The number of wagons that joined the Evans/Cherokee

[320]Pyeatt letter, Pueblo, June 20-22, 1849.

[321]Captain Barber's (Barke's) mixed company of wagons and ox teams arrived
June 23 at Pueblo and continued on to Greenhorn, where the party split to
follow different routes. Barry...West...pp 858-59. [Col. Congreve] Jackson's
train of Waggons was on the upper Arkansas on June 15. The James Kirker-
piloted Illinois men traveled up the Arkansas to Pueblo; on to Greenhorn; and
from there a detachment of 50 men explored for gold on "Sangre de Cristo
creek." Eventually, some of the company, without Kirker, took the Gila route
to California. Dr. A.M. Heslep, of that train, in a July 8 letter from
Greenhorn, wrote about a third company "June 27 [at Pueblo], the Ithaca
company has been alternately in advance or rear of our company." Barry...
West...p 857. The Ithaca and California Mining Company pack-mule train,
captained by Charles V. Stuart, arrived at Pueblo in late June. The captain
wrote of obtaining a guide: "not finding a guide at Bents Fort we dispatched a
party to Taos New Mexico to procure Kit Carson [instead] we got a Mr.
[Charles] Kinney an old Mountaineer & a reliable brave Gentleman. After
consulting with him as to our course & having encountered some of Col Fremonts
men frozen and returning...we changed our course from the White River
[headwaters of the Arkansas River] to the more northerly pass on the Cach
Lapoudre or what is called the Medicine bow & Larrime plain, crossing Green
River at Brown's hole & thence by Fort Uinte to Utah Lake & Great Salt Lake."
Hafen & Hafen..."Stuart's Trip" Journals of Forty-Niners (Glendale, Calif:
Arthur H. Clark Co. 1961), vol. 15, p 18. Joseph Milner arrived at Taos on
June 20, departing north on June 23 "accompanied by Kit Carson, a few miles."
On June 30 Milner's group arrived at Pueblo, after crossing the Arkansas
River, and left the next day following the same route, perhaps with the Ithaca
company. MS 1449, Joseph Milner Papers, Univ. of North Carolina at Chapel Hill
Library, Historical Collection. Milner was with a company he did not identify
which had departed from Memphis by boat for Fort Smith on March 18. They left
Fort Smith April 1, got to Little River on April 25, arriving in San Miguel
[New Mexico] on June 4. They proceeded to Santa Fe [June 8], departed June 15.
Two weeks after leaving Pueblo, Charles Pancoast, traveling south, wrote of
meeting a Louisiana company who intended to go north toward Pueblo, then up
the "western borders of the Rocky Mountains to the Platte River...thence take
the northern Route to California." Anna Paschall Hannum, ed. A Quaker Forty-
Niner: The Adventures of Charles Edward Pancoast (Philadelphia, Pa: Univ, of
Pennsylvania Press 1930) p 211. According to Grant Foreman, Capt. Robert
Harris and his company from Washington and Crawford Counties, Arkansas, left
Fort Smith April 11, proceeding directly up the Arkansas River, planning to
cross the mountains near its head. Foreman Marcy...p 92. Barry, whose
objective was to mention everyone who traversed any part of Kansas, did not
mention this trip. The Fort Smith Herald, which solicited companies and their
rosters, did not mention the departure from that city, either during the time
period or after. Therefore it is conjecture to say they did or did not travel
the route they anticipated. Some have suggested it was Black Harris, who was,
however, dead of cholera in St. Louis by June 7, 1849. Fort Smith Herald 27
June 1849, vol 2, no 45. One Robert Harris was in one of the 1850 companies on
the Cherokee Trail.

Company during their four-day recruit at Pueblo is unknown. If
Lewis Evans left Pueblo with twenty-eight or twenty-nine of his
original wagons, as stated by two company members, then between
eleven and nineteen additional wagons joined his train, since both
forty and forty-seven wagons were later noted by members of Howard
Stansbury's Expedition.[322]

The Evans/Cherokee Company still led the way north, in two
divisions--packers and wagons. On June 22, the reduced wagon
company, enlarged by the addition of remnants of the Helena
(Arkansas) and perhaps other emigrant companies, turned north from
Pueblo, away from the Arkansas River for good. The turnbackers
headed home the same day. The packers, also expanded by recent
arrivals from Santa Fe, left within the following two days.

---

[322]Howard Stansbury *Exploration of the Valley of the Great Salt Lake*
(Washington, D.C.: Smithsonian Institution Press Reprint 1988). Stansbury
topographers Lt. John W. Gunnison noted forty wagons; Albert Carrington noted
forty-seven.

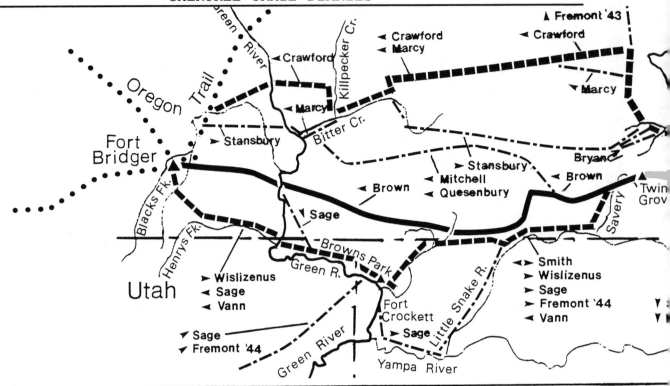

The Cherokee Trail
Bent's Old Fort to Fort Bridger

Showing some of the pre-1859 expeditions that traveled portions of the various branches of the Cherokee Trail.

Major Stephen H. **Long**, 1820:   U.S. expedition to the Rocky Mountains
Col. Henry **Dodge**, 1835:   Expedition of Dragoons to the Rocky Mountains
Elias Willard **Smith**, 1839:   Architect & civil engineer, pleasure trip
Frederick A. **Wislizenus**, 1839:   German physician, pleasure trip
Rufus B. **Sage**, 1842:   Traveled the West from 1841 - 1844
Cpt. John C. **Fremont**, 1843 - 1844:   Topographical engineer, his 2nd expedition
Francis **Parkman**, 1846:   Writer, scholar of American Indians
James Sawyer **Crawford**, 1849:   Member of the Lewis Evans Cherokee Expedition
James **Vann**, 1849:   Member of the Cherokee "Packers" group
John Lowery **Brown**, 1850:   Cherokee expedition to California
James **Mitchell**, 1850:   Cherokee expedition to California
William **Quesenbury**, 1850:   Cherokee expedition to California
Cpt. Howard **Stansbury**, 1850:   U. S. expedition returning east from Salt Lake City
Lt. Francis T. **Bryan**, 1856:   U. S. War Department expedition to Bridger Pass
Cpt. Randolph B. **Marcy**, 1858:   U. S. expedition from Fort Union to Fort Bridger

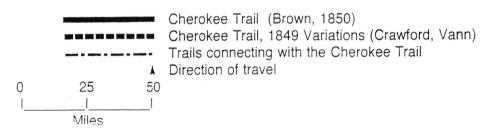

Cherokee Trail (Brown, 1850)
Cherokee Trail, 1849 Variations (Crawford, Vann)
Trails connecting with the Cherokee Trail
Direction of travel

0   25   50
|_____|_____|
Miles

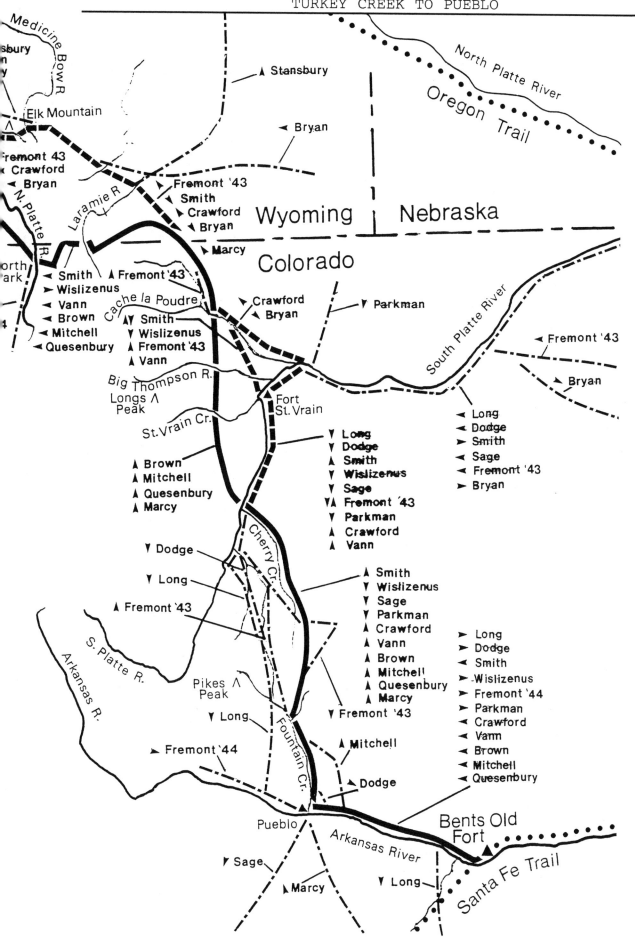

Chapter 6. PUEBLO TO GREAT SALT LAKE

Evans/Cherokee Company Packer Route

> we...passed over Laramie Plains to the headwaters
> of Yampah river, down said river to the Vermilion
> mountains, across said mountains to Brown's Hole,
> from thence to Bridgers.
>
> --James Vann, Cherokee

Information available at the time they were writing led Grant Foreman and other researchers to conclude that the Evans/Cherokee Company split at Pueblo, some members going north and others going south to Santa Fe.[323] The Crawford diary, and recently found letters from members of the Company reveal that no company members continued to Santa Fe. Secondly, Foreman gave the packer route as "past the present city of Laramie...westward through Bridger Pass."[324] However, in 1849 the Bridger Pass route did not exist.

In separate entities, both the Cherokee/white packers and the wagon group of the California-bound Company embarked north from Pueblo. The route had been for hundreds, perhaps thousands of years, a north-south travel corridor. Known as the Great North Trail, it ran on the east side of the Rocky Mountains from Alaska to Mexico. In the 1800s the portion from Pueblo to Fort Laramie became known as the Trappers Trail, or the Divide Trail.[325]

Travelers on that trail stayed near the foothills east of the Front Range of the Rocky Mountains because the area was less susceptible to the winds and blizzards of the plains. The wooded bottomlands along the trail's rivers and streams, protected for the most part by the mountains, offered an abundant variety of game as well as year-round cottonwoods for winter horse feed, fuel, and shelter. In addition, the corridor offered a more or less "safe" haven between the mountain dwelling Utes and the

---

[323]"one faction turning north instead of continuing with the remainder of the company to Santa Fe." Foreman...*Marcy*...p 75.

[324]Ibid. p 76. Bridger Pass was not explored until September 1850, by Capt. Howard Stansbury. 31 Cong. 1 sess. H. Exec Doc 5, Serial 569 p 307. Appendix B: Bureau of Topographical Engineers. Orders were written 11 April 1849.

[325]Whiteley "...Trappers Trail..."

Indians of the Plains.[326]

Fur trappers worked the rivers and streams of the Rocky
Mountains from their headwaters to their junction with the Platte.
Consequently, a series of trading posts sprang up along the South
Platte. In the 1830s, within three years, four posts were built in
a fifteen mile stretch of the South Platte: Fort Lupton;[327] Fort
St. Vrain;[328] Fort Jackson;[329] and Fort Vasquez.[330]

---

[326]The state of Colorado lies between meridians 102° and 109° west longitude.
The 105th runs through Fort Collins, Denver, Colorado Springs, Pueblo, and
Trinidad, and roughly marks the boundary between the plains and the mountains.
The part east of 105° is a treeless plain; mostly lower than 6,000 ft. and
without conifers, except for the Arkansas/Platte Divide, which is covered
mostly by yellow pine. Ellsworth Bethel "The Conifers or 'Evergreens' of
Colorado" *The Colorado Magazine* vol 2, no 1, (January 1925). Ponderosa Pine is
also called Western Yellow Pine (*Pinus ponderosa* Laws.) The Rocky Mountain
variety is *P. ponderosa* var. *scopulorum* Engelm. Preston...*Rocky Mountain*...p
19. Cottonwoods of the corridor were Narrowleaf *Populus angustifolia* Ibid. p
103 and Plains *Populus sargentii* Ibid. p 111.

[327]West Point graduate Lancaster P. Lupton was with Col. Henry Dodge and his
dragoons up the South Platte River in 1835. After resigning from the military
he went west to Fort Laramie, followed the Trappers Trail to the South Platte
River, where Vasquez and Sublette already had a post for trade. In 1836 Lupton
built an adobe/cottonwood fort 35 miles north of Cherry Creek and carried on a
very successful trade. His success motivated Fort Laramie and Fort Bent to
build branch posts. In 1839 David Adams was working for Lupton at "Fort Plat
at the mouth of Larima [River]." Charles E. Hanson, Jr., ed. "The David Adams
Journals" (Chadron, Nebr.: Museum of the Fur Trade 1994) p 2. In 1847 Lupton
moved to Hardscrabble (CO) south of Pueblo; from 1846 to 1848 he was involved
in the mail to and from Bent's Fort. In 1849 Lupton joined the gold rush to
California taking his family the Northern route. The 1850 California census,
Calaveras County, Calaveras Dist. listed L.P. Lupton-45, wife Thomasa-35,
John-13, Platte-11, George-9, and Elizabeth-3/12. Lupton's net worth $1,300.

[328]Built by Bent and St. Vrain, called Fort Lookout and Fort George before St.
Vrain. Harvey L. Carter, "Marcellin St. Vrain" LeRoy Hafen, ed. *Mountain Men
and the Fur Trade* vol 3, pp 273-78. Born October 17, 1815 in Spanish Lake,
Missouri, Marcellin came to Bent's Old Fort on the Arkansas about 1835. All of
Marcellin's first wife's children were born at Fort St. Vrain: Felix 17 June
1842; Charles 17 October 1844; Mary 9 March 1846. In 1848 Marcellin was ill;
taken to St. Louis in a Dearborn carriage accompanied by Wm. Bent and
Alexander Barclay. Marcellin came back well with Elizabeth Jane Murphey as
wife; they had ten children, the first born in 1851.

[329]Built by Peter A. Sarpy and Henry Fraeb in 1837 in response to the building
of Fort Lupton. Fort Jackson was sold to Bent and St. Vrain in 1838 and
subsequently abandoned.

[330]Built by Louis Vasquez and Andrew W. Sublette in 1837, Fort Vasquez was
sold to Lock and Randolph in 1840 or 1841 and "evacuated" in 1842 following a
business failure. Vasquez went into partnership with Jim Bridger to trade on
Blacks Fork of Green River, then Fort Bridger at its present site. LeRoy R.
Hafen "Louis Vasquez" Hafen... *Mountain Men*...vol 2, pp 321-38. Also LeRoy R.
Hafen, "Mountain Men-Louis Vasquez" *Colorado Magazine* vol 10, pp 16-19 (1933).
In summer 1849, Vasquez was east of South Pass in Wyoming encouraging
emigrants to go to Fort Bridger. On June 10, emigrant William G. Johnston
wrote, "near to the camp was a temporary trading post, established within a

Wislizenus wrote in 1839:

> We remained in the neighborhood of the forts [St. Vrain, Vasquez, Lupton] for about three days....Goods are usually transported to this place in great ox-team [from] Missouri.[331]

On July 4, 1843, Fremont stopped at Fort St. Vrain. Farther up the South Platte he noted the remains of two forts (Forts Vasquez and Jackson) and his arrival at Fort Lancaster (Lupton) ten miles south of Fort St. Vrain.[332] In 1849, Captain Evans relied on Fremont's journal writings.

In 1845 William Franklin traveled south from Fort Laramie, describing the fort locations and abandoned status:

> we passed St. Vrain's Fort and 6 miles further another old one....A few miles brought us to Luptons Fort and we passed two others during the day. These are all deserted now, the trade having become too small to support them....All of the forts are built like Fort Laramie....St. V's and Lupton's forts are both larger than Fort Laramie.[333]

The 1849 Evans/Cherokee Company members mentioned only the remains of Forts Lupton (called by them Fort Sabre) and St. Vrain.

Most literary references to this portion of the gold seekers' journey state the groups traveled "Pueblo to Bridger's," or the "South Platte to the Green River," as if there were a clear and easy path between the two. The route from Fort St. Vrain northwest to the Cache la Poudre River, north to the Laramie Plains, then west to Fort Davy Crockett at Brown's Hole had been used by explorers, trappers, and traders with their pack animals, and various plains and mountain Indian groups seasonally hunting. But it was a rigorous and dangerous route, subject to the vagaries of weather and unpredictable presence of Indians.

Split off from the wagon Company, the thirty Cherokee/white packers left Pueblo for the Green River on June 23 or June 24, 1849. With experienced guide Dick Owens they expected to travel

---

week past by Mr. Vasquez." He operated a ferry across the Green River and also opened a store in Salt Lake City in 1849. By 1859 Vasquez was in business in the new town of Denver, Arapahoe County, Kansas Territory.

[331]Wislizenus...*Journey*...p 138.

[332]J. C. Fremont, Brevet Captain of the Topographical Engineers. "Report of Exploring Expedition to the Rocky Mountains in the year 1842, and to Oregon and North California in the years 1843-45." Doc No 166 (Washington: Blair and Rivers, Printers, 1845). Jackson and Spence...*Fremont*...pp 436-45.

[333]Schubert...*South Pass*...p 25.

faster and easier on their intended route. Joining them were members of the Helena, Arkansas group who had traveled via Fort Smith to Santa Fe. The *Fort Smith Herald* noted the intended route of the Helena Company from Santa Fe:

> Twenty of us are going through from Taos with a Lieutenant who has been ordered to California as an aid to Gen. Smith. We expect to go north of the Old Spanish trail.[334]

Previous researchers have interpreted this statement to mean the company took the Old Spanish Trail. But they did not.

The "Lieutenant" was Alfred Pleasanton. His June departure from Santa Fe was noted in the *Cherokee Advocate*:

> Lt. Pleasanton, 2d Dragoons, Aid de Camp to Gen. Persifer P. Smith, with an escort of ten men from company H 2d Dragoons, left Santa Fe on the 9th [June] for California, via the South Pass.[335]

The assumption was that they would go to Fort Laramie. But that was in Santa Fe, before they knew Dick Owens would guide them. Pleasanton had traveled with Dick Owens in February and March of 1849 from Santa Fe to the Arkansas River and back again.[336] Pleasanton, after being assigned to California in June, chose to go with Owens, who had experience over the routes. Owens had been over this 1849 packer route to the Green River many times.[337]

These 1849 gold-seeking Arkansas and Cherokee "packers" were the least experienced group of any who had ever followed the trail that lay ahead of them. From Pueblo the route led north from the Arkansas River over the Arkansas/Platte Divide to the South Platte

---

[334]*Fort Smith Herald* 8 August 1849 vol 2, no 51, p 2. Letter written from Santa Fe on June 2. Also Ralph P. Bieber, ed. *Southern Trails to California in 1849* Southwest Historical Series (Glendale, Calif: Arthur H. Clark Co. 1937) vol 5, p 308 citing *Southern Shield* 31 August 1849.

[335]*Cherokee Advocate* Monday 30 July 1849 "Arrival from Santa Fe."

[336]Harvey L. Carter, "Dick Owens" Hafen...*Mountain Men* ...vol 5, p 288.

[337]In spring 1839 Kit Carson and Dick Owens were hunting in the Wyoming Black Hills, between the North Platte and the Laramie Plains. This trip also took them to Fort Hall; then south to Brown's Hole. In 1843 Owens was at Bent's Fort. In spring 1845 Owens was in Taos with Carson where they began to farm. However, when John C. Fremont came along in August, both sold out and went with Fremont--again. Subsequently Fremont would name the river and lake in California for Dick Owens. In 1846 Owens was Captain of Company A in Fremont's Battalion of Mounted Riflemen in California. He accompanied Fremont to Washington D.C., prepared to testify at Fremont's court martial. In January 1848 Owens was back at Taos, and was living there with Carson at his home when Fremont arrived there from his fatal winter trip in the Rocky Mountains.

at the present city of Denver. Continuing north, the trail stayed
on the east side of the South Platte River as far north as Fort
St. Vrain, near the junction of St. Vrain Creek and the South
Platte River.

Here the pack mule trail ran northwest toward Fort Davy
Crockett[338] at Brown's Hole, and later to Fort Bridger. This supply
and fur trading route was heavily used. Mountain men and travelers
visited the Brown's Hole area via this trail from 1825 to 1844,
many making notes about the "fort." Ashley in 1825; Colonel Bean's
trapping expedition the winter of 1831-2; Kit Carson, 1832. Carson
and three other trappers trekked from the Green River to North
Park; down the "corridor" from the Laramie Plains to the South
Platte River.[339] Robert Newell in 1837 left Sublette and Vasquez'

---

[338]Fort Davy Crockett in Brown's Hole was operated by Phillip Thompson,
William Craig and Prewitt Sinclair. LeRoy R. Hafen "Fort Davy Crockett, Its
Fur Men and Visitors" *Colorado Magazine* vol 29, (1952) pp 17-33. William Craig
settled in Brown's Hole in 1836. Fort Davy Crockett was reported to be the
social center of the Rockies. Built of log, it had three wings and a dirt roof
and floor. In 1837 Kit Carson and seven men went to Brown's Hole, joining
Thompson and Sinclair on a trading expedition to the Navajo Indians where they
traded for 30 mules, which Thompson took to Sublette & Vasquez at Fort
Vasquez. In 1838 Thompson joined Jim Bridger. Thompson, with other mountain
men reportedly went to California to steal horses in 1840.
The builders, owners and operators of Fort Davy Crockett were gone by the mid-
1840s; William Craig to Fort Walla Walla. James W. Bashford *The Oregon
Missions* (N.Y.: Abingdon Press 1918) Appendix 1, p 292 lists Craig among the
Oregon Pioneers. William Craig. a Mountain man with a Nez Perce wife, settled
at Lapwai, American Board missionary Henry Harmon Spalding's mission on the
banks of the Clearwater River at the mouth of Lapwai Creek in November 1839.
Mary Richardson Walker first mentions Mrs. Craig while all were at the
Rendezvous at Popo Agie in 1839, p 98. Mrs. Spalding records Craig "settled
here" p 214. The editor notes Craig's wife was "a daughter of Old [chief]
James, took a homestead about eight miles up the valley from Lapwai," and in
1845 "the wheat was however stacked except a portion let on shares to Mr.
Craig" p 283, indicates Craig was still in the area of Lapwai (present
Lewiston, Idaho). C. M. Drury *First White Women Over the Rockies...Six Women
of the Oregon Mission who made the Overland Journey in 1836 and 1838*
(Glendale, Calif: Arthur H. Clark Co., 1963) vol 2. Phillip Thompson went to
Oregon in 1842; Prewitt Sinclair to California in 1843. "Pruett St. Clair" is
listed as a member of "The Bean-Sinclair Party of Rocky Mountain Trappers,
1830-32" LeRoy R. Hafen, *Colorado Magazine* vol 31, no 3 (July 1954). A reduced
number of the original group set out from New Mexico in September 1831,
eventually going into winter quarters at Brown's Hole on Green River.
Prewitt's brother Alexander was killed by Indians at the Battle of Pierre's
Hole in July 1832. After that incident, the trapping party disintegrated. By
1839 Prewitt was one of the three owners of Fort Davy Crockett. Sinclair
settled in Santa Cruz County, California becoming an important citizen.
[339]Martin H. Schloo, "History of the Cherokee-Overland Trails; 'Fort Collins
and LaPorte, Colorado North to the State Line'" (Fort Collins, Colo.: 1995).

fort on the South Platte River on May 19 with two men, traveling to the Laramie Fork; then to the head of Little Snake River, bound for Fort Davy Crockett.[340]

T. Biggs from Fort Vasquez and C. Warfield from Fort St. Vrain in 1839 accompanied the Peoria (Illinois) Party. Their route, on advice of A[ndrew] W. Sublette and P[hilip] F. Thompson, had been the Santa Fe Trail to Bent's Fort where the party split. From there under the leadership of Robert Shortess, diarist, the party of eight proceeded over the Divide Trail to Fort St. Vrain on the South Platte and on to Fort Davy Crockett.[341] The other group included Thomas J. Farnham and four others who hired a trapper named Kelly to guide them across the Rockies via the headwaters of the Arkansas River. The party made their way to Fort "David Crockett" on Green River and subsequently to Oregon.[342]

E. Willard Smith joined a party of thirty in 1839 under Messrs. Vasquez and Sublette, owners of Fort Vasquez, who were transporting goods from Independence, Mo., by wagon, for their trading establishment on the South Platte. Philip Thompson, part owner of Fort Davy Crockett, was also in the party, transporting goods on twenty-seven mules to Fort Crockett. Along the Santa Fe Trail, near the Kansas/Colorado border, they overtook the oxtrain of Lancaster P. Lupton who was carrying goods to his trading Fort (Lupton) on the South Platte. From the Arkansas River, all took the Divide Trail to the South Platte. Smith accompanied Thompson's party leaving Fort Vasquez, traveling northwest to the Cache la Poudre; then north through the "corridor" to the Laramie Plains. There they went west, crossed the Medicine Bow mountains near the Colorado/Wyoming border, crossed North Park and the north-flowing North Platte river, and struck west to Fort Davy Crockett.[343]

---

[340]LeRoy R. Hafen, "Robert Newell" Hafen...*Mountain Men*...vol 8, pp 261-62.
[341]LeRoy R. and Ann W. Hafen, ed."The Peoria Party-Shortess" *To The Rockies and Oregon 1839-1842 with Diaries and documents* (Glendale, Calif: Arthur H. Clark Co., 1955) pp 104-05.
[342]Thomas J. Farnham, *An 1839 Wagon Train Journal: Travels in the Great Western Prairies The Anahuac and Rocky Mountains and in the Oregon Territory* (N.Y.: Greeley & McElrath 1843; republished by Northwest Interpretive Association 1983). Farnham described the fort on p 56.
[343]During winter 1839, between Brown's Hole and the North Platte, Smith and party killed and dried 100 buffalo, and bagged six grizzlies. Hafen and Hafen *The E. Willard Smith Journal* Far West...Rockies and Oregon... (Glendale,

Between September 1839 and April 1840 Smith traveled both ways over the route.[344] This route was virtually identical to that of the 1849 packer groups.

Kit Carson spent the winter at Fort Crockett in 1840; Rufus B. Sage in 1842. Sage described his route, which closely resembles the packer route of 1849 in reverse.[345] John C. Fremont saw the remains of Fort Davy Crockett in June 1844.[346]

The forts at both ends (St. Vrain and Davy Crockett) had active commercial lives during the 1830s. Fort Bridger flourished after the 1840s, trade shifting to the supplying of emigrant travelers to Oregon and California.

Crossing the South Platte at St. Vrain, the 1849 Packer route struck northwest intersecting the Cache la Poudre River near the mouth of Boxelder Creek, east of Laporte. The route (today's U.S. 287) went north from the Cache la Poudre over the divide between the waters of the Poudre and the Laramie Rivers onto the Laramie Plains, where it turned west.[347]

Passing through the south portion of the Medicine Bow Range, the route turned northwest through North Park to the North Platte River. Crossing the north-flowing North Platte, it ran northwest along the eastern base of the Sierra Madre Mountains, crossing the Encampment River and Jack Creek. Continuing in a westerly direction it crossed the Continental Divide at the Twin Groves (elevation 8,100 ft.). The route turned south along Savery Creek.[348] From there it went to the Little Snake River, west along

Calif.: Arthur H. Clark Co. 1955) vol 3. Also Hafen, "Journal of E. Willard Smith" *Colorado Magazine* vol 27, no 3 (July 1950) pp 166-88. Baptiste Charbonneau, son of Sacajawea was in the party as designated hunter for the Thompson party to Fort Davy Crockett, and for the spring journey east. Barry ...*West*...pp 378, 413.

[344]Baptiste Charbonneau, boated furs with seven others, including Smith, down the Platte, taking 700 buffalo robes and 400 buffalo tongues to St. Louis. Wislizenus...*Journey*...1839 pp 131-38.

[345]LeRoy Hafen and Ann W. Hafen, eds. *Rufus B. Sage: His Letters and Papers 1836-47 with...reprint of his "Scenes in the Rocky Mountains and in Oregon, California, New Mexico, Texas, and the Grand Prairies"* Far West and the Rockies Series (Glendale, Calif: Arthur H. Clark Co. 1956) vol 5, pp 183-85).

[346]Efforts to establish the exact location of Fort Davy Crockett are ongoing.

[347]The 1850 Cherokee/white goldseekers began building a wagon road westward from here (Willow Creek near present Tie Siding, Wyoming).

[348]Named for a trapper of Jim Bridger's era. Mae Urbanek, *Wyoming Place Names* (Boulder, Colo.: Johnson Publishing Co. 1967).

it, then to Vermilion Creek. Following the creek south the route entered Brown's Hole on the Green River.[349]

Five days behind the Evans/Cherokee forty-niner packers was the Ithaca Packing Company. Evans arrived at Pueblo on June 18, departed June 22; Ithaca Co. was mentioned at Pueblo on June 27. They hired Charles Kinney Mountain man for $700, choice of three mules, and two wagons. Janet LeCompte states he went through in thirty-eight days from Pueblo. The arrival date in Salt Lake would have been about August 2. While Kinney traveled the same route as Owens' as far as Brown's Hole, he then took the party southwest through the Uintah Mountains to Fort Uintah instead of north-northwest from Brown's Hole to Fort Bridger. Kinney was following (in reverse) Fremont's route of 1844 to Fort Uintah; Kinney then proceeded north to the Great Salt Lake. Charles Kinney was back in Greenhorn in 1850.[350]

Dick Owens led the combined Arkansas, Cherokee, and military packing company north from Brown's Hole along the Green River. Crossing the Green River proved disastrous. A "skin" raft was used to ferry the packs and supplies across the river. Company member James Garvin, who was ill, was put on the raft with the packs of Hiram Shores, Aaron Tyner, and the Morrow boys. Before reaching the west shore, the packs and Garvin went down, "to rise no

---

[349]Brown's "Hole" now called Brown's Park is a "...valley some forty miles in length along the Green River bounded on the south by Diamond Mountain [Uintah Range] and on the north by Cold Spring Mountain...[it] lies roughly half in Utah and half in Colorado with some of the northern extremities reaching into Wyoming...Nature provided mild winters which...provided ideal shelter for ...men...and...[animals]..." William L. Tennent, *John Jarvie of Brown's Park* (Bureau of Land Management Cultural Resource Series No 7, Utah State Office 1981, 1982, 1984) p 4.

[350]Janet LeCompte, "Charles Kinney" Hafen...*Mountain Men*...vol 4 pp 169-72. For details see Hafen and Hafen...*Journals of Forty-Niners*...vol 15 "A. Charles V. Stuart's Trip" pp 17-19; "B. Statement of W.C. Randolph" pp 20-22; and "C. Account by Judge H.S. Brown" pp 23-26. In the early 1830s, Antoine Robidoux built a trading fort in the Yampa (Bear) River area; he named it Fort Uintah (also called Fort "Winty" or Fort Robidoux). Frederic J. Athearn *An Isolated Empire: A History of Northwestern Colorado* (Denver, Colo.: BLM 1982) Cultural Resources Series Number Two p 22. From Pueblo, the Ithaca men took an "unusual route-via the Cache La Poudre, Laramie Plains, Browns hole, and Fort Uintah to Utah Valley." (quoting historian Dale L. Morgan). It was this route that George Withers and others of Captain Barber's company also traveled. Barry ...*West*...p 857. What is "unusual" about this route, if anything, is that Charles Kinney took the Ithaca Company from Brown's Hole west to Fort Uintah rather than northwest to Fort Bridger.

more."[351] The packers continued northwest to Fort Bridger, where
they struck the main California Road.

As this assemblage of packers approached Fort Bridger they
caused some excitement. Kansan Lorenzo Dow Stephens, emigrant
stopping at the fort, wrote:

> At the first fort [Laramie] there were twenty soldiers; and at the
> latter [Bridger] only Bridger and some Indians....Several of us boys had
> gone ahead of the train and were enjoying ourselves asking Bridger
> questions. He was an old mo[u]ntaineer and could give us good advice.
> While we were talking, Indians began to pour in from different quarters,
> very much excited and saying Indians were coming. Everybody hustles
> around, the Indians flocked in, the doors were barred, rifles made ready
> for the scrap, when a pack train hove in sight. It was an emigrant train
> from Arkansaw, and being the first one from that direction, from a
> distance, it was natural to infer they were Indians.[352]

The approach to Fort Bridger from the east or southeast was very
different from the approach used by the South Pass emigrants,
which was from the Northeast. Stephens did not know that a portion
of the "train from Arkansaw" were Indians--Cherokee.

The exact route taken by the combined packer company was
unknown until November 1994. Company member James Vann responded
to the following report in the 31 August 1853 *Cherokee Advocate*
which devoted nearly two full columns to the article "William
Claude Jones's Route to the Pacific--Highly Important Statement."
In an earlier letter to St. Joseph newspapers, Jones announced the
discovery of a "new" Railroad route to the Pacific:

> Mr. Jones...has set before the American people what no other man has yet
> pretended to do. [he] is the first man to describe a practicable route
> [railroad]....he describes minutely an easy passage through the
> mountains. [Jones wrote:] Crossing the South Fork [South Platte River]
> above St. Vrain's Fort, the route will skirt the base of the
> mountains...and enter a pass where the South Fork of the *Cache a la
> Poudre* bursts from the mountains. Then...through a prairie valley and
> over an elevated plain to the Medicine Bow mountain[s], near the source
> of Laramie river. This mountain is...covered with a dense forest of
> excellent timber for the construction of a road, some fifty miles south-
> east of the Medicine Bow Butte [Elk Mountain]. Emerging from this
> forest, it enters the North Park, passes the North Fork of the Nebraska
> or Platte, skirts the base of the main range [Sierra Madre], and crosses
> through a low prairie divide [Twin Groves], about two degrees south of
> the South pass, on the head waters of the North Fork of the North Fork
> of the Yampah river [Little Snake River], and enters the desert valley

---

[351]Oliver W. Lipe letter to his wife from Salt Lake, August 15, 1849. *Cherokee Advocate* 21 January 1850.
[352]Lorenzo Dow Stephens, *Life Sketches of A Jayhawker of '49* (San Jose, Calif.: Nolta brothers 1916).

of the Upper Colorado of the West [Green River]....It will not be
necessary to cut a solitary tunnel. Nature has graded the road....The
highest point of the pass is about 7,000 feet, and the ascent from the
east is gradual....On the west, it descends to Green river....The valley
of the Colorado [Green River] is desolate, except on the immediate
margins of the stream, and a group of detached mountains east of Brown's
Hole; yet it is rich in coal, this mineral being found in many
localities, and in large bodies...

Thence there are three routes that can be pursued--one by Ford[sic]
Bridger--one by the Winta [Fort Uinta] and Utah Lake, and the other more
central, up Henry's fork, and by the head of Webber river to the Great
Salt Lake City.[353]

The newspaper article indicated Jones had been over the route
himself, but did not divulge when or with whom.

On the Route map of the Stansbury Expedition of 1849-1850 to
and from Salt Lake an "1850 Jones Route" was drawn.[354] Much
research has been devoted to Jones' identity, speculation as to
the possible source of his knowledge, and how the route came to be
included on the official government map.[355] It appears that the
Jones Route was added after 1850, but prior to Lt. William
Gunnison's completion of the map for publication in 1852.

James Vann responded in the same edition of the *Cherokee
Advocate* to Jones' prospective railroad route:[356]

Of a part of the route as described by Jones we had ocular
demonstration. We crossed the South Platte at St. Vrain, entered the
mountains where Cache la Poudre burst forth from its mountainous
confines, bore a little north towards the Medicine Bow mountains,
crossed the mountains into the Parks, passed over Laramie Plains to
the headwaters of Yampah river, down said river to the Vermilion
mountains, across said mountains to Brown's Hole, from thence to
Bridgers: during our whole time in the mountains we did not see any
of these ascents over which rail roads can be built as if by magic. If
this route is so far preferable to any other, it is strange than it is

---

[353]In 1853, Lt. John William Gunnison left Fort Atkinson July 19 with
instructions to survey between the 38th and 39th parallel for a possible
railroad route. Was his assignment based on William Claude Jones' report?

[354]Howard Stansbury, *Exploration of the Valley of the Great Salt Lake* (Reprint
Washington, D.C.: Smithsonian Institution Press, 1988) Original title:
*Exploration and Survey of the Valley of the Great Salt Lake of Utah, including
a reconnaissance of a new route through the Rocky Mountains.* 1852.

[355]Another Jones, John Wesley, was by 1850 a Captain in the cavalry who
escorted immigrants from Fort Laramie to California. Ultimately he developed
the "Pantascope," a traveling exhibit derived from daguerreotypes and
sketches. Material held by the California Historical Society Vault MS 36 (82-
414). Diarist William Quesenbury (1850) traveled with Jones on his return trip
from California in 1851.

[356]James Vann, editor of the Cherokee newspaper prior to the 1849 California
trip, was a member of the Evans/Cherokee pack group. He resumed his editorial
chair December 23, 1851, following his return from California.

not the favorite route of Col. Benton, as it is one of Col. Fremont's
trails, as we were told so by our guide Owen, who was also Fremont's
guide along the same route. It is true we saw much beautiful and grand
scenery--fine water--but we saw none of the fine timber as described
(that is in great quantities,) but we saw that which is not spoken of by
Jones. We on the fifth of July saw and passed over...*snow*. If those
mountains were passed...without being tunnelled, many hundred
miles would be added...by running around them."

William Claude Jones described the 1850 Cherokee wagon
company route. Perhaps he traveled as a member of one of the four
Cherokee/white companies.[357] Jones resided in southwest Missouri
where members of both 1849 and 1850 Cherokee/white companies
originated. Ironically, when the railroad was built through
Wyoming years later, it followed much more closely the 1849
Evans/Cherokee Wagon Company route.

The combined packer company guided by Dick Owens entered Salt
Lake (City) on July 24, 1849. They happened onto the first Mormon
celebration of Brigham Young's 1847 entry into the valley. Company
member Cherokee George W. Keys described the festive event.[358]

> City of the Salt Lake,
> July 15th [25th],[359] 1849.
>
> Dear Brother:--I avail myself of the present opportunity of
> writing you a few lines to let you know that we are all well at
> present, we got here yesterday about 10 o'clock where we found five
> or six thousand Mormon inhabitants assembled at a feast or
> celebration, where they had met to celebrate the day of their arrival
> in the valley of the great Salt Lake two years ago.[360] This performance
> was very much like one of our temperance meetings. They marched

---

[357]See vol 2 *1850 Another New Route to the California Gold Fields.*

[358]The letter was preceded by: "The following is an extract from a letter of
Geo. W. Keys to his brother L.H. Keys. Mr. Geo. W. Keys, and others from this
neighborhood left about the 20th of April and joined Capt. Evans' Company, and
traveled in it to Publo, the foot of the Rocky Mountains. From thence they
have been travelling by pack horse."

[359]The date as printed is in error. The first Mormon celebration of Brigham
Young's arrival in the valley was July 24, 1849. Perhaps a typo in the
newspaper, the erroneous date has been copied by many researchers.

[360]Research in Mormon archives revealed: "July 23...Some emigrants for
California furnished 75 lbs. of powder for firing salutes." *Journal History*,
Church of Latter-Day Saints, Salt Lake City. The July 24 entry describes the
celebration in detail, but no reference to emigrants or the presence of
emigrants is made. At least these Cherokee and white packers, along with the
powder-provider emigrants, appreciatively participated in the consumption of
food. John Edwin Banks, member of the Buckeye Rovers company, noted: "Those
who came by Salt Lake say that the celebration of the 24th of the July by the
Mormons was a grand affair. All were invited, not less than five thousand
dined." Howard L. Scamehorn, ed. *The Buckeye Rovers in the Gold Rush, An
Edition of Two Diaries* (Athens, Ohio: Ohio Univ. Press 1965) p 62.

around their shed several times--the land [band?] of music in front
then 24 young men in white uniform with swords, in their hands,
then came 44 young ladies in white, followed by 12 old men bearsing
[bearing] flags or banner. After speaking, singing, and parading
round firing cannon &c., they sat down to as fine a dinner as you
would find any where--which to us was not bad to take. They had
lots of beans and peas, and potatoes &c. We have been about one
month coming from Pueblo to this place, a distance of about 100
miles[361] over one of the worst roads in the west, with several large
rivers to cross; we had them to swim and raft...We have passed a great
many emigrants since we struck the Northern road, besides what have gone
ahead and still behind. A great many of them have died with the cholera-
-We have heard that the company of Cherokees[362] that came by the way of
Independence have lost several of their men from the cholera[363] &c.
Flour and Bacon is worth 15 cents per lb here and scarce at that--The
News from California is very encouraging indeed--the Mormons tell us
that any man that will work can make from one to three hundred
dollars per day:

  From this place to California is about 800 miles,[364] we expect to
get there about the first of Sept. I must stop as the mail is about
ready to leave.[365]--I remain your affectionate brother until death
                                                C[G].W. KEYS. [366]

The combined Cherokee/white pack company led by Dick Owens
completed the Pueblo to Salt Lake journey in approximately one
month. The guide-less Evans/Cherokee wagon group took almost twice
that long, building wagon roads over quite a different route.

------

[361]An error; it is geographically impossible. The 1849 Evans/Cherokee wagons
went approximately 680 miles to cover the distance from Pueblo to Salt Lake,
albeit a different and longer route. This 100 mile figure was picked up by
Oakley p 56 and other researchers.

[362]Dr. Jeter Lynch Thompson's party traveled via the Independence-North Platte
route in company with Missourians led by Judge Tully. Struck by cholera, at
least 8 died--Samuel W. Bell, Brice Martin, William Parks, Elijah Blythe,
James Henry, ---Purly, Markham, and Judge Tully. See *Cherokee Advocate* 20
August 1849 and 21 January 1850.

[363]On June 9, George Gibbs, member of the Mounted Riflemen bound for Oregon
described the Cherokee illness and some deaths while camped in a ravine near
O'Fallon's Bluff east of North Platte, Nebraska. Raymond W. Settle, ed. *The
March of the Mounted Riflemen From Fort Leavenworth to Fort Vancouver May to
October, 1849 as recorded in the Journals of Major Osborne Cross and George
Gibbs and the official report of Colonel Loring* (Glendale, Calif: The Arthur
H. Clark Co. 1940) p 311. Burial was aided by some other emigrants. "When they
arrived four were dead....They dug a grave large enough for seven... covered
[the four]...and came away." James Eaton account, F.D. Calhoon, *The Lassen
Trail* (Sacramento, Calif: Cal-Con Press 1987) pp 46-47.

[364]The Evans/Cherokee wagon company traveling from Salt Lake to the Cosumnes
River via the Hastings Cut-off and Carson Pass, was measured by Pyeatt's
roadomiter as 775 miles, recorded by diarist James Sawyer Crawford.

[365]Almon Babbitt arrived in Salt Lake with mail July 1; left Salt Lake for the
East with the mail July 27. Barry...*West*...p 870.

[366]*Cherokee Advocate* 12 November 1849.

WYOMING

NEBRASKA

North Fork

Cache la Poudre R.

CHEROKEE

Boxelder Cr.

LATER CALIFORNIA
CROSSING

OREGON
TRAIL

South Platte River

0   15   30   45

Miles

FORT
ST VRAIN

'PACK'

1850 ROUTE

TRAIL

1849 ROUTE
OLIVER 1850

EASTERN
COLORADO

RALSTONS
CREEK

ROUTE OF THE CHEROKEE
1849 ROUTE

ROCKY   MOUNTAINS

South Platte R.

Cherry Cr.

RUSSELLVILLE

POINT OF ROCKS

PLATTE-
ARKANSAS DIVIDE

Big Sandy Cr.

Black Squirrel Cr.

JIMMY
CAMP

PIKES
PEAK

Fountain Cr.

CHEROKEE

Arkansas R.

Chico C.

MITCHELL
1850

TRAIL

SANTA FE TRAIL

BIG
TIMBERS

KANSAS

PUEBLO

BENT'S OLD
FORT

Arkansas River

TAOS TRAIL

△ GREENHORN

MOUNTAIN BRANCH

Timpas Cr.

Purgatoire River

SPANISH
PEAKS

SANTA FE TRAIL
CIMARRON
CUTOFF

NEW MEXICO

OKLAHOMA

Chapter 7. PUEBLO TO GREAT SALT LAKE

Evans/Cherokee Wagon Company Route

we sout out from this place [mouth of the Cache la Poudre] without road trail or guide

--John Rankin Pyeatt

Of the original Evans/Cherokee wagon Company, four wagons had turned back for Arkansas from Pueblo, and thirty members stayed over, preparing to "pack." On the morning of June 22, 1849, the remaining "29 wagons and 91 men"[367] started north from Pueblo joined by eleven to eighteen wagons gathered from other companies.[368] Their route followed the Divide, or Trapper's Trail, toward abandoned Fort St. Vrain. That segment was identical with the Packer Route.

Hiram Davis captured the beauty of the moment:

> We leave the [Arkansas] river today and take our way up the Boiling Spring River which has its rise in Pike's Peak as you will see from the map. This peak is 40 miles...and we travel directly towards it...you would suppose you could reach it in half an hour on horseback. The view...north and west is most grand and magnificent--the crown of Pike's Peak as well as the Taos (Tous) Mountains in the south is covered at this time with snow from 5 to 10 feet deep and as it glitters and flashes in the sunbeams reminding you of the gloomy days of December when people hang themselves. The beautiful green earth at your feet carpeted with various kinds of luxuriant grasses will remind you of May and the time of sweet flowers that are your especial delight and admiration. I have seen no beautiful flowers on this road. Perhaps if I had you along to tell me their names and point out their beauties, I could appreciate them more. I must not think of you and the flowers or I shall not be able to finish this letter.[369]

Pyeatt blacksmithed until the last minute, then hurriedly finished a letter for one of the turnbackers to deliver.

> now I am afinishing my letter whill the wagons ar getting reddy to start and all in confusion...on this ocasion as we are aleaving our friends in the wilderness   they will not start before tomorrow or next day   one worde more and I am don   that is Andrew [son] has the name of being the best boy in the company   he is very attentive to bisness and his

---

[367]Davis letter to his wife from Pueblo June 22, 1849, *Flashback* vol 1, no 1, (May 1959). Washington County Historical Society, Fayetteville, Arkansas.
[368]Gunnison, with the Stansbury Expedition noted forty wagons of Evans' company. Albert Carrington noted September 14th: "Evans' road (made with 47 wagons in /49)." Brigham D. Madsen, ed. *Exploring the Great Salt Lake: The Stansbury Expedition of 1849-50* (Salt Lake City: Univ. of Utah Press 1989) p 655.
[369]Davis letter, Pueblo, June 18-22, 1849.

helth is very good   this is the case with all the company with out
exception as far as I [k]now   may the Lord Bless you and children and
seport you in all your trials and dificultyes is my sincear prair giv
my lov and respects to all inquiring friends
To Elizabeth Pyeatt
                                        John R. Pyeatt[370]
                                By the favor of Thomas Tiner[371]

Hiram Davis finished his letter poignantly:

the wagons have started 2 hours ago and I must hurry to overtake them.
It may be some time before I will have a chance to write to you again,
my dearest Elizabeth, but I shall think of you none the less--I fear too
much. I am too full to say more than to advise you to take good care of
your sweet little self until the return of him that loves and adores you
above all things in heaven or earth. The dear children, say many kind
things to them for me and don't let them forget they have a father.
Write.

                                        Your affectionate
                                        Husband Hiram

     Leaving Pueblo on the Trapper's or Divide Trail, the Company
began a gradual ascent from 4,660 ft. elevation, toward the 7,520
ft. watershed Divide between the Arkansas and Platte rivers. The
Divide is a high plateau which projects east/west, perpendicular
to the main Rocky Mountains. An 1839 traveler, E. Willard Smith,
noted the change in elevation:

7th [September] We have been going up hill all day, & have reached some
high ground and have a splendid view of the plain below. We can see at
least eighty miles in either direction...We ate our dinner at a creek
called Fontaine Quibouille, boiling Spring, called so on account of the
manner in which it boils from the mountain.[372]

Diarist Crawford resumed keeping the 1849 mileages.

"friday 22 [June] Fountain qui buit. 21 1/2 [miles]"
       [approximately 9 miles south of present Fountain,
                   El Paso Co., Colorado]

     The next camp, Jimmy's Spring, also called Jimmy Camp, lies
approximately 20 miles east of Pikes Peak, and was one of the most
heavily used camps on the Divide or Trappers Trail. Crawford:

"Saturday 23 [June] Jimmy's springs 21 3/4 [miles]"
        [8 miles east of present Colorado Springs,
                   El Paso Co., Colorado]

---

[370]Pyeatt letter, Pueblo, June 20-22, 1849.
[371]Thomas Tyner, a turnbacker, took this letter with other letters and goods,
back home to Arkansas with him. Thomas' son Aaron continued to California from
Pueblo as one of the thirty Company packers. Aaron and others would lose
everything when a skin raft turned over crossing the Green River .
[372]Hafen and Hafen...*Smith Journal*...p 165.

Sage, 1842, described Jimmy's Camp:

we reached an affluent of Fontaine qui Bouit, called Daugherty's creek.....the creek derives its name from [James] Daugherty, a trader who was murdered upon it several years since....Here we remained for three or four days, to procure a further supply of provisions...An abundance of grass.[373]

Sunday the Company reached the Arkansas/Platte Divide. Crawford:

"Sunday 24 [June]   Peninsula Prairie   15 [miles]"
[near Point of Rocks on the Arkansas/Platte Divide
4 miles NW of Eastonville, El Paso Co., Colorado]

Sage had described the area as:

an interesting plateau, furrowed at intervals by deep canons, enclosing broad bottoms of rich alluvion, and ridged upon either hand by high hills of pine and ledges of naked rock...a rough country, interspersed with high piny ridges and beautiful valleys, sustaining a luxuriant growth of vegetation...known as the Divide. [it is] a sweet little valley enclosed by piny ridges.[374]

One of the features of the immediate area is the Black Forest, named from the appearance of the dense Ponderosa Pines.

To-day & yesterday we passed through some strips of pine timber, the first I have seen in this part of the country. It is quite a relief after having seen nothing but cottonwood along the prairie streams.[375]

The 1849 company moved north across the plateau onto the headwaters of Cherry Creek. Crawford:

"monday 25 [June]   Cherry Creek   21 [miles]"
[Two miles north of Castlewood Canyon State Park,[376]
Franktown, Douglas Co., Colorado]

Cherry Creek is characterized by steep-sided bluffs or cliffs near this campsite. Sage described the Creek and valley in 1842:

---

[373]Hafen and Hafen...*Sage*...pp 71-72.

[374]Ibid. pp 70-71.

[375]Hafen and Hafen...*Smith Journal*...1839. The 1845 party of Stephen Kearney, traveling toward Bent's Fort from Fort Laramie described the Black Forest area: "Near the head of this stream there is fine timber....for one day's journey, a part of the road, six miles in length, led through the pine forest." 29 Cong. 1 sess. 1846 vol I, Senate Doc., Serial 470 p 214.

[376]In August 1933, after a series of intense rains, the Castlewood Dam, built in 1890 across one of the narrow canyons three miles south of Franktown for irrigation and to hold back the periodic floodwaters of Cherry Creek, burst-- sending water, houses, barns, livestock and personal goods down the creek to inundate the city of Denver. Jack E. and Patricia A. Fletcher, *The History of Glendale, Colorado*. (Denver, Colo.: City of Glendale 1983) p 69.

This stream is an affluent of the Platte, from the southeast, heading in a broad ridge of pine hills and rocks, known as the 'Divide.' It pursues its course for nearly sixty miles, through a broad valley of rich soil, tolerably well timbered, and shut in for the most part by high plats of table land, - at intervals thickly studded with lateral pines, cedars, oaks, and shrubs of various kinds.

Sage described the stream characteristics and gave the reason for its name:

[Cherry Creek] gradually expanding its banks as it proceeds, and exchanging a bed of rocks and pebbles for one of quicksand and gravel, till it finally attains a width of nearly two hundred yards, and in places is almost lost in the sand. The stream derives its name from the abundance of [choke] cherry found upon it.[377]

Parkman, in 1845, also noted:

we reached Cherry Creek. Here was a great abundance of wild cherries, plums, gooseberries, and currants. The stream, however, like most of the others which we passed, was dried up with the heat, and we had to dig holes in the sand to find water for ourselves and our horses[378]

Descending from the Divide plateau into the broad sandy valley, they camped near the intermittent stream.[379] Crawford:

"tuesday 26 [June]   Camp Hand   20 [miles]"
[Cherry Creek Reservoir State Recreation Area,
Arapahoe Co., Colorado]

During the next day's travel, the Company descended to the junction of Cherry Creek and the South Platte River, where the city of Denver presently stands.[380] Though previous researchers have written that gold was discovered near here in 1849, Crawford's diary, as well as the Pyeatt and Davis letters, confirm that no time was spent in looking for gold near the site of the future city of Denver. Rather, Cherokees panned for and found gold

---

[377]Hafen and Hafen...*Sage*...p 69.
[378]Parkman...*Oregon*....p 256.
[379]"Though Cherry Creek is an intermittent creek, more often a river of sand than water, the real wealth lay not on the surface but deep in the sands of the bed. There a pure, large stream of water flows throughout the year." In July 1887 from the sands of dried-up Cherry Creek, the gravity flow provided the city of Denver with "nine million gallons of water a day." Fletcher and Fletcher... *Glendale*...pp 51-52. "An average of two to five million gallons a day was extracted from its sands until the 1950s when the wells (called galleries) were closed because of upstream landfill pollution." Ibid. p 69.
[380] The company descended from 7,520 ft. on the Arkansas/Platte Divide to 5,180 ft. elevation at the junction of Cherry Creek and the South Platte River.

north of this site in 1850 after crossing the South Platte.[381]

Remaining on the east side of the river, the Company traveled northeast down the Platte. Crawford:

"wednesday 27 [June]   Camp Platt.   22 [miles]"
[approximately one mile upstream from present
Henderson, Adams Co., Colorado]

**"thursday 28 [June]   Old fort Sabre [Lupton][382]
16 1/2 [miles]"**
[1 mile north of present Fort Lupton, Weld Co., Colorado]

The company rolled past the remains of two other trading forts, Fort Jackson and Fort Vasquez, to Fort St. Vrain. Crawford:

"...friday 29 [June]   St. Vrain   13 [miles]..."
[1 mile north of the St. Vrain Creek and South Platte River
junction, Weld Co., Colorado]

Pyeatt's letter: "from Pueblo to St. vrain on the sout fork of the Platt a distance of 140 miles we had good road."[383]

Fort St. Vrain was the largest fur-trading post along the South Platte Valley. It was 125 ft. long and 100 ft. wide, with walls two ft. thick and fourteen ft. high constructed of adobe. Its location halfway between Bent's Fort and Fort Laramie made it a well-known meeting and trading place.[384] Parkman found in 1846:

> At noon we rested under the walls of a large fort, built in these
> solitudes some years since by M. St. Vrain. It was now abandoned and
> fast falling into ruin. The walls of unbaked bricks were cracked from
> top to bottom. Our horses recoiled in terror from the neglected
> entrance, where the heavy gates were torn from their hinges and flung
> down. The area within was overgrown with weeds, and the long ranges of
> apartments once occupied by the motley concourse of traders, Canadians,
> and squaws, were now miserably dilapidated.[385]

---

[381]Discovery by Lewis Ralston in 1850 led to exploration by Cherokee in 1858.

[382]The reason Crawford gave it this name is unclear. It was built by Lancaster P. Lupton and abandoned by 1849. The old Fort Lupton is currently being reconstructed.

[383]Pyeatt letter to his wife, "Salt Lake, California" August 12, 1849. Diarist Crawford recorded 150.75 miles from Pueblo to Fort St. Vrain.

[384]Marcellus (Marcellin) St. Vrain ran this fort. Kit Carson called it Fort Bent in 1843. Brent N. Petrie, "Map Showing Outstanding Landmarks in the Boulder-Fort Collins-Greeley Area, Front Range Urban Corridor, Colorado." USGS Misc. Investigations Series, Map I-855-F.1975. Fremont used the fort in 1843; found abandoned by Kearny's "March to South Pass" troops in 1845. Hamilton Gardner "Captain Philip St. George Cooke's March in 1845" *Colorado Magazine* vol 30, no 4, (October 1953) p 263. Also Schubert...*Franklin*...1845 p 25.

[385]Parkman...*Oregon*...p 255.

In 1849 it was still importantly mentioned by emigrants as a "place," perhaps because it appeared on the maps and in the reports of John C. Fremont. The Evans/Cherokee Company had Fremont materials in their possession and depended upon them for travel. In a reminiscence, Company member James Pierce noted: "we followed the Fremont trail via Pueblo, Cache Le Poudre and Cherry Creek."[386]

The skeletal remains of Fort St. Vrain had important value to the company. Pyeatt:

> we made a ferry boat at St vrains f[or]t out of plank that w found thear (the fort being dserted for sometime back) and took it...down the platt...17 miles...to the mouth of another stream [Cache la Poudre River] that runs in on the other side of the Platt....we had to go below the mouth of this stream...down to the crossing...to avoid having It to fery it and the platt both being swiming....this boat was large enough to cary the largest of our wagons without unloading them.[387]

Finding both rivers high, the "ferry boat" was necessary in saving time; wagons didn't have to be dismantled. Captain Evans obviously preferred to cross only one river--the South Platte, after its confluence with the Cache la Poudre. Crawford:

"Saturday 30 [June]   Cache la poudre 17 1/2 [miles]"
[junction of Cache la Poudre and South Platte Rivers,
five miles east of present Greeley, Weld Co., Colorado]

Crossing the entire company took four days. Having done all the work building their raft and using it, they left it. Pyeatt explained: "when we ware don crossing we drew the boat out on the North side of the river and left it for the bennefit of the nex that should com along this road."

From their position, they would have seen the Rocky Mountains directly west of them. Pyeatt's letter described what they saw:

> [we] was in sight of a considreable fall of snow about the last of June it fell on the mountains one day about twelve o clock and was plain to be seen the next day.

---

[386]*Salt Lake Tribune* "The Find on the Desert" Sunday 11 May 1902 p 31.
[387]Pyeatt letter, Salt Lake, August 12, 1849. Fort St. Vrain is often described as having adobe-walled construction. It is obvious from Pyeatt's description of the use of the "planks" for a ferry, that there was sufficient and large lumber or boards at the deserted fort. Pyeatt's wagon, for instance, held his entire blacksmithing equipage including a forge. Not having to unload was important to him. Clearly a rather large ferry was constructed, and floated downstream to the confluence of the Cache la Poudre and South Platte.

The Evans/Cherokee wagon company proceeded west along the north side of the Cache la Poudre. William H. Ashley traveled this portion of trail up the Poudre in 1825.[388] Whether he took a wagon this far is debatable. In February, 1825 Ashley wrote: "the scene around us was pretty much the same as when we arrived, everything enveloped in one mass of snow and ice."[389]

The Evans/Cherokee Company was pioneering again. They were the first to build a wagon road the entire distance between the South Platte River Crossing east of Greeley (Colorado), and the North Platte River near present Pick Bridge in Wyoming. This road was known as the Cherokee Trail until at least 1862.

Company member Pyeatt's following statement shows very clearly that 1) they were having to cut and build their own road for wagons and 2) the company did not hire a part-Osage guide at Pueblo as has been reported in past research:

> we sout [set] out from this place [at the mouth of the Cache la Poudre] without road trail or guide through the plains and hills   we succeded very well from 15 to 20 miles a day for sometime.[390]

From Greeley west to Laporte and then north to the Laramie Plains, the company would ascend more than 3,400 ft. in elevation within seventy miles of travel. Only in their travel from Pueblo north to the Arkansas/Platte Divide, did they have a comparable ascension in such short distance. Crawford recorded two days:

"June [July] monday 2   Mosquitto[391]   **10 1/2. [miles]"**
[approximately 5 miles west of Greeley, Weld Co., Colorado]

---

[388]Harrison C. Dale, *The Ashley-Smith Explorations, The Ashley Narrative* (Glendale, Calif: The Arthur C. Clark Co. 1918) p 128. The name of the river is reportedly derived from this Ashley expedition when it became necessary to temporarily cache or store powder in the bank of the river. Harvey L. Carter "Ewing Young" Hafen, *Mountain Men...*vol 2, pp 383-84. Col. Dodge mentioned "Cache de la Poudre" in 1835. "A Report of the Expedition of the dragoons under Colonel Henry Dodge, to the Rocky Mountains, during the summer of 1835, &C." (Washington D.C.: 1836). Smith, 1839 "18th [September] We encamped last night on a small stream, Cache-la-Poudre, called so because powder was hidden there some time since." Hafen...*Smith Journal*...vol 3, p 169 n.
[389]Dale...*Ashley*...p 128.
[390]Pyeatt letter, Salt Lake, August 12, 1849.
[391]The company members were accustomed to the malarial anopheles of the lower Arkansas and Missouri rivers. They might have been unfamiliar with the lesser damage these insects might inflict. The campsite was named for the abundance of mosquitoes, also noted in 1850 on this river.

"tuesday 3 [July]   Crow Camp, Boxelder[392] **20 [miles]"**
[Junction of Box Elder Creek with the Cache la Poudre,
east of present Fort Collins, Larimer Co., Colorado]

The morning of July 4, traveling west along the Cache la
Poudre downstream from its constriction by the mountains, the
Evans/Cherokee Company passed present Fort Collins and Laporte.
Laporte was the most notably used crossing of the Poudre River.
Trappers and traders had used it for over two decades in their
pack train travels between the Rockies and the forts along the
Platte and Arkansas.[393]

The 1849 wagon company traveled over the same ground Fremont
had. Evidence today indicates that Fremont did not travel up the
main stream of the Poudre River, taking instead the North Fork.[394]
Evans probably explored the possibility of taking Fremont's route
up the North Fork, finding it impassable for wagons. By evening
the two routes converged. Fremont's "we camped near the end of the
pass at the mouth of a small creek [Lone Pine Creek]" is the same
place as the Evans/Cherokee July 4 campsite.

---

[392]"Boxelder creek is formed by several smaller streams, notably one rising in
Wyoming and another in Larimer county [Colorado].when it comes out on the
Plains it sinks in the sand to rise again further down and for some distance
forms a running stream, then again loses itself in the sand." Ansel Watrous,
History of Larimer County, Colorado. (Fort Collins, Colo.: The Courier
Printing and Publishing Co. 1911) p 203.

[393]Joseph Antoine Janis (Jaunisse), employed by the American Fur Company in
the 1830s, was known to be at this Cache la Poudre crossing, arriving from
Taos in 1844. In 1859 he returned with his family and built a cabin at what
would become Laporte, Colorado. Barry...*West*...pp 231, 415. Fremont crossed on
July 28, 1843 traveling northwest after leaving Fort St. Vrain. "from Fort St.
Vrain west over the Laramie Plains....A few trappers had been in that country
before....Ezekiel Williams and his companions in 1807...fleeing before hostile
Indians. Jacques Laramie...ten or twelve years later...paid for his daring
with his life." C.G. Coutant, *The History of Wyoming* (Laramie, Wyo.: Chaplin,
Spafford & Mathison, Printers 1899) Chapter 20, p 279.

[394]"Fremont's second expedition went through the Livermore country in July of
1843. The expedition camped near what is now Ted's [Ted's Place was a local
cafe, store and gas station at the intersection of U.S. 287 and Colorado
Highway 14] and, finding they could not go up the main Poudre, Kit Carson
guided the party over a low gap....Fremont's party dropped down on the North
Fork above the present location of Fort Collins City waterworks. Thinking they
were on the main Poudre, they came up the North Fork as far as its junction
with the Pine (Creek) and then followed practically the same route as the
present highway to Virginia Dale and over the divide." Gertrude G. Barnes
"History of Silver Bow Ranch, Livermore" *Colorado Magazine* (July 1951) p 281.
"The description of the journey of 29 July seems to describe the canyon on the
North Fork of the Cache la Poudre, above Fort Collins." Jackson and Spence...
Fremont...p 455, on Ms. Barnes research.

Crawford:

"wednesday 4 [July] Independence, Boxelder 18 [miles]"
[present Livermore, Larimer Co., Colorado]

Fremont noted he subsequently traveled:

along a kind of vallon, bounded on the right by red buttes and
precipices, while to the left a high rolling country extended to a range
of the Black Hills....in the afternoon travelled over a high country,
gradually ascending toward a range of buttes, or high hills covered with
pines, which formed the dividing ridge between the waters we had left
and those of Laramie river.[395]

This aptly describes the Evans/Cherokee traverse toward present
Virginia Dale, Colorado. Crawford:

"thursday 5 [July]   Big grass Camp   15 [miles]"
[later Virginia Dale stage station, Larimer Co., Colorado][396]

The forty-niners crossed the present boundary into Wyoming,
entering the Laramie Plains at an elevation of 7,700 ft. George
Frederick Ruxton described the Laramie Plains:

the extensive bend of the Platte which incloses the Black Hill range on
the north, and which bounds the large expanse of broken tract known as
the Laramie Plains, their southern limit being the base of the Medicine
Bow Mountains.[397]

A Company member reminisced they were supplied with game:

From the Little Arkansas to the Laramie plains we were scarcely ever out
of sight of buffalo, an our larder was always stocked with five or six
kinds of wild game.[398]

On the Laramie Plains in present Wyoming, Crawford noted:

"friday 6 [July]   Big willow grove   14 [miles]"
[Willow Creek, south of present Tie Siding,
Albany Co., Wyoming][399]

The Company proceeded northwest across the Laramie Plains
camping near Fremont's camp of six years earlier.

---

[395]Fremont...*Report*...p 122.

[396]Named for his wife, the place was made famous by Jack Slade, Overland Stage
Station Manager and sometime outlaw. It remains a Colorado Historic Landmark
site near the Colorado/Wyoming border.

[397]George Frederick Ruxton, *In The Old West* (Oyster Bay, N.Y.: Outing
Publishing Co. 1915) p 131.

[398]Pierce...*Tribune*...1902. There are some areas within this description which
were known to be destitute of buffalo in 1849.

[399]Today's name derived from a much later railroad tie collection point. Ties
cut from "The Black Forest" were hauled to the site over the Cherokee wagon
road cut through in 1850.

Crawford:

"Saturday 7 [July] South Larime [River], main fork
16 [miles]"
[eight miles SW of present Laramie,[400] Albany Co., Wyoming]

The wide use of the name "Laramie" has added much confusion and misinterpretation regarding locations of the Cherokee Trail. *Laramie* has been interpreted variously as referring to Fort Laramie, the present city of Laramie, Laramie River(s), or Laramie Plains. Only the Laramie River(s) and the Laramie Plains should be considered in describing the Cherokee Trail routes. Crawford:

"Monday 9 [July]   Middle fork Larime   19 [miles]"
[Little Laramie River 18 miles NW of present Laramie,
Albany Co., Wyoming]

Toward the north end of the Medicine Bow Mountains traveling became more difficult for the forty-niners. Pyeatt wrote: "[when] we got with in som 40 or 50 miles of the North fork of the Platt...the hells became worse and we had to detain more time hunting out the rout and working it ."[401] Fremont, 1843: "we took our way directly across the spurs from the point of the mountain, where we had several ridges to cross."[402] The Company probably took comfort in the fact that Fremont had traveled and camped here not many years before.

Now working the road more, the Company moved on. Crawford:

"Tuesday 10 [July]   Godards Creek   18 [miles]"
[approximately 7 miles SE of Arlington, Carbon Co., Wyoming;
one mile west of the Carbon/Albany county line]

"Wednesday 11 [July] Medicine bow Creek   15 [miles]"
[approximately 6 miles south of present town of Elk Mountain,
on Medicine Bow River, Carbon Co., Wyoming]

The dominant physical feature of the landscape before them was Elk Mountain. Fremont noted that "Medicine Butte" appeared

---

[400]All uses of the name Laramie are derived from the same source. Jacques la Ramie (French Canadian) according to Jim Bridger, came to the area as head of some independent trappers, including Bridger, around 1817 to trap the Platte and north of there. In 1820 la Ramie went up the river which would later bear his name, and was killed by Indians. It "is variously spelled as la Ramee, la Ramie, Larame, and Laramie." Lola Homsher, "History of Albany County to 1880" *Annals of Wyoming* vol 21, nos 2 & 3 (July and October 1949) n p 183.
[401]Pyeatt letter, Salt Lake, August 12, 1849.
[402]Fremont...*Report*...p 124.

isolated and to be about 1,800 ft. above them, with snow "reaching from the summit to within a few hundred feet of the trail."[403] He turned left and entered the pass on a broad trail that quickly deteriorated to ravines and thick aspen groves. South of Elk Mountain, he noted present Pass Creek and Coad Mountain.[404] The wagon company moved south around Elk Mountain just as Fremont had. Crawford:

"Thursday 12 [July]   Medicine butte   11 [miles]"
[4 miles SW of Elk Mountain (Medicine Butte), north of Coad Mountain on Pass Creek, Carbon Co., Wyoming]

Fremont, in 1843 described the approach and camp on present Pass Creek: "Continuing our way over a plain on the west side of the pass, where the road was terribly rough with artemisia, we made our evening encampment on the creek, where it took a northern direction."[405] The 1849 Company approached the same place. Crawford noted the camp:

" Friday 13 [July]   Camp Fremont   8 [miles]"
[Pass Creek, 10 miles NE of Saratoga, Carbon Co., Wyoming]

Captain Howard Stansbury was sent by the federal government in 1849 to survey the Salt Lake country.[406] In 1850, work done, he returned east along Bitter Creek with Jim Bridger as guide, noting various places along their route where the 1849 Evans/Cherokee Company intersected or paralleled their path. At Pass Creek, topographer Carrington noted, "we arrived...at a small stream...which Fremont passed in 18 [left blank] & afterward Evans team of 47 wagons." Lieutenant Gunnison, topographer, recorded forty wagons in Evans' company.[407]

---

[403]Ibid. p 125. The Elevation of Elk Mountain is 11,156 ft.; the 7,500 ft. contour line is at its base.

[404]Pass Creek was named by Howard Stansbury in 1850.

[405]Fremont...Report...p 125. Ashley, in the area in 1825: "We used as a substitute for fuel an herb called wild sage. It resembles very much in appearance the garden sage but acquires a much larger growth and possesses a stock of from four to five inches in diameter. It burns well and retains fire as long as any fuel I ever used." Dale...Ashley...p 133.

[406]31 Cong. 1 sess. H Ex doc 5, Serial 569, p 307 Appendix B: Bureau of Topographical Engineers. Stansbury was also instructed to employ another topographer (Albert Carrington) and other men "who know the area." Carrington: "Fremont had represented this pass as very rough & Bridger declared it extremely difficult for wagons." Madsen...Stansbury...p 654.

[407]Ibid. p 655.

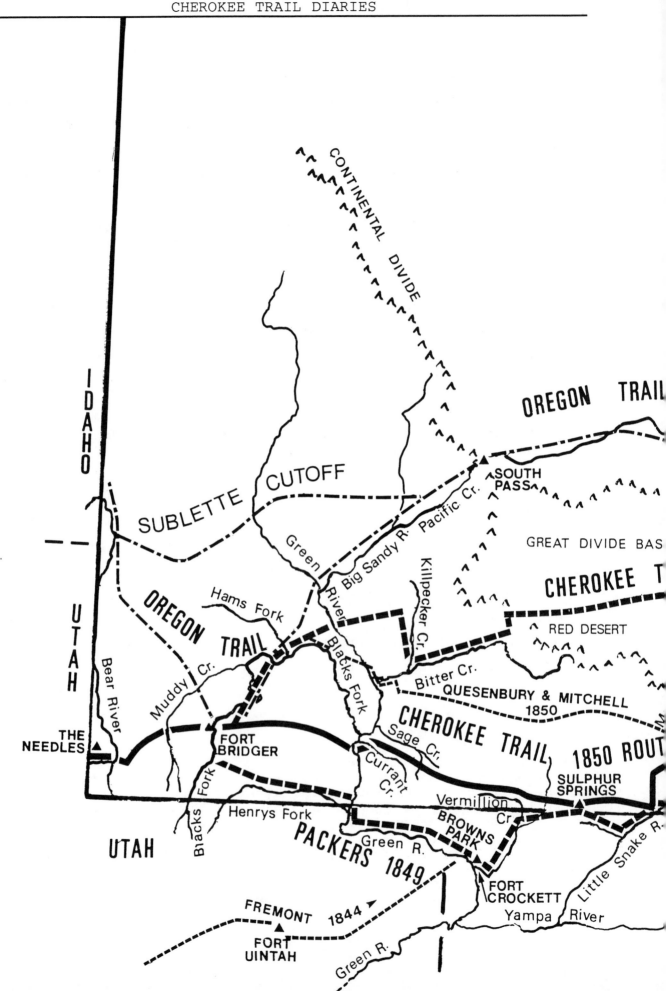

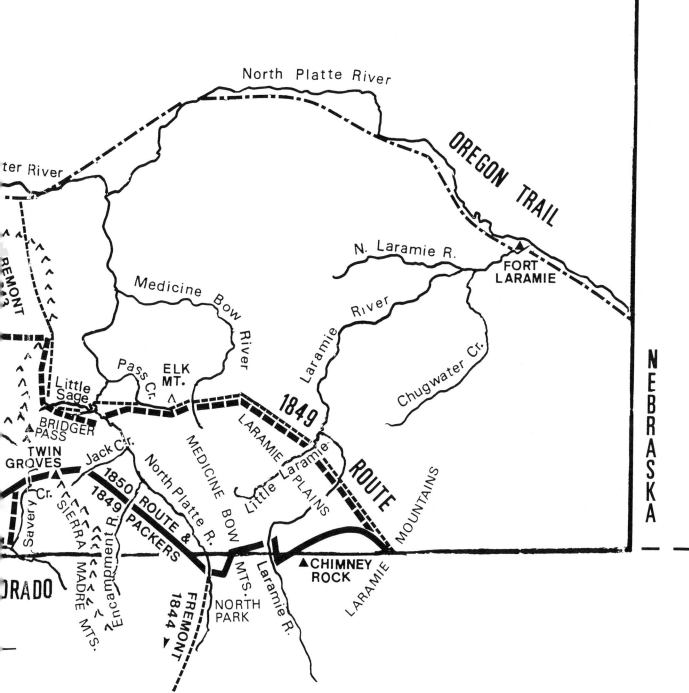

SOUTHERN
WYOMING

ROUTE OF THE CHEROKEE
1849 ROUTE

0   15   30   45
Miles

Leaving Camp Fremont at Pass Creek, the 1849 wagon company worked the road west to the North Platte River. Crawford:

"Saturday 14 [July]   North Platt   12 [miles]"
[7 miles NW of Saratoga, Carbon Co., Wyoming]

In its upper reaches, the North Platte flows north from the Colorado mountains into Wyoming, as far north as Casper. Passing north around the Laramie Mountains (known then as the Black Hills) the river turns east to Nebraska. It is along the banks of this east-flowing portion that the Oregon-California emigrants traveled. Both the 1849 and 1850 Cherokee Trails crossed the North Platte River in its upper reaches.

Pyeatt's letter described their river arrival and crossing:

we got to this stream [North Platte] on Satrday evning and I[n] tending to spen the sabath hear but oing to hevy cloud that lay upe the river we became afraid the river would rize and it being scarcely foardiable we htched up and crossed the river on Sunday evning.[408]

Crawford:

"Sunday 15th [July] Crossed the North Platt"[409]
Immediately upon crossing, Captain Evans sent out the Company scouts, as was his consistent policy. Pyeatt, "on Sunday evning having a prty out [to] look out [scout] the route [they] retrned on Sunday evning to guide us on to the next camping place."

Crawford records moving west from the North Platte River:

"Monday 16 [July]   Mud Creek[410]   12 [miles]"
[Sage Creek, Carbon County, Wyoming][411]

_____

[408]The Evans/Cherokee wagon company crossing in July was during the annual "runoff" from the Rocky Mountains on the south and Sierra Madre Mountains on the east hence Pyeatt's "scarcely fordiable." The 1849 Company crossed south of the mouth of Sage Creek; Fremont in 1843 crossed north (downstream) of the mouth of Sage Creek.

[409]Captain Stansbury, crossing in September 1850, found the North Platte seasonally low. "The river in its present stage is one hundred sixty feet wide and two feet deep; the bed consisting of gravel, rolling pebbles, and boulders." Stansbury...*Exploration*...p 244.

[410]Not to be confused with Muddy Creek, west of Bridger's Pass, explored by Stansbury in 1850.

[411]Lt. Francis T. Bryan noted on Wednesday, August 13, 1856: "Leaving the North Platte, and following the beaten road (Evans',) for about twelve miles, we come to a narrow stream running between steep banks, which we supposed to be Sage Creek." *Report of the Secretary of War* "Report of Lt. Francis T. Bryan. Fort Riley to Bridger's Pass 1856." 35 Cong. 1 sess. Senate Ex. Doc. 11, Serial 920 pp 455-81.

Pyeatt reported their efforts to find a way across the Continental Divide:

> here we sout out to cross the divede between the Atlanttic and the Pasiffic...next day the ballance of our men returned and reported that we cound not git through for the lack of water and grass.[412]

Pyeatt's letter clearly indicates that the Company explored present Bridger Pass as a possible route, but found insufficient water and grass to sustain them. Seven years later, ordered to find Stansbury's 1850 Bridger Pass, Lt. Francis T. Bryan found the same problem. He went west over the Pass for one day, quickly concluding he would lose all the stock should he move on. He hurried back over the pass. Additionally, Bryan reported "none of the guides had ever been through [the pass] though they had been long in the mountains and in that part of the country."[413]

Had the Evans/Cherokee Company been able to proceed directly west on July 17, they would have opened Bridger Pass, the pass "discovered" by Stansbury fourteen months later.[414] Many reputable researchers attempting to chart the route of the 1849 Cherokee Trail have assumed Evans' company crossed Bridger Pass. This error has been perpetuated by virtually every subsequent researcher. The actual building of the Bridger Pass road for wagon travel took place in 1858 as a military response to the so-called Mormon War.

When they found they could not get through present Bridger Pass, the forty-niners went west around the base of Sheep Mountain and then turned north toward present Rawlins. Pyeatt described:

> we then turned north down [parallel to] the platt for the road near the South pass and traveled one day.[415]

Crawford's diary noted their next campsite:

**"Tuesday 17th [July] Artimecia [Artemesia] Creek
11 [miles]"**
[south of present Rawlins, Carbon Co., Wyoming]

---

[412]Pyeatt letter, Salt Lake, August 12, 1849.
[413]Bryan..."Report"...1856.
[414]On September 20, 1850 Stansbury with his packing company and one little wagon, led by Jim Bridger, crossed Bridger Pass from the west, seeing the Medicine Bow Butte (Elk Mountain) in the distance to the east.
[415]Pyeatt letter, Salt Lake, August 12, 1849.

On July 18, still on the track of Fremont, the Company found it necessary to make a decision--to go west as planned or go north, as Fremont had, toward the Sweetwater and the main California Trail. Company members feared there would not be water and grass to sustain them on a westerly path. Pyeatt:

> the captin not being willing to give up the rout acros to Green river stopped the train and took 2 men to look the rout furthe[r] himself the captain returned in the night having foun water an grass a suitable distance for camp having sent the other two men on to look out another place for camping
> when the capt returned he found apart of the company determined to go to the south pass any how and apart of them being connected with others that did not want to go that way.[416]

Those who felt safer following Fremont's track, using his maps and journals, wanted to break off and proceed north. They probably came to that decision because they believed that not even Fremont would cross the desert route west.[417]

If they continued reading Fremont's report, they would note that he said conditions between present Rawlins and the Sweetwater in August were unpleasant with very poor encampment, little water, scanty grass, and "Within fifty miles of the Sweet Water, the country changed into a vast saline plain."[418]

Out of deference to those who wanted to proceed north, Captain Evans accompanied them for one day. Pyeatt:

> he thot best to go with them one day further to let them settle thear bisness for a division of the company ....this they don.

Pyeatt reported what happened as the larger number of the Company

---

[416]Ibid.

[417]Fremont, on August 6, 1843, from near Rawlins, Wyoming: "From an eminence, in the afternoon, a mountainous range became visible in the north, in which were recognised, some rocky peaks belonging to the range of the Sweet Water valley; and, determining to abandon any further attempt to struggle through this almost impracticable country, we turned our course directly north, towards a pass in the valley of the Sweet Water river." Jackson and Spence...Fremont...p 464. William H. Ashley's party members of 1824-25 were also unfavorably impressed by this terrain: "28th [March 1825] The country was such as to prevent me from continuing my course W....The country generally--is becoming very much cut to pieces by ravines or dry hollers." Morgan...Ashley...p 104. Morgan identified Ashley's position at the end of this day as four or five miles east of Rawlins. n p 265. Fremont went north from present Rawlins, while Ashley had not gone as far north as the Sweetwater, but proceeded west across the Red Desert, more northerly than the 1849 Evans/Cherokee wagon company.

[418]Fremont August 7 and 8, 1843.

started west from present Rawlins:

> we went on that day with the expection of a seperation next morning but
> to our surprise they...continued with us to green river. [they] did not
> ovetake us for two days.[419]

Here then, at or near Rawlins, the Fremont journals and maps came
to their last use by the Company.

During travel on July 18, the forty-niners went north toward
Rawlins, then southwest.[420] In this area in 1858, Captain Randolph
B. Marcy wrote: "We again intersected Evans' trail at this
point...we followed Evans' road."[421] For all of the turmoil among
the company about which route to take, Crawford recorded only day,
date, campsite, and mileage:

"Wednesday 18 [July]   Canon   12 [miles]"
[approximately 5 miles SW of Rawlins, Carbon Co., Wyoming]

The general Company health had been good. It began changing
after crossing the North Platte River. Pyeatt:

> we got along very well till we got to the North fork of the platt hear
> Mathis [J.M. Mathews] got lost from the train and lay out in the snowy
> mountains in his shirt s[l]eaves, affter which he had a sevear spell of
> sickness and had to be hald in a wagon....Porter [Pyeatt, John's
> brother] has had a bad sepel of sickness [but] was able yet to ride on
> horsback....we have had considreable sickness...with many others myself
> not exempt   my Andrew [son], John Kellum, James Carnahan and John
> Carnahan are all of our mess that has not bin sick more or less since we
> left the Arkansas river   many others of the company has been sick
> allso.[422]

Lipe's letter commented on the sickness:

> Since we crossed the North Platt, there has been much sickness in our
> company; the disease is Mountain Fever. Of us Cherokees, Daniel [Gunter]
> myself and [Martin] Schrimsher, have been sick, but are well again.[423]

---

[419]Pyeatt letter, Salt Lake, August 12, 1849.

[420]A notation on the Wyoming topographic map indicates "hogback" in this area.
Also Hogback Lake. On the south of the lake is the 7,000 ft. contour line.
USGS "State of Wyoming" 1:500,000. Present Interstate 80 from Rawlins to Rock
Springs, Wyoming approximates the 1849 Evans/Cherokee Trail.

[421]*Report of the Secretary of War* "Letter from 'Camp Scott, Utah, June 28,
1858'" 35 Cong. 2 sess. 1858-1859, Sen Ex Doc 2, Serial 975 p 110. In 1867
Grenville M. Dodge's Engineer's Report for the Union Pacific Railroad made
several references to their use of the Cherokee Trail west of Rawlins,
Wyoming. "General Dodge's Report" 40 Cong. 2 sess. 1867-1868, House Ex Doc
331, Serial 1346, pp 7, 12-14.

[422]Pyeatt Letter, Salt Lake, August 12, 1849.

[423]O. W. Lipe to Mrs. Lipe from "Mormon City, Salt Lake," August 15, 1849.
Cherokee Advocate 21 January 1850. Mrs. Lipe was Catherine Gunter. Her father

The Company had at least one doctor with them when they left Arkansas--Dr. W. R. Cunningham. No mention was made by Lipe, Davis, or Pyeatt[424] in letters, or by diarist Crawford, as to whether the doctor was capable or whether his services were necessary or utilized.

Many diaries, earlier and later, in this mid-Wyoming geographic area mention persons contracting mountain fever. On the Cherokee Trail it appears to have happened consistently after crossing the North Platte River. In 1924 Dr. R. R. Parker wrote about mountain fever:

> The designation likely included, among other diseases, Rocky Mountain spotted fever, but the one most frequently concerned appears to have been the tick-borne infection now known as Colorado tick fever. At present [1942] this occurs mostly in a strip of mountainous country extending from the eastern limits of the Rocky Mountain system in northern Colorado and southern Wyoming westward to include the Sierras in California.[425]

The 1849 Company had been traveling on Parker's "eastern limits of the Rocky Mountain system" since their arrival at Pueblo on June 18. A more recent investigation also concluded, "The most likely cause of mountain fever...was Colorado Tick Fever."[426]

When the Company began traveling on July 18, it would be to trek across the Great Divide Basin and Red Desert Basin, and they would pioneer another new wagon road which would have continued use. The absence of primary material has perplexed researchers for decades about this 1849 traverse of Wyoming. Most concluded the Company went over the not-yet-existent Bridger Pass route. Some assumed the Company went southwest from the North Platte River, to

---

John was a Welchman who operated a powder mill in the Cherokee country in 1814. Her mother was Catherine of the Oolootsa group of Cherokee. Emmet Starr...*Old Cherokee Families*...pp 367, 368 and 472.

[424]Pyeatt apparently favored natural medicine. Later, in California, he was requested to give aid for scurvy: "by applying the botanic practes strictly he [A A Crawford] was soon on his feet....this shoes [shows] the superiority of the Botanic practis over the Mineral practice." Letter to Elizabeth Pyeatt Children and Friends" from "Cosumenes Califonia" February 17, 1850.

[425]Georgia Willis Read, "Diseases, Drugs, and Doctors on the Oregon-California Trail in the Gold-Rush Years" *Missouri Historical Review* vol 38, p 260, n 17 p 267.

[426]Jay A. Aldous and Paul S. Nicholes, "What is Mountain Fever?" *The Overland Journal* vol 15, no 1 (Spring 1997) pp 18-23 referring to the Mormon Vanguard Company and on the Portnuef River.

cross the Continental Divide where the 1850 company crossed at Twin Groves. The Crawford diary and letters, coupled with the Pyeatt letters, make it clear the 1849 Company crossed the Great Divide Basin and Red Desert Basin. This route is further documented by the 1850 Stansbury, 1856 Bryan, and 1858 Marcy military report entries and map notations about the "Evans" route.

Crawford's scanty 1849 diary indicates short mileage for the next day. The time was spent waiting for the return of Captain Evans and the wagon party who had wanted to proceed north on the Fremont route. They were unaware they had crossed the Continental Divide during the day.

"Thursday 19 [July]   Devid betwixt N Platt and green River
Back on the way 2 or 3 miles"
[approximately 8 miles SW of Rawlins,[427] Carbon Co., Wyoming]
For the Continental Divide crossing on this route, the highest elevation is 7,150 ft. at the east entrance to the Great Divide Basin. Rawlins is 6,769 ft. Since the general terrain is high plateau interspersed with mountains, the crossing is barely perceptible. Crawford's realization of crossing the divide came after the traverse. The diary entry shows it was an afterthought.

The next day's journey is recorded by <u>Crawford</u>:

"Friday 20 [July] Red Bluff incampment fine Spring
14 [miles]"
[approximately 7 miles NW of present Bridger Pass,
Carbon Co., Wyoming; south end of Red Rim]
Crawford here included a short narrative of the terrain, water, and game. He listed the variety of available game.[428]

> From this place Back to the Medicine Bow river is a verry big and Broken Belt of cuntery with but little grass[429] but generaly, most excelent

---

[427]Sugar Creek, an intermittent stream, flows north at this location. During most of the year it probably doesn't flow at all. But 1849 was a wet year, snow visible as well as close, as noted several times by Pyeatt.

[428]WPA files in Cheyenne reveal: "There were a few buffalo on the Red Desert west of Rawlins in the early [18]90's." E.C. Peryam, "Indians and Old Trails--The Past and the Passing in Encampment History."--nd

[429]"The Northern portion [of the Red Desert] is an almost unknown region, barren of vegetation, and almost without water, but said to contain several alkaline ponds." Arnold Hague and S.F. Emmons, "Descriptive Geology by Clarence King U.S. Geologist" *Report of the Geological Exploration of the Fortieth Parallel* Professional Papers of the Engineer Department No. 18, U.S. Army. Under the Direction of Brig. and Bvt. Maj. Gen. A.A. Humphreys, Chief of

Springs; the main ledge of the rocky mountains is betwixt this place and
and the North Platt. the game on this part is Buffalow, Bear, Elk, Deer,
Antilope, mountain Sheep, goats, Porcupines and other small game.

Another who mentioned game was Company member James Pierce in his
reminiscence, "[we went] across the Laramie Plains to Green river,
and our trail led through the greatest game country of America."[430]

Conditions worsened as the company traveled west across the
Great Divide Basin. Crawford begins writing more:

"Satu[rday] 21 [July] Salt Pond or Snipe Pond
13 1/2 [miles]

at this place the train lost [blank] head of Cattle from drinking too
much Salt Watter or some other cause."

[South of Interstate 80 at State Highway 789, Carbon Co., Wyoming]

Pyeatt reported the effects of the water on both men and animals,
as well as three dead oxen:

When we star[ted] from this camp we had now [no] camp picked out, and
being thrown of our cours we went on to Inter cect our course again and
that night we had to camp at a salt lake with out any fresh water only
what we had in our caggs (this lake is called bitter Lake by the
mountainiers)   this water had a poisnous affect on man and beast
hear the company lost three oxen that died and many other that was sick
for days that they was not fit for service   in aword evry animal in
the train was affected with it more or less   one of the Carnahan boys
best oxen was left hear being one of the 3 that was lost by this
lake.[431]

Crawford noted later there had been frost and ice on both of these
days in the desert. Crawford:

"Sund 22st [July] Muddy Pond and no grass 16 [miles]"
[south of Wamsutter, Sweetwater Co., Wyoming]

The pond may have been temporary, created by runoff.[432] The
situation, which had become quite serious, caused these Christians
to travel on Sunday.

The next day there was not even water. Crawford:

"Mon 23d [July] Camped in a plain, no water or gras
15 1/2 [miles]"
[Near Tipton, Sweetwater Co., Wyoming]

Engineers (Washington: Gov't. Printing Office 1877) vol 2, p 211.
[430]Pierce...*Tribune*...1902.
[431]Pyeatt letter, Salt Lake, August 12, 1849. The lake is unidentified.
[432]Capt. Randolph B. Marcy when crossing this desert June 1, 1858 noted:
"Standing water in ponds in many places in these flats...would probably dry up
in midsummer." "Itinerary of a march...New Mexico to Camp Scott, Utah
Territory." 35 Cong. 2 sess 1858-1859, Sen Ex Doc 2, Serial 975, p 201.

Pyeatt noted another problem--rough terrain:

> our rout now lay through dry land regin [region] and dry loose dirt and
> very ineaving [uneven] that made it very hard pooling [pulling] and all
> the water that we got was very bad   one nigh we lay without watter
> intirely for our animals   we our selves had som in our caggs [kegs].[433]

The Company wagon train was moving west over the Great Divide
Basin. Conditions became nearly desperate. Diarist <u>Crawford</u>
records the scarcity of water and their perilous situation:

> **"Tues 24th [July] Camped at a ravine...10 [miles]**
> ...with some rain watter   We have crossed no water since yesterday
> morning and men and Beasts are almost famished for watter-----"
> [NW of Tipton, Sweetwater Co., Wyoming]

They had come nine days west from the crossing of the North
Platte River. It would be another nine days before they camped on
the east bank of the Green River preparing to cross it. While they
and their stock were suffering, the Company packers on the same
day were enjoying a good meal in Salt Lake City during the Mormon
celebration.

Ashley had crossed this terrain on March 30, 1825, more
northerly than the Evans/Cherokee Company. He emphasized:

> This would be a difficult Country to travel through at any other time
> than when the snow was melting as it would be entirely destitute of
> water is a poor grass country Entirly a bed of sand.[434]

Pyeatt described their crossing and efforts to find water:

> we traveled on nex day the most of the men with out a drop of water till
> in the evning say one oclock all thee men out huntin watter that had
> horses to ride....those riding returning and find now [none]...
> when one of the men that was a foot found water.

Imagine their jubilation at finding the water. Pyeatt:

> this water was from a heavy s[h]ower of rain that fell 2 day before and
> woueld not las more then 2 days longer   had it not bin fer this water
> we must have suffered conssidrable for we did not find any more [water]
> till next night som 18 or 20 miles further.

The campsite name reflects their thankfulness. <u>Crawford</u>:

> **"Wednesday 25 [July]   Camped on the head of a Branch of
>   green river   Camp Providence   16"**
> [NE of Point of Rocks, Sweetwater Co., Wyoming]

---

[433]Pyeatt Letter, Salt Lake, August 12, 1849.
[434]Morgan...*Ashley*...p 104. Morgan identifies the area as the Great Divide
Basin (n 77 p 265) and a campsite due north of Tipton (n 79 p 265.)

For Pyeatt there could be only one source of the water:

> many of our company hear acknowledged that this water was sent by God
> for our bennifit   thankes be to his name for the kind protection that
> he has afforded us from day to day   hear in this desert we began to
> git sick no dount from having to drink so much bad water and cook our
> provision with a bitter srub that grows in abundance hear and is ver
> troubleson to travel through (it is called artimitia or wild sage).[435]

During the next day the Company crossed Tenmile Draw going northwest, turned west/southwest, and then southeast down Deadman Wash, bringing them again to Tenmile Draw. Crawford:

**"Thursday 26 [July]   Came 15 miles round through the
Cliffs and camped 5 miles from last Knights camp"**
[Point of Rocks, Sweetwater Co., Wyoming]

At this camp they struck Bitter Creek, down which they would travel four days. The Pilot Butte, northwest of present Rock Springs, Wyoming, became evermore distinct.[436] Crawford:

**"Friday 27 [July]   Moved 11 miles and camped
on the same Branch   11 [miles]"**
[West of Thayer Junction, Sweetwater Co., Wyoming]

**"Satuarday 28 [July] moved 8 miles and camped on
the Same Streem   8 [miles]"**
[2 miles NE of Baxter, Sweetwater Co., Wyoming]

In September 1850, Stansbury and company topographers William Gunnison and Albert Carrington noted the places where the Evans 1849 trail crossed, or was identical to, their route, notably on Bitter Creek and west of the North Platte River.[437]

---

[435]Pyeatt letter, Salt Lake, August 12, 1849.

[436]Stansbury, returning east noted on September 12, 1850 : "we came in sight of a huge butte...some forty miles distant: a landmark well known to the traders, and called by them Pilot Butte." Stansbury...*Exploration*...p 231.

[437]Evans reached Fort Bridger on August 8; Stansbury August 11, 1849. Members of Stansbury's party returning east in 1850 noted Evans' route along Bitter Creek. The Stansbury "Table of Distances" noted: "Sept. 14 EVANS'S TRACE...This is a trace made by a part of emigrants from Arkansas, in 1849, which continues north of Bitter Creek to Bridger's Fort. The grass on this part of the route is very limited, and sage the only fuel. Water slightly brackish and sulphurous." The next day "Sept.15 FORD--Cross to the left bank; Evans's Trace on the right; creek 80 feet wide, and 6 feet deep; banks steep. SULPHUR SPRINGS...The springs are on the right bank, and issue from the base of high bluff rocks of gray sandstone. Evans's Trace takes the north-east branch, and joins, [us] near the [North] Platte River." Stansbury p 282. Again on September 21 after crossing Bridger Pass the day before: "Sept. 21 "EVANS' TRACE--Direction from the camp is toward the Medicine-bow Mountains. Evans' Trace from Bitter Creek here crosses Sage Creek valley." Stansbury p 284. Gunnison noted Evans route on September 14, 15, and 21 when "our

The morning temperatures hovered at freezing. <u>Crawford</u>:

**"Sunday 29 [July]   mooved 4 miles and camped
on the Same Streem [4 miles]**
...This morning and the 21st Or 2nd of this inst [July], their was
frost and ice Plenty in Camps."
[6 miles east of Rock Springs, Sweetwater Co., Wyoming]

At this campsite Crawford wrote:

From this Place Back 75 or 80 miles[438] is a pore dreary, Rough and Hilly
Country, destitute, (almost) of grass, and no timber of any Kind except
the Artemecia Shrub. with visible Signs of Volcanic eruptions in a grate
many place, Stone Cole is abundent in this part of the World. But 2
Springs have Béen Seen in the last named distance; one Calebrate...[439]
the other Pure White Sulpher."

<u>Crawford</u>:

**"Monday 30 [July 1849] We remained in Camp to day
on the account of a good Patch of grass"**
[6 miles east of Rock Springs, Sweetwater Co., Wyoming]

Captain Evans and his scouts investigated the route ahead,
finding the way straight west impassable for wagons. The Company
members were too worn down to construct a wagon road through the
narrow canyon between present Rock Springs and Green River,
Wyoming. Captain Evans turned the company north up Killpecker
Creek. <u>Crawford</u>:

"Tuesday 31st [July] [15 miles]...
moved six miles down the Same Stream [Bitter Creek] and turned a
northwest Course and camped 15 miles from last nights camp near a good
Spring."
[9 miles north of Rock Springs on Killpecker Creek,
Sweetwater Co., Wyoming]

Crawford's more lengthy entries may indicate he feels the worst is
over for this portion of the journey.

---

course...finally left Evans branch." Carrington noted Evans on September 14:
"Evans' road (made with 47 wagons in /49)," 15, and 21. On Stansbury's map,
the "Evans Route" is speculative, not based on a visual reconnaisance. Wheat
noted: "Another feature of outstanding interest on this map is what it shows
of the early evolution of the Cherokee Trail. An "Evans Route," followed to a
considerable extent by Stansbury from Fort Bridger to the North Platte, had
been opened by a party of 47 wagons from the Cherokee Nation in 1849, with the
result, as [Mormon] Carrington tells us, that the road was called by the
Mormons the Arkansas route." Carl I. Wheat, *Mapping the Transmississippi West*
vol 3 1846-1854. (San Francisco: Institute Historical Cartography 1959) p 125.
Stansbury, Gunnison and Carrington noted Evans' trace at both the west (Bitter
Creek) and the east (Sage Creek) intersections of the Stansbury route.
[438]Measured by Pyeatt's roadomiter, it was 79.5 miles from this spot back to
their "Muddy Pond and no grass" camp of Sunday, July 22.
[439]Chalybeate=Mineral. Crawford used the phrase on two Arkansas River camps.

The Company turned west around White Mountain and Pilot Butte and went through present Skunk Canyon toward the Green River. Crawford:

"Wednesday August the 1st 1849 moved 14 miles and camped in a hollow"
[12 miles north of the city of Green River, Sweetwater Co., Wyoming]

The long sought Green River was reached the following day. Crawford:

"Thursday 2nd [August] moved 8 1/2 miles...
and Camped on the East Bank of Green River. We remained on this Streem until monday following   this is a Butiful Streem, well ansering To its name in appearance."
[Approximately 15 miles NW of the city of Green River, Sweetwater Co., Wyoming]

Later Pyeatt declared about the desert traverse, "we was near three weeks acrossing this divide which has hurt our animals worse then all the rest of the trip." The primary concern when crossing the desert had been for the survival of both humans and animals.

Though perhaps of little concern to them at the time, the Evans/Cherokee Company had pioneered another wagon road.[440] Theirs was the first wagon train to cross this Great Divide Basin and Red Desert. Even Fremont in 1843 had decided it was too harsh and had turned north at Rawlins toward the Sweetwater River. Also worthy of mention, the Evans/Cherokee Company saw no other wagons at the Green River because they were some fifteen miles south of the Oregon-California Trail crossing. Nor had they seen any other emigrants since leaving Pueblo (Colorado) June 22.

It is unclear just when they crossed the Green River.[441] Having safely reached a haven with plenty of wood, water, and grass, the company could be expected to take care of the business

[440]Mormons called it the "old dry route," Ellen Hundley, "From Utah to Texas in 1856" Kenneth L. Holmes, ed. *Covered Wagon Women* (Glendale, Calif: Arthur H. Clark Co. 1988) vol 7, pp 132-55. They also called it "the Arkansas Route" as noted by Carrington. This route was used for years afterward by emigrants, military and for overland stock drives until the 1880s.
[441]Crawford noted their arrival at the east bank on Thursday. Pyeatt did not mention when they crossed. He did indicate finishing work on Saturday. It was the custom to cross the rivers and streams when first approaching them, near night, rather than waiting until morning. Overnight weather often changed the condition of the waterways.

of wagon and equipment repair. Pyeatt:

> when we got to green rive we rested 3 day   thear put up the black
> smith tools and don som repairs on the wagons   having arived on
> thirsday evnin we got don our work on Saterday.

As captain responsible for the entire Evans/Cherokee wagon
company of up to forty-seven wagons, Lewis Evans was determined to
keep the company moving. He knew there was an opportunity to stop
not many miles distant at Fort Bridger, and another at Salt Lake.
Captain Evans started west from Green River with the bulk of the
company on Sunday August 5, 1849. But Pyeatt, a hard-working
opinionated man, evidently insisted his group not go. Five wagons,
including that of diarist Crawford, stayed at the Green River over
Sunday. Pyeatt:

> a Sonday the company started [to move]   all with the xception of five
> wagons our 2   the Carnahan boys James [the diarist] and Andrew Crawfords
> and the [John M.] Whams and Emistons boy [John Thompson and Andrew
> Edmiston] wagons.

Repair work finished on the Green River, there was time for
attending to what Pyeatt believed important--giving thanks on this
Sabbath, especially since others had been spent haphazardly.

> we staid and In joyed one quiet Sonday   the first sin[ce] we left home
> for when we did not travel the day was spent shooting washing working
> of evry discription which made me all most dred to see the Sabath com
> for fear that God would send som judgment on the company for thear
> weekedness   but thankes be to his name he has bestoed blessings on the
> company while the[y] war aprofaining the Sabath and taking his name in
> vain   but the Sabath on green river was spent differently   it was
> spent in sing[ing] the prais of his name that had protected us throug
> this desert   Indeed this was a sabath of injoyment   It dos my Soal
> good when I think of it   O that all of our Sabaths would be as
> pleasant as this one.[442]

Having vented his feelings about the company, Pyeatt was
rejuvenated by the stopover. On Monday, August 6, 1849, the five-
wagon Pyeatt/Crawford group moved west from their glorious and
prayerful Sunday celebration on the bank of the Green River. The
Crawford diary chronicles resumption of their journey:

> **"Monday 6th [August 1849] moved 18 miles**
> and Struck the Salt Lake Road East of Bridgger's Fort on a Butifull
> Streem Called Blacks Fork of Green River."
> [4 miles W of Granger, near Uinta/Sweetwater Cos. line, Wyoming]

---

[442]Pyeatt letter, Salt Lake, August 12, 1849.

The Pyeatt/Crawford group had arranged to meet Captain Evans and the rest of the company at the main road on Monday. However, before reaching the main road--(variously called the California Trail, the Salt Lake Road or Independence road)--they encountered Captain Evans and eleven wagons of the Company train. Pyeatt:

> we arose early a monday and Started for the road which was som 8 mile of but to save distance we traveled twelve before we reachedth it   a mile or 2 before we got to the road we came to a leven of our wagon waiting for us.

As usual, Pyeatt took this opportunity to voice his opinion.

> the captin hear being unwilling to leave us and a po[r]tion of those weekest retchs was unwill[ing] to stay so the captain gave them leave to go on and we have not seen them since   all and thankes be to God for thear departure for the bulk of them ar of the loast clas of beings that aint fit to liv or di.

In so doing Pyeatt gave important information about those who left the Company and were not seen again on the journey.

> they ar the cherikees and Fayettvill trash such as [George C.] North [Dr. William Riley] Cunningham [Christian, Edward, Herman, Hermina and Barbara Freyschlag] Fresklau[443] and others of like stripe all to gether 12 wagons   they came on to bridgers fort and thear many of them got drunk on whiskey at $1 dollar apint and cut up tall shines.[444]

O.W. Lipe with the "cherikees" wrote: "When we arrived at the Independence road, we Indians quit the company and went ahead."[445] No primary materials have been found to document the further route of these twelve Cherokee/white wagons. They did go to Salt Lake, because Lipe wrote home from there. Calvin and Henderson Holmes, in the group, traveled the Lassen Trail into California. [446]

---

[443]Freyschlag is an early resident name Allen and McLane, *Arkansas Land Patents*, Washington County (1991) p 71. The members of the Freyschlag family were brothers and sisters. A special spring wagon had been made for the trip by wagonmaker Peter Van Winkle. At least two members of the family taught at the highly-acclaimed Sophia Sawyer Female Seminary: Herman, Art, and/or was Dancing Master; and Hermina, Instrumental and Vocal Music. It is obvious that these were respected citizens and that Pyeatt is being rather reckless in his designation of "Fayetteville trash." Edward stayed in California for two years, returning to Fayetteville area where he lived to be ninety. Christian settled in "the west." Another Freyschlag, George, remained in Fayetteville where the family from Germany had settled in approximately 1833.
[444]Pyeatt letter, Salt Lake, August 12, 1849.
[445]Lipe letter, Salt Lake, August 15, 1849. Even though Lipe was born in New York, he married a Cherokee, and he refers to himself as part of "we" indians.
[446]Holmes' diary notes mileage on the Lassen route and arrival on November 8.

Pyeatt continued his letter with some sad news--the first death in the wagon company:

> Just as we got to the road one of our company Died   a man by the name of Nathen Tharp[447] a son en law of John VanHouse [Van Hoose] of white river   he has bin labering under a disease from a child[hood] and this disease being agravated by exposeer and the bad water no dout s[h]ortened his life thus we buried him the morning after we got to the road.

Lipe's letter also noted the death: "We have had one death in our company, a man by the name of Thorp from White River, he died from an old disease."[448] Crawford wrote, "one Mr. Tharp Died with what the doctors call Diabetus."[449]

There had been no cholera deaths, and no maurauding by "wild Indians." The stock losses, aside from the forty-plus on the Arkansas River, were three oxen left in the Red Desert. The party was in very good condition as they joined the main road to California.

The Company, minus the twelve Cherokee/white wagons, resumed travel east of Fort Bridger. <u>Crawford</u>:

> **"Tuesday 7th [August] moved 17 1/4 miles**
> and camped on Hams Fork of Black River [Blacks Fork] a butiful Streem runing out of the Eutaw mountains."
> [7 miles Northeast of Lyman, Uinta Co., Wyoming]

> **"Wednesday 8th [August] moved 12 miles to Bridgers**
> **Fort on the Same Streem**
> this is a butiful valey of Land watered by Hams Fork of [Crawford is writing around a diagonal ink spill] Green River."
> [present Fort Bridger, Uinta Co., Wyoming]

Crawford occasionally had small spills of ink on his diary pages. A large spill on this page is so pervasive that it shows through many pages, and he wrote around it.

Fort Bridger, built by traders Jim Bridger and Louis Vasquez, has a long history in the area. By 1849 Bridger was conducting business at the fort, while Vasquez was along the main California Trail near South Pass.[450]

---

[447]Nathan was 21 years old, having married Mary Van Hoose.
[448]Lipe letter, Salt Lake, August 15, 1849.
[449]Crawford Letter to wife Harriet from Salt Lake, California August 16, 1849.
[450]For a description of Vasquez and his 1849 whereabouts see William G. Johnston *Overland to California* [1849] (Jos. A. Sullivan. Oakland, Calif:

At Fort Bridger Pyeatt got news of the pack company members.

When we got to Bridgers fort we heard of our Pack Boys   they ware
about 20 day ahead of us[451]   they left a letter for the captain thear
they had bad luck acrossing green river   they got one man drownded by
the name of Gaven and lost many of thear packs saddles bridles and
gunns   [Hiram] Shores [Aaron] Tiner and the morrow boys [Hugh, James
and William] lost all the money they had   betwee[n] $300 and $500
dollars   they came on to Bridger and thear got provision saddls and
othe[r] thing they had need of at a very hy[high] price   som of thear
horses had giv out and the most of them looked bad so we ware told.

Lipe, member of the Cherokee/white twelve wagon breakaway party,
wrote of the Green River drowning on August 15 from Salt Lake:

The packers who left us at Pueblo had a man drowned in Green River by
the name of Garvin, from Benton County, Ark. Garvin was sick, and was
crossing on the raft made out of skins, the raft sank with all the
baggage it contained, and G.[arvin] also to rise no more. There was no
timber, consequently a craft out of skins. One of the packers remained
here [Salt Lake] who gave us the report the Cherokees with the packers
sustained no damage.[452]

The 1849 Evans/Cherokee Company pioneered the first
continuous wagon route from Bent's Fort to Fort Bridger. Besides
California and Mormon emigrants, Captains Loring and Marcy
traveled over this route in 1858 with U.S. military men and
stock.[453] News of the newly-built and successfully used route was
transmitted to the folks back in Arkansas. Pyeatt:

this Bridgers fort is 48 miles from green river and 440 miles from the
sout fork of the Platt   36 milles of this distance we had had a rode
and the balance we had to make our own road with out trail or guide
through mountains and plains   thus you will see why we have bin so
long gittin hear   but we a[re] told that we have plenty of time to git
thear [California] yet.[454]

Lipe wrote from Salt Lake city to Cherokee Nation with details of
the new route:

We traveled from Pueblo by the following route: Fort St. Vrains on South
Platt--crossed South Platt at the mouth Cache A La Pudre--up said stream
thro' the mountains to Laramie Plains; thence crossed Laramie rivers
near the mountains, crossed Medicine Bow river, passed Medicine Bow

Reprint Biobooks 1948) pp 93-94. Fort Bridger has been faithfully restored as
a State Park by Wyoming. New interpretive signs mention the Cherokee Trail.
[451]Evans/Cherokee Company Packers arrived at Fort Bridger on July 19 according
to Pyeatt's information.
[452]Lipe letter, Salt Lake, August 15, 1849.
[453]Randolph B. Marcy, "Itinerary 25" The Prairie Traveler: Handbook for
Overland Expeditions. Published by Authority of the War Department (N.Y.:
Harper & Brothers 1859) pp 323-26.
[454]Pyeatt letter, Salt Lake, August 12, 1849.

Mountains; crossed the North Park and North Platt, Green river, south of the South Pass, and intersected the Independence road on Black's Fork, about 14 miles west of Green River.

Over these ruts trod thousands of emigrants and many thousands of cattle, horses, and sheep. Portions of it were used as the Overland Stage Trail beginning in 1862, and later the Union Pacific Railroad, two interstate highways, and numerous state and county roads. It was known as the Cherokee Trail for decades.

and that part of it from Latham [near the confluence of the Cache la Poudre and the South Platte] to Fort Bridger was to become a thoroughfare as frequently traveled as the Oregon Trail.[455]

Before the discovery of the Crawford diary, researchers had too little documentation to map or describe the 1849 route, which was therefore inaccurately described by them.[456] Their inaccuracies were copied and perpetuated by subsequent researchers. Some researchers tried to fit the 1850 diary of Cherokee John Lowery Brown to the 1849 route. However, two more 1850 diaries with additional information now confirm that Brown did not take the 1849 trail in Wyoming that was pioneered by the Evans/Cherokee Company. The 1850 route in Wyoming was more southerly.

Crawford continued keeping mileage in his 1849 diary, but had no more need of naming the campsites since they were now on a common and well-used highway. As the company moved west, away from Fort Bridger, toward Salt Lake, he began writing more narrative, including descriptions and incidents of the trail. Crawford:

> **"Thursday 9. [August] moved 22 miles**
> throug a very Hilly Cuntery But not rocky; With Several good fresh watter spring, and two others which they call Soda springs we encamped for the night on the divide Between Green and Bear rivers this night was Cold enough to lye Comfortable under 3 or 4 Blanket."
> [near railroad station marker Altamont, Uinta Co., Wyoming][457]

---

[455]W. J. Ghent, *Road to Oregon: A Chronicle of the Great Emigrant Trail* (N.Y.: Longmans, Green and Co. 1929) p 157.

[456]Ralph P. Bieber, ed., "The Cherokee Trail" *Southern Trails to California in 1849* Southwest Historical Series (Glendale, Calif: Arthur H. Clark Co. 1937) vol 5. Grant Foreman, *Marcy and the Goldseekers* (Norman, Okla.: Univ. of Oklahoma Press 1939). Ghent...*Oregon*...p 156 erred in assuming the Bridger Pass route was used. Margaret Long, "The Cherokee Trail" *The Smoky Hill Trail* (Denver, Colo: Kistler Stationery Co. 1953) vol 1. Muriel H. Wright, ed. "The Journal of John Lowery Brown, of the Cherokee Nation en Route to California in 1850" *Chronicles of Oklahoma* vol 12, no 2 (June 1934).

[457]The altitude near Altamont is 7,500 ft. The name means high mountain.

Late in the day the wagon company passed the Wyoming/Utah border to camp at a well-noted place called the Needles.

"Friday 10 [August]   [17 1/2 miles]
we imbarked this morning and traveled about 7 miles in a S.W. direction and came to a Splendid Spring South of the Road, from thence 2 miles further and nooned on Bear river a very Butifull Streem interlocking with the waters of Green River. from thence we traviled 8 1/2 miles further through a butifull Hilly Cuntery, and camped at the mouth of a canion, this is on a Small streem Called Willow Creek, the grass from Fort Bridger to this place is verry fine"
[beneath the landmark rock formation called "The Needles,"
Uinta Co., Wyoming/Summit Co., Utah]

The cold nights and early mornings continue. Crawford:

"Saturday 11 [August]   22 [miles]
last night was verry Cold, there was Plenty of Frost this morning. We traviled to day through a Hilly part of the world, our course being S.W.Camp in a Deep Canon."
[Echo Canyon, Summit Co., Utah]

Pyeatt in a letter noted the cold and the sometime advantages of ice and snow the Company had experienced:

the wather has bien very col   we had a sma[r]t frost night before last and last night we had Ice...we have not bin out of sight of snow for near two months only when we ware in some deep hollow   I have not seen an oxens tung out with heat...nor appier to be distresed withe heat...since we left the arkansas river   we have frost and Ice very frequetly   we had snow in our camp to eat in July brot from the mountains by the company   we alsow camped one night the last of July [toward the western edge of the Red Desert, Wyoming] with in one half mile of snow and ice   this will appier strange to you that we should be so near the snow and have grass but this is the cas in the valies and on these sonow[sic] mountains   whear the snow is off thear is grass and one of our company says he was whear he could getheer [gather] snow with one hand and pluck flowers with the other the same tim   It has been universly the cas that we found the best grass near the snow mountains [and] all the best water.[458]

Crawford described Echo Canyon where they rested:

"Sunday 12 [August] we remained in Camp to day.
the Bluffs of Rock, on our right, for a considerable distance are perhaps 3 or 4 hundred feet high the rocks of a redish color."

Pyeatt's letter of August 12 recounted their mileage:

we are now writtin 45 milles of [from] the Salt lake where the Mormons live and we travel from 17 to 23 miles a day on this road thow the mountains are worse hear then any part of our Journy   we have bin in the road since monday evning last   the last week we traveled 110 miles and rested one half day to repar a broken wagon.

---

[458]Pyeatt letter, Salt Lake, August 12, 1849.

Life was good, for the moment. But the rumor mill along the trail was as active as ever, with conflicting information on the availability of grass. Pyeatt:

> the only difficulty is the gras bein eat ou before us which we ar informed can not be   it is so plenty that it can not fail   we have had plenty...of the very best...ever since we got to the [main] road the grass in this cuntry is much better then in Arkansas   it contain so much seed that it is all most equal to grain for cattle.

Evidently at Fort Bridger the company had received more news about the main emigration. Pyeatt:

> Thear are a great many more emigrants on the road behind us   the number is said to be over one thousand wagons by good authority   I close my letter for the presant for I cant mail it till I git to the Sault lak at the Morman town and proby I may have something more to rite thear....Capt. Evenes is sick at this time.

The company moves down the canyon over rough road. <u>Crawford</u>:

"Monday 13 [August]   20 [miles]
we traviled to day 20 miles over the worst road that we have seen since we left home, we moved 7 miles and came to Webers fork of Bear river, we traviled down Some distance and Crossed it and made the Balance of our days travil through a verry rough country, with plenty of good Water, and Plenty of a Brackish or salt tast, last on this morning their was a heavy Frost, and Plenty of Ice in our Buckets and Pan."
[Approximately 7 miles SW of Henefer, Morgan Co., Utah]

"Tuesday 14 [August]   Traviled 17 1/2 miles
to day over the highest hill that we have traveled over since we left home, throug Some verry deep and rough Canions, with Considerable of the Balsomwood on the Sides of the mountains. to night we camped on the Canion that leads to the mormon City."
[Emigration Canyon, east of Salt Lake City, Salt Lake Co., Utah]

**"Wednesday 15th [August] We traviled 12 miles
and came to the grate Mormon City."**

Pyeatt described the road conditions as they neared the "mormon City":

> We arived hear yesterday about twelve o clk after travling ove some of the worst roads that we have had yet and the dust   the worst I eve saw in my life   indeed it is hard to conseive of the lik un less you could have seen it....I never seen the lik of dead oxen in my life   w pass on[e] evry litte bit and frequently severl in sight of each other   this distruction is from the dust and hard driving   thus hole trains all most hav bin distroyed yet our teams hold out tolerable well.[459]

---

[459] Pyeatt's letter to wife Elizabeth at "Boons Boro Arkansas State." from "Morman town Saut Lak" written August 16, 1849 was included with his letter written August 12.

Diarist Crawford penned a letter home from Salt Lake.

The Common Report is, that their are about nine thousand Waggons a head
of us, and about 1,000 on our rear; Altho all the Emigrants that we hear
talk, admit that we came exactly the right way...Yet perhaps not one
fourth of the Emigration passes this road: The grater part go the upper
or Fort Hall road...The Emigrants have Suffered very much with the
Colera   I heard one man Say that he knew that their must be at least
one grave for every mile on the north rout [via the South Pass] for 7 or
800 miles.[460]

The emigrants were no doubt curious to see the newly-settled
valley, barely two years old. The pack company had been witness
to, and perhaps participants in, the first July 24 celebration of
Brigham Young's entry into the valley. O.W. Lipe, member of the
Cherokee/white twelve-wagon breakaway group, wrote glowingly of
Salt Lake on August 15:

The Mormons have a beautiful country, it is almost entirely
surrounded by mountains -- some of which are covered with perpetual
snow. Their town is regularly laid off and finely watered. Water is
conveyed through every street for the purpose of irrigation, as it is
the only means of successful farming--as it scarcely ever rains here in
the summer. The valley is fine for irrigation, as the mountains afford
numerous small streams of the purest water--the Mormons seem to be here
a happy people...
   I must state to you that I have had some water melons, radishes,
and beets in this place. The people here are just done with their
harvest; they have raised fine crops of wheat--some think they
have raised 40 bushels per acre...
   A man reported here that he found gold in the streets of this city--
he seemed to be a man of truth. I have no doubt but gold is plenty in
this country...The Mormons are coining gold at this place. They report
gold very abundant in California.[461]

Diarist Crawford was favorably impressed with Salt Lake, and
said so:

this is a regularly layed off City for the purpose of farming; evry man
has a lot of 1 1/4 acres of ground layed off to face on some of the
Streets that run through the City which Streets run E and W N and S, the
Bishop then points out each mans Block for his dwelling and guardning
they then have a part of the ground layed off in 5 acre Blocks nearest
the City for the use and convenience of Mechanics. Then Still further
Back they have the ground layed off in 20 acre Blocks, for the use of
regular farmers, this the farmers draw for by lottery Their City is
Butifully Situated west of Some high Mountains, and East of the Eutaw
Lake or outlet on the Jordon of the west as the Mormons Call it.   from

---

[460]Crawford letter to wife Harriet from "Mormon City, Salt Lake, California"
August 16, 1849.
[461]Lipe letter, Salt Lake, August 15, 1849.

the City to Jordon is about 2 miles which distance we traviled on this
Eavening and camped on the west Bank of Jordon. they erigate their land.

While the others praised Salt Lake, Pyeatt was not impressed.

                                    Morman town Saut Lak August the16th
We arived hear yesterday about twelve o clk.... I think we ar mostly don
with It [dust] for we had afine rain to day and it is probly that we
will have a shower every week or so so as to keep down the dust....we
will star[t] to morrow fr the gol diggins   we have heard from them
since we got hear that one man freekenlly makes $200 a day   if this be
the cas we will make som if we git thar and keep our health   we are
all well at presant but James Carnahan   he let the wagon run ove his
foot yesterday morning and hert him very bad so that he cant walk.

Pyeatt reacted to prices, routes, grass, "harvist of the emigrants," and his ability to avoid being "chiseld."

Squire mares [Marrs] has bot a small wagon to day for $30,00 worth $80
or $100 and has sold the body of his for $10   whether he can sell the
balance or not I dont now   wagons ar worth nothing hear thear are so
many teems that has givout and the oners have sold them for little or
nothing and packed through....We hear many report hear about the rout
the mormons tell us that we cant go throug this season for a man has
returned and sayes the grass is all eat up and burnt and the oxen and
horses ar astarving to deth and many other such tails to git us to leave
our wagons and by [buy] thear poneys and mules for anor[mous] prices
mules $200 to $250   Indians payes $100 to $150   thus they hav made a
harvist of the emigrants this year   but they cant com it over these
boys   We understand them too well to be chiseld by them.

O.W. Lipe continued his letter (parts already quoted):

                    Mormon City, Salt Lake Wednesday, Aug. 15th, 1849.
    We have got this far, a distance from home of 1420 miles. We arrived
here on Monday [August 13] and expect to leave this evening....[462]
    Since I commenced writing this, the others [of the twelve
Cherokee/white wagons] have come in, but in two separate companies, so
we have put off starting until morning, and we go with one of the
companies--so our train will be 12 wagons. On this road we often see one
wagon traveling to itself. The wagons on this road are so numerous that
it seems like one continual train.
    The distance from here to Sutter's is said to be 800 miles, and the
Mormons discourage the emigrants as much as possible. They wish the
emigrants to remain six weeks and take a southern route to San Diego,
and intersect the Fort Smith route; many will go that way....Hundreds
have come here from Santa Fe, and go the way we intend going. There is
no road from here to the southern route, the emigrants will have to make
their road and pay a Mormon $1,000 to show the way...
    Great many cattle have died on this road--as yet we have not lost
any. Our cattle have done well--it will yet take us at least seven
weeks to get to the gold diggins...

---

[462]The pack company, guided by Dick Owens, had arrived July 24. See Geo. W.
Keys letter from Salt Lake.

Some emigrants for California leave here afoot with their provision
on their backs--others start with a pack on an ox or a cow--so you
find that some are perfectly afoot, what a struggle for gold!...

We will be much longer on our journey than I had expected -- our
journey will be about six months.[463]

Pyeatt noted the options he knew about for further travel:

if we go south of the lake not quite so long as it I[s] som 100 or 150
miles nier [nigher=nearer] but thear is a sault plain to go through som
80 and som 45 miles that we will hav to hall watter and hay for our
animals   we have not detrmined which rout we will go yet   the captin
is--making inquiry at this time to now which rout we had best go   what
the result will be I do not not know thow I expect we will go south of
the lake...[the Hastings Cutoff]   but I must close my letter for I
don't know when to qut riting I could rite as much more but I don't
know whether you will git it or not   So I clos by asking the blessing
of God on you all and requesting your prairs for

                                         John R. Pyeatt...
I had for got to tell you that Andrew [their son] has continued well all
the time with the exception of slight head ache a few times and is very
attentive to bisness, more so than ever I saw a boy of his age in my
life I believe   nothing more J.R.P.

Crawford's letter from Salt Lake (parts already quoted):

                         Mormon City, Salt Lake, California Aug 16-1849
Dear Harriet
I now take this opportunity to let you know that I and the Balanse of
us, are well; and have been with slite exceptions on all the rout Since
we left home, perhaps by the time you git this letter, you will have
heard a grate many falce rumors, Conserning our fate. But with the
exception of loosing our oxen, and the Roads being a good dail further
than I expected I have not at all been disapointed: our: road has been
verry good, except about 300 miles, that is from the North Platt to this
place;...

We have: camped 2 miles west of the City on the west Bank of the
Jordon of the west; this is a beautifull streem runing from the Eutaw to
the Salt lake-the part of the valey in which this City is Situated is
about 30 miles wide and about 200 miles long. this is a verry
Picturesque Place...The prospicts, according to the accounts, ahead of
us is gloomy--But this has been the case all the time.

Crawford, like Pyeatt, wrote of the routes they could select
and the distances they had to cover:[464]

But we now have to fall in behind this vast Emigration or go Some other
rout....I have Strong hopes of gitting to California this winter, The
mormons Say it is about eight hundred miles from this place to Suters

---

[463]Lipe Letter, Salt Lake, August 15, 1849.
[464]The letters from Pyeatt and Crawford were both postmarked October 11 from
Salt Lake. It appears they had missed the mailman by about 20 days. Almon
Babbitt had carried a U.S. mail west to Salt Lake, arriving July 1; leaving
for the East again July 27. Barry...West...p 870. After August 16, the next
service was apparently in early October from Salt Lake.

[Sutter's Fort]; We have a road viamiter attached to one of our waggons Which by measure makes the distance from Fayetteville to this a little over fifteen hundred miles.

I think that no people or train, ever had more reason to be thankfull than we have. Our teems are in verry good order....I am now in Morman Citty, in the house of a verry Cleaver old gentleman and lady.[465] The mormons Seem to live in a Cientific maner....he [the farmer] has to cultivate every foot of the lands that he takes: evry man has to live by the Sweet of his own Brow....the Citizens appear to be verry Kind: and obliging: I have Just dined at a verry good Table: loaded with Plenty....I must Conclude my letter   I Cannot write all that I want to write   Harriet Be as contented as you Can; if I ever get home this trip will do me the Balance of my days: Kiss Emmy and the Boy for me Farewell   Harriet Crawford   James S. Crawford NB give my Respects to Father and mother and all the Connexion, till [tell] Kinnibrugh his Cane [an ox] is leader of the train   JSC

Pyeatt cautioned against rumor:

It will not do for Emigrants to beleave tai[l]s they hear   for example we hear the distance is from 350 milles to 868 to the gol diggins thus the tails go   I think from the bes Iformation that we can git it will take us twenty five or thirty dayes[466] yet to git theear.

It remained only for Capt. Evans to find the best route for the wagon company to follow. The information and decision took less than forty-eight hours. On August 17, the Company left Salt Lake.

---

[465]At the end of the James Sawyer Crawford diary on an otherwise blank page is the following: "Citizens of Mormon Town Mr. Pierce and Lady   Mrs Judith Higbee   Mrs. Eliza R Snow   Mrs Augustis Cobb."
[466]It took Pyeatt sixty-six days, from August 17 to October 22, to get from Salt Lake to California.

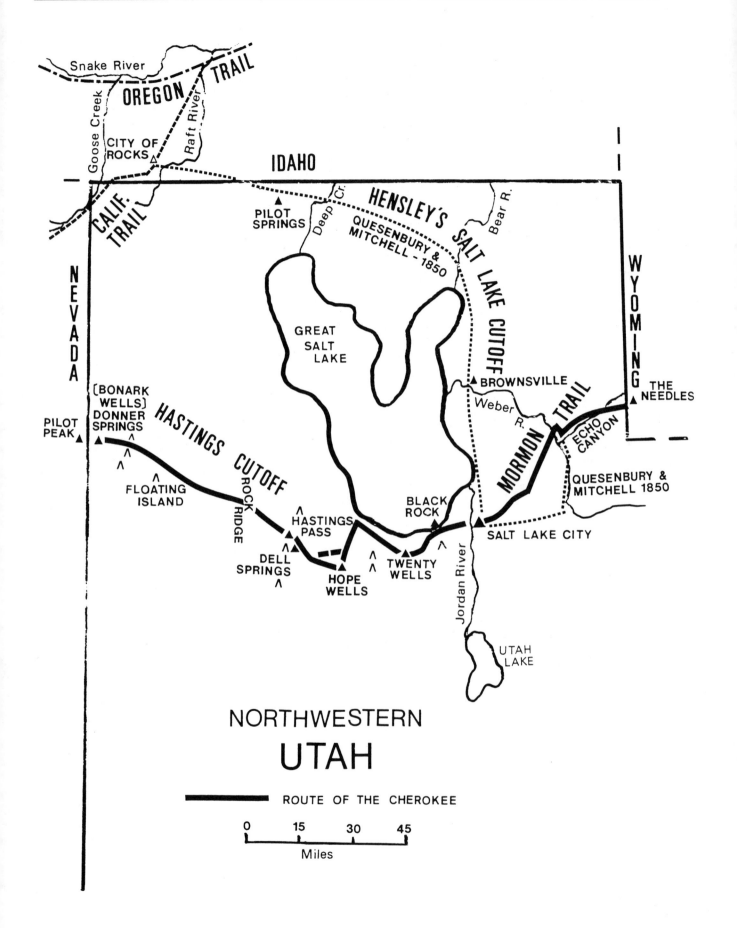

NORTHWESTERN
UTAH

—— ROUTE OF THE CHEROKEE

Miles

Chapter 8. GREAT SALT LAKE TO CALIFORNIA

> we moved...round the south end of the lake [and]
> struck out...through a miserable Desert
> > --James Sawyer Crawford

By the time the original Evans/Cherokee party, which left the Grand Saline on April 21, 1849, reached Great Salt Lake, the Company was divided into three identifiable groups. Two groups of Cherokee and whites--the packers, and the breakaway company of twelve wagons--took the Hensley Cutoff. It was the main route, north around the Great Salt Lake, and previously assumed to be the only route used in 1849. The third group was the larger Evans/Cherokee wagon company, which traveled the Hastings Cutoff over the Great Salt Desert.

THE HENSLEY CUTOFF

In the first group were the thirty Evans/Cherokee men who "packed through" from Pueblo. The packers had been joined at Pueblo by Lieutenant Pleasanton, his dragoon escort, some of the Helena, Arkansas Company, and perhaps others. Guided by experienced mountain man Dick Owens, they arrived at Salt Lake city on July 24. Although their progress and route from Salt Lake City to California is not documented by packer company members, they were seen by other emigrants. On August 1 T. J. Van Dorn, at Thousand Springs Valley on the California Trail, saw them and wrote:

> The valley was filled with teams and pack mules--one...Mr. Owen[s] at their head who charges us to be careful of the Digger Indians.[467]

The packers were seen again on August 9, near Little Humboldt River Meadows on the Humboldt River, 66 miles east of the Lassen Cutoff. Amos Josselyn noted:

> Late last evening [August 8] a train of pack mules came up and encamped near us. They had come by the way of Santafee and had to leave that rout and come this way on account of high waters and the scarcity of grass. Gov. Smith's staff of California [including Lt. Alfred Pleasanton] was in this train.[468] [Dick] Owens was their guide.[469]

---

[467]"T.J. Van Dorn Diary," Typescript. Yale University Library, p 30.
[468]"Lt. Pleasanton, 2d Dragoons, Aid de Camp to Gen. Persifer P. Smith, with

The Owens-led packer group had been in Salt Lake on July 24 and 25. Based on the above two sightings of the pack company, the Owens pack company used the Hensley or Salt Lake Cutoff. In one week the pack train passed over the cutoff from Salt Lake to City of Rocks, and in one more week, they traveled up the Raft River and down the Humboldt.[470] Josselyn's wagon party arrived in Sacramento September 11. However, no specific notice of the Owens packers' arrival in Sacramento has yet surfaced, either in military correspondence or reports, or the newspapers.[471]

Dick Owens had traveled across the Salt Desert with John C. Fremont in 1845 over what became known as the 1846 Hastings Cutoff. The adversities of that trip on the Salt Desert traverse probably encouraged Owens to lead his pack mule train over the Hensley route, around the north end of the Great Salt Lake.[472]

The second group--twelve wagons--split off from the main Evans/Cherokee Company at the main California Road east of Fort Bridger. They arrived at the Great Salt Lake August 13; left there on August 15. Their route from Salt Lake to California via the Hensley route is not yet documented by primary sources. However, on the Applegate/Lassen Cutoff, J. Goldsborough Bruff noted seeing Cherokee and Arkansas emigrants, probably from this group.[473]

---

an escort of ten men from company H 2d Dragoons, left Santa Fe on the 9th [June] for California, via the South Pass." *Cherokee Advocate* 30 July 1849 copied from "Santa Fe papers."

[469] J. William Barrett II, ed. *The Overland Journey of Amos Platt Josselyn Zanesville, Ohio to the Sacramento Valley April 2, 1849 to September 11, 1849* (Baltimore: Gateway Press, Inc. 1978) p 41.

[470] Owens' packers covered about 430 miles in fourteen days, an average of 31 miles a day. Correspondence with Roy Tea (Oregon-California Trails Association, Utah Crossroads Chapter) verified these mileage estimates.

[471] 31 Cong. 1 sess. Sen Ex Doc 1, Serial 549, p 159, Ltr 26 August 1849 from Bvt. Maj. Gen. Persifor Smith (Commander of the Pacific Division, U.S. Army) has no mention; p 173, Ltr 30 August 1849 from Bvt. Brig. Gen. Bennett Riley states: "The detachments of dragoons...the escort of the [customs] collector [Collier] [Santa Fe Trail to Santa Fe; then Gila Route] and with the Arkansas emigrants, have not yet arrived."

[472] Stansbury...*Exploration*...p 111.

[473] Georgia Willis Read and Ruth Gaines, eds. *Gold Rush: The Journals, Drawings, and other Papers of J. Goldsborough Bruff* (N. Y.: Columbia Univ. Press, 1944. Excerpts reprinted with permission of the publisher. (P5[A], Sept. 15, 1849); Critical Notes H1 pp 569-70. References are quoted from both journals--H1 and P5. Calvin Hall Holmes' diary includes mileages on the Applegate/Lassen route. Original diary held by California Society of Pioneers.

THE HASTINGS CUTOFF[474]

The third party of the 1849 Evans/Cherokee Company, the main wagon group, could have numbered as many as thirty-five wagons.[475] Still captained by Lewis Evans, they arrived at Salt Lake August 15 and departed August 17, proceeding straight west on the Hastings Cutoff across the Great Salt Desert.

During the two days in Salt Lake, Captain Evans spent considerable time obtaining information on the routes from Salt Lake to the goldfields of California. The route north of the Great Salt Lake, later called the Hensley Cutoff, though only a year old, was the main one. Why it was not taken is unknown. The lateness of the season, and the resulting lack of grass for the oxen, may have been a major factor. The information that no previous company had taken the Hastings that season meant there would be grass available.[476]

No doubt the Evans/Cherokee wagon company had a copy of the T.H. Jefferson map[477] and used it.[478] Jefferson traversed the Salt Desert in 1846 as a member of the Hastings and Harlan Young party. He produced a guide, "*T.H. Jefferson's Guide...*" *(map and "Accompaniment")*, and published it in 1849. When or where Lewis Evans obtained his copy is unknown. In March 1849 a book dealer in St. Louis advertised several guidebooks for California, including Jefferson's.[479]

---

[474]Rush Spedden, "The Hastings Cutoff" *Trailing the Pioneers: A Guide to Utah's Emigrant Trails 1829-1869*. (Logan, Utah: Utah State Univ. Press 1994) "The term 'Hastings Cutoff' was used historically for the general route from Fort Bridger via the south shore of Great Salt Lake to the Humboldt River....the section...became known west of Salt Lake City as the Hastings Road. In the last few decades, the Hastings Road has been referred to more commonly as the Donner-Reed Trail, or simply as the Donner Trail." Oregon-California Trails Assoc. Utah Crossroads 1994 Convention Tour Booklet D p 2.

[475]Company member James Pierce much later in his life reported 14 wagons in his group alone--those of the related members of John Rankin Pyeatt.

[476]Dale L. Morgan, *The Great Salt Lake* (Lincoln, Nebr.: Univ. of Nebraska Press Bison Book 1986) p 228.

[477]George R. Stewart, ed. T.H. Jefferson *Map of The Emigrant Road from Independence, MO., to St. Francisco, California* (San Francisco: California Historical Society Reprint 1945) p 20.

[478]Personal Correspondence with Roy D. Tea, 1993: "Apparently the Cherokee Trail emigrants had a copy of T.H. Jefferson's map of 1846."

[479]Barry...*West*...p 800. Jefferson's background has been the subject of much speculation. Rush Spedden "Who was T.H. Jefferson?" *Overland Journal* vol 8, no 3 (1990) pp 7-8.

Crawford, diarist for the main Evans/Cherokee wagon company, recorded the company's stay in Salt Lake and what, for him, must have been a reluctant departure west, away from the bounty of the valley, and the hospitality he had enjoyed there. Crawford:

"Th[ursday] 16 [August]

we lay by to day and recruited our oxen and traded Some with the Mormons."
> [at Salt Lake City, on the west bank of the Jordan River
> or "Eutaw Outlet" Salt Lake Co., Utah]

In 1902 James Pierce (Pearce), a member of the main Evans/Cherokee wagon company (and nephew of John Rankin Pyeatt), was living in Park City, Utah. Pierce wrote:

> Our party left the rendezvous at Ross's salt works in the Cherokee nation [in] April, 1849...
> We started west from Salt Lake the latter part of August, 1849, with an outfit of thirty-five men, twenty-one of our original party, ten of the Pomeroy and Preble[480] outfit and four packers, under the command of John R. Pyatt....Our train consisted of fourteen wagons drawn by horses, mules and oxen, and well loaded with supplies and all kind of tools for placer mining.

It was natural for sixteen-year-old Pierce to remember his uncle John Rankin Pyeatt as captain. Even though neither appointed nor elected, Pyeatt showed he had leadership and clout. When Pierce claimed that fourteen wagons were in the company, he was referring to the Pyeatt contingent.[481]

The only documentation of company membership is names appearing in the Crawford diary, in the letters of Pyeatt and Crawford, and in the reminiscence of James Pierce in 1902. These men were all related. And while they certainly did not consult one another about their writings (their divergent points of view were already demonstrated) the writings alone give no reliable estimate

---

[480]Barry...*West*...p 806. "On May 9 one company...set out [from Old Fort Kearney] Pomery 33-wagon...mercantile train...with...groups...[including] Peebles' party." The further progress of this company is unknown. Stansbury reported that on September 12 he left Salt Lake city for Fort Hall with pack mules accompanied by "Mr. T. Pomeroy, merchant from St. Louis, on his way to California." Pierce's reminiscence indicates a portion of Pomeroy's mercantile train went west over the Hastings Cutoff.

[481]When they reached California, seventeen related members built and resided in a dwelling--two houses connected by a dogtrot. The building was large enough and unique enough so they were able to offer "intertainment," that is food and lodging for travellers, at a rather handsome price. Pyeatt to wife Elizabeth Children and friends from "Cosumenes Califonia" February 17, 1850.

of the total company as it existed west of Salt Lake city. The total number of wagons from the Company using the Hastings Cutoff is estimated to be thirty-five, until the Lewis Evans journal or other primary documents surface giving more information, .

Usually Crawford noted the daily mileage, but in the first day's move away from the settlement at Salt Lake, he did not. Made in the evening, the move was just far enough away to get the company to themselves. <u>Crawford</u>:

"Friday 17th [August]

we struck camp this eavening and moved Some distance out to ward the South end of the Salt lake. "

[West Valley City, Salt Lake Co., Utah]

Crawford's entry on August 17 confirms that this Evans/ Cherokee wagon company, whatever its size, was moving west on the Hastings Cutoff. This is perhaps the first diary which verifies that wagons were used on this route in 1849.

In the absence of primary material, researchers have maintained that no wagons had come this way since 1846--the year of the Donner/Reed tragedy. For instance, Dale Morgan wrote that Captain Stansbury, while under orders to survey the Salt Lake and crossing the Salt Desert at night on November 3, 1849, found remains of emigrant wagons and belongings, "probably sad remains of the Donner party, for the forty-niners had not taken Hastings' Cutoff."[482] Again, Morgan: "none are known to have crossed the Salt Desert [in 1849] except Stansbury's pack party."[483]

The 1849 diarist's record over the next two days includes much more description and positive comment about the country. <u>Crawford</u>:

"Saturday 18.[August]...12 1/2 miles...

we moved to day...round the South end of the lake, this is the most Beutiful Sheet of water that I ever saw in my life. its water is as Clear as the pure are, and as Salt as water can be made with salt Their is, in this lake 3 Islands [Antelope, Fremont, Carrington Islands]. on which their is Some verry high mountains, on."

[near Black Rock, Lake Point Junction,
Tooele Co., Utah]

---

[482]Morgan...*Salt Lake*...p 228.
[483]Ibid. p 258.

During the day the company traveled southwest, then west across the Tooele Valley. Crawford:

"Sunday 19 [August]...21 miles
we moved to day...and camped at good frish water, which has not been the Case befor since we left Jordon [river]: Their being nothing but large Salt Springs on the road till this nights camp."
      [Twenty Wells, at Grantsville, Tooele Co., Utah
              Jefferson's "Hasting Wells,"]

During the day's travel they indulged in an activity that delights residents and visitors today. Crawford:

on this day several of us went in the Lake to bathe: This watter Can not be waded in whin it is up to the Armpit: in Spite of all your efforts you will rise, and you cannot Sink your self in it at all. You may float on your back and hold up, and wash your feet at the same time, on this Lake.

Crawford described another too-common trail incident:

this evening a young man (([left blank] and his partner both from Missouri) in drawing a Rifle from the waggon musel[muzzle] foremost, was Shot through the Arm; The Ball passing Through his arm and then betwixt the Thumb and finger, then through the Arm and into the breast of his companion. This evening we camped a verry good Spring.

Crawford never mentioned if the Missouri men lived or died, but this diary excerpt reveals that more than Arkansans and Cherokees took wagons over the Hastings in 1849--there were also Missourians.

The next day they went northwest. Crawford:

"Monday 20 [August]...19 miles
We Struck Camp to day, and moved..Still South of the lake, Passing now and then large Salt Springs and but verry little fresh Water. Camp to night at Salt Spring."
      [north end of Stansbury Mountains; present Timpie Spring/
              Timpie Point, Tooele Co., Utah]

Next day they moved south, away from the Salt Lake. Crawford:

"Tuesday 21 [August] We moved 9 miles to day.
and passed Some verry large and pretty Salt Springs   this day we left the Lake and have traviled nearly a South Course."
[South in Skull Valley to Cedar Springs, SE of Horseshoe Springs,
      Tooele Co., Utah. T.H. Jefferson map notes "Cedar Sp."]

Jefferson wrote in the very helpful "*Accompaniment* [to] *MAP OF THE EMIGRANT ROAD*:"

North-east of Hope-Wells, upon the mountain, about two miles from the road, is situated Cedar spring. It affords an abundant supply of delightful water, has cedar trees and some bunch grass near it.

Crawford took time during the hay cutting to comment on visitors.

> Yesterday and to day We have been visited, by Several Indians of the
> Piute or Eutaw tribe, they are the most filthy Beaings that I ever Saw.

The Company made preparations to cross the Salt Desert. <u>Crawford</u>:

"Wedens 22nd [August] we lay by today to Cut grass
to Hall for our oxen through a wilderness of about 80 miles"

Jefferson called this "the fearful long drive 83 Miles no grass
nor water," and his map noted:

> To accomplish the long drive grass & water must be carried from Hope
> Wells and the journey performed night and day making short & regular
> camps. Not more than five waggons should go in company and the cattle
> should be continually guarded.

In his "Accompaniment," Jefferson wrote:

> Take in a supply of water and green grass at Hope-Wells. Three or four
> gallons of water per ox is enough. Water is more important than grass...
> don't hurry the oxen; make a regular camp about every 20 miles. Remain
> at each camp two hours or more, and measure out the water to each ox in
> a basin. Unyoke at each camp and leave the cattle loose....Adhere to
> these rules and you will go through safe.[484]

In 1846 Jefferson also had crossed in mid-August. The 1849
Evans Company appears to have gone nearly straight west from Cedar
Springs, not south to Hope Wells first. Pierce:

> We went out by the point of the mountain, through where Grantsville now
> is and on to Skull valley, which was the last place for water this side
> of the desert. At that point we filled our water barrels, one for each
> wagon, and started across the desert, which our odometer...showed to be
> ninety miles in width, and which we were three days and two nights in
> crossing.[485]

Crawford began to use the campsite and physical feature names
from the 1846 Jefferson Map, verifying the map's use by the
Company. Beginning with a thirty-mile overnight march, <u>Crawford</u>
chronicles the desert crossing:

"Thursday 23 [August]...30 miles
We Started to a west course...a cross a valey or Salt Plain, and Crossed
over Scorpion mt
[present Cedar Mountains,
Jefferson's "Scorpion Mountain"]

---

[484]Stewart...*Jefferson*...p 20.
[485]"The Find on the Desert" *Salt Lake Tribune* Sunday 11 May 1902 p 31, col 4-
7. Reprinted by Robert Hoshide in "Crossroads Quarterly Newsletter" Utah
Crossroads Chapter, Oregon-California Trails Association vol 5, no 1, (Winter
1994.)

leaving the Dell Springs [present Redlum Springs, Jefferson's "Dell
Spring"]...at the East Base of the [Cedar] mt on our left, this is a
rugged Mountain 9 miles over [Hastings Pass] which we crossed about an
hour after night and by Brake of day we halted at the foot of Rock
ridge...making the distance of to days travel 30 miles."
[Grayback Mountain, Tooele Co., Utah, Jefferson's "Rock Ridge"]

Pyeatt wrote of the six days' travel from Salt Lake and their
entry into the desert:

we left the Mormon town on the 17th day of August and got to the desert
on the 23th 64 miles hear having cut grass in the time above mentioned
and supplyede ourselves with watter....we started through the desert 67
miles through the desert on the 23.[486]

Pierce remembered that their water fell short:

The second day out made it plain that our supply of water was entirely
inadequate, but we struggled as best we could.

Crawford records the most disastrous event of their journey--
another day and night crossing, the oxen giving out, and the
abandonment of the wagons on the desert. Crawford:

"Friday 24 [August]...22 1/2 [miles]
we Struck out to day through a miserable Desert Where in many places we
could not see the least vestage of vegitation of any Kind for many miles
round us, we continued our Journey through the day making in this day
and night travil about 22 1/2 miles, Though we camped...[east of
Floating Island, Tooele Co., Utah] 2 hours before day   about this time
the wind rose and blew from the north which almost Chilled us through
The letter part of this nights travil, a good many Cattle gave out and
we had to leave our Waggons or double teems and go [o]ut to Water and
grass, [Donner Spring area] which is 21 miles from This place, we took
our teem and Went out to water leaving one ox which we got out the next
day."

Pierce's reminiscence of the desert crossing includes their
emergency decisions and actions to save themselves and animals:

so many of the stock perished that it was impossible to proceed further
with the train. A consultation was held and it was decided to take the
strongest of the animals with four of the lightest wagons and make a
dash for the water known to be on the west of the desert. Each man was
allowed to put on his blankets, one change of clothes and his gun, and
in addition enough food was selected as the company thought to carry us
through....This unburdened we again started and within a few hours it
became evident from the actions of the stock that we were approaching
water, as they would sniff the air and hurry forward without urging, and
about sundown of the third day we struck the longed-for springs.[487]

Pyeatt wrote of their efforts--double-teaming with half of
their wagons to reach water, then returning to recover the stock,

[486]Pyeatt letter to wife Elizabeth children and friends from "California,"
November 11, 1849.
[487]Pierce...*Tribune*...1902.

and leaving his big wagon, with the others, to the desert:

> we ware ablige to double teams and go out with half of our wagons after
> gitting our teams to the gras and resting aday we again cut grass and
> took one wagon back to hall the grass and water   this was the carnahan
> boys wagon we having made arangement with them to join with them and
> leave our big wagon in the deser   this we don putting the load in
> thear wagon and came out in two days more.[488]

The final tally of loss, in their little "connexion" group alone,
is given in Crawford's diary. They recuperated for five days at
Donner Spring.

"Saturday 25 [August]
> We got our oxen and Waggons all out with the exception of one Waggon and
> four or five oxen, at this place we lay by 5 days and recruited our
> oxen."

>   [Present Donner Spring area, 22 miles north of Wendover,
>   Box Elder Co., Utah; Jefferson's "Bonark Wells"]

In dry weather, the desert's salt crust might have supported
the wagons. But after a rain, the crust was easily broken to
reveal mire. Bryant, in 1846, found it to be "a composition of
salt, sand, and clay...our mules sometimes sunk to their knees."[489]
Pyeatt had previously mentioned in a letter from Salt Lake that it
rained. He was pleased because the rain settled the clouds of dust
on the California trail. The recent rain nearly spelled disaster
for the company on the desert. The additional effort expended in
the mud flats decimated their animals, both horses and oxen.
Pyeatt considered the group's losses:

> [we] got a part of our wagons through on the 25th leaving the rest of
> them in the desert 21 miles from water and grass, our teams giving out
> from the hard pulling in the mud....we got all of our oxen out (but som
> of them has bin of very little us to us since thos [though] we have got
> them all but one to this place) [Consumnes River, California]....(thear
> ware many of the company that did not get thear oxen all out of the
> deser)....(we had left evrything that we thot we could do with out after
> we got through the big desert and put oxen to the little wagon, the
> horses havi[n]g given out).[490]

James Pierce, in his 1902 reminiscence, responded to a story
in the *Salt Lake Tribune* that claimed forty-niners died in the
Great Salt Desert. He related his experience pertaining to

---

[488]Pyeatt letter, California, November 11, 1849.
[489]Roy Tea...*Hastings*...booklet p 15, quoting from Edwin Bryant *What I Saw In California in 1846 and 1847* (London: Richard Bently, 1849.)
[490]Pyeatt letter, California, November 11, 1849.

crossing the desert in a newspaper article.[491]

> Park City, May 9.[1902]---"I noticed in the Tribune of April 30th an account of the finding of remains of a prospector on the desert west of Skull valley and near the abandoned emigrant wagons...But the press and public are both in error regarding the fate of the party who abandoned those wagons. As a matter of fact not a single person in the outfit failed to reach California...[after the Salt Desert was crossed] all the rest of our supplies, tools, camp equipage and ten wagons were left on the desert to be destroyed by the elements...
>
> How do I know? Well, I was a member of the party and though only sixteen years old at the time, the hardships endured on that trip have fixed its occurrences so firmly in my mind that I can recall nearly every incident in that journey.

Pyeatt also wrote they left "the rest of them [wagons] in the desert." He further indicated that one wagon, his "big one," was also left in the desert.[492]

Capt. Howard Stansbury returned from surveying around the Salt Lake three months later. In early November 1849, traveling east across this Salt Desert, he discovered:

> During the night...five wagons and one cart, which had stuck fast in the mud, and been necessarily left by their owners, who, from appearances, had abandoned every thing, fearful of perishing themselves in this inhospitable desert. Great quantities of excellent clothing, tool-chests, trunks, scientific books, and, in fact, almost every thing...had been here left strewn over the plain. Many articles had not even been removed from the wagons. The carcasses of several oxen lying about.[493]

Pierce recalled later asking about the Evans Company wagons:

> In 1866 I met Maj. Egan in Salt Lake who told me he had been out to our abandoned wagons, some of which he burned for the purpose of securing the iron, which was in the early days was [sic] very scarce in Salt Lake.
>
> Maj. Egan stated to me that he had concluded from the number of wagons, and the skeletons of the animals lying about that the entire train had perished, and I presume that is how the report of our death was started, but it was a mistake.[494]

Robert Hoshide in a contemporary article presented some very interesting insights, new information and controversial findings about the wagons in the desert.[495] The following is excerpted from

---

[491]Pierce...*Tribune*...1902.

[492]Pyeatt noted several times during the trip unloading his big wagon and setting up shop to do blacksmith repairs: at Fort Mann, at Pueblo, at Green River, at Fort Bridger, and at Salt Lake City.

[493]Stansbury...*Salt Lake*...p 114. November 2-3, 1849.

[494]Pierce...*Tribune*...1902.

[495]Robert Hoshide "Salt Desert Trails Revisited" *Crossroads Quarterly*

his documented unpublished version of the article:

> page 3: I shall review the when and where wagons were abandoned on the Salt Desert through November 1849, when Howard Stansbury on his 1849-1850 government expedition passed abandoned wagons during the night. Next, I shall survey the 1849 Salt Desert crossings and demonstrate how the Pearce account and other facts impact on previous conclusions based on the archaeological record [of 1986-1988]. I shall conclude by showing why many relics found at the Donner-Reed Excavation sites were not left by the Donner Party."
>
> page 10: "There are no [former] records of wagons being left on the Salt Desert in 1847 or 1849."
>
> page 14: "The physical evidence confirms that artifacts found by the Donner-Reed Excavation probably [came] from the Arkansas parties."
>
> page 16: "Firearms--Pearce mentions leaving weapons in the desert, while no mention is made by the Donner Party...Wood--...Puzzling are wood fragments such as White Pine and Douglas Fir that did not come from Illinois or Arkansas, but probably from the Wasatch Mountains in Utah. A member of the Arkansas group traded for a wagon in Salt Lake City." [Pyeatt letter 16 August from Salt Lake: "Squire Marrs has bot a small wagon to day for $30."]
>
> page 17: "Tracks and ruts"; continued on.
>
> page 18: "Forty-niner J.R. Pyeatt is the only one who describes extreme difficulty going through the mud..."[Pyeatt also stated "we had a fine rain today" on August 16 in Salt Lake].
>
> page 18: "Conclusion...Recent excavations in sites labeled '42To467-42To471' are probably from the Arkansas parties mentioned in this paper rather than Donner-Reed wagons which has been previously supposed. The archaeological assemblage found at the Donner-Reed."
>
> page 19: "excavation sites fits much better with the Arkansas parties than with the Donner-Reed Party."[496]

On Thursday, August 30, after four days spent at Donner Spring, Captain Evans and most of the 1849 company members resumed traveling. Crawford, Pyeatt, and Pierce stayed behind and laid by for an additional day recruiting the men and animals. Pyeatt:

> heaving rested agan [at Donner Spring area] in a few day we started to tak the next desert 25 or 26 miles though the company [Evans] leaving us [leaving Pyeatt's extended family] one day before withe [with] the Crawford boys and one other wagon Making in all 5 wagons. [Evans] was to wait for us at the nex water and grass.

Crawford never mentioned the temporary split but continued notations of the five wagons as they moved west from the Donner Spring area. The small company traveled into Nevada on the Hastings Cutoff.[497]

Newsletter Utah Crossroads Chapter, Oregon-California Trails Association vol 5 no 2 pp 5-9 (Spring 1994.)
[496]Ibid.
[497]James Pierce noted: "At this point the four packers left us, and after resting up a little we pushed on."

Crawford:

"Friday 31st [August]...20 miles

We struck out to day over an other 30 miles Desert   we traviled 20 miles over a plain and up a considerable mountain Called Bonicks[498] mt...and about mid night we camped for the remainder of the night."
[present Silver Zone Pass, Toano Range, Elko Co., Nevada]

Crawford noted another trail encounter with Indians:

"September the 1st 1849 Saturday...10 miles

We moved early this morning and by 2 aclock we reached Childes Cache a Verry Pritty encampment, here we have been viseted by a port of the Showshownee Tribe of Indians which are a tolerable good looking tribe."
[Present Big Springs,[499] 5 miles south of Oasis, Elko Co,, Nevada; Jefferson's "Chiles Cache" at "Relief Springs"]

They expected to find the Evans/Cherokee Company waiting for them. Pyeatt's reaction at not finding Evans there was, "they [Evans] did not [wait] it being Saterday when we got thear and they knowing we would want to rest on the Sabat."

The main Company had spent four days (Pyeatt's group five days) at Donner Spring recuperating from crossing the Salt Desert. Considering the country through which they still had to pass, Captain Evans could not wait. He moved on, aware that Pyeatt would insist on stopping on Sunday. That further angered Pyeatt.

> and they [Evans] as I beliave wanting to compell us to travel on sunday being now in the midst of the Indians and they astealing everything they could.

One of the five wagons left them and went ahead. Pyeatt:

> but we rested on the Sabath [September 2] thus falling behind the company two days   the one wagon...left us leaving but 4 wagons and 22 men.[500]

Crawford seemed rather calm about the Shoshone seen on the Sabbath, then recorded a very busy Monday moving across rugged terrain.

---

[498]The T.H. Jefferson map shows "Bonark Wells," "Bonark Mts.," and "Bonark Indians." A National Geographic "Indians of North America" map of 1972 shows the southern boundary of Shoshone-Bannock (Bonark) Indians to be a nearly east-west line in the latitude of Ogden, Utah as far west as a branch of the Owyhee River in Nevada.

[499]The first wagons through this section of the Hastings Cutoff were of the Bidwell-Bartelson Party in 1841. At this location they abandoned their remaining seven wagons and packed through. Roy Tea "Hastings Longtripp a Hastings Cutoff Trail Guide from Donner Spring to the Humboldt River" p 14.

[500]Pyeatt letter, California, November 11, 1849.

Crawford:

"Sunday 2nd [September] We lay by to day

and we were visited by 12 or 15 of the Showshowne tribe they appear to be friendly, and they are verry much of Beggers..."

"Monday 3d [September]...25 miles

We Struck camp to day...and moved 11 1/2 miles South and Nooned at the Warm Springs . [Flowery Lake Springs; Jefferson's "Warm Spring"]. from thence we Struck a West Course and Crossed Childes Mountain [Pequop Mountains via Flowery Lake Pass; Jefferson's "Bonark Mts."] and the Valey West of it [Independence Valley] and camped at Mound Springs making in this days Travil 25 miles, this Spring is Some What Sulphurius. Grass is becoming More plenty here than Some distance East of this."

[Mound Springs, approx. 2 miles So. of Chase Springs,
Elko Co., Nevada; Jefferson's "Mound Spring"]

Edwin Bryant, 1846, wrote of this place "another small oasis, of an acre or two of green vegetation, near the centre of which were one or two small springs or wells of cool fresh water"[501]

Crawford continued his 1849 diary from Mound Springs as the company moved out early, hurrying to catch up with Evans:

"Tuesday 4th [September]...13 1/2 miles.

We left this morning and Crossed the Warm Spring Mt [north end of Spruce Mountain Ridge] and the Vally west of it [Clover Valley] and encamped at Mill Spring. This is a beutiful Spring afording a grate Water Priviledge We made 13 1/2 miles to day."[502]

"Wedensday 5 [September]...15 miles

We moved early this morning [west along Hwy 229] and Crossed over a gap of Mill Spring Mt [southern end of East Humboldt Range] which Was 9 miles a cross, Thence a cross a pretty vally 6 miles [Ruby Valley] and Camped at a beautiful branch Coming out of the East Side of a Mt. on our front, or west of us   this is a beautiful Valley, and fine grass, and ecellent Water, runing in beautifull branches from the Mt out East, a grate manny Indians have been Seen today of the ShowShownee Tribe, our travil to day has been 15 miles..."

[40 miles sw of Wells, Elko Co., Nevada;
T.H. Jefferson's campsite of "29-30 August" 1846]

"Thursday 6 [September]...20 1/2 miles

we left Camp to day, and Struck A South Course along the Same mt; This Mt is verry high and rugged with now and then Snow on its Summits; This days Travil of 20 1/2 miles has bien a long the West Side of Fountain Valley [Ruby Valley; T.H. Jefferson's "Valley Of Fountains"] one of the most Beautifull valleys that I ever Saw in my Life watered with the

---

[501]Tea..."Hastings Longtripp"...p 18. A 1996 field trip to the area proved that the two mounds with springs beneath were still there. Participants were invited to jump up and down on the mounds in order to feel the springing action and see the water produced by that.

[502]T. H. Jefferson's 1846 pack party recorded on his map a distance of 12 miles from Mound Spring to Mill Spring. The 1849 party was a wagon company.

finest Springs running out from the East Side of the mt: and Spreding through the richest vallys of grass. Antelop are in large gangs in this vally and the Mt Pheasant or Sage Cock, are plenty here   Their is no timber here but, Some Scrubby white Cedar or Junper, and Pine on the mts we camped to night with out water or grass."
              [Jct. of Harrison Pass Road; Elko Co., Nevada]

The valley, with its numerous springs, which they had passed through, is now The Ruby Lake National Wildlife Refuge.

     As they moved toward the south end of the Ruby Mountains, Indian encounters became more numerous. Crawford:

                "Friday 7 [September]...11 1/2 miles
we moved today early, and continued our Course South, passing Some of the most beautifull Springs that I ever Saw   We passed to day 45 Springs of different Sises.   these we passed to day in the Space of 11 1/2 miles, which is our days travil   to night We were visited by a good many Shoshonies. We gave thim Som presents of Tobacco;"
                   [Near the south end of Ruby Lake,
                    Elko/White Pine cos. line, Nevada]

     According to Pyeatt's letter they remained separated from the main wagon company following their insistence to rest on the Sabbath. Indian theft from the small company forced them to seek the protection of the larger Evans/Cherokee group:

     we set out on monday [September 3] and got on very well through the week till Friday night [September 7] got within 5 or 6 miles of the company hear the Indians Stole three horses and one mule from us some of them being tied cloast to the tents   the horses they stole was red but bit ross [color description] a mare of Bob Epperson and the mule I got from Calb   the mule they brot back nex day and I think that we could have goten the rest of them if our little company had all bin to gether but all the boys that could be spared from the wagons was hunting the stolen horses   thus we found it nessary to over tak the [Evans] company again and stay with it   this we don that night.[503]

As they rounded the south end of the Ruby Mountains. Crawford's diary corroborates the stock thefts, the reason for rejoining the main company:

                "Saturday 8 [September]...21 [miles]
we lost 3 mares and one mule last night which were stolen by the Indians. we Started on our Journey this morning and was met by Some Shoshonies bringing Back the Stolen mule   after going 7 miles South This morning we Turned west and crossed a mt [Overland Pass] and camped on a Small Crick; on the East of the Mt we [had] passed perhaps 25 or 30 springs today."
                [west of Overland Pass, White Pine Co., Nevada]

Crawford's letter identified the owners of the stock:
"Eprosons, J.R. Pyeatt, and A.B. Crawford had...a nag a piece,

---

[503]Pyeatt letter, California, November 11, 1849.

Stolen from them...in Fountain Valey."[504]

     After rejoining the main company Pyeatt commented on the lost
stock, and the Company not wanting to wait while recovery was
attempted. He was continuously angered by taking the road on
Sunday and he questioned the leadership of Capt. Lewis Evans:

> we then got along tolerable well   the company wouldn't wait for us to
> go back to try to git our horses but started again on Sunday   (I
> mention this circumstance to show the necesity of A company starting to
> know what sort of leaders they have and not put thos in that has a name
> to live while they or ded [are dead] in trespasses and in sins).[505]

The entire group went north into Huntington Valley. Crawford:

"Sunday 9 [September]...20 miles
we Started a north course to day down a Small Streem Called glovers
Crick [present Huntington Creek]. this is a verry pretty vally
[Huntington Valley] and we made 20 miles to day."
[SW of Jiggs, Elko Co., Nevada; Jefferson's "Glover Creek"]

"Monday 10 [September]...10 miles
We Started North this morning and Continued our Journey down the Same
Streem   This valley is narrow, but a good valley of land   Their is
no game in this part of the Countery Except Antelope, and a few Black
Tail Deer and Pheasants of Different Kinds. we made 10 miles to day."
[Near the junction of Cottonwood Creek and Huntington Creek,
NW of Jiggs, Elko Co., Nevada]

"Tuesday 11 [September]...12 1/2 miles
we Left Camp Early this morning and passed through Some verry good land,
Still Keeping a North Course, and after making 12 1/2 miles Encamped on
the Same Streem after passing a larger Crick Coming in on our right."
[South Fork of the Humboldt River, south of Elko,
Elko Co., Nevada]

     On this day, September 11, Missourian Alfred Oliver, packer
from the Evans/Cherokee Company, wrote a letter from Sacramento
which appeared later in the *Fort Smith Herald*.[506]

> Oliver of Newton county, Missouri..."Travelers that started here, never
> have nor never will reach here. The distress and loss of life on the
> road cannot at this time be ascertained. It will be one month yet,
> before we can learn anything caertain, but, that there has been a great
> loss of life there is no doubt." Mr. Oliver is a man we are well
> acquainted with, and confidence may be placed in what he writes.[507]

_____

[504]James Sawyer Crawford letter to wife Harriet & Children from "California
thirty miles East of Sacrimento City...Nov the 18th 1849."
[505]Pyeatt letter, California, November 11, 1849.
[506]O. W. Lipe wrote: "[May 15] At little Arkansas [river] we over took a wagon
with four persons from the northern part of Missouri." Oliver could have been
with this wagon.
[507]*Fort Smith Herald* 26 December 1849 vol 3, no 18, p 1. Oliver returned to

The Company's last day on the Hastings Cutoff was consumed by the difficult trip through the narrow canyon of the South Humboldt River. Crawford:

"Wedens 12 [September]...12 miles
we proceeded on our Journey on a west Course, and entered a rough Canion [So. Fork of the Humboldt] which Continues about the Spac of 8 miles: in This distance we had to travil in the bed of the creek at least one fourth of the time; thier not being Room for a road on neither Side: The Bluffs in places being, perhaps 500 feet hig   We made 12 miles to day and encamped on the Humbolt or Marys River, in Sight of the main Road."
[approximately 8 miles southwest of Elko, Elko Co., Nevada]

Another important junction was reached--the main California Road. Pyeatt: "We got to the road on the 12th of Sept., 193 miles from the desert."[508]

The Evans/Cherokee wagon company had traversed what no other recorded 1849 companies had--the Hastings Cutoff. No other wagon company experienced the hardships and difficulties of the twenty-six days on the Hastings from Salt Lake to the Humboldt River. While they experienced no disease or death, they lost wagons and some oxen on the Salt Desert. And a few horses were taken in Ruby Valley. But they weren't the only ones to take the route.

Cherokee Dr. Jeter Lynch Thompson, with slaves, (not part of the Evans/Cherokee Company), left Cherokee Nation traveling the main California Trail along the Platte.[509] After being joined by Judge Tully's Missouri Company, they were afflicted with cholera while on the Independence Road.

some of our friends who started for California last spring, by way of the upper rout [Platte], from Independence...cholera prevailed among them, but not to a very alarming extent, and from the communication lately received in this nation from Dr. Jeter L. Thompson that 14 persons belonging to his company concluded that they would go on ahead of the main company, and after the 14 persons had got two or three days ahead of the main company, a little beyond Platte River, they were

---

Arkansas in February 1850 with Lewis Evans' Journal. He captained an 1850 train over the Evans/Cherokee trail as far as the Laramie Plains.
[508]Pyeatt letter November 11, California. The Crawford diary mileages total 191 from Donner Spring area to the end of the day's journey on September 12, "in Sight of the main Road."
[509]Dr. Jeter Lynch Thompson was one of the first Cherokee medical doctors. He went to Texas in 1845 with Cherokees looking for suitable places to emigrate. In California by late 1849, he set up a ranch twenty-five miles from the Feather River mines for beef and "next year's" vegetables. He developed a plan for his slaves to work in exchange for freedom. By 1855 he was back in the Cherokee Nation, as Senator from the Delaware District.

attacked with the Cholera, and eight out of 14 died; viz: Samuel W. Bell, Brice Martin, William Parks, Elijah Blythe, James Henry, ---- Purly, Markham, and Judge Tully, of Mo.[510]

They died near North Platte, Nebraska. News of the deaths was communicated to the Evans/Cherokee groups at Salt Lake city.[511] The remnants of Thompson's Company traveled west from Salt Lake city over the Hastings Cutoff. According to the reminiscence of a member of Dr. Thompson's company, the doctor himself was afflicted with cholera. They made a swing out of a buffalo robe up in the wagon bows, and left him in the middle of "this 90 mile desert [with] one wagon and four men...and also the tools to dig his grave with." Four days later as they were waiting in camp [at Donner Spring?] they saw the doctor's lone wagon in the distance. They surrounded it to hear of the doctor's last hours "but instead were transported with joy to see the Doctor himself much improved in health."[512]

---

[510]*Cherokee Advocate* 20 August 1849.
[511]Packers arrived in Salt Lake on July 24; splinter group of 12 wagons, mostly Cherokee on August 13; and the main wagon company on August 15.
[512]Foreman...*Marcy*...pp 82-87.

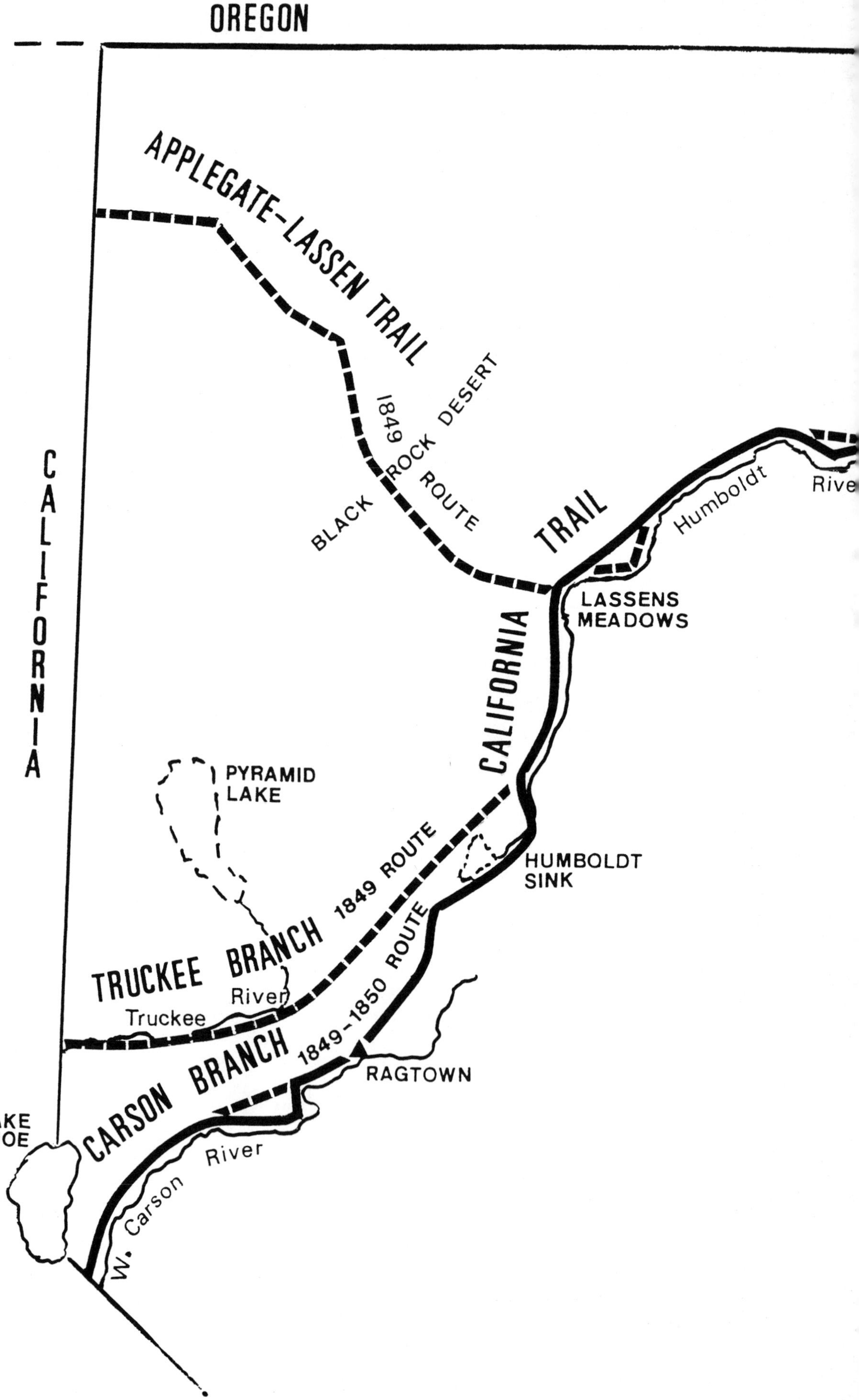

OREGON

APPLEGATE-LASSEN TRAIL

1849 ROCK DESERT

BLACK ROCK ROUTE

CALIFORNIA

CALIFORNIA TRAIL

Humboldt River

LASSENS MEADOWS

PYRAMID LAKE

HUMBOLDT SINK

TRUCKEE BRANCH 1849 ROUTE

1849-1850 ROUTE

Truckee River

RAGTOWN

CARSON BRANCH

LAKE TAHOE

W. Carson River

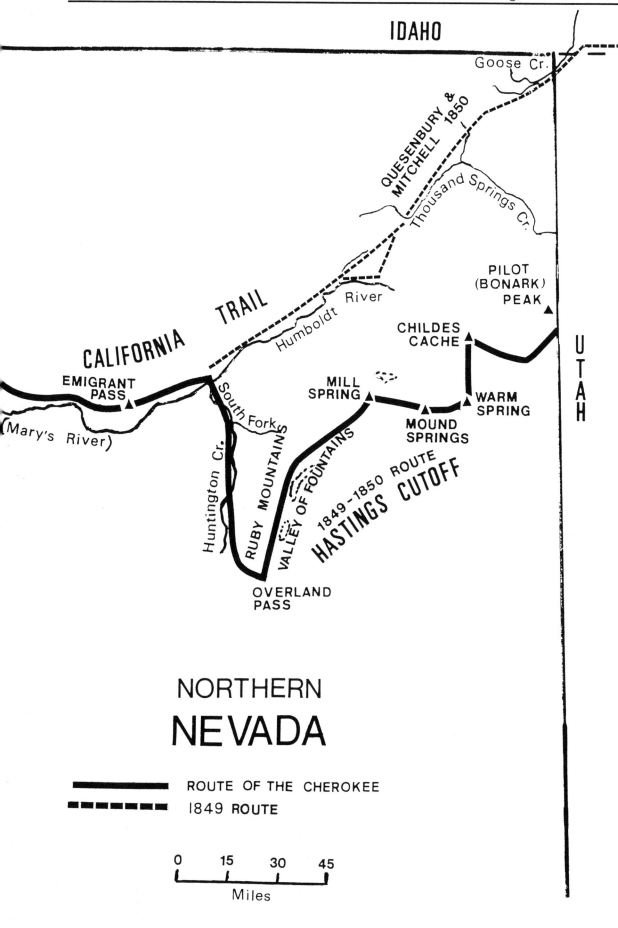

IDAHO

Goose Cr.

QUESENBURY & MITCHELL 1850

Thousand Springs Cr.

PILOT (BONARK) PEAK

CALIFORNIA TRAIL

River

Humboldt

CHILDES CACHE

EMIGRANT PASS

(Mary's River)

South Forks

MILL SPRING

WARM SPRING

MOUND SPRINGS

UTAH

Huntington Cr.

RUBY MOUNTAINS

VALLEY OF FOUNTAINS

1849-1850 ROUTE

HASTINGS CUTOFF

OVERLAND PASS

NORTHERN

NEVADA

ROUTE OF THE CHEROKEE

1849 ROUTE

0   15   30   45

Miles

ALONG THE HUMBOLDT RIVER

The 1849 Evans/Cherokee Company moved from the Hastings Cutoff into the mass migration on the main California Trail. They traveled west on the north side of the Humboldt River. Members lightened their loads daily, leaving a wagon because the oxen gave out. Crawford:

"Thurs 13 [September]...17 1/2 [miles]
We moved early this morning and Struck the [California] road; [The T.H. Jefferson Map calls it "Road from Fort Hall to California & Oregon"] and found a good many emegrants incamped on the river; we found the grass grately diminished by advanced imigration, This is a beautifull river [Humboldt] runing through Some Fertil Land. We nooned to day on the river, and Struck out across the hills, [Greenhorn Cutoff] which makes near twenty miles of a rough and dusty road before we struck the river again; about half way through this mountain one of our oxen and one of [John M.] Whams and one yoke of [John A. and Hiram] Summers gave out, and we Camped for the night; we made to day 17 1/2 miles."
[Emigrant Pass, SW of Carlin, Eureka Co., Nevada]

Condition of the grass on the main road and the Humboldt itself was later written about by Pyeatt:

hear we found the grass eating to the ground in a word we found but very little grass   from that on to near the sink of the humbolt river, a distance of 244 miles...it dos not diserve to be called a river.[513]

They continued to throw away all but necessities; left another wagon. Crawford:

"Friday 14 [September]...12 miles
our oxen all being recruited we Started this morning, after throwing out 100 lbs of Tobacco and a good many other things: we traviled 12 miles to day and Camped on the Humboldt once more."
[Approximately halfway between Beowawe and Dunphy, Eureka Co., Nevada]

"Satur 15 [September]...15 miles
[John] Wham & [Andrew E. and John Thompson] Edmiston left their waggon this morning and put their Cloths and bedding in our Waggon and Some Flour and Corn meal; we moved on to day and after makeing 15 miles encamped on the Same Streem grass is verry scarse on this part of the river."
[North of Argenta Point, east of Battle Mountain, Lander Co., Nevada]

"Sunday 16 [September]...17 miles
we moved early to day and continued down the Same Streem 17 miles and Encamped for the night, we have passed Several graves on this Streem."
[NW of Battle Mountain, Lander Co., Nevada]

---

[513]Pyeatt letter, California, November 11, 1849.

More horse theft occurred. The losses resulted in further hardship. <u>Crawford</u>:

"Monday the 17 [September]...12 miles

last night the Indians Stole one horse of Capt Evans one of Esqs [Gus A. and Leonard] Shulars one of Jas McKinneys and one of mine. five of us followed their trail afoot about 10 miles Back on the Humboldt But, we could not over take them   we returned and got to Camp Some time in the night. Our train traveled 12 miles to day and Encamped on the Same Streem."

[north of Valmy, Humboldt Co., Nevada]

Crawford's letter identified the owners of stolen stock:

my horse, two of Capt. Evans [Robert Epperson] Eproson, T. James [McKinney?] Andrew Edmiston, James Devin, and myself, followed them...10 miles...but we could not over take them afoot.[514]

The companies had been on the road since April. Folks at home wondered why letters were not received. Besides accidents and death along the trail, there were other mishaps reported at home.

Many of the friends of the overland emigrants to California, by the Missouri and Arkansas routes, have been expecting for a long time letters from them. The cause of their disappointments, probably, is that at a recent fire in St. Louis, a mailbag, containing several thousand letters, was so damaged by fire and water as to be illegible. The mail agent in St. Louis has done all he could to dry the letters and send them to their proper destination, but the superscription of many of them has become obliterrated.[515]

The Company moved early each day, steadily down the Humboldt River. <u>Crawford</u>:

"Tuesday 18 [September]...17 miles

we moved quite Early this morning and Continued down the Same Streem, our road being verry good to day and the two last days. We made 17 miles today and Encamped on the Same Streem."

[NE of Golconda, Humboldt Co., Nevada]

"Wedens 19 [September]...15 miles

We moved Early this morning a West Course and had but little grass today, or rather their is but little grass left on this road; this Season the Emigration has been So large to the west   We made fifteen miles to day and camped on the same Streem; this day we Crossed over an other mountain which is the 2nd Cut off Since we Came to this river."

[NW of Golconda, Humboldt Co., Nevada]

The road became tougher on the animals as they approached the vicinity of present Winnemucca.

---

[514]Crawford letter, California, November 18, 1849.
[515]*Cherokee Advocate* 17 September 1849 p 2.

Crawford:

"Thursday 20 [September]...14 miles
We Started Early this morning and traviled over a bad sandy road a West Course on the Same Streem, and made 14 miles and and Encamped on the North Side of the Same river."
[Approximately 3 miles North of Winnemucca, Humboldt Co., Nevada]

"Friday 21 [September]...13 miles
We left Camp Early this morning and continued our Course down the Humbolt. the Mts on Either Side are verry sandy the road in the Bottom Was good to day   We made 13 miles to day and Encamped on the river. No grass to night--."
[SW of Winnemucca, Humboldt Co., Nevada]

"Saturday 22 [September]...11 miles
We mooved Early to day down the Same Streem occasionally Crossing Some verry Sandy Points which Put into the River. This part of the river is Poor and without grass. We made 11 miles to day and Encamped on the Same Streem."
[north of Mill City, Pershing Co., Nevada]

"Sunday 23d [September]...17 1/2 miles
We Started on our Journey this morning and Continued down the Same Streem; passing the Oregon road today, which road Crosses the Siera Mountain to the North of our rout   We made 17 1/2 miles to day; Passing but Little grass on our rout to day. and none to night."
[Rye Patch Reservoir, west of Imlay, Pershing Co., Nevada]

This "Oregon road" noted in Crawford's diary became known as the Applegate Trail.[516] Some who had traveled the Cherokee Trail, perhaps all of the twelve wagon breakaway party of the Evans/Cherokee Wagon Company, took the "Oregon road." Premier diarist and sketcher J. Goldsborough Bruff turned onto the "Oregon road" on September 15, eight days ahead of this main body of the Evans Company. Bruff mentioned meeting Cherokees on that cutoff on September 21.

Calvin Hall Holmes and his brother Henderson were members of the twelve wagon breakaway party from the Evans/Cherokee Company. Holmes' scant diary lists their mileages "From Humboldt" over the Applegate and Lassen Trails.[517]

---

[516]The Applegate Trail was pioneered in 1846 by Jesse Applegate (who led the famous Cow Column to Oregon in 1843), Levi Scott and thirteen others as a shorter, less troublesome route from Fort Hall to the Willamette Valley. William R. Sampson, ed. *John McLoughlin's Business Correspondence, 1847-48*. (Seattle: Univ. of Washington Press 1973) p 66 ns 123-4. Published in cooperation with the Washington Historical Society.

[517]Holmes diary page 1.

The Lassen Meadows, located at the turnoff, were mentioned by other travelers as a source of grass. However, the main Evans/Cherokee Company traveled late in the season when most of the grass had been eaten or harvested for hay. Crawford noted "little grass" until the next day, and further south. His weariness is evidenced by unusually pessimistic remarks. <u>Crawford</u>:

"Monday 24 [September]...11 1/4 miles

We Started quite Soon this morning and Continued our Journey Through the Same desert, and after making 11 1/4 miles we found a Small Patch of grass on the river, where we Camped for the purpose of recruiting our oxen. This is the most miserable, Worthless, poor, Sandy, dusty and hatefull Counterys (with a few exceptions) that any white man ever saw, or ever will See till he Comes and Sees this Sand and dust."
[north of Rye Patch Dam, Pershing Co., Nevada]

Pyeatt wrote they had to find other forage for the stock:

the large body of emigrants that had past before us had consumed the grass all most intirely so that our teams had to liv mostly on willow bushes this being all most the only shrub on this stream, for it dos not diserve to be called a river.

The Company clung to each spot of grass as they moved toward Humboldt Sink. <u>Crawford</u>:

"Tuesday 25 [September]...4 miles

We remained in Camp to day till about three oclock this eavening; We then mooved 4 miles down the river Where we found a Small patch of grass; by driving our Cattle three miles off of the road: This is Still a poore and dreary region."
[south of Rye Patch Dam, Pershing Co., Nevada]

"Wedens 26 [September]...14 1/4 miles

We gathered our Stock Early this morning, and Continued our Journey west through a poore region of Countery, with little or no grass at all, and after making fourteen miles & 1/4 we encamped for the night on the Same Streem, Where we found Some tolerable good grass. This Country on either Side of the river is verry rugged and mountaineous; with no appeerence of timber Except an occasional Shrub, or the Artimicia [sage]."
[NE of Lovelock, Pershing Co., Nevada]

Within the next day's travel, a decision had to be made about which route to take across the Sierra Nevada. The right hand road led across Truckee Pass. The left hand road was the Carson route.

If pioneers chose the Carson Road, they were led across the dreaded forty-mile desert, totally waterless and strewn with abandoned wagons and dead livestock.[518]

---

[518]Jeanne H. Watson, "The Carson Emigrant Road" *Overland Journal* vol 4, no 3 (Summer 1986) p 4.

Captain Evans' apparent choice of the Carson route could have been based on Fremont's writings. Fremont explored the area. Evans had already used Fremont's journals in choosing his routes. Jefferson, whose map Evans had used on the Hastings Cutoff, had traveled the Truckee route, and admonished:

> Those who expect to cross [California Mountains] in safety must reach the Truckey Pass by the 1st of October...If you arrive late...and encounter snow, do not attempt to cross the mountain (as Reed's party did)...[snow] does not usually begin falling till November.[519]

It was nearly October 1, and they were still east of the last desert. The company hurried on, leaving camp early and traveling late. <u>Crawford</u>:

"Thursday 27 [September]...13 1/2 miles
We left Camp this morning and continued down the Same Streem. we passed over some verry pretty Bottom land, with no vegitation, except Some Large bunches of grees [greasewood], and Salt wood   this river assumes a new appearance here, by Its Spreading over the land and Sinking   we made 13 1/2 miles to day and encamped in fine grass; this is near the sink of the River."
[SE of Lovelock, Pershing Co., Nevada]

Though the monotony of the terrain and the drudgery of travel were evident, the company stayed together and continued to rise early and travel as far as possible each day. Two weeks had passed since they reached and traveled on the Humboldt River. In that time they went 203 1/4 miles, an average of 14 1/2 miles daily.

Finding good grass, they stopped to cut it. The company had not stopped traveling since September 13, and two Sundays were ignored. This day's stop must have been welcomed, even though it was still a workday. Here they made their first contact with Paiute Indians. <u>Crawford</u>:

"Friday 28 [September] We lay by to day
and Cut grass for Crossing the Desert: A good many Indians visited us to day, of the Piute tribe   they appear to be verry honest and friendly."

Pyeatt wrote:

> hear [at Humboldt Sink] we fond plenty of grass   the grass is confined to the river botoms and in small bodyes....we got to the sink on the 29th...hear resting and cutting grass for the next desert a distance 43 miles   we started on.[520]

---

[519]Jefferson's "Accompaniment..."p 21. The reference to Reed is to the Donner/Reed party of 1846.
[520]Pyeatt letter, California, November 11, 1849.

The Company started, at night, to cross the desert. <u>Crawford</u>:

"Saturday 29 [September]...15 1/2 miles
We left Camp to day in the eavening and we Soon entered the Desert and about ten aclock Camped at the Pool or Sink of the Humboldt River after making fifteen and a half miles."
[SE edge of Humboldt Sink, Churchill Co., Nevada]

"Sunday 30 [September]...21 miles
we moved Early this morning and at the distance of eight miles we nooned at what is Called the Sulpher Wells. We watered our cattle here and in the eavening we continued through the Desert and after traviling till 11 oclock we camped after making 21 miles to day. no water or grass to day Since we left the wells."
[approximately 15 miles north of Fallon, Churchill Co., Nevada]

Pyeatt's letter included an entry for the desert traverse:

we started on and before we got through we had to leave our wagons and go to water and grass som two miles from the road   the last part of this desrt som 12 miles was deep Sand and very hard pulling   hear the Carnahan boys [James and John, nephews of Pyeatt] left thear wagon
    having now [none] but our little wagon we war compelled to leave evrything but provision to do us through and our cloathing one tent and a few of our tools   hear we left our trunkes boxes in a word we left evrythin of the kind but my trunk it being the lites [lightest]   we took it to keep our little things in and went on to carson river.[521]

Crawford, distressed at the dead animals they constantly passed, described the two-day effort to find water and grass for their own animals. Two of them didn't make it. <u>Crawford</u>:

"Monday October the 1st...13 miles
We moved early this morning through this Miserable Desert; passing carcases of, Oxen, Mules, and horses, evry few hundred yards. I Saw as many as nine ded Oxen one mule and one horse, to day; the two furthest apart, not more than 75 yards. I Suppose we passed today and part of yesterday, near 100 ded bruits on this Desert:[522] We made thirteen miles to day and the boys Camped in this awfull Desert once more; and drove their Cattle to a Curies Lake South of the Road a mile or two: [Soda Lake, Churchill Co., Nevada]...This Lake looks as tho it had been made by a volcanoes bursting a hole out of an Elevation 2 or three hundred feet above the River (Salmon trout or Carsons River) which is about 3 miles from this Lake: This water tasts Strongly of Alkalie, or as Something else. Their is some grass on the margin of this Lake: Our oxen remain here till Wedensday, and we took our oxen and waggon out and moved out to the river, which was 4 1/2 miles from where our waggon was: (On monday night I and two more of the boys went...to the river with packs on our Backs) We made eight miles and 1/2 to day by 9 oclock in the night. and Camped on Salmon trout a beautifull Streem about 15 or 20 Steps wide: we left two oxen in the Desert, Larry and Lyon."
[Approximately 3 miles west of Ragtown, Churchill Co., Nevada;
        Ragtown site is eight miles west of Fallon]

---

[521]Ibid.

[522]Crawford would later write in a letter November 18, 1849 from California "we never were out of sight of the carcasses of Oxen or horses."

Many of the Arkansans, and others, named their oxen. They spoke of them as dearly as they would long-time friends. Jefferson advised "[oxen] should be young...domesticated, and well broken ...learn the oxen to go by speaking and calling their names."[523]

James Pierce recounted many years later:

[we] met with no great trouble until we reached the Humboldt desert, forty miles in width, which we had to cross almost without water as our barrels had been abandoned on the Skull valley [Utah] desert.
    About this time our provisions ran short and several of the [unnamed] oxen were slaughtered for food.[524]

Neither the diary nor letters note that any of their oxen were slaughtered for food. Who could eat Larry and Lyon?

Crawford's diary continues as the men move up the Carson River with some unexpected companions, including Chief Truckee:

"Thursday 4 [October]...15 miles

we Started early this morning up the [Carson] river, their being but little grass where we Camped last night, and after Crossing a Sandy ridge 10 or 12 miles and Striking the river again and Keeping up Some distance we Camped for the night after making fifteen miles to day: At the Lake in the Desert their was [had been] a Small Band of Pyute Indians which has traviled with Capt. Jones (from [left blank]) who has been in Company with us for Several days ever Since we left the Alkutim lake; old Truckey[525] is the Capt of this Band of Indians."
[3 miles east of Silver Springs, near county line of Lyon and Churchill Cos., Nevada]

Sarah Winnemucca, the daughter of Chief Winnemucca, grand-daughter of Chief Truckee, wrote in her later book that she was on this trip to California as a young child with her mother and a number of other tribal members. According to Sarah, Chief Truckee met John C. Fremont, who gave him the name Truckee. Subsequently, Truckee and twelve of his men went to California with Fremont, returning after the Mexican War. Truckee was very impressed with his white brothers, and subsequently, until his death in 1859, declared no hand was to be raised against the whites.

Captain Evans left with the bulk of the 1849 wagon company. Crawford and Pyeatt chose to stay back and take advantage of the grass and to lighten their loads.

---

[523]Jefferson..."Accompaniment"...pp 14-15.
[524]Pierce...*Tribune*...1902.
[525]Sarah Winnemucca Hopkins, *Life Among the Piutes: Their Wrongs and Claims.* Mrs. Horace Mann, ed., (N. Y.: G. P. Putnam's Sons 1883) Sarah said Truckee's name "is an Indian word; it means all right or very well." p 9.

Crawford:

"Friday 5 [October] we lay by to day

their being good grass here, to rest our teems, Capt Evans and the balance of the Company except [Squire] Marrs, [John and Hiram] Sumner, [also McKinney] [John Rankin, son Andrew, and JR's brother H. Porter] Pyatt, and [James and John] Carnahan, mooved on to day, taking a right hand road a cross an other ridge: Our teems being verry weak, we layed out Some more of our loading and prepared to pack Some on our backs, which by the by is getting to be verry common and fashionable on this road."

Pyeatt's letter tells of their dilemna:

the [larger Evans] company hear left us again in the desert   we however over took them again [in a] few days   but the Crawford boys[526] oxen had given out and they could not go on with out help so we staid and rested a day and helped them along   the company leaving us again and we did not overtake them any more.[527]

Here, for the third time, Pyeatt and Crawford and their Arkansas "connexion" were separated from the main Evans/Cherokee Wagon Company. The other two separations resulted from disputes over Sunday travel: the first at the Green River in present Wyoming; the second on September 1 at present Big Springs, Nevada on the Hastings Cutoff. This time the companies saw each other no more.

Crawford and Pyeatt with the much smaller company, joining others, continued toward the Carson Route south of today's Lake Tahoe. Crawford:

"Saturday 6 [October]...12 [miles]

we Started this morning with Capt Dickys train and Capt Jones,[528] on a left hand road up the river, and after Crossing a Sandy ridge of 9 miles, and going up the river Some three miles we Camped in the verry finest Kind of grass. This morning Pyatt left his Roadomiter.[529] We now have to guess at the Distances   This morning We left H[iram] Sumner & James McKinney at Camp. they Spoke of leaving Their Waggon and packing through."
[near Fort Churchill Historic State Park, Lyon Co., Nevada]

---

[526]There are three or four Crawfords in this company: Andrew Alexander, Andrew Buchanan, the diarist James Sawyer, and William, who is questionable.
[527]Pyeatt letter, California, November 11, 1849.
[528]Captains Jones and Dickey are undocumented entities.
[529]Research to date has turned up no other mileage indicator in the Evans/Cherokee "Washington County Emmigrating Company."

Crawford and Pyeatt continued up the Carson River.

"Sunday 7 [October]...14 miles

We left Camp this morning early and proceeded up the river, this river runing from the Siera Nearly an East Course, we have passed but little grass to day, our road being tolerably good: the Mountains being rugh and high on Each Side of the river. We made about 14 miles to day and Camped on the South Bank of the Same river in some Scattering bunches of Grass. "

[West of Table Mountain, NE of Dayton, Lyon Co., Nevada]

Some of the men from the Evans company packed from here, choosing the 1848 Mormon route from the Carson River north to the Truckee on today's Alternate U.S. 50 and 95.[530] John Chandler, part of the rescue effort, met them on "Trucky River on Middle route" noting on October 18 that a "Pack train from Salt Lake Capt. Evans."[531] had received necessities. Rescue parties from California were already on the way on all incoming routes, but found very few to aid on the Truckee route.

Captain Kilburn and myself [were] under the impression that all the emigrants on this route with wagons had already reached the western side of the mountains [September 27].[532]

Crawford and Pyeatt continued on the Carson River. Crawford:

"Monday 8 [October]...16 miles

We started early this morning and after going 4 miles, Crossed over to the north Side of the River where we Struck the road, which Capt Evans took; here our road left the River and made a Cut off a cross a point of a mountain some ten miles over: Here the Spurs of the Siera, Raise their Rugged heads in gloreing [glorying?] view before us, both on our right and left, and in front. We made 16 miles to day and--Camped on the North Bank of the river."

[Two miles east of Carson City, Carson City Co., Nevada]

Crawford, in spite of the travails of the journey, managed to maintain a very optimistic attitude, appreciating the valley. Some emigrants behind them were being harried by Indians. On October 10, they crossed into California.

---

[530]Many California miners would later return to the Virginia City area located on this road.

[531]Rucker Report "Names of persons...relief was issued." cited in Read and Gaines...Bruff...H1 Critical Notes p 569.

[532] "General Smith's Correspondence, California "Relief Reports from Lassen's Cut-off, 1849" (John H. Peoples and Major D.H. Rucker) 31 Cong. 1 sess. 1850 Sen Ex Doc 52, Serial 561 vol 13. John J. Chandler letter to Major Rucker p 110. Chandler and Kilburn subsequently went over the mountains to the Carson Route to aid emigrants.

Crawford:

"Tuesday 9 [October]...15 miles

we moved early this morning and Crossed over a Sandy ridge and Continued
up the valey of the River; here we found the Best quality of grass, This
is a beautifull valley of grass. Their is a kind of grass in this valley
which generally grows near waist high, and the Blades on the Same is
about 2 1/2 feet high, thickly Set on the main Stem. The blads resemble
the blades of our nimble Will. It has a head a little like a wheat head,
and a grain Simular to an oat grain. Their is thousands of acres of it
here as thickly Set as Timothy posibly Can grow. This is a Beautifull
valey with fine water (on todays travil) and Plenty of Pine Timber on
the Sides of the Mountains. This part of the vally lyes from S.W to N.E,
we made fifteen miles and Camped on the North Side of the River   The
River, Near the foot of the mountains Which is cuverd with Pine Timber:
on yesterday [John M.] Wham & [J.W.] Hastings went Back 7 miles for a
Knife, left on the River and met Some Emigrants who we left behind a few
days ago; the Emigrants turned out their oxen to noon, and In a few
moments 6 of their oxen were Shot by the Diggers, with Arrows. They were
not Killed, but wounded."
[near Genoa, Carson Valley, Douglas Co., Nevada]

"Wedens 10 [October]...11 miles

we moved early this morning and Kept up the River Near the mt, a S.W.
Course passing some fine Springs, for machinery, and Splended grass and
land in the vally, and timber on the mountains Plenty. we made 11 miles
to day and Camped North of the River at the foot of the mountains."
[Approximately 3 miles NE of Woodfords, Alpine Co., California]

Pyeatt: "had very good grass to the mountain a distance of 102
miles   we got to the mountain on the 10 of oct."[533] On October 10
it snowed on the high Sierra. the first snow of the season. There
would be grim evidence of it for the Crawford and Pyeatt party to
see in a few days. Crawford:

"Thursday 11 [October]...10 miles

we Started Soon this morning and after slopeing round the Spur of a Mt
we entered the mouth of a Canion, out of which the Salmon Trout runs,
from Nearly a West Course, with grate Rappidness   Here is fine timber,
of the Pine Kind, it is from 1 to 6 feet over, and tall at that the
Mountains on Each Side of the Canion are verry high with Snow on their
Summits. This is the ruffest place that I ever Saw a waggon pass. We
have got through the rugh part of the Canion and Camped after making ten
miles."
[Hope Valley, approximately 7 miles west of Woodfords,
Alpine Co., California]

Crawford passed through Carson Canyon. "Here the west fork of
the Carson River flows over rocks between high walls."[534] It took
most of the day to accomplish the few miles.

533Pyeatt letter, California, November 11, 1849.
534Watson..."Carson"...p 6.

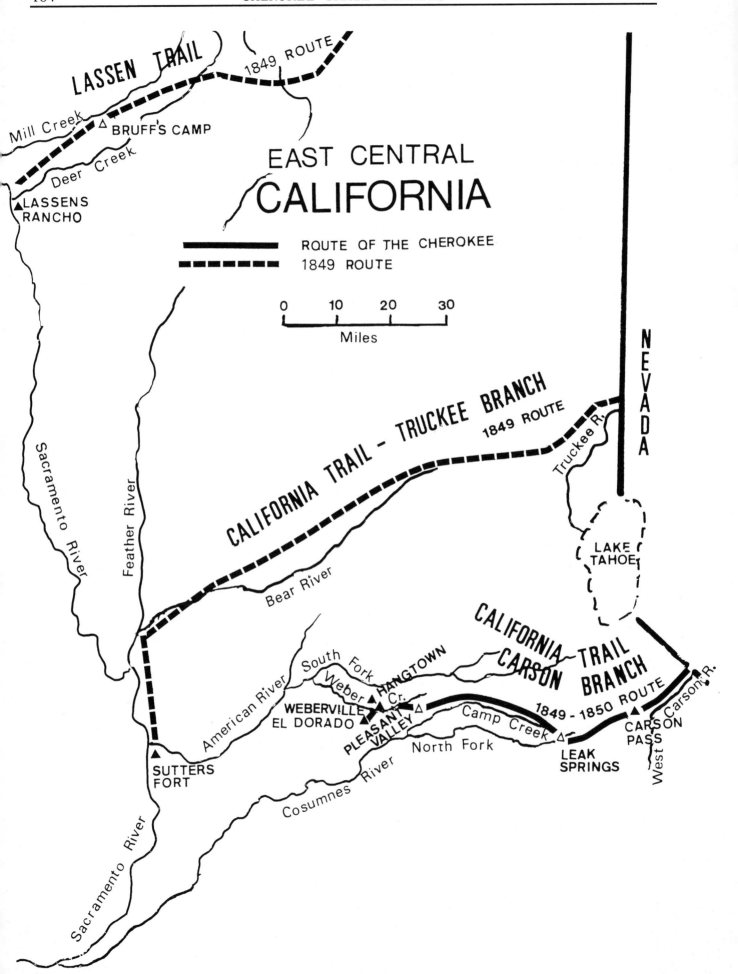

EAST CENTRAL
CALIFORNIA

ROUTE OF THE CHEROKEE
1849 ROUTE

0   10   20   30
Miles

Crawford:

"Friday 12 [October]...7 miles.

We Saw the most frost this morning that I ever saw this Early, The frost remained on the ground till nine aclock   We Started at 8 aclock this morning, and Kept a South Course, Still up the Salmon Trout River, the road being verry good to day, the valley being generally Covered with pine of Different Kinds: Some of which are 6 or Seven feet through Their is also what Some Call Juniper timber here. I think I Saw one 7 feet through to day, We have made 7 miles today and camped in full view of the Back Bone of the Siera Mts   at the foot of this Mt-Their is a Small Lake [Red Lake]...Which is Mirery round the edges."

[One mile east of Carson Pass, Alpine Co., California]

They saw the first snow and the results of it as they struggled over the rugged mountains in terrible weather. Crawford:

"Saturday 13 [October]...6 1/2 miles

We Started this morning and Crossed the first Ridge of the Siera [Carson Pass] We Cross this on a West Course. This is the most Rugged Road that I ever Saw. Their fell a Snow Some three days ago   It, in Places is 3 inches deep on our Road   Thier was a heavy freeze, and frost, last night. The Snow is White over the Mountains, Their is verry fine Timber on this Mountain: We Camped on the 2nd and Main Devide of the Siera. We are not yet more than half Way to the top of the Ridge; Their is a grate destruction of property on this road; one mile ahead of us, Their was 4 yoke of oxen and two or three horses frozen in the last Snow 2 or three days Since; We made Six and ahalf miles to day."

[south of Caples Lake, Alpine Co., California]

"Sunday 14 [October]...9 miles

We moved early this morning and continued up the mt till We Came to the Top: I never felt the wind blow So hard in any place, as it did While Crossing this Mt, It was all we could do to Keep from being Blown off by the wind. Some of our boys had to crawl, to keep from Being Swept away. We got over and Camped in a rugged Bottom after making nine miles. Their was Snow plenty, and the ground was Frozen."

[along Squaw Ridge behind and above present Plasse resort, SW of Silver Lake, near Amador/El Dorado Cos. line, California]

Pyeatt described the efforts to save one of their few wagons:

we cossed the Sumit on the 4th day after we started up it   this is the worst mountain that I ever saw   many places it looked like it was imposable for wagons to git along   whill we ware crossing the sumit the wind blew all most like a tornado   it had lik to have taken one of our wagons of[f] but by locking both wheels and the help of the oxen we saved it from going over and down a bluff   the wind blew severl of the men down sow that they had to hold to rock to save themselves   all so som of the week oxen ware blown down but non hurt   thear had bin some snow before we crosed the mountain   it fell to the depth of 6 or 8 inches...It had melted out of our way before we got thear and we had very prity weather all...[except]...the wind above s[p]oken of and that did not last long...the weather on the mountain was clear and plasant during the day and the nights was cold with heavy frosts, ice freezing over one and ahalf inches thick.[535]

---

[535]Pyeatt letter, California, November 11, 1849.

James Pierce remembered this fearful part of their journey:

Carson canyon, where we were caught in a snowstorm which left about two feet of snow on the ground...and for a time we feared the same fate which overtook the Donner party, whose trail we followed across the desert; but fortunately the storm abated and we crossed.[536]

Sarah Winnemucca wrote:

At last we [Piute under Chief Truckee] were camped upon the [Carson] summit, and it snowed very hard all night, and in the morning my grandfather [Truckey] told his people to hurry and get their horses, and travel on, for fear we might get snowed into the mountains. That night we overtook some emigrants who were camped there to rest their oxen.[537]

The Sierra mountain trek continued. <u>Crawford</u>:

"Monday the 15 [October]...6 miles
We moved at 8 o clock this morning, and continued our Course through a rugged mountaineous Countery., the Hill Sides tolerable Rich, and the finest Timber immaginable, of the Pine Species   grass and Water occasionally in the Vallys, We made Six miles to day, and Camped on a high ridge, with grass and Water on the South Side of the Road."
[East of Leek Spring Hill, El Dorado Co., California]

<u>Crawford</u> received some welcome help from government rescuers:

"Tuesday 16th [October] we lay by to day.
and gave our oxen a little rest, Here we met a Government train of Oxen going out to help the Emigrants a cross the Siera. This I think to be a laudeble Charity from Uncle Sam; The Col let us have two yok to assist us in gitting out."

Pyeatt described how the rescuers helped him too:

After we had got over the sumit of the mountain one days travel we met a government train of oxen that was agoing to help those that needed help and the Crawford boys got 2 youk [of oxen] from them   this helped us as much as them for we had to let them have from 2 to 4 oxen all the time to git them along and then they could hardly git allong.[538]

"The Col" who came along at the right time was Col. Ferris Foreman, sent out as leader of one of the relief companies under Maj. Daniel Rucker. In his report, Ferris wrote:

most of the emigrants needing work and beef cattle were in and about the carrivan and summit [Carson Pass route]. I have divided my oxen... sending the strongest over the summit.[539]

With two new yoke of oxen for their wagon, Crawford, with Pyeatt's small company went on. He was still amazed at the trees.

---

[536]Pierce...*Tribune*...1902.
[537]Hopkins...*Piutes*...p 25.
[538]Pyeatt letter, California, November 11, 1849.
[539]*Smith's Correspondence*...Foreman's Report was written November 7, 1849.

And the worst was over. <u>Crawford</u>:

"Wedensday 17 [October]...15 miles

We mooved Early this morning and Continued our Journey a West Course, along a Deviding Ridge, which was covered with the Prettiest Timber that I ever Saw, I Saw a fallen Pine of Some Kind today, which was 75 steps long. I think we have Seen Several today, that are 200 feet high   The ground on which the Pine grows is verry loose and dry. Their is a grate many that are 6 feet in Diameter Some perhaps 8 feet; Sine of Deer to day, Plenty, for the first time in Some time, We mad 15 miles to day and Camped in a hollow, on a branch With out grass, We cut the Aspin Popplar for the Cattle to Brouse."

[Along Camp Creek, El Dorado Co., California]

Truckey's Paiutes were noted again. Crawford was able to relax under a tree while on guard duty. <u>Crawford</u>:

"Thursday 18 [October]...12 miles

We Started at eight oclock this morning and Kept a West Course along the Same Ridg, the ground not So Rockey as usual, the Soil appearantly good, With as handsom Timber as a man Could desire; Capt Truckey and his Band have been With us off and own ever Since we lef the Desert. After making 12 miles, We Camped to night on the Same ridge without water or grass and have cut down a quantity of oak timber for our cattle to brouse on, which is the first oak we have Seen for the last 1500 miles, we made 12 miles today and I am now Setting under a Pine near 8 feet over, writing this Journal by fire light, and also guarding our oxen   my [guard duty] Tour beaing near out, it is twelve aclock."

[SE of Pollack Pines, El Dorado Co., California]

Crawford was still impressed by the size and amount of the timber. Next day they saw their first gold diggings. <u>Crawford</u>:

"Friday 19 [October]...10 miles

We started Soon this morning and Continued our Course West - along the Same ridge, Continually passing as Pretty timber, as I ever Saw, I think their is many Sticks [trees] ove 200 feet high on this Road. We made 10 miles to day and Camped on the Same ridge, with Water in the hollow on either Side of the Road."

[8 miles east of Placerville, El Dorado Co., California]

The Arkansans wasted no time in prospecting. <u>Crawford</u>:

"Saturday 20 [October]...8 miles

We moved early this morning and after going Some few miles, We Sloped down into the vally, amongst the first gold diggings that We have Seen, We Went on some distance and Came to the Suberbs of a little vilage caled Weaberville,[540] We Camped in the valey after making 8 miles, it being quite early   Some of the boys, Prospected and found a Small portion of gold out of a Small Branch."

[Placerville, El Dorado Co., California]

They were not satisfied to stop--not yet. Crawford continued

---

[540]Gold was discovered on Weber Creek in 1848 by Charles M. Weber, also the founder of the city of Stockton. *Overland Journal*, Vol 6, No 4 1988 p 33. Crawford has written the name phonetically, giving the proper pronounciation.

his diary for two more days. <u>Crawford</u>:

"Sunday 21 [October]...15 miles

...we Started this morning, and turned South, and traviled some fifteen miles, through a broken Country and Camped for the night on the left of the road. with but little grass or water for our oxen. The timber to day is low, beaing diferent kinds of oak, with as fine mast[541] as I ever Saw."

[south of El Dorado, El Dorado Co., California]

"Monday 22 [October]...14 miles

We left Camp this morning and Kept a South Course, through a verry Similar Countery to that passed yesterday. and after making Some fourteen miles we Camped on a Streem Called Cozumas River."

[west of the junction of North and South Forks of the Cosumnes River, on the El Dorado/Amador County Line, California]

Thus ends the diary of James Sawyer Crawford on his 1849 journey from Arkansas to California.[542]

Preparation for winter was essential. The Pyeatt party, including Crawford and about fifteen other men stayed together on the Cosumnes River, building two winter cabins 16 ft. square, with a dogtrot between.[543] Pyeatt described their activity:

In two weekes we have dug gold bilt a cabin hunted deer mooved 4 miles   in all made by diggin and selling venison to the Indians 35 ounces of gold   we have killed 21 deer sold them from 5 to 23 dollars apiec   if this bisness would keep up this will be a better bisness druring the winter then mining.

The remaining forty-niner Cherokee and Arkansans arrived in California on all three routes: Carson, Truckee, and Lassen.

---

[541]mast=nuts accumulated on the ground.

[542]Crawford kept another diary of his homeward journey in 1851. He started home via ship to Panama, crossed the isthmus on foot, and took another ship to New Orleans. Sadly, he never saw his home in Cane Hill, Washington County, Arkansas again, his health failing him within 30 miles of Fayetteville.

[543]James Pierce [Pearce] was one of the 17. Others have been identified as James and John Carnahan; Andrew A., Andrew Buchanan, William, and James Sawyer Crawford (diarist); James Crawford Devin and Matthew A. Devin; Andrew E. and John Thompson Edmiston; Robert Eproson [Epperson]; J. W. Hastings; T. J. Kimbrell [Kimbrel]; Squire Marrs; H. Porter, John Rankin and son Andrew E. Pyeatt [Pyatt]; and John M. Wham.

Chapter 9. APPLEGATE and LASSEN TRAILS "CHEROKEE CUT-OFF"

> **One might not go far wrong in surmising that Cherokee were among the first converts to take the north trail at the bend of the Humboldt--a surmise which is arresting in view of its bearing there the name of "Cherokee Cut Off"**
>
> --Read and Gaines

Due to the importance of the name Cherokee Cutoff, noted by J. Goldsborough Bruff, a brief account follows for all known Cherokee parties that took the Applegate and Lassen Trails in 1849. Bruff noted meeting various groups of Cherokee in late September.[544] Which of these Cherokee groups is responsible for the *Cherokee Cutoff* name at the junction of the California and Applegate Trails is uncertain.

Evidence indicates the Cherokee and white packers led by Dick Owens traveled at least partially on the Applegate route. Other probable early Cherokee travelers were Dr. Jeter Thompson Company members, who arrived via the Independence and Hastings routes. The number from the Evans/Cherokee Wagon Company included the twelve wagon breakaway group. Member Calvin Holmes noted mileages.[545]

On the Humboldt River east of the Applegate cutoff on August 27, Elisha Perkins referred to a Cherokee party, perhaps one of those mentioned above:

> A very fair hoax was played off this afternoon opposite our camp by the Capt of the Cherokee train which was some two or three miles back. He had been forward to look for grass & was returning when he met at our camp several trains which had stopped for water & was Being dressed in half Indian costumes, with buckskin pants, moccasins &c, & rather dark complexion, he was taken for a French mountaineer...& was immediately beset by a crowd of Emigrants anxious to learn the latest news from the "diggings." In answer to their inquiries he told them that...Gold was plenty....After a number more such yarns he left them as he was in a great hurry....Everything of course become more & more exaggerated the more it was repeated. We happen to know the Capt as we had passed his train.[546]

---

[544]Read and Gaines...*Bruff*...(P5[A], Sept. 15, 1849); Critical Notes H1 pp 569-70. References are quoted from both journals--H1 and P5.

[545]Holmes Diary "From Humboldt"

[546]Jerome B. Howard of the 1849 Ithaca (N.Y.) Pack Mule Company. Thomas D. Clark, ed. *Gold Rush Diary: Being the Journal of Elisha Douglas Perkins on the Overland Trail in the Spring and Summer of 1849* (Lexington: Univ. of Kentucky Press 1967) pp 109-10.

APPLEGATE TRAIL

Hubert Howe Bancroft wrote about the route:

The Applegate correctly termed the South Road, [for Oregon] was
pioneered in 1846 by Levi Scott, Jesse Applegate and thirteen
others...from the Willamette Valley...across northern California to the
Humboldt River and on to Fort Hall.[547]

John McLoughlin, former Chief Factor at Fort Vancouver, noted the
desirability of this route to Oregon immigration:

the Best Route from Fort Hall to this place [Willamette Valley] is by
the Road Explored Summer 1846 by Mess Applegate and party as the
Immigrants who came by it this Season were here long before those who
came by the Old Route [Oregon Trail] and as it passes out of the Range
of the Nez perces Cayouses and Walla Walla tribes...Every Exertion ought
to be made to get the Immigrants to pass by this Route.[548]

In reference to the Applegate/Lassen route Bruff wrote:

The Oregon & California roads fork at a large bend of the [Humboldt]
river, where the R. turns directly S.-- The Oregon road here leaves it,
and runs on a W. course towards a gap in the mountains.[549]

The route was very attractive to California emigrants. The
crossing of the Sierra Nevada mountains via Fandango Pass was at a
much lower elevation than crossing via either the Carson Pass or
the Truckee routes. Moreover it was rumored to be a shorter route
to the goldfields.

LASSEN TRAIL

In 1846, the same year that Applegate and Scott explored
their route, Peter Lassen guided U.S. Navy Lieutenant Gillespie's
pack group north over the mountain road to Klamath Lake to meet
John C. Fremont. This route later became the Lassen Cutoff.

Peter Lassen arrived in California from Oregon in 1840.[550] By
1845 Lassen established his ranch on the Bosquejo Rancho Mexican

---

[547]Hubert Howe Bancroft (the works of), *History of Oregon* (San Francisco: San
Francisco History Co. 1886-1888) vol 1, pp 544-62.
[548]Letter to Secretary of War William L. Marcy, October 16, 1847. McLoughlin
also noted the need for a fort at "Rogues River Valley...to keep...the
Communication open Between this [Oregon City] and Fort Hall and this and San
Francisco." William R. Sampson, ed. *McLoughlin's Business Correspondence 1847-
1848* (Seattle: Univ. of Washington Press 1973) pp 66-67. McLoughlin's use of
Applegate rather than any other name for the route may be related to Jesse
Applegate's having surveyed McLoughlin's property in Oregon City.
[549]Read and Gaines...*Bruff*...pp 1209-10 Appendix 8.
[550]In May 1839 Lassen with others, including missionaries, left the states for
the Columbia River. James W. Bashford, *The Oregon Missions* (N.Y. & Cincinnati:
The Abingdon Press 1918) p 291.

land grant, the 1849 "Lassen's Ranch," in present Tehama County.[551]

In 1847 Lassen returned to Missouri to bring two things to California: a hoped-for train of emigrants and a Masonic Lodge charter.[552] The Grand Lodge of Missouri issued the Masonic charter for *Western Star* Lodge, No. 98 on May 10, 1848 to Peter Lassen, to be located at Lassen's new settlement, Benton City, Upper California.[553] Lassen traveled west from Missouri in Joseph B. Chiles' company with Samuel J. Hensley.[554] Ignorant of the California gold finds, Lassen started west to Benton City with his Masonic charter and twelve wagons from Fort Hall via the Humboldt, Applegate, and Lassen's 1846 trail.

Meanwhile, the Applegate Road south from the Willamette Valley led Oregonians to California for gold. Oregon Chief Justice Peter Burnett, with 140 men in fifty ox-drawn wagons, left Oregon City in September 1848. At Goose Lake they turned south toward Sacramento onto a wagon trail very recently pioneered by Peter Lassen's Company. A newspaper account:

"LASSEN'S RANCH, Oct. 27, 1848."
"The first wagon train ever to cross from Oregon Territory to California has...arrived safely in the Sacramento Valley...
Shortly before reaching their destination the Burnett party caught up with a group of eastern emigrants piloted by Captain Lassen, and gave them assistance in completing their long trek...
they met the wagon trail of the Lassen party, which had passed about 25 days ahead of them. They followed this trail, and finally overtook the emigrants about 40 miles from the Sacramento Valley and 35 miles past the summit of the mountains...
"Where we overtook the Lassen party," Judge Burnett declared, "the only obstruction to the passage down the mountain was fallen timber and

---

[551]In 1881, Leland Stanford became the owner of 9,000 acres of the "Vina" ranch. By 1885 he had acquired fifty-one more parcels of it. Vina Ranch eventually covered 55,000 acres. Stanford University sold it in 1943. Personal correspondence March 1999 with Patricia White, Archives Specialist, Stanford.
[552]Edwin A. Sherman 33°, comp. and ed. *Fifty Years of Masonry in California* (San Francisco: George Spaulding and Co. Publishers 1898) vol 2.
[553]Notice of the first Masonic meeting was published in the *Alta Californian*, San Francisco 23 August 1849. Sherman...*Masonry*...p 47. Lassen didn't know that a Masonic Charter had been granted October 17, 1846 from the Grand Lodge of Missouri, to be called "Multnomah Lodge, No. 84 to be located at Oregon City, Oregon Territory." That charter came across the plains in a trunk and reached its destination September 11, 1848. Bro. Joseph Hull, The Master, and several other brethren of that Oregon lodge were in Burnett's Oregon Party that overtook Lassen's group near the end of his new Trail. Ibid. p 53.
[554]Barry...*West*...p 748. The total company was forty-seven wagons and eighty men in addition to at least seventy-five women and children.

loose rock on the surface. Ten or 15 men cut out a road in one day as far as timber was concerned, for 15 miles, and did it as fast as the wagons could follow. Only two of our wagons broke down from the rocks."

The pass through the mountains is a good natural one, according to the Oregon leader, with ascent and descent both gradual. Little labor would make it an excellent road.[555]

Burnett and the Oregonians brought the first news of the gold finds in California to the Lassen-led emigrants. The newspaper reporter additionally surmised:

Captain Lassen had gone out to meet the incoming immigration from the United States. He induced several wagon families to come to California by his new route.[556]

Research shows that Peter Lassen did not go "out to meet the incoming immigration" as has so often been reported, notably by Hubert Howe Bancroft. Lassen was on his way back from the States with the first Masonic Charter for California. Burnett reported Lassen's wagon route was nearly completed, needing only one day or fifteen miles of road clearing.

Many emigrants who were members of fraternal organizations continued their membership in California. Bruff wrote to the settlements in winter (1849) noting by symbol which correspondents were Masons. A significant number of the Evans/Cherokee Company members were Masons. The same year the California Charter was granted, and Oregon received the Multnomah Charter, Masonry was brought to Tahlequah, Cherokee Nation. The Grand Lodge of Arkansas granted the Cherokee Lodge No. 20 Charter November 8, 1848.[557] The Cherokee had become Masons in the eastern United States (Georgia, Alabama and Tennessee) before their Removal to present Oklahoma. In Fayetteville, Washington Lodge No. 1 was founded in 1835, the oldest in Arkansas state. In Benton County, the first lodge was chartered in 1847.[558]

---

[555]Dudley T. Ross, "The Centennial Gazette '100 Years Ago Today'" p 87, Native Daughters of California #3 *Scrapbook*. Modoc County Museum, Alturas, California.

[556]Ibid.

[557]Officers were installed July 12, 1849. C.W. West, *Tahlequah and the Cherokee Nation 1841-1941* (Muskogee, Okla.: Muscogee Publ. Co. 1978) p 25.

[558]Oscar E. Williams, "Washington Lodge No. 1, F & A Masons" 24 page booklet, 1951. Sherman...*Masonry*...p 42 notes the Grand Lodge of Kentucky granted a dispensation for Arkansas Lodge at Arkansas Post in 1818, before statehood.

THE CUTOFF

Dick Owens, guiding the 1849 Cherokee and white pack company met the party of Amos Josselyn on August 8 and 9 on the Humboldt.[559] Owens may well have given the company enough information to convince them to take the Applegate Trail. On August 13 Josselyn's party turned onto it, making no mention of letters, notices, or other inducements to take the route, which were noted by later emigrants.

Owens was familiar with the Sierras. He had been over them with Fremont in 1843 and 1845-46. It is probable that Owens took his Cherokee and white pack company over a route similar to Fremont's that followed the present Applegate Trail--to Rabbithole Springs, then to Mud and Pyramid lakes, and west into California's golden valleys--a route mentioned by Israel Lord.

Sept. 9, 1849...Report here says that there are four routes, the old one, across the desert; another, striking Truckey River...; a third north of Pyramid Lake...crossing over to Feather River; and a fourth, still farther north, called the Government Road. The last two leave the road...at the next great bend of the river. The first of these two is called the Cherokee route....A Cherokee who resides in California has been through to this point, and started back with the great Cherokee train.[560]

Those who did not meet Dick Owens got information from another source--military troops. Alonzo Delano, traveling behind Owens' Cherokee and white packers, met a train from Oregon on August 23 near High Rock Canyon on the Applegate

[who were] going to meet the troops on the Humboldt with supplies [troops of the Oregon Mounted Rifles had wintered at Fort Hall]. we learned that there was a good and feasible wagon road, leading from Goose Lake...to California, which was opened last season; that the passage of the great mountain [Sierra Nevada] was not difficult....The best news of all was, that we should reach the gold diggings on Feather River in traveling a little over a hundred miles.[561]

559J. William Barrett, ed. *The Overland Journey of Amos Platt Josselyn: Zanesville, Ohio to the Sacramento Valley April 2, 1849 to September 11, 1849* (Baltimore: Gateway Press Inc. 1978) p 42.

560Necia Dixon Liles, ed. *"At the Extremity of Civilization"* (Jefferson, N.C.: McFarland & Co. Inc. 1995) p 109.

561Alonzo Delano, *Life on The Plains and Among the Diggings...*(Auburn and Buffalo: Miller, Orton & Mulligan 1854; Time-Life Reprint 1980) p 198. Lt. George Hawkins left Oregon City in June with supplies for Fort Hall.

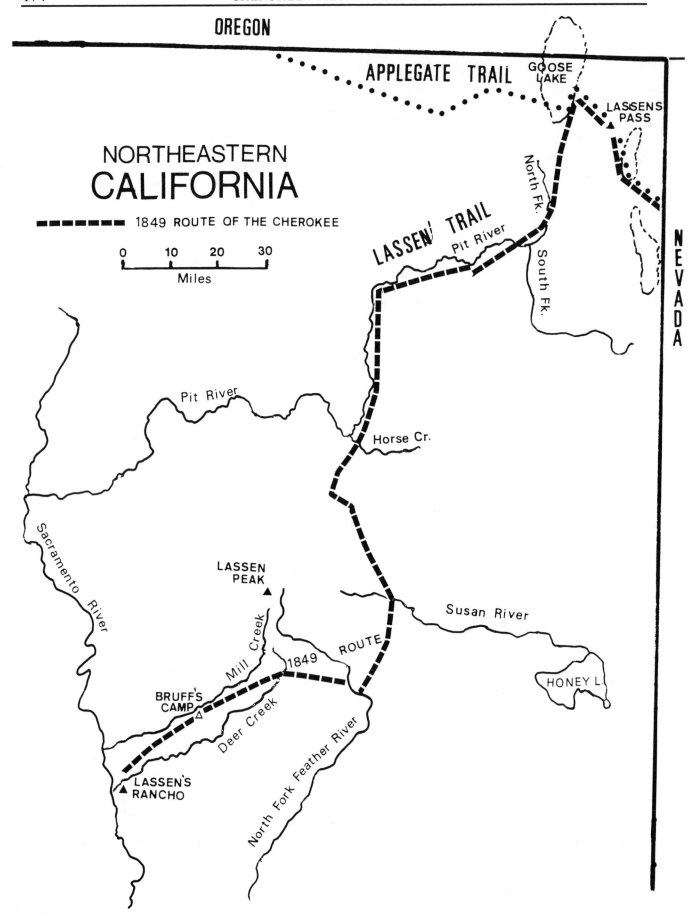

OREGON

APPLEGATE TRAIL

GOOSE LAKE

LASSENS PASS

NORTHEASTERN
CALIFORNIA

▪▪▪▪▪▪▪ 1849 ROUTE OF THE CHEROKEE

0   10   20   30
Miles

LASSEN TRAIL

North Fk.

Pit River

South Fk.

NEVADA

Pit River

Horse Cr.

Sacramento River

LASSEN PEAK

Susan River

Mill Creek

ROUTE

1849

HONEY L.

BRUFF'S CAMP

Deer Creek

North Fork Feather River

LASSEN'S RANCHO

The troops with the government supply train obviously had not been over the Lassen Trail they gave information about. This erroneous mileage information was passed on to many emigrant parties along the cutoff as well as on the main Humboldt River route and was repeated both verbally and in written notes placed on the trail at the cutoff, by both the military and the emigrants themselves.

Emigrant Samuel Murray Stover, who turned off a week after Delano, called the Applegate/Lassen the "new route." He saw an overabundance of emigrants on it, and encountered the Oregon relief train: "A train from Oregon City came in this evening with supplies for the troops at Fort Hall and those on the way to California."[562] Stover, in the first small wave of emigrants found a good road and had no trouble from Indians.

On August 26 Captain Warner and party were sent out from Sacramento to survey the best route to the Humboldt River. Working north along the Lassen route, they met the Applegate Trail and turned east on it. On September 12, Stover "found some soldiers with flour, etc. for the troops who were out exploring."[563] The soldiers were support troops for Captain Warner's survey party.

James Tolles, who had been among "300 teams...making hay [on the Humboldt] to go over the cutoff" saw notices written by the surveying crew on September 14 at the junction of the Applegate and Lassen trails. They found a "guide written by government surveying crew nearby, stating 287 [miles] to gold diggin's. Road gets longer as we go."[564] For the first time, the emigrants had accurate, newly-measured mileage for the Lassen Trail from Goose Lake south.

---

[562]*Diary of Samuel Murray Stover Enroute to California 1849* (Elizabethton, N.M.: H.M. Folsom, Carter County 1939) p 34 and Samuel Murray Stover "Westward Bound 1849" MS 81, University of Oklahoma, Diaries 1849-50.

[563]Stover diary p 37. On August 26, Bvt. Maj. Persifor Smith, commander of Military Department 11, Northern California and Oregon, had sent Captain Warner, surveyor, to find the best route from Humboldt River to Sacramento. By October 9 Major Rucker had heard that Warner had been killed by the Indians.

[564]Doris Beard (Granddaughter), ed. Reprinted in a series "Trails and Trials of '49'" in the *Marysville Appeal-Democrat. Appeal* vol 137, no 28; *Democrat* vol 45, no 28, 5 February 1930. Not all issues in the series were found.

THE CHEROKEE CUTOFF

As early as September 14, the turnoff from the Humboldt River was called the "Cherokee Cutoff." Kimball Webster:

> The left hand road is the old trail and leads down the [Humboldt] river to the "Sink," as it is called....The distance from this place to the Sacramento valley, according to the best information in our possession, is about 300 miles.
> The other, or right hand road, is called the Cherokee Cutoff, and the distance is said to be but 180 miles from this place to the Feather River gold mines....
> The question arose, which of the two roads shall we pursue--follow the old road--...or shall we risk the new one....
> The question was submitted to a vote of the company, and it was in favor of trying the "Cutoff," as it is called, with scarcely a dissenting vote.[565]

Clayton and Rebecca Reeve from Tennessee sent letters home, in which Rebecca called the cutoff route "The Cherokee Cutoff."[566]

Another trail description that appeared in the *Daily Missouri Republican* was written by a party who knew they didn't want to take the Lassen, and yet ended up traveling over it. Company members Ames and Donovan noted the cutoff had another name attached to it--"Cherokee Pass."

> "Travel Across the Plains"...Our intention was...to proceed on the old road of the Truckey route, but were unfortunately induced to take the new road about 70 miles above the Sink, by the report that this, The Cherokee Pass, would take us into Sacramento Valley via Feather River Valley much sooner, the ascent up the mountains being much easier.... After traveling on this route we shortly discovered that we were traversing the course which must bring us to the Lawson [Lassen] Pass of the Sierra Nevada, which we could not have been persuaded to do with our eyes open, for we knew before we left Mary's River that we should have to go too far north of our course, so much so as to be at least one month longer on our journey.[567]

BRUFF'S CHEROKEE GUIDE

Bruff's diary contains the only known written copy of a "Cherokee Guide."[568] This is in the form of a way bill giving directions, names and places, mileages, notes on water and grass, etc. to the Northern California goldfields.

---

[565]Kimball Webster, *The Gold Seekers of '49.* (Manchester, N.H.: Standard Book Co. 1917) pp 82-83.

[566]Merrill J. Mattes, *Platte River Road Narratives* (Urbana, Ill.: Univ. of Illinois Press 1988) MS 601, p 202.

[567]*Daily Missouri Republican* 22 February 1850.

[568]Read and Gaines...*Bruff*...P4, facing p 277. "[BRUFF'S VERSION OF APPLEGATE'S WAY BILL, CALLED BY HIM ELSEWHERE (IN ABBREVIATED FORM) "CHEROKEE GUIDE"]." p 1209, Appendix 8.

In the authors' search for a written *Cherrokee Guide*, many
special collections libraries were contacted. George Miles,
Curator of Western Americana at The Beinecke Rare Book and
Manuscript Library, Yale University answered our query. "As far as
I am aware no copy of the Cherrokee Guidebook has yet been
found....I assume it remains an uncovered piece of Americana."[569]
Read & Gaines conducted their own research on the "Guide":

> By comparison with the "Way Bill from Fort Hall to Williamette Valley,"
> recently [ca 1944] discovered by Miss Nellie B. Pipes, Librarian of the
> Oregon Historical Society...it will be seen that the Way Bill must have
> been the original of both the "Cherrokee" and the [New York] "Herrald"
> guides....the distances from Goose Lake to the "Sacramento" are links in
> the Oregon, not the California trail.[570]

Whatever the origin, Bruff, noted for his detail and
accuracy, called it the "Cherrokee Guide." From a position fifty-
eight miles above the Humboldt Sink, Bruff recorded the following,
later adding the October 19 date.[571]

---

[569]Miles, Personal Correspondence November 11, 1985. "I enclosed for your
information an entry from the third edition of Henry Wagner's *The Plains and
the Rockies* [Located in "1851" no 196, p 262] which suggests that the guide
may have been written by Jesse Applegate and first published in the *Oregon
Spectator*, April 6, 1848....the most recent edition of *The Plains and the
Rockies* makes no mention [it.]" The *Oregon Spectator* was first issued at
Oregon City 5 February 1846 as a bi-monthly. The first editor was Col. W. G.
T'Vault, an Oregon pioneer of 1845. He was born in Kentucky and was a lawyer
by profession. It is said that he had acquired some editorial experience in
Arkansas. George H. Hemes "History of the Press of Oregon 1839-1850"
Quarterly, Oregon Historical Society vol 3, no 4 (December 1902).
[570]Read and Gaines...*Bruff*...p 1212 Appendix 8.
[571]Bruff Proctor Journal no 5, called P5 by Read and Gaines.

CHERROKEE GUIDE

"September 15, 1849 - October 19, 1849 The Lower Humboldt
to Deer Creek Meadows:
Here to forks -- Cherrokee Guide
Forks to gap or pass in mountains...........12
(Springs 1/2 m. to left of road)
Thence to Rabbit Hole Springs...............13
"   "   Black Rock, &c..............20
(7 m. beyond B.R. Boilg Spg. plenty --)
[Thence to] Mud Lake.....................20
About 5 m. S. of R. Hole Springs are hot sprgs. &
grass plains. If the road could go that way it would
be longer, but probably better.
[Thence to] Last Hot Spring...................3
"   "   Salt Valley................. 2
"   "   1st Camp in Hight [High] Rock Canon.10
Up H.R. Canon...................................20
Thence to Little Mountain Pass..................18
4 m. from the last water of high rock creek to a good
camp at a running brook; 2 m. more, on left of road,
are springs: Grass & water both sides of pass.
Thence to Warm Springs.......................12
Summit of Sierra Nevada
Plenty of grass & water all
Around a lake [Goose].........................20
Canon Creek (Pitt River)........................8
Down Do [ditto]...............................10
Goff's Springs (warm).........................8
Big Spring....................................4
Shallow Lake.................................10
Sacramento River (long drive)...................20
Crossg do (Rock Bridge).......................4
Being 84 m. down valley at a settlement, & about 75 from
Feather R. mines, or 95 from Sacramento City."572

Though Bruff recorded it as "Cherrokee Guide," the above is
obviously the Applegate and Lassen route. His entry "About 5 m.S.
of R[abbit] Hole Springs...If the road could go that way" is
perhaps the route west identified by Lord as the third route (of
four): "north of Pyramid Lake by Mud Lake, crossing over to
Feather River."573

572Read & Gaines...*Bruff*...pp 286 and 288. "Bruff evidently took time at
'Grass Camp' (20 miles above Mary's River ford, the 'Here' of the Cherrokee
Guide) while his company made hay for the "Dry Stretch" (between the Humboldt
turn-off and Black Rock), to study...the two routes to California....namely
the new Lassen Cut-off and the Truckee. .The first turned...from the Humboldt,
the Truckee followed down the Humboldt some eighty miles to its Sink.
Apparently Bruff received hereabout new information on the Lassen route in the
shape of two guides. One was the guide herewith, transcribed by him and
called...the Cherrokee Guide....It is probably the 'printed guide' referred to
by Bruff and cited by Delano." Ibid. p 1211 Appendix 8.
573Liles..."Estremity"...p 109.

Bruff traveled the Applegate and Lassen route among Cherokee, making entries in his journal about them.

> Sept. 21, 1849 In about 5 1/2 ms from Springs...Passed a camp of people from the Cherokee country, who had sent their cattle back to the Springs to water. [p 183 and p 293]...
> September 22...The trail was a circuitous one, on account of springs & marshes. A Straight line, from this to Black Rock, Boiling Springs about 8 ms. the rock bears, SE by E from this camp. There are many companies camped here--10 P.M. Dr O'Brian & family came up, and camped....Here are Missourians, Illinoisians, Cherokees &c. [p 187]...
> September 23, 1849...The companies camped here, moved off to-day, except the Cherokees and an Arkansas company.[p 188]...Surrounded by camps:-Missourians, Cherokee, packers &c.[p 296]...All...moved off in afternoon, except Cherokees & Arkansas men.[P 297]

Bruff noted on September 23, "Cherokees & Arkansas men" were the last to leave the camp. The Evans/Cherokee twelve wagon breakaway party included members of the original Fayetteville (Arkansas) Gold Mining Company.[574] Cherokee members included Lipe: "we Indians quit the company."[575]

Bruff again noted Cherokee:

> September 24, 1849...Here we are opposite the natural fortress [he named Fremont's Castle] and near the S.W. Side of the valley, [p 297]. Here found the 2 Doctors and their families, I dined with the Cherokees[p 189]...Left Cherokees & Arkansas men, pack mule squad, N. Yorkers, &c behind at last camp, with several other companies. [p 298] Dined with Cherokees."

When Bruff "dined with the Cherokees," it could have been with O.W. Lipe, a New York-born white married to a Cherokee, who had bragged about his culinary skill while on the Santa Fe Trail.

On September 25, Bruff entered High Rock Canyon.[576]

> September 26...The Cherokees came up this morning.[p 193] and...This morning an ox train, Cherokees, Dietz & Young, &c. came in.[577]

Bruff did not mention any Cherokee for several days. Then on September 30, camped at the base of the Sierra Nevada mountains

---

[574]Officers of the Fayetteville Gold Mining Company included Dr. W. R. Cunningham. Others from Fayetteville were the five-member Freyschlag family, two Beans, two Sanders, two Holmes, North, Simms, McRoy, Mallet, Cline, Chew.
[575]Those who quit the Company in addition to Lipe were his relatives: Daniel Gunter (nephew), and Martin M. Schrimsher (brother-in-law), and brothers George Washington and Richard N. Keys. Cherokee Joseph Sturdivant sent his stock on the Applegate/Lassen with members of the main Evans/Cherokee wagon company, which may have included the five unnamed slaves. Sturdivent himself traveled another route, either the Carson or the Truckee.
[576] Read and Gaines...Bruff...p 300.
[577]Ibid. p 301.

Found here, several Missouri companies, the Cherokees, &c. Major Horn and Coy and Dietz & Young came up late in the afternoon. [p 199]...(Fine grass & mtn Stream edge of S.W.) Found Mo Cherokees, & sevl other camps: camp'd here.[578]

Among the "Cherokees & Arkansas men" noted by Bruff were Calvin H. Holmes and his brother Henderson. Part of a diary kept by Calvin notes mileages "From Humboldt" on the Applegate and Lassen trails ending at Sutter's Fort, with a total of 483 miles. Calvin gave his date of entry into California as November 8, 1849.[579] The Holmes brothers left Arkansas with the Evans/Cherokee Company. With eleven other wagons they left the main wagon company at the junction of the Cherokee Trail and the California Road east of Fort Bridger. Company member Pyeatt called the twelve-wagon breakaway group "cherikees and Fayettevill trash."

Bruff had agreed as company captain to stay as guardian at "Bruff's Camp," surrounded by the wagons and effects abandoned by his company and others as they hurried on toward Lassen's Ranch. He was faithful to his agreement. And as a bystander, he faithfully chronicled those who watered, nooned, camped, or stopped to talk.[580]

Between September 30 and October 28, a lot happened--early snows coupled with late emigrants. The twelve-wagon breakaway group, and members of the main Evans/Cherokee wagon company were caught with the rest.

The next Cherokee Bruff saw was Senora Hicks, on October 28, coming out from the settlements with Maj. Daniel Rucker and the government emigrant relief party. Bruff:

> October 28, 1849 11 A.M...I also proceeded down [to a spring with a Sergeant] a few hundred yards in the same direction, to meet the Major [Rucker] who was in company with Mr. Hicks, the Cherokee.[p 244] the Maj. & Mr. Hicks a Cherokee. [p 345] I met the Major and Mr. Hicks, (Cherokee chief) They hurried on.[581]

---

[578]Ibid. p 306.

[579]It is not clear if the date Calvin gave means arrival within the borders of California, or at the settlements. The Society of California Pioneers' membership required arrival in California before January 1, 1850.

[580]Bruff occupied his camp until the dead of winter, moving slightly down in elevation, where he stayed until March 1850, when he walked in to the settlements.

[581]Read & Gaines...*Bruff*...p 612.

Read & Gaines attempted to identify the Cherokee "chief."[582] Bruff himself made the notation of "chief." Whether Bruff assumed by the importance given Hicks by Rucker, or was told this by Rucker in order to give more credence to Hicks, is not known. Read & Gaines stated: "At least 'Mr. Hicks' was a person in whom Major Rucker placed absolute confidence."[583]

In either case, the person in question was not George Hicks, and not a Cherokee chief, but Senora Hicks. Though not nominally a Cherokee Chief, Rucker may have made the statement because of his intimate knowledge of chiefs in Senora's family.[584] Senora and his younger brother Charles Renatus Hicks left for California in 1849 with the Dr. Jeter Lynch Thompson Company via the Platte River route. They were early arrivals.

Bruff's diary continues on November 1, the day after a tree fell on and killed the Allford men in camp.

> Capt. Pierce, of the Weston Company, with a party of his men, and some Cherokees, returned from their camp, to hunt about the neighboring vales for lost cattle.[p 254]
> Capt. Pierce, and a party of his men & some Cherokees, came back armed, looking for cattle, in the valleys on each side of the hill.[p 352]
> Nov. 2nd...This morning the Weston & Cherokee party, started off early to look for cattle and Hunt deer. The Allfords moved off also.[585]

Read and Gaines, with limited primary resources available in 1944, tried to clarify and identify the Cherokee parties seen by Bruff. As this source is too valuable to ignore, or to leave in its present state, the authors feel that both the time and space are well justified to make corrections.

---

[582]"It is a temptation to identify this Hicks, (Cherokee chief) with George Hicks, Sr., 'a lawyer by profession...a notable man among the Cherokees,' quoting Bancroft's *History of Colorado* p 364."

[583]Read and Gaines...*Bruff*...p 612.

[584]Senora Hicks was first cousin to Flora Coody, Maj. Daniel Rucker's first wife, who died at Fort Gibson in 1845. Senora's grandfather, Charles Renatus Hicks was a Principal Chief. Upon his death, Charles' brother William Hicks was elected Chief, serving until 1828. At that time, Senora's uncle John Ross, (his mother's brother) was elected Principal Chief. John Ross served as Cherokee Principal Chief until his death in 1866.

[585]Read and Gaines...*Bruff*...p 255.

In "CRITICAL NOTES" H1, editors Read and Gaines stated:

54. It is particularly regrettable that Bruff, usually careful to note names gives none to the Cherokee. There were several parties of Cherokee en route to the gold fields in 1849. One went from Fort Gibson, presumably the "pack mule company" whose safe arrival at the gold diggings is noted in the *Cherokee Advocate* of Dec. 3, 1849, and after a passage of "exactly four months and twelve days," was at work in the Stanislaus River diggings on September 17 (letter of Lovely Rogers, *Cherokee Advocate*, Jan. 8, 1850); another reached Sacramento July 1 (letter of George E. Grymes, *Cherokee Advocate*, Jan. 8, 1850).

1. The Fort Gibson pack mule company--Letter (from Tuolumne River written September 17) by Lovely Rogers is correct. The company, the Cherokee and Mississippi Company captained by J.N.A. Carter and A. M. Wilson, followed Lt. Buford's route from Fort Smith along the Canadian River to Santa Fe, then proceeded to California via the Gila River route. Members included Finney Chisholm, S. B. Cordrey, George E. Grymes, Lovely Rogers, Thomas Scott, ---Shaw, A.D. Wilson, G.W. Wilson "and other Cherokees and white men," and Captain Carter.

2. George E. Grymes was not in another Cherokee party, but a member of the same party as Lovely Rogers.

Bruff Critical Notes:

a third was led by Colonel Black, reaching its destination prior to July 1 (*Cherokee Advocate*, Oct. 22, 1849; Jan. 8, 1850).

3. Colonel Black did not go to California in 1849, but led prospecting parties and reported gold strikes on Walnut Creek (Kansas).[586] His parties rendezvoused on the Grand Saline, and were made up of both Cherokee and whites.[587] Because of the similarities in the organization and the place of starting, it was natural to assume their destination was California.

Bruff Critical Notes:

yet another, with a detachment of which Major Cross fell in "June 9, about five miles below the Forks of the Platte" (Cross, Report, p 146), took the "Independence route," and reached "the valley of the Sacramento on the 28th October, being on the journey six months and ten days" (letter of Jeter Thompson, *Cherokee Advocate*, Feb. 9, 1850).

4. For the Jeter Lynch Thompson party noted by Cross, the route is correct--the northern or Independence route.[588] D. Jagger,

[586]*Cherokee Advocate* Monday 9 July 1849.
[587]*Cherokee Advocate* Monday 3 September 1849.
[588]Raymond W. Settle, ed., Major Osborne Cross, *The March of the Regiment of*

non-Cherokee emigrant said they met a "company of civilized Cherokee Indians." while traveling along the Platte.[589]

David Carter, editor of the *Cherokee Advocate* noted:

Sad News.--The latest news from some of our friends who started for California last spring, by way of the upper route, from Independence. ...soon after the California companies commenced their march from Independence...the cholera prevailed among them, but not to a very alarming extent, and from the communication lately received in this nation from Dr. Jeter L. Thompson...14 persons belonging to his company concluded that they would go on ahead of the main company, and after [they] had got two or three days a head of the main company, a little beyond Platte River, they were attacked with the Cholera, and eight out of 14 died: viz. Samuel W. Bell, Brice Martin, William Parks, Elijah Blythe, James Henry,---Purly, Markham, and Judge Tully, of Mo.[590]

Major Cross noted on June 9 they were:

within five miles of the junction of the North and South Forks of the Platte, and sixteen miles from where the emigrants make their first crossing on the South Fork commonly called the lower crossing....On the right of the road, and not far distant, we passed the encampment of a party of Cherokees, who had broken up their party....It consisted, a few days ago, of fourteen persons; since yesterday six had died with the cholera. One was dying at the time they were visited, and the remainder were too ill to assist in burying the dead. Among the whole of this party there was but one man who really was able to render any assistance to the others.[591]

The one Cherokee reported by Cross able to obtain assistance for the burials, did so. Help was rendered by a company that included eighteen-year-old James Eaton, who wrote in his memoirs:

after having dinner, we saw an Indian come riding....we waited for him to come up with us. He could speak English well and told us that several men of their Company had the cholera and that before he could get back, that another one would be dead, and he wanted some of us to come and bury them, as so many of their men were sick that they were unable to do it....Harris...and Mr. Campbell said [they] would go, so it was arranged that they go and bury the dead. The Indian companies were nearer the river and our men had to cross an Alkali pond that was between the two camps before they could reach the Indian camp....When they arrived, four were dead, but the man which the messenger had said would be dead was better and afterwards got well, but a man whom he thought was safe was

---

Mounted Riflemen First United States Military Expedition to travel the full length of the Oregon Trail from Fort Leavenworth to Fort Vancouver May to October, 1849 as recorded in the journals of Major Osborne Cross and George Gibbs and the official report of Colonel Loring (Lincoln and London: Univ. of Nebraska Press 1940, Bison Book 1989) pp 73-74.

[589]Mattes...*Platte River*...p 174.

[590]*Cherokee Advocate* 20 August 1849. Others in the party were John Lynch Adair, William W. Buffington, Dennis W. Bushyhead (later Cherokee Chief), Tom Clark, Charles and Senora Hicks, Joseph Lynch Martin (who turned back when cholera appeared), and John Martin Thompson, brother of Jeter.

[591]Settle...*Cross*...p 74.

dead. They dug a grave large enough for seven and put the four in it, covered them up, and came away.[592] These Indians...were dressed like we were and were quite civilized. It was thought that they had brought the disease on themselves through their own carelessness. We afterwards saw the same Indians several times while on the route, and when I got to California, I saw the messenger there.[593]

George Stewart noted the number of deaths.[594] Hulbert queried: "But what about those who are here rubbing shoulders with us, and dropping, like those Cherokees, into unknown and unmarked graves."[595]

In Read & Gaines' *Bruff...* The *Cherokee Advocate* edition listed as January 8, 1850 should be dated January 7; and that of February 9, 1850 should be dated February 4, 1850.

Bruff Critical Notes:

most pertinent for us, and famous in the history of trail making, is the company of Capt. Lewis Evans, of Fayetteville, Ark., to which, we surmise, Bruff's Cherokees belonged.[596]

5. Captain Lewis Evans noted by Read and Gaines is generally correct. The Cherokee mentioned by Bruff were originally from the Evans/Cherokee Company. The remainder of the wagon group, which took the Hastings Cutoff, further divided and traveled into California over three routes: the Carson, Truckee, and Applegate/Lassen.[597] Cherokee Joseph Sturdivant wrote on November 20 from California: "The balance of the [Evans/Cherokee] train took the northern route on Humbolt River, and my team with them."[598]

DISASTER ON THE LASSEN

Emigrants from all trails arriving in Sacramento in late summer informed U.S. military officials of impending disaster. There were many others still behind them in desperate straits, as

---

[592]Burial was east of present North Platte, Nebraska.

[593]F.D. Calhoon, *The Lassen Trail: The James Eaton Diary* (Sacramento: Cal-Con Press 1987) pp 46-47.

[594]George R. Stewart, *The California Trail* (N.Y.: McGraw-Hill Book Co. 1962) p 228.

[595]Archer Butler Hulbert, *Forty-Niners: The Chronicle of the California Trail* (Boston: Little, Brown and Co. 1931) pp 119-20.

[596]Read and Gaines...*Bruff*...p 567.

[597]Documentation for the Carson route is in the James Sawyer Crawford Diary and letters; the John Rankin Pyeatt letters, and the James Pierce reminiscence. For the Truckee route, the Crawford diary and Joseph Sturdivant letter in *Cherokee Advocate* 11 March 1850; Sturdivant also documented the use of the Lassen by a large portion of the company.

[598]*Cherokee Advocate* 11 March 1850.

far back as the Humboldt River, who would be dangerously late in trying to cross the mountains. Worn-out and footsore oxen contributed to an even slower pace. The abandonment of provisions increased as emigrants moved west toward the Sierra.

In response, Gen. Persifor Smith "took the responsibility of ordering pack mules and supplies to be provided at the expense of the Government[599] and gave Major Rucker orders to dispatch relief companies."[600]

On September 16 Rucker dispatched Captain Kilburn, with civilian John Chandler, to aid the emigrants on the Truckee route. Rucker: "if the whole of the supplies should not be required on the Truckey route...take or send them over to the Carson route." One emigrant wrote on October 1 from Sacramento to Major Rucker: "Dr. Worthley...passed 140 wagons on Carson River, many of which had returned from the Truckey route." Correspondence to Major Rucker from "Captain in charge of Party on Carson river route" Robert W. Hunt stated the reason for the lack of emigrants on the Truckee and Carson:

> On the 14th [October, on the Carson route] we met Captain Kilburn...who informed us that the emigration was not so large as we had been led to expect, as much the greater portion of those who were behind, had been induced by Lieutenant Hawkins[601] and several others to take the extreme northern or old Oregon route [Applegate/Lassen], which, owing to the lateness of the season, was considered the safest.[602]

On September 13, having come in over the Oregon or Lassen route. emigrant Captain Craig told Rucker "a notice had been put up at the forks of the road" stating the distance to be much less than other routes. Emigrants had therefore "thrown away all their

---

[599]$100,000 was allocated from the Port of San Francisco, the only revenue which could be quickly accessed.

[600]Bayard Taylor, *Eldorado* (Lincoln: Univ. of Nebraska Press 1949) p 215.

[601]Lt. George W. Hawkins, Member of the Mounted Riflemen. Read and Gaines..*Bruff*...p 538. *The Fort Smith Herald* carried notice of Hawkins' orders on 20 September 1848, vol 2 no 7 "to repair to Fort Leavenworth, and there await the orders of the lately appointed Governor, Gen. Lane, for Oregon. The company will leave Jefferson Barracks to-morrow." In Settle...*Cross*...p 129 n Hawkins wrote Colonel Loring he would leave Oregon City for Fort Hall June 24 with supplies; p 337 Hawkins started from Willamette Valley via the Southern [Applegate] Route, which placed Hawkins traveling toward and along the Humboldt River, going the reverse direction of the emigration.

[602]*General Smith's Correspondence, California,* (Daniel H. Rucker and John H. Peoples) "Relief Reports from Lassen's Cut-off, 1849" 31 Cong. 1 sess. Sen Ex Doc 52, Serial 561 (Washington, D.C.: 1850) vol 13 pp 111-14.

provisions, except what they thought to be sufficient to last them to the Sacramento." The distance was much greater than the signage indicated, and Craig was sure the emigrants would be out of provisions.

Webster, arriving October 19 over the Cherokee Cutoff, implied that Lassen was the source of misinformation:

> It was currently reported and probably with truth, that some time early in August, after the immigrants had begun to pass down the trail on the Humboldt River, a man with a party was sent out over the mountains and deserts by Lassen, whose ranch was located on the Sacramento River, to induce so much of the immigration as possible to take that route and which he called the "Cherokee Cutoff," and represented the distance to be but 180 miles to the Feather River mines, with a good road to travel over with many superior advantages over the old trail.[603]

As previously noted, it was the members of the Fort Hall-bound supply train from Oregon, and not Lassen, who gave poor advice and incorrect mileages to many along the Applegate route, and along the Humboldt River. So far as is known, the only circular sent out over the Lassen Trail was the one from Major Rucker, who noted the bearer, Senora Hicks, had been over "the whole of the route to Lassen's."

On October 4 Rucker was on the Lassen trail.[604] Under the date of October 13, he sent Senora Hicks with the following "circular" to the rear of the emigration on the Lassen, two days after the heavy snows on the Feather River:

---

[603]Webster...*Gold Seekers*...pp. 97-98.
[604]Rucker..."Report"...p. 100.

> *For the information of all emigrants on the Lawson's [Lassen]*
> *or Northern route.*
>
> > *Camp on the left branch of Feather river, Oct.* 13, 1849.
> > The undersigned is on this road with provisions for the
> relief of all emigrants who may be in a starving condition.
> These supplies have been forwarded by order of General Persifer
> Smith, the military commandant of this country, to be furnished
> only to those who are in a destitute state. I have a few beef
> cattle, (some thirty head,) some hard bread, flour, pork, and a
> little rice.
> > The bearer of this, Mr. Hicks, has passed over the whole
> of the route to Lassen's, in the valley of the Sacramento, and
> will give any information to the emigrants that is necessary
> for the preservation of their stock or their speedy progress. I
> would advise all families who may be in the vicinity of the
> Sierra Nevada, or whose teams are not in fine condition to
> throw away all heavy articles that they can possibly do
> without, and push on to Feather river valley, where there is
> plenty of grass, and to remain there one or two days to recruit
> their animals, also to cut grass sufficient to last their stock
> from Deer Creek valley to Lassen's, which is about fifty-three
> miles, over a very hilly and rocky country, without a blade of
> grass for the whole distance.
> > I believe that it is important that all the families
> should move on to the utmost of their abilities, as the season
> is far advanced, and the danger of being caught in the snow in
> these hills by no means slight. For that reason I have advised
> that those who are far in the rear, and have light teams, to
> throw away all heavy and useless property; to keep only their
> provisions and actual necessities.
> > The distance from Feather river valley to the valley of
> Deer Creek, is about fifteen to twenty miles. In Deer Creek
> valley there was grass sufficient for the stock to eat during
> the night, but not of sufficient length to cut for hay: hence,
> the necessity of cutting on Feather River.
> > Respectfully,   D.H. RUCKER,
> > > > > *Brvt. Maj. 1st Dragoons.*[605]

On October 21 civilian John H. Peoples wrote to Rucker, who
had become ill and returned to the settlements:

[On Pitt River] I met Todd's [relief] party and Mr. Hicks...he [Todd]
has given away all his provisions, and seen the last of the emigration
over the mountains....he left the wagons on the...16th, and passed not
more than 40 wagons on the road.[606]

---

[605]Ibid. p 102.
[606]Ibid. pp 126-27.

The winter weather season on the Lassen route began with a drizzling rain on October 30, turning to snow by the following morning. Peoples noted in his report some extreme difficulties in attempting to get the rear of the emigration in to the settlements.[607] There seemed to be no sense of urgency on the emigrants' part.

> loaded from the bed to the top of the bows; no argument of mine could induce them to abandon a thing, and they would drive their poor oxen till 12 o'clock at night to catch up with my train...the storm continued....I saw at once, that if my animals were not quickly hitched up they would freeze....I started off the wagons, pack mules and beef cattle...without breakfast...and urged upon the owners to do the same, but some of them were foolish enough to remain there...
>   The next morning the storm was raging and the snow deeper on the ground than ever, I of course hurried the mules up to the wagons and had them started at once, telling the drivers not to stop till they got into Feather river valley.[608]

Bruff noted he saw Cherokees out looking for their cattle on November 1 and 2. It continued to snow heavily. John Peoples made little progress, urging emigrants to leave their possessions.

> On the morning of the 4th [November] I started with all the women, children and helpless men in the valley....before getting into the first hill, my animals in the wagons began to fag...and I was forced to encamp....Here it snowed all night, and the next day....with the utmost difficulty [got] over Deer Creek valley. Every man was on foot, including myself...every man pushing against the hinder parts of the wagons.[609]

The anguished Peoples described what he left behind:

> Major...for 20 miles back, wagons are buried in the mud, up to the bed, and cattle lying all around them....I left eight men, teamsters, with the families, with instructions to help them with fires, and anything they may need.

Still in his mountain camp, Bruff saw the relief party on November 21 and noted that the government relief party "came from the rear with two wagons, 3 yokes each, filled with women and children."[610]

On November 27, Peoples brought in the rear of the emigration, which had been his charge since September 15.[611]

---

[607]Peoples' Report was dated December 12, 1849.

[608]Ibid. p 132.

[609]Ibid.

[610]California State Archives. Bruff deposition in "Claims for emigrant services 1849 Lawson [Lassen] Rd 11/16/50."

[611]Peoples..."Report"...p 122. Contrary to general belief, apparently not all were rescued by government teams, and not all were off the trail by November 27. Several testimonials appear in the California State Archives corroborating

However, Bruff, Captain of the Washington City and California Mining Association, noted on December 2 that civilian Joseph Petrie appeared in Bruff's Camp on foot and left on December 4 for Davis' Rancho. Bruff:

> After the means and exertions of the Government Relief party had been expended, there remained Several families, Supposed close enough to The Settlements to get in without difficulty...Leut. [General] Wilson sent in to The Settlements for mules to get his family in.--and Petrie being there, and noticing great difficulty about procuring the mules, and animated by compassion for the un-fortunate females and children, hired, at his own expense, 21 mules, for 9 days, at $5 per day; and likewise paid for, out of his own purse about $230 for provisions.--...Among these were the Alfords [612]-- old mother and two daughters.... Petrie... got them in Safe-- Lastly, at "Steep Hollow" [he] employed five days labor...getting in Several other families.[613]

Members of the Evans/Cherokee wagon company reached the settlements in the last week of October and the first week of November on the Lassen Trail. There are no reports of Cherokee or Arkansans from any company dying from their stormy weather entry into California. Nonetheless, their loss of animals was high. Cherokee Joseph Sturdivant wrote on November 20 about the Evans/Cherokee wagon Company's losses:

> I am now in camp with Wm. Shores and Capt. Evans, who arrived here about three weeks ago with about half the Arkansas teams. The balance of the train took the northern route on Humbolt River, and my team with them. I learn from Lieut. Rucker who has been with supplies to relieve the emigrants that they [Evans/Cherokee company members] had been caught in a snow storm, and have lost all the stock that belonged to the train. The Government lost all of their mules and every thing else except some Beef cattle. So my team, wagon and every thing else is gone to the d--l.[614]

The *Cherokee Advocate* continued to publish many reports of disasters that befell the 1849 emigrants. In early 1850 editor David Carter made many more statements intended to dampen the enthusiasm of 1850 would-be emigrants. But he was unsuccessful. Cherokee were laying plans for the 1850 journey to California.

---

the statements submitted by one Joseph J. Petrie for use of his own animals, equipment, and provisions to rescue emigrants.

[612]Read and Gaines...*Bruff*...pp 214-15. Bruff noted that Allfords had the large 2-story "steam-boat" wagon, and a month old infant in the wagon.

[613]Bruff..."Claims"...

[614]Letter, Joseph A. Sturdivant to wife Arie from California November 20, 1849. *Cherokee Advocate* 11 March 1850 p 2. Sturdivant remained with the Evans company.

ᏣᎳᎩ, ᎤᏕᏲᏗ ᏕᎦᎵᏲ, ᏓᏁᏫᏓᎥ

CHEROKEE TRAIL DIARIES

Vol. II 1850—Another New Route to the California Gold Fields

1850 Introduction

This volume is based primarily on three diaries: William Quesenbury, James Mitchell and John Lowery Brown.

William Quesenbury--artist, schoolteacher, church representative and experienced long distance traveler--wrote, sketched, hunted, and fished along the entire route to California. He began his trip with the Cane Hill (Arkansas) California Emigrating Company. However his actions would show that he did not want to be permanently attached to any group. Quesenbury simply did not fit well with the responsibilities of group travel.

William Quesenbury was an educated man. His diary is complete with proper spelling, grammar and punctuation, while most other diaries of the period were written with less attention to those items. Even in the field, while traveling under arduous conditions, his writing is complete, concise, clear.

His diary was published in 1979 in issues of *Flashback*. However, his sketchbook from the 1850 trip to California along the Cherokee Trail, and his return in 1851 via the Oregon/California Trail was lost. Inquiries to Arkansas institutions as well as to Duke University where other Quesenbury materials are held, yielded no knowledge of this sketchbook, which was obviously with the diary in 1850. In 1994 the sketchbook (in the same large format as the diary) surfaced in private hands and was purchased by the *Omaha World-Herald* Foundation for the Nebraska Historical Society. Permission has been obtained to use several of the 1850 sketches in this book.

Quesenbury began his California diary entries on Tuesday, April 9, 1850, the day he left home for California. He arrived in El Dorado County, California on August 19, sketching frequently along the way. The sketches documented the route taken, which in southwest Wyoming did not match any of the then-known routes. Quesenbury lost his way and came to the Green River at the present city of Green River, Wyoming. His sketches of the magnificent rock formations, notably that of Tollgate Rock, are perhaps the first done in the area.

The James Mitchell diary is published here for the first time. Mitchell, with "queshinbery," started the trip as a member of the Cane Hill California Emigrating Company. Once on the road, he showed his impatience with the pace of the slow-moving wagons, fairly quickly working his way to the front of this combined "caravan," to travel part of the way with the lead ox train captained by a Mr. Edmonson. Once over the Continental Divide, he and thirteen others left the ox train and traveled cross-country toward the Green River. Throughout, Mitchell's diary entries exhibit his considerable knowledge of natural history. Mitchell stopped writing July 27 on the Humboldt River, and entered eastern El Dorado County, California with Quesenbury on August 19, 1850.

John Lowery Brown's diary was the only previously available work chronicling an 1850 trip from Cherokee Nation to California. The Brown diary was first published in 1934 in the *Chronicles of Oklahoma*. Research safely places diarists Quesenbury and Mitchell in the traveling companies concurrent with Brown's, and on the same trail, at least as far as Twin Groves, the crossing of the Continental Divide in Carbon County, Wyoming. Brown, a Cherokee, was with the horse/mule wagon company under captains Mayes, then McNair, and lastly Taylor. Brown remained with this Cherokee company for the entire trip, even through the changes of leadership and different modes of travel. This group tarried at present Denver, Colorado, where enough gold was found to warrant some Cherokee members and their relatives returning in 1858 to prospect further, precipitating the Pikes Peak Gold Rush.

Brown began his "Journal kept by J.L. Brown of the Cherokee Nation" on April 20, 1850 about 22 miles east of Tahlequah in present Oklahoma. Brown arrived in eastern El Dorado County, California on September 21, a month after Mitchell and Quesenbury, but a month earlier than the Evans/Cherokee emigrants had arrived in 1849.

1850 Chapter 1. DECISIONS

While the 1850 would-be emigrants from Arkansas, southwest Missouri and Cherokee Nation were deciding whether to go to California or stay home, the weekly *Cherokee Advocate* was full of reports of dreaded conditions and diseases on the trails. At the same time these negative stories often reported new strikes and wonderful riches. The following three articles are examples.

col. 3 A GOLD HUNTER'S EXPERIENCE

Mr. Riley was one of...forty eight [that] on arriving in Sacramento lost eight men from the effects of the scurvy and the fever of the climate, and twelve or fourteen afterwards returned home sick....The prevailing diseases are dysentery and chills and fever...

Mormon Island...on the north fork of the Sacramento...has been made an island by cutting a canal across the main land...to turn and drain the bed of the river, [and] still continues to yield great quantities of gold. The Mormons realized millions of money from this island, and have gone back to Salt Lake immensely rich. It is the general opinion that about one-third who go to california realize fortunes. The reports concerning the inexhaustible quantities of gold to be found are confirmed...

The cities are reported to be crowded with young men, who cannot obtain employment, and are in the most destitute situation. Great mortality is said to exist among the emigrants...for the want of attention....Many are left to die on the bare ground...it is said that men who in the States had a seeming degree of christianity about them, turn perfect fiends and brutes from...the unclean love of lucre, which is...exalted to the highest degrees.[615]

COL.4 FROM THE NEW ORLEANS PICAYUNE OF THE 5TH.
FURTHER FROM CALIFORNIA

The *Alta California* of the 31st December contains a long account of matters and things at the mines....the snows have descended, and operations have ceased....The streams of the Sierre Nevada are swollen ....the cold rain falls, leaving no hope of resuming mining until the ensuing spring. On the American river [they] have been compelled to abandon the field. The Georgetown washings...have been very productive. On Trinidad river, the success...has been limited; but on Feather river, South Fork, new washings have been worked with immense success....vast numbers of people are in winter quarters, generally in health, high hopes and spirits.

It is a prevailing opinion, that the mining season of the next year will prove more flatteringly productive to the majority of diggers than has any...[616]

Lucky Gold Digger-- A correspondent...writing from Pleasant Valley,[617] California, in November, states that one man, [near] Webber's Creek, took from the mines $17,000 in the short space of 14 days.[618]

---

[615]*Cherokee Advocate* 11 March 1850 p 1.
[616]Ibid.
[617]John Lowery Brown would arrive at Pleasant Valley on September 23, 1850.
[618]*Cherokee Advocate* 18 March 1850 p 1.

Many letters from the 1849 emigrants advised people to stay home, but did little to discourage people from their determination to go to California. Col. Jonathan Mulkey wrote such a letter. He and his son James had traveled in the 1849 Jeter Lynch Thompson "cholera" company. Mulkey's letter arrived in Cherokee Nation too late to help stem the 1850 departure.[619]

> I now want to say something for the benefit of our friends, who were wise enough to stay at home in our happy country: That is to remain there contented and never to think to come here to make a fortune easy; for should they come with all the good health and good luck that they could posibly wish, yet when they get here, the privations, troubles and disappointments to be suffered, will outweigh all the gold they dig, for it is by digging it must be obtained--much the hardest labor to be performed.[620]

Newspaper editors nationwide reported concerns about depopulation and the anticipated shortage of men.

> *The California Emigration.* The large numbers of citizens who are making preperations to emigrate to California this spring, have awakened the apprehensions of some our folks, who say the country will become depopulated..."there will not be more than one man to seven women" left ...From all we can learn, between four and five hundred will go from Washington county. Many will go from all the surrounding counties... --*Arkansas Intelligencer.*[621]

Emigrants had more options for travel in 1850. Not only were there improved roads and routes, there were also entrepreneurs who promised easier travel for the emigrants. These would go south.

> **Ho! For California**.--A gentleman of this place, of known integrity, proposes to take persons from Fort Smith to California for $200 each, paid in advance. The mode of conveyance will be *pack mules*, with a good substantial wagon to every ten men....Should a man get sick, the wagons are ready to haul him. The calculation would be for the wagons to travel from 20 to 30 miles per day. Each man will be required to furnish himself with a gun, pistols, ammunition, &c; also blankets and clothing. All other things furnished.
>   Send in your names. If 60 good men will enter into the arrangement, we will start between the 1st and 15th of April.
>   Send your names to this office--*Fort Smith Herald.*[622]

---

[619]Jonathan Mulkey's Prussian name was Von Moltke. His wife, Maria Ross, youngest sister of Chief John Ross, died in 1838 either on the Trail of Tears or shortly after arrival in present Oklahoma. Mulkey's sons James, Lewis and William were apparently cared for by an aunt, Eliza Ross, until the 1850s. Grant Foreman Collection, Oklahoma Historical Society, Oklahoma City.

[620]*Cherokee Advocate* 16 July 1850.

[621]*Cherokee Advocate* 1 April 1850 p 2.

[622]*Cherokee Advocate* 4 March 1850 p 2.

Other entrepreneurs guaranteed to make the trip dependable and timely, in contrast to the uncertainties of individual or group travel experienced in 1849. A plan for transporting emigrants with certainty and facilities was presented in another newspaper issue. This company would follow the route on the north side of the Platte.

> *Ho! for California.*--S. Roundy & Co. proprietors of the Great Salt Lake Carrying and Transporting Company, give notice in the St. Joseph *Gazette* that they are prepared to transport 500 passengers from Iowa and Deseret Depot, 2 miles below the mouth of the Great Platte River, where they have permanently established a warehouse and ferry, to Sutter's Fort, in the gold mines of Upper California. Through tickets $200.[623]

A little later in the spring, another idea was presented:

> Novel Enterprise.--Another mode of Conveyance to Califoronia.-- Considerable of a stir was created in Baltimore a few days ago by the arrival of a herd of eleven Syrian camels at that port....Sands & Howes, the well known enterprising circus proprietors, are about to establish an overland line to California with them, which is to leave Independence, Missouri, directed for San Francisco, early in June. These gentlemen have already, Thirty-one camels....the brig Catherine...on her passage...to New Orleans, has on board twenty two more; making in all fifty-three....a caravan of twenty-five or more, will leave each point once a month. *N.Y. Herald.*[624]

If the emigrant still wanted to transport himself, there was helpful news including comments from trusted correspondent Colonel Russell, on the extent of the gold and the route:

> LATE CALIFORNIA LETTERS
> extracts of a letter by Col. Wm. H. Russell[625]...dated Pueblo De San Jose, Nov. 9, 1849.
> *My Dear Sir*:...I...reached Sutter's Fort...and to my surprise at this landing on the Sacramento I found a large town or city, where I left two years ago an unbroken forest....
> The accounts received at home of the marvelous amount of gold...have

---

[623]*Cherokee Advocate* 18 March 1850 p 1.

[624]*Cherokee Advocate* 13 May 1850 p 4.

[625]Russell, of Callaway County, Mo. captained an 1846 company which included, for a time, the Reed/Donner group. Near Fort Laramie, Russell resigned command; traded wagons for mules and went ahead, reaching Sutter's Fort on August 31, 1846. Louise Barry *The Beginning of the West, Annals of the Kansas Gateway to the American West 1540-1854* (Topeka, Kans.: Kansas State Historical Society 1972) pp 583-85. Russell left California on March 25, 1847 with a company of 16-17 traveled east on southern routes and the Santa Fe Trail, arriving Independence, Mo. on July 2, 1847 with dispatches from Commodore Stockton and Lt. Col. Fremont. Ibid. pp 693, 699. Russell captained a large 1849 party which left April 24 from Mo. proceeding up the Platte. Russell, with company remnants reached Sutter's Fort August 8, 1849. Ibid. p 833.

not been much exaggerated, if at all....

In the precise ratio that gold is plenty, so are the prices....every meal...ever so common, costs $1.50, and sleeping on blankets $2....in addition to eating...it requires the most rigid economy to keep the ends together, and if you happen to get sick....you are ruined....

We make...extracts from a letter...by Wm. B. Royall[626]...dated Dry Diggingsville, December 8th 1849:

...I believe this to be a great country for all young men of steady and industrious habits....Leave St. Joseph the 15th April with forage to last about two weeks. Mules are much preferable to oxen. The grass will be better as you advance.--

Take Sublet's Cut-off before you get to Green river, and at Bear river valley take Hedgpeth's [Hudspeth's] Cut-off, leaving Fort Hall to your right--at the sink of Mary's river take the Carson route. These are the principal landmarks of the route.[627]

All who read the above certainly believed themselves to be "of steady and industrious habits" and therefore able to do well in the gold fields.

This second year of travel would be different in a number of ways. Cherokee and white emigrants knew that three land routes were available: 1) The main California route from Independence could be reached by going north to that road via Fort Scott. It would be the most crowded. 2) The route from Fort Smith to Southern California via present New Mexico and Arizona known as the Marcy, or Southern Route, would be less used but drier. 3) The third known route was that taken by the 1849 Evans/Cherokee Company. It would be less crowded than either of the other routes. And therefore would provide more grass and less danger of cholera. Only two men died in the 1849 Evans/Cherokee pioneering company: one from drowning while crossing Green River, and one "as a result of an old disease [diabetes]."

The 1850 groups would try cutoffs from the 1849 Evans track for better, shorter, or more improved wagon-road conditions. Local entrepreneurs lost no time on the one hand in assisting the process, or on the other, in debunking the merits of such cutoffs. At least one advertised.

---

[626]William B. Royall with Missouri volunteers from the Mexican War made trips along the Santa Fe Trail in 1847 and 1848. Barry...West...pp 728, 748, 751, 757-59, 778; left Missouri early May 1849, arriving Sutter's Mill August 20. Ibid. p 839.

[627]Cherokee Advocate 18 March 1850.

FERRY!

P AY no attention to new humbugs as new established Ferries--new cut
roads--new bridges and new high cuts.

Keep the old well established and plain road to my Ferry on Grand River,
ten miles below the Grand Saline,[628] where you will find a good and safe
boat to cross in, careful and obliging Ferrymen, and charges as cheap as
the cheapest. Drovers will find this the best and safest point to cross
stock at on Grand River. I will ferry at all stages of the water, and
all times except Sundays and night--I will not ferry *then* only in cases
of great emergency.

> JOHN H. McINTOSH
> Cherokee Nation.
> Saline Dist. Dec. 6 1849.[629]

Many 1850 travelers were convinced to take the 1849 Evans/
Cherokee route by evidence of its success. The 1849 Crawford diary
showed that Captain Evans tried to keep his wagon train traveling
at the speed of 20 miles per day. Military Capt. Abraham Buford
had written a glowing account of the Evans' trace road and his
rapid travel over it from the Santa Fe Trail to Fort Gibson, which
was reported in the *Fort Smith Herald* and other papers.[630]

John C. Wheeler, editor of the *Fort Smith Herald,* printed
Buford's report.[631] He was a leading proponent of Marcy's Southern
Route--Fort Smith to Dona Ana (New Mexico); thence over Cooke's
Wagon Road to California. Wheeler printed many columns of negative
reports about trails other than the Southern route. His purpose
was to ensure that the Fort Smith to Dona Ana route would be so
heavily used that it would become part of The National Road.

Wheeler had read the account of travel over the entire
Evans/Cherokee route from Arkansas to California in Captain Evans'
journal. Alfred Oliver brought it back and took it to the office
of the *Fort Smith Herald.*

---

[628]The 1849 emigrants rendezvoused at the Grand Saline.

[629]*Cherokee Advocate* 7 January 1850 p 4.

[630]*Daily Missouri Republican* 30 June 1849.

[631]Wheeler married Cherokee Nancy Watie, sister of Stand Watie. According to
Wheeler's son, Will Watie Wheeler, Sr., his father was "the first man that
ever set a Cherokee type. He made the fonts for the distribution of the type,
and after George Guess completed the alphabet Mr. Wheeler, in company with
Messrs. Leonard Wooster and Butler...missionaries...went to Cincinnati, Ohio,
and arranged to have type cast. Mr. Wheeler became a type-setter on the
Phoenix, [1828] a Cherokee national paper." D.C. Gideon, *Indian Territory* (N.Y.
and Chicago: The Lewis Publishing Co. 1901) pp 451-52. In 1843 the family
moved to Fort Smith, where John "established the first newspaper west of
Little Rock, Arkansas."

Editor Wheeler did not publish the Evans Journal, writing only:

> we had the pleasure of looking [it] over. Each day's travel is marked
> and the nature and face of the country is set down minutely.[632]

Wheeler later explained his refusal to print the Evans Journal:

> We...will positively never publish any thing that is calculated to
> injure the interest of Arkansas....we have a road leading to California
> ...that is far superior to...any one that runs in that [north] direction
> ...we have evidence that the Southern route by Dona Ana is far, very far
> superior to the one marked out by *him*.[Lewis Evans].[633]

Alfred Oliver kept the Evans Journal, giving information
from it to others in the 1850 wagon trains. Diarist William
Quesenbury was already on his way to California camped west of the
Verdigris River, on cold and blustery April 18 when he copied into
his diary a brief general narrative, and the mileage and campsite
part of the Evans Journal. The Evans diary has never resurfaced.

In the northwestern part of Arkansas, from the very same
areas where at least 23 men joined the 1849 Evans/Cherokee
company, another party formed for the 1850 trek. Chaired by the
Rev. J. J. May, meeting on February 13 they adopted their
resolutions, naming their company The Cane Hill California
Emigrating Company. J. T. Craig, later elected captain, acted as
Secretary writing the resolutions. They resolved to start early
and travel Evans' route "to some point which they may think most
suitable to leave it, to intersect the Independence road this side
of the Rocky Mountains."

While they did not discourage packers, they wanted every four
or five men to have a "two horse wagon to be drawn by four good
mules or horses." Those wagons were to carry no more than 1,000
lbs. Initially they appointed a committee to physically inspect
each wagon, with power to reject any wagons which were
unsuitable.[634] At the second meeting on March 16, the committee
reported that it proved to be too impractical to inspect the
widely-dispersed wagons.

There were instructions for company members. Each was to have

---

[632]*Fort Smith Herald* 9 March 1850 vol 3, no 28, p 2 col 2.
[633]*Fort Smith Herald* 23 March 1850 vol 3, no 30, p 2 col 2.
[634]The Wagon inspection committed was composed of Isaac P. Spencer, J. A.
Hagwood (Hagood), James Mitchell, and George Crum.

a good gun, 2 lbs. of powder, 4 lbs. of lead or shot, flints and percussion caps. Each man was to carry no less than $25 cash.

The newspaper carried a report of their resolutions of February 13 and their subsequent meeting on March 16, at which William Quesenbury performed duties as clerk. This second meeting at Boonsboro set the place of rendezvous as "near Lewis Ross' beyond Grand River...6th day of April." Quesenbury entered: "A number of Cherokees having expressed a desire to join this company, it was agreed to receive them as members."[635]

In February 1850 Harriet Crawford wrote to her husband James Sawyer Crawford from her home near Boonsboro. Crawford, the 1849 diarist, was in California: "there is a good many persons talking of going to California in the West. Moses Edmiston[636] and all the Mayberries."[637]

Meanwhile, in Cherokee Nation, fifty people reportedly enrolled in the Cherokee Emigrating Company, which first met at Mrs. Susan Coody's home on Bayou Menard, southwest of Tahlequah near Fort Gibson.[638] Three of the organizers were William L. Holt, Richard Drew, and N. B. Hawkins.[639] The company planned a rendezvous on April 20 on the west side of the Grand (Neosho) River opposite the residence of Lewis Ross. The *Advocate* carried an editorial about the meeting, and subsequent March 25 meeting.[640]

---

[635]*Cherokee Advocate* 25 March 1850 p 2.

[636]Three Moses Edmistons lived in the area. Moses James Edmiston died before August 1845; his son Moses Ewen died in 1851; a third, Moses A. Edmiston was born 1822 and died 1857. Relationship of the above to "Captain Edmonson" is unknown. Captain Edmonson's identity remains unknown.

[637]Harriet Crawford letter to husband James Sawyer Crawford, from "Washington Cty. Februay the 9th 1850"; mailed from "Boonsboro Arks 22th Feby."

[638]Grant Foreman, *Marcy and the Gold Seekers: The Journal of Captain R.B. Marcy, with an Account of the Gold Rush over the Southern Route.* (Norman, Okla: Univ. of Oklahoma Press 1939, 1966) p 98. McArthur...*Arkansas*...states they left Tahlequah on April 22. *Cherokee Advocate* 29 April 1850 p 2 col 1. Susan Coody is not to be confused with the Widow Coody at Coody's Bluff noted by 1849 diarist Crawford. Bayou Menard flows into the Arkansas River 3/4 mile below the Neosho (Grand) River.

[639]Richard Drew married Jennie Bushyhead, sister of forty-niner and later Principal Cherokee Chief Dennis Wolfe Bushyhead. At least one of Jennie's brothers, Edward Wilkerson Bushyhead, went to California in 1850. Though William L. Holt and Richard Drew were both in this company, which joined Clement Vann McNair on May 7, no mention of N.B. Hawkins, Creek Indian, was found in any sources relating to the 1850 journey to California.

[640]*Cherokee Advocate* 18 March 1850 p 2; and 1 April 1850 p 2.

The editorial report of the second Cherokee meeting and the resultant resolutions included a recommendation for the Cane Hill and Cherokee companies to unite:

> Just previous to this we published some of the proceedings of the Cane Hill meeting Arkansas; in which an invitation was given to any Cherokees that might wish to join them, to do so. In this we publish to day, the Cherokees give the invitation to any citizens of Washington, Crawford and Benton Counties Arks. to join them; and should they all unite and make one company we would like to know by what name it will be christened.

California Emigrating Company had previously been chosen for the Cherokee company name. The leaders, like those of the Cane Hill Company, wanted to make sure the wagons would make the trip. A mandatory inspection was written in. None would be allowed "unless they are...good and sufficiently strong and new." Each 1,000 lb. wagon should be able to carry 1,500 lbs.; the 1,500 lb. to carry 2,000 lbs.

Each emigrant was to provide 75 lbs. of bacon, 100 lbs. of flour and "one peck of salt to each man" in addition to sugar and coffee "and other necessaries to last." Each should have a good gun, 2 lbs. of powder and 6 lbs. of lead.[641]

At least two Cherokee merchants took the emigration seriously, inserting ads in the paper asking folks to pay up.

Keep Your Credit Up.
All persons indebted to the undersigned either by Note or Account [are] requested to come forward and make settlement.

GEO. M. MURREL.
Tahlequah, C.N.,
Feb. 15th[642]

George stayed in Tahlequah. His concern was that the emigrants settle up before they left. In the same paper was:

Pay up your Debts!
All persons indebted to the undersigned are requested to come forward and make payment, without fail, as I am anxious to settle up my business.

G.M. MARTIN.
Saline District, C.N.
Nov. 22nd, 1849."

---

[641]*Cherokee Advocate* 1 April 1850 p 2.
[642]*Cherokee Advocate* 4 February 1850 p 4.

Gabriel M. Martin (called Gabe) wanted to settle up so he could become an emigrant. His brother Brice had been a forty-niner, getting only as far as near present North Platte, Nebraska on the Platte River where he and his brother-in-law Samuel W. Bell, were among the nine who succumbed to cholera.[643] The deaths of his relatives seemed to deter Gabriel only from taking that northern route. Martin traveled in the 1850 emigration with relatives on the Evans/Cherokee route.[644]

The following groups began the trip in Arkansas, Cherokee Nation, and Missouri. They eventually made up the four main wagon companies and one pack company of the 1850 emigration on the Cherokee Trail.

1. Cane Hill California Emigrating Company. Diarists James Mitchell and William M. Quesenbury started with this company.

2. Captain Edmonson's ox train company.

3. Return Jonathan Meigs' Cherokee group.

4. Robert Harris' group.

5. Samuel Houston Mayes' Cherokee group. Diarist John Lowery Brown started with this group.

6. Captain Clement Vann McNair's Cherokee Company.

7. Cherokee Jonathan Wolfe's group, the Cherokee California Emigrating Company.

8. Captain Holmes' ox train company.

9. Captain Alfred Oliver's ox train company.

10. Thomas Fox Taylor's (last) Cherokee group.

11. T. J. Mims (Mimms) & Co. Cherokee pack group

---

[643]Samuel W. Bell married Rachel Martin, Gabriel's sister.
[644]Gabe's oldest sister Martha married George Washington Adair, who made the trip; sister Susannah married Clement Vann McNair, elected Captain of the united company at the beginning of the 1850 trip.

Chapter 2. THE 1850 RENDEZVOUS

All the Other Companies has gone Evins's Route
--Lewis Riley

The 1849 Evans/Cherokee Company left the Grand Saline as a united group. The 1850 emigrants were a loose coalition of Cherokee and white groups that traveled together for unscheduled and unregulated periods of time. The groups and company compositions changed fairly frequently. Lack of, or finding, adequate grass, dissimilar pace of travel, and dissatisfaction with leadership all contributed to these changes.

Moreover, the need for cooperation and manpower in building a road was gone; the Evans/Cherokee Company had blazed it in 1849. The trail was known and plainly visible for them to follow. Additionally, there was no hostility from the plains Indians in 1849. They had no reason to remain a large and united company.

The stated intent of the Cane Hill and Cherokee companies was clear: they both intended to make the trip to California; each invited the other to join them. Both stated they would rendezvous at the same place as the forty-niners--the Grand (Neosho) River near Lewis Ross'. However Cane Hill set April 6 for a rendezvous date; the Cherokee set April 20. In keeping to their respective schedules, the Cane Hill men crossed Grand River and proceeded onward to the Verdigris River, where they waited until the end of April for the Cherokee. These two companies did not unite until May 5. The delay and the foul weather led to hard feelings.

In early April the *Advocate* reported unfavorable weather:

> April 5th, the weather was cold and wintery, and spitting snow in the fore part of the day; setting farmers and Californians back.[645]

All the newspaper stories printed so far indicated the rendezvous of companies would take place at the Grand Saline, where the forty-niners rendezvoused. As late as April 18, four wagons with travelers left Tahlequah "to join others...and the Washington and Benton county emigrants who are to meet them on the

---

[645]*Cherokee Advocate* 8 April 1850 p 2.

west side of Grand River, and form the train for the far west."[646]

However, the first letters from the departing emigrants that were printed in the newspaper confirmed that the majority of the 1850 Arkansas, Missouri and Cherokee companies did in fact rendezvous and depart not from the Grand (Neosho) River, but farther west, on the west bank of the Verdigris River.[647]

ROUTES TO THE RENDEZVOUS

All of the 1850 emigrant groups crossed the Grand (Neosho) River at the same place--at Lewis Ross'store and postoffice, but at different times.

Captain Edmonson's route to the Verdigris River is unknown. Edmonson himself remains unidentified.

The Cane Hill California Emigrating Company, including diarists Quesenbury and Mitchell, was on the road to California about 20 days before the Cherokee company including diarist John Lowery Brown. The Cane Hill Company traveled north from Cane Hill, crossed the Illinois River, northwest for a few miles, west over the frontier border of the state of Arkansas, and through Flint to the Grand (Neosho) River.

The Cherokee California Emigrating Company, whose proceedings were reported by the newspaper, preceded diarist Brown's company on the route from Tahlequah north/northwest to Grand (Neosho) River.

John Lowery Brown, with Cherokee citizens Mayes', Adairs, and Bells traveled from near Stilwell (Oklahoma) northwest to Tahlequah, then north/northwest to the Grand River.

Missourians who joined the emigration traveled nearly due west from Honey Creek to the Grand (Neosho) River.

All companies proceeded at different times from the Grand River northwest toward the Verdigris River on much the same route, most crossing the Verdigris at or near Coody's Bluff.

The planned rendezvous of all companies to meet at the same

---

[646]*Cherokee Advocate* 22 April 1850 p 2.
[647]*Cherokee Advocate* 6 May 1850 p 2.

place at the same time didn't happen--not at Grand (Neosho) River; not at the Verdigris. In fact, the ox trains of Edmonson, Holmes, and Oliver; the horse/mule trains of Cane Hill, Cherokee Emigrating, and Brown's Cherokee Mayes/McNair group never traveled all together. Edmonson's last encounter with any other group was at the Verdigris when they offered help crossing the river to the original Cane Hill company. The company refused the help because they would not bind themselves to Edmonson for the entire trip.

Two of the three diarists began the journey as members of the Cane Hill Emigrating Company. Their diary narrations appear first.

"California, California, California, California."

begins the William Quesenbury diary. The diary measures 31 x 19 cm (about 12 1/4" x 7 1/2") which was about the same size of his sketchbook. He kept both diary and sketchbook through the trip. The first entry here shows the actual line length in the diary, as well as the composition of pages throughout. Quesenbury:

"**April Tuesday 9 [1850]**   Left Uncle Mark's after breakfast with Mrs. Mitchell. Came on to Cincinatti.[648] Drunken place. Got me a buckskin.
    To Illinois.[649] Wagons two hours ahead. Pushed to get to the shop where Crum's[650] wagon had gone to get the tire welded. Wagon already gone. Followed. Found it had got lost and had gone three or four miles out of the way. At length got into the right road, and overtook our company[651] about a mile from Tower's mill."

---

[648] One of the border towns that sprang up (approximately 9 miles north and a little east of Cane Hill in Washington County) to trade with the Cherokee following Removal from the Eastern U.S. Most were intentionally set as close as possible to Indian Territory. The north/south highway connecting the towns from Van Buren, Arkansas to southwest Missouri (present Highway 59 in Arkansas; Highway 20 in Oklahoma; Highway 43 in Missouri) was called by some the "Whiskey Road," "Military Road," and "the Stage Road." A portion of the "Trail of Tears" came through northwest Benton and Washington Counties.

[649] The Illinois River starts in NW Arkansas (south of Sylvan Spring, north of the Washington/Benton Counties' line) and runs southwest into Oklahoma.

[650] George Crum is mentioned often in the diaries of both Quesenbury and Mitchell. Crum was one member of a small committee whose original responsibility was to inspect each wagon of the Cane Hill California Emigrating Company for fitness.

[651] The Cane Hill company consisted of twenty four men and six wagons. Crossed into present Oklahoma.

James Mitchell also started his diary on April 9, 1850. In contrast to the very large Quesenbury diary, Mitchell's is a commonly used size which fits in the hand, or in the jacket or shirt pocket. Only this first entry shows the actual line length of this small diary. <u>Mitchell</u>:

> "left on cane Hill
> washington county
> ark on the 9th april
> 1850 on a trip to the
> gold digings in Calif
> orna Wm queshin
> =bery and me tog
> =eather a cold wet
> day we overtook
> our --es that even
> =ing that had Started
> the day before in w
> =aggons on flint[652]
> about 34 miles from
> home at camp near Bower's mill."
>   [near Flint, Delaware Co., Oklahoma]

Virgil Talbot wrote about the mills on Flint Creek:

> the old mill race took off from the main course of the stream [Flint Creek]. Said to have been built when the first mill was built sometime in the late 1830's or early 1840's, it was probably built with slave labor belonging to Jeremiah Tower[s][653]

The "Early Mills of Washington County" does not mention any Bowers Mill.[654]

---

[652]Virgil Talbot, "Memories of Flint Creek" *The Goingsnake Messenger* vol 7, no 2 (May 1990) "Flint Creek begins in Benton County, Arkansas in the community of Springtown, where a large spring feeds clear water into the small stream that meanders southwest into Oklahoma....it was known as Flint Creek shortly after the Cherokees came here...in the early 1840's it became the boundary line for a few miles along the northern edge of Goingsnake...District." The creek runs through Sections 13, 23, 24, 25, 26, and 35, T20N-R24E where it joins the Illinois River.

[653]Talbot..."Flint"...The mill location is Sec. 24, T20N, R24E. It was said when Stephen Hildebrand acquired the mill and enlarged the mill race, he paid $2000 in gold for the work. Stephen was married to Pauline Beck niece of Jeremiah Towers. Her brothers John and Jeffrey Beck were in the 1850 Cherokee company to California. Jeffrey wrote back they found gold at the foot of the Rocky Mountains, near present Denver and that if he lived to get back from California he would "make a trial for it." That discovery, credited to Lewis Ralston, was the basis for the Colorado Pikes Peak gold rush of 1858-59. Ralston and the Becks went back in 1858. Stephen Hildebrand was also a first cousin of Brice and John (Jack) Hildebrand and Barbara Hildebrand Longknife. All three were in the 1850 company of travelers to California.

[654]Bobbie Byars Lynch, "Early Mills of Washington County" *Flashback* vol 25, no 1 (February 1975) and no 2 (May 1975.) The mill referred to would have been in present Oklahoma. The only reference found to a mill of this name, which seems to have done business from the Missouri line south to Van Buren, Arkansas, is:

Quesenbury had clearly written "Towers mill." Mitchell had just as clearly twice written "Bower's mill."

Mitchell and Quesenbury began the trip together. Whenever they traveled together, their diaries indicate inescapable differences in observation. They often appear to be in different circumstances with totally unrelated surroundings.

In this volume their diary entries appear together for the duration of time they traveled together. The identification of their location for each end-of-day follows the Mitchell entry. Their diaries continue on the second day of travel. Quesenbury:

> **"Wednesday 10 [April]** Mule hurt yesterday. Couldn't travel. Put Prince in. Worked well. Crossed a prairie and camped. One of Ross' negroes with a mule team camped with us. He was going to mill."[655]
>
> Mitchell:
>
> **"10 wendsday [April]** a cleer day, with a little frost Strickler[656] and me got corn & fodder at Bower's mill   each of us paid $1   we took the wrong road toward Fort Gibson we Saw an old indeans packer   camped on a wet post oak[657] Branch."
> [near the Delaware/Mayes Cos. line, Oklahoma]

During the next day they arrived at Lewis Ross' store and camped nearby. Quesenbury briefly noted his interests--those which would occupy him for the entire journey--hunting. But Mitchell indicated the first hint of dissatisfaction in their company. The issues were the waiting, and the grass, subjects which ultimately occupied many pages of diary notations throughout the journey to California.

"Bower's Mills, Spring river, Mo. [with the] long experience of 26 years in manufacturing flour, recommends that the...mills when they send off loads of flour, despatch with them certificates of the miller, so that the merchants may not be imposed upon...'Bower's Mills' send out good flour." *The Arkansas Intelligencer* (Van Buren) 16 May 1846 vol 5, no 14, p 2.

[655]Lewis Ross had a license from the Cherokee National government to process and sell salt at the saline on the Grand River. The entries mentioning this mill indicate it was west from Flint and close by the road.

[656]Strickler is identified only with a single name throughout both diaries. Interestingly, his name does not appear on the agreement to pack from Pueblo, but he remained with Quesenbury throughout the journey until August 20, 1850.

[657]Post Oak *Quercus stellata Wang.* "A small tree with often leathery leaves....frequently grows with Blackjack Oak." George A. Petrides, *A Field Guide to Trees and Shrubs*, Peterson Field Guide Series (Boston: Houghton Mifflin 2nd ed. 1972) pp 216-17. In this part of Oklahoma the travelers were near the western limits of hardwoods.

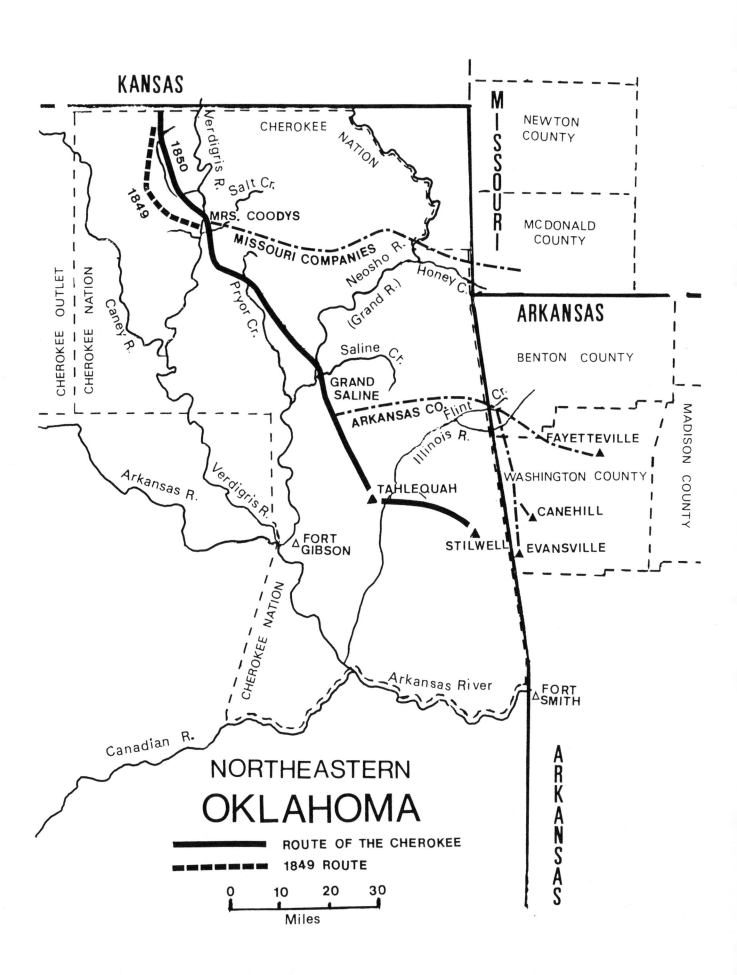

KANSAS

CHEROKEE NATION

Verdigris R.

Salt Cr.

1850

1849

MRS. COODYS

MISSOURI COMPANIES

Pryor Cr.

Neosho R.

(Grand R.)

Honey C.

MISSOURI

NEWTON COUNTY

MC DONALD COUNTY

ARKANSAS

BENTON COUNTY

CHEROKEE OUTLET

CHEROKEE NATION

Caney R.

Saline Cr.

GRAND SALINE

ARKANSAS CO.

Flint Cr.

Illinois R.

MADISON COUNTY

FAYETTEVILLE

Arkansas R.

Verdigris R.

TAHLEQUAH

WASHINGTON COUNTY

CANEHILL

FORT GIBSON

STILWELL

EVANSVILLE

CHEROKEE NATION

Arkansas River

FORT SMITH

Canadian R.

NORTHEASTERN
OKLAHOMA

ARKANSAS

ROUTE OF THE CHEROKEE

1849 ROUTE

0   10   20   30

Miles

Quesenbury:

"Thursday 11 [April]. Went on and got to Martin's.[658] Then to Ross. On the way to day some of the boys got a squirrel up a tree and killed it. Camped down below [Lewis] Ross' store."[659]

Mitchell:

"11 Thursday [April] in 3 miles got in our right road and could See wagons a head who belonged to our company   we got to the Grand Salt works and intended crosing Grand river but our company would not because they said the grass was to Scarce when in my opinion the real cause was waiting for more company for fear of indians   crum & me Bought 14 bush[el] corn   crum paid 5 and me 2 dollars for it."
[near Salina, Mayes Co., Oklahoma]

According to Grant Foreman, a company of men from Crawford and Washington counties in Arkansas left April 11 captained by Robert Harris.[660] Harris initially traveled with the Cane Hill Company on the Evans/Cherokee Trail. Still on the east side of the Grand (Neosho) River, the Company held elections.

Quesenbury:

"Friday 12 [April] Waked up and found my pony gone. Stolen of course. Hunted---couldn't find him. Hay[661] also hunted. Some of the boys found a lake. Several of us went down to it. Great many water hens.[662] None Killed by those in the boat. Nothing on pony."

Mitchell:

"12 Fryday [April] crum & me went 2 miles to Martins and [bought] 3 bushels of corn and a tinn bayler for which I paid $2.25   we held our election at night   cregg & parks[663] were made our officers."
[near Salina, Mayes Co., Oklahoma]

---

[658]Judge John Martin, member of the Cherokee Constitutional Convention of 1827 at New Echota (Georgia) was first Treasurer of Cherokee Nation East in Georgia. He moved to Cherokee Nation West in 1837, settling at Saline in Saline District (south of Salina, Mayes County, Oklahoma). Elected the first Justice of the Supreme Court of the Cherokee Nation in 1839, he died in October 1840 at Fort Gibson. It would be logical to think that at least one of his seventeen children was living near Salina in 1850.

[659]A postoffice was licensed to his son Robert and had been operating at this location since 1849. Lewis Ross was a brother of Principal Chief John Ross.

[660]Foreman...*Marcy*...p 92 wrote that Captain Robert (?) Harris was an "experienced mountaineer who had spent half his lifetime in the Rocky Mountains." Harris planned to proceed directly "up the Arkansas River, planning to cross the mountains near its head." Robert Harris was elected lieutenant of the eighteen-wagon John Wolfe company which split from the main group on May 17 near the Santa Fe Trail. Quesenbury also went with Wolfe.

[661]This is probably Henry Hays, who disciplined Quesenbury's horse once, and who packed from Pueblo.

[662]Probably American Coot, *Fulica americana*.

[663]J[ames] T. Craig and Perry Park were the elected officers; Craig, Captain.

The areas adjacent to the Grand (Neosho) River near present
Salina, Oklahoma are now under the waters of Hudson Lake.[664] The
lake Quesenbury mentioned could be the original lake.

The Company had already spent two days waiting at the
scheduled rendezvous place (Ross'), then spent one day crossing
the river, and another waiting for the Cherokee companies.

Quesenbury:

"Saturday 13...1850...April[665] Spent a long day in crossing
Grand river. Got over at length and came out in the prairie two miles or
more to a camping place."

Mitchell:

"13 Sattureday [April] a beautiful frosty morning all made ready
to cross grand river   all appeared good umered [humored] and ready to
assist each other   our waggon was first over there being only 6 of
them in all   our little company made a gentiel appearence in the high
prararie   we camped on a beautifull branch 2 1/2 miles west of the
river only 24 men in company."
     [west of Grand (Neosho) River, Mayes Co., Oklahoma]

Quesenbury:

"Sunday ~~15~~ 14 [April] Laid by today. Wrote letters back home."

Mitchell:

"14 Sunday [April] a windy morning with the appearence of rain
here we remained the day and a long day to me   I wrote a letter back
to my family."
     [west of Grand (Neosho) River, Mayes Co., Oklahoma]

After crossing the Grand (Neosho) River, the 1850 groups (and
1849) turned northwest. The Cane Hill Company made good mileage on
April 15, overcoming the problems of wrong road and a bad creek
crossing, and finding the grass was indeed not yet up. Mitchell
had noted scarce grass as a reason given for not crossing the
Grand (Neosho) when they first got to it on April 11.

Quesenbury:

"Monday   ~~16~~ 15 [April] This morning we got a good start.
Came on without much interruption till we got to Pryor's Creek. About a
mile before we got here we took the wrong road, an came to a bad bank on
the creek. We should have taken the right hand. Got back into the right
road, and soon afterwards came to an Indian's house where we got more
corn. Camped on Pryor's[666] Creek, two miles from the Indian's."

---

[664]Salina is Oklahoma's oldest city.
[665]At the top of each page, Quesenbury wrote the year and month.
[666]Southeast of Pryor, Mayes County, Oklahoma, Pryor's Creek was named for

<u>Mitchell</u>:

"15 [April] monday ...20 miles cleer and beautifull   all made a Soon Start in hopes of geting to good grass which appeard so very desirable to all   we got about 20 miles to a branch of Pryors creek and camped neerly without grass."
        [between Adair and Chelsea, Mayes Co., Oklahoma]

The spring weather played havoc with departure of the Cherokee groups behind, reported by the Cherokee newspaper.

The California Company that is making up here and at Fort Gibson, and from the adjoining State, calculate to rendezvous on the 20th inst., on the other side of Grand River--some have already passed on, from Washington County probably, and will be joined by others as soon as they can get ready.

We are apprehensive that the backwardness of the spring will make very much against them, as their stock cannot do well without prevender[sic], and they will not be able to carry enough to last them any distance. The first week in May would suit much better for a starting period.[667]

The Cane Hill Company was one that had "already passed on."

The 1850 companies experienced the same problem crossing the Verdigris River that the 1849 Evans/Cherokee Company did--steep and muddy west banks. A high west bluff opposite the original Coody's Bluff (approximately 640 ft. elevation) hindered the 1850 crossing. An ox train had crossed ahead of them. <u>Quesenbury</u>:

"Tuesday ~~17~~ **16 [April]** Today has been a hard one on our teams. Mud holes and banks very bad. At length we came to the Verdigris River. The west bank was by far the most difficult we have seen yet. Got two wagons over--ours & Shipley's.[668] The ox team Company assisted some by pulling at the ropes. They have unasked proffered to help us with a hundred yoke of oxen if we want them. Fiddling in the ox team company tonight.[669] Sam Coody[670] in the prairie to day driving up a large drove of cattle. He has five hundred young calves this spring."

Nathaniel Pryor, Sergeant in Lewis and Clark Expedition's 1804-06 Corps of Discovery. Pryor eventually moved to this vicinity, near the creek bearing his name, where he died June 10, 1831. Grant Foreman, "Historical Phases of the Grand River Valley" *Chronicles of Oklahoma* vol 25, no 2 (Summer 1947) p 152.
[667]*Cherokee Advocate* 15 April 1850 p 2.
[668]Houston and Jess Shipley were both in the company. Both signed the agreement to Pack from Pueblo.
[669]Mitchell mentioned sixty men in Captain Edmonson's ox team company.
[670]Coody is a well-respected name in the Cherokee Nation. Emmet Starr *Old Cherokee Families* Reprinted from *History of the Cherokee Indians and their Legends and Folk Lore* (Norman, Okla: Univ. of Okalhoma Foundation 1968) pp 433-34. Samuel Coody married Sallie Riley. Sam's brother-in-law Wiley Forrester was in the 1850 Cherokee company. Sam's first cousins George Washington Keys and Richard R. Keys went to California in 1849 with the Evans/ Cherokee Company. There were two Coodys in the 1850 emigration; Joseph, and Susan Coody, who was from Bayou Menard, between Tahlequah and Fort Gibson.

<u>Mitchell</u>:

"16 [April] a rainy warm morning   we got to the verdigrees &
attempted to cross   the banks being bad 2 of the wagons got over with
great difficulty and had the offer of ox teams to help to the rest of us
over next morning if we was to wait till morning   we waited and in
vain."
     [west bank of Verdigris River between Nowata and Delaware,
                    Nowata Co., Oklahoma]

Despite the offer of help in crossing the Verdigris River,
and the conviviality of fiddling the night before, there were
strings attached to the offer made by the ox train. Mitchell was
more upset than Quesenbury about the conditions attached. The
sixty man ox train, the lead 1850 train, was captained by a Mr.
Edmonson.[671]

Along with the elections, the Cane Hill Company probably had
produced a set of regulations that included the responsibility of
guard duty.

<u>Quesenbury</u>:

"Wednesday 17 [April] The ox team company have refused us the
assistance they promised last night unless we bind ourselves to join
their company and stick to them all the way. Don't accede. Got the
wagons over without assistance or trouble. Got a new camping place,
about three hundred yards from the ox teams. Went a fishing in the
evening with Oliver, Got & Bean.[672] Caught nothing. Saw Beaver-toter in
the bottom to day; he had a Cherokee with him on a pony which I tried to
buy. He said he would be back and let me know. Guard tonight for the
first time."

----

[671]The name has been well-known in Washington County, Arkansas since at least
the 1830s. Augustus Van Edmondson married Cherokee Martha Nannie Thompson,
sister of Jeter Lynch Thompson; he would have been the right age. In Tuolumne
County, California "Index to Claims 1850-54" one J. Edmonson and partners Ira
and Henry Rose made a claim on April 12, 1852. James Mitchell's diary later
mentions a Rose in the Edmonson company. Two Edmonsons, Andrew and John T.
were with the Evans/Cherokee Company in 1849. Edmiston, Edminston and Edmonson
are variant spellings.
[672]One William Oliver, a member of the Harris contingent, was perhaps the son
of Missourian Captain Alfred Oliver. (See John L. Brown Diary). Another
William Oliver was a pioneer of Evansville, Arkansas and married Mary Jane
Smith February 21, 1850. John Gott, a Cherokee, was later elected Sergeant of
Guard under the Captaincy of Clement Vann McNair. The only Bean listed on the
1850 trip was Talbert (or Tolbert), a Cherokee. His mother, Elizabeth was a
sister of Captain McNair. Tolbert, with the Cane Hill group above, was noted
by Quesenbury nearly three weeks before the McNair and other parties united on
May 5. Tolbert died on September 9 east of Carson's Creek in present Nevada.
Communications from McNair descendant Elizabeth Fischer in California states
that another nephew, William Bean, (Tolbert's brother) accompanied McNair on
the trip. In 1850 Clem McNair was enumerated at Placerville in El Dorado
County, California.

The small company shows its determination. <u>Mitchell</u>:

> **"17 wendsday [April]** cold and cloudy   60 men with ox teams[673]
> were a cross the river in Sight of us who offered to & assist in crosing
> the river last evening and refused to help this morning unless we would
> Join their company and p[l]edge our Selves as honerable gentlemen to not
> leave it   this give us double vigger and we Soon got over without
> assistence   the most of our men wer in favor of remaining here till
> grass got better and Some of [them] went off 5 or 6 miles after corn &
> returned without any   could not get it for $1 a bushel   plainly See
> the main cause of the detension is waiting for more men to overtake us
> and go with us."

[west bank of Verdigris River, NE of Nowata, Nowata Co., Oklahoma]

This is the first of several instances of showing independence and
intent to keep themselves separated from the other groups. The
Cane Hill Company camped out in the prairie. From this point on,
dissension grew in the company. Only the first two 1850 groups had
crossed the Verdigris River: the Edmonson ox train; and the Cane
Hill California Emigrating Company horse/mule company.

    <u>Quesenbury</u>:

> **"Thursday 18 [April]** Wind blowing cold from the N. Prospect of
> very bad weather."

Continuing on the same page, Quesenbury departed from his style of
daily recordkeeping. He had somehow obtained access to the 1849
Lewis Evans Journal sent back from California with Alfred Oliver.
It is obvious that he copied the following general narrative (from
the Grand Saline to beyond the Green River in present Wyoming)
from Lewis Evans' journal. <u>Quesenbury</u>:

> Our road from the Grand Saline to the Santa Fe road is good with a few
> unimportant alterations. Here I will suggest that the best way to
> save distance would be to steer a straight course to Ft. St. Vrain. All
> those acquainted with the region say there is no impediment. This would
> shorten the distance not less than 200 [miles] in 600. from here to Ft.
> St. Vrain. The S. Platte would probably be to ferry. Taking a W. course
> probably 20 m. to Box Elder a tributary of the Cache de la Poudre. Here
> our trail enters the black hills and after passing a bluff several
> hundred feet high on the right of the road and on a small tributary of
> the Cache [la Poudre]. Probably a mile or more the stream forks we took
> the left hand but it was ascertained the right hand is the best and
> leads into the Laramie plains, and by keeping nearly N. would strike our
> trail some ten miles in the plains, but would miss some good springs

---

[673]There are three known ox team companies traveling this route in 1850. The
one above is captained by Edmonson, who was in the lead of the separated
groups, and with whom James Mitchell would travel for quite some time. Another
ox train was captained by a man named Holmes, who may have been a relative of
Calvin and Henderson Holmes, forty-niners from Bentonville, Arkansas. The
third ox train, captained by Alfred Oliver, was from southwest Missouri.

that we passed in those deep ravines. Our trail is probably on the best
route from here to Medicine Bow Creek. After crossing the Creek take to
the right and leave the Medicine Bow butte [Elk Mountain] to the left
and steer nearly N.W...crossing N. Platte which will probably be to
ferry, and leave the SweetWater Mts. to the right and passing as near to
there on the left as possible until they enter the Alkaline Plains, then
steer nearly west to the Pilot butte a mountain in shape like a wash
bowl inverted. From this it is probably 25 m. to Green river which is
close to the road.

Mid-page, at the conclusion of the narrative Quesenbury
copied mileages and campsites from the Evans Journal, and/or from
Crawford's. The mileages and campsites of the 1849 Crawford diary
very nearly match as far as "Providence" camp.

Rendezvous at Grand River	65		
Prior's Creek	15		
Caroll Camp	5		
Divide	15		
Verdigris	10		
Red-buck Creek	6		
7th South Camp	20		
Eighth Camp	20		
Pond Camp	20		
Fish Camp	20		
Rabbit Camp	7		
Elm Branch	12		
Pererco? Branch	15		
Spring Creek	12		
Rivers Creek	20		
Cotton Wood Fk. of Arkansas	20		
Wild cat Creek	20		
Bois de vache	18		
Wolf camp	20		
Little Turkey Creek Santa Fe Road	15		
Big Turkey Creek	10		
Little Arkansas	15		
Big Cow Creek	15		
Osage camp Bank of Arks	22		
Little Ash Creek	25		
Pawnee Fork of Arks	10		
Elk Camp Bank of Arks	22		
Island " " " "	22		
Fann " " " "	25		
Camp Joy	22		
Tarapin Camp	20		
Lower Chalybeate wells	20		
Upper " "	20		
Sand hill Camp	20		
Hail Camp	21 1/2		
Camp Decision	18		
FitzPatrick	20 1/2		
Picket ware Camp	20		
Ft. Bent	11	592	
Long reed	19	282	
Camp 41	16	874	
Camp 42	18	To Cherry Creek	
Pueblo	20		
Fontaine qui bouit	21 1/2		

Jimmy's Springs	21 1/4
Peninsula Prairie	15
Chry Creek	21
Camp Ham	20
Camp Platt	22
Old Ft. Saber	16 1/2
Ft. St. Vrain	13
Cache de la poudre or Ferry Platte River	17 1/2
Musgintoo Camp [Mosquito]	10 1/2
Crow camp [Box Elder]	20
Independence	18
Big Indian Grass Camp	15
Big Willow Grove	14
S.Laramie or main fork	16
Middle Fork [Laramie]	19
Godard's Creek	18
Medicine Bow Creek	15
" Butte	11
Camp Fremont	8
N. Platte	12
Mud Creek	12
Artimisia	11
Coon Camp	12 1/2
Rocky Mountain	3
Red bluff canon	14
Alkali Pond	13
Muddy water pond	16
Dry Camp	15 1/2
Providence	10
Ravine	16
Sulphur Spring	18
Piter [Bitter] Creek	11
Norris Camp	8
Clay bluff	4
Mountain bluff	15
Dry Valley	4
Green River	8 1/2
California Road	13
Caross? Swamp	5
Fork of Black river	17 1/2

A comparison of the 1849 Crawford diary with the above mileages and camps shows that only after the camp called "Providence" above, the following seven entries are names not used by Crawford.

On his next page Quesenbury concluded his entry for the day.

"1850   18 [April] Still **lying by**. Horses grazing. Rain at night. No game.

On the same day Mitchell wrote:

"18th [April] Thursday   cold & cloudy   rained towards 12 we had chickens for diner."
                    [west of Verdigris River, NE of Nowata,
                        Nowata Co., Oklahoma]

As the Cane Hill Company moved west of the Verdigris River,
one of the Cherokee companies was just beginning to travel
westward from Tahlequah, the capital of Cherokee Nation. The
Cherokee Advocate noted:

> On Thursday, April 18th, our little town [Tahlequah] was quite in a
> bustle with the California Emigrants, they (the emigrants,) making
> preparations to start their long and tedious journey, and their friends
> assisting them, and waiting to bid them farewell and to wish them great
> success in their undertaking. Four wagons and their accompaniment of
> persons leave this place today, to join others who have gone ahead, and
> the Washington and Benton county emigrants, who are to meet them on the
> west side of Grand River, and form the trail for the far west. They
> calculate traveling Capt. Evans' Route, except where they may shorten it
> by cut offs.
>
> May peace, prosperity, and health attend them.[674]

The Cane Hill Company continued to wait for the Cherokees on
the cold, wet prairie. The elected company leaders were out
seeking a "cutoff" from the 1849 Evans/Cherokee trail. Quesenbury:

> **"Friday...19 [April]** Mr. Craig and others went to view out our
> way ahead. Got my horse ready to go with them. Wouldn't let me ride him.
> Head today. Hays[675] rode him after Perry[676] whipped him down into the
> timber. Went up with Crum and others to graze the animals in the bottom.
> Rained hard. Built a fire. Some of the ox team company came to us. Back.
> Dinner. Today Perry [Parks] and myself commenced cooking."

Mitchell:

> **"19th [April] Fryday** cold & rainy   I took a land walk a
> beautifull farming country good land timber & water   Our captain[,]
> gott & Rogers[677] went to look out a neirer way than the Evans trale
> determined to Start tomorow on our Jurney   I have to ceep the
> Strongest lookout to ceep my mare from leaving me."

[west of Verdigris River, NE of Nowata, Nowata Co. Oklahoma]

The Cane Hill Company moved northwest to California Creek.
Mitchell made no diary mention of wanting to go directly to
Council Grove, which would take emigrants toward the main
Oregon/California Trail. Mitchell was, however, extremely anxious
to be away, and grew increasingly agitated.

---

[674]*Cherokee Advocate* 22 April 1850 p 2.
[675]Henry Hays is mentioned here and as a signer of the Agreement to pack from
Pueblo (Colorado).
[676]Perry Parks. In the James Sawyer Crawford letters exchanged in 1849 and
early 1850, Harriet Crawford wrote her husband: "there is a good many persons
talking of going to California in the Spring [1850] Isaac Spencer H Hanks
Perey Parks Craig the merchant James West."
[677]"Captain" is James Craig, "gott" is John Gott, Cherokee, who later became
Sgt. of the Guard in the McNair company. Rogers is not yet identified.

Quesenbury:

"Saturday 20 [April] Got ready and started. Ox teams off also. On the top of the hill in the prairie we left Evans' trail [by] taking to the right. Waited twenty minutes for the Tennesseeans who have actually joined us. Came on without trouble till we got to a creek[678] about four miles from Verdigris where we were camped. Crossed two forks of it and camped. On the last fork we worked some.[679] Some went a fishing nothing but little perch I caught 32. Started with Craig to day to view out the way. The little black mule followed some distance but turned back. I came back to camp in search of it. Then went a fishing. An express from Meigs[680] got up. I wish Meigs had never been heard of as connected with this company. Mitchell talks of taking a straight shoot for Council Grove."

Mitchell:

"20 [April] Satureday all made ready to Start on our Journey the ox company Started first. 3 men from Tenessee Joined us which made our company 27 Strong we took a cut Said to be nearor than the road travele last year [Evans'] and we would gain 2 days travel in 5 days we Stoped in 3 miles to grase [graze] and Send men ahead to look [for] a camping place our men returned and reported that there was good grass in 5 miles ahead our capt concluded that it was to late to go to it that evening and we Stayed here till monday a rich low overflowed country on a creek that routs in to the verdigrey this unessary delay I profisied would harm when our lookouts Started in the morning that it was only done to blind to decieve and in fact to wait for more company late in the evening here come a cherocee runer informing us that there company [was] comeing on and they wished [us] to wait I Saw at one [once] it pleased Some of our leading men and they were determined to wait for them I determined to not wait and [instead to] go on it being 8 days Since we left the Branch on Grand river & only have traveled about 40 miles. we could of traveled in the Same time 80 miles at least and our animels in as good a condision as they are and of had as much corn & provision as we now have."
[on California Creek SW of Delaware, Nowata Co., Oklahoma]

Both Quesenbury and Mitchell expressed negative feelings about Return Jonathan Meigs, in the company catching up to them. Neither of them ever explained why. Perhaps because Meigs was a son-in-law of Cherokee Chief John Ross. If most of Quesenbury and Mitchell's Cherokee friends were from either the "Treaty Party" or the "Old Settler" groups, there would be animosity toward Chief John Ross

---

[678]Mormon Creek and California Creek. Both were appropriately named for those that passed this way. Mormon Creek was named following 1853, when a company of Texas Mormons wintered in the vicinity.
[679]They had to "work" the banks i.e., dig them down to get the wagons across.
[680]Return Jonathan Meigs, wealthy trader, was grandson of longtime Indian Agent (1801-23) Return Jonathan Meigs. The younger R. J. married Jennie Ross, daughter of Chief John Ross. A "gang" burned his Park Hill home late in 1845. Early in 1849 he advertised in the *Cherokee Advocate* to sell out, intending at that time to travel by ship via Panama to California. There were two Ross-named men also on this 1850 trip: H. and Jonathan.

and members of his group.[681] They may have resented Meigs because
he was well-to-do, a businessman in Tahlequah, or residing in Park
Hill in Cherokee Nation. Mitchell and Quesenbury attributed the
delay to Cherokee in general, and Meigs in particular.

On Sunday April 20 Cherokee diarist John Lowery Brown left
his aunt's home east of present Stilwell, Oklahoma. Distance alone
means that Brown was not part of the Cherokee company that Return
J. Meigs was a member of, which was approaching the east side of
the Verdigris River.

Quesenbury and Mitchell, with the Cane Hill boys, were
obliged to wait again, over Sunday and yet another day before
starting on the journey. They wrote on as they waited for the
other companies. While Mitchell was seething and impatient to get
underway, Quesenbury seemed to be taking everything in stride.
Both made good use of the Sunday.

Quesenbury:

"1850 April 21. Sunday. Laid by to day. Some are still
discontented and talk of leaving. Mr. May thought of preaching in the
evening but declined.[682] Wrote letters back home."

Dissension in the Cane Hill Company grew, over issues
including whether to "pack" or stay with wagons. Mitchell and
Strickler wanted to pack so they could travel faster. Robinson was
annoyed because he carried in his wagon goods belonging to both
the others. Here is another example of not wanting to be bound to
any company or any other individual. Mitchell:

"21 [April] Sunday warm   a little rain in the morning   wind
wind brisk from the South   our Cheracee who come up with us last
evening Started back with 2 of our men with him to See if the [Meigs]
company had got to the river   I talked Strong of Starting on in the
packing with my 2 poneys   Strickler was Strongly in faver of going on
also   Robinson[683] appeared very angry at us and urged that we Should

---

[681]Quesenbury recorded a trip to Texas in 1845-46 with anti-Ross Cherokee.
[682]Rev. J.J. May was listed in the 1850 census as 23 years old living in Cane
Hill. Many wives or heads of families listed their husbands and/or sons as
living in Arkansas even though they were on their way to or prospecting in
California. In this group were William May, Peter May and and J.J. He is
listed in the 1852 California Census at "Mary's Diggins" with William May,
Hicks, A. Delano, J. Delavan, and Capt. Wilson.
[683]Robinson is identified only with a single name throughout the diaries. He
did own a wagon, in which both Mitchell and Strickler put some goods. Later he
threw the belongings out on the prairie, going ahead with Edmonson's company.

bind our Selves before we went any further to continue with the waggon
under any circumstances   we give him a positive refusel without he
would bind himself also to travel a constant dayly gate [daily gait] to
the mines.   I put on a cleen Shirt for the first time after leaving home
our men returned back from the river   the...long looked for great &
much esteemed Megs &co had not yet arrived at the [river] to great
disapointment of Some of our leating [leading] men   Some women are
Said to be coming with them who it is Supposed will be very desirable to
some of our leading men..."

[On California Creek, SW of Delaware, Nowata Co., Oklahoma]

The thought that women would influence decisions on the journey
west was repugnant to Mitchell. The women in question were from
the Cherokee California Emigrating Company which had its initial
meetings at the home of one of them, Susan Coody.

Foreman quoted a letter dated May 7, 1850 about the women in
question:

California has drawn a good number of the people of Bayou Menard off
this spring. Mrs. Susan Coody, M[argaret] Merrell, James Colston's wife,
M[argaret] Scott, and E[lizabeth] Terrel[684] among the lot. M[argaret]
Scott left walking with her all on her back.[685]

While the Cane Hill company waited, they went fishing.

Quesenbury:

"**Monday 22 [April]**   Went a fishing down the creek. Caught two
small trouts and three fine cats [catfish]. Mr. Mitchell brought me a
biscuit. He and Strickler fished with me. Went as far as the mouth of
the creek."

Mitchell:

"**22nd Monday [April]** extrmely cold and blustry   Strickler
cush[686] & me went a fishing & caut a fine mess of fish for Supper
Robinson eat Some   news come to us from the river that part of company
we were staying here for had got to the river and were waiting for our
assistance to get over and Join us   the women Spoken of who were to of

---

But he also managed to leave signs and signatures along the trail, in rock and
wood, that were seen by others.

[684]the wives of James Colston, Sam Coody, ---Merrill, Lige Terrill, and
Sanford Scott. Starr...*Cherokee*...p 433 lists a Susie Fields married to
Charles Coody. A brother-in-law Wiley Forrester was in the 1850 group. Another
possibility is Sam Coody, same family, who was on the trip, who was married to
Sallie Riley. Ibid. p 455. Margaret Merrell, youngest child of Benjamin
Merrell and Nannie Thompson. Ibid. p 447. Margaret Scott married Joseph Kell,
whose aunt Elizabeth Kell (p 442) was married to Lewis Ralston, a member of
the 1850 party, credited with the gold find on Ralston Creek north of Denver,
Colorado on June 22, 1850.

[685]Letter from Lewis Riley to John Drew. Authors were unable to locate these
letters at the Oklahoma Historical Society in Oklahoma City, or during an
earlier visit to the Thomas/Foreman Library in Muskogee.

[686]This is the first time in his diary that James Mitchell refers to William
Quesenbury as "Cush," a nickname used by Arkansans then and now.

been with them were not along and had Joined another company at Fort Gibson and went up the ark river. with great Satisfaction we learned the great and venerable Megs had arived here at the river and was waiting for assistince to cross next morning."

So much for waiting for the women. Mitchell must have been pleased. He exulted in not having to assist the Meigs party cross the Verdigris River, and seemed satisfied with the captain's assurance that they would proceed the next day. On the other hand, the waiting began to rankle even Quesenbury. They both fished as they waited. The fish were an additional source of food.

Quesenbury:

"Tuesday 23 [April] Lying by yet eating up our provisions. I went up the creek to day with Got, who soon left me. I went higher up, and caught four of the very finest kind of trouts. Meigs and Cunningham[687] got up this evening. Fished again at night with May[,] H Shipley[,] Got.[688]   Shipley caught a gar.   Got a cat."

Mitchell:

"23rd [April] Tuesday cold and frosty   Soon one man out of each mess was detailed out to assist the venerable Megs &co in giting over the river   I had the good luck to escape this labor and went a fishing again. on ariving at my hook that I Staked out last evening there was a fine cat fish on it plenty for our dinner   Osage Indians in our camps   crum and me got a buffelow robe from them to ly on $2.25 price   our capt assures us that when thes men at the river gits up with us that he will proceed on regular and wait no more for back company to overtak us   2 of these long lookd for waggons Joined us late in the evening and Megs with them   4 more waggons were gone to another crosing five miles up the river who we expected to git with us tomorow."

[California Creek, SW of Delaware, Nowata Co., Oklahoma]

Quesenbury went fishing again; then built a raft.

"Wednesday 24 [April] Several of us went up again a fishing H. Shipley and myself headed the long hole. Jo Williams[689] and myself made a raft. and floated about on it. I caught a trout, Brought my raft down to the old sycamore and left it."

Some folks from home caught up with the train attempting to recover property. Mitchell sent letters back with them. Despite

[687]Meigs and Alfred Cunningham were both with the Cherokee party. Meigs was Alfred's uncle. Another uncle, Andrew Ross Nave, married Meigs' widow after Meigs' death on the Hastings Cutoff. Cunningham died in Sacramento on about February 19, 1851.

[688]Would be more clear if Quesenbury had written Shipley *and* Gott. "Got a cat" means Mr. Gott caught a catfish.

[689]Joseph Lynch[?] Williams is noted only four times in Quesenbury's diary; but one of those is his name on the agreement to pack from Pueblo. Joseph's cousins William Wirt Buffington and John Lynch Adair, and Tom Clark, were forty-niners in their cousin Jeter Lynch Thompson's party.

the captain's assurance of the day before, they again waited, for
four more wagons, which would make the company, including Meigs,
thirteen wagons and forty-nine men.

Mitchell:

"24th [April] wendsday more frost   Some of my acquaintances
overtook us after a mule from John [J.J.] May   John would not give up
the mule   we Sent back letters by them   fish did not bite well this
day   we learn that our company will be 49 men Strong and 13 waggons[690]
when these last naimed 4 waggons Joins us   sufficient to go on."
[California Creek, SW of Delaware, Nowata Co., Oklahoma]

Cherokee and others continued to arrive. On Thursday
Quesenbury and Mitchell and the Cane Hill Company moved slowly. At
the campsite, Quesenbury committed what would prove to be an
almost disastrous act involving the Osage who had come to their
camp the day before. Quesenbury:

"Thursday 25 [April-6 miles][691] Started and came on till we
met Coody He then guided us to the present camp. Eleven wagons are at
the river. Went down to a drove of Osage horses. An Indian was washing
them in the creek. There was only one good mule. Back and camped. Broke
a stick over an Osage's head. Considerable excitement in camp about it.
Thought I had more enemies than friends, though my friends, few as they
were, were worth a prairie full of travelers such as opposed me."

The "considerable excitement" brought on by Quesenbury's
indiscretion was based in historical experience. Cherokee and
Osage had a sometimes uneasy peace since territorial disputes of
1821. In 1841, Major Ethan Allen Hitchcock, inspecting the Indian
Territory for fraud involved with the Removal of tribes, said in
his report that tribes in the area had never been any danger to
the frontier or to U.S. citizens but:

the Osages...have committed more depredations in Missouri than all the
other Indians together....These are the Indians... that require to be
over-awed by the presence of a Military force.[692]

Quesenbury's indelicate act was not even mentioned by

---

[690]The original Cane Hill Company was six wagons and twenty-four men. Four men
from Tennessee joined, presumably with one wagon. Meigs came with two wagons;
four more wagons brought the total to thirteen wagons and forty-nine men.
[691]Quesenbury begins to add the mileages traveled each day in the left margin
under the current date.
[692]Grant Foreman, ed. *A Traveler in Indian Territory: The Journal of Ethan
Allen Hitchcock, late Major-General in the United States Army* (Cedar Rapids,
Iowa: The Torch Press 1930) p 247.

<u>Mitchell</u>:

> **"25th [April] Thursday...8 miles** we Started   cleer
> morning and warm   we expected [to] find our 4 waggons five miles above
> here in hopes they had crosed the river last evening   we lerned they
> had not crosed and would not cross before tomorow   we went to a large
> creek about 8 miles and, Stoped to wait again   our capt and others
> went Back to the [river] to learn when the other waggons would cross
> he returned Bringing news that they would cross next day and part of
> them ox teams[693] not suited to travel with us."
>
> [California Creek, southwest of Lenapah, Nowata Co.,Oklahoma]

Here we are spectators of an immediate result of Quesenbury
breaking a stick over the head of an Osage. Either Quesenbury and
Mitchell were in different places (one gives mileage as six; the
other as eight) or Mitchell simply did not pay attention to the
deed. This was not the last of the company's encounters with Osage
over the act. They would see them again on May 2. News of
Quesenbury's incident traveled back to the *Advocate*. On May 5 "Our
(Cherokee) California Emigrants" wrote, as they were traveling:

> They were considerably surprised by a company of forty Osages, who
> offered some violence to one or two of their company who were out some
> distance from the camp grazing their horses. But when the Osages
> ascertained that the company was composed principally of Cherokees, they
> desisted from further violence, and hoisted the flag of peace. They
> suppose that the reason the Osages ordered any violence, was in
> consequence of the ill treatment some had received from Capt. Craig's
> company [Cane Hill], supposing them [Cherokee] to be some of the
> same.[694]

Another incidence report made its way to the newspaper:

> Report says, that some of the company have had a brush with some of the
> Indians, but no mention is made of it in the letter. We presume it
> cannot be so, unless it happened since they wrote.[695]

Meanwhile other companies were behind, traveling toward the
anticipated rendezvous. Samuel Houston Mayes of Muddy Springs was
the assumed captain of one group. Foreman lists Samuel Houston
Mayes and sons George Washington Mayes and John Thompson Mayes;
Richard Fields; Looney L. Rattlingourd; James Shelton; Edward E.
Bushyhead and brother Daniel Bushyhead, Sam Lasley, Will Goss,
William Holt, Charley Holt, Ben Goss, Ben Trott, Zeke Byers, Bose

---

[693]The Holmes ox company, since Edmonson was ahead and Oliver did not leave
Missouri until April 27.
[694]*Cherokee Advocate* 27 May 1850, editor's column p 2 col 1.
[695]*Cherokee Advocate* Monday 24 June 1850, editor's column p 2 col 1.

Simcoe, Lige Terrill, Devereaux Jarrette Bell and wife Juliette Vann.[696] Cherokee diarist John Lowery Brown left home with Jonas, a black, joining other Cherokees from around Stilwell, which included the Mayes and Adair family members. Brown's diary begins:

"Journal kept by J.L. Brown of the Cherokee Nation Route
From Grand Saline (C.N.) to California June 3d, 1850.[697]
Off for California
April, 1850

"20 April...12 miles Left Mrs Packs[698] & came to Mrs Gilbreaths-"

"21 [April-Sunday]   Lay by all day --"

"22 [April]...10 miles... Brought the waggon to Lewis Meltons. Staid at Grandfathers [699]--"

The next day this company, headed by Samuel Houston Mayes Sr., passed through Tahlequah, the capital of Cherokee Nation. They were five days behind a four-wagon Cherokee group noted in the *Cherokee Advocate* as leaving on April 18.

Brown:

"23 [April]...1 mile... Came on by to Tahlequah and on to Mothers[700] -."
            [Cherokee Co., Oklahoma]

"24 [April] Lay by all day."

"25 [April]...25 miles... Started with the waggon and left it & came on to Grand River --."
            [south of Salina, Mayes Co., Oklahoma]

---

[696] Foreman...*Marcy*...p 110.

[697] On June 3, Brown's company, Captained by Clem Vann McNair was at Camp 27 east of Deerfield, west of the Kearny/Finney Counties line, Kansas. They had just come through the great Indian/Trader gathering conducted by Indian Agent Thomas Fitzpatrick. Brown may have purchased his pocket-sized diary there.

[698] John's mother Rachel Lowery's first cousin Elizabeth Lowery married William Shorey Pack. Starr...*Cherokee*...p 367. Mrs. Pack lived a mile east of Stilwell (Oklahoma) on the side of a hill. Nearby Muddy Springs (Adair County) was a rendezvous for emigrants on their way to California during the gold rush. Samuel Mayes and family lived at Muddy Springs. Foreman...*Marcy*...p 110.

[699] George Lowery Jr. was John's maternal grandfather. He was born in Tennessee; was a major and veteran of the War of 1812; and was elected assistant Principal Chief in 1847.

[700] Rachel Lowery Brown Orr. Her first husband David Brown, John Lowery Brown's father, was born in 1801 and died in 1829.

Brown:

"26 [April] the waggon came on with Adairs.[701] I staid at Clarks."[702]

Written on April 27, a letter noted other departures and the routes taken, including an important statement about travelers over the 1849 Evans/Cherokee route:

Jinings [Jenings?][703] has left for California....The Tah-le-quah California Company leaves this place tomorrow; [April 28] and a company from the Creek Nation will leave the fifth of next month. This company will go the Southern Route, and I believe that all the other companies has gone Evins's Route.[704]

Brown crossed the Grand (Neosho) River.

Brown:

"27 [April] Crossed the [Grand River with the] waggon [corner Journal worn, writing faded]."

Brown had barely left home, traveling only forty-eight miles from April 20 to 27. He spent that time going from relative to relative, including his grandfather and mother. The diary mentions only Adairs as co-travelers during those few days. The Mayes company rendezvoused with Cherokee Thomas Fox Taylor and Devereaux Jarrett Bell at the Grand (Neosho) River. Here Brown began numbering campsites, a practice he would keep up throughout the entire journey to California. The campsite numbers and locations are shown on maps in Appendix A in this book, indicated by an arrow and the number.

---

[701]George Washington Adair and his oldest son, twenty-year-old William Penn Adair traveled in this group with John Lowery Brown. G.W. Adair's brothers-in-law were Brice Martin, who died from cholera near North Platte, Nebraska in 1849; and Gabriel Martin, who traveled with this party in 1850, dying before reaching California. G.W. Adair's sister-in-law Susannah Martin was the wife of Clement Vann McNair, captain of this party at the beginning of the trip. When they united with the Clement Vann McNair party, they were traveling with cousins Mayes, Trott, Goss, and Candy. These cousins appeared in the 1850 California Census in El Dorado County, all in the same house.

[702]Joseph Henry Clark married Mary Polly Ward, whose mother was Lucy Mayes, sister of Samuel Houston Mayes, Sr.

[703]An Anderson Crittenden Jennings was married to Martha Jane Landrum, first cousin once-removed of both Elizabeth Kell and Emily Duncan, whose husbands Lewis Ralston and John Beck were in the 1850 Cherokee company.

[704]Lewis Riley to John Drew, April 12 and 27, 1850. Letters reportedly at Thomas/Foreman Library, Muskogee, Oklahoma.

The next three days' travel took the company from the Grand (Neosho) River to the Verdigris River. Brown:

"**April 28 [15 miles]** Left Grand River in company with T.F. Taylors[705] & D. J. Bells[706] waggons....Gentle Rolling Hills.... Camped on the first prong of Pryors creek, which shall be called --**Camp 1st**."
    [west of Adair, Mayes Co., Oklahoma]

"**29 [April]...18 miles**...Camped on Salt creek near Mrs. Coodeys[707]....**Camp 2.**"
    [about six miles east of Nowata; south of U.S. 60 two miles; Nowata Co., Oklahoma]

"**30 [April]...8 miles** Crossed Verdigrice River and camped on the west Bank **(Camp 3d)** --."
    [two miles east of Nowata, Nowata Co., Oklahoma]

"**May 1st Lay bye** all day --."

This small, mostly related Cherokee group was on the way to join the main 1850 Cherokee emigrating company. They did not catch up to the main company until May 5. Two days ahead of diarist Brown and Mayes' company, was the main Cherokee company. No diarist has been found for the early part of the journey of the Clement Vann McNair group.[708] Once united, Brown was diarist for the whole Cherokee company for the entire journey.

From southwest Missouri came another group, primarily an ox train, led by Captain Alfred Oliver.[709] Besides the now-and-again

---

[705]Thomas Fox Taylor was born in Tennessee and was perhaps 37 years old. His sister Mary Jane married Dr. Jeter Lynch Thompson, captain of the ill-fated 1849 Cherokee "cholera " company. Thomas Fox Taylor's sister Eliza Christine was married to Jeter's brother Johnson Thompson, who left for California by boat early in 1850.

[706]Devereaux Jarrette Bell's brother Samuel W. Bell died in 1849 of cholera near North Platte, Nebraska on his way to California with Jeter Lynch Thompson. Devereaux' sister Sallie Caroline was married to Stand Watie. Devereaux' wife Juliette Lewis Vann traveled with him to California in 1850, where they stayed for at least five years. His cousin George Washington Adair with his son were along in 1850 too, as was Samuel Mayes, his cousin's husband.

[707]Daniel Ross Coody and his family had lived there for some time. He married Amanda Drew, Sarah Ross, a cousin, and Eliza Levisa Bennett. William Shorey Coody was his brother; a sister Flora married army man Daniel Henry Rucker, leader of the 1849 rescue in the California Sierra snows. Starr...*Cherokee* ...pp 410-11.

[708]Some of the men of the original California Emigrating Company joined Captain McNair's group, including Richard Fields, William L. Holt, and John H. Wolfe. Wolfe would captain a breakaway wagon group May 17.

[709]One Alfred Oliver erected a 3 1/2 story distillery, one of the first

mentions in the John Lowery Brown diary, only an obscure reference
has been found to indicate the existence of the Oliver train. No
record of company members has been found. Company member Cherokee
Barbara Hildebrand Longknife provided a glimpse of the beginning
of the 1850 emigration in Oliver's train. Longknife:

> My husband [William Longknife] and I started for California the 27th day
> of April 1850 from Stand Watie's[710] on Honey Creek. Stand Watie
> accompanied us to the Verdigris the place appointed for the start. Capt.
> Oliver a Missourian took command.

Barbara, 22, was pregnant at the time the trip began. Her first
daughter Mary Jane was born "at the foot of the Sierra Nevada"
before they reached California on October 6.[711] Barbara's brother
John Hildebrand, called "Jack," was also on the trip.[712]

Fort Smith Herald editor Wheeler printed the route he thought
Oliver planned to take:

> California Emigrants from Missouri going the Fort Smith route.
> Mr. A. Oliver, with a company from the south-west corner of Missouri,
> intends taking the Fort Smith route to California. Mr. O. arrived from
> California a few days ago and is now about returning. The great quantity
> of emigrants on the Missouri route deters him from going that way. He
> says that the forage along the road cannot support the number of animals
> that will be taken that route, and that a great deal of suffering will
> be the consequence. Look to it ye emigrants.[713]

When Alfred Oliver had returned from California to Fort Smith with
Lewis Evans' Journal of the 1849 trip, editor Wheeler refused to
print it. Captain Oliver was still in possession of the journal as

---

establishments in McDonald County, Missouri. Olivers settled along Patterson
Creek in the early 1840s. J. A. Sturgess, ed./comp. *Illustrated History of
McDonald County, Missouri* (Pineville, Mo.: 1897) p 45. The 1840 Missouri State
Census lists Alfred Oliver in Marion Township, Newton County; in 1844 the
election place was moved from Alfred Oliver's; Alfred was a road overseer; in
1845 he was authorized to keep a ferry at Elk River. In the 1850 McDonald
County Census there were four Olivers. One Alfred Oliver was listed as 46
years old, a farmer whose net worth was $2,000. Of his eight children, a son,
William H. was old enough to accompany his father to California in 1850. A
second Alfred in the census was 35, from Tennessee. There is an Oliver's
Prairie (50 square miles of rich land--the county's first settlement), and an
Oliver Cemetery in Newton County, Missouri.
[710]Stand Watie was one of the 1835 Removal Treaty signers; and a Confederate
General in the Civil War. He and his family lived and are buried in Southwest
City, McDonald County, Missouri. Stand Watie would have known Alfred Oliver.
[711]In late 1865 Barbara took her two daughters, Mary Jane and Anna Diane, to
Hawaii. Barbara is buried in Nuuanu Cemetery in Honolulu.
[712]John Hildebrand died in California in 1852.
[713]*Fort Smith Herald* 4 May 1850 vol 3, no 36, p 2.

he set out for California, not on the "Fort Smith route to California" as editor Wheeler printed, but on the 1849 Evans/Cherokee Trail.

When Captain Oliver's Missouri company crossed over the Verdigris, all of the major 1850 Cherokee/white companies were on the 1849 Evans/Cherokee Trail toward the Santa Fe Trail. They traveled as a loose caravan the entire trip, sometimes catching up with and passing one another. Perhaps it was as well because of the sometimes scarce wood, water, and grass.

The Cherokee Trail would again prove to be a healthy trail, remaining disease-free for 1850 travelers.

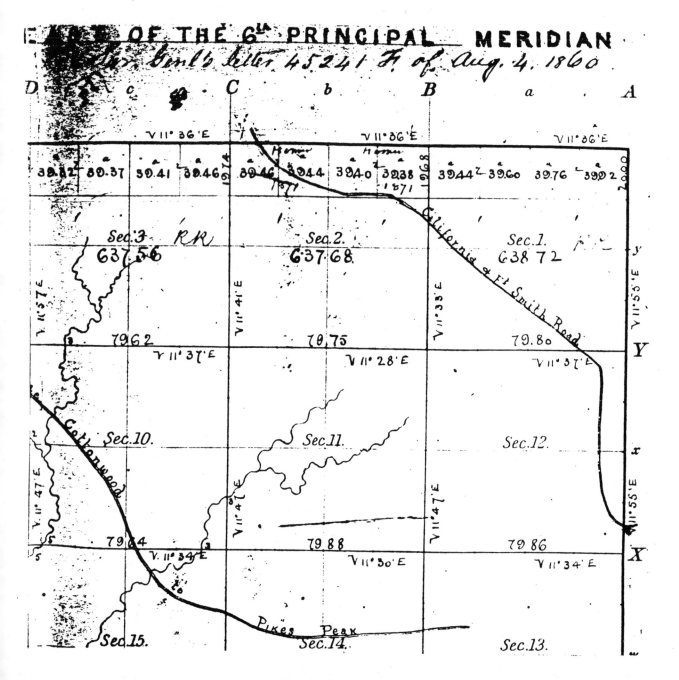

Chapter 3. VERDIGRIS TO TURKEY CREEK

**The Cherokees have gone Male and Female to join in
this Golden scramble, with families [left] behind**
--Cherokee Advocate 10 June 1850

No journal has been uncovered for the first 1850 company to cross the Verdigris River--the Edmonson ox train, which was reported by diarists William C. Quesenbury and James Mitchell to be sixty men and one hundred yoke of oxen. The composition of the company is uncertain. Few names are available from printed sources. The Edmonson Company proceeded at a consistent pace west from the Verdigris River.

Diarists Mitchell and Quesenbury were with the second group to cross the Verdigris River--The Cane Hill California Emigrating Company. It started out as six wagons and twenty-four men, some of them Cherokee, and was later joined by three Tennesseans.

There were four other groups that subsequently crossed the Verdigris to join in a loose association for the journey to California. The Return Jonathan Meigs' Cherokee group crossed first, with a reported six wagons and twenty-two men, increasing the Cane Hill California Company total to thirteen wagons and forty-nine men. Mitchell wrote on April 26 : "Our expected company come up with us this day and was ready to Start with us next morning." West of the Verdigris River the enlarged Cane Hill Company proceeded slowly for eight more days waiting for the McNair/Wolfe combined Cherokee companies to catch up.

Captain Holmes' ox train's crossing of the river is unknown, but was perhaps that referred to on April 26 by Mitchell "part of them [are] ox teams not suited to travel with us." Cherokee diarist John Lowery Brown later reported: "a Train of ox waggons, 20 waggons, came up this evening" on May 27 (near present Garfield, Kansas). This was evidently Holmes' train.

The Clement Vann McNair Cherokee group, joined by the John Wolfe Cherokee party crossed the Verdigris on April 28.

Diarist Brown reported that Sam Houston Mayes' Cherokee party of twelve wagons and twenty men crossed on April 30, and caught up with the combined Cherokee McNair/Cane Hill companies on May 5.

Brown stated on May 6 "Left Tom [Fox] Taylor to wait for another crowd" which was an eight-horse wagon group that finally joined them May 26 at Brown's Camp #21 near Garfield, Kansas.

Capt. Alfred Oliver's ox train from Missouri also joined the caravan. Leaving southwest Missouri on April 27, they were reported in a letter to the *Cherokee Advocate* "[joined] by a party from Missouri and Arkansas, of about forty persons."[716]

Waiting with their Cane Hill Company on today's California Creek, the Quesenbury and Mitchell diaries continue the day after Quesenbury hit an Osage over the head with a stick. Mitchell was sent out to look for the 1849 Evans/Cherokee trail, and Quesenbury had another incident with the Osage.

Quesenbury:

"Friday 26 [April] Coody came over just after an Osage had run his horse against me. They wanted to Swap. Wouldn't do it. Perry went back with Coody. May, Mitchell and some others went ahead to view out the way. At night Perry came back with a poor, blind Dun colored mule that he had given the Hank mare for. He got four buffalo skins y cinco pesos[717] to boot."

Mitchell:

"26 {April] Fryday a beautifull morning   John Gott Cuningham & me were detailed out to go ahead that day & find Evans trail Supposed 15 or 20 miles beyond us   we Started and had a hard day of it not even took time to graze our horses and took us till after dark to get back to camps   we found Evanss trail about 18 miles ahead and and looked out way to cross the creek and raveens   we wounded a deer and Saw 3 elk our expected company come up with us this day and was ready to Start with us next morning."
                    [wagons stayed on California Creek]

The long-awaited start of the newly-enlarged company was hardly mentioned by Quesenbury.

"Saturday 27 [April...15 miles]   Started tolerably early. Cunningham[718] lagged back but we got him along. Some of the new comers that came last night lost a mule. John Pierce[719] was in their crowd.

---

[716]*Cherokee Advocate* 27 May 1850 p 2.

[717]"y cinco pesos" means "and five dollars." Mexican silver was common currency of the time. Quesenbury was familiar with it from his 1845 trip to Texas and his participation in the War with Mexico.

[718]Alfred Cunningham, soon to be wagonmaster.

[719]John's brother James Pierce [Pearce] made the 1849 trip with the Evans/Cherokee Company. They were perhaps the first to cross that desert with

There are two ox teams, four cows and three bulls. Camped along the same stream we came to day before yesterday. Meigs, Cunningham, and others below us. Fished in the evening for trout, caught none. A chap of the last crowd fished with me with cheese for bait."

Now that he knew the location of the Evans trail to the west, Mitchell couldn't help being sarcastic about their slow pace.

"27 [April] Saturday...about 12 miles...all Started 13 waggons and traveled about 12 miles and camped near the head of the Same creek we left this morning to remain till next morning Buchanan saw a wolf cetch a turkey and took it from the wolf that is a Shame..."
[headwaters of California Creek, east of Wann,
Nowata Co., Oklahoma]

In the 1849 company, John Rankin Pyeatt had attached a "roadomiter" to one wagon. Evidently there was not yet a mileage measuring device in this 1850 group. Quesenbury wrote 15 miles; Mitchell wrote 12. The company waited again. Quesenbury:

"Sunday 28 [April] Laid by. Some of the new comers went a hunting. In the evening at 3 o'clock Mr. May preached. Nearly all our crowd atended."

Mitchell spent another day reconnoitering the Evans trail.

"28 [April] Sonday cold & winday I took a trip Back to the Evans trail to try and discover a _ _ _? and better way than we looked out [found] the other day and found a better and nearor way to the trail and much better   our back company all come up 49 men."
[headwaters of California Creek east of Wann,
Nowata Co.,Oklahoma]

On this same Sunday the Jonathan Wolfe Cherokee group crossed the Verdigris, and wrote letters. The *Cherokee Advocate* editor reiterated some incidents of the trip, including the Osage help they hired to cross the swollen Verdigris River.

We received a few lines from our California friends[720] who left here on the 18th ultimo. They wrote from the west side of the Verdigris River on the 28th [April]. They were all well and in good spirits--they had been laying by five or six days; partly, in consequence of being convenient to corn for their teams, as the grass was rather short and young to subsist on.
They also state that they will cut off 25 miles, by leaving Evans' route about one mile this side of Mrs. Coodey's, and crossing the Verdigris six miles above at a place called the "Hickory Bluffs," and intersecting the Evans' trail again some twelve or fifteen miles from the crossing.[721] By traveling a northwest course the road is a good level, prairie way; and the ford at Verdigris is said to be the best on

wagons in 1849. James was in Park City, Utah in 1902.
[720]Unfortunately editor Carter did not identify these "California friends."
[721]The newspaper editor has confused the reader. The letter writer has already crossed the Verdigris.

the river. The river was past fording when they got to it. They were consequently compelled to employ some Osages, that were encamped near the crossing, to assist them in getting over. The Osages soon constructed a water-craft out of buffalo skins, and crossed their baggage safely. After which they were able to get their wagons and teams over without much difficulty. At this place they[722] were joined by C.V. McNair--making their company thirty-five strong. Mr. Craig and [enlarged Cane Hill] company was some twelve miles in advance.

On the morning of the 29th, our friends expected to take up the line of march for the golden region of the far west. So we presume they have left the west banks of the Verdigris after having exhilarated their appetites, as they say, with "an excellent pot of turtle soup"-- some of their own cooking--"very excellent"[723]

On Monday April 29, the McNair and Wolfe groups held elections and wrote a Constitution. The Constitution was adopted and sent with the letter to the *Advocate*. Constitutional Articles were tested before the company reached the Santa Fe Trail.

Fifteen Mile Creek,
May 1st, 1850.

Mr. Carter--*Dear Sir*:--It is made my duty as Secretary to the Cherokee California Emigrating Company, to forward to you for publication, the rules and regulations as adopted by them, for their government during their journey via the Prairies, together with their officer names, and also the names of all the men composing said company,[724] which you can give a place in the Advocate if you please for the gratification of our friends which we have left behind. (I presume it will be interesting to some, to learn who our officers are, and what kind of rules we have adopted, for our government and protection.)

Constitution of the Cherokee Emigrating California Company

Art.1st. This company shall consist of the following officers, viz.: One Captain, one Lieutenant, one Sergeant of Guard, one Wagonmaster, a Committee of twelve persons to transact business, and a Secretary, all of which shall be elected by a vote of the majority of the Company, to serve during good behavior.

Art. 2d. The duty of the Captain shall be determined when the company shall start their manner of traveling, &c., &c. And he shall see that the laws and regulations of this company be strictly and rigidly enforced on all occasion, and in short, have a complete oversight of all the movements of the company.

Art. 3d. The duties of the Lieutenant shall be to perform all the duties of the Captain in case of inability or absence, and otherwise be subject to the direction and order of the Captain.

Art. 4th. The duties of the Sergeant shall be to mount the guard, and visit the same at least once during each night, at an hour most convenient to himself. He shall each night have one relief Corporal.

Art. 5th. The duties of the Wagon Master shall be first, to see that all wagons belonging to the company are kept in good repair. Secondly,

---

[722]This is John Wolfe's group. The Clem Vann McNair party crossed on April 28. This party "were joined by C.V. McNair."

[723]*Cherokee Advocate* 6 May 1850 p 2.

[724]Apparently editor David Carter either thought the company members' names unimportant, or he didn't have enough room to print them. Unfortunately none have been found in any editions of the *Cherokee Advocate*.

see to the arranging of the wagons whilst traveling and to all other duties which properly belong to a Wagonmaster.

Art. 6th. The duties of the Committee of Twelve, shall be, to have complete jurisdiction of all offences, and misdemeanors which may be committed by any of the company during our campaign. But in case of any person being found guilty of committing a capital offence, then on appeal shall be granted by the Committee of Twelve, upon application of the convict, or his or their counsel, to twenty-four other men, who shall be chosen from among the company, by a majority of said company, whose decision shall be final.

The Committee shall also pass the by-laws which shall be approved of by a majority of the company.

Art. 7th. Any three persons belonging to the company may call a meeting of the Committee of Twelve in case of any aggrievances.

Art. 8th. The duties of the Secretary shall be, to keep a correct record of all the proceedings of the company, keep all public papers belonging to the company, and also act as Secretary to the Committee of Twelve.

The foregoing Constitution was read and unanimously adopted, on the 29th day of April, 1850 at camp on Elk Creek.

After which, Jno. H. Wolf was called to the chair and an election went into; which resulted in the election of the following officers, viz:

C.V. McNair, Captain; Robert Harris, Lieutenant; Jno. Gott, Sergeant of Guard; Alfred Cunningham, Wagon Master; Jno. H. Wolf, Secretary.[725]

This Cherokee Emigrating California Company was composed of the McNair, Wolfe, and Harris groups. The now-enlarged Cane Hill Company, including diarists Quesenbury and Mitchell, was twelve miles ahead and would cross into Kansas next day. The festering discontentment erupted. Quesenbury:

"Monday 29 [April...15 miles] Excitement about going ahead. Some are disaffected. A meeting was called. Cunningham elected wagon master. Meigs, Got and others refused to go on. Our same old crowd [Cane Hill] except Shipley went with us. Crossed the creek just at our camps-- (fifty or a hundred yards above) and struck N.W. for Evans' Trail. Came to it in about 3 miles, just opposite a long mound.[726] Came on about twelve miles and camped, i.e. 12 m. from where we struck the trail. Camped to the right of the road on a branch. The [Edmonson] ox teams had been there before us. No game yet. Rogers wagon tongue broke to-day."

Mitchell was disgusted with those they had waited so long for, and who now broke off from them. The newly-enlarged Cane Hill Company began to split up.

Mitchell:

"29 [April] monday [20 miles] a meeting cal[l]ed and more than half of our company droped off from us who we had been waiting for and who had been Send us word to wait for them   But all this I anti[ci]pated that when they come up with us they would [drop off]

---

[725]*Cherokee Advocate* 27 May 1850 p 2.

[726]They struck Evans Trace approximately four miles east of Wann, Nowata County, Oklahoma.

even the venerable Megs John Ross Son in law left us   we prooceed on mad and Last and camped on deep Branch 20 miles."
[Onion Creek, SE of Wayside, Montgomery Co., Kansas]

Later the *Fort Smith Herald* printed an exaggerated and incorrect story of splits within the Cane Hill Company. Editor Wheeler couldn't help adding a comment on their choice of route:

> We are informed, by good authority, that the company of California emigrants, that left Arkansas, to go the northern route, split up at the Verdegris river, and have taken different routes. The praries, on the frontier of Missouri, are represented to be entirely destitute of grass--nothing but a bleak waste...It is thought, that owing to the want of grass, and other difficulties, that a portion of the company will endeavor to turn across and fall into Capt. Marcy's road.
> If this company had taken the advice of friends, they would have been, by this time, five hundred miles upon the Southern, or Fort Smith road.[727]

The 1849 Evans/Cherokee trail must have been plain to see and easy to follow; the Cane Hill Company began to increase mileage to twenty a day. Quesenbury's comment about keeping on the dividing ridge supports the statement of 1849 company member Hiram Davis.

> The travel was on the divide[728]...which we found to be exclusively of high, dry, rolling prairie slopes, offering no obstacles whatever to any number of wagons.[729]

Quesenbury comments unfavorably on the use of the 1849 "waybill" he copied while in camp on April 18. Crawford's campsite names and mileages closely match those copied by <u>Quesenbury</u>:

> **"Tuesday...30 & L.[730] {April]...20 miles** Country rolling. Evans kept all the the divide he could find. Crawford's way bill useless as we do not know the names of his camps from the landmarks. We pass about two camps a day of the [Edmonson] ox team company. Camped on the S. Side of the road. Water Down in the hollow. Black jack timber."[731]

<u>Mitchell</u> noted geologic formations and vegetation. Packers join.

> **"30 [April] Tuesday** cold and windy we went over high rocky hills Stop on a Black Jack ridge to noon good grass   pased curious lime

---

[727] *Fort Smith Herald* 18 May 1850 vol 3, no 38, p 2.
[728] Divide between the waters of the Verdigris River and the Caney River.
[729] *Cherokee Advocate* 30 July 1849 from *Daily Missouri Republican* 4 July 1849.
[730] Quesenbury notes the "L." or "Last" to identify the last day of each month.
[731] Blackjack Oak (*Quercus marilandica* Muenchh.) A low to medium-sized tree often growing with Post Oak (*Quercus stellata* Wang.) George A. Petrides, *A Field Guide to Trees and Shrubs* Peterson Field Guide Series (Boston: Houghton Mifflin Co. 1972) p 219. Bark thick; nearly black; divided into rough, square blocks. Richard J. Preston, *North American Trees* (Ames, Iowa: The Iowa State College Press 1950) p 197.

Stone   camped on a high ridge   timber in Sight on each Side abundent
2 men with packs from union county over took us and camped with us."
[NW of Hale, Chautauqua Co., Kansas]

Both Mitchell and Quesenbury began to write about the
advantages of packing. Quesenbury:

"May 1...Wednesday...20 miles Got a mule from Craig to work in
the wagon. Very wild. Hays and myself staid back packing. The little
black mule hard to drive. Our way is still on the divide.
     Came to a spot of timber and camped on the right of the road. The
pack men who joined us on Monday morning are still with us."

From the time he crossed the Grand River, Mitchell had written of
the necessity to make more mileage, which "packing" would achieve.
Now he has proof. Mitchell:

"1st May Wendsday a frosty cold morning   timber scarce   rock
points high   pased Some rich limeStone praararies   the road very
crooked in consequence of many Branches to cross   a beautifull Still
day   after 8 oclock we nooned on a branch runing north good grass and
that very desirable   our men all Still and good umered [humored]
when we are going ahead I ride on before with a led animal with me and
Stop 2 or 3 miles to graze waiting for the waggons to come up   this
gives me time to write my memorandoms to rest and is a proofs that packs
can travel greatly faster than waggons   we camped on deep guly
grass not good   high hills to our left."
[near Mound Branch, NW of Moline, Elk Co., Kansas]

The indiscretion committed by Quesenbury against the Osage on
April 25 continued to affect the company's safety. Quesenbury:

"Thursday 2...May...1850...6 [miles]
     Early start. Our road is crooked very. Sometimes south and southwest,
still on divide. Got to Evans' old camp. No grass. Came up the Creek.
     Raining all day at intervals. Craig and myself went ahead to find a
camping place. Ascended very high land. Rained cold wind high. Went on
till we believed the chance for camping bad.Turned back and camped about
two miles above Evans' camp to the left of the road. Soon after we got
here three or four Osages came into camp. Presently others came and in a
short time sixty or seventy more. Our camps were in a perfect hubbub.
Perry ran and brought our animals and tied them to the wagon.The animals
of some of the others were frightened off,but after about three quarters
of an hour they were brought back, two or three of our men and several
Osages having gone after them. Great talk, high talk, smart talk, simple
talk, all kinds of talk in our camps now. The Osages came two or three
hundred yards above us. Rained all night. Moved wagons and tents down."

Mitchell was suspicious of the captain's motives for camping so
near to the previous night's camp--six miles. Company members were
frightened by the wild and noisy behavior of the increasing
numbers of Osages, and for the first time Captain Craig corralled
the wagons for the night.

<u>Mitchell</u>:

"2nd [May] Thursday Started   cregg our capt went ahead   after going five or 6 miles to See if there was good camping places a head he returned with a report that in his oppinion we could get to no good camping place that day and had better Stop till next day. I believed when the capt Started that the intension was to detain us waiting again for more company   it rained   in the evening an Osage indian come to us with a flag of peace and to us more of thim were coming   in a few moments 4 more were in camps with there flags telling us their chief was coming to See us   we were camped close under a bluff and in a few moment more there appeared near 100 [Osage] charging on us with there bell ratling and them making a great nois   a general Stampeed took place among our horses   I saved mine by hard work from giting away our capt was assured that the indians come to Kill us and take our horses from us   he cus great String him and park after Seeing that there was no dainger   the capt forted[732] with the waggons that night and could not be convinced that there was no dainger."

[near the west border of Elk Co., Kansas]

Officers of the corralled Cane Hill company decided to wait for the Cherokee companies that were coming behind. All waited except Mitchell and his mess. <u>Quesenbury</u>:

"Friday 3 [May] Our red brethren went off this morning. Those that came to see us, had on dry blankets. Mitchell and his mess left us this morning and went ahead. The wind blows extremely cold from the N. I believe it is decided to remain here till the [Cherokee] Company behind comes up. Our wagons are close together, and three of our messes cook at the same fire. Wind continues cold; the Indian talk continues unabated. Rained at night."

James Mitchell, with Crum, Strickler, and Robinson (who still had his wagon) left the main Cane Hill California Emigrating Company, charging ahead to overtake the Edmonson ox train, still in the lead. Mitchell doesn't explain his reason for leaving. Perhaps he was disgusted over the result of the Quesenbury/Osage incidents, or the company leadership that held them back to swell their numbers, or simply the slow pace. <u>Mitchell</u>:

"3rd [May] Fryday cold and wet the indians at their worship in Sight   our Brave capt [Craig] and [Perry] Parks their guns in their hands expect an attack every moment--my mess left the crowd as they refused to go on till they got more company   we roled ahead a long distance and camped at an Elem log on a branch with poor grass no timber in Sight only a little Brushy Elm."

[Little Walnut River near Leon, Butler Co., Kansas]

---

[732]Beginning with Josiah Gregg, the description is of a circle, each wagon tongue pointed near or overlapping the rear wheel of the wagon in front. Animals are placed inside the circle, in the corral.

MITCHELL GOES AHEAD TO THE SANTA FE TRAIL

The fresh tracks of Captain Edmonson's 100-yoke ox train simplified travel for Mitchell's small, fast-moving group.

<u>Mitchell</u>:

"4th [May] Saturday cold and windy   Started Soon and camped on a large creek named Arkansas[733] to grase and eat   here we found that the ox teams we were trying to overtake had camped the last night   we pushed on and camped again on a little Elm creek[734] mixed with hackbury."

[SE of Potwin, El Dorado Co., Kansas.

Encouraged by the closeness of the Edmonson ox teams, Mitchell and his men pushed on early the next day, crossing the Whitewater River near present Potwin, Kansas. Here they overtook and joined Edmonson's company, which evidently had no problem about traveling on Sunday. <u>Mitchell</u>:

"5th Sunday [May]...5 miles+ very cold and windy   we traveled about 5 miles to cottonwood[735] and here overtook and united with the Ox teams [Edmonson] we were trying to overtake who had not yet left there camps   they met us with Shouts and welcomed us into there camps   we proceeded on and after leaving this Streem not even Saw timber fo[r] the day   our men Kiled a Buffelow[736] and the Indians Kiled one by the road Side   we seen it fall   we camped and used Buffelow chips for fuel."

[NE Harvey Co. near the Marion Co. line, Kansas]

One of the major inconveniences of open prairie camping with tents is the havoc wreaked by the high prairie wind and rains. Santa Fe trader Josiah Gregg had warned against using tents. <u>Mitchell</u>:

"6 [May] Monday Started Soon   travel over beautiful level country withot timber entirely   we had to use the Buffelow chips again for fuel   we saw antilopes and Some Buffalow But our men ciled none we camped again without timber   it rained the wind blowed and turned very cold   our tend blowed down."

[six miles SE of Galva, McPherson Co., Kansas]

The rain also affected the packers' fires; they had no way to keep the buffalo chips dry. The company was pleasantly surprised to reach the Santa Fe Trail so soon the next day.

---

[733]Walnut River, at present El Dorado, Butler County, Kansas.
[734]Rock Creek, four miles southeast of Potwin, Butler County, Kansas.
[735]Whitewater River, Butler County, Kansas.
[736]First and easternmost Buffalo reported in either 1849 or 1850 companies.

<u>Mitchell</u>:

"7th [May] Tuesday we could Start no fire and consequently cook none as the Buffelow chips were all wet   we Started ahead to try and get to timber   I went ahead   crum got very angry about his gun geting tramped on by oxen without cause as he Should of taken care of his own gun   to our Surprise we Struck the Santifee road[737] in 2 or 3 miles us expecting it to be at least 25 miles distant from us[738]   ths was encouraging thoug the day was ____?   the Son appeared about 9 oclock   our men Kiled a buffelow and Stoped to Save Some of it. I found of[f] the road a little   while we were Stoped   the remaines of a land reck   a good wool matrass larg enough for all four of us to bed on and it clean and nearly new. [near] by layed 2 Spanish Saddles Some pieces of carpet   a Grass Sack   and part of Irons of a burned down waggon. a layed 30 Steps from the pille with bullet hole Shot threw it   off about a 100 yards lay the remains of a dead horse   I found als[o] a good iron picked [picket] Stak with ring in it near the pile we camped again without wood though good grass."

[south of McPherson, McPherson Co., Kansas]

Several of the items found proved to be very useful to the travelers. They were remnants of the violent snowstorms of the prolonged winter of 1849-50. In 1849, as the Evans/Cherokee Company reached and traveled along the Santa Fe Road, O.W. Lipe wrote they found:

waggons and irons of every discription are strewd all along...tons of iron could be picked up, it seems as if the waggons are first left and afterwards burned for fuel by others passing and the iron remain.[739]

THE CANE HILL COMPANY JOINS THE CHEROKEE COMPANY

In 1849, one reason to travel with the Cherokee had been put forth; that there would be no trouble with their red brethren. And in 1849 after a boisterous emigrant/Osage Saturday night dance there had been no further contact with Osages. In fact, only four Indians were seen before the company reached Pueblo (Colorado).

In 1850, however, William Quesenbury's early encounter with the Osage had set the stage for multiple incidents. Captain Craig had corralled the wagons following a noisy, flag-waving, invasive

---

[737]Running Turkey Creek, McPherson County, Kansas.

[738]Apparently the Edmonson ox train company did not have the benefit of maps or journals from the 1849 Evans/Cherokee company. First, they were looking for timber; second they were surprised at how close they were to the Santa Fe Road. There was at least one more time when this company would stop and, with confusion reigning, wonder how to proceed.

[739]*Cherokee Advocate* 30 July 1849 letter from O. W. Lipe written May 27.

demonstration by 100 Osage. Craig and Perry Parks decided it was critical to wait for the larger Cherokee Emigrating California Company to overtake and strengthen their group.

Quesenbury's 1850 diary resumes on May 4 near the west border of Elk County (Kansas) the day after Mitchell and his three companions left the Cane Hill wagon company behind.

Quesenbury:

> **"Saturday 4 [May] 1850** Wind continues cold,- has veered a little to the E[ast]. Potts made a discovery of wagons and Wm. Oliver and Jo Williams of a spy, both of which discoveries proved false.[740] We are disagreeably situated. It is uncertain when the wagons will get up. There is some talk this morning half earnest, half joke, about going back. No one hunts, in fact, it is useless to do so as the deer must be lying down and the turkies are squatted. No animal of our climate can stand this wind and thrive."
>
> [still in camp on west border of Elk Co., Kansas]

The Osage Indian scare of two days previous, the miserable cold and rainy weather, and little or poor grass all contributed to the uncertainty and misery. Now the situation was compounded by the rumor that some might turn back home. Quesenbury:

> **"Sunday...5 [May]** Some talk about going back. As far as I am concerned, I shall not. Rogers and McQuorter[741] went off to day and returned with the news that they had found fine grass. Geared up and went to it. Two miles and a half off. The Creek near here is a head branch of the Verdigris.[742] Water very clear. Went down and grazed the animals. In suspense about the future--have no confidence whatever in any management such as we have, affecting anything."
>
> [still near the west border of Elk Co., Kansas]

This was a great place on the trail for the Cane Hill Company to wait. Quesenbury's considerable knowledge about plants, birds, animals, their habits and habitats are displayed in the following entry. Quesenbury:

> **"Monday...6 [May]** Early this morning heard a turkey gobbling up the Creek. Started for him but two others started also. Quit the hunt and got after prairie hens. Killed none. After breakfast Mr. May and McQuorter left us to hunt up the rear wagons.[743] Henry Hays and myself took our guns, went over the ridge and shot a time or so at prairie hens. Made for the creek. Found an excellent fishing hole. Fished some,

---

[740]There is another diary mention of Potts. Jo Williams is mentioned twice.

[741]This is the second mention of Rogers. McQuorter, only mentioned once, accompanied the 1845 Cherokee group to Texas and Mexico searching for possible lands for emigration. Quesenbury also made that trip.

[742]Clear Creek, tributary of Elk River.

[743]The Cherokee California Emigrating Company captained by Clem McNair.

but they wouldn't bite. On our way back we killed three squirrels. Hays clomb [climbed] for one. Saw a gang of partridges. The growth of the bottom on this creek is walnut, overcup,[744] hickory, pecan, buckeye,elm, hack berry, and perhaps some few others. There have been bee trees here, and perhaps we might find some if the weather would permit. A rat was chased on the side of the hill over the branch among the rocks. Cooked the squirrels by boiling. Field larks continue in great numbers; also plovers and blackbirds. One of pack companions report the good grass continues all the way Down the creek as far as he went. He saw some deer. Weather variable. Sometimes sunshine, sometimes sprinkling rain.

Speculations about Mitchell and Crum--The Osage battle at times is as exciting as ever. Just before sunset Mr. May and McQuorter got back from the [Cherokee] wagons. Houston Shipley came with them. The other Company will be here tomorrow. Doubtful. McQ. and May were chased by a detachment of the Cherokee crowd."

[still near the west border of Elk Co., Kansas]

Quesenbury writes more about hunting, and lightening his load.

"Tuesday 7...May..1850 Disturbance in camp last night caused by an Indian or a wolf. Guard doubled. Rained hard after day and continued till nine or ten o'clock. Overhauled things in wagon. Threw out a box or so. The wind this morning was intensely cold, but after the rain ceased, it became pleasant. In this evening about three quarters of an hour before Sunset, Houston Shipley and myself went a squirrel hunting in the bottom. Houston killed one; I, three. On our way back we came across Hays who had lodged a squirrel. Shot it out."

[still near the west border of Elk Co., Kansas]

Captain McNair's Cherokee company, coming up from behind, sent word to the Cane Hill boys making it very clear that they could travel anywhere they liked. However, they were not to have voting rights, nor representation in the leadership. McNair's resolve not to include the Cane Hill Company was based on Quesenbury's encounter with the Osage, and the subsequent hostility of the Osage toward the Cherokee. Quesenbury:

"Wednesday 8...May This morning Craig and Shipley went back to meet the wagons. Nearly all the others are off grazing the animals. I'm baking bread. This is the most backward spring I ever experienced. Some of the trees are in full bloom, and some have scarcely budded. The nights are chilly; the wind tolerably constant, either from N. or S. and equally as cold from one point as the other. At about eleven o'clock several Osages visited us. They had buffalo meat, and were travelling to their towns.[745] Perry tried to trade for a pony, but did not succeed. One of the Indians tried to ride the little black mule, but he couldn't.

---

[744]Overcup Oak (*Quercus lyrata* Walt.) Rough acorn cup is unique, enclosing nearly all of globular nut; only very tip visible. Petrides...Trees...p 216.
[745]The Great Osages' "towns" nearby were in the "Verdigris District;" Little Bear's town was located some 10 miles above the junction of Fall river with the Verdigris; Chetopa, headwaters of Chetopa Creek; Elk-town on Elk Creek; and at least one more between the Verdigris/Caney Creek junction. A full listing of Osage Towns of 1850 and later. Barry...*West* ...pp 944-46.

Buckner[746] gave them his dog but they wouldn't take it off. Went a fishing up the creek. Caught nothing. Craig came back. The other company is willing that we travel before, behind, or with them. They are camped near or at Evans' camp last year."[747]

[Clear Creek, headwaters of Elk River, near west border
of Elk Co.,Kansas]

The Cane Hill Company was made to camp outside the corral. <u>Quesenbury</u> knew who to blame.

"Thursday 9 [May] ...15 [miles] Started about 8 o'clock. Saw the wagon train of the other company going on. Got with them at the foot of the hill near our old camp. We now have thirty-five wagons along.[748] Bought a horse from Merrill[749] to day. Camped about a mile and a half west of the ox team[750] camp. Our whole Cane Hill crowd are stationed outside the lines of encampment. This is Wagon Master Cunninghams work."

[NE of Latham, Butler Co., Kansas]

BROWN TRAVELS WITH THE MCNAIR/WOLFE CHEROKEE COMPANY

On May 2, one hundred Osages had come into the camps of the Cane Hill California Emigrating Company, which prompted the company to stop and wait for the larger McNair/Wolfe Cherokee Emigrating California Company. The same day, Cherokee diarist Brown, with Mayes' group, left the Verdigris River.[751] Continuing northwest from the river <u>Brown</u> notes:

"2 [May]..15 miles Traveled 15 miles. 10 waggns alltogather. camped on a small creek **(camp 4)."**
[on California Creek, west of Lenapah, Nowata Co., Oklahoma]
The next day two more wagons joined.

----

[746]Buckner's first name is William. He spent considerable time with Quesenbury throughout the trip.

[747]Mound Branch of Elk River.

[748]Foreman...*Marcy*...p 101. "John Beck, Weatherford ('Ludge') Beck, Brice Hildebrand, Joe Spears, Eagle and John Clark, Cherokees, were members of the party."

[749]Merrell (various spellings) traveled with his wife Margaret.

[750]Captain Oliver of Missouri's ox train. Captain Holmes' ox train caught up with the McNair/Taylor company May 27.

[751]Samuel Houston Mayes and sons, George Washington and John Thompson Mayes; Devereaux Jarrette Bell and wife and Juliette Vann Bell; George Washington Adair and William Penn Adair; Benjamin Franklin Goss; Benjamin Trott; Edward Wilkerson Bushyhead and Daniel Colston Bushyhead; Zeke Byers; Richard Fields; Charley Holt and William Holt; Samuel Lasley; Looney Rattlingourd; James Shelton; Bose Simcoe; and Lige Terrell with wife Bet (Elizabeth) Terrell.

Brown:

"3d [May]...8 miles   Traveled 8 miles. 12 waggons [?]
alltogather **(Camp 5th)."**
[north of Wann, south of Kansas border, Nowata Co., Oklahoma]

"4th [May]...15 miles   Travelled 15 miles [corner Journal worn]
camped in two hollows [corner Journal worn] the gap of the
[corner Journal worn] **[Camp 6]."**
                [near Wayside, Montgomery Co., Kansas]

The Osage were still on the trail and angry because of the
Quesenbury incident. Brown notes catching up with the McNair/Wolfe
Cherokee Emigrating California Company--and the Osage. Brown:

"May 5th...[Sunday]15 miles   Traveled 15 miles and caught up
with the company commanded by Clem McNair. a war party of Osages came
into camp, causing great excitement **(Camp 7)."**
                [near Hale, Chautauqua Co., Kansas]

Members of the McNair/Wolfe Company wrote home that they were
joined by Taylor and Adair (Brown-Mayes'). Captain Oliver's forty
person Missouri ox train joined the same day. A war party of forty
Osage surprised them. The *Cherokee Advocate* editor commented:

> Our California Emigrants write to us from the South Prong of East
> Verdigris, under date of the 5th inst.
>   They still complain of the shortness of the grass--consequently
> making but short drives per day. They were apprehending that they would
> be compelled to lay by in order to wait for the grass to get better. The
> weather was still cold and disagreeable; so much so that they had to
> wear their overcoats. They were joined on the day they wrote, by Messrs.
> T.F. Taylor, G.W. Adair, and other Cherokees, numbering about twenty--
> also by a party from Missouri and Arkansas, of about forty persons[752]--
> making the wole [sic] number one hundred and twenty-three strong--
> besides the ladies who number twelve. They were also expecting to be
> joined shortly by seven or eight wagons from near Fort Gibson. They were
> considerably surprised by a company of forty Osages, who offered some
> violence to one or two of their company who were out some distance from
> the camp grazing their horses. But when the Osages ascertained that the
> company was composed principally of Cherokees, they desisted from
> further violence, and hoisted the flag of peace. They suppose that the
> reason the Osages ordered any violence, was in consequence of the ill
> treatment some had received from Capt. Craig's company,[753] supposing
> them to be some of the same.
>   They state their whole company to be in the best of health, not even
> a bad cold among them.
>   All that compose the company send their best respects to their
> friends and acquaintances."[754]

After Mayes' group was "numbered into" the McNair/Wolfe

---

[752]Members of Oliver's ox train left Honey Creek in SW Missouri April 27.
[753]Quesenbury broke a stick over an Osage's head on April 25.
[754]*Cherokee Advocate* 27 May 1850 editor's column p 2, col 1.

Cherokee Emigrating California Company, the total was 123, plus twelve ladies. Thomas Fox Taylor went back, rejoining the company later, after which he played an important leadership role. Brown:

> **"6 [May]...[Monday] 10 miles** our crowd of 12 waggons Joined and were numbered into McNairs Company   the company numbering 32 waggons travelled 10 miles.   Left Tom Taylor and 5 men to wait for another crowd **Camp 8 --"**
>   [SW of Elk Falls near county line, Elk Co., Kansas]

> **"7 [May] Lay By** all day --."

> **"8 [May]...10 miles** Traveled 10 miles. camped [?] By a spring of very cold [water?] **Camp 9th."**
>   [Mound Branch, Elk Co., Kansas]

Quesenbury knew the Cherokee company was nearby and wrote: "They are camped near or at Evans' camp last year." Crawford, 1849 diarist, had called it "Spring Creek."

     Diarist Brown with the Cherokee company:

> **"May 9th...20 miles** Traveled 20 miles on what was supposed to be waters of Arkansas River--**Camp 10th**."
>   [Rock Creek, NE of Latham, Butler Co., Kansas]

Throughout his diary, Brown included additional information around the main text, including the following marginal notes on the Cane Hill emigrants joining, and their total strength. Brown:

> **May 9** The Company was joined on Thursday by, five waggons and 21 men, which [corner of Journal worn] [rai?] sed the number of persons [corner of Journal worn] to 105 men, 15 negroes and 12 females all under the command of Clem McNair --

The joining of the companies was recorded by Quesenbury:

> Saw the wagon train of the other company (Cherokee) going on. Got with them....We now have thirty five wagons along

     The entire combined Cherokee Emigrating California Company under Capt. Clem McNair, Captain Oliver's forty person ox train, and the Cane Hill California Emigrating Company traveled more or less together for a few days. The daily entries of Quesenbury (Cane Hill) and Brown (Cherokee) are shown together.

     Quesenbury savored everything--except their position in camp.

> **"1850...Friday 10 May...4 [miles]** Some animals lost this morning. [Mr.] Got, with a detachment went ahead to look out a place of encampment. Doubtful as to our leaving here to day. Rained last night. Another norther is blowing. Cold as usual. Some of the elms on

this branch are budding, some are not. The red buds[755] are in bloom. The spade that Mr. Mitchell had of Rogers &Co was found in the road sticking up as he left it. Yesterday a prairie dog[756] was heard barking. This is the first sign of them. The detachment reported grass about four miles ahead. Geared up and went to it. Found it excellent. Tonight we are placed just in the pass way. More of Cunningham's work."[757]

Brown:

"10 [May]...5 miles Started after dinner and Traveled five miles **Camp 11th --."**

[headwater branch of Hickory Creek, Butler Co., Kansas]

The contrast in diary-keeping is nowhere more evident than on the May 10 entries. Brown's entry presented bare facts. Quesenbury, the observer, recorded everything he saw and his reactions.

The second "message" left by the company ahead is recorded by Quesenbury:

"Saturday 11 [May]...18 [miles] Got off about 9. This days travel has been over the best road I have seen since we left. The country is becoming more level. About eight miles from last night's camp we crossed a creek [Little Walnut River] as large as the one we camped on. Nooned without much chance for water. Got a cup of cold flour from Noon Bean.[758] Came on ahead of the Company to a creek. Saw the ox teams had camped in the bottom. Some names and dates were left on trees. This creek we call Cotton Wood. Evans called it Shores' Creek.[759] Camped on the opposite side, from home."

Brown:

"11 [May]...18 miles Traveled 18 miles. Crossed a creek about 12 oclock and camped at night on a large Creek, the Bottom of which was covered with walnut growth. **Camp 12 --."**

[Walnut River, two miles south of El Dorado, Butler Co., Kansas]

Quesenbury does not identify his messmates, but seems to have

[755]Redbud (*Cercis canadensis* L.) A small tree with showy redding springtime flowers that appear before the leaves. Petrides...*Trees*...p 208.

[756]Black-tailed Prairie dog (*Cynomys ludovicianus*) prefers short-grass prairies. The crater-shaped mound around the burrow entrance is up to 2 ft. high x 4 in. diameter; the tunnel narrows and goes down steeply 3-16 ft. before turning horizontal, where the grass-lined nest chamber is in a side branch. That the Prairie Dog, rattlesnake and Burrowing Owl (very often mentioned in trail diaries) live together in harmony is a myth, since rattler and Owl eat young 'dogs' and 'dogs' eat Owl eggs and young. Many of their towns formerly included hundreds of square miles. Ralph S. Palmer *The Mammal Guide* (Garden City, N.Y.: Doubleday & Co., Inc. 1954) pp 170-72.

[757]Wagonmaster Alfred Carroll Cunningham was the grandson of Susannah Ross, sister of Chief John Ross and Lewis Ross. By marriage Alfred was related to Return Jonathan Meigs. Alfred Cunningham made the 1845 trip to Texas.

[758]Cherokee Tolbert Bean and his brother William were on this trip.

[759]Crawford's diary called it Cottonwood Fork of Arkansas. Capt. Alfred Oliver had the Lewis Evans journal, from which "Shore's Creek" could have been taken. Hiram and William Shores were 1849 Evans/Cherokee Company members.

had difficulty in sustaining personal relationships.

> **"Sunday 12 [May] 1850 Laid by.** Attending to my own animals. Circumstances have become so unpleasant that a separation in our mess becomes necessary. Since I left home there has been a constant disturbance about everything in the world that was to be done. Cooking can't be done right; pallets can't be made right nor anything else. Such a state of things render the trip most unpleasant. Mr. May preached about 11 o'clock. I did not hear him. John Pierce and myself had taken a walk down the creek. A great many of the Company are off hunting and fishing. Some black squirrels[760] have been killed. Patilla[761] killed the first turkey[762] yesterday evening. Vegetation seems somewhat more advanced here, but the red buds are not out of bloom."

Brown:

> **"May 12   Lay By (Sunday)"**

[Walnut River, two miles south of El Dorado, Butler Co.,Kansas]
The combined companies had at least two good reasons for laying by. Judging from the initial Cherokee hesitancy to move without adequate grass for the animals, the stopover was considered a necessity. Here there was water, wood and grass. Also it was Sunday, and there was at least one preacher in the combined companies--J. J. May.

On Monday, Quesenbury was ready to go again. Instead, he went hunting, while a crisis rocked the company. Quesenbury:

> **"Monday May 13** Still at the same camp. Will not move today on account of some one's sickness. Merrill was caught asleep on guard last night.[763] Went down about sunrise with my horses to the bottom. Back to breakfast. About eleven o'clock Houston Shipley went with me up the creek to graze horses and hunt. Got after a squirrel which ran into a hole in an elm, at the ground. Smoked it out. Houston broke the ram rod of his gun and we came back to camp. Jones[764] came by us in the bottom with four squirrels--two of which were black. Some are in a notion to go back home. Hope they will, that I may send letters by them."

---

[760]There is not enough description for discriminating between the Eastern Gray Squirrel (*Sciurus carolinensis*) which in parts of its range can have many melanistic (black) individuals; and Eastern Fox Squirrel (*Sciurus niger*) which also has melanistic individuals. Either species could be in this range. Palmer...*Mammal*...pp 186-88, 190-91, plate 24.

[761]Unidentified person. Patillo signed the agreement to pack from Pueblo.

[762]Wild Turkey (*Meleagris gallopavo*) is the largest upland game bird; the species from which all domestic turkeys are descended. Jay Ellis Ransom, ed. Harper & Row's *Complete Field Guide to North American Wildlife* Western ed. (N.Y.: Harper & Row 1981) pp 65 and 73. The eastern race is native to eastern Oklahoma and eastern Kansas. Paul A. Johnsgard *Birds of the Great Plains* (Lincoln: Univ. of Nebraska Press 1979) p 125.

[763]Probably caught by John Gott, Sergeant of the Guard, whose duty was to mount the guard and visit each of them once every night.

[764]The only mention of Jones in any diary. Perhaps William Claude Jones of southwest Missouri.

Though there had not been any night raids or stampedes since the unification of the companies, sleeping on guard was a very serious offense. This camp was located at or near the traditional Osage crossing of the Walnut River. Local records state the crossing was so well used it was worn into rock. The guards were absolutely necessary.

Brown's diary entry did not even mention the company crisis:

"May   13   Lay By."

[Walnut River, two miles south of El Dorado, Butler Co., Kansas] With the Brown diary alone the trial was unknown. He mentioned nothing about Merril's trial, or the resignation and re-election of Captain McNair. The addition of the Quesenbury manuscript fills in the details. There was a leadership crisis. The 1850 Cherokee Emigrating California Company Constitution articles had spelled out the responsibility and method of trial.

> Art. 2d...the Captain...shall see that the laws and regulations of this company be strictly and rigidly enforced on all occasion...

> Art. 6th...The duties of the Committee of Twelve, shall be, to have complete jurisdiction of all offences, and misdemeanors which may be committed by any of the company during our campaign.

There was much ado, but no changes were made. Quesenbury:

> **Tuesday 14 [May]...15 [miles]** Merril was tried last night for sleeping on post. Found guilty but the Committee [of Twelve] remitted his fine. Capt. McNair resigned on account of the proceedings. This morning a new election was held and McN. elected again. Got off about 9 o'clock. Ox team started in advance. Came to a small crick where Mitchell and Crum had camped, and we nooned on the far side. Passed two or three creeks to day that would have made good camping places. Stopped an hour and a half before sunset. The ox teams had camped on the other side of the creek. This morning has been the first that was comfortable without fire. The day has been warm."

For the third time Quesenbury saw evidence of Mitchell and Crum's passage. It would not be the last. Emigrants carved on trees, and wrote and carved on rocks along every trail across the land. It was probably very reassuring to find that friends had passed this way alive.

Brown:

> **14 [May]...about 15 miles** Traveled about 15 miles crossed two creeks and camped at night on Shoare's Creek **Camp 13th --.**"
> [crossing of Whitewater River, one mile NW of Potwin,
> Butler Co., Kansas]

This hardwood bottomland proved useful in wagon repair. Ahead were more treeless plains and the buffalo country.

Quesenbury:

"Wednesday 15 [May]...18 [miles] Old Man Dean[765] broke his axle tree yesterday.[766] Making a new one this morning. The bottoms on this creek are small. The wild rye is not abundant as it has been. Vast quantities of gooseberry bushes are in bloom; - they are precisely like our tame ones. Left at about half past ten. The road is level enough for a railroad.[767] No timber within several miles of the road at any point. Water very scarce. In a dry time, none can be had. Buffalo skeletons begin to appear. Antelope[768] are seen and chased. At two hours by sun made "Bois de vache" Camp.[769] Found piles of buffalo chips that Evans' Company had gathered last year. Left my pipe where I grazed to day. After I had gone a mile, I missed it. Turned back and got it. Shot at a striped prairie rat[770] on the way but missed it. The pony jerked my arm as I fired. At about 8 o'clock an order came to bring our horses closer tonight. Brought mine up closer and staked them. Buckner discovered fresh Indian sign not far off, which was the cause of the present order. The water at this camp has a taste as disagreeable as Glauber salts. All our victuals taste of it. At about ten a row was raised among the horses. All hands jumped up. Some horses loose. In a short time order was restored."

Both diarists noted signs of Evans' 1849 passage. Brown:

"15 [May]...20 miles Traveled all day without any timber in sight 20 miles and without any water until night [corner of Journal worn] Camped at Evanes old [1849] camp ground used Buffalo Chips for wood, this is the place that Capt. Evans called Buffalo Chip Camp **Camp 14 --."**
     [Doyle Creek, NE corner of Harvey Co., Kansas]

---

[765]The only mention of Mr. Dean, who remains unidentified.

[766]A most fortunate place to break an axletree; the next day and for days more, wood was so scarce that both 1849 and 1850 emigrants had to utilize buffalo chips for fuel.

[767]The Missouri Pacific Railroad now runs over the trail in this area, from near Oil Hill (NW of El Dorado) to Potwin; also Kansas state highway 196. The Oklahoma, Kansas, and Texas Railroad crosses the trail near Elbing in the NW corner of Butler County. In 1886, a charter was filed for the Fort Smith, Eldorado and Northwestern Railroad Company which was to run within three miles of this trail, from SE Chautauqua County through Elk, Cowley, Marion, Harvey, and McPherson counties. The Railroad never materialized.

[768]This is the furthest east mention of antelope--Pronghorn (*Antilocapra americana*) in 1850. In 1849, letter writer Hiram Davis wrote they had seen "many antelopes" before getting to the Santa Fe Trail. Modern range maps for this species do not include any part of Kansas. Palmer...*Mammal*...pp 306-07.

[769]Evans' name for this 1849 campsite approximately ten miles E. & N. of present Walton, near Doyle Creek, in the NE corner of Harvey County.

[770]Probably Thirteen-lined Ground Squirrel (*Spermophilus tridecemlineatus*) Ransom...*Wildlife*...p 310. The only striped Ground Squirrel within its wide range. The period below ground (hibernation) lasts from fall until March or April. They're at home on Grassy prairies, rocky areas and brushy timber margins. Palmer...*Mammal*...p 177.

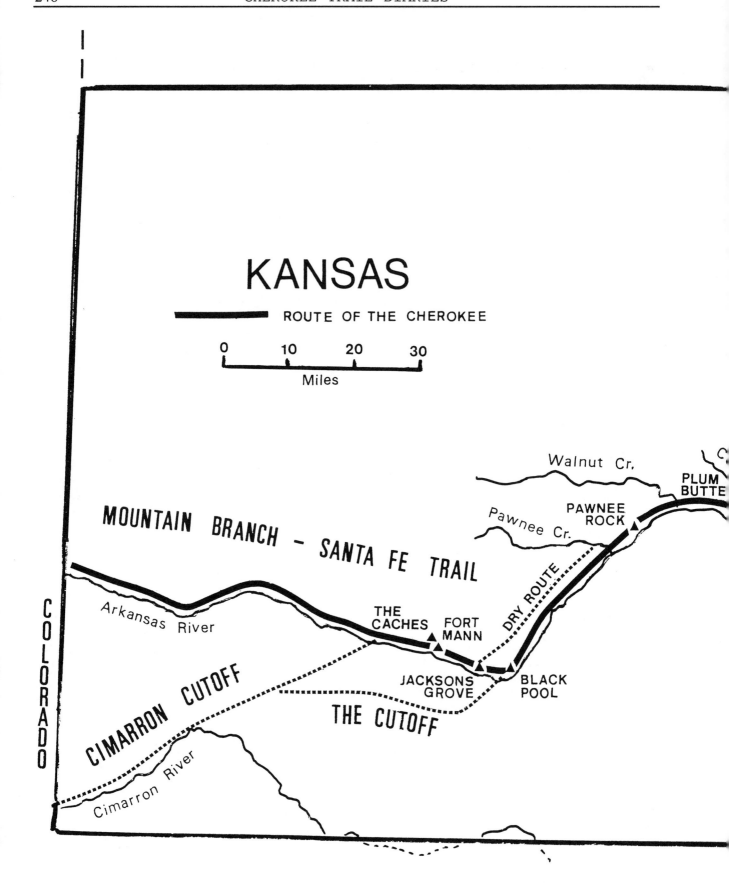

KANSAS

ROUTE OF THE CHEROKEE

0   10   20   30
Miles

MOUNTAIN BRANCH – SANTA FE TRAIL

Arkansas River

THE CACHES

FORT MANN

DRY ROUTE

Walnut Cr.

PLUM BUTTE

PAWNEE ROCK

Pawnee Cr.

JACKSONS GROVE

BLACK POOL

CIMARRON CUTOFF

THE CUTOFF

Cimarron River

COLORADO

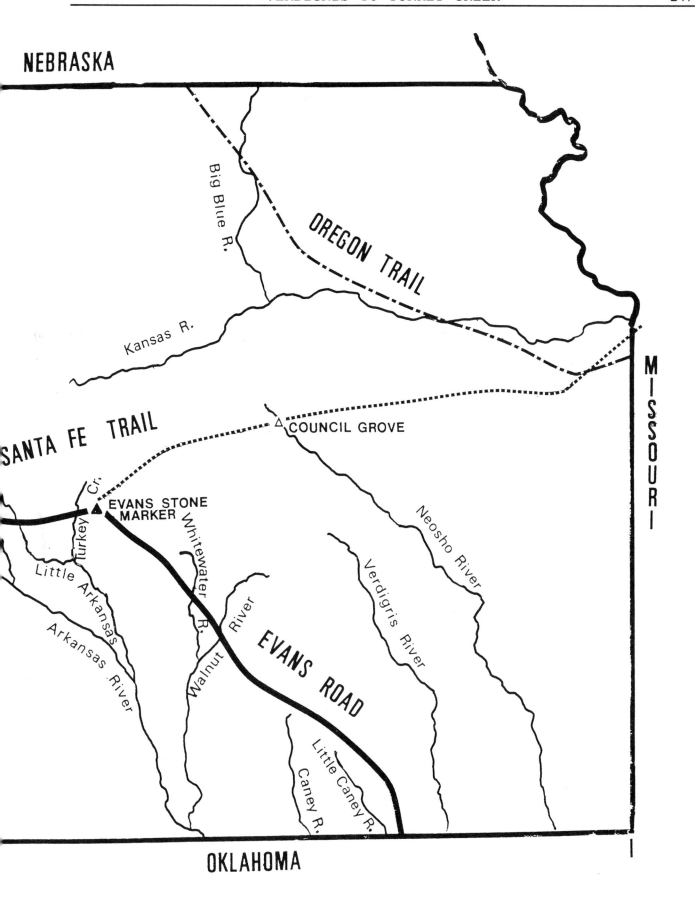

The absence of trees and talk of a company split are again noted. The night ended with a most welcome fandango. <u>Quesenbury</u>:

"Thursday 16 May...1850...14 [miles] Got a tolerably early start. Country barren and destitute of timber. One tree a mile and a half from our camp this morning, and another some three miles from the road to the left, were the only trees we have seen to day. Houston Shipley and myself came ahead. Two Antelopes crossed the road just before us and came galloping round to cross back. Houston waited for them to stop, and just before they did an inconsiderate chap banged away just behind Houston, and frightened them off. Saw two buffaloes to day: they were about three miles off. The old Negro Harry[771] entertained me for a long time with Indian war tales, and a great many things that I knew to be lies. Stopped at a sluggish stream, but the water is incomparably better than that we had last night. The wagons came up in about three hours. Camped. This is one of Evans' Camps.[772] <u>Bois de vache</u> [773] tonight and not a sprig of grass to mix with it. Patilla and some others have killed some very large bull frogs[774] with which, they are being epicures, intend to have some dainty eating.

At night a disturbance arose about a separation in the company. A meeting was called. Every body excited. Some determined to go ahead; some to lag back. About ten a considerable fandango[775] was in full operation in the Square. Grass is short here. Some few stunted prickly pears.[776] Rushes are shooting up on the slopes of the prairie.[777]

The ~~old~~ camp fires of Evans' Company left traces that are perfectly visible so plain that I thought the Ox teams had camped here."

The fandango created the illusion that perhaps differences were settled; in fact it was more a bon voyage celebration. The twelve women from various trains, never mentioned, must have been immensely popular at the fandango. Two are identified from primary sources: Juliette Vann Bell, wife of Devereaux Jarrette Bell; and Barbara Hildebrand Longknife, wife of William Longknife.[778] <u>Brown</u>:

"May 16th...15 miles... Traveled all day No timber in sight yet...Camped on a sluggish stream of very cold water   the same place that Evans camped at **Camp 15."**
[Middle Emma Creek, one mile south of Goessel, Marion Co., Kansas]

---

[771]It is unfortunate that negroes and women were not considered important enough to write about. This is the only mention of Harry.
[772]In 1849 Crawford called it "Wolf Camp."
[773]Both Bon de Vache and Bois de Vache are used to mean Buffalo Chips.
[774]Bullfrog (*Rana catesbeiana*) The largest frog in North America; up to 8 inches. Ransom...*Wildlife*...p 494.
[775]Fandango is a commonly used Spanish term for dance or party; men became familiar with Spanish terms when they fought in the 1846-48 war with Mexico.
[776]One of several varieties of cactus.
[777]The company entered the McPherson Lowlands. Permeable Sand and Gravel account for the dryness; a scattering of marshes account for the rushes.
[778]Others previously mentioned include Susan Coodey, Bet Terrell, Margaret Merrell, Margaret Scott, and James Colston's wife.

But in his margin Brown noted: "still using Buffalo chips for wood Great excitement in camp   danger of dividing."

All knew they were nearing the Santa Fe Trail, a widely-used thoroughfare. The combined companies had traveled together from May 9 to the morning of May 17, when eighteen wagons went ahead, away from the combined companies, and Quesenbury with them. His first day traveling with them they reached the Santa Fe Road, where trade and mail were carried on. Quesenbury again caused a great inconvenience, this time to his new company. Quesenbury:

"Friday 17 May...1850...15 [miles] This morning the Company separated. Eighteen wagons broke off and went ahead--Ours with the rest. At about ten o'clock we spied wagons on the Santa Fe road. Nearly all the outriders broke off and went to them--I among them. Travelled about four miles across the country before we reached them. They were returning to the U.S. Saw another train nooning about two miles further on where Evans' trace enters the Santa Fe road, at Little Turkey Creek.[779] Dr. Palmer was the owner of it. He furnished me with writing material and I wrote a letter, a short one, back home. Our train in the mean time nooned at a branch a quarter of a mile from the Santa Fe Trader's.

After I had written my letter I got into a swap with Dr. Palmer[780] for a mule. He asked mex $20[781] to boot. Wouldn't give it. We started on and after I had gone a mile Palmer came back, and swapped. Whilst I was writing in the wagon to day some of our Company were killing buffaloes. I looked out of the fore end of the wagon and saw them chasing a calf. They had killed a bull.

We came about four miles from the junction of the roads and camped. Water bad, but grass good. I gathered some weeds to cook with. On going to my wagon a team got frightened at the weeds I was carrying and stampeded, breaking a wagon tongue and axle tree. The owners went to some timber to the left of the road about four mi[l]es, and brought back a hackberry[782] log. Lent my pony to help bring the timber.

---

[779]The 1849 Evans/Cherokee Company erected a large stone where their trail intersected the Santa Fe road. See Vol I. Evans left letters there to be mailed. By 1855 this junction in Empire Township was C. O. Fuller's Ranch, the earliest identified white residence in McPherson County, which provided accommodation for travelers on the Santa Fe Trail. U.S. Government surveys beginning in 1856 in Meridian Township, Secs. 1, 2, and 12 have the "Cherokee Trail" marked; in Empire Township, on the line between Sec. 34 and 35 at the south is marked "Fuller's Ranch;" in Spring Valley township, Secs. 25, 36, 35, 34, 27, and 28 show an unnamed trail which orientation approximates the Cherokee Trail.

[780]The only Dr. Palmer listed by Barry...West...p 830 died at Independence, Missouri of cholera on May 14, 1849. Identification of this Palmer is unknown.

[781]Mexican coin. The returning Santa Fe Traders were usually carrying large amounts of specie and bouillon from their business in Santa Fe.

[782]Either American Hackberry (*Celtis occidentalis* L.) or Lowland Hackberry (*Celtis laevigata* Willd.) The wood is similar to ash; and is of commercial value. Petrides...*Trees*...p 209.

The other train passed us and camped a mile ahead.[783] Tonight we have buffalo meat for the first on the trip. We use mush for bread. Rogers came by and ate supper with us.

At night held an election for officers of the company. Wolf was elected captain; Harris Lieutenant, Buckner Sergeant, Dennis, wagon master, Craig, Secretary..."

[Turkey Creek, four miles SE of McPherson, McPherson Co., Kansas]

Brown stayed behind, writing on the first day of separation:

"17 [May]...18 miles today Today at 12 oclock Traveled 10 miles and came to the Santa fee Trail to Independence. Traveled about 8 miles after entering the Trace and camped on a small stream of water, Turkey creek. still using Buffalo chips for wood This morning the company devided. part of the company, 19 waggons, started ahead, independent of Clem McNairs. we passed them this evening about 2 miles   it is said to be 175 miles from this place to Independence & five hundred and fifty miles to Santa fee --...**Camp 16th."**

[Dry Turkey Creek, three miles south of McPherson, McPherson Co., Kansas]

This division in the company was also reported to the *Cherokee Advocate*. Again the editor "interpreted."

We have been permitted to read a few hasty lines from John H. Wolf, member of the California Company from this place:

The letter is dated on the 17th May last, at the intersection of the Independence and Evan's route...

The evening before writing the letter, the company agreed to divide; in as much as some of the horse and mule teams out traveled the others, which was principally composed of oxen.

Mr. Meigs, Jno. Ross; and mess, Jos. Coody and mess, Ben Sanders and mess, and others numbering 16 wagons, compose the company. They are traveling a head of the others, and will form the advance guard, while the rest will bring up the rear, as fast as the nature of the case will admit. They had had the pleasure of killing two or three Buffaloes, which was quite fine sport, and quite fine eating no doubt. They represent themselves as quite well, and in fine spirits--buoyant with the prospects before them.[784]

Whether it was sixteen, seventeen, or eighteen wagons, the company's division into two units was not along white and Cherokee lines. There were Cherokee and white in both groups. Those who left were later recorded in the William Quesenbury diary. With Capt. Jonathan H. Wolfe went: W. G. Barker, Manley Bates, --- Black,---Blake, J. Riley Buchanan, William Buckner, Ed and Dan Bushyhead, Joseph Coody, James T. Craig, Alfred Cunningham, Dennis----, Sam Dick, Wiley Forrester, J. Gonder, James Hagood, Robert Harris, Henry Hays, Jack Hildebrand, ----McCurdy, Charles McDaniel, J.J. May, Peter May, William May, R. J. Meigs, ----

---

[783]Dry Turkey Creek near McPherson, McPherson Co., Kansas.
[784]*Cherokee Advocate* 24 June 1850 editor's column p 2, col 1.

Merrell [and wife Margaret?], George W. Nave, William Oliver, Perry Parks, ----Patillo, J. Peck, Jonathan Pierce, ----Potts, Henry Prescott, Jim Pyeatt, William Quesenbury, Rick---, Samuel Riley, H. Ross, Jonathan Ross, Ben Sanders, Houston Shipley, Jess Shipley, Tom Smith, D. Wafer (Hafer?), Hampton Williams, Jo Williams, William Williams, and ----Yates. At least twenty-two of these forty-nine were Cherokee, including elected leaders John Wolfe and Robert Harris. The Wolfe and McNair companies met again at Pueblo (Colorado).

Captain McNair's company, and Captain Oliver's ox train, brought up the rear. Cherokee diarist Brown remained with McNair. As they reached the Santa Fe Trail, McNair's Cherokee/white company was ten days behind Edmonson's lead company. Captain Edmonson's train of sixty men and 100 yoke of oxen was one day east of Fort Mann near present Dodge City, Kansas. Diarist James Mitchell was with them. Edmonson remained in the lead the entire distance to California, and did not see the other trains again.

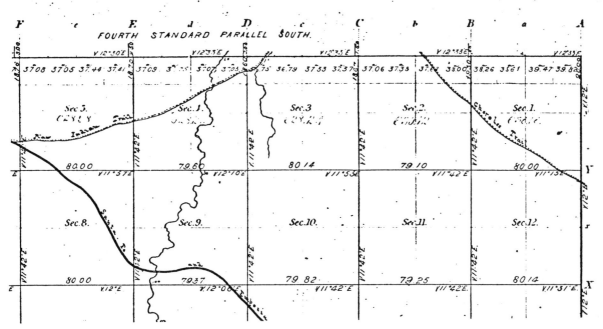

Chapter 4. THE SANTA FE TRAIL CORRIDOR

Evans calls it 125 miles from this place
[Little Arkansas River on the Santa Fe Road]
to Fort Mann and 390 miles to Pueblo
--John Lowery Brown

Since crossing the Verdigris River on April 16, Edmonson's lead ox train traveled consistently every day, putting mileage between themselves and the other companies. The Mitchell diary, the only known journal of this train, serves not as mileage keeper, nor even campsite marker, but as a chronicle of the ox train's activities. Traveling west and nine days ahead of the other companies, the traffic, the mail, Santa Fe traders, and the military are subjects of Mitchell's notes.

"8th [May] wendsday a fine morning   the mail pass from Santifee[785] before we Starte   I prevail on it to Stop a few minuts till we could write a few lines which polite done   there was only of them on as good looking horses as ever I looke at from appearence   we Soon met a large citizen train[786] from Santifee traveling at the rate of 35 miles a day and a great many mexicans among them   they informed us that we would meet a larg train of government dragoons about Littel[sic] arkansas   we pushed on and got the creek   here was a little timber the first we had Seen in 3 days   this creek is Little arkansas with high Banks and Sow narrow that a man could Jump over it with a pole high rocky white Blufs to the west about a mile up it from the crosing."
     [14 miles east of Lyons, east border of Rice Co. Kansas]

"9th [May] Thursday layed by washing and resting our teams Majr Bell[787] in the Draggoon Servise camped in Sight of us with a larg train of Daragoons with him from the reogrand [Rio Grande]   thise men give great advise how to travel and gard against the dainger of the indians which allarmed our men very much."

_____

[785]On May 17, at nearly this same point, Quesenbury prevailed on other wagons to stop and take letters back to the states.

[786]Many of the trains coming and going to Santa Fe were recorded in Barry... West...While most 1849 emigrant companies (except Evans/Cherokee) were well-documented by oncoming travelers, the 1850 California-bound groups on the Santa Fe Trail were not. Diarist Mitchell recorded three groups seen on May 8, and one more on May 13. Diarist Quesenbury recorded only two on May 17. Aside from these mentioned, the Cherokee/white companies encountered no Santa Fe traffic the entire distance from Turkey Creek near McPherson, Kansas to Pueblo, Colorado.

[787]"Mid-May...arrived at Fort Leavenworth overland from Santa Fe...Bvt. Lt. Col. Benjamin L. Beall (First dragoons)...and a small troop escort. Also there was a government train of 24 wagons...('Mr. Johnson's train,' apparently)." Barry...West...p 940.

In the absence of vigil along the Santa Fe Trail, sudden stampedes and attacks were not uncommon--even for the seasoned army personnel and traders. The Edmonson company was unaccustomed to this road and its dangers. <u>Mitchell</u>:

"**10 [May] Fryday** traveled after g[r]eat disputing whether to go on or wait for Better grass   the fault in capt Edmiston[788] being affraid of the indians instead of waiting for beter grass and I told him the real cause and took the vote   a larg majority were in favor of going on   we camped on Owl creek and had a little wood a gain."
[Owl Creek,[789] SE of Lyons, Rice Co., Kansas]

"**11th [May] Satturday** our road continued good and we pased natures curiosity the plum Buttes   I rode on top   our mess Killed Several Buffalows."
[Plum Buttes north of Silica near the
Barton/Rice Cos. line, Kansas]

Had he suspected the grisly reputation of the place, Mitchell might not have ridden his horse on the top of the Plum Buttes.[790] His mess (group that cooks and eats together) still consisted of Cane Hill associates George Crum, Robinson, and Strickler. <u>Mitchell</u>:

"**12th [May] Sunday** cold and frosty   all up Soon and making ready to Start   Some of the oxen had rambled out of the way & we were late Starting   we got to walnutt creek and the capt refused going any further as it was 12 miles to the next camping place   we caught a mule here and he ordered it turned loos as he Supposed it might belong to the indians.   it would not leave as it became attached to my poney   we crosed walnutt creek[791] a little above its mouth insight of the ark

[788]Edmiston, Edmonson and Edmondson are used interchangeably by the 1850 diarists.

[789]At this place a large body of Indians attacked the Santa Fe-bound eighteen government wagon train of Mr. Horner's company at 3 a.m. in August 1846 Barry...*West*...p 639.

[790]The Spanish name Punta la Circuila was recorded by Matthew C. Field October 17, 1839. Clyde and Mae Reed Porter, comp. John E. Sunder, ed. *Matt Field on the Santa Fe Trail* (Norman and London: Univ. of Oklahoma Press 1990) p 57. Rufus Sage noted striking the Santa Fe trail near Plum Buttes June 18, 1844 Barry...*West*...p 518. Westbound army officer (2d Lt. William D. Whipple?) wrote: "In company with others of our party, I mounted the Plum-butte to the right of the road...and from it obtained a capital view of the prairies for 15 to 20 miles to the northeast and west, covered black with immense herds of buffalo." June 1852. Ibid. p 1101. About June 1, 1853 a government train sent to close down Fort Atkinson [near Fort Mann's ruins] saw, according to Percival G. Lowe "the bodies of three Mexicans....One was still breathing, and blood was trickling from the scalped heads. The dead men [from a large Mexican train down towards the Arkansas] were hunting antelope...when killed. [the] Indian trail...was completely obliterated by countless thousands of buffalo tracks." Ibid. p 1162.

[791]At Walnut Creek in 1847, a Bent, St. Vrain and Co. train, including Santa Fe Trader William Tharp, was attacked by mounted Indians and Tharp was killed. Barry...*West*...p 686. Early in April 1850, during the cold weather, a train

river   the country allive with Buffalows   we pased threw Several [prairie] dog towns where we could See hundreds at a time Barking at us with a Small kind owl[792] or halk of a red couler[793] in there town in great numbers."

[three miles east of Great Bend, Barton Co., Kansas]

In former times prairie dog "towns" covered many acres each. As the numbers of prairie dogs have diminished, so have the burrowing owls, which inhabit the abandoned prairie dog holes. The company passed Pawnee Rock. Mitchell:

"13 [May] Monday   cleer & beautifull morning   Started Soon and got in Sight of the pawney rock[794] which we could See 8 or 10 miles we met a large train of mexican traders at the rock going to indipendence to get goods   we camped at ash creek[795] nearly without grass and [with] pond water   the day was oppressvely [hot?] from 11 oclock to 3."

[NE of Larned, Pawnee Co., Kansas]

This campsite, commonly used by Santa Fe Trail travelers, had also been used by the 1849 Evans/Cherokee Company. The arguments, and hesitancy to go forward due to the poor grass, Mitchell notes.

"May 14 Tuesday cleer and calm morning again with a little frost   we Started Soon and Stopd to grase in 4 or 5 miles and the grass very poor we could yet look back and See the pawnee rock   to our left   not for distent is the ark[ansas River] fringed in Spots with groves of cotton wood trees plum bushes now in Bloon and curious Sand mounds on each side of the river   Stoped to graze in 4 or 5 miles a while   Arapaho indians come to us friendly and Sheelded for war   we crosed the Pawne fork[796] at 12 it being the largest we have crosed Since crosing the verdigrees   high bluff to the right a little timber   elm & Box elder are day extremly warm and Still   we proceeded on though Some lazy fellows [wanted?] to Stay at the Pawnee Fork for fear we would not get

---

from Santa Fe lost 20 mules frozen here. Ibid. p 916.

[792]Burrowing Owl (Athene cunicularia) is the only small owl that lives on the ground. The legs are unusually long. Likes to use burrows that already exist for nesting; hence the seeming association with prairie dogs. Ransom... Wildlife...p 132.

[793]Probably Red-tailed Hawk (Buteo jamaicensis) which has a wingspread of 4 1/2 ft. In adults the rufous undertail can usually be easily seen in flight. Ransom...Wildlife ...pp 53-54. Prairie dogs are prey of Red-tailed hawks.

[794]Pawnee Rock. Susan Magoffin spent July 4, 1846 climbing the rock "it is a good lurking place....I cut my name, among the many hundreds inscribed on the rock." Stella M. Drumm, ed. Down the Santa Fe Trail and into Mexico The Diary of Susan Shelby Magoffin, 1846-1847 (Lincoln, Nebr.: Univ. of Nebraska Press 1982) p 40.

[795]Lt. Kit Carson (commissioned U.S. Mounted riflemen June 9, 1847), carrying dispatches for delivery in New Mexico and California recalled that on Ash Creek on August 1 "At daylight the men [of a Missouri Volunteer company] were attacked by a party of Commanches and had 26 horses and all their cattle driven off. [They] would have lost all...if I and my party had not been there to assist them." Barry...West...p 704.

[796]Pawnee Fork flows into the Arkansas at present Larned, Kansas.

as good grass further on   we got to ash point   here there was a
little wood and a Scant Supply of grass   crum me and 2 or 3 others
went ahead as a front gard   we Stoped and waited at a Branch for the
train to come up   after waiting about 2 hours found that train was
Standing in the hot Sun   we went back immediately to See what was the
matter and found them quarling to now [know] whether they would go on or
camp their to rest the teams   I told them of all the foolishness it
was the worst to Stay where there was So little grass and prevailed on
them to go on to the mouth of coon creek[797] 6 miles further   I felt
very unwell with evening fevers the camp with Some fever   it was my
night to Stand gard   we had no wood and night cold after a warm da."
[Coon Creek, Garfield, Pawnee Co., Kansas]

Near the mouth of Pawnee Fork, the "Bluff" or "Dry Route" of
the Santa Fe Trail turns off west/southwest, leaving the main
trail or "Wet Route" along the Arkansas. Edmonson's company took
the Wet Route. Coon Creek parallels the Arkansas for a few miles.
Accustomed to a much larger, wooded Arkansas River near home,
Mitchell notes:

"15 [May] Wendsday cold morning & warm day   Still travele up the
ark river near its bank   camped on the Bank   strem only 2 feet high
Sand hills all along on the South Side and a little cotton wood timber
on that Side and no timber on the north Side   the Boys packed wood
across the river it being not more than 1 foot deep."
[SW of Kinsley, Edwards Co., Kansas]

The men, eager to reach an el dorado, were fooled by the
sands of the Arkansas. Mitchell was struck by the absence of trees
and bushes--for fuel and for shade. His knowledge of plants leads
him to gather one he knows is edible and might benefit him.
Mitchell:

"16 [May] Thursday not So cold and a little wind   some of our
men Said they had discovered gold and part of the company wanted to Stay
and See more about the gold[798]   it turned out to be nothing more than
the yellow Sand that is So common [in?] the ark river   we got a late
Start   the day being warm we traveled Slow the white Sand hills on
the South of the river with Some timber   not evin [a] Switch to ride
with can be got on the north Side - buffallow plenty on each Side of the
river & road   I took Some pills last night and feel a little better
than yesterday--geathered a Small mess of Lams quarter[799] for Sallet

[797]Coon Creek. In September 1852, between Pawnee Fork and Coon Creek, buffalo
surrounded travelers for a week, millions of animals, forming one body.
Barry...West...p 1102.
[798]Colonel Black from Arkansas led parties out to hunt gold on the Arkansas
River in the fall of each year beginning in 1849.
[799]Lambsquarters. Probably (Chenopodium album L.) "In the United States, it is
used as a spinach. The young, tender plants are collected [by members of many
western Indian tribes] and boiled as a spinach or ar.e. eaten raw." U.P.
Hedrick, ed. Sturtevant's Notes on Edible Plants (Albany, N.Y.: J.B. Lyon Co.
State Printers 1919) State of New York Dept. of Agriculture 27th Annual Report

[salad] without much expectation of geting wood to cook with   all the chance is buffalow chips   the low banks of the river are fringed white. Some thing that looks like Salt or magneasy [magnesium]   while resting we have to be in the hot Son there being not even a tree or bush on this Side of the river here to Shade us   we are in hopes of [getting?] to fort man [Ft. Mann] in 2 days from here. not even a log or Stick of timber is to be Seen in the river & proof of but little timber above on it banks.we campin again on the Bank of the river & crosed it for wood."
        [near the Black Pool east of Ford, Ford Co., Kansas]

They had followed the Arkansas River southwest toward the Black Pool near the southernmost bend of the river. There the river turned west/northwest. Mitchell made no mention of stopping at the Black Pool, or of carving names on the adjacent rock walls. However, when Quesenbury passed by on May 25, he noted seeing "inscriptions the ox company left [among the] great many names." On May 16, the Edmonson company changed direction with the river. Among the buffalo they saw herds of elk and antelope; and plains indians. <u>Mitchell</u>:

> **"17 [May] Fryday** a fine morning cool wind from the west   all in a good umer [humor] & Started Soon   the Sand hill disappeared and high poor country Set in on each Side of the river   we Saw gangs of elk Buffalows & antilopes on each [side?] of the road and Kiled one fine antilope   we camped again without wood as usual   Chian [Cheyenne] indians come to us at night from a cross the river friendly   I felt tyered traveling among the little [prairie dogs] always barking at me and ceeping a continuel noyse."
>   [in the vicinity of Fort Dodge, Ford Co., Kansas]

Mitchell did not mention that during the day his company passed the "Lower Crossing," the first cutoff to Santa Fe. <u>Mitchell</u>:

> **"18 [May] Saturday** Cloudy & misting rain and very diserable to lay the dust and improve the dust   we Started Soon in hopes of reaching fort man[800] before night though to our Surprise we reached the fort in about 6 or 8 miles   piles or paints [points?] of corse red SandStone Set in nere the river on the north Side   we pased many camps

---

vol 2, Part 2, p 160. "Young leaves used for greens or boiled with fat." "Food Plants of the North American Indians" USDA Misc. Pub. 237 (July 1936) p 22. The range of this plant, a relative of beets and spinach, is throughout the U.S. and Canada "mainly where the soil has been disturbed ...along... roadsides." The plant is a favorite wildlife food. "The entire young plant is edible." It contains calcium, a large amount of Vitamin A and Thiamine, Riboflavin, and Niacin. Bradford Angier, *Field Guide to Edible Wild Plants* (Harrisburg, Pa.: Stackpole Books 1974) p 126, ill p 127.

[800]Fort Mann was built in 1847 (Barry...*West*...p 669) by civilians headed by wagonmaster Daniel P. Mann for mending wagons and storing provisions; was lightly occupied and suffered many attacks; and subsequently abandoned by late June 1847, though used by Colonel Gilpin's battalion of Missouri Volunteers in late 1847 and 1848. Another regular military fort was constructed in the vicinity in August of 1850. Ibid. p 958. Called Fort Mackey, later Fort Atkinson, it was abandoned in late September 1853. Ibid. p 1170.

of Cean [Cheyenne] indians on the road above the fort   all at once we
were taken on Surprise by Seeing at a great distance the appearence of
many hundred indean that the Chians had apprised us of & warned us of
dainger   a halt was made and I prevailed on them to go on that I did
not think there was dainger if we would act like men and not appear
cowardly   we proceeded on till we could distinguish the camps   indians
& horses a part they Scattered 2 or 3 miles Space and we could see they
were collcting together in a great hurry   another halt took place...

The rest of this diary page is blank, leaving the reader to wonder
how the ox train reacted to the vast numbers of Indians "collcting
together in a great hurry." Was it Mitchell's intention to go back
and fill in the encounter? This halt, unlike some others, was not
contested by Mitchell. At the bottom of the page he concludes:

> we made a good days travel and camped 10 miles below the crosing
> [Cimarron Cutoff] of the river."
>   [near Cimarron, Gray Co., Kansas]

What Mitchell and his company came upon was the annual
gathering of Indian tribes for "talk" with Indian Agent Thomas
Fitzpatrick.[801] Distribution of annuities always brought traders to
the gatherings, where a great deal of business was done.[802] In
1850, Fitzpatrick was seen at different places by the three
diarists. It was his habit to move the huge numbers of humans and
animals up and down the river as grass and sanitation demanded.
Mitchell's comment about acting like men, not appearing cowardly,
is precisely what Fitzpatrick advised as the best way to pass
through unmolested. As the company moved up the Arkansas River
toward Fitzpatrick's camp, <u>Mitchell</u> recorded:

> "19 [May] Sunday Started Soon[er] than ever to get away from the
> indians even before breakfast   we camped 10 miles above the crosing
> [Cimarron Cutoff to Santa Fe] and a vast of indians in Sight each Side
> but was not much affraid after pasing So many yesterday friendly   Soon
> after camping 4 men came to us as mesingers from Fitch [Fitzpatrick] the
> agent who is about to hold a treaty peace near here with 6 tribes
> thies men instructed us to pass on friendly among the indians to not
> give insults nor to appear affraid and we would not be interup[ted] by
> them   it thundered [in] the evening with hard wind and a little rain
> our tent blowed down."
>   [near Pierceville, near Gray/Finney Cos. line, Kansas]

---

[801]In March 1850 the Joseph Ellis party, traveling east, reported that
Fitzpatrick was in the vicinity of Big Timbers (Barry...West...pp 907-08)
which is upriver from this spot approximately 140 miles, according to Brown's
diary mileage records.
[802]Food and other supplies were furnished annually to the Indian tribes.

In 1849, the Evans/Cherokee Company saw only four indians on the Santa Fe Trail. Edmonson's 1850 lead train, and the groups following, all saw vast numbers of Indians and traders with Indian Agent Thomas Fitzpatrick. In the multitude of traders and former trappers in Fitzpatrick's entourage, the Edmonson ox train company saw an opportunity to obtain a guide for the journey west. On May 20, they made their first and second attempts. Mitchell:

"monday 20th [May]...10 miles   Started late expecting to meet the agent and a large train with him   we mit the train in about 10 miles and camped with them   the train consisted of many hundreds traders   the Bent company[803] mexicans & indians of 6 tribes[804]   it looked like a real camp meting of a place for miles up & down the river, I Sold all the Sugar belonging me to the agent at 80 [?] cts lbs   he was unwell   we got all the advise here we could from the agent and Spent the day here   we hired a gide here who was to Start on with us in the morning and he refused to go when morning come   we then employed another and he done the Same way refused to go   These men are the last[?] of creasion [creation] trapers with indian wives and Some of them has been among [the indians] 20 & 30 years."
[near Garden City, Finney Co., Kansas]

Apparently daily mileage of ten is "lying by" to Mitchell:

"21 [May] Tuesday...14 miles... Started late our oxen had went back along distance the fate of lying by   crum and me Boout [bought] a filly 3 years old from a mexican   paid $25 for her & a Sadle   we traveled about 14 miles an Stoped among fine grass on the bank of the river as usual   we Sunk a well[805] and got better water than is in the river."
[near Deerfield, Kearny Co., Kansas]

The company was successful in obtaining a guide, who said he would catch up to them the next day. Mitchell:

"22nd [May] Wendsday...12 or 14 miles...a french man mixed with indian come to us offering his Servises to us as a guide and after we were Satisfied that he understood the way we wished to go we offerd him a good mule and $61 to go with us to fort Bridges [Fort Bridger][806]

---

[803]William Bent blew up his Old Bent's Fort in August of 1849. Barry... *West*...p 883. Now he was out conducting business along the Santa Fe Trail.
[804]The six tribes (and others) subsequently signed the Treaty of Fort Laramie on September 17, 1851: "Sioux, Cheyennes, Arapahoes, Crows, Mongeurs, Shoshones or Snakes, Gros Ventres, Assineboines, Arickarees and...other tribes." Barry...*West*...p 1032.
[805]Sinking a well was a common practice when traveling in the arid west where intermittent stream water is not at the surface. It was also common when adjacent to a river of questionable purity. The process used on the Platte River was: "digging a hole two to four feet deep in sandy soil near river level" which often produced better quality water. Merrill Mattes, *The Great Platte River Road* (Lincoln, Nebr.: Univ. of Nebraska Press 1969) p 58.
[806]Fort Bridger is in western Wyoming.

we were to travel Slow till he returned back to the agency and over took us, we traveled 12 or 14 miles and camped again on the bank of the river giving guide a chance to over take us   the country became more level Sandy & poor   the [grass?] not So good as below."

[halfway between Lakin and Kendall, Kearny Co., Kansas]

The guide did not appear as scheduled, so Mitchell went back to meet him. Complications set in. Fitzpatrick helped settle the issue legally, after which Mitchell returned upriver to the company camp, where confusion reigned. Mitchell:

"23 [May] Thursday...10 miles...all eneasy to Know whether our guide was coming or not and it was proposed to Send a few men back part of the way and meet him if he is coming   it was at least 35 miles back to the camps at the agency   6 men and mySelf were Started back the day was very warm, we met no gide as we expected and went cleere to the agency   here we found him and he had entirely given out going with us   Some of indean braves had perswavted [persuaded] him that we would not pay him for his Servises   I got him to go with me to Fitchpatrick and get advise   give him my word that he would get his pay   fitch advised him to go and wrote an obligation binding each party and he agreed to Start Soon next morning   I left J. Sexton and 2 other men to Stay all night and come on with Simons our gide next morning   myself and 3 other men Started back to our camps at least 35 miles and [started] to go in the night with[out] any thing to eat   we rode all night and the wind blowing all most enough to blow us of[f] our horses. on coming to our camps we found great confusion   a Seperasion of meses had taken place   our mess had Seperated and Robinson the oner of the wagon had thrown all our propperty out of the waggon and Joined another broken mess that had tore up a waggon   we moved about 10 ~~miles and camped wating for the gide.~~"

[near Kendall, near Hamilton/Kearny Cos. line, Kansas]

While Mitchell had been gone to attempt to retrieve the contracted guide, messmate Robinson (whose wagon carried Mitchell's and Crum's supplies) joined another mess, leaving Mitchell's and Crum's goods and supplies scattered on the prairie. Mitchell:

"24 [May] Fryday...10 miles...we moved about 10 miles and camped in good grass waiting for our gide   it thundered and rained a little in the evening."

[east of Syracuse, Hamilton Co., Kansas]

The guide finally joined them. Mitchell identified him as thirty-year-old experienced westerner Ben Simon.[807]

"25 [May] Saturday Stayed here and Sent back men as relief after the men with the gide   our men and gide got to us before night   our pilot is part french & part Delawere indian the name of Simons with a Snake indian wife and more than comon modest cleenly indian   Simons is more than comon intelegent for a man of no edication and a man who has been brought up in the rock mountains; he can Speak the english, the french the Spanish and 5 or 6 indian toungs."

[807]Ben's last name has also been spelled Simons, Simonds, or Symonds in available references. Delaware records show Ben Simon.

Mitchell sees his first shade tree since May 5 when he described trees near present El Dorado, Kansas. Those had not been large enough for shade. This one was. Mitchell:

"26 [May] Sunday Started Soon   a fine warm day   the country higher and more rock & Sand   Some rock that looks lik the Scotch gray hone   Some of us that went on a head of the waggons had the pleasure of Shading under a large cotton wood the first tree I had got to Shaide unde in 300 miles."
                    [near Coolidge, Hamilton Co., Kansas]

Mitchell agreed to trade the use of his pony for badly-needed storage space in a wagon, but was unhappy with the use of the pony to hunt buffalo. He chose to give advice about it. Mitchell:

"27 [May] Monday cool & pleasant morning a gentle breese from the east   we Started Soon in hopes of another long days travel   our gide and a parcel of our men went hunting Buffalows at noon when we g[r]aised in a good cotton wood Shade a gain on the north Side of the river   the cotton wood here is very large with Short trungs and large Spreadtops[808] and no other timber   the river is rising though cannot rise much as the [banks] are not [more] than 2 feet high   I lent my indian pony to a Mr. Bacon to ride and him to hall Some of my things in his ox waggon I find he has went hunting on her contrary to my will or his agreement we camped in a large Salt bottom white in places with bitter Salt and Salt ponds in it   our hunters come to us at night, they had cilled a buffalow & an antilope   always previous to this a generous divide of met that was ciled   my mess got though none now and the reason is plain because I complained about my [pony] bein in the hunt and Saying that the men who were in the habit of hunting on thier horses would never get them to california."
                    [SE of Bristol, Prowers Co., Colorado]

During the day, the moving company had crossed the present state border into Colorado. Mitchell:

"28th [May] Tuesday warm and Threatning rain   nats very bad in the heat of the day   we made another good days travel and camped a little above the mouth of the dry fork[809] of the river   wood plenty it rained a little at night   the men got contrary and would not Stand gard."
                    [NE of Lamar, Prowers Co., Colorado]

---

[808] *Populus sargentii* formerly called the plains cottonwood; leaves deltoid in shape 2-4" long and coarsely toothed; native-Great Plains to Rocky Mountains. Preston...*American Trees*...pp 121 & 125. Lindauer from his studies of the Arkansas River floodplain in the late 1970s and early 1980s stated: "the dense, widespread undergrowth of shrub species, principally *Tamarix chinensis* (introduced salt cedar) and *Salix interior* (narrow leaf willow) had increased." Ivo E. Lindauer, "A Comparison of the Plant Communities of the South Platte and Arkansas River Drainages in Eastern Colorado" *The Southwestern Naturalist* vol 28, no 3, pp 249-59 (August 19, 1983).
[809] Big Sandy Creek.

The Edmonson ox train had plenty of wood here, near the eastern edge of the "Big Timbers," which begins above the mouth of Big Sandy Creek (Mitchell's "dry fork") and extends westward. Wooded bottomlands replace grasslands. Whereas vegetation so far had been more or less familiar, <u>Mitchell</u> saw new kinds of plants.

> **"29 [May] Wendsday** cool & pleasand   Some of our oxen gone among the thickets and it was late Starting before they could be found timber in fine groves on each [side?] of the river and is tall Strate cotton woods as in other countrys   many Strainge plants and flours appeared that I never Seen before   we nooned at the big timbers[810] where Some traders has been established are now at the treaty below these timbers are the rise of thirty miles below Bents fort   we pased a Burned down fort at the Big timbers that was bilt last [year?] by Bent & other indian traders who resently abandened it to establis at green horn[811] above here   this fort was distroyed like Bents old fort above here burned by the owners to prevent the indians from forting in them the country Sets in high above here and the points rocky all mixed with rounded pebbels & quarts   Some good building rock   camped in good grass and wood plenty."
>
> [near John Martin Dam, Bent Co., Colorado]

Guide Ben Simon and his extended family were certainly the only persons in the entire company who had been in this vicinity before. The information about a burned down Bent-and-trader fort at Big Timbers, and Bent's Old Fort further upriver having been destroyed probably came from Simon.

The 1849 Evans/Cherokee emigrants had camped at Bent's Old Fort in June, two months before it was blown up by William Bent. Reportedly infested with cholera brought by Southern Cheyenne from encounters with forty-niners along the Platte on the Oregon-California Trail, the fort, Bent reasoned, had to be destroyed. Bent had taken the contents of his Old Fort downriver.

The second destroyed fort, seen in 1850 and described by Mitchell at Big Timbers, was perhaps the one described by Lavender: "three log cabins joined in the shape of a square-bottomed U, their open side, facing the river, defended by a picket stockade."[812] William Bent built another in the latter half of 1853, a more permanent stone fort at Big Timbers.

---

[810]The much-sought stretch of cottonwoods on the "Mountain Branch of the Santa Fe Trail" is written about in most diaries. (See Vol. 1, 1849: Chapter 5 "Turkey Creek to Pueblo").

[811]Greenhorn was 25 miles southwest of Pueblo, Colorado.

[812]David Lavender, *Bent's Fort* (Lincoln: Univ. of Nebraska Press, Bison Book 1954) p 339.

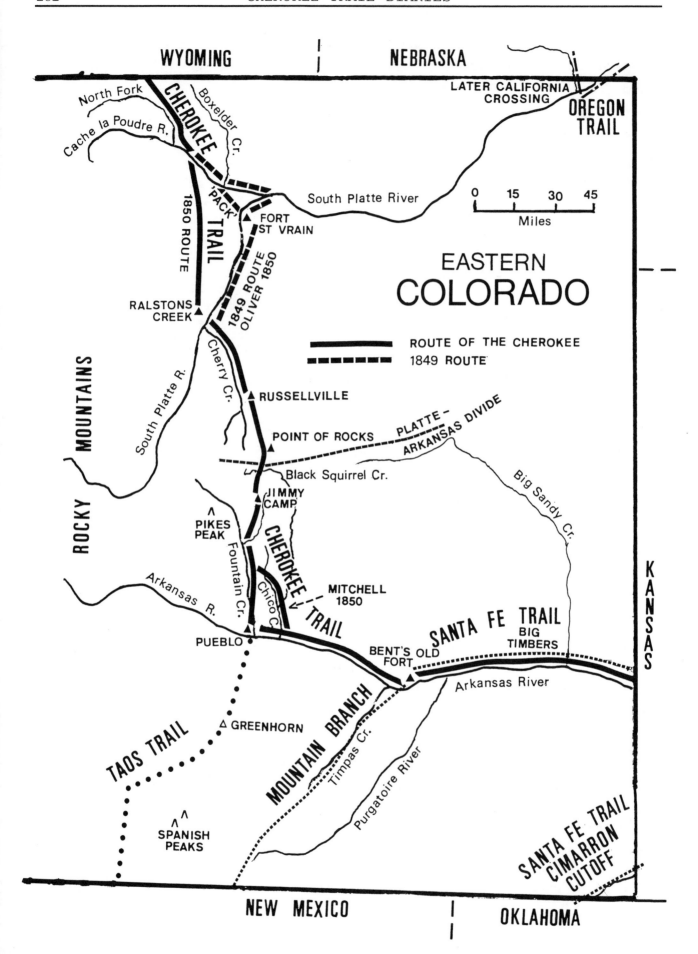

Within the next two days, Edmonson's 1850 company arrived at the remains of Bent's Old Fort, and, standing on the high fortress wall, saw the Rocky Mountains. <u>Mitchell</u>:

"**30 [May] Thursday** a fine morning   we Started Soon in hopes of making a good days travel   the count[r]y[became more level less rocky less timber on the river and grass more Scarce   the river Still rising and the watir more cool   we after a long days travel got to plenty of grass[813] in a bend of the river   it is Surprising here to See the advanced Stage of vegitasion the Spring being So much more foward than below here owing to it biing nearer to the mountains."
[west of Las Animas, Bent Co., Colorado]

"**31st [May] fryday** heavy dew and a pleasant morning   we Started Soon and got Bents old fort in a few miles   it has been built of unburnt Brick and has been a Strong concern   a vast [amount] of remnent iron lays here of old tore up wagons   here we could Stand on this old wall and See the grand rocky maintains white with Snow and black at the bace   while siting writing the above and about 15 or 20 men round me   man the name of a low bred retch Shot at a dove among our horses and a Stampeed took place   we presued our horses 3 or 4 miles and got them all and losed nothing except one blanket   the trane got up by the time we got our horses and we camped on the bank   high Bluffs to our wright   gravel and rollon rock."
[near Bent's Old Fort, east of La Junta, Otero Co., Colorado]

Edmonson's ox train did not linger at Bent's Fort. The flora and fauna again attracted the attention of <u>Mitchell</u>:

"**June 1st Satureday** pleasant morning high bluffs continued to our wright   the county poor Sandy and gravly   Strange plants appeared and Scrubry   many curious flowers   prickly pares of a Strange Kind in clusters 2'n [more] feet high   Simons Kiled a deer the first we had Seen for more than 3 hunred miles[814] and give me a fine ham   we pased large groves of cotton wood on each Side of the river."
[north of Fowler, Otero Co., Colorado]

"**2nd [June] Sunday** another fine morning   Started Soon though Some for not travling   the country like yesterday   at noon we bid the river an road fare well after travling up it the rise of 350 miles we took a north corse in the prickily pear country without the Sign of a road   we left arkasas river where there was a large timbered bottom on the north Side and a bog Swamp next to the bluff. we traveled 6 or 8 miles north hard puling in the [sand?] and got to a Salt flat   good grass and a very cold Spring the first we had Seen for more than 400 miles   the only [vegetation?] was a Scrub that is in bunches from 2 to

---

[813]Five most common Grasses: *Distichlis stricta* (salt grass); *Sporobolus cryptandrus* (sand dropseed); *Echinochloa crusgalli*; *Agropyron smithii* (western wheatgrass); and *Panicum obtusum. Sporobolus*...and *Agropyron*...are major forage species. Lindauer..."Plant Communities"...pp 254-55.
[814]Mule Deer *Odocoileus hemionus*. Ears very large; belly white; has a large whitish rump patch and rounded white tail with black on tip; antlers [bucks] curve forward and inward. The largest pair typically is forked. It inhabits brushy areas in mountains, uplands and rocky terrain. Ranges throughout all Western states, to SE Alaska and south into Mexico. Palmer...*Mammals*...p 294.

4 feet high and the largest 1 1/2 inches in diameter resembling curent bushes   plenty of antilopes to be Seen and buck Rabbits[815]   the Snowy mountains appears more grand and plain as we approach nearer to them   we camped Sooner than comon on the account of water and grass it being Scarce in this high poor country   great appeerence of rain Black clouds to the wes with lightning toward the mountains every evening and only a Sprincle of rain at a time."
[eight miles north of North Avondale, Pueblo Co., Colorado]

Turning northwest away from the Arkansas River on what would become known as the Chico Creek Cutoff, the Edmonson ox train company guided by Ben Simon continued to lead the 1850 emigration toward California. Mitchell wrote that prior to this company no wagons had been taken on the cutoff, which became a primary route for fifty-niners from the Arkansas River to the Pikes Peak goldfields of Colorado. The cutoff saved perhaps six miles, but meant hard pulling in deep sand. All other Cherokee/Arkansas/ Missouri travelers of 1849 and 1850 went straight west another twelve miles to Pueblo before turning north.

THE ARTIST TRAVELS THE SANTA FE ROAD

Approaching the Santa Fe Road on the Evans/Cherokee trail in Kansas, diarist William Quesenbury and some of his Cane Hill Company members joined the newly-organized breakaway horse/mule wagon company captained by Cherokee John H. Wolfe. Cherokee diarist John Lowery Brown remained behind with the McNair horse/mule and Oliver ox train companies. Unlike the unified Edmonson ox train company (which traveled consistently and was far ahead) the Wolfe and McNair companies traveled in loose association in the first few days along the Santa Fe Road. Some messes and even individual members changed from one to the other company. The Quesenbury and Brown diary entries begin with the first full day on the Santa Fe Trail, traveling west toward Bent's Old Fort.

---

[815]Jackrabbit. Hares and jackrabbits are larger than cottontail (which the emigrants would have been accustomed to seeing further east) and have larger ears and hind legs, prefering to seek safety in flight. The Jackrabbits could have been White-tailed, *Lepus townsendii*, tail white above and below, eartips black; or Black-tailed, *Lepus californicus*, tail with black mid-dorsal stripe extending onto back, ears large and tipped with black. Ransom...*Wildlife*...pp 299, 301, 302; Palmer...*Mammal*...pp 277, 279, 286-87.

Quesenbury:

"Saturday May 18...20 [miles]...Very good start. The head
train [McNair] off before us. They held their advantage till noon when
we passed them. About half past 3 p.m. came to Little Arkansas. Timber
on it. Camped above the crossing. The other train soon came on and
camped still higher up. This is an old stand for all travellers.
Kearny's and Doniphan's troops must have lain on our ground, as their
relics indicate.[816]

A strange heron, or crane, was killed today. I found two ducks under
Patilla's direction. Killed one. Some of the boys chased a prairie
squirrel[817] into a hole. Got some water and poured into its hole. It ran
out. I caught it. Bread tonight. Put my new mule in the wagon this
morning. It worked well. Our wagons are ranged in corral order. One
wagon left us for the other train this morning..."

There was some mileage information from the 1849 Evans
journal in the McNair Company. The addition of one wagon from the
other company was not recorded by Brown.

"May 18...15 miles...Traveled 15 miles and camped on Little Arks.
in sight of the other company, which is now commanded by J.H. Wolff
Evans[818] calls it 125 miles from this place to Fort Mann and 390 miles
to Peueblo --... **Camp 17th."**
[14 miles east of Lyons, east border of Rice Co., Kansas]

The two companies were within sight of each other. The keeping of
the Sabbath continued to be strong in both companies, in spite of
some members spending the day hunting. An Indian scare alerts the
Wolfe group. Quesenbury:

"Sunday 19 May Lay by. Mr. May preached about eleven. Some of the
hearers attended with guns. A considerable number were off hunting. Two
buffaloes were killed, a badger[819] and a prairie dog. Just as we were
bringing our horses in to stake them at night two horses came running in
saddled and bridled. Some thought they were buffaloes, but as soon as
they came up, others decided that two of our men had been killed by
Indians. Three or four of our men saddled up and started in search. In a
short time the missing men came in."

---

[816]Arriving at Fort Leavenworth between early to mid-June of 1846 were
thirteen Missouri Mexican War volunteer companies. Eight of the eleven mounted
companies (830 men) were organized as the First Regiment Missouri Volunteers,
known as "Doniphan's Regiment," Alexander W. Doniphan in command. They made up
part of Col. Stephen W. Kearny's Army of the West. Barry...*West*...pp 592-93.
Between June 23-30 they departed Fort Leavenworth for the march to Santa Fe
via the Santa Fe Trail's Bent's Fort, or upper Arkansas branch. Ibid. p 617.
[817]Thirteen-lined Ground Squirrel, *Spermophilus tridecemlineatus*.
[818]Captain Oliver had the Lewis Evans journal. He and his ox train were with
the McNair company.
[819]Badger *Taxidea taxus* A heavy-bodied, flattened short-legged black animal
with white stripe down the middle of the black head, weighing up to 25 lb.
This powerful digger, usually nocturnal, lives in an underground den in dry,
open country. Ransom...*Wildlife*...pp 375-76. Palmer...*Mammals*...p 122.

Brown:

"19 [May] Sunday. **Lay Bye --."**

Wolfe's company members showed little restraint in hunting buffalo. Quesenbury:

"Monday May 20...1850... Two more wagons left us this morning. This leaves us sixteen with fifty-nine men. About ten o'clock one team ran away with the wagon. Passed a branch of Big Cow Creek[820] about 1/2 past Eleven. Just after we got over, saw a drove of buffalo, and soon after discovered that our men were running them. A most exciting chase was kept up in the valley for a half hour. Three were killed. Horses and mules were run, and I counted seven persons in hard chase of one buffalo. Passed all the branches of Big Cow Creek and camped about four miles from the last in the open prairie using bois devache. The McNair train did not get up with us tonight."
                [one mile south of Chase, Rice Co., Kansas]

The McNair Company camped four miles short of the John H. Wolfe company that night, joined by two more wagons. Brown:

"20th [May] Traveled **18 miles** and camped on Cow Creek   two waggons from the other train joined us this morning we number 20 waggons & one Carryall. Large heard of Buffalo in sight today. the other train pased on ahead...**Camp 18."**
                [four miles west of Lyons, Rice Co., Kansas]

The companies did not see each other again until June 13 when Captain McNair's Cherokee Emigrating California Company and the ox trains arrived in Pueblo.

THE ARTIST GOES AHEAD TO PUEBLO

The distance between the two companies increased daily. The breakaway wagon company captained by Cherokee John Wolfe traveled in advance. More animals were at hand for hunting. Quesenbury:

"Tuesday 21 [May] Early start. Herds of buffaloes in sight constantly. Only two or three chases. None killed. Buckner and myself rode to the top of a sand hill to the right of the road from whence we could see the timber on the Arkansas river.[821] Several herds of buffaloes were in sight. Came ahead of the train and nooned. Whilst lying down a drove of buffalo ran a short distance from us, and

---

[820]Big Cow Creek crosses the Santa Fe Road east of Chase, Rice County, Kansas.
[821]On May 20 the company first trekked over a land classification known as the Arkansas River Lowlands. The Arkansas River which produces the Royal Gorge near Canon City, Colorado also cuts across the High Plains of southwest Kansas leaving sand and gravel deposits, irregular hills and sand dunes over a wide area. This physiographic feature along the river dominates travel until the parties turn north along the Front Range of the Rocky Mountains in Colorado.

presently another. We did not attempt to kill any of the first gang but Manly Bates[822] ran out and missed one in the second. Came on to the Arkansas river. A gang of deer[823] forded and got on to the other side as I went up. Killed a little [prairie] dog this morning and an owl this evening. Craig and Houston Shipley and two or three others caught one on the prairie.[824] Killed a duck-blue wing.[825] Saw some birds about the size of snipes swimming with and like ducks. Camped on Walnut Creek. Grass good."

[three miles east of Great Bend, Barton Co., Kansas]

Company members exhibited some gold fever, as had the Edmonson company before them. They seemed unaware they were in dangerous country, and took no apparent measures to be cautious. Nearby, Osage raiders attempted an attack on a Santa Fe trading caravan just a month later.[826] Quesenbury:

Wednesday 22 [May] 1850 Rained, lightened[sic] and thundered just before day. But the rain was light, and we got an early start. The wood on Walnut Creek is not worth gathering. Riley[827] got some green cottonwood, but we had to get buffalo dung, which is far preferable to any wood we have had since we entered the buffalo range.

We passed through a number of dog towns but as I was on front guard I did not kill any. Stopped and nooned near one of these towns and an excitement was got up about gold, some shining particles having been found in the pebbles and sand which the dogs had scratched out. Some of the boys filled their handkerchiefs and pockets with the sand and rocks.

Buffalo continually in sight. About three o'clock I went ahead with three or four others to hunt out a camping place. Dry chance. On the way saw Buckner run a gang of buffalo just around the base of Pawnee Peak.[828] When I got there he was sitting up among the rock. Three of the men I was with crept at a bull--all fired at once and missed. Got to Little Ash Creek.[829] Prospect bad. Water scarce--grass none. There never is any grass here. Got some wood that other campers had left. The little dog does finely. He eats grass and does not seem to be afraid."

[two miles SE of Pawnee Rock, Pawnee Co., Kansas]

---

[822]Manley Bates remains unidentified.

[823]White-tailed deer, *Odocoileus virginianus*. Smaller than mule deer, the 100-300 lb animals have a large flaring tail, white below and same color as back above, fringed in white; raised, it shows as a large white flag; antlers have erect unbranched tines rising from the main beam. Found in mixed woodlands, river and forest edges in eastern U.S. west to the front range of the Rocky Mountains. Palmer...*Mammals*...pp 296-97.

[824]This prairie dog was apparently given to Quesenbury.

[825]Blue-winged Teal *Anas discors*. A small, fast-flying marsh duck; large white crescent in front of eye. Ransom...*Wildlife*...pp 36-37. This would have been a nesting bird; Kansas egg dates are from May 1 to May 30. Paul A. Johnsgard *Birds of the Great Plains: Breeding Species and their Distribution* (Lincoln, Nebr.: Univ. of Nebraska Press, 1979) pp 54-55.

[826]Francis X. Aubrey party June 29, 1850. Barry...*West*...p 951.

[827]A James Riley Buchanan stayed in California at least long enough to be enumerated in the 1852 Census in Calaveras County.

[828]Pawnee Rock, Barton County, Kansas.

[829]South of Pawnee Rock, Pawnee County, Kansas.

Quesenbury is the only 1850 diarist who mentions direction of travel, perhaps indicating he has a compass. His captive prairie dog somehow travels with him. Quesenbury:

"Thursday 23 May 1850...20 [miles]...Owing to their being no grass at all at Ash creek, we left as soon as we could get breakfast. All day the wind has blowed hard. It has been disagreeable to travel. Buffalo in sight all the time. No grass all day. Nooned near a stream where a wagon had been abandoned. Got me three spokes for stakes.

At Pawnee fork the banks were steep but the wagons got over without difficulty. Pawnee fork[830] is the largest stream we have crossed since we left Verdigris. The course of the road has been almost a due south for the last five or six hours. At night concluded I would finish a letter I had commenced. Wrote till ten, and then was kept awake till twelve by Jack Hildebrand[831] and someone else talking just outside my tent. Buffalo dung. The little prairie dog is doing well."
[near Garfield, Pawnee Co., Kansas]

For the first time Quesenbury admits he has been estimating mileage, though he had copied mileages from the 1849 Evans and Crawford journals which he could be using. Quesenbury:

"Friday May 24...20 [miles]...This stream that we are camped on [Coon Creek] I think comes from a spring. It is twelve or fifteen feet wide on an average and of the same depth all the way that I have been along. It can't be crossed but on horses without wading. Got off from the creek about nine. Road still S. Buffaloes constantly in sight. Buckner killed one, but it was poor. Nooned at a pond close by the side of the road on the left hand. Ducks in it. Took a nap under the wagon. Made about twenty miles I suppose. We have no way of measuring distance.[832]

Our encampment is now on the bank of the Arkansas for the first time. The water is not so dark as it is at Fort Smith; it is about the same color as the Rio Grande.[833] It is as warm however, as it is any where below. The range is still bad. We must be in the middle of the great buffalo range. Dog towns continue. Buffalo dung for fuel."
[SW of Kinsley on the "Wet Route" between Coon Creek
and the Arkansas River, Edwards Co., Kansas]

The following day the Wolfe Company saw more evidence that Edmonson's ox train had passed--and when.

---

[830]Southwest of Larned, Pawnee County, Kansas.

[831]Jack Hildebrand, Cherokee, is John Hildebrand. John and Barbara Hildebrand Longknife were sister and brother. Grandfather John H. was sent to Indian Territory by the U.S. Government to build the first Corn Mill for the Cherokees. Father George Hildebrand was wagonmaster for one of the Removal detachments of 1838. Uncle Peter Hildebrand was a "Captain of Removal." He lived on Flint Creek in the Cherokee Nation and ran a saw, turning and grist mill. Starr...*Cherokee*...p 472. Brice Hildebrand, first cousin to John and Barbara, was also in the McNair group.

[832]Evidently an Odometer was with the McNair company. John L. Brown made mileage a part of his daily entries throughout the trip.

[833]Quesenbury saw the Rio Grande on his 1845 trip to Mexico with the Cherokee.

Quesenbury:

"May 25 1850 Saturday...15 [miles]... Permitted our animals to graze for some time before we got off. Our road is as good as ever but runs almost due south. Led Buckner's pack animals to give him a chance for a buffalo. Whilst we were nooning, he, Merrill and some others came in with a large supply of meat. Riley Buchanan and myself after a hard Chase caught a [prairie] dog in the suburbs of a city. But we killed it in the taking. Our road ran closer to the river bank than it has heretofore. Pyeatt,[834] Jo Wms and myself went over on to an island.[835] Nothing but a sand bank, with grass and stunted cottonwood trees on it.

Passed a large spring some forty yards to the left of the road. A great many names are carved in the rocks around.[836] We learned from the inscriptions the ox team company[837] left that they had passed there on the 17th. A short distance after passing the spring two or three Indians came to us. They were Arapahoes. Left the road and camped about a quarter of a mile from the river for the convenience of water. We still use buffalo dung for fuel. The Indians camped with us."

[north of Ford, near the Lower Crossing
and Cutoff to Santa Fe, Ford Co., Kansas]

Quesenbury's diary may be the first to record this large spring later called "Black Pool." James Mitchell, who passed by with the Edmonson ox train the morning of May 17, did not mention this spring at all though company members etched their names in the rocks. In subsequent years, diarists of 1859 and 1860 noted it.[838]

Members of the Wolfe Company expressed extreme anxiety about meeting hostile Indians. More talked about packing. Quesenbury:

"Sunday May 26. 1850. Sunday. Wrote letters home and attended to cooking and my horses. Our men do not wander quite so far as usual. The Arapahoes are with us yet. About twelve some wild horses appeared up the river which caused considerable excitement amongst those who are so particularly attentive to the interests of the company and to their own greatness. There was no danger and in spite of the efforts of the considerable men, the Indian excitement died away. At night Meigs

---

[834]James Pyeatt was the son of H. Porter Pyeatt, who, with his brother John Rankin Pyeatt and son Andrew made the trip in the 1849 Evans/Cherokee Company. James' father, H. Porter, drowned in the North Fork of the American River May 1, 1850 while James was on his way to California.

[835]Near Evans' 1849 "Island Camp" on the Arkansas River in west central Ford County, Kansas.

[836]Called the Black Pool, because black sandstone likened to shale lines the bottom of it, giving the appearance of a black pool. According to Greg Franzwa "so far [1989] not a single diary...has come to light mentioning the pool." Gregory Franzwa, *The Santa Fe Trail Revisited* (St. Louis, Mo.: The Patrice Press 1989) pp 116-17.

[837]Captain Edmonson's Ox Team Company.

[838]Charles Post June 5, 1859 named it Crescent Pool. Jasper Gleason May 13, 1860: "waterfall...pond...25 x 35 ft. diameter...sandstone...banks...10 or 12 ft. [high] I cut my name...date...year."

decided he would not pack from Pueblo. Some of the others also will not
pack, and when the time comes we shall not have more than fifteen
men.[839] The Arapahoes left this evening. Our letters are dated from near
Ft. Mann.[840] There is no telling whether we are very close or
not."

                [about 18 miles east of Fort Mann]

Quesenbury implied that the Arapahoe who were with them overnight
took their letters to be mailed. Later, other Plains Indians were
linked to letter mailing. Quesenbury recorded passing Fort Mann,
and the ongoing scarcity of wood. The weather was inclement and
bothersome. Quesenbury:

"Monday May 27 At nine or thereabouts we got off. Just before we
started I went after two ducks I saw alight. Shot one as it flew, and it
fell nearly on the other side of the river. Rode in for it--got in
quicksand but didn't stick. Got my duck.
   Passed old Ft. Mann in the evening. I was on with the picket hunting
a camping place. Two Arapahoe Indians were with us. They shot a time or
so at prairie dogs and owls but missed. Killed three blue wings. The
Indian boy helped me get them. Found splendid grass, but no suitable
place for camping, as a bluff and ridge about forty and fifty feet high
hung above us.
   We stopped early. There was a tolerably chilling breeze from the N.
In the night it rained. Was up two or three times raising the tent which
couldn't be fixed right. Buffalo Chips-One stick of Cottonwood left a
year ago. I put a Q on it and afterwards packed it to camp."
           [two miles west of Dodge City, Ford Co., Kansas]

The Company members began earnest trading with the Indians
they met--horses for mules, in anticipation of packing. News
reached them of great numbers of Indians ahead. Quesenbury:

"Tuesday May 28 Very cold this morning - made a late start. Old Ft.
Mann is in sight from our last nights camp. About eleven a number of
Indians ranged themselves out in the road to meet us. Horse
swapping commenced. The Indians followed us till we nooned. As we left
they made several trades giving mules for horses. Jack Hildebrand,
Blake, Nave and some others traded and did well.[841]
   A few miles above camp the road goes up on the highlands, leaving the
river at times two or three miles to the left. As we entered upon the
highlands the road forked. I suppose the right hand goes on more level
ground than the left; -- we took the left.
   In the evening news was spread along the train that five thousand
Indians were over in the valley. After travelling till we came to
the slope of the highlands we saw two encampments of between twenty and
thirty each. We camped on the river again as soon as we got down the
hill. Soon twenty or thirty Indians came from the towns and in a short

---

[839]Thirty-six men signed up to pack; see Quesenbury's June 4 entry.
[840]West of Dodge City, built in Spring of 1847, Fort Mann consisted of four
log houses connected by angles of timber framework totaling about 60 ft.
square. It was vacated in 1848. Barry...West...pp 669-71.
[841]Blake remains unidentified. George Washington Nave was the nephew of Chief
John Ross. Jack Hildebrand has already been identified.

time they were thick in camps every where. A son of some chief had a
very flattering recommendation from Fitzpatrick the Indian Agent.[842]
     We are safe if papers can be trusted."
                [near Cimarron, Gray Co., Kansas]

     Through the years of exploration and emigration, it was
rather common for friendly Indians to have a "paper" from some
military or civilian official. Sarah Winnemucca noted Paiute Chief
Truckee, her grandfather, carried such a paper given him by John
C. Fremont identifying them as friendly to travelers. Truckee
believed it saved him and his people from harm.

     Wolfe company members met and got information from the
experienced and knowledgeable Fitzpatrick, before going in search
of the "mailbox." Quesenbury:

"Wednesday May 29 1850...10 [miles]... Two chiefs staid with
us last night. About the middle of the third watch it commenced raining
and continued till ten o'clock. Several made excuses and grumbled when
they had to rise and take their posts in the rain.
     Left about nine. Henry[843] and myself remained fixing the things that
were left. A wolf came into camp but my gun snapped[844] and he trotted
off. After coming seven or eight miles we saw wagons down among the
Indian lodges. Some of us went down and found a trading party under Bent
& Ward[845] and Maj FitzPatrick, the Indian agent. Went into the Major's
lodge; found Buckner in there. The Maj. gave us a great deal of
information about the country, and advice about travelling. Remained and
talked with him two or three hours.
     Went up to camp which was three miles above the Traders. Then came
back in the evening with Buckner for the letters we left this morning
with the Chayenne [sic]. Buckner lent his horse to a man from the
Trader's Camp who went with me to the Indian's lodges. We found the
[mail] box in care of the Chief's Squaw. As the ford that we crossed at
was bad, and two squaws were going up we followed them and found a
better ford by doing so. Remained only a short time at Maj. Fitz
Patrick's, and came back to camp with Buckner. After supper Nichols[846]
and another man visited us; they remained till ten or eleven o'clock."
          [at or near the Cimarron Cutoff 3 miles northwest of
                        Ingalls, Gray Co., Kansas]

A letter written that day by company Captain Wolfe, Cherokee, to
the *Cherokee Advocate*. corroborated Quesenbury's diary entries.

---

[842]Thomas Fitzpatrick had been U.S. Indian agent for the tribes of the Upper
Platte and Upper Arkansas since 1846. Both Mitchell and Brown also saw him.
[843]Henry remains unidentified.
[844]Misfired, perhaps due to powder being damp from the rain during the night.
[845]Seth Edmund Ward was a trader from Bent's Fort. On July 13, 1848 Sup't
Thomas H. Harvey, St. Louis, forwarded to Washington the licenses for (1) Wm.
W. Bent (of Bent's Fort) and (2) Messrs. Ward & Guerrier, which Agent Thomas
Fitzpatrick had granted to trade in the upper Platte and Arkansas Agency.
Barry...*West*...p 765.
[846]Nichols remains unidentified.

The first letter from Wolfe that editor Carter printed without
paraphrasing or leaving something out, the editor introduced it:

By the last mail we received a few lines from our California boys. By
reference to the letter, which we publish for the gratification of all
concerned; it will be seen that they are journeying on finely. All well
and in good spirits--and probably commenced their march over the
mountain about the first of June. Their advice to those who may wish to
go hereafter, is to "pack." But our advice would be not to go at all.
But read the letter, it is quite interesting.

                                        Indian Resort, May 29th, 1850.
Mr. Editor:
    Dear Sir,-- Having an opportunity to send you a few lines, I shall
avail myself of the same.
    At this time we are encamped on the bank of the Arkansas River,
thirty miles above Fort Mann. At present, we all enjoy good health; and
were blessed this morning with quite a refreshing shower of rain, the
first we have had for some time, which, I assure you, was received by us
quite thankfully, as the dust had become very oppressive. We have been
traveling the road from Independence to Santa Fe for the last two weeks,
but fortunately we left that road [Cimarron Cutoff] this morning and are
now traveling a road less dusty. Since we left the Osage hunting
grounds, we have seen several bands of other tribes. To-day, about noon,
we came to a point which had been set apart by Maj. Fitzpatrick, (Indian
Agent,) for several of the Northern tribes to meet in council. The Agent
was on the ground. To whom I had the pleasure of being introduced this
evening, and from him we have obtained some valuable information, in
regard to the several routes and passes through the mountains. He is a
man of extensive information; and has accompanied Fremont in two of his
tours through the mountains--besides that, he has made several tours
independent of those.
    Maj. Fitzpatrick, the Agent, informed me, that the object of the
council was to give the Indians a friendly talk and make some presents,
and if possible, to prevail upon the several tribes to send on a
delegation to Washington city, for the purpose of treating with the
Government of the United States, which though, he presumed would not be
effected, on account of their being no interpreters. Up to this time, I
presume, there is no treaties existing, between the United States and
these tribes, who have been requested to meet in council. Five tribes
have come in, and one or two more looked for.-- Those present are
Aporohas [Arapahoes], Apaches, Chienne [Cheyenne], Soux [Sioux], and
Comanches. I should judge there was two thousand present--all appear
perfectly friendly, and the Agent informs us that we need not fear any
thing from Indians--this side of the mountains. But warns us against one
tribe, which roams on the mountains, the name of which I have forgotten.
    In case the Agent succeeds in getting those several tribes to send on
to Washington a Delegation, and treaties are entered into, it will be
greatly to the interest of the emigrants traveling this route. At
present we have to guard our stock, day and night, but as yet we have
sustained no losses, or encountered any difficulty whatever with the
Indians. We find, though, that the Indians are quite annoying, they come
to our camps and we have to give them something to eat, before we can
get rid of them--though we have no great room for complaint, as they
have a great many very fine mules, and we have succeeded in trading the
most of our horses to them for mules, which I think will be greatly to
our advantage, especially if we pack through from Green Horn, which
place is south of Pueblo twenty five miles. It is the intention of the
greater part of this company to pack from that point.

I would advise all persons, from my little experience, to pack, and never start with wagons, as there is a certain time only to make the pass through the mountains, failing to make that time suffering is the consequence.

We have had some very poor grass which is in consequence of there being so many Buffaloes, we are scarcely out of sight of them during each day.

You may hear from me again from the Great Salt Lake.

I am yours Respectfully,

JNO. H. WOLFE.[847]

Cherokee John Wolfe was contrasting the stage of government relations between these plains Indian tribes and those of the Cherokee, who had been "treating" with the U.S. government since just after the American Revolution.

The routing of this letter is interesting to imagine. Quesenbury said that letters were in a box in care of the "Chief's squaw." From there, the mail might have found its way to a mail carrier the Indians would meet at the Cimarron Cutoff. However, this month the regular mail from Santa Fe was delayed by an Apache attack at Wagon Mound.[848] The delayed return mail left Las Vegas, N. M. on May 27, arriving at Fort Leavenworth June 18. However, it took Wolfe's letter nearly two months to get to the *Advocate*.

Due to his childish antics, the skilled but self-centered Quesenbury missed an opportunity to record more in-depth observations about the assemblage of Indians, forerunner of the 1851 Fort Laramie Treaty. Quesenbury:

"Thursday 30 May...20 [miles]...Several of our company went back to the Traders. I sent another letter back. Got a tolerably early Start - say nine o'clock. After coming perhaps nine or ten miles we saw a cloud of Indians ahead. Some of them came and met us. Rode in advance with Wolf and two or three others with the Spokesman of the [Indian] town. The Indians were pitching their tents or lodges. The train passed and some in front of it drove a ground squirrel along for some time till it appeared tired. I then got down to catch it, but it outran me and tired me down. Jo Wms came to my releif [sic] but it out did him. Coody then came and it outran him and got into a hole.

Nooned two miles above the Indian Town. Our camp was soon overrun with Indians. Horse swapping commenced. One chap got a mule with the sorest back imaginable. The Indians swapped saddles bridles and all, without taking them off. After the train got ready to start, Perry and myself went back to the Indian town, to get a mule an Indian-had promised, but after delaying there a long time he wanted a pistol and

---

[847]*Cherokee Advocate* "Monday July 23, 1850." (Monday, the usual printing day, was July 22) p 2 cols 1 and 2.
[848]Apaches attacked, killing all ten of the mail party bound for Santa Fe. Bodies were found on May 19. Barry...*West*...p 947.

some coffee to boot. Overtook Black[849] and two or three others trading for a mule, which they succeeded in getting. On our way got down to shoot a wolf. Fired and missed. Black shot his pistol also which frightened a led horse and made him jerk a chap off his horse. Tolerable grass. Buffalo chips and wood mixed."
[near Garden City, Finney Co., Kansas]

Dissension continued to brew over travel routes, despite the specific information obtained from Fitzpatrick. Quesenbury:

"Friday last-of May 31...1850... The road leaves the river and does not touch near again for twelve miles. Soon after we started we came across an antelope Johnson[850] had killed and laid in the road. He had placed his hat on it to keep wolves off.[851] Met a Cheyenne with three horses which he had stolen from the Utah's. He had stampeded the horses and killed a man that pursued him. He had a scalp to show that he had done so.

Considerable excitement about roads. There will be another split in our company in less than ten days. The most absurd things are adduced as arguments in favor of ways and routes, besides a large amount of lies. I rode to the river just before nooning to water my horse. Found two large snipes there. Killed them. They were white, marked regularly with black, brown neck, bill three or four inches long curved slightly upwards long blue legs, and webfooted.[852] Meigs says they are [blank] but his ignorance on other matters makes me doubt his knowledge on this. Camped on the river. Wood very scarce. Craig took umbrage at some of us talking about antelopes. Simple. Meigs is determined not to pack."
[near Lakin, Kearny Co., Kansas]

Mammals and birds continued to be plentiful on this Mountain Branch of the Santa Fe Trail. But dust, heat, and bad grass added to the disagreements, making travel very unpleasant. Quesenbury:

"Saturday 1 June...25 [miles]...At a little before daylight hobbled out my pony and soon after waked up every body. Strong wind from S.W. Nooned at about 1/2 past 11. Took off my saddle by a large cottonwood. This is the first tree Shade I have injoyed for a long time.

About an hour before we got to our Encampment for the night Wiley Forrester[853] shot at an antelope which jumped a few rods and fell dead. At night he divided it, giving each mess a mess. Harris killed an antelope also, and Buckner a buffalo; of the latter but little was brought in but Harris' antelope was divided like Wiley's.

---

[849]Black remains unidentified.

[850]Johnson is mentioned only once and remains unidentified.

[851]Any article of clothing that was worn could be used, as it was thought that the "smell of man" kept the wolves away. Not to be confused with the Coyote *Canis latrans*, or Brush Wolf, The Gray Wolf *Canis lupus* "almost exclusively used buffalo for food." Eugene D. Fleharty *Wild Animal and Settlers on the Great Plains* (Norman: Univ. of Oklahoma Press 1995) p 299.

[852]American Avocet (*Recurvirostra americana*) inhabit freshwater shorelines. This was probably a breeding pair.

[853]Wiley Forrester was married to Elizabeth Coody, sister of Samuel and Charles Coody, both on this trip.

Our encampment is near a clear slough. Grass bad but plenty.[854] Our pioneers were misunderstood by the Capt. because one of them showed him the wrong ground. The others had found a most excellent place a mile off on the river. The day has been warm and the dust disagreeable. Dog towns still continue. New kinds of vegetation appear. Larks continue as they have all along the way in great numbers. But those here sing differently from those at home,-and at all hours of the night."[855]
[near Syracuse, Hamilton Co., Kansas]

One of the Wolfe company went to sleep on guard duty. The entry indicates this company was still operating under a set of rules like those established at the outset of the journey by the larger Cherokee Emigrating California Company, of which Capt. Wolfe had been an elected officer.

Sunday was partly a traveling day, but also used for rest and recreation, including sketching and playing in the sand hills along the river. Quesenbury:

"**Sunday June 2.** Before sun rise we commenced gearing and by three quarters of an hour of sun, we reached the place found by the pioneers yesterday. Some grumbled as they do at every thing. Some talk about McDaniel's[856] going to sleep on post last night. He wrote an impudent note to Buckner to day, bullying him and the Committee.
Went down to the river and took a sketch of the sand hills opposite. Mr. May went with me, but he remained only a short time. A great number of our men were in a swimming. After dinner Mr. May, Henry Hays, and myself went over the river to the sand hills. We crossed by wading. The water varied in depth, every few steps--sometimes it was up to our waists and in ten feet only knee deep. We walked over the hills awhile scratching our initials in the sand, besides tramping them with our feet. I made a Q which is plain from Camp half a mile off.
Returned and McDaniel was tried for sleeping on post last night. He acknowledged it but swore he wouldn't submit to the decision of the Committee, which was, that he should stand double the usual time."

Despite the continued tension, they moved on. Quesenbury:

"**Monday 3 June 1850** Left after an early breakfast. Couldn't find my powder flask. Went back to the Saturday evening's camp for it. Couldn't find it. James Pyeatt and myself went out on the prairie to the right. Got fooled by carrion crows. We thought they were pheasants. In the evening an antelope ran through our lines although a great many shots were fired at him. Merrill killed him afterwards. In the evening later I noticed some large birds of the snipe kind that Patillo calls Curlews.[857] Bad prospect all the evening for a Camping place. At length camp was pitched near the mouth of a sandy run. Wood very scarce. By

---

[854]*Distichlis stricta* (salt grass).
[855]Probably Western Meadowlarks *Sturnella neglecta* at this location.
[856]Charles McDaniel was the son of James McDaniel and Rachel Riley. Charles died west of Fort Bridger, Wyoming.
[857]Long-billed Curlews (*Numenius americanus*) are found on the Great Plains short grasslands during the breeding season. Extremely large brown shorebird 20" to 26" long with a 5"-7" long bill.

chance Peck[858] and myself found an old Indian camp and we took the willows for wood. It has rained in showers to day. Once while we nooned. The evening is most disagreeable."
[near Holly, Prowers Co., Colorado]

On June 4, Quesenbury wrote a longer than usual narrative. No doubt Fitzpatrick had told them that the Edmonson company was led by an Indian. There is no mistaking his attitude in the discourse on passing "Dry Creek," the supposed cutoff taken by the Edmonson ox train. In the days to come they would find evidence, including another message from one of Edmonson's men, that Edmonson went farther west before cutting off. Wolfe's company began to fall apart. The weather was miserable--wet, windy and cold. Men were not abiding by the rules. Discontent with the entire situation led to the final resolve of the company members to pack. Quesenbury:

"June 4 Tuesday. This morning twenty three agreed to pack from Pueblo.[859] Buckner, myself and two or three others will start ahead of the crowd for that place tomorrow. Some of the boys said they saw snow falling just before we left Camp. It was certainly most disagreeably cold. A drizzling rain from the E. fell on our backs for a half hour, but by noon or long before the day had become pleasant.

At noon we halted on famous Dry Creek. This Creek has since the foundation of the prairies remained unnoted. But on account of a large indelible wagon road made by numberless traders, but more lately by the ox team Company guided by an Indian, this Creek Dry Creek has sprung into Celebrity, notoriety and even fame. The disaffected of our company intended to take this big wagon road, and make a nigh cut on us of a hundred and fifty miles. Hamp Williams was sent ahead to have the road ready. He reached the creek, but-but- when the disaffected chaps got to Dry Creek they were a dry set of fellows. There was no right hand whatever, not even a buffalo trail.

Came on with Buckner and Harris. Two antelopes ahead of us were fighting a wolf. We all shot at them but missed. They were too far off. Found an excellent camping place on a slough where the Traders camped awhile back. Wood plenty.[860]

This is the third night Meigs has kept his wagon out of the corral. After passing dry Creek, Cunningham drove out into the prairie to the right and got ahead of the train. All regularity and order among the wagons has been abandoned. Wind blowing hard from N. since 4 p.m. At night cold drizzling rain. H. Shipley in the rain on the first W[atch]."
[near Lamar, Prowers Co., Colorado]

On the next page, Quesenbury wrote what would be the only list of the J. H. Wolfe wagon company. At best this constitutes probably a maximum of one-half of the members of the company. Until other

---

[858]Known only as J. Peck; signed the agreement to pack from Pueblo.

[859]The list on page 185 of Cush's original journal contains 36 names; 22 of them written by Quesenbury.

[860]This stretch along the Arkansas River in Colorado was called Big Timbers for the number of larger trees, principally cottonwood.

primary sources come to ligh, this stands as the partial company
list. The first part is the Agreement, written in Quesenbury's
handwriting. He also wrote the first twenty-two names on the mixed
Cherokee and white list.

June 4th 1850

We the undersigned agree and are resolved to pack and travel to
California from Pueblo; and we contemplate securing a guide on reason-
able terms, and of making our route direct through the mountains to the
Mormon City; but in case of failing to get a guide we still shall travel
by packing on the Evans' trail. And Wm. Buckner is hereby empowered to
select men to accompany him to Greenhorn to make suitable preparations
for our contemplated business.

1 J. H. Wolf.   22 Bates.
2 J. Craig.   [Ink Smear] Blake.
3 J. P. Parks.   24 W. G. Barker.
4 Patillo.   25 Wiley Forister.
5 Buckner.   26 Saml Riley.
6 Quesenbury.   27 Merrell.
7 Buchanan.   28 J Gonder.
8 Hays.   29 Jno Pierce.
9 May.   30 Joseph Coodey
10 Smith (Tom).   31 D. Wafer.[Hafen?]
11 Wm Wms.   32 Ben Sanders
12 Jo. Williams.   33 H Ross.
13 Oliver.   34 Sam Dick.
14 Yates.   35 McCurdy
15 Hagood.   36 J. Peck.
16 Potts.
17 Jno. Ross.
18 Bushyhead.
19 Pyeatt.
20 J. Shipley.
21 H. Shipley.

Buckner selected Quesenbury, Robert Harris and Prescott from the
Wolfe company to go to Greenhorn, assigned to find and employ a
guide. The trip was recorded by Quesenbury.

"June 5... Harris, Buckner, Prescott and myself started ahead for
Greenhorn.[861] We had not gone far before we discovered what we took to
be horses on a side of a hill. Approached them behind a tree when we
[got?] a good and fair look, the horses turned out to be rocks. Nooned
after passing over a barren and high country. The road left the river
some two or three miles to the right. At our nooning place two large
wolves-lobos, came by. Passed a dry creek or so and took to the

[861]Greenhorn, 25 miles south and west of Pueblo, reportedly named for Comanche
Chief Cuernoverde in the early 1700s. The trail from Fountain Creek (Pueblo)
to Greenhorn joined the Ute Trail. Through the 1840s settlements at Pueblo,
Hardscrabble and Greenhorn were inhabited by mountain men, single as well as
those with families. Most traded with Taos to the west and south. In 1847 some
were killed in the Taos Uprising; others served as enlistees to apprehend the
killers; served as Sheriff and Grand Jury to convict the Insurgents. Utes and
Apaches were both trading partners and subjects of concern.

river where we camped. The river is rising fast. After supper and we had started we got a view of the Rocky Mountains--just above the horizon but plainly discernable. In a few minutes we saw other points to the left. Camped in the brush. Fine place for grass."

[one mile east of Bent's Old Fort, Otero Co., Colorado]

Before reaching Bent's Old Fort, the four Wolfe company members stopped long enough for Quesenbury to sketch it. At the fort they again found evidence of the Edmonson ox train company. Quesenbury:

"June 6 Thursday.   Got off much earlier than the train usually does. We were again on high ground; the day was dry. We turned aside to the left as the road did not appear to approach the river. Harris tried to shoot an antelope but failed. I was near shooting Buckner's dog in the brush for some animal. Nooned in a thickety bottom. Immense quantities of turtle doves. They are now laying & hatching.

We had not proceeded far before we came in sight of Ft. Bent[862] -- in fact we discovered it from camp this morning --about a mile below. Stopped and sketched Ft. Bent. Saw Robinson's name[863] on the door. His company passed May 31."

[north of Fowler, Otero Co., Colorado]

More evidence of the Edmonson ox train was plain to see, as the four Wolfe company members proceeded toward Pueblo. Quesenbury:

"June 7 Friday. Good start. Saw ox team sign[864] soon after. Their date was June 1. Shaved a cotton wood stick and wrote on it for the benefit of the company. The ox teams turned off soon after making towards Pike's Peak, which is perfectly visible, and has been since yesterday morning. Nooned and travelled as usual. Passed some old adobe buildings in the evening.[865] Camped and cooked an hour by sun as usual. Then travelled on to Fontaine qui bouit[866] which had been high, but had fallen sufficient for fording. Crossed and turned to the left. Stopped under a large Cottonwood. Our horses near us; grass plenty but not of a good quality. Saw some deer this evening; too wild to get a shot at. After night on our way we turned off to look at a singular shaped bluff of rocks or sand, I couldn't tell which, that looked like an old castle."

[Pueblo, Pueblo Co., Colorado]

---

[862]Old Bent's fort, a National Historic Site today, is seven miles east of La Junta, Otero County, Colorado.

[863]Robinson, former messmate of Mitchell, was in the Edmonson ox train company one week ahead.

[864]Diarist James Mitchell, with the Edmonson company, did not mention leaving any signs for the trains following them.

[865]Probably remnants of Gantt's Fort (Fort Cass) built by John Gantt in 1832, abandoned about 1834, the year Bent's Old Fort was built further downriver. Barry...*West*...p 288.

[866]Fountain Creek flows south from present Fountain (Colorado) entering the Arkansas River at Pueblo. The "Fountain that Boils" is from chemical effervescence, not temperature.

The Wolfe company advance men turned south from Pueblo, and
proceeded to Greenhorn to procure a guide. <u>Quesenbury</u>:

"June 8 Saturday Off soon again. We camped last night within a
mile of Pueblo,[867] where we arrived an hour by sun. Crossed the river
just below. Very deep fording-almost swimming. At 11 o'clock got to St.
Charles Creek.[868] A single old adobe building two lodges, and a wagon
body form the residences of the inhabitants of this settlement.

Just before we got to the Creek we saw a woman and some dogs and very
soon after an Indian lad with bow and arrows galloped up on a point to
our left. The chief man was out hunting. He soon came in with an
antelope. There was considerable joy among the children. In a few
moments some of the meat was boiling. Before it got done it was set out
in tin pans on the floor. Sweet milk and cornbread both filthy as well
as the antelope constituted our meal. I couldnt eat but the others made
up. After dinner we left Marsaline[869] and the St. Charles. Stopped and
grazed our horses. About half past three we got a view of Greenhorn[870]
in the valley ahead. It disappointed us. Two rows of buildings of three
or four rooms each enclosed by corrales made the town. A strip of
patches irrigated by ditches to the left of the buildings below and
above were the only indications farming we saw. Some cattle and horses
were grazing in the valleys. We rode up to a man setting by a ditch. He
said his name was Poisel.[871] We had letters to him and others. At his

[867]A Spanish word for town or village. In 1806 Zebulon M. Pike (for whom Pikes
Peak is named) erected a crude log building near the site; in 1822 Major Jacob
Fowler, trapper and trader, built a log cabin here. Mathew Kincaid had a sheep
ranch at the mouth of the Fountain in 1841-42, by which time trappers and
traders had constructed an adobe fort. Mountain man Charles Town was there in
1842; also when Fremont stopped by in July 1843, after which he went with
Fremont to California. Fort Pueblo was also called Fort Spaulding. Charles
Autobees, working for the Turley distillery at Arroyo Hondo brought liquor
from Taos and used Pueblo for storage; on return from a "liquor run" he loaded
furs at Pueblo to take to St. Louis. Pueblo was called "Robert Fisher's fort
on the Arkansas" by Turley in 1843. Archibald Metcalf lived at Pueblo trading
with Utes, Arapahoe & Cheyenne in late 1845. Near Fort Pueblo the women and
children, along with the sick and disabled men of the Mormon Battalion (under
General Crook they were on their way to California as enlistees for one year's
service in the Mexican War) wintered in 1846. The 1849 inhabitants of Pueblo
were discussed in Vol I. In 1854, Pueblo inhabitants who did not escape were
killed by Utes on Christmas Day. A group of Cherokee teamsters, sent by
employer Charles Autobees to collect and bring possessions out of Pueblo, were
also killed. Any record of their names has so far not been found.
[868]After the killing of Simeon Turley in the Taos Uprising of 1847, Alexander
Hicklin bought $498.75 worth of oxen, buffalo robes, coffee, wheat, and
clothes from the Turley estate, collected $475 due him, and moved to the Taos
Trail crossing of the San Carlos (St. Charles) River, 10 miles south of Fort
Pueblo. There he started a bottomland farm on land granted to Gervasio Nolan,
who gave it to Charles Autobees. Ralph C. Taylor, *Colorado, South of the
Border* (Denver, Colo.: Sage Books, 1963).
[869]Marceline Baca. Another prominent Marcellin, St. Vrain, ran a trading fort
on the South Platte until the 1840s.
[870]Farming at Greenhorn was carried on by Marcelino Baca "Marcellin" where he
raised cattle, corn, wheat, beans, and watermelons for trade to Indians.
[871]John Poisal was Thomas Fitzpatrick's father-in-law. Alexander Barclay with
George Simpson and Joseph Doyle started a settlement at nearby Hardscrabble in
1844, where 70 persons lived. Dick Owens was in Greenhorn during the passage

invitation we put up at his house.   Staked our horses on the hill.
Slept out of the house, by the front wall. Kinney[872] couldn't be
obtained for a guide. Took supper with him. Maj. FitzPatrick's wife or
squaw looks sleepy and doesn't begin to come up to previous
descriptions."

[Greenhorn, Pueblo Co., Colorado]

Thomas Fitzpatrick married Margaret Poisal in 1849. Sixteen-year-
old Margaret was about five months pregnant when Quesenbury saw
her, accounting for her looking "sleepy and doesn't begin to come
up to previous descriptions." Their first child, Andrew Jackson
Fitzpatrick, was born October 8, 1850.

William Quesenbury created five or six sketches during the
few days of arranging and rearranging to pack from Pueblo. The
sketch mentioned here is Spanish Peaks, the Wah-To-Yah, executed
while Quesenbury was at Greenhorn. Quesenbury:

"**Sunday 9 June.** Took a walk about three miles. Sketched some
mountains to the left of the main range of the Rocky Mountains. Back.
Looked at the corn and wheat. Corn just peeping up."

Quesenbury and companions were unsuccessful in obtaining a guide,
and prepared to leave Greenhorn, but not before he described the
inhabitants. Quesenbury:

"**Monday 10 [June].** At eight or thereabouts started back for
Pueblo. Poisel, Burke and Gerry[873] were along. Came to St. Charles. Deep
fording as the other day. Got dinner again. Same as before. Marsalin
joined us. Henry Prescott and myself rode behind. Those before went to
the upper ford. Followed them. They were afraid of it and took the lower
ford. Saw the train from the highland camped. Deep as before at the
ford. Sorry I'm back.

---

of the 1849 Lewis Evans company; he guided those who elected to pack to
California. John J. Burroughs and Briggs, farmers and stock raisers at Pueblo
and Hardscrabble, also went to California in 1849. Archibald Charles Metcalf,
said to be one of the first settlers on the Greenhorn (John Brown, William New
and Marcelino Baca the others) succumbed to cholera in 1849, so was not there
in 1850. LeCompte...*Pueblo, Hardscrabble, Greenhorn*...In 1850 Kit Carson was
back from California, noted at the Upper Platte Ferry on the North Platte
River on June 13 "here with a drove of horses and mules for sale." Eleazar
Stillman Ingalls, *Journal of a Trip to California By The Overland Route Across
the Plains in 1850-51* (Fairfield, Wash.: Ye Galleon Press 1979) p 40. Carson
was also reported at Fort Laramie on June 5 "arrived here a few days since
from Santa Fe, with a band of thirty horses and mules....he holds a grand
levee from morning till night....Guide books and maps of the road have no
chance against his word." *Cherokee Advocate* 17 September 1850.
[872]Charles Kinney guided the Ithaca Pack company members to Salt Lake, leaving
Pueblo after the Evans/Cherokee packers guided by Dick Owens. In 1850 Kinney
was again at Greenhorn. Janet LeCompte, "Charles Kinney" Hafen...*Mountain
Men*....vol 4, pp 169-73.
[873]Burke is unidentified. Perhaps one of the following three persons was
"Gerry:" Vincent Guion, Francois Guerin, or Gervais Nolan.

This Greenhorn[874] is a place singular because of its mixture of American, Mexican and Indian manners. The farming is on the Mexican style; the language-all kinds;-the houses Mexican imitation excepting an Arapaho or Blackfoot lodge or so. Some eight or ten different languages are spoken. The children seem to talk with each other in all of them."
[Pueblo, Pueblo Co., Colorado]

Meanwhile, the rest of the Wolfe company had arrived in Pueblo. Altogether nineteen men with five wagons determined to continue north immediately. Robert Harris, part of the team sent to Greenhorn, was among them.[875] Forty men including Quesenbury remained at Pueblo preparing to "pack." Quesenbury:

"Wednesday [Tuesday][876] **11 June** Vast preparations for packing. Meigs has determined to pack. Five wagons left. We sold ours for pack saddles. Marsaline and Burke remained, Poisel went home-and Gerry. Wolf and three or four others went also. All busy preparing. Gerry has promised us four pack saddles with rigging complete for our wagon. To night put the horses in the Pueblo enclosure, with Shipley's wagon at the door."

Although many people have described Pueblo, there are few sketches of it. Quesenbury's is therefore quite important. The sketch is included in this volume. Quesenbury:

"Thursday [Wednesday] 12 [June]...Still all hands are busy preparing. Pack saddles are turned out fast. River rising. Mr. May went with me to his hook below Pueblo. I afterwards took a sketch of the place. In the evening Mr. May and myself went up and wrote letters under a cottonwood by the pond. It is doubtful that our letters will ever reach home."

Toward midday on Thursday, the McNair/Taylor Cherokee Emigrating California company members were seen coming from the east. Quesenbury:

"Friday [Thursday] 13 [June] Sleepy this morning. After breakfast walked over to the Fontaine qui bouit hunting antelopes. Took down it to the road. Saw nothing. At eleven some of the McNair's men began to come in. Presently the whole train came. They meet us friendlier than they left us."

---

[874]Located within the Vigil & St. Vrain Spanish Land Grant of 1843-44, Greenhorn was always a scattered settlement. It became known as Hicklin in 1859 when Zan Hicklin took possession with wife Estefana Bent, daughter of the massacred Charles Bent, New Mexico's first Territorial Governor. Taylor... *Colorado*...and *Colorado Magazine* vol 4, (1927) pp 186-87; vol 6 (1929) p 81.

[875]June 19 these five wagons caught up with Edmonson's company at the Cache la Poudre River.

[876]Quesenbury error. June 11 was a Tuesday. The next two days' dates are correct; the days should be Wednesday June 12; and Thursday June 13. Quesenbury picks up the right day and date on "Friday June 14."

CHEROKEE DIARIST BROWN TRAVELS THE SANTA FE TRAIL

Cherokee Captain McNair held his horse/mule company and Oliver's ox train company back on Cow Creek. Two more wagons from the Wolfe Company had joined them on May 20. The delay put them one full day behind Captain Wolfe's group. Brown:

"May 21st [Tuesday] Lay Bye all day [Camp 18]."
        [four miles west of Lyons, Rice Co., Kansas]

The next day they moved on, striking the Arkansas River, camping on Walnut Creek. Brown:

"22 [May] Traveled about **20 miles** & (Arks. River) camped on Wallnut creek **Camp 19."**
        [east of Great Bend, Barton Co., Kansas]

An additional day of laying by put the McNair company two full days' travel behind the Wolfe company. There was no reason given for laying by on May 21 and again on May 23, unless it was anticipation of the arrival of the Thomas Fox Taylor horse/mule wagon group. A large herd of buffalo provided an opportunity for fresh meat. It also meant the grasses were cropped short. Brown:

"23 [May] Lay Bye all day. Large heard of Buffalo & grass scarce."
        [still east of Great Bend, Kansas on Walnut Creek]

McNair's company left Walnut Creek, traveling two full days to reach camp on the Wet Route of the Santa Fe Trail. Brown:

"24 [May] Traveled **20 miles.** passed pawnee Rock and camped on ash cr. grass bad --...**Camp 20"**
        [two miles SE of Pawnee Rock, Pawnee Co., Kansas]

"25 [May] Traveled **18 miles,** crossed Pawnee fork, quite a large stream with high Banks. camped on Arks River. **Camp 21."**
        [SW of Garfield, Pawnee Co., Kansas]

"26 [May] (Sunday) Lay Bye all day. Captain T.F. Taylors[877] company consisting of eight horse waggons came up with us today with the intention of joining us --."

McNair always stopped on Sunday.[878] Diarist Brown noted fifty-nine

---

[877]On May 6, Brown noted: "Left Tom Taylor and 5 men to wait for another crowd."

[878]McNair was a long-time strong and active Christian in Cherokee Nation. Opposite this page in Brown's diary is: "Untill the awakening Trump of the Archangel Shall Summon them from a sleeping oblivion into the bright presence of our heavenly father."

men and sixteen wagons in the McNair company on May 20. Taylor's
eight wagons would bring the total of horse/mule wagons to twenty-
four. If the average number of four persons to a wagon held true
in the Taylor Company, there was a minimum total of ninety-one
emigrants in the twenty-four wagons. The Taylor company was
"admitted" into the McNair company May 29.

Captain Oliver and his ox train had been traveling with the
McNair Company for quite some time. The companies lay by again on
Monday, May 27. Another ox train caught up, this one captained by
a Mr. Holmes. For the first time they met Plains Indians. Brown:

> **"May 27   Lay Bye** all day a Train of ox waggons, 20 waggons
> came up this evening. A comp[any?] wer visited by 9 Arapahoes   Indians
> who camped in sight --."

> **"28 [May]** Traveled **15 miles** and camped on the Ark-Riv.
>   **Camp 22** --."
>   [SW of Kinsley, Edwards Co., Kansas]

> **"29 [May]...18 miles**   T.F. Taylors company was admited into Mc-
> Nairs co this morning   an election was held for Lieutenants   T.F.
> Taylor was elected first, and J.M. Reace[879] second Lieutenant   today we
> traveled 18 miles camped on the river **Camp 23** --."
>   [near the Black Pool, east of Ford, Ford Co., Kansas]

While McNair's company was accepting new members on May 29,
Captain Wolfe was three days ahead on the Santa Fe Trail, writing
his letter at the "Indian Resort." Following Taylor's admittance
into the company, McNair increased the daily mileage. Brown:

> **"May 30th**   Traveled **25 miles**, passed the Ruins of Ft. Mann and
> camped 2 miles above on the Bank of the River **Camp 24th** --."
>   [four miles west of Dodge City, Ford Co., Kansas]

The McNair/Taylor company arrived at the Indian gathering May
31. Brown had very little to say. Brown:

> **"May 31**   Traveled **25 miles**, came to the crossing of the Santa
> fee Road   Maj. FitzPatrick, Indian Agent, was there paying Indian
> annuities to the different tribes --...**Camp 25.**"
>   [at the Cimarron Cutoff three miles NW of Ingalls,
>   Gray Co., Kansas]

The next day's reduced mileage was probably due to passing
slowly through the Indian gathering, where a great deal of trading
no doubt took place.

---

[879]A John C. Reese is listed in the extended Grant family by Starr...*Cherokee*
...p 324. Distant cousins Beck, Fields, and Taylor were in the 1850 companies.

Brown:

"June 1st 10 miles Started at 12 oclock and Traveled 10 miles.
Camped on the Bank of the River **Camp 26** --."
                    [east of Pierceville and the Finney/Gray
                              Cos. line, Kansas]

McNair and Taylor resumed their high mileage travel, which
did not deter yet another company from overtaking them. Brown:

"2nd [June] Sunday...25 miles... Traveled about 25 miles
Camped on the River. Today at noon T.J. Mims & Co. Caught up with the
crowd   12 days from home...**Camp 27** --."
[east of Deerfield, and the Kearny/Finney Cos. line, Kansas]

Brown's note "12 days" is the time it took "Mims & Co." to reach
the McNair/Taylor company. From the Grand (Neosho) River crossing,
the distance measured by Brown was 419 miles. Mimms' average daily
travel was approximately 35 miles, indicating his was most
certainly a pack party and not a wagon group.[880] Brown:

"June 3d[881] **(Monday)   Lay Bye."**

The company passed the Upper Crossings of the Santa Fe Trail,
and embarked on the Mountain Branch toward Bent's Fort. Brown:

"4. [June] 20 miles Traveled about 20 miles and camped on Bank of
the River in a cottonwood grove, very hard rain **Camp 28** --."
    [halfway between Lakin and Kendall, Kearny Co., Kansas]

"5 [June] Traveled **18 miles** camped on Bank of River
Camp 29 --."
            [east of Syracuse, Hamilton Co., Kansas]

The McNair/Taylor company crossed the modern border between
Kansas and Colorado. Brown:

"6 [June] Traveled **25 miles** camped on the River.
Camp 30th --."
              [near Holly, Prowers Co., Colorado]

"7 [June] Traveled **20 miles** and camped on Bank of River
Camp 31st --."
    [near the mouth of Big Sandy Creek, seven miles east of
              Lamar, Prowers Co., Colorado]

---

[880]Emmet Starr lists two John Mimms, father and son. The elder married Nannie
Collins. At least two of her cousins were forty niners--Lovely Rogers and
Seaborn Cordery. Starr...*Cherokee*...pp 391, 395.
[881]This date appears with the title on the front half-page of the John Lowery
Brown Journal.

Unlike other diarists, Brown made no mention of the Big Timbers area, through which they passed on June 8.

"8 [June]...20 miles Traveled about 20 miles today, about 10 oclock passed a grave of Indians who fell in Battle   sign posted 3/4 miles to the Right of the Road...**Camp 32."**
            [north of Able, Bent Co., Colorado]

"June 9th...15 miles Sunday Lay Bye part of the day. Started 12 oclock and traveled 15 miles. Camped on the Bank of the River. **Camp 33 --."**
            [Fort Lyon, Bent Co., Colorado]

Finally they got their first glimpse of the rockies before reaching Bent's old Fort. Brown:

"10th [June]...25 miles...this morning saw mountains at a great distance covered with snow   supposed to be a spur of the Rocky Mountains, at noon reached Bents Fort. Traveled on until night. Made 25 miles. Camped on the River. **Camp 34 --."**
            [north of Swink, Otero Co., Colorado]

In the left margin. Brown wrote: "the snow mountains that we saw today proved to be the Spanish Peak."[882] Brown:

"11 [June] Traveled **25 miles** Camped on the River **Camp 35 --."**
[NW of Fowler, near the Crowley/Pueblo Cos. line, Colorado]

McNair/Taylor next camped where Edmonson's ox train company had turned northwest on June 2. Brown didn't mention the cutoff.

"12 [June] Today made **20 miles** Camped on Bank of River high mountains to the left covered with snow **Camp 36 --."**
[Chico Creek, west of North Avondale, Pueblo Co., Colorado]

McNair/Taylor's horse wagon company and the two ox trains arrived at Pueblo within two days of one another. They celebrated the second day with another fandango. Brown:

"June 13...12 miles...today snow toped mountains in view plainly. Traveled 12 miles and at noon reached Peueblo found J.H. Woolfs company there preparing to "Pack" --.**Camp 37."**
            [Pueblo, Pueblo Co., Colorado]

"14 [June] Lay Bye all day. The ox Train consisting of 33[883] waggons came up and camped near, at night had a big dance --."

---

[882]Also called Wah-To-Yah, which impressed Quesenbury enough he sketched them.
[883]There are two distinct ox wagon companies--Captain Oliver's and Captain Holmes.' Holmes' company of 20 ox wagons joined the McNair and Taylor Companies on May 27, southwest of Garfield, Pawnee County, Kansas.

All companies that left the Verdigris River had arrived at
Pueblo except one--the Edmonson Ox Company, which took the later-
called "Chico Creek Cutoff" twelve miles east of Pueblo.

While on the Santa Fe Trail, Mitchell had seen the mail, one
group of military, two trader trains, and Fitzpatrick with the
traders and Indians. Quesenbury, with the John Wolfe company, saw
two trader trains, one of which took mail, and Fitzpatrick, the
traders and the Indian tribes. John L. Brown, with the McNair/
Taylor company, noted seeing only Fitzpatrick handing out
annuities to the plains Indians.

The companies were in excellent shape. They had no disease or
serious illness, no depredations, and no loss of stock, despite
encountering large numbers of Indians.

The McNair/Taylor company, along with Oliver's and Holmes' ox
trains, left Pueblo on June 15 after laying bye only a day and a
half. The Wolfe company had spent more time in the vicinity of
Pueblo and Greenhorn, trying to find a guide, trading, and
preparing to pack. Wolfe's forty packers left Pueblo on Saturday,
June 15, after committing one final grandiose act described by
Quesenbury.

WILLIAM M. QUESENBURY SKETCHES ON OPPOSITE PAGE

    TOP:

"Pueblo from the East"

    Sketched June 12, 1850 from the Arkansas River.

    BOTTOM:

Pikes Peak, sketched June 17, 1850 from top of Point of Rocks.

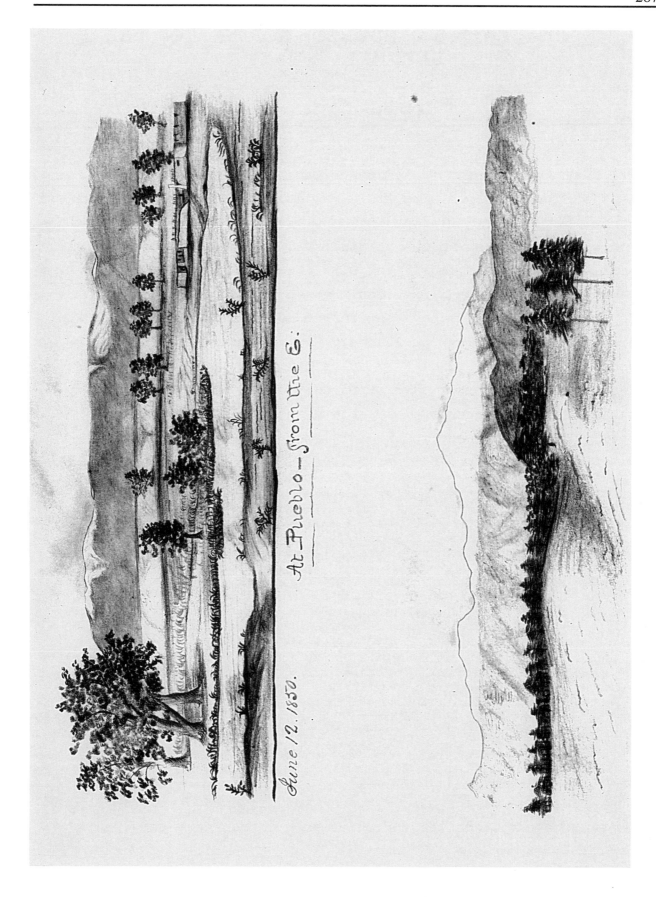

At Pueblo – from the E:

June 12. 1850.

Chapter 5. PUEBLO NORTH TO THE LARAMIE PLAINS

Lay Bye. Gold Found
--John Lowery Brown 22 June 1850

Captain Edmonson's (Edmiston, Edmondson) ox train, with the mess of diarist James Mitchell, George Crum, Strickler, and one other, did not linger at Bent's Fort after May 31. Former messmate Robinson had broken up the original Mitchell mess group a few days earlier by unceremoniously throwing the others' clothes out of his wagon all over the prairie. The Edmonson company moved away from Bent's Fort. The next day they turned northwest, away from the Arkansas River toward the Fountain River "without the Sign of a road." The Company, including guide Ben Simon and his extended family, pioneered what came to be called the Chico Creek Cutoff, making it possible to avoid Pueblo altogether. Edmonson's was still the lead company in the 1850 emigration from Arkansas, Missouri and Cherokee Nation. <u>Mitchell</u>:

> **"2nd [June] Sunday** another fine morning   Started Soon though Some for not travling   the country like yesterday   at noon we bid the river an road fare well after travling up it the rise of 350 miles we took a north corse in the prickily pear country without the Sign of a road   we left arkasas river where there was a large timbered bottom on the north Side and a bog Swamp next to the bluff.   we traveled 6 or 8 miles north hard puling in the [sand?] and got to a Salt flat   good grass and a very cold Spring the first we had Seen for more than 400 miles   the only [vegetation?] was a Scrub [shrub] that is in bunches from 2 to 4 feet high and the largest 1 1/2 inches in diameter resembling curent bushes   plenty of antilopes to be Seen and buck Rabbits[883]   the Snowy mountains[884] appears more grand and plain as we approach nearer to them   we camped Sooner than comon on the account of water and grass it being Scarce in this high poor country   great appearence of rain   Black clouds to the wes[t] with lightning toward the mountains every evening and only a Sprincle of rain at a time."
> [North of North Avondale, Pueblo Co., Colorado]

Two men strayed from the new route and became disoriented, but finally found their way back to the camp. The company members, now accustomed to the daily thunder and lightning, were about to experience a violent weather phenomenon common near the Front

---

[883]Jackrabbits. *Lepus townsendii* or *californicus*.
[884]The Rocky Mountains in this case. The term seems to have been applied to any mountain with snow along the western trails.

Range of the Rocky Mountains. <u>Mitchell</u>:

"3rd [June] Monday Cloudy & cool   2 of our men left the train about 3 oclock last evening and has not returned yet   it is fierd the indians has got them   the Train Started on and Sent out men to hunt Rose and Carter our lost men   after Some time their Sign was discovered going South towards the river   it was then evident that they were lost and trying to find us   we traveled on 8 miles Due north and camped to find out more positively the fait of our lost [men]   our camp here is on a little cleer creek runing South the water Brackish the country poor plenty of prickly pears   antilopes in abundence and Buck Rabbits   the latter feeds on the prickly pears   about 12 oclock our lost hunters returned after great fatiegua they having rambled back to the river and took our trail where we left it yesterday   our gide Says it is 17 or 18 miles from here to the next water too far to travel to day and we Stayed here   to day it clouded thundered and lightened all evening and a heavy hail Storm and rain fell about dark   many tents blowed down and the men got very cold and wet."
[on Chico Creek, North of North Avondale,
Pueblo Co., Colorado]

"4 [June] Tuesday plenty of hail yet remaining on the ground from last evening   the darkest cloud rising to the west that ever I Seen with heavy thunder and bright flashes of lightning   about the time we were ready to Start it looked allarming and a hea[v?]y Storm comence[d] hail wind and heavy rain   the Storm continued 1/2 the day and the coldest that ever I felt in June   tents blowed down and the [men?] Suffered greatly with cold   the creek we camped on rose in a few hours past fording and we were compeled to Stay here the remainder of the day on the account of the high water and the quick Sandy country that will mire a horse or waggon whin it is wet   there is Some cotton wood on this creek and great appearence of Stone coal along the creek Bluffs Some hard lime Stone mixed with Sulpther   it rained all evening and till in the night   it was so dark all day that the mountains could not be Seen."
[on Chico Creek]

As wild as this storm was, it was not unusual in this area of the Arkansas/Platte Divide. In an early May 1858 storm, lives of many animals and a few men were lost by Col. Loring's military company on their way with supplies for the Utah "war."

The 1850 company travelled on. The devastation from the hailstorm was everywhere. <u>Mitchell</u>:

"5th [June] Wendsday cleer and cool, the creek down. the mountain [Pikes Peak] plain to be Seen and white with Snow to the bace   from appearence it having Snowed on it when it rained on us   after Starting we Soon come to worse than quick Sand waxy morter like it was mixed with lime withe a little gravel in it like lime Stone mixed with Sulpher. it was hard puling on our anamals generaly the morter a foot deep   there is Scarce any vegitision on this formasion except the prickly pear   we Soon found that it [was?] well for us that we did not travel yesterday as there had been a great hale Storm bfore us   we found patches of hale lying yet not melted more than a foot deep although the day was very warm and it had layed more than 24 hours   we found rats dead that boroughs in the ground and had been forced from Their dens be the emence

rain and Kiled be the hail   these rats are of a Strange cind if rats
they may be cald   these must be of the Kangeroo race with long tails
long hind legs and Short fore legs its couler gray.[885] we found also a
drowned prararie dog and lots of Birds Kiled by the hail. we only
traveled 8 or 10 miles and a hard travel at that and camped on a large
creek huckel-bur in English its name in French [blank][886]   Some
goosbery bushes are to be Seen on this creek   the dwarf Rose in bloom
a Srub chery[887] and varous other bushes that are Straing to me   the
cotton wood tree on its banks and a tree resembling the quacan asp."[888]
[Fountain Creek 15 miles north of Pueblo, Pueblo Co., Colorado]

The detailed description of Ben Simon and extended family is
best seen in the next entry. There were other revealing details
yet to come. Mitchell:

"6th [June] Thursday a fine Still cleer morning and cool   we
Started Soon a north corse   road good and pased fine grass   we
continued up the creek on the east Side approaching nearer the mountains
pikes peak in plain view of us   large willows appeared along the
bottoms of the creek   plum thickets[889] in abundance   we camped in
good grass wood and watter   our gide Shewed where there was an indian
beried last year and Said there was $20 in cash in the grave with him
Some of our men undertook to take him up to get the money and [were?]
Shaimed out of it by hard perswaision   our gide is too good a man for
to comit So bace an act although he is part Delawere indian and part
french   his wife is withe us and appears to be a modest woman raised
in Santifee by Spanyard. and her mother is with us a full Snake indian
This daughter the wife is half Spanyard   She [mother] has with a Son
older than the daughter a full Snak indian   the old woman appears to
[be?]very brisk[?] and Smart   a distent relation is along with us of
the old womans   a girl 10 or 11 years old who the old woman corects and
Seems to have a desire to bring up decent and industros   they are
dr[i]ving cattle with them and milks every morning. They all dress after
the fashion [of] white folks."
[Town of Fountain, El Paso Co., Colorado]

Edmonson's ox train reached and began traveling on the long-

---

[885]Kangaroo rats have small front feet and legs, extremely long hind legs with
a very long tail. Most make mounds, from mere handfuls of dirt up to 15 ft. in
diameter and 4 ft. high, with many entrances. They inhabit dry areas, with or
without brush or trees, some preferring loose soil or even rocky soil. The
young are darker(more slaty) than adults, which are usually pale sandy to dark
brown. Only the Ord's *Dipodomys ordii* has a range in Colorado. Palmer...*Mammal*
...pp 211-13. This nocturnal animal runs by leaping like a kangaroo. Ransom
...*Wildlife*...p 325.
[886]Fountain Creek (Fontaine-qui-bouit) had many variants of its French name.
[887]Chokecherry *Prunus virginiana*--a shrub or small tree with small red to
black astringent fruits; widely distributed in North America. Preston...
Trees...p 261.
[888]Quaking Aspen *Populus tremuloides*. In wind, the leaves appear to tremble.
[889]American Plum *Prunus americana*. A shrub or small tree 25-30 ft, usually
divided near ground, spreading by shoots from the roots into dense thickets.
Richard J. Preston Jr. *Rocky Mountain Trees* (Ames, Iowa: The Iowa State
College Press 1947) p 189.

used, north/south Divide or Trapper's Trail.[890] The 1849
Evans/Cherokee company, both packers and wagons, traveled directly
north from Pueblo on this trail as would the other 1850 companies.

Members of the Edmonson ox train had their first exciting
encounter with Grizzly. Mitchell:

> **"7 [June] Fryday** fine morning   Started Soon expecting to travel
> 25 miles   we crosed a pine ridge with large pine[891] timber on it and a
> good Spring [892]   in this grove are thickets of curents[893] some formed
> Some in Syellow bloons, drawf cherys and the Straingest flowes   we
> pased near a hot Boiling Spring at base of pikes peak[894]   3 of our men
> went hunting   they found 3 grisly Bears[895] 2 miles from the train
> all of them the bears were Kiled   one of them after it was Shot took
> after canon[896] from Madison county & persued 2 miles to the train. Canon
> was So exosted [exhausted] that he was not able to Stand when the bear
> was Shot and him releaved   in a few rods more it would of had him
> we got to an extensive pinery after crosing a ridge   we camped on a
> Small creek east of the road with high bank in prararie near the pine."
>   [Black Squirrel Creek, El Paso Co., Colorado]

Perhaps due to the excitement during the day, James Mitchell's
narration of June 7 is somewhat jumbled in sequence. The passing
of a boiling spring "at base of pikes peak" would have occurred as
they reached Fountain Creek on the evening of June 5. His "good
Spring" was Jimmy Camp Spring further east. His "pine ridge with

---

[890]Lee Whiteley, "The Trappers Trail: 'The Road to Fort Laramie's Back Door'"
Overland Journal vol 4, no 4. (Winter 1998).

[891]Ponderosa or Western Yellow Pine *Pinus ponderosa*; a tree 150-180 ft. high
and 3-4 feet in diameter, with deeply furrowed bark. Preston...*Rocky
Mountain*...p 19.

[892]Jimmy Camp Spring, eight miles east of downtown Colorado Springs, Colorado.
Most travelers camped at the spot.

[893]There are both black and yellow currant varieties. Both were much used by
the Indians of Colorado and Utah. The golden currant was taken "by Lewis &
Clark from the Rocky Mountains" back to the east for cultivation. U.P.
Hedrick, ed. *Sturtevant's Notes on Edible Plants* (Albany, N.Y.: J.B. Lyon Co.
State Printers 1919) State of New York Dept. of Agriculture 27th Annual Report
vol 2, part 2, p 495.

[894]Mitchell's reference is to Fountain Creek. The "boiling" is caused by
effervescence rather than temperature. Saying they were "passing near"
indicates Simon was telling them about it, rather than the company actually
seeing it. The "boiling spring" is upstream (northwest) at Manitou Springs,
Colorado. The spot where they rejoined the north-south Divide Trail was near
the present town of Fountain.

[895]Grizzly Bear *Ursus horribilis*. A large thickset bear, with dished-in facial
profile and maned hump on shoulders; front claws often twice as long as hind.
Adult males usually weigh about 500 lb. Presently lives in uplands and
mountains to above timber line extirpated from extensive plains areas it
formerly occupied. Only a few hundred remain in the contiguous U.S., mostly in
Montana and Wyoming. Palmer...*Mammal*...pp 83-85.

[896]Canon was from Madison County, east of Washington County, Arkansas.

large pine timber on it" should be followed by "we got to an extensive pinery after crosing a ridge" which brought them to their camping spot on Black Squirrel Creek June 7.

The next morning, still on the Divide, they got an early surprise. <u>Mitchell</u>:

"**8 [June] Saturday** at the dawn of day the indians came charging on horse back near our encampment. they Shot of[f] a number of low guns at us yelling at the Same time in a most frightfull manner. of all the tumbling of lines tearing up Stakes and Snaping laretts [lariats] it beat it all. a way went more than 2/3 of our horses   all that Sucseeded in breaking loose run after the indians and not Slow away went more than 2/3 of our horses after the indians   all that got loose except 5 which the indians got were Saved   as good luck would have it they run in a natural pen and could not get out without Jumping down a bluff more than 20 feet. the indians lost a large brass pistel 2 pr Mocasons a bullet proof Shield and a mountain Sheep Skin a parcel of us percued them   in a few miles they took of[f] in different directions in the pine timber and we found that it would be useless to Spend time any longer after them   we made a late Start on consequence of this Stampeed and yet made a good days travel   we pased a vast [amount] of pine timber[897] more timber than we had pased in one day for more than Six hundred miles   we pased rocky points [including Point of Rocks] large mases of nacid [naked] rocks about the divide between the Platt and the ark rivers."
            [near Russellville, Douglas Co., Colorado]

Point of Rocks was a regular campsite for travelers, including the 1849 Evans/Cherokee Company. The "Black Forest" was noted by virtually every writer who went across this 7,500 ft. watershed divide. The pine would help build the city of Denver a few years after Mitchell traveled through. The vegetation on Cherry Creek is interesting to <u>Mitchell</u>:

"**9th [June] Sunday** Started Soon and [got?] to where the water run north on a creek[898] that we went down all day the waters of Platt oak timber[899] of a curious Kind   golden willow[900] and various Scrubs that I am unacquainted with   we camped on this creek and camped Soon on the

---

[897]From the appearance of the Ponderosa Pine *Pinus ponderosa*, the area is known as the Black Forest.

[898]Cherry Creek was named for the chokecherries found along its banks. Many of the names of the creek branches of the South Platte River were communicated to Lieutenant Fremont in 1842 by the officers of the American Fur Company and their trappers; subsequently most were adopted by the U.S. Authorities. A description of Cherry Creek was written by Parkman in the summer of 1846. Francis Parkman, *The Oregon Trail* (N.Y.: Grosset & Dunlap 1927) p 305.

[899]Gambel Oak *Quercus gambelii*. A shrub or small tree up to 25-35 ft. high, 6-10" in diameter; dry foothills and canyon walls; the only abundant deciduous oak tree in the low Rocky Mountain Forest. Preston...*Rocky Mountain*...p 153.

[900]*Salix* spp. Thirteen Rocky Mountain species attain tree size. Preston...*Rocky Mountain*...p 114.

account of it raining a little   good land is in the valies of this
creek and plenty of good pine timber in the high lands in Sight   we had
a fight in camps this evening   nothing Strange on Such a trip as this
we are now camped near the South Platt."

[on Cherry Creek in Douglas or Arapahoe Co., Colorado]

Before reaching the South Platte at the site of Denver, Ben
Simon and his mother-in-law showed their ability to communicate in
a variety of Indian languages. <u>Mitchell</u>:

> **"10th [June] Monday** rained a little   one of gard saw 2 indians
> last night and Snaped at one   the tracks wer plain to be Seen this
> morning   our old Snake [woman] went out and made a Speech to them in
> the Snake tougne   the gide also made another Speech to them in
> different tongues advising them to desist and be friendly that the
> whites would distroy them. we made a late Start on the account of oxen
> being gone   we got to the platt river this evening about 3 oclock and
> went to hunting a crosing place in hopes of fourding it but found it to
> deep as far as we Serched   the river is less than the Ark[ansas]
> purer water and a Stronger curent more timber on the banks than the ark
> cotton wood and willow and country more high. a vast of elk Sign and
> deer are to be Seen   our men kiled a fine deer   here appears to be a
> great hunting ground and a place resorted by traders   3 old forts now
> abandoned are not far below here.[901] it is plain to be Seen that all who
> travel here are on the watch out as all the old camping places are off
> from the timber and bluffs an evidence of fear   it rained in the
> evening."

[Denver, Denver Co., Colorado]

It is not clear whose "old camping places" Mitchell saw. The 1849
Evans/Cherokee Company had camped northeast of Denver near
Henderson Island.

The Edmonson men worked two days to build adequate watercraft
and to successfully cross the South Platte. This may be the first
recorded crossing of the South Platte at Denver by white men and
wagons.[902] <u>Mitchell</u>:

> **"11 [June] Tuesday** cleer & warm   about half the men went to work
> making 2 canoes to cross and the others garded as we expected an attack
> from the indians at this place   we are it is Supposed 40 or 50 miles
> above where Evans crossed this river last Season.[903] and will Save that

---

[901]Fort Lupton, Fort Vasquez, Fort St. Vrain, and Fort Jackson all did brisk
business in the 1830s on the South Platte River downstream from Denver. This
1850 company did not see these abandoned forts.

[902]In 1858, Capt. Randolph B. Marcy wrote: "we continued on upon the "Cherokee
California trail," skirting the eastern base of the Rocky mountains, and
crossing small tributaries of the South Platte, until we reached the 'Cache la
Poudre' creek." *Report of the Secretary of War* 35 cong. 2 sess. (1858-1859)
Sen Ex Doc 2 Serial 975 p 193.

[903]The 1849 Evans/Cherokee Company crossed the South Platte near the Cache la
Poudre River's confluence with the South Platte River, east of Greeley,
Colorado, 54 miles north/northeast from Denver. The Trappers Trail followed
down the South Platte from Denver to the trading forts of Fort Lupton, Fort

much distance or more by crosing here   I Stayed at camps as a gard and
Said but little about the mode of crosing the river as I new but little
about it   the canoe makers Soon made a little baby canoe and Spoiled
another   they tryed crosing in the one they finished with 3 men in it-
-over it turned and ducked them well in the cold water. then a dispute
took place and part of the men undertook making a raft   they had it in
the river and considered it Sufficient   on trial however it was found
to be too Small and a larger one had to be made the day was Spent and
in a manner nothing done of any advantage   Some fine deer   some wild
gees[904] Sumers and hatches here."

"12th [June] Wendsday cleer and warm   all hands Seemed more
united and went to work Soon finishing the canoes and rafts with the
intension of crosing this day   they Spoiled one of the canoes and Soon
had the other ready for crosing. the crosing was comenced on a Small
Scale with a Single canoe taking over flour Bacon cloathing and other
Small articles   the [raft] was put in the water and answered a good
purpose though it was hard to manage   waggons could be taken over 2 at
a time by taking them a part or one at a time all together   it was a
hard days worke and took till dark for all to get over   2 of my poneys
when we attempted to Swim the horses a cross got back to the Same Side
with others and I never expected to get them again   a Mr. Cox had an
indian poney in gang that he undertook to crees.[905] he Shot too low and
kiled him   after making many efforts to get mine with help I went
alone and Sucseeded in throwing a Larette over one of their heads and
the other followed in and I caught it at camp."

The Edmonson Company camped on the west side of the South Platte
River. The road they pioneered went north from Denver toward the
Cache la Poudre River at Laporte, Colorado. The other 1850
companies, except Oliver's ox train, followed this new wagon road.

Next day, the first stream they noted is now called Clear
Creek. Upstream is the mouth of Ralston Creek.[906] Mitchell:

"13 [June] Thursday cool   Started without a road nearly north
and Soon got to another bad Streem   after Spending Some time hunting a
ford we got a cross all Safe by proping up Some of the waggon beds   we
continued our cors till night a little west of north the Snowy mountains
close on our left and black hills   the grass very good   water good
Soil generaly good and but little timber   it thundered in the evening
a dark cloud appeared before us & a great roar   (we crossed the Platt
it is Supposed 30 miles above fort Saber[907] or more) we Stoped at 12 to
graze and water and part of our train were opposed to the Stop and went
on contrary to order becaused we detained So long crossing the creek[908]

Jackson, Fort Vasquez and Fort St. Vrain, then went northeast to Fort Laramie.
[904]Canada Goose *Branta canadensis*. Those of the Rocky Mountain area are of the
largest of this species. Johnsgard...*Birds*...p 81.
[905]Crease=a common practice to stun and capture an animal by creasing the head
with a bullet.
[906]On June 22, nine days after the Edmonson ox train crossed, Lewis Ralston
discovered gold there, delaying the McNair/Taylor Cherokee company two days.
[907]Fort Lupton; written "old fort Sabre" by 1849 diarist Crawford.
[908]Boulder Creek. Until further research reveals who the members of Edmonson's
ox train were, one cannot rule out that this time might also have been spent

towards Stoping time we could account for the roaring before us, we come to where the earth was white with hail as large as bird eggs   it appears to rain every day under these mountains along here."
[north of Lafayette, Boulder Co., Colorado]

The first creek of the next day was St. Vrain Creek; the second "daingerous bad creek" was Little Thompson River. Guide Ben Simon had been over this route before. Mitchell:

"14 [June] Fryday a Soon Start in hopes of a good days travel and in a few miles was detained again by another bad creek   we all got over again without loss   our crse north aggain   we were Scarce ever out of Sight of antilopes and 10 ["Several" crossed through] of them were kiled   our gides Brother in law a young Snake indian got hurt badly by his faling with [while?] in presuit of a wounde antilope   in the evening we had another daingerous bad creek to cross   the gide calls it Sadly because he found a Saddle on it long ago   we camped up in the edge of the mountains on little creek runing east, the water cold from the Snow."
[Little Thompson River near Berthoud, Larimer Co., Colorado]

In paralleling the Front Range of the Rockies between Denver and Laporte, they were compelled to cross the streams and rivers at right angles. Impressed by the massive mountains Mitchell wrote:

"15 [June] Saturday cleer and cool   all in the umer [humor] for traveling and Started Soon   Bordering on the mountains great mases of cleer I Suppose Silax[909] quartz and blocks of grinite appears on our way at noon we came to another large creek and found a good ford to cross it is caled Thomsons river [Big Thompson River]   long befor night we were Stoped by another large creek [Cache la Poudre] forming out of the mountains and no chance of fording it and looked daingerous to raft we here got to a point that we had been Steering to for 2 days and the rainge drops lower & west."

The Edmonson ox train reached the Cache la Poudre River near present Laporte, Larimer County, Colorado. The crossing proved difficult, like most others along the Front Range. Mitchell:

"16th [June] Sunday Sent men and went up and down the river to find the best place to cross   I went up the river betwen the mountains and on one as high as I could get betwen the cracks of the rocks Stood a large beautifull flour the only one I ever Seen of the Kind   wild chery bushes were on the Side of it   currents, goosberys, plums and a Strange bery that I never Seen before   Crum one of my mess and Robinson drawed [knives?] and guns at each other   it took all to make our raft."

Unable to find a ford at hand, they camped, leaving their task of raft-building for the next morning.

River conditions changed overnight. Still in hope of finding

panning for gold, although Edmonson seems to have been determined to move at a fast pace, no doubt urged on by guide Ben Simon.
[909]Perhaps Silica, a type of quartz.

a ford, Simon, with Mitchell and others, went west to explore
upriver. Mitchell:

"17th [June] Monday all hands at the raft making ready to cross
as Soon as posable   the river yet gradualy rising   cotton wood
quaken asp and Box elder[910] is the groth in the low lands and Scattering
pine on the mountains   another Seperation of messes took place and a
waggon was Sawed up for timber and picket Stakes   unfortunate Robinson
who Sepperated from our mess had to join another mess with no assurence
that he would be taken all the way   our raft was entirely unmanageble
and it landed 1/2 [mile?] below. we then made a smaler lighter one and
the gide   myself, crum and pedegrw was Sent up the Streem to discover
[a?] pass up the creek in the mountains on the South Side or a ford
above that we could cross   we went about 8 miles up the creek among
the mountains up hill neerly all the time and with some difficulty got
to the highest peak of this range So that we could see perhaps 100 miles
before us in the Larame plains,   a waggon can not be taken to this peak
by teams and it is even difficult and daingerous to lead a horse up in
places   many new plants are to be Seen on the peaks Strange to me   the
lilack in bloom and 2 small trees of great curiosity to us all and the
grandest Sight that ever I have Seen   the river had perpendiclar
cliffs [Poudre Canyon] in places Several hundred feet high and looked
frightfulle to look down at - we found 4 miles above the last place we
could apperoa[ch] the river, a place where we thought we could ford the
river at a wide place   Some of our men went up next morning to examine
the river had rose 6 or 7 inches and they considered the curent to
Strong to venture."

Having explored the river west, upstream to its negotiable limits,
and finding no ford, the Company concluded to use the raft to
cross. Upriver, birds nested in the canyon, as they still do.
Mitchell described them in some detail.

"18th [June] Tuesday we comenced crosing with our light raft it
answered a better purpose than I expected   the [river] had fell on the
account of weather being more cool[911]   Some of us went up 3 miles to
See if it could be fourded, it was yet too deep   we found a Swarm of
byrds in a high bluff Sheltered by a progecting rock   perhaps
thousands of these little birds could be Seen at a time going to and
from their nests like bees   they biuld their nests of mud and in
regular order.[912] the byrd makes a noys like the martin and its Shape is
like the martin though its [blank] and couler differs   it is Smaler
and more handsom   we Saw a pheasant [Grouse]."

---

[910]Boxelder *Acer negundo*. Mitchell would have been accustomed to a variety of
this Boxelder in Arkansas. Preston...*Rocky Mountain*...p 233.

[911]Rivers that originate in high elevations where the overnight temperatures
are below freezing send less water downstream, especially early in the day.
The Cache la Poudre is such a river. The 12,000 ft. elevations of its
headwaters are "subject to freezing temperatures and snow for eight or nine
months of the year and still contain...melting snowbanks by the time of the
first snows of September." Howard Ensign Evans and Mary Alice Evans, *Cache la
Poudre: The Natural History of a Rocky Mountain River* (Niwot, Colo: Univ.
Press of Colorado 1991) p 22.

[912]Cliff Swallows nest in both the upper Poudre Canyon and the North Fork.

After four days spent searching for fords and building rafts they finally crossed the Cache la Poudre. Meanwhile, some other wagons caught up. <u>Mitchell</u>:

> **"19 [June] Wendsday** we finished crosing and Started   we were haled by a company coming on the other Side of the river wishing assistance & help a cross the river   we remained here all day and got them across 19 men, 5 waggons[913]   part of these men we left on the verdigree."

These were former John H. Wolfe Company members, who left Pueblo June 11 after the rest of the company members decided to pack and subsequently got rid of their wagons. Mitchell wrote he had last seen "part of these men" on the Verdigris River (on April 20). Unfortunately, Mitchell did not record names of the nineteen men.

The enlarged Edmonson Company traveled north from the Cache la Poudre River in the vicinity of today's Highway 287 in Larimer County, Colorado. <u>Mitchell</u>:

> **"20 [June] Thursday** Started Soon, entering the black hills to get into the Laramee plains as soon a[s] posable-we made a good days travel and a good way through the gaps in the hills on an old indian trace[914] it rained in the evening."
> [near base of Steamboat Rock, Stonewall Creek,
> Larimer Co., Colorado]

The Edmonson Company crossed the present Colorado/Wyoming state line the next day and struck the Laramie Plains. Delaware guide Ben Simon turned them west, away from the 1849 Evans/ Cherokee Trail that continued north. <u>Mitchell</u>:

> **"21 [June] Fryday** we Started Soon the morning cool & cleer   in the evening we got over the hills into the Larame plains, our men Kiled a fine buffalow   we pased a waggon trail Supposed to be Evans trail made last year   our gide woule not trvel it far because he thought he could go a nearer way   we pased a high Spur[915] in the evening covered with ceder or Juniper   we camped on a cold water creek   one of our gard busted a cap at an indian that was trying to Steal a hors."
> [Lone Tree Creek, west of Boulder Ridge, Albany Co., Wyoming]

Simon had packed through here before, probably many times. Now he led the Edmonson ox train over a new wagon route almost due west

---

[913]The five wagons and 19 men traveled 168 miles in eight days (using Brown's diary mileages) from Pueblo to the Cache la Poudre River via present Denver following the new wagon road north pioneered by the Edmonson Company.

[914]For descriptions from previous travelers, see Vol I. Chapter 7. The 1849 Evans/Cherokee Company pioneered the wagon road from the mouth of the Cache la Poudre west to Laporte, then north to the Laramie Plains.

[915]Boulder Ridge, Albany County, Wyoming.

across the Laramie Plain, entering the Medicine Bow Range near the
Colorado/Wyoming border. The remaining 1850 companies, parties,
and individuals from Arkansas, Missouri, and Cherokee Nation
followed Edmonson's new wagon road. This marks the building of the
Southern branch of the Cherokee Trail through Wyoming.

THE ARTIST AT PUEBLO

Up to forty members of the John H. Wolfe Company, including
diarist William Quesenbury, delayed at Pueblo for several days in
preparation for the next part of their trip. Out on the plains, on
June 4, they had signed an agreement to pack from Pueblo. The
following days Quesenbury, Harris, Buckner and Prescott had gone
to Greenhorn, southwest of Pueblo, in an unsuccessful effort to
obtain Charles Kinney as guide for the packers. They traded for
animals, pack saddles, and equipment, making arrangements for
delivery to Pueblo. The rest of the company meanwhile continued
west along the Arkansas River to Pueblo, meeting Quesenbury's
group June 10, returning empty-handed from Greenhorn.

Nineteen men in five wagons chose to go north immediately,
hoping to catch Edmonson's lead ox train; the rest packed.
Quesenbury recorded the next several days' preparation necessary
to their departure. His own activity included sketching.

"Wednesday[916] **[Tuesday] 11 June** Vast preparations for packing.
Meigs[917] has determined to pack. Five wagons left. We sold ours for pack
saddles. Marcaline and Burke remained, Poisel went home-and Gerry. Wolf
and three or four others went also. All busy preparing. Gerry has
promised us four pack saddles with rigging complete [in exchange] for
our wagon. To night put the horses in the Pueblo enclosure, with
Shipley's wagon at the door."

"Thursday [Wednesday] 12 Still all hands are busy preparing.
Pack saddles are turned out fast. River rising. Mr. May went with me to
his hook below Pueblo. I afterwards took a sketch of the place.[918]

---

[916]June 11, 1850 was a Tuesday. The next two days' dates are correct; the
days should be Wednesday June 12; and Thursday June 13. Quesenbury picks up
the right day and date on "Friday June 14."

[917]Quesenbury (and Mitchell early on) often mentioned Return Jonathan Meigs in
diary entries. There is no reason given for this continued emphasis. Meigs
kept his wagon and joined the Cherokee McNair/Taylor company, not yet arrived
in Pueblo. Meigs did not survive the trip to California.

[918]Sketch reproduced in this volume. Quesenbury also sketched Bent's Old Fort.

In the evening Mr. May and myself went up and wrote letters under a cottonwood by the pond. It is doubtful that our letters will ever reach home."

Quesenbury recorded the arrival of the McNair/Taylor Company at Pueblo. For several days, they had traveled somewhat together, noted earlier in the Quesenbury and Brown diaries. Quesenbury:

> **"Friday [Thursday] 13 [June]** Sleepy this morning. After breakfast walked over to the Fontaine qui bouit[919] hunting antelopes. Took down it to the road. Saw nothing. At eleven some of the McNair's men began to come in. Presently the whole train came. They meet us friendlier than they left us."

Cherokee diarist Brown, with the McNair/Taylor Company, recorded the meeting of companies at Pueblo. Brown:

> **"June 13 [1850] 12 miles** today snow toped mountains in view plainly. Traveled 12 miles and at noon reached Peueblo   found J.H. Woolfs company there preparing to "Pack" --**Camp 37.**"

"Preparing to pack" must have been a state of activity and confusion such as these men had rarely, if ever, witnessed. Both diarists note the arrival of the Holmes and Oliver ox trains. Quesenbury describes the final preparations to pack.

> **"1850   June 14 Friday...**Our pack saddles were brought over last night about dark. This morning all hands of us are busier than ever fixing them. The ox train got in this morning. They camped above the McNair Company. Gambling has commenced in open daylight. Heretofore it has been more secret."

> Brown:

> **"[June] 14** Lay Bye all day. The ox Train consisting of 33 waggons[920] came up and camped near, at night had a big Dance --."

Again, neither diarist mentions the women of the company, twelve at the start. Which of the companies the women traveled with, what their names were, and what they did throughout the journey is uncertain. Surely they participated in the "big dance" at Pueblo.

The McNair/Taylor company traveled on after spending one and a half days at Pueblo. Leaving early in the morning, they did not see the final deliberate acts of destruction by members of Cherokee John Wolfe's packing company. Nor did they see Wolfe's company that first night.

---

[919]"Fountain that Boils." Fountain Creek flows into the Arkansas at Pueblo.
[920]Capt. Holmes' 20 ox teams had joined the McNair company on May 27 at Coon Creek in Kansas, Brown's Camp 21. Capt. Oliver's ox train joined earlier.

Brown:

"**[June] 15 [1850] 15 miles...**Traveled North along the north
Bank of a large Creek [Fountain] which emptys into Ark R Below Peueblo.
Left the Pack company preparing for Packing. Made 15 miles.
Camp 38 --."
     [south of the Pueblo/El Paso Cos. line, Colorado]

     Quesenbury and the pack company were not quite ready to leave
Pueblo. Before departure one more big event took place, a willful
act of destruction described by Quesenbury:

"**Saturday 15. 1850 June 8 [miles]** Still fixing packs. All
near about ready. Several of us were engaged an hour or two this morning
in destroying the remnants of the conveniences we had with the wagons.
Trunks, boxes, &c were laden with small articles, consigned to the
river, and then sunk by pelting them with stones. Iron bound casks and
many such useful things were treated in the same way.
     But the most destruction happened in a pile which was built by our
whole company, of tent poles, axes, spades, guns, buckets, lanterns-
coats-every thing appertaining to a California trip. Jim Pyeatt rolled
the remnant of his wagon on the top. We packed our animals and as we
started from Pueblo, I took the brands of three tent poles and set fire
to the heap."

Quesenbury listed nearly every item destroyed or thrown in the
river and consigned to the fire--everything, except why they did
it. The motive for the wanton destruction is a matter of guessing.
In both 1849 and 1850 emigrants were angered by the Pueblo area
traders' low exchange value placed on their wagons and the high
prices of pack animals and equipment. John Rankin Pyeatt wrote
"som sell, or rather give away thear load and wagons"[921] while
fellow traveler Hiram Davis called the residents "the most
abandoned set of thieves, Mexicans, Indians, halfbreeds that ever
disgraced any spot of earth."[922] Apparently the Wolfe company
packers could not bring themselves to leave anything behind which
might be of use to the traders, mountain men, or plains Indians.

     The minimum amount of supplies mandated by the Cherokee
company regulations, for instance, were "75 lbs. of bacon, 100
lbs. of flour...one peck of salt to each man...in addition to
sugar and coffee...and other necessaries to last." The foodstuffs
were supplemented by the game animals procured along the trail:

---

[921]John Rankin Pyeatt letter to wife Elizabeth from Pueblo June 20-22, 1849.
[922]Judge Hiram Davis letter to his wife from Pueblo June 18-22, 1849.
Flashback vol 9, no 1, (May 1959). Washington County Historical Society,
Fayetteville, Arkansas.

buffalo, antelope, deer, rabbit, prairie dogs, ducks, shorebirds, hawks, owls, turtles, and fish. Much of the food hauled from home became surplus at Pueblo.

Following the "ceremony" of destruction, the Wolfe pack company moved north from Pueblo. <u>Quesenbury</u>:

> "**[June 15]** It was between 12 and 1 o'clock when we left Pueblo. Some few of the mules behaved badly, but the majority of them rolled on without trouble. Jess Shipley's mule stampeded and was near throwing him. Camped on the Fontaine qui bouit. The grass was large and good, but not very abundant. There was a great deal of sand over the whole [river] bottom, which made it fatiguing for the horses to graze upon. No guard tonight. Took my gun and blankets and went down to some cottonwoods where I slept with my horses tied by me. Warm tonight for the first in some time. Tom Smith[923] and two or three others slept in the cottonwoods above me."
>
> [Fountain Creek, Pueblo Co., Colorado]

Wolfe's packers passed McNair the next day, as the companies jockeyed for position along the road. <u>Quesenbury</u>:

> "**Sunday [June] 16. 1850 14 [miles]**...The Company determined this morning to travel. This is the first time we have broken the Sabbath by travelling. The grass is bad and we are inconveniently situated. A good many places offered to day at which we might have stopped but the Company went on. Passed McNair's Company. Nooned on a slope. The Ox team [Capt. Holmes'] ahead about half a mile--the McNair's about a quarter below. In two hours the Ox train under Oliver came up and passed on following McNair's Company that left a short time before. Our company and the other ox train remained for the night.
>
> Rogers and McQuorter joined us whilst here, but soon after went on to get their mules shod at the foremost train. Mr. May left also for the McNair company. He joined Jno. Brown's mess.
>
> At six o'clock an election for Sergeant was held in place of Buckner who resigned the morning we left the company for Greenhorn."

Quesenbury's notations of June 16 give a clear account of the several separate companies. The diary entry next includes a summary of the vegetation he had seen across the country.

> "From the time we struck the Arkansas river where the Santa Fe road crosses it, the timber has been cottonwood and willow.[924] The grass has been sufficient for our different trains, but not such as we find in the prairie at home. Some of it was green, along the river but on the

---

[923]There are two Thomas Smiths connected to Cherokee: one married Sarah Fields, cousin of company member Richard Fields; one married Susie Fawling, cousin of the Martins and Lowreys. Starr...*Cherokee*...pp 310-11, 368.

[924]Cottonwood is *Populus* Genus; there are approximately a dozen species in North America. Eastern Cottonwood (*P. deltoides*) is east of the 100th meridian in Arkansas and Kansas; the Plains Cottonwood (*P. sargentii*), is the common tree of stream banks west of the 100th meridian. Preston...*Trees*...p 125. On the Arkansas both Peachleaf Willow *Salix amygdoloides* and Narrowleaf Willow *S. interior* occur in mixed stands. Lindauer..."Comparison..." p 252.

highlands, it was short, fine, and dried up.[925] In the buffalo range and on the dog town country it was much poorer than elsewhere.[926] This kind of country extends from the Turkey Creeks[927] to the Santa Fe Crossing of Arkansas.[928]

On the Fountaine qui bouit, I noticed the first Bitter Cottonwoods.[929] These are found on this stream all the way up from its mouth. The common cottonwood also prevails. Rushes grow from Verdigris river to the head of the Fontaine qui bouit. Prickly pears of three or four different kinds are found. Some currant bushes and cherry, are found. Wild sage abounds from thirty miles below Ft. Bent to this place. Prairie roses I first saw near Verdigris. They are plenteous yet."[930]

Quesenbury finished his daily entry noting the new position he's been elected to.

"Sunday 16 June   I-myself was elected Sergeant in Buckner's place. Placed the guard at night. In the latter part of the night and early in the morning the wind blows cool from the N. About 9 or 10 it changes and comes from the S."

Quesenbury noted the Wolfe company traveled on Sunday, the first time they had done so. This may have resulted in the loss of Rev. J. J. May to McNair's company. Reverend May was probably much more suited to this company. The fact that May quit the Wolfe company is corroborated by Brown's note in the left margin of his diary: "today J.J. May of Cane Hill, Arks quitt the pack Co--and joined my mess." Brown:

"16 June...15 miles... Traveled along the creek 15 miles. No buffalo since the 30th of May. Bear sign Plenty, one killed today[931]
Camp 39 --."
                 [Town of Fountain, El Paso Co., Colorado]

On the left hand page opposite his entry for June 16, Cherokee

----

[925]This area, known as the short-grass prairie, consists primarily of native buffalo grass *Buchloe dactyloides* and Blue Grama *Bouteloua graciles*. Both are short but despite their small height these grasses are the two most important year-round forage grasses of the Great Plains. R. W. Pohl, *How to Know the Grasses* (Dubuque, Iowa: Wm. C. Brown Co. 1953) pp 131, 143.

[926]Quesenbury is very observant; the poorer grass is False Buffalo Grass *Munroa squarrosa* with a very low forage value. The plants grow on overgrazed (or disturbed) soil, blow-out, prairie-dog towns, corrals, etc. Ibid. p 131.

[927]Turkey Creeks are east of and near McPherson, Kansas.

[928]The Cimarron Cutoff, which is near the 100th meridian.

[929]Narrow-leaf Cottonwood *Populus angustifolia* occurs along streambanks in the Rocky Mountains at altitudes of 5,000-10,000 ft. Fountain Creek, on the Cherokee Trail, is 5,550 ft. elevation.

[930]Plains Cottonwood *Populus sargentii*; Rushes-*Juncus* spp; Prickly Pear-*Opuntia* spp; Currant Bushes-*Ribes* spp; Cherry-Western Choke Cherry *Prunus virginiana*; Wild Sage-Sagebrush *Artemisia* spp; Prairie Rose-*Rosa setigera*.

[931]James Mitchell recorded grizzlies northeast of the Pikes Peak region on June 7. Brown's was probably a black bear *Ursus americanus*.

diarist Brown made some mileage notes:

from Grand R	674	to Peueblo
" Peueblo	499	to Green River
	1,173	
" Green River	158	to Mormon City
	1,331	
	331[932]	
	1,662	

Quesenbury, after their first long distance day, sketched again, this one probably from the top of Point of Rocks (see page 287). Restless to go on and evidently weary of the responsibility of Sergeant of the Guard after two days, he made arrangements to go ahead of the other packers. Quesenbury

> **"Monday 17 June. 30 [miles]** The [Holmes] Ox train got off before us. However we passed all trains[933] during the day. Stopped for a moment at a spring [Jimmy Camp Spring] on the right hand of the road. Water good. Farther on three or four miles water was found in ponds to the left, along a branch. Camped near a beautiful hill, partly bare and partly covered with pine.[934] Bucker[sic] Wolf, Barker and myself went to the top. Sketched Pikes' Peak again from it.
> At night agreed with Perry to divide provisions. Riley Buchanan concluded to go with me. Placed the guard-the 2nd and last night of my Sergeantship. Buckner Riley and myself will make a start to morrow morning for California."
> [Point of Rocks, El Paso Co., Colorado]

Traveling north from Fountain, Colorado with the McNair/Taylor company, Brown continues his diary:

> **"June 17...20 miles...**Traveled north, leaving the Creek. Traveled over Sand hills, pine Timber. passed Pikes Peak which is covered with snow. camped at cold spring of water [Black Squirrel Creek]--made today about 20 miles **Camp 40th."**
> [Four miles east of Black Forest, El Paso Co., Colorado]

Pikes Peak is the most easily recognized pilot point on the Mountain Branch of the Santa Fe Trail, and the Cherokee Trail. All travelers mention its dominance in the landscape. It is the undoubted indicator of the route traveled. In the reminiscences and diaries from subsequent years, the question of route followed is often resolved by the mention of passing Pikes Peak.

A large and wealthy 1857 Arkansas company, the Baker/Fancher

---

[932]Brown did not indicate what this figure represents.

[933]Holmes' ox train, Oliver's ox train, and McNair's horse/mule wagon company, in that order.

[934]Point of Rocks, El Paso County, Colorado.

train, took this route, as evidenced by the following quote of a
member who traveled with the train as far as Salt Lake. "The route
taken was up the Arkansas River in the vicinity of Pikes Peak and
from this location on the middle emigrant trail to Ft. Bridger."[935]
(Adult members of this company were methodically killed by Mormons
and Indians in southern Utah, in what became known as the Mountain
Meadows Massacre.)

Quesenbury had left the Wolfe pack company at Pueblo to
overtake Mitchell, who was with Captain Edmonson's lead ox train.
On June 18, Mitchell and company were crossing the Cache la Poudre
River on the raft they had constructed. Quesenbury, meanwhile, was
descending Cherry Creek Valley to the South Platte River.

"Tuesday 18 June...35 [miles]...Buckner, Riley and myself got
ready and Started. After going three miles I got down and shot at an
antelope. Lost my bag of shot which I had to go back for a mile and a
half. Merrill overtook me and wanted to go with us. Didn't accede. Saw
great numbers of antelopes. Buckner shot at one very close. Missed. I
shot with buckshot. Missed. Nooned at Cherry Creek as Evans called it,
and according to his count we have made twenty-one miles to day to this
place.[936] Whilst nooning found that I had left my tobacco and tin tube
with the company behind. As we were packing up, they came, and we
travelled with them till they camped, when I got my tobacco and tube.
Buckner, Riley and myself made about two miles and stopped and cooked.
Showered a few minutes. Went on after dark three or four miles. Crossed
the Creek and laid down in a thicket with grass around half-leg high."
[near the Douglas/Arapahoe Cos. line, Colorado]

The McNair/Taylor company camped on Cherry Creek where Quesenbury
nooned. Brown:

"[June] 18 Traveled **25 miles**. Camped on a Bold Running, Clear
stream of water. waters of the Platt. Good grass & wood
Camp 41 --."
[Near Franktown, Douglas Co., Colorado]

Brown added a note in the left margin: "today we crossed the
dividing ridge between the Arks & Platt."[937]

[935]Roger V. Logan, Jr., ed. "The Mountain Meadows Massacre" *Mountain Heritage:
Some Glimpses into Boone County's Past After One Hundred Years* (Harrison,
Ark.: Times Publishing Co., 1969) pp 25-31 Harrison Jr. Chamber of Commerce.
[936]From Point of Rocks to Franktown the distance is 21 miles. The 1849 Evans/
Cherokee wagon company camped on Cherry Creek near present Franktown, Douglas
County, Colorado, about six miles east of Castle Rock.
[937]"The most prominent feature in the profile of the plains is the 'Divide', a
high main ridge, approached by a series of lesser ridges with a mesa-like top
which rises to an elevation of 7,500 ft. On each side the bed of whitish-
yellow and reddish sandstone appear like fortifications, holding a nearly
horizontal position."*Rocky Mountain Directory and Colorado Gazatteer* (1870).

WILLIAM M. QUESENBURY SKETCH

"June"

Steamboat Rock sketched June 23, 1850.

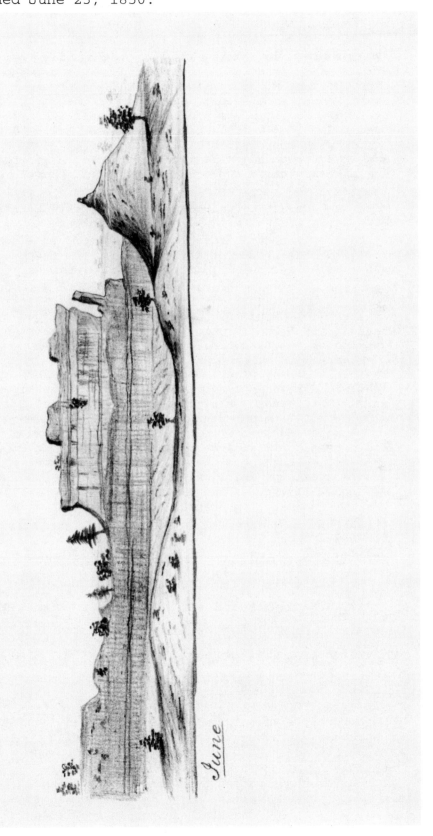

Quesenbury, off on his own with Buckner and Riley, continues to keep mileage records, based on his copy of the 1849 Evans/Cherokee journey. They followed Edmonson's trail to the Platte, and crossed, where the 1849 journals became useless. Quesenbury:

"Wednesday 19 June 1850 ...25 [miles]... Slept much later this morning than we intended. When we got off the sun was two hours high. Buckner wounded an antelope. Saw a pheasant just after we left camp. Nooned among some cottonwoods on the right of the road. Hot day. Near our nooning place the ox train under Edmonson turned off down the creek. The road went over the divide. We followed the new trail.

Saw some deer near the timber on the left which Buckner tried to get a shot at, but they were very wild. We soon afterwards found one of the ox train camps and saw they had staid there a day or so. Followed the trail and came to the Platte about half a mile off.[938] Saw a raft or some water craft on the other side. [Robert] Harris[939] had passed on the 16th at 10 o'clock.[940]

Buckner rode Arab into the river to try it--found it swimming in a few yards. He went over. I, then, tied the hatchet to his mule's neck, after Riley and myself had unpacked the animals; The hatchet was needed to break apart some cross pieces that bound a canoe[941] between two logs --the water craft we saw on the other side. I then put in on Pony, whilst Riley drove the other animals in. All got across safely. Made three trips with the canoe before we got all our packs over. Found some gearing on the bar which will make good girths.

Started and got about three quarters of a mile. Looked back and saw the pack company. They shouted to us--little dreaming of the trouble they would have in a short time. In about six miles we came to another stream that caused us a great deal of trouble [Clear Creek]. We were already wet from a hail and rain that had fallen on us after crossing the Platte. Buckner tried the stream, and thought it fordable, but it was not half crossed. We could not, on account of the deep and swift current get out where the ox train did. Buckner found a shallower place just above, over which he took our packs on Arab, by making two trips. We then went over with the animals excepting two which turned back. Buckner and myself went back and brought them over. It is wet and cold at our camp to night. We built a fire and risked the Indians--our horses grazing just in the outer edge of the thicket we are in."

Quesenbury and his two traveling companions camped northwest of Denver near Clear Creek. The direction of travel changed to cross the various creeks and eroded ravines which emanate from the Rocky Mountains on the west, running east toward the Platte River. The companies traveled perpendicular to these impediments.

---

[938] Confluence of Cherry Creek with the South Platte River at present Denver.
[939] With the five wagons which had left John H. Wolfe's company at Pueblo June 11, Harris had written or carved the date which Quesenbury saw on a rock or tree. Harris was with Quesenbury trying to procure a guide at Greenhorn.
[940] On June 12 Mitchell, with Edmonson's ox train, crossed the swift South Platte River using canoes and rafts they fashioned; Harris crossed June 16.
[941] Mitchell's canoe makers built "a little baby canoe" on June 11, and on June 12 they were "Soon finishing the canoes and rafts."

The three men put progressively more distance between themselves, the Wolfe pack company, and the wagon groups. The next few entries follow them north toward the Laramie Plains. Quesenbury

"**June 20. Thursday 30 [miles]**...Sun two hours high when we started. Followed the same trail as yesterday over a very rolling country. Antelopes continue very abundant. The road is very winding- for a long time going N.W. and then turning E.N.E. for two or three miles.Nooned on a sluggish branch [Coal Creek]. Made coffee as the water was not fit to drink. Buckner cooked a curlew which I killed on the way. It hailed tremendous hard and large--staked our animals to prevent them stampeding in the hail. I killed a pheasant [grouse] near a stream [Boulder Creek] which we crossed a few miles from the branch we nooned on, and after coming about a mile further Buckner shot a deer down. Took the hams. Stopped and cooked in a little hollow to the right of the road. There was water, but it was unfit to drink. As soon as dark came on we struck N.E. for some timber we observed before night. Found grass there nearly waist high."

"**1850 June 21 Friday 30 [miles]**...The longest day in 1850. Got breakfast. Buckner's mule took a small fly round at an antelope before we started. Went up the creek [St. Vrain Creek] hunting a ford. With difficulty found one. Passed two or three fine streams [Little and Big Thompson Rivers] and nooned to the left near a bare rocky ridge thrown up in triangular form, to the left of the trail. Late in the evening Buckner discovered a grizzly bear down in the valley just below us. He was feeding. Buckner shot at him, but he only reared on his hind legs, looked round, and went to feeding again. Buckner then mounted Arab, gave chase, and shot at him again as he ran over a ridge. Cooked where we got off our horses for the bear. Water in the gourds gave out. We have but two. Rode on after night and found timber which gave us a good sleeping place as far as security was concerned, but a most dismal one as far as comfort was the question--There were millions of ravenous musquitoes, singing round us. The grass was not as good as it was last night. Not a drop of water, although plenty of timber."

"**June 22 Saturday 20 [miles]**...No water this morning and of course no coffee. Ate venison and bacon. Rode about ten miles before we came to water which was as we suppose Cache de la Poudre.[942] Worked hard making a raft. Got it completed and our things on it. Riley and myself rode into the river and Buckner drove the horses in after us. Pony wouldn't swim. He after several surges threw me off, and I swam to bank. I never was in as cold water before. The horses got over, and Buckner then brought the raft across. It was near swamping when it struck land. Got our things off--untied our ropes from the raft--let the logs go.[943] Spread out our things to dry--cleaned up our guns as they had got wet. Cooked and ate. About 3. P.M., as we were saddling up, two men appeared on the trail behind. They proved to be Merrill, and Tom Smith who hearing our guns thought the Indians had attacked us and had put off to our rescue.

---

[942]Approximately four miles northwest of Fort Collins in Larimer County, Laporte is situated near the opening or portal where the river emerges from the mountains into the broad Poudre valley; thus the name.
[943]In contrast, the 1849 Evans/Cherokee Company left their raft at the Cache la Poudre "for the bennefit of the nexthat should com along." John Rankin Pyeatt letter to his wife from Salt Lake, August 12, 1849.

As I had been expecting for a day or so past Riley Buchanan got faint hearted and decided to stay with the pack company behind. Divided our provisions and left him. Buckner and myself went alone. Followed the river a mile or so, when the trail turned to the right up a valley with red bluffs on the right and high sloping hills on the left. At every fifty yards we went up a rise and immediately into a hollow.[944] This continued for about ten miles when we camped on the right in a gorge made by a small branch [Owl Creek] passing through the red bluffs. Grass not very good. Water in a hole just below us."
[Owl Canyon, 3 miles SE of Livermore, Larimer Co., Colorado]

The Front Range here is a series of uplifts like parallel rows of spines, facing west, as though resting upon one another. Erosion between the uplifts has produced north/south U-shaped valleys, one of which they traveled through. Quesenbury:

"Sunday June 23 1850 30 [miles] Started tolerably early. The road for eight miles or thereabouts, very much like that of yesterday bad for wagons. At twelve came to the Ox company's camp. Nooned just above. In the evening passed through the wildest--most broken country I ever beheld. Rocks of all sizes piled in all shapes. Many places risemble the ruins of Stonehenge that we see represented in pictures.[945] Saw traces of a wagon way at two or three different points this evening. Rocks rolled out of the way, blazes, etc.[946] Turned from the road to the left, and camped on a branch running east between pine hills; the N. side of the S. hill thickly timbered with pines. This evening has been drizzly, cold, and disagreeable."
[probably Mud Creek, Tributary of Dale Creek, three miles NW of Virginia Dale, Larimer Co., Colorado]

During the noon stop, near the site of the later Cherokee Stage Station, Quesenbury sketched Steamboat Rock, marking it simply "June."[947] The rock's resemblance to his sketch is clear. Quesenbury entered the Laramie Plains.

"June 24 Monday 30 [miles]...At an hour and a half of sun we struck out. The road kept to the right of a range of hills, but turned over them in the course of four or five miles. A large valley opened before us. The range of hills that the road crossed runs into it, rather dividing it. Came to the Ox company's camp [Lone Tree Creek]. A wagon and an oven remained."

---

[944]The Front Range here is a series of uplifts like parallel rows of spines, facing west, as though resting upon one another. Erosion between the uplifts has produced north/south U-shaped valleys, one of which they traveled through.
[945]This is an excellent description of the country between Livermore, Colorado and the Wyoming border along U.S. Highway 287.
[946]Traces of either the 1849 Evans/Cherokee wagon company; and/or Edmonson's 1850 ox train just a few days ahead.
[947]Cherokee Stage Station was on the Overland Stage Line, beginning in 1862. Also called Ten Mile, and Stonewall Station, located on Stonewall Creek, near confluence with Ten Mile Creek, west of Steamboat Rock. Martin H. Schloo, *Research of the Cherokee-Overland Trails Fort Collins and Laporte, Colorado North to the State Line.* (Fort Collins, Colo: Self-published 1996) pp 44-45.

William Quesenbury and his companion William Buckner continued traveling by themselves, with their packed animals. They turned west to follow the Edmonson ox train toward the North Platte River. Wolfe's pack company was close behind.

THE CHEROKEE WAGON COMPANY TRAVELS NORTH

John Lowery Brown remained with the McNair/Taylor company. Traveling with them, ahead or behind, were Captain Oliver's ox train and Captain Holmes' ox train. As they all traveled down Cherry Creek, from Franktown toward Denver, <u>Brown</u> recorded:

"[June] 19 20 miles... Continued down the above mentioned Creek 20 miles   Good Grass, water & timber **Camp 42** --."
[near present Cherry Creek Reservoir, Arapahoe Co., Colorado]

Brown added a weather note in the left margin: "very hard storm this evening hale from the size of a Birds to a hens egg." The company followed the Edmonson track to the South Platte. <u>Brown</u>:

"June 20th ten miles to-day Took a left hand trail down the Creek, which was made by Capt Edmonson about two weeks ago. about 10 oclock came to the South fork of Platt River. Made a Raft and commenced crossing the waggons. camped on the bank of Platt. **Camp 43** --."
[confluence of Cherry Creek and South Platte River
site of Denver, Denver Co., Colorado]

Additional notes beside Brown's entries for June 27-29 indicate confusion reigned during the South Platte River crossing. For the first time, Brown embellishes his usual brief entry:

"Sayings of the Boys while wrafting the Platt --
No one speak but the Captain [Clement Vann McNair]--Will you hold your tongue you scoundrel--hold on, pitch on to that raft fellows a dozen or two of you--push it off--now she rides--Let her swing--hold to the rope to the right you Rogues--Run out to the right with the rope--Cordelle there on the Left Rope. pitch ashore my lads--all Right--Let her come --now she Rides--Get off the Rope there Behind--I cant pull the Raft and you on the Rope. Get away Bill from behind, you'r so short, you pull down instead of along--who did that? There now the rope is Broke--Back she goes--Pull her up--stop that fellows mouth and hear what the Captain says--I'll spill you into the River the first thing you know--Look out I'll see if I can throw a rock over. who saw a Kan Karen--he did? who killed a deer with a Black tail--oh it was a sheep--no it was a Goat-- No it was a "Donkey"--That was a good one by Gum--George pull my finger why didn't they marry. now is the time to hold your tater--Into it Dugen--&c &c."

At the junction of Cherry Creek and the South Platte River was another division of companies, albeit a temporary one.

Captain Oliver, who had Lewis Evans' 1849 journal, continued with his ox train down the South Platte River, not crossing until he came to the confluence with the Cache la Poudre, exactly as the 1849 Evans/Cherokee Company had done. After crossing, Oliver's company of perhaps twenty ox wagons then traveled westward along the north bank of the Cache la Poudre to Laporte. There Oliver turned north away from the river. There he reappeared in Brown's diary, having made the trip faster than those who took the newly-pioneered 1850 wagon trail north from Denver to Laporte.

Captain McNair continues north after the crossing of the South Platte at Denver. <u>Brown</u>:

> "**June 21 [Friday] 6 miles...**finished crossing at 2 oclock
> left the Platt and traveled 6 miles to Creek Good water grass & timber
> **Camp 44 --.**"
>   [Ralston Creek, Arvada, Jefferson Co., Colorado]

> "**[June] 22 Lay Bye. Gold found.**"

Brown added a note in the left margin: "we called this Ralstons Creek because a man of that name found gold here." Lewis Ralston knew the Georgia goldfields.[948] In 1835 he was living on the Etowah River. The censustaker noted "Lumpkin County has extensive gold mines."[949]

The *Cherokee Advocate* printed a report in early September:

> Report has reached this place, that a portion of our Californians who left here this spring by way of Capt. Evans' route, have stopped at the foot of the Rocky Mountains in a full placer of gold. We do not believe this report, until we hear something more confirmatory.[950]

---

[948]In the Lewis Ralston household were "Five Quarterblood Indians and one white marriage. They owned a ferryboat." James W. Tyner, ed. *Those Who Cried* (Chi-ga-u Inc. 1974) p 50. Lewis Rolston [sic] married Elizabeth Kell; their 14 children included #6 Lewis Rolston [sic] who married Eliza Postell. Starr ...*Cherokee*...pp 42 and 47. Another Georgia source noted: "Lewis Ralston married Elizabeth Kell, daughter of Alex and Emily; went to Colorado...made a settlment on Ralston's Creek; returned to Lumpkin Co." Mary B. Warren and Eva B. Weeks, eds. *Whites Among the Cherokees: Georgia 1828-1838 Written by the Participants* (Danielsville, Ga: Heritage Papers 1987) p 237.
[949]Dahlonega, Georgia, in Lumpkin County, was the site of a branch mint established to handle deposits from the Georgia gold rush which began in 1828. Deposits from California began in 1850 and continued through 1861, peaking at $359,122 in 1853. Deposits from Colorado were made between 1859-61. "Bullion Deposits at Dahlonega Branch Mint" *The U.S. Branch Mint at Dahlonega, Ga: Its History and Coinage* (Easley, S.C.: Southern History Press, Inc. 1984) Table V, p 85. It was after the 1828 gold discoveries in Georgia that the push for mandatory Indian Removal to the west began in earnest.
[950]*Cherokee Advocate* 3 September 1850 p 2.

The Cherokee newspaper had to wait a few more months for further confirmation of the gold discovery in the Rocky Mountains. Company member Jeffrey Beck wrote of it. The editor commented:

> copy of a letter, from California, [from]...Jeffrey Beck...He and his company discovered gold on this side the Rocky Mountains as they went out--and should he live to get back, he intends making a trial of it. He thinks it would be more profitable than working in California[951]

Jeffrey and John Beck, as well as Lewis Ralston, traveled in the 1850 McNair company.[952]

Of the emigrating groups from Arkansas, Missouri and Cherokee Nation, McNair's company was last to pass through. None of the preceding groups had noted either stopping or prospecting. In 1858, Cherokee, Georgians, and others returned to the area to explore for gold. Those who stayed found the traces they were seeking, precipitating the Pikes Peak Gold Rush of 1859.

While the 1850 company continued to prospect on Ralston's Creek Brown entered in his diary:

> "**June 23**   this morning all except 3 messes who traveled on concluded to stay and examine the Gold. Bell Dobkins[953] & R.J. Meigs traveled on."

Devereaux Jarrette Bell and wife Juliette Vann were in the first mess Brown mentioned, with probably two or three other relatives. The McNair Company moved north on Edmonson's new road, Brown:

> "**June 24th 26 miles...**Left Ralstons Creek and made 26 miles. Rainy & very mudy. Camped on creek plenty water, wood, & grass
> **Camp 45 --.**"
>   [St. Vrain Creek near Longmont, Boulder Co., Colorado]

Brown wrote in the left margin: "only 14 waggons   snow toped mountains in view today." For the first time, Brown noted the number of wagons in the McNair/Taylor company. Once they were all together again, there were at least 17 wagons in the company. In two days, they got to the Cache la Poudre River. Brown:

> "**[June] 25** Traveled **16 miles** and camped on a Creek. plenty good water, wood & grass   **Camp 46 --.**"
>   [Big Thompson River near Loveland, Larimer Co., Colorado]

---

[951]*Cherokee Advocate* 25 February 1851 editor's column p 2 col 1.
[952]A John Beck married Emily Duncan, a cousin of Elizabeth Kell, whose husband Lewis Ralston was credited for the 1850 gold find near Denver.
[953]A John Robert Dobkins is listed by Starr...*Cherokee*...pp 385 and 446.

"[June] 26 Traveled **15 miles** and came to a large Creek where we found the ox train [Capt. Holmes'] and the [3] horse wagons that had left us preparing to "Raft." good water, wood & grass **Camp 47**--."
[Cache la Poudre River, Laporte, Larimer Co., Colorado]

Brown's margin: "Black Tailed Deer killed today Cashla poodra."

The Company spent another day building the raft, which they used to cross the river. Brown:

"June 27 Lay Bye all day. finished a Raft --."

"**[June] 28**   this morning Both Trains united and "Rafted" to-gather. finished, and Camped on north Bank of Cashe La Poudre River Clem McNair having resigned, T.F. Taylor the Lieutenant took command of the Co as Captain   **Camp 48** --."
[north bank Cache la Poudre River, Larimer Co., Colorado]

Without knowing what actually precipitated the change of command, only speculatation is possible. Clement Vann McNair was elected captain of the company on April 29 on the west bank of the Verdigris River in Oklahoma. He tried to resign once--on May 14, on the Walnut River near El Dorado, Kansas, but he was immediately re-elected, and continued as captain. Whatever happened on or before reaching the Cache la Poudre River, McNair resigned and Cherokee Thomas Fox Taylor took command. He would remain captain until the company reached California.

The company moved north, discovering Captain Oliver's ox train. Brown:

"June 29 20 miles. Early start. Traveled up north Bank of the Cashe La Poudre River 3 miles, when we left the River turned north into a Pass through the hills. 12 miles since morning and we came to a small creek [Owl Creek] the first water since Leaving the River. This evening passed over rough Road. Camped half a mile to the right of the road on a hill by the side of a large, steep Red Mt. after leaving the Road to Camp, we crossed Evans old Trace, which had just been passed over by Capt Olivers ox train, whom we left at the River Platt, and who had continued down that stream on Evans Trace. & we making a Cutoff being delayed at the Cashe La Poudre in crossing, he had got ahead of us. Made today 20 miles **Camp 49."**
[near Steamboat Rock, Larimer Co., Colorado]

The Holmes and Oliver ox trains, and the Taylor/McNair horse/mule train left their campsite near Steamboat Rock and proceeded to the Laramie Plains. Brown:

"June 30th Sunday 20 miles. Traveled West today over tolerably wild sage   good Road plenty Water. Camped on a small Running stream foot of hills. high winds & cold. Made today 20 miles **Camp 50**--."
[Willow Creek near Tie Siding, Albany Co., Wyoming]

With a change of leadership from McNair to Taylor, the company for the first time did not stop for the Sabbath. During the day, the companies passed the site of Virginia Dale, future Overland Stage station site.

Next day Captain Taylor, like the others, turned off to follow Edmonson westward. <u>Brown</u> wrote:

"July 1   Entered the Larrima Plain. **Left Evans Trace**."
This is the last 1850 diary entry that mentions the Evans Trace. From this point on, the 1850 emigrant companies, beginning with the Edmondson Ox train guided by Delaware/French Ben Simon, traveled west toward the Medicine Bow Range and the North Platte River, blazing the Southern Cherokee Wagon Trail in Wyoming.

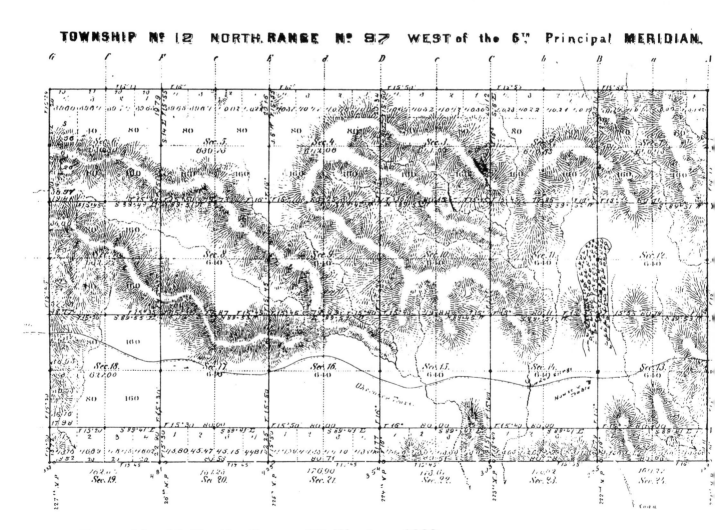

Township 12 North, Range 97 West.   1882.

The "Cherokee Trail" is shown passing "Powder Spring" in section 14. This is known today as Lower Powder Spring and was Brown's "Sulphur Spring" / campsite 62.

ELEVATION CHART, 1850 Edmonson/Cherokee Trail

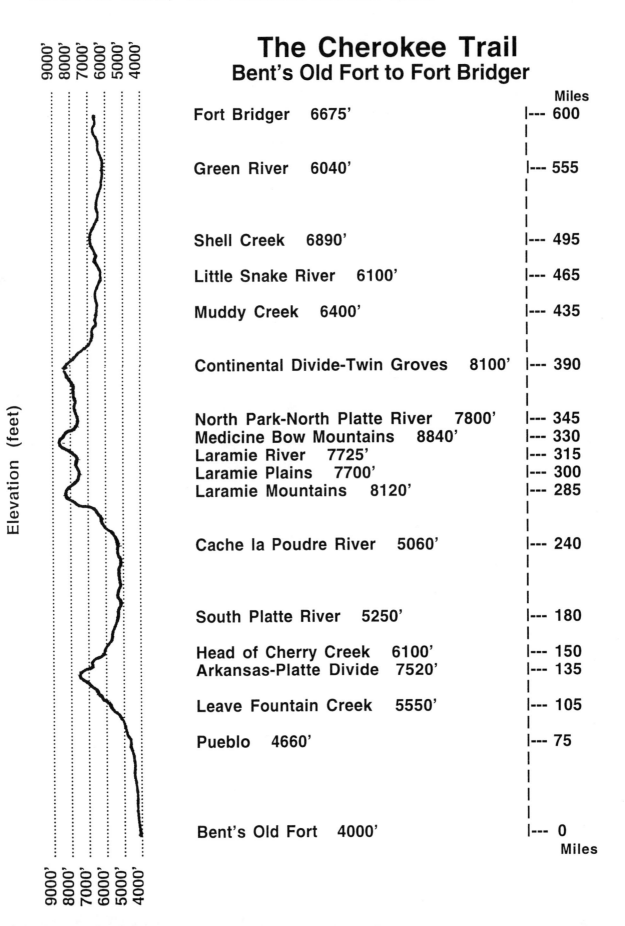

The Cherokee Trail
Bent's Old Fort to Fort Bridger

Miles

Fort Bridger   6675' |--- 600

Green River   6040' |--- 555

Shell Creek   6890' |--- 495

Little Snake River   6100' |--- 465

Muddy Creek   6400' |--- 435

Continental Divide-Twin Groves   8100' |--- 390

North Park-North Platte River   7800' |--- 345
Medicine Bow Mountains   8840' |--- 330
Laramie River   7725' |--- 315
Laramie Plains   7700' |--- 300
Laramie Mountains   8120' |--- 285

Cache la Poudre River   5060' |--- 240

South Platte River   5250' |--- 180

Head of Cherry Creek   6100' |--- 150
Arkansas-Platte Divide   7520' |--- 135

Leave Fountain Creek   5550' |--- 105

Pueblo   4660' |--- 75

Bent's Old Fort   4000' |--- 0
                                                         Miles

Elevation (feet)

9000' 8000' 7000' 6000' 5000' 4000'

Chapter 6. EDMONSON/CHEROKEE (SOUTHERN) TRAIL

Laramie Plains to the North Platte River

Edmonson's Company had to Cut a Road Through the Timber
--William Quesenbury

Mitchell, Crum, and Strickler were with the Edmonson ox train a few days ahead of the other trains. Ben Simon had guided the Edmonson company as they crossed the South Platte River, making a well-defined trace, a new wagon road north. All the companies but Oliver's ox train followed that trace along the Front Range of the Rocky Mountains to the Cache la Poudre River. Failing to find a route west through the Poudre Canyon, the Edmonson party crossed the Cache la Poudre at Laporte (Colorado) and proceeded north to the Laramie Plains, where Simon turned them west, saying he could take them "a neerer way" than the 1849 Evans/Cherokee route.

The Edmonson company, first wagon train on the route, turned west to the Laramie River and crossed it, where they had to begin cutting the road. Mitchell's diary documents the route from Lone Tree Creek, west of present Tie Siding, Wyoming. Mitchell:

> **"22 [June] Saturday** we Started late owing to a Seperation in a mess and another waggon was left. a gun was left [and] Some bake ovens &c we traveled we had a good way to travel though we went South in consequence of a deep fork of the Larame and no timber on it to make a raft we camped on nor[t]h bank of the Lareme in the mountains near the Snow our gide Kiled an antilope and a Bufelow and his dogs caught 3 young antilopes."

> **"23rd [June] Sunday** cool morning we Started late not expecting to travel far owing [to finding] the way to look out through the mountains in the pine timber[954] 2 waggons were left again and various other property with thim we traveled about 4 or 5 miles & Stoped to look out the way before us the gide & other men and myself went in the mountains the tallest pine timbr & Stratest is here to be Seen that has been on our way the Bolsom pine is here quakin asp and another Sort of pine."[955]

---

[954]Mitchell evidently means they had to spend a lot of time finding the way through the timber.

[955]Pine species possible at this 7,725' location include: Limber Pine *Pinus flexilis*, which is 25-50 feet tall, with plumelike, often drooping branches (which means it could not be the "tallest pine timber and Stratest" described above by Mitchell; Lodgepole Pine *Pinus contorta* which can grow 70-80 feet

The throwing away of goods and abandoning of wagons, while unfortunate, left a plain track of debris for the individuals and companies following them over this trail, which had not seen emigrant wagon trains before. Heavy timber impeded their progress. <u>Mitchell</u>:

> **"24 [June] Monday** Started Soon and Sent men a head cuting out the road the country heavy timbered in the Spurs of the mountains and well watered   we traveled about 15 miles and got near the north fork of Platt. we pased an encampment of indians   they left when we come in sight or hearing which is evidence that they are hostine[956]   a heavy cold rain in the evening."

Cherokee diarist Brown would later note Indian problems. The old trails in and out of North Park, and the huge piles of buffalo heads, bones and horns were noted by <u>Mitchell</u> as the company approached the North Platte River.

> **"25th [June] Tuesday** cold & rainy   we Started in the rain and wound about on an old indian Trail pasing in Sight of the white clay a noted place among indians in the east rim of the north park[957] or Buffalow pen[958] the indians calls it   here we Kiled an elk and Buffalow   more old plain trails are to be Seen here leeding into and out of this park than ever I Seen on the Same ground   Several hundred heads of buffalows are here piled in one pile, a pile of bones on one Side of it and a pile of horns on the other Side   our gide could give no account of the caus of these piles   we got to the nor[t]h platt at the upper enterence of the great canion 40 miles in length[959]   we comenced geting timber for a raft to cross next day   the river is wider than South platt with a more jentle curent, very rocky."

---

tall having a long, slender bole; and Ponderosa Pine *Pinus ponderosa* which can grow 150-180 feet tall and 3-4 feet in diameter. Preston...*Rocky Mountain*...pp 11, 19, 25.

[956]Mitchell evidently means hostile. The indians could just as well have been frightened at seeing an entire ox train in their territory. Ben Simon no doubt gave Edmonson's company information about Indian skirmishes in the North Park area between tribes, and with whites in previous years.

[957]The only reference found describes not a clay, but "Carboniferous limestones...recognized at only one locality...upon the northeast side, where they lie up against the Medicine Bow Range, inclined at a low angle [that] measure, at least, two or three hundred feet in thickness." Arnold Hague and S.F. Emmons, "Descriptive Geology" *Report of the Geological Exploration of the Fortieth Parallel Under the Direction of Brig. and Bvt. Maj. Gen. A.A. Humphreys, Chief of Engineers, by Clarence King, U.S. Geologist Vol II.* U.S. Army, Professional Papers of the Engineer Department No. 18 (Washington: Government Printing Office 1877) p 114.

[958]Buffalo Pen was historically widely used to describe North Park, where large numbers of the animals spent the winters. Fremont noted the translation of the Indian name for North Park meant "cow lodge."

[959]The North Gate Canyon of the North Platte starts five miles north of Cowdrey, Jackson County, Colorado and runs 20 miles north and northwest into Wyoming, ending 18 miles southeast of Encampment, Carbon County, Wyoming.

No other source found (including the two other 1850 diarists coming along behind) mentions these large piles of skulls, bones and horns. The remains attest to the great number of buffalo killed in North Park. The Edmonson company endured a cold crossing of the North Platte River. <u>Mitchell</u>:

> **"26 [June] wendsday** cold and a little frost   we finished our raft Soon this morning and comienced crosing   we were intirupted in a Short time by a hail Storm which is comon in these mountains   all got over Safe about night and camped on the west making wood of our raft."

Meanwhile, diarist Quesenbury and Buckner, traveling alone to the Laramie Plains, turned off to the west toward the Laramie River. They easily followed the debris-strewn trace made a few days earlier by Edmonson's ox train. <u>Quesenbury</u>:

> **"June 24...Monday...30. [miles]**[960]   At an hour and a half of sun we struck out. The road kept to the right of a range of hills, but turned over them in the course of four or five miles. A large valley [Laramie Plains] opened before us. The range of hills that the road crossed runs into it, rather dividing it. Came to the Ox company's camp.[961] A wagon and an oven remained.
>
> The road was somewhat better after we left this camp for twelve or fifteen miles, as it passed over a level plain of sandy soil. Much of the road today however has been up [stream] branches with muddy crossings that gave us considerable trouble, as the mules disliked to enter them. Passed a small creek which was rising.
>
> Saw some ponds with encrustations around the edges like salt. Some of the ponds had dried up, leaving an incrustation [alkali] resembling snow on ice.
>
> Came to a lake about a mile long and a quarter broad.[Sportsman Lake] Not a tree or shrub around it. There was no outlet to its waters. A single bluff of old red sandstone rose on the south bank from the water about 20 ft. high and forty yards long. At the west end of the lake there is a range of red sandstone about as high as the bluff spoken of. The road runs between this and the water. Vast quantities of ducks were swimming on the water.
>
> Turned off the road to graze to the right. Saw an antelope feeding. Went towards it, to shoot it. But having got its curiousity excited it came to me. As it ran I shot it with the shot barrel. Broke its hind leg. Buckner's dog soon caught it. Went over and shot it in the head with my pistol. Took a ham. Commenced raining and continued till night. Came to a stream [Laramie River]. The Ox Company had camped on it. They here had left two wagons. Buckner tried the ford, but it was too deep for safety. Turned up the river and camped on an island. Two horses near us--the rest over on the flat.

---

[960]As long as Quesenbury traveled with a wagon train of some sort, his mileages might be taken as accurate. But he was not with any wagon from Pueblo, Colorado to his joining the California Road east of Fort Bridger.
[961]Edmonson camped at Willow Creek, near present Tie Siding, Wyoming.

Wet and cold--stream high--impracticable to raft,--we must remain here till the stream falls."

Quesenbury's camp on an island in the Laramie River was upriver from the ford used by the Edmonson wagons. Spring "runoff" was in high gear. His campsite choice proved unfortunate. Quesenbury:

"**Tuesday...June 25...1850** The river this morning had got into our pallet. It rose two or three inches last night. Determined to stay till the river falls sufficient to permit us to ford. The whole day has been unpleasant. Cold drizzly rains have succeeded one another every hour. Baked bread. A couple of antelopes have been feeding and straying around our camp all day. Buckner went out in the evening and shot at one whilst they were fighting.

I have thought more about home since last night than I have during the same period of time since I left. I dreamed of home last night. Saw friends--but this morning sorrow returned and
        The voice in my dreaming ear melted away.
In the evening late Buckner went down to the ford, and left a note for the Packmen.[962] The river has fallen about an inch today. There have been very heavy rains in the N. and I think some showers toward the S.

On this island strawberries are in bloom. Willow, currants, and about a dozen different plants grow on it..."

They remained on the island in the Laramie River, their situation becoming progressively worse. Finally moving off in the afternoon, Quesenbury described the difficulties he was sure Mitchell and the Edmonson ox train had experienced over this ground. Quesenbury:

"**June 26...Wednesday...15. [miles]** The river rose a half inch last night. This is disheartening. We must try and make a raft to day. Something has delayed the company behind a long time. They ought to have been here yesterday. At about one o'clock the river having fallen only about a half inch, we concluded we would wait no longer. Went down again to the ford. Buckner found that by crossing a little lower down it would not wet our packs. Left a little bag of cold flour where the road goes into the stream for the benefit of whoever gets it first. At two trips on Arab, our things were safely crossed. Struck out on the trail which goes near an Indian's grave not more than a half-mile from the river. Got on very rolling ground. Found two wagons the Ox Company has left. The road continued on very bad ground for wagons. Went through pines for several miles. There trees were not large but as thick as they could stand.[963] Buckner snapped [shot] at a deer in the pines. Saw two grey squirrels among them.

The road through the pines is a horrid one. Steep slopes and miry mudholes and rills at the foot of each of them.[964] Edmonson's company had to cut a road through the timber. Came to the steepest place I ever saw a road go down. I cannot imagine how the wagons ever succeeded in doing so; it was about a quarter of a mile down.

---

[962] The John Wolfe pack company.
[963] Lodgepole pine grows thick after a fire, a condition called "dog-hair."
[964] Boswell Creek area, eight miles southwest of Woods Landing, Albany County, Wyoming.

Entered a valley[965] full of Indian trails, one of which had very lately been travelled. Camped to the right of the trail.[966] Saw two bears just at dusk and before we camped. Wet camping place. It has rained on us all the evening. Afraid to build a fire. Did without."

"Thursday...27...June...1850 Heavy frost last night. Corners of the blankets froze this morning. Cooked and left. But before we started we heard two guns. Supposed Indians about or the Ox train just ahead. Our road ran south then W. [into North Park] then N.W. till it struck a stream about the size of Cache la poudre, [North Platte River] but not near so swift or cold. Edmonson's company had made a raft but it was gone.[967] They left some pieces of timber, Aspen logs, which we cut in two and tied together for a raft. Put our things on. Buckner went to the mountain for a pole; he then Swam Arab and I drove the other animals in after him. All got across safe. Started myself on the raft. Beat down a long way but got over. Went up and led the horses down. Arab fell broadside with me in the slough that makes from the river on the N. Cooked. Saddled up and came ahead. Smoke at the river. The other Company is not much over a half a day ahead.

Saw some large birds which proved to be pheasants [grouse]. Shot my shot barrel and wounded one and killed another dead. I then shot my rifle barrel and killed another. Night came on and we were compelled to turn in. Found a good camping place to the left. Built no fire. Slept in a very secure place among thick aspens."

Quesenbury's gun must have been either a side by side, or an over and under combination. One barrel is a rifle, the other a shotgun. Quesenbury and Buckner had traveled from the Laramie River, through the Medicine Bow Mountains to North Park and the North Platte River. They were still behind Edmonson's ox train and diarist Mitchell.

Behind Quesenbury and Buckner were the Holmes and Oliver ox trains, and Thomas Fox Taylor's horse and mule train (formerly captained by Clement Vann McNair) which included Cherokee diarist John Lowery Brown. They all turned west away from the 1849 Evans/Cherokee trace, following the 1850 wagon road recently built by Edmonson's wagon company. Brown's Diary is the only one to record the entire Southern Cherokee wagon road across Wyoming.

Cherokee diarist Brown, with Taylor, entered the south end of the Laramie Plains on July 1, nine days behind Edmonson; seven days behind Quesenbury. From the Willow Creek campsite, southeast of present Tie Siding in Albany County, they turned west, passing Sportsman's Lake and Boulder Ridge.

---

[965]Valley of Lawrence Creek, north of Kings Canyon, Jackson County, Colorado.
[966]North of Kings Canyon.
[967]Mitchell wrote the Edmonson company built a raft, used it to cross, then camped "making wood of [burning] our raft." June 26 entry.

Brown noted the turnoff:

"July 1st...25 [miles] Entered the Larrima Plain. Left Evans
Trace & followed the Trace made by Edmonsons Co. which runs to the left
of Evan's--   passed a large Lake, full of fish, [Sportsman Lake]
Traveled across the L[aramie] Plains and Camped in a hollow, at a good
spring--the ox Co's near. Made today 25   **Camp 51--."**
                    [South of Woods Landing, Wyoming near the
                              Wyoming/Colorado border]

Crossing the Laramie River, which had been very troublesome
and high for Quesenbury, Brown noted Edmonson's road work.

"July 2...16 miles   Crossed Larrima River.   Struck into the
hills. Pine & better Cottonwood timber. the Road had been opened by
Edmonsons Co.   hilly Country. Muddy, Boggy Road in the timber, which
was very hard pulling for the Mules. Camped at foot of hill in a hollow.
the ox Company's near. plenty timber and water.   Grass scarce. Made
miles 16   **Camp 52--."**
                    [near Wyocolo, Carbon Co., Wyoming]

Brown wrote in the left margin on July 2: "today we cross the
waters of west Platt. Many cold springs." The combined ox and
horse/mule wagon companies continued south and west, entering
North Park. Brown:

"[July] 3...[10 miles]... Traveled to the left through a
pass.[968] Entered a plain [North Park] & turned to the Right down the
North fork of the Platt. Came to the crossing at noon found 2 small
rafts which had been left by Edmonsons Co. & the Pack Co.   Home's Co.[969]
took the rafts and commenced crossing... (Oliver's Co. built a raft, we
also built one) Capt's Taylor & Oliver Joined their forces togather and
built a Raft. we all camped on the River. **Camp 53--."**
                    [three miles NW of the junction of Colorado Highways
                              127 and 125, Jackson Co., Colorado]

Brown wrote in the left margin on July 3: "wild sage   today there
was a R.[ocky] M.[ountain] Goat[970] killed."

    The exact timing of the John Wolfe pack company from the
Laramie Plains is unknown. Cherokee diarist Brown mentioned seeing

---

[968]Near Kings Canyon, Colorado. This was erroneously identified in the editing
of the John Lowery Brown diary in *Chronicles of Oklahoma* vol 12 pp 177-213,
(June 1934) n pp 192-93 as located east of the North Platte River near Elk
Mountain, Carbon County, Wyoming. The Mitchell and Quesenbury diary entries
clarify the location in the northern part of Jackson County, Colorado,
approximately 50 miles south of the site identified in 1934.
[969]Captain Holmes' ox train company.
[970]Rocky Mountain Goat *Oreamnos americanus* is actually a goat-like antelope
closely related to the Chamois. Range maps of today indicate they live only in
Idaho, Montana and Washington state. More probably this was a Bighorn Sheep
Ovis canadensis, which still ranges in Wyoming and Colorado. Palmer...
Mammal...pp 314, 316.

their traces on July 3 at the North Platte River. They were all following the route used by the 1849 Evans company packers led by Dick Owens.

The first theft of the trip was recorded on Independence Day after they crossed the North Platte River and camped. Brown:

> **"[July] 4th 6 miles**   Crossed the River and traveled 6 miles. Camped on small Branch. Water & gras. wild sage for fuel. Capt holmes Co. 4 miles ahead on creek. good water, grass & wood   about ten oclock tonight about 25 head of horses & mules, were stolen from our Co. by Indians, and 4 or 5 head from homes Co making 30 alltogather **Camp 54."**
>
>   [Six mile Creek, north of Colorado/Wyoming border
>   Carbon Co., Wyoming]

Brown wrote in the left margin that his losses from theft were one horse and one mule. The Edmonson ox train company diarist Mitchell had noted indians in the area on June 24:

> near the north fork of Platte, we pased an encampment of indians   they left when we came in sight or hearing of which is evidence that they are hostine [hostile]

On June 26, packers Quesenbury and Buckner were traveling west in the same vicinity of the North Platte River and recorded:

> Entered a valley full of Indian trails, one of which had very lately been travelled...Wet camping place...Afraid to build a fire. Did without.

All the 1850 companies from Arkansas, Missouri and Cherokee Nation reached the North Platte River with no disease or death. The hostile encounters were limited to one promulgated by the act of Quesenbury with an Osage early in the journey, and this theft of thirty horses.

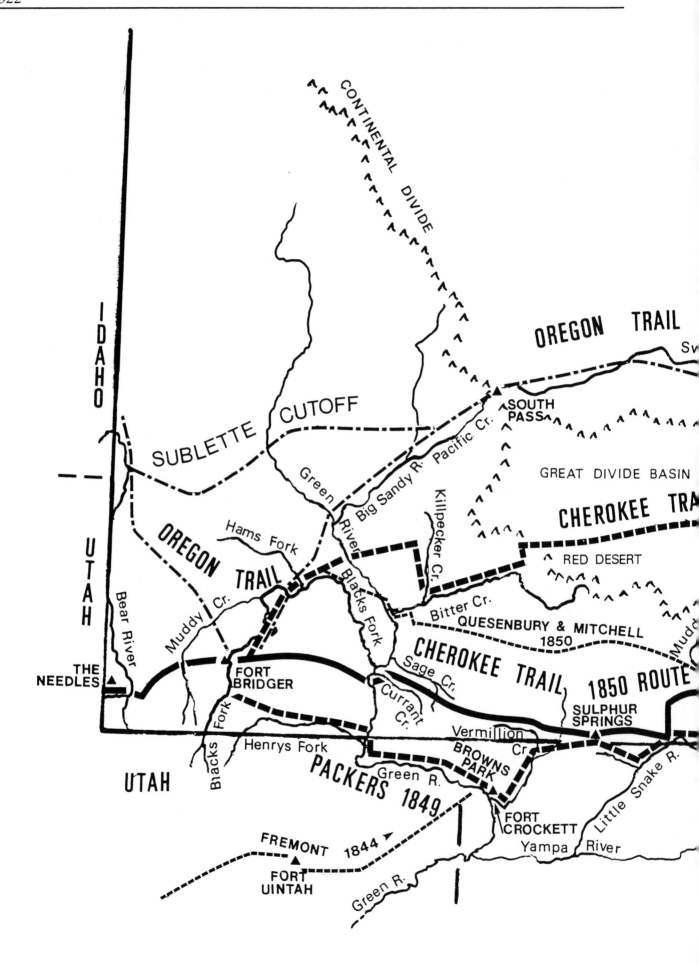

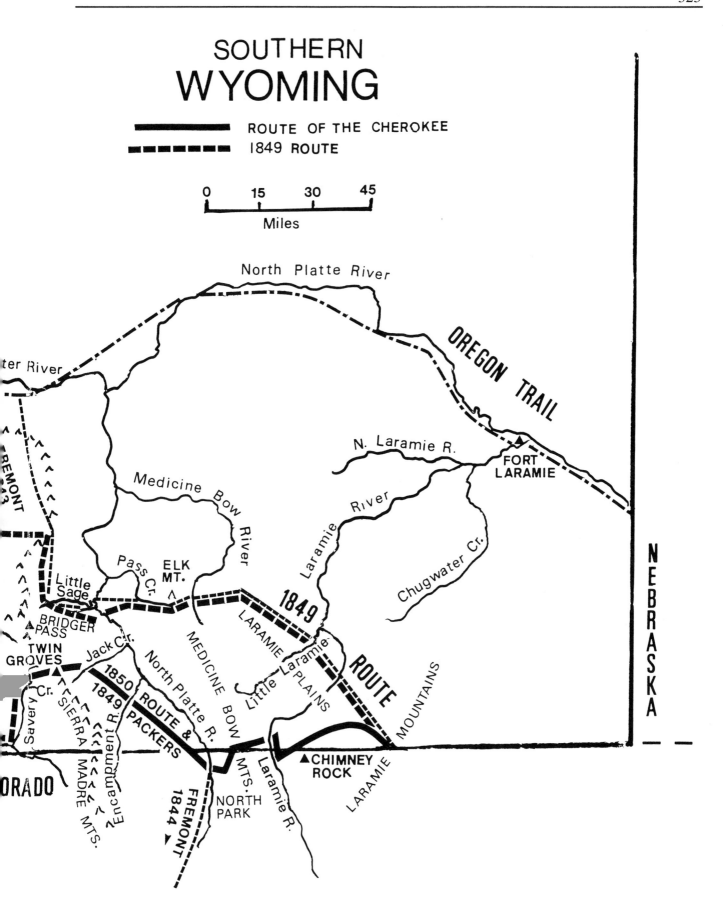

SOUTHERN WYOMING

ROUTE OF THE CHEROKEE
1849 ROUTE

0   15   30   45
Miles

Chapter 7. EDMONSON/CHEROKEE (SOUTHERN) TRAIL

North Platte River to the Green River; to the Independence/California Road; to Salt Lake.

The Worst Road that we have Traveled Over since we left Home
--John Lowery Brown

From the crossing of the North Platte River, James Mitchell continued traveling with Edmonson's ox train--for one more day.

Mitchell:

"27 [June 1850] Thursday   frosty & cleer   we Started a little west of north Bearing out from the [North Platte] river - in a beautifull valey and nooned on a bold creek[972] runing out of a canion from the mountain its corse north east   we camped on another creek runing the Same near the piny mountains."

On June 28, while Quesenbury and Buckner were rapidly making their way westward toward the Edmonson ox train, Mitchell was leaving it. Though he had traveled with Edmonson since early May, he and thirteen others became impatient with the pace of the ox train and struck out on their own. None of Mitchell's party had ever been over this route. Prior to departure they obtained as much information as possible from company guide Ben Simon. Leaving Simon and the Edmonson company, "another bad creek" that the Mitchell company of packers crossed was the Encampment River at present Riverside, Wyoming.[973]

Mitchell:

"28 [June]   14 of us left the [ox train] and determined to try and get to the mines Sooner than the waggons could go-we Soon got to another Bad creek to cross forming from the mountains   we found a ford & all got over Safe and cept our corse a little north of west betwen the mountains. the great divide covered with Snow on the South and the mid Bow[974] on the north   we crosed ma[n]y little creeks forming from the mountains on our left entering into canions. we Killed 2 Sage hens

---

[972]Big Creek, Carbon County, Wyoming.

[973]Encampment was called "Camp le Grande" by Bridger, Sublette, Fitzpatrick, Carson, and Baker who traded goods with Indians there. Mae Urbanek, *Wyoming Place Names* (Boulder, Colo: Johnson Publishing Co. 1967).

[974]Sierra Madre Range on the south; northern mountains of the Medicine Bow Range on the north. The Medicine Bow Butte of the time, now Elk Mountain, may have been visible as the party moved up out of the North Platte River valley.

much like the prararie hen only larger   about 2 oclock we could See
the gap in the great divide & turned our cors a little more South   we
Kiled 2 Sage hens larger than our hens   we camped near the gap in the
mountain   we had fine grass, would & water   plenty of Bufalow in
Sight nearly all the time and antilopes."[975]
                [near Twin Groves, T16N, R87W, 20 miles SW of Saratoga,
                                Carbon Co., Wyoming]

On the same day, Quesenbury and Buckner caught up to the Edmonson
ox train. After receiving directions from guide Ben Simon, they
forged ahead. Unfortunately, this is the last recording of the
1850 Edmonson ox train company. <u>Quesenbury</u>:

"Friday...28...June...25.[miles]   Late start this morning on
account of cooking our sage hens or pheasants. They were fine eating. In
six or seven miles we came to the Ox team camp. The smoke was still
flying from their fires. Pushed on. On the way Buckner took time to
shoot an antelope, and I, a large rabbit. Came to a considerable Stream
as large or larger than the main fork of Laramie river[Encampment].
Forded, but got my coffee wet. Nooned and dried my things. Cooked.
     Struck out and in an hour saw the train ahead. Came to an old
squaw,[976] and a child with a packhorse or so. She came on with us to the
train which we overtook at a creek. Saw our friends, they told us that
Mitchell, Crum and some others had Struck out without a guide for
California. We immediately resolved to follow their track and overtake
them. They had left that morning.
     Saw the pilot Ben Simons, who took us to a rise and showed us the
direction he had told Mitchell to go. Found the trail of the horses, and
pushed on as fast as we could. Got bothered once or twice in finding the
right tracks but continued ahead without much delay. Buckner's mule
Stampeded and kicked the pack off. Fixed, and pushed on. Just as it was
getting so dark that it was unsafe to trail tracks any longer, we
thought we discovered Smoke ahead. But we had no idea of venturing
towards it except on the trail; so we turned to the right and camped
without fire in a very secure place for ourselves, and in a good place
of grass for our horses."

Diarists Mitchell and Quesenbury have both seen the last of
the ox train and guide Ben Simon. Quesenbury stopped at dark,
fearful of traveling onward, exercising caution by camping without
a fire. The next morning Mitchell and Quesenbury met again. They
had not seen each other since May 3. <u>Quesenbury</u>:

"Saturday...29...June... By the first peep of day we were up and
cooking. Got off at sunrise. Pushed on. What we thought to be Smoke last
night was Smoke. Saw it distinctly from the top of a hill, and we
Shouted, and were answered. Came up and found Mr. Mitchell and our

---

[975]During a stop just east of Twin Groves in 1996, the authors'
photodocumenting party counted 60+ antelope in two large herds.
[976]This lady could have been Ben Simon's mother-in-law; his extended family
was traveling with Edmonson's ox train. However, Mitchell made it a point to
note about Simon and family: "They all dress after the fashion white folks."
Mitchell Diary June 7. Other Indians could have been Arapahoe, Cheyenne, Ute.

friends. They were saddling up. Rolled on. Saw numbers of buffaloes. Two of our men wandered off after them. Waited three hours for them and just as we were under headway they came in sight.

This morning about half past ten o'clock we got fairly over the great divide between the waters of the Atlantic and Pacific Oceans. The water came from snow banks and springs. I knelt down and drank where the stream we were crossing was not more than a foot wide,-cold and clear.

Got disagreeably cold in the evening, which was cloudy. A cold drizzling rain beat in our faces which compelled us to Stop. An antelope with more than ordinary curiosity came around us, fighting the dog. I shot it and killed it to prevent more delay.

Our route has been through a sea of wild sage. Towards night we began to doubt finding water, but found very good, and plenty of grass. No stakes for our horses. Burnt wild sage for fuel. The wind blowed cold. The night Chilly, requiring all the cover I could get."

The reunion was also described by Mitchell:

"29 [June] Saturday   frosty cold   while Sadling to Start we were Surpprised by a loud yell on a high east that we crosed last evining and Seen 2 men coming that we left in creggs[977] company on the verdigree, Cush[978] & Buckner   I never Seen a man more glad than queshinbury appeared to be when he come up with us   we proseded on threw the gap it being very bad   So many little hills and bad branchis Buffalows and antilop plenty   2 of our men left among the buffalows Soon this morning and had not returned at noon   our 2 men returning after us wating Several hours with a fine load of fat Buffalow meat we went on & camped on a Branch   our corse has been this day a little South of west and very [bad?] country   emence Snow Banks in places."

The daily entries of Mitchell and Quesenbury can be compared as they moved west from the 8,100 ft. Continental Divide at Twin Groves (Wyoming) toward the Green River. These packers were no doubt given information by guide Ben Simon about line-of-sight pilot points.[979] The first was Five Buttes, which is visible from Twin Groves; the second was North Flat Top Mountain, visible from Five Buttes. The "object west" described was likely Five Buttes. Seven men left the party. Mitchell:

"30 [June] Sunday frosty and plenty of ice   we took an object west at a great distance west to travel to and had great trouble in getting to it   Too many bluffs & bad branches in the way   in the evening we got out of the mountains & got to a bad Swampy creek runing South[980] Supposed to be a fork of elk head [Little Snake]   7 of our men were dissatisfied with the corse we were travling & left us taking a more South corse[981]   the nine of [us] left together camped in a high dry valy without water and poor grass   hors mired."

---

[977]James T. Craig was Captain of the Cane Hill California Emigrating Company.
[978]"Cush" is the name used for Quesenbury by Arkansans.
[979]In 1849 Lewis Evans used both Medicine Bow Butte (Elk Mountain) and Pilot Butte (north of Rock Springs) for pilot points in his more northerly path.
[980]Muddy Creek, north of Baggs, Wyoming.
[981]The 1849 Evans/Cherokee packers went south to the Little Snake River.

<u>Quesenbury</u>:

"1850...Sunday...30...June...and last [day]...25
[Miles]...Got off early. The wild sage continued as thick and as
troublesome as ever. Nothing but a barren, destitute country around.

Nooned on a sluggish branch; where my pony mired in a few minutes
causing considerable trouble to my friends who helped me out with him.
He was dragged out with ropes. Continued on after we crossed the branch,
which we did with difficulty in the same destitute barren country. Every
sign betokened scarcity of water, but we came to a miry muddy stream
running towards the S. We after hunting up a mile found two places which
afforded bad crossing places, but we got our animals over safely.

Struck out for the highlands. Bad prospect for grass and water, but
we found the latter in sufficient quantities for the animals in a
flat. Had to do without water but we cooked and ate nevertheless."

After crossing Muddy Creek, the Mitchell/Quesenbury pack
company left the track which would be taken by the guide Ben Simon
and the Edmonson ox wagon company, followed by the other three
groups. From Twin Groves west, the exact route of the Mitchell/
Quesenbury packers is difficult to determine. With no guide and no
way to check mileage, the party literally rambled on in basically
a northwest and west direction toward Green River. On April 18
while still in present Oklahoma Quesenbury had copied information
about Pilot Butte (near Rock Springs, Wyoming). Perhaps they
expected to easily find it. Their search for water and the route
west from Twin Groves begins with this description by <u>Mitchell</u>:

"July 1st Monday cool & cleer   we Started Soon due west and
about 8 oclock come to Some alkaline ponds and a little poor grass
here we cooked and eat a little and Started our corse and about 12 or 1
oclock we got to a curious Set of bluffs that we had been Seeing and
Steering to for more than 30 miles   we appeared to be on a great
divide between maries river & elk head and no appearence of watter
all the country Sandy and Shely [shale-ly] rocks cheefly without
vegitasion   on the west Side of these bluffs we found the trail of the
7 men that left us yisterday Stering north west evidence that they had
abandoned their South corse   we saw the appearence of low lands South
west and took that corse to a dry creek   we found nothing [but] dry
Sand in the bottom of this creek and left it after going down it a long
distance   we took our west corse again dintermined to travel near all
night or find water   after going 10 or 12 miles we come to a mountain
we could [not] get down and Stoped with [no] grass wood or water all
tired and hongry."

Mitchell's "great divide" is between Muddy Creek and Little Snake
River to the east; and Bitter Creek and Green River to the west.
His "maries river" is Green River. The same day and night's search
and travel is recorded by Quesenbury.

Quesenbury:

"July..1...Monday...30. [miles] At daylight we got up, and by sunrise or a little after we were under way. In four miles we came to little ponds in a small branch, at which we stopped and cooked.

Seven of our party broke off yesterday evening; they were not pleased with our method of travelling, nor the direction.

The country became more destitute today than yesterday. We rose very high ground after leaving the water. Pushed on, without any prospect of getting water, but in ardent hopes of it. The country was cut up with gullies; the soil loose, nothing but dusty sand and hard mud all cracked in millions of different ways. Clay bluffs some-times heightened the miserable looking country. They were washed in various shapes. Sometimes a tower; sometimes pillars, steps, domes etc.

At an hour by sun[982] we turned our course, S.W. and hunted down a dry stream--in vain. Grazed a few minutes and struck directly towards W. After sunset took the evening star for our guide and after it went down took two other stars. Passed through some very high sage bushes at times, up hill and down hill, till at length we were stopped by a sudden jump off. One man went down, but the place was decided to be impracticable for our animals. Turned back to the first sage bushes and laid down, tieing our animals around us, without grass or water...."

Quesenbury and Mitchell have both described a geologic formation known as The Haystacks, near Dug Springs on the later Cherokee/ Overland Stage Route, 15 miles south of present Tipton, Wyoming (and Interstate 80) in Sweetwater County. Quesenbury, always the artist, took time to sketch. He dated it and named it "Scenes in the Alkaline Plains."[983]

July 1 had to be a low point in their journey. They were lost; they were tired and hungry; they had neither water nor grass. Both continue recording their search for water. Mitchell:

"2nd [July] Tuesday Steered a little Southwest to Snowy peak to get water all without breakfast and our horses tide up without grass about 10 oclock before we got to Snowe mountain we found Some bad water and a little poor grass   we even rejoysed to get this alkaline water we cooked here & eat   a fight here took place betwen 2 of our men   one wanting to go on and find better grass and then graze and the other wishing to graze here   after cooking here in about 2 hours we took our west corse again threw this nacid [naked] Sandy hilly country and camped again without water or grass in a maner[?] on a dry branch with Scatering Bunches of grass."

Quesenbury:

"July...2...Tuesday...1850...15. [miles] This morning early Mr. Mitchell came into Camp if camp we may call it from a high point to the N. as we were getting up, and reported a bad prospect ahead. We

---

[982]An hour before sunset. Robert Hendrickson, *Happy Trails: A Dictionary of Western Expressions* (N.Y.: Facts on File, Inc. Dictionary of American Regionalisms 1994) vol 2, p 128.

[983]The sketch is not included due to limitations on the Quesenbury sketches.

saddled up and followed the ridge some five miles, going down at the
S.W. point, the only place we could get down in that distance. Found
water like that of yesterday morning but running.

Cooked and let our animals pick the scattering grass. Then after a
stay of some two hours and a half we started keeping up a branch that
runs into the one we stopped on. Had some difficulty in crossing it.
After getting over we struck our old course W. over as desolate a
country as ever--dreary, dry, and apparently boundless.

Stopped for the night after going six or eight miles without water,
as last night. Our course this morning was directed to a level hill in
the distance S.W. that had white spots on it that was evidently snow.
Our finding water prevented our going further towards it.

I am now writing in a country dreary and desolate, and from
appearances waterless for a great distance, but whilst I write a number
of mosquitoes are singing around. They must have been blown by a western
breeze to this place."

The search for drinkable water intensified for both men and
animals. They were hungry. The situation was dire. <u>Mitchell</u>:

"3 [July] Wendsday Started Soon west again over a hilly Sandy
nacid [naked] country full of curious bluffs   Some of them with a
little ceder on them though mostly nacid   about 2 oclock we found
water bad again   we could Scarce hold our anamals from it when they
come to it. crums broke loose and plunged in & had to be haled out with
ropes   not one blaid of grass could be Seen about here and we left
without cooking   Some of our men had eat nothing Since yesterday & ar
complaining of hunger   we Soon got to good grass and water worse then
ever So bad that we were affraid to drink it or let our horses drink of
it   4 of our men went from here a foot in Serch of water while our
horses graised under a Snowy mountain not [more] than 4 or 5 miles
distant   they returned with Snow in their pans & good water in their
Jugs. they reported good grass and water and wood under the Snow   we
went up & camp here   our poor horses filed up here with good water &
grass and we cooked to do us a day or 2 prepairing for another Scarcity
of water & grass which which we f[e]lt the next day."

<u>Quesenbury</u>:

"Wednesday...3...July...20. [miles] We got up and saddled
our animals as soon as it was light enough to do so. Struck out W, our
old course. The country became no better as far as water was concerned.
Passed some remarkable scenery of rocks but we were in no condition to
enjoy such things.

At one o'clock we came to a miry little stream of alkali water.
Watered my animals with Crum's bucket. Ate a snack with Mr. Mitchell.
There was no grass on the branch, so we left after we got our animals
across which we had difficulty in doing. After travelling three or four
miles our course was stopped by a bluff. Turned N. and found a going
down place. Stopped at the bottom and grazed our horses for a little
while, but came on and found good grass a little further over.

Took off our packs. There is water below this place about a hundred
yards, but Mr. Mitchell who tasted it thinks it a mixture of every thing
vile,-alum, copperas, arsenic etc. He says it is too mean to drink, to
taste, or even to look at. Ford and three others, Crum included have
gone to some snow banks on a mountain S.W.[984] They have taken jugs, and
expect to reach it in a mile and a half.

---

[984]Possibly Quaking Asp Mountain, Sweetwater County, Wyoming.

Whilst waiting for the snow men, Mr. Mitchell lost his pistol which we found after a short hunt in the grass. Presently the snow men came back. The bank was four miles off. They brought two jugs of water, and a pan or so of snow. They reported a camping place above, to which we went, finding there good wood, and tolerable water and grass."

Finding wood, water, and grass relieved the tension in the small company. Next day the party found its way to Bitter Creek, and to the Green River, initially misidentifying it. Mitchell:

"4th [July] Thursday   we Started over a bad rocky mountain all our horses could do to get down it   I lost my pistole going down it & and had to go back & clime it again after it   we found a cold good Spring under the west Side of this mountain but too Soon in the day to benifit us   we continued our corse among the the mountains west as near as we could   the country curiously bluffed and all a Sandy & Salty foundasion   we pased on the high lands large groves of Juniper in the evening we got to a Stree[m] runing west without grass or watter fit for use all crusted with Salt & Some poisones matter   we continued down this Streem west among cliff juting up to the river So that we had to clime larg Steep hills Sometimes from the Streem on the account of these cannions on the Streem being impasable[985]   we had a plain indian trail to gide us   late in the evening when we were on a high hill we could See this Streem imtyed into a larger Streem   we Supposed the larger to be Mary river though when we got to it found it to be a larger Streem than we expected runing South. all agreed it must be green river fine grass was here in the river bottom and good
water & wood."

Quesenbury:

"July...4...Thursday...20. [Miles] The Glorious Fourth! Dry times with us. Left early, going over rolling ground as usual. Went down a high steep slope. After going about a mile and a half--Mr. Mitchell discovered that the mare had shaken off his pistol again. I turned back with him and found the pistol about two thirds up the steep slope we had passed. Found our men at a spring in the high prairie on the side of a slope. The spring was exceedingly cold, clear and pure. Rested here a few minutes, and then went on. Dreary prospect ahead.
    Travelled several miles down a hot, dry valley which was tolerably in our course, Struck over a ridge and came to another valley running W. with water running in it. Followed on several miles and came in sight of a stream running apparently E. It seemed from the high lands where we were to be small--not more than twenty steps across.
    Descended the highlands to the stream and camped. Before we had been here long several began to suppose we were at Green River.
    We were delayed a while this evening by Crum's mule stampeding."

The "Stree[m] runing west...all crusted with...poisones matter" described by Mitchell is Bitter Creek, which runs west along Interstate 80, into the Green River. The junction with Bitter Creek was west of present Rock Springs.

---

[985]The 1849 Evans/Cherokee wagon company left Bitter Creek at Rock Springs to go north along Killpecker Creek and around White Mountain, avoiding the rugged route between the present cities of Rock Springs and Green River.

The Mitchell/Quesenbury pack group saw no other company after they left the Edmonson ox train near the Continental Divide east of Twin Groves. Here at the Green River, they were south of the 1849 Evans/Cherokee crossing; and north of the other 1850 companies' crossing. Traveling north, they found a way to cross.

Mitchell:

> **"5th [July] Fryday**   we Sent men to examine the river and See if there was any posability of foarding it as their was no timber here on the river fit for to make a raft   we could See that our poor animals were much worster travling through this desert and has great need of rest   this green river is at least 300 yards wide and runs Stronger than I expected   high hills on every Side of the Salt formasion. the bottoms narow with cliffs juting in to the water edge. So that it can not be traveled up or down without frequent crosing or going over these high hills   after a Serch for a Suitable place to cross we Started up the river with the intension of going up to great imegrant trail[986] to cross   after going up a few miles we discovered a good Small canoe across the river on an Iiland   quesenbery Swam over and brought the canoe   we tied a log on each Side and comencd crosing
> plenty of Musketoes are here & horse flies, Some fine flours [flowers] the wild rose in a bundance   all got over Safe about dark with great toil and labor only loosing one puter plate."

Quesenbury confirms they are using a spyglass.

> **"1850...July...5...Friday.** All agreed this morning we were on Green river. Crum went back and found his coat which he lost yesterday.
>   Waited awhile for Strickler who tried to wade. Found it impracticable. Packed and started up the river. Went about two miles, before I overtook the most of the Company. Thought I saw a canoe in the willows on the other side. Some of the men were of the same opinion. Mr. Mitchell came up and we determined to go back and examine with the spy glass. One look satisfied us that it was a canoe.
>   Strickler and myself made a paddle and started over by swimming. We got us chunks [wood] to swim on in case we should be beaten below by the current which drawed to the N. bank. I got over safe but Strickler turned back. Found the canoe a small one. Paddled it over, and the others got a couple of logs to put to the sides.
>   We made seven trips before we got everything over. Our horses were disinclined to enter the water, but after a couple of hours hard work we made them all swim. Camped just below our landing place in the cottonwoods. Good grass. Left some of our things above."

Mitchell and Quesenbury, with seven other men traveling with pack horses, struggled for a week from the North Platte River to the Green River.[987]

---

[986]The Oregon/California Trail from the South Pass crossed the Green River approximately 24 miles northwest of the town of Green River. The 1849 Evans/Cherokee wagon company crossed approximately 18 miles northwest of the town at the railroad bridge at 41°42.31N, 109°42.44W. (Sec. 22, T20N, R109W).
[987]Crum, Strickler, and Ford have been named; Buckner was with Cush since Pueblo; it is known that there were two named Ford; two others are unknown.

July 4. 1850.

Near Green River.

WILLIAM M. QUESENBURY SKETCHES

Upper

"July 4, 1850 Near Green River"

Lower

Tollgate Rock (also sketched on July 4)

Close scrutiny of the two sketches executed by Quesenbury in this area confirms the pack group's approach to the Green River from the east. The upper sketch, titled "July 4, 1850. Near Green River" is of a series of bluffs jutting up from the highlands south of present I-80, east of the town of Green River, Wyoming. The main formations are identified as Pulpit Rock in the center of the sketch, and Kissing Rocks on the right. Quesenbury sketched it as he traveled west over one of the hills "the high lands where we were" along Bitter Creek.

The second Quesenbury sketch, untitled, is Tollgate Rock, a more famous formation.[988] It is one of a series of formations on the east side of the river, which tower over the present city of Green River.[989] William Quesenbury may have been the first to sketch these formations. The famous landscape artist Thomas Moran began painting Tollgate Rock in 1871.

Though they encountered no indians, they were in a depleted state, suffering the want of good water, grass and wood. At the Green River, they were seventeen days ahead of Cherokee diarist John Lowery Brown and the Thomas Fox Taylor-led companies.

As they left the Green River Mitchell wrote:

"6 [July] Satturday Started late owing having our bundles deranged yesterday crosing   we took our corse again west and in about 12 miles come to another river runing nearly east   we nooned here & Supposed it to be the black fork of green river   the [river] made a turn in its corse a short distance above and we were well perswaded it was the black fork of green River   late in the evening dust was seen in long Strings at a great distance   we Supposed it to be emegrants on

---

[988]Correspondence with Marna M. Grubb, Green River (Wyoming) City Clerk.
[989]In 1996, the authors matched both sketches with their respective places. The "July 4, 1850 near Green River" site is three miles east of Green River on the south side of Interstate 80. Tollgate Rock was sketched from the west bank of the Green River, one-and-a-half miles northwest of downtown Green River.

the indipendence trail   when we camped we were in Sight of wagons not
more than 2 miles from us   we had good would and grass & water again."

Along this short stretch of travel, they were on the 1849
Evans/Cherokee Company route. They consulted the map. Their
approach to the main trail was also recorded by Quesenbury.

"Saturday...July...6...25. [miles] Got a late start. Went up
the river but had to leave it as it was on account of bluffs impossible
to follow. Turned out and struck our old course veering a little N. At
twelve came to a stream as large as N. Platte which from the map[990] must
be Black Fork. Nooned. I cooked bread. Whilst engaged at it there blew
up a very hard gale of wind. Passed a pond near the river, in which were
a good many ducks. They were as wild as if they had been hunted a great
deal.
        In the evening about four o'clock we came to a trail evidently made
by Californians. Followed it to the river [Black's Fork]. Looked ahead
and saw clouds of dust rising from the main road, about six or seven
miles off. Camped about a mile and half below the road. We could see the
wagons from our camp.
        We are at the Independence Road at last"
                [NE of Granger, Sweetwater Co., Wyoming]

Quesenbury and Mitchell could see wagons on the California trail.

THE CHEROKEE COMPANY FOLLOWS THE EDMONSON TRACK

Meanwhile, the Cherokee/white, horse/mule and ox wagon trains
continued west from the North Platte River, following the Edmonson
company's trace toward Twin Groves. Cherokee diarist Brown with
Captain Taylor's horse/mule wagon company, along with Oliver's and
Holmes' ox trains, were camped six miles northwest of the North
Platte River after crossing on July 4. At about 10 p.m., thirty
head of horses and mules were taken from the Taylor (twenty-five)
and Holmes (five) companies "by Indians." Following the horse and
mule thefts Brown's daily narration continues noting all three
companies, with Cherokee in each, who were still traveling more or
less together. Brown:

"[July] 5...4 miles...a Co of men under Capt Taylor went in
pursuit of the stolen horses. Our Train & that of Capt Olivers which
came up this morning moved on 4 miles to the creek where Capt homes
company were.   Camp 55--."
                [on Big Creek, Carbon Co., Wyoming]

---

[990]Considering the difficulty this packing party had in getting to the Green
River from the North Platte, a map was not thought to be in hand. However,
since Quesenbury's original mileages and information had come from the 1849
Evans/Cherokee Company, their map would only now have become useful.

Township 13 North, Range 81 West. 1880   (GLO Map)

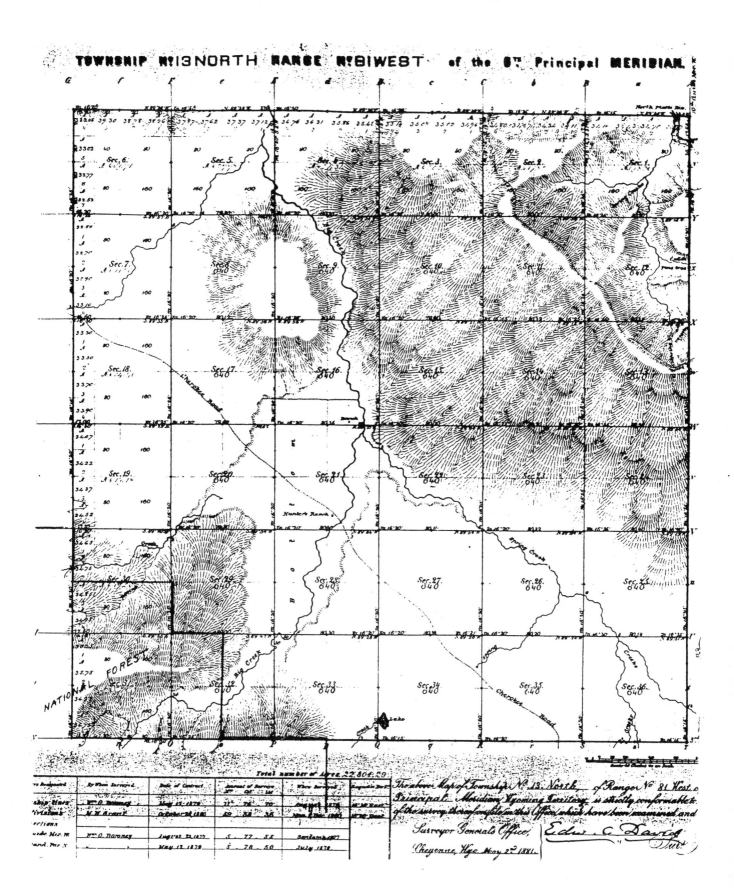

Township 14 North, Range 83 West. 1889   (GLO Map)

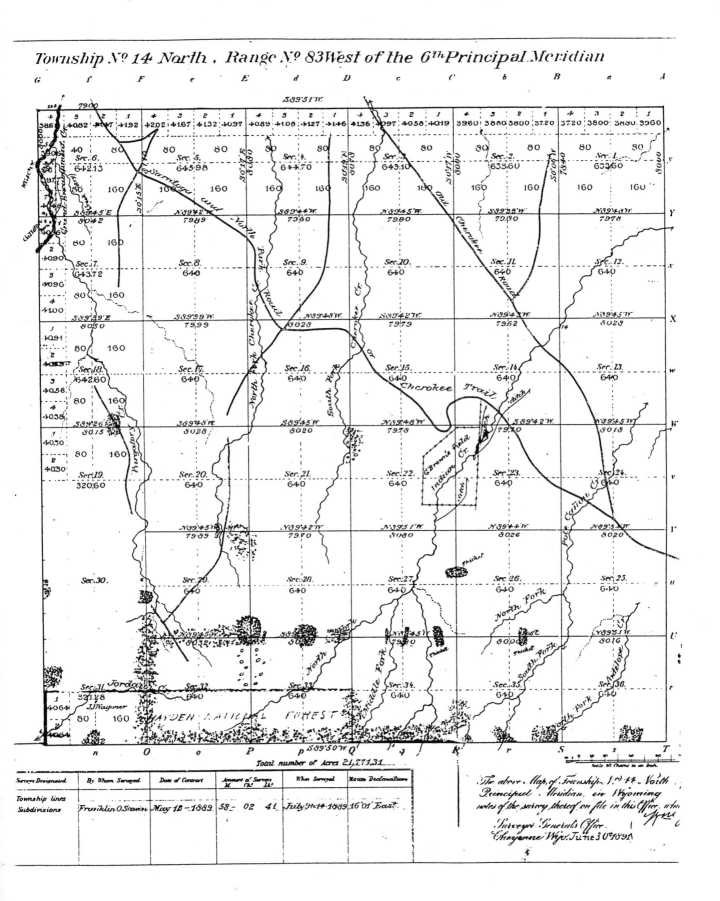

In the left margin, Brown noted an unfortunate incident: "a Spanish Boy[991] was mistaken for an Indian tonight and shot by one of the guards. his life is dispaired of."

The company stopped on July 6, which gave them time to bury the Spanish boy. They were also awaiting the return of Captain Taylor, who was in pursuit of the horse thieves. Brown:

"[July] 6 The Train **Lay By** all day--[992]."

The next day, Sunday, they traveled on without Captain Taylor.

"[July] 7...20 miles...today the Train moved on assisted by the Ox Co and camped on the first large creek, which was called Eagle Creek [Encampment River]. 20 miles. this evening Capt. Taylors Co. returned without overtaking the "Rogues." they found one horse, belonging to Capt. Taylor, having been left or lost by the Indians. **Camp 56--."**
[Present town of Riverside, Carbon Co., Wyoming]

And in the left margin: "Bad Traveling on account of wild sage." The companies traveled on together for security. The ready availability of wood, water and grass permitted it. Brown:

"July 8...20 miles... Today the two ox Co. and our Train move on togather. only ten horse teams, the rest ox,[993]   ours & Olivers train & traveled 20 miles, and Camped on small Branch 1/2 mile to the rite of the Road good water, grass & wood   Capt homes Co moved fa[r]ther on ahead--**Camp 57--."**
[Willow Creek, Carbon Co., Wyoming]

Brown's margin note: "very Bad Road."

The three companies proceeded on Edmonson's track, crossing the Continental Divide at Twin Groves.
Previous editing of the Brown diary, and subsequent Cherokee Trail literature, erroneously placed Brown's 1850 crossing of the Continental Divide farther north at Bridger Pass. Brown again commented marginally on their traveling conditions: "very Bad Traveling on account of Bad Road & wild sage."

Brown:

"July 9...20 miles...today at 10 oclock we crossed the dividing Ridge between the waters of the Atlantic & Pacific Oceans. Bad Road Traveled 20 miles. crossed Elk head creek [Savery], and camped on small branch tolerable good grass   **Camp 58--."**
[Little Savery Creek, Carbon Co., Wyoming]

---

[991]Identity of the Spanish boy is unknown.
[992]This was Saturday; normally the train would stop on Sunday.
[993]Captain Holmes' and Captain Oliver's. The number of ox wagons that got into Pueblo the same day as and after the McNair/now Taylor company was 33.

More than two months after all of the 1850 Cherokee/white emigrants traveled over the Continental Divide at Twin Groves, Howard Stansbury recorded the Bridger Pass location for the first time. On September 20, 1850, Stansbury described traversing what became Bridger Pass: "grass and water were scarce, and the growth of artemisia very thick, making it somewhat difficult to pass our little wagon over it."[994] Stansbury experienced difficulty with one little wagon. Certainly no large wagon trains such as traveled the Cherokee Trail in Wyoming in either 1849 or 1850 traveled Bridger Pass. No wagon emigrants used it, and no further work was done on this pass and route until 1856, when Lt. Francis Bryan was sent by the government to examine it.

Arriving from Elk Mountain via Pass Creek, Bryan crossed the North Platte River. The next day "[gave] an opportunity to make a reconnoissance of the country ahead....none of the guides had ever been through 'Bridger's Pass,' though they had been long in the mountains and in that part of the country."[995] Bryan completed the inspection over Bridger Pass to Muddy Creek and back, but was continually fearful about the lack of forage, and the abundance of sage, which made travel exhausting. The 1849 Evans/Cherokee Company, exploring the pass, found "we cound not git through for the lack of water and grass."[996]

Who, then, did improve Bridger Pass? And when?

Actual building of the Bridger Pass road for wagon travel took place in July 1858, as a U.S. military response to the "Mormon War."[997] In 1859, during the Pikes Peak gold rush, there was heavy use by travelers from Denver to Salt Lake. Ben Holladay further increased the traffic in 1862 by moving his Overland Stage Line south, from the then dangerous South Pass route, to the Cherokee/Overland route over Bridger Pass.

In 1850, diarist Brown was instead on a newly pioneered wagon road some 16 miles southeast of Bridger Pass, having crossed the

---

[994]Stansbury...Report...pp 241, 242.
[995]Report of the Secretary of War 35 Cong. 1 sess. Sen Ex Doc 11, Serial 920 pp 462-63.
[996]John Rankin Pyeatt letter to his wife from Salt Lake August 12, 1849.
[997]Report of the Secretary of War 35 Cong. 2 sess. (1858-59) Senate Ex Docs, Serial 975 pp 206-12.

Continental Divide at Twin Groves. <u>Brown</u>:

> **"[July] 10...25 miles**...Traveled 25 miles today without finding
> water untill night, when we camped on a Branch of Elkhead creek. Very
> Bad Road. Grass scarce water not good **Camp 59--."**
>   [Muddy Creek at mouth of Cherokee Creek, adjacent to
>   Wyoming Highway 789, Carbon Co., Wyoming]

During July 11, the trains traveled west around the North
Flat Top Mountain, no doubt a pilot point, before turning
southwest and south toward the Little Snake River. <u>Brown</u>:

> **"July 11th...20 miles...**Today we had very good Road for a few
> miles and then the rest of the way, the worst Road that we have Traveled
> over since we left home. No water or Grass or Timber. The Road Dry &
> Dusty & pached [parched]. No game, Sage Grass scarce.
> at Sundown we reached the dry Bed of a large Creek where we got water by
> digging holes. the water tasted of Salaratas, salt. Grass scarce. Made
> today 20 miles--**Camp 60--."**
> [Sand Creek, near the Sweetwater/Carbon Cos. Line, Wyoming]

>   Perhaps apprehension of the Snake Indians convinced the
company to use the "corral" system, a circle with stock inside.
The last place it was used was on the Santa Fe Trail, when
thousands of Plains Indians were in the vicinity. <u>Brown</u>:

> **"July 12...5 miles...Camp 61...**We traveled 5 miles and came
> to where Capt Home's Co. were camped which was 1 1/2 miles from the
> Yamper River.[998] A great many Indians were coming into camp as we got
> there which caused great excitement. They came up Friendly. They proved
> to be the Snake Indians. Capt Homes reported that he had been 8 or 10
> miles and could find no water or grass, so we all concluded to stay
> where we were we carelled togather. [illegible] carried our stock[999] to
> the R[iver] to graze and packed water from the same place 1-1/2 miles."
>   [One and one-half miles NE of Little Snake River, north of
>   Cherokee Rim, Sweetwater Co.,Wyoming]

The companies lost no time in leaving the Little Snake area. They
went up over Powder Rim for about ten miles, then turned southwest
past Powder Mountain to Lower Powder Spring.[1000] Next to a 12-15
ft. high sharp cliff at that location a small spring presently
runs off to the south, creating a narrow band of vegetation
including cattails and grasses. <u>Brown</u>:

---

[998]Little Snake River, which flows southwestwardly into the present Yampa
River about four miles east of Dinosaur National Monument in Colorado.
According to John C. Fremont in his *Report...1842-3-4*, p 124 "Yampah" was the
Snake Indian name for this river and also the name of a plant, the root
gathered in the region annually by the Snake Indians.
[999]"carried" here probably means drove and watched.
[1000]41°00.56N, 108°17.67W.

"July 13...25 miles... Traveled today 25 miles very Rough Road. No grass wood or water. Traveled untill sometime in the night when we came to Sulphur Springs. Not fit for man or Beast to drink. No grass **Camp 62**--."
[Lower Powder Spring, near Colorado border,
Sweetwater Co., Wyoming]

Brown's margin note: "horses and oxen failing." The companies continued, traveling nearly straight west from Lower Powder Spring. Brown:

" **[July] 14...5 miles**   Traveled 5 miles and came to Salt water with little grass. Camped. **Camp 63**--."
[two miles north of Colorado border, T12N, R98W,
Sweetwater Co., Wyoming]

W. A. Richards, Wyoming southern boundary survey crew member working nearby in 1873, noted on August 16:

It behooves us to make good time to Green River fifty miles away.... supplies...low....No game here...but rabbits. An old road runs west about 20 ch[ain]s north of this camp. Suppose it to be the old Cherokee trail....It runs nearly west and we must follow it to get through the country.[1001]

In an inhospitable landscape, the 1850 companies were in dire straits. The good health of the company came to an end. Sickness struck animals and men. Brown:

" **[July] 15...20 miles**...Man & Beast sick. Caused by drinking the water that we have been drinking for several days. Traveled today 20 miles and came to a narrow swift Branch[1002] of good cold water with tolerable good grass   **Camp 64**--."
[Vermilion Creek, near Wyoming Highway 430,
Sweetwater Co., Wyoming]

"July 16   Lay Bye--."

Since two of the three requisites for camping were at hand, the company stopped an extra day to recruit the sick emigrants and animals. The companies proceeded along Sage Creek, crossing a branch near the present site of the 1852 Malinda Armstrong grave. Returning with her family to Texas from California on the Cherokee Trail, Malinda became ill. Shortly afterwards, the Armstrong family buried their daughter on Trout Gulch.[1003]

[1001]"Diary kept by W. A. Richards in Summer of 1873 Survey of South Boundary of Wyoming" *Annals of Wyoming* vol 8, no 1 (July 1931) p 492.
[1002]In the 1934 editing of the Brown diary, this was incorrectly identified as Bitter Creek, which is located some 30 miles farther north.
[1003]The gravesite and marker has been maintained by the Ramsey family. "The

The 1850 Cherokee/white companies hastened toward the Green River. Brown:

> **"[July] 17...20 miles**...Traveled 20 miles over tolerable good Road. Camped in deep hollow on little Branch. Good grass. Sage for fuel Snow mountains in view on ahead **Camp 65--."**
> [headwaters, Sage Creek, near U.S. Highway 191,
> Sweetwater Co., Wyoming]

Continuing on the south side of Sheep Mountain between Sage Creek and Currant Creek, the emigrants reached the Green River, where more illness confronted them.

> Brown:

> **"[July] 18...20 miles**...Several cases of sickness in the Co. Very Rough Road Camp on Branch of Green River, one mile from the River[1004] Made today 20 miles wild sage as usual **Camp 66--."**
> [Currant Creek, Sweetwater Co., Wyoming]

> **"July 19...2 miles...**Home's Co moved 3 miles to the crossing of Green River. Olivers & taylors Co. Camped along the River. Great many preparing to "pack" from this place **Camp 67."**
> [east bank of the Green River, near the mouth of
> Currant Creek, Sweetwater Co., Wyoming]

The short mileage day gave Brown time to write a brief summary of the terrain they had traveled over since the crossing of the Continental Divide at Twin Groves. Brown:

> 499 miles from Peueblo to Green R
> This is the most desolate looking country that I ever saw. Since we crossed the deviding Ridge on the 9th the Ground has been dry & parched & very dusty. Salt water except now and then you find good water Grass very scarce. No game.
> Nothing much Except wild sage growing in this part of the Country Wild and Rugged hills (very Bad Roads)--.

The first of the two ox trains, Holmes', crossed the Green River. Others waited. Brown:

> **"[July] 20...we lay Bye**   Today Capt Home's Co Rafted their waggons across the River. R.J. Meigs drowned one of his mules.--."
> [east bank of the Green River, near the mouth of
> Currant Creek, Sweetwater Co., Wyoming]

Return Jonathan Meigs was mentioned for the first time in a long while.[1005] The second ox train crossed the next day. Brown:

Story of a Pioneer" *Quarterly Bulletin* vol 1, nos 1 & 2 (August 15, 1923) p 19 State of Wyoming Historical Department, Cheyenne.
[1004]Campsite now under the waters of Flaming Gorge Reservoir in the Flaming Gorge National Recreation Area.
[1005]Meigs started the journey by catching up to the Cane Hill California Emigrating Company after crossing the Verdigris River. On May 17 he joined

"**[July]   21...lay Bye**   Capt Olivers Co--Rafted over the River. Taylors Co. not crossed but preparing to pack--."
            [east bank of the Green River, near the mouth of
                    Currant Creek, Sweetwater Co., Wyoming]

Barbara Hildebrand Longknife and husband William Longknife were among the Cherokee members of Oliver's ox train. Barbara's subsequent letters from California unfortunately do not include much information on the journey.

Brown, frequently leaving out explanations which would be helpful to readers, did not say that he, as a member of Taylor's horse/mule wagon company, was also preparing to pack. Preparation consisted of unloading and leaving their wagons, while choosing goods and loading or "packing" the horses and mules which had been pulling their wagons. Companies that "packed" from places such as Pueblo had the opportunity of purchasing Mexican mules and packsaddles. Here at the Green River there were no pack animals available to buy. It took two more days for Taylor's company to get ready and cross, while the other companies went ahead. Brown:

"**[July]   22...lay Bye**   This morning Capts Oliver & Home's Comps Traveled on. Capt. Taylors Co. here yet. Expect to cross the River tomorrow."
            [east bank of the Green River, near the mouth of
                    Currant Creek, Sweetwater Co., Wyoming]

"**[July]   23 lay Bye**   This morning we commenced crossing the River By Riding our horses and Carrying the Packs on our shoulders as the water was very deep. by 12 oclock we were all safe across and camped on the west bank of Green River   **Camp 68**--."
            [west bank of the Green River, Sweetwater Co., Wyoming]

Taylor's packers, as well as Holmes' and Oliver's ox trains, crossed the Green River near present Buckboard Crossing in Flaming Gorge National Recreation Area.

Taylor's Company spent five days laying bye, resting and recuperating and preparing to pack from the Green River. While on the west bank of the river, Brown wrote a more detailed description of the river and surrounding country. Brown:

Green River is about [blank] yards wide, with numerous Islands upon which Good Grass Grows into which we drove our horses & mules The

Cherokee John Wolfe's breakaway wagon Company near the Santa Fe Trail. He left Pueblo with Captain McNair's Company. Here at the Green River he is identified with Captain Holmes' ox company.

Timber is cottonwood & willow. The water of the River is good, though
not so cold as that of the Platt or other Mountain Streams which we
crossed. The country along the Banks of the River is very rugged, looks
Dreary & Desolate, with high Bold Bluffs on the west Bank--.

The layover gave company stock a much-needed rest. The country
immediately west was similar to that they had already come over.
Taylor's company was the last to leave the Green River. Brown:

"**[July]   24...25 miles**   This morning about 10 oclock the Pack
Co. left Green River and Traveled Due west over very desolate looking
country, Destitute of vegitation of any kind & water. After Traveling
about 25 miles, we came to and camped on a small stream of Muddy & very
Bad tasting water. **Camp 69--.**"
   [Big Dry Creek about halfway between McKinnon Junction and
        Lyman near the Uinta/Sweetwater Cos. line, Wyoming]

Brown's left margin note was: "Snow topped Mountains near by."
Former company captain McNair[1006] became ill, unable to ride. With
no wagon available for transport, they were forced to stop.

   Brown:

"**[July] 25...12 miles**   Today we traveled over country the same
as before Rugged & Rough. No grass Bad water. after Traveling about 12
miles we came to a large creek of good water, with plenty good grass. We
stopped for the day, Clem McNair being sick.[1007] **Camp 70--.**"
   [Smith Fork, four miles east of Lyman, Uinta Co., Wyoming]

"**[July] 26**   Today we **lay Bye** McNair being unable to travel
light showers, every day since we came to Green River."

   Taylor's pack company reached Fort Bridger the next day.
Continuing past the fort, they joined the vast emigration, and
recorded the first Cherokee death. Brown:

"**[July] 27...20 miles**   After traveling this morning about 8
miles we came to Bridgers Ft. on Black Fork of Green River. At this
place the Trace from Independence to the Salt Lake passes. a large Train
of waggons were in sight bound for California. we were told by the
inhabitants at this place & also by Emegrants that Thousands of persons
were dying on the upper rout which leads by Ft Hall of the Colara. we
were also told that about 8 miles ahead, Olivers Co had camped & one of
the Cherokees belonging to the Train had died, they could not recollect
his name. we traveled on, came to the grave By the side of Road & found,
by some writing on a board, that it was Charles McDaniel who had died.
we traveled on a few miles fa[r]ther & camped 1/2 mile to the left of
the Road. good water & grass Made today 20 miles **Camp 71--**
we find this Trace to be crowded with Emegrants to the Gold diggins.
We are har[d]ly ever out of sight of waggons."

[1006]McNair was elected Captain of the original Cherokee Emigrating California
Company. At the Cache la Poudre River Thomas Fox Taylor became Captain.
[1007]In both 1849 and 1850, sickness identified as "mountain fever" was
mentioned after crossing the North Platte and Green Rivers.

[Muddy Creek, north of Piedmont, Uinta Co., Wyoming]
Brown wrote further in the margin: "113 miles from this place to
the Salt Lake   Snow mountains to the Left   many springs of
cold water   12 miles from [beyond] Bridger."

Bringing up the rear of the 1850 Cherokee/white emigrants who
traveled the Southern Cherokee Trail through Wyoming, Brown began
to record people of the much larger emigration which they joined
at the California Road. Brown was somewhat shocked, or fascinated,
by the number of deaths on this larger emigration trail. For a
time, he recorded them opposite his diary.

Graves we have passed since Intersecting the Independence Route
1. C. McDaniel--July 25, 1850
2. J.A. Drake Died at this place July 15, 1850 St. Charles, Mo.
3. Horatio Morse July 17, 1850 Marcy Co. Mo.
4. M. Harris died July 18, 1850, Franklin Co Dublin Ohio
5. A Grave on the left side of the road with some writing on
    the head board, stating that he had been found by the
    road so [word illegible] that they could not ascertain
    who he was or where he was from--. dated 19th July,
    1850 & signed An Emigrating Company--

Thankfully, their own four companies lost only one man, Charles
McDaniel, not on the Cherokee Trail but after reaching the "trace
from Independence." McDaniel was the first of several Cherokee to
die before reaching California.

In 1849, when the Evans/Cherokee wagon company reached the
California road they lost one man, Nathan Tharp, from Diabetes.
The 1849 pack company also lost one man, James Garvin, who drowned
crossing the Green River.

The illness in both years was mainly Mountain Fever. But none
had the dreaded cholera. Both the 1849 Evans/Cherokee Trail across
the Red Desert, and the 1850 Edmonson/Cherokee, or Southern
Cherokee Trail, proved to be free of cholera.

Perhaps the absence of cholera was a major factor in the
continued usage of this Cherokee Trail by emigrants from Cherokee
Nation, Arkansas, Missouri, and Texas to California, Oregon, Utah,
and later to Idaho and Montana.

ALONG THE CALIFORNIA ROAD TO SALT LAKE CITY

Mitchell, Quesenbury, Buckner, Strickler, Crum, at least two
men named Ford, and two other "packers" reached the Independence

or the California Road July 6, twenty-one days before Cherokee
diarist Brown. Mitchell called it "great trail;" Quesenbury sighed
"at last." Immediately, the two diarists recorded the many sights,
sounds, and challenges confronting them. Mitchell:

> "7 [July] Sunday a Soon Start and got to these waggons on the
> great trail   we pased in travling 17 miles 60 waggons or more
> dead oxens horses and mules lay here & thair all a long   we nooned on
> a Spot of good grass and pushed again nearly South 18 miles up the black
> fork and camped 2 miles from the road in tolerable good grass again,   we
> pased many more waggons this evening   people were camped all round us
> Some had layed here all day ceeping Sonday."

The many emigrants they passed seemed intent on their journey, and
not at all friendly to the packers. Quesenbury continues to note
mileage,though they have no way to "measure" it. Therefore, only
the known landmarks can be used to chart their progress;
individual campsites can only be speculated. Quesenbury:

> "Sunday...7th...July...30 [miles]   Saw bunches of wagons
> all along ahead of us. Passed among the emigrants till noon when we
> turned to the river and grazed. These Emigrants seem to mind their own
> business--they never take the trouble to raise their heads or speak as
> we pass them.
>   Continued passing trains till we turned off the road. One of the
> Fords broke his gun off at the breech by jabbing his horse with it.
> Camped on Black Fork again, two miles below Bridge's Fort. The grass had
> been tramped and grazed upon everywhere before we came here. There are
> trains above. Two or three men came down with hooks and lines fishing,-
> one of whom stole a box of matches as he lit his pipe at the fire."

What first impressed both were the vast numbers of wagons and
people, the condition of the grass from so many animals, and for
Quesenbury, an observation of petty theft. They did not linger.
Once again the diaries reveal different perspectives. Mitchell is
faithful to the physical surroundings, while Quesenbury adds the
rumors and speculation. Mitchell:

> "8 [July] Monday...27 miles   the coldest morning ever I Saw at
> this Season of the year   we rose a hill & saw fort Briges [Bridger] 2
> or 3 miles from us resembling a Strong horse pen to our left   our road
> went winding among bad hills & Snow all white in the mountains to our
> left [Uinta mountains] and patches all round us on the north Sides of
> the hills   great groves of juniper[1008] is on these hills. Some cotton
> wood asp, and willow of various Kinds[1009] are on the low lands   the

---

[1008]Either Rocky Mountain Juniper *Juniperus scopulorum* Sarg. or Utah Juniper
Juniperus utahensis (Engelm.) Lemm. Both grow in bush and tree form.
Preston...*Trees*...pp 111, 113.

[1009]For Mitchell to know there are "willow of various kinds" is a testament to
his powers of observation and knowledge of plants. This is probably Peachleaf

willd drawf chery here is now in bloom   we traveled 27 miles [camping]
on a little hollow on the mountain Side   here people were camped again
in every direction insight again."

    Quesenbury:

"Monday...8...July...1850...27 [miles] Got a late start
this morning. My mules were unruly and gave me trouble in passing
trains. Ford, Buckner, and the others left before we did, and we have
not seen them but once to day, which was as we nooned. We stopped on the
W. slope of a high ridge we came down, above the road;
they grazed about three quarters of a mile further on, beyond a branch.
    A report has been passing among the Emigrants to day that twenty-
seven Indians had been killed a day or so ago by a party ahead. There
are a hundred different ways of telling the tale, all of which are
contradictory. Indians have probably been killed, but of the circumstances we cannot judge.
    Camped on the side of hill about a quarter of a mile from water, and
timber, quaking asp about the same distance above. The country is
becoming more broken--more like the W. slope of the Rocky mountains."

They continued to pass the slower trains, sometimes with
difficulty. During the next day they crossed the present Wyoming/
Utah border. For the first time Mitchell recorded seeing the dead.

"9 [July] Tuesday...25 m[iles] frosty   took the winding
road again and had great troble in pasing these trains betwen the hills
in 9 miles we crosed a large rapped creek fordable runing to our right
here we pased a number of these waggons that we had been trying to pass
we grased on a branch runing west-rocky Bluffs to our right   we camped
in this branch. Small trains wer on it above & below us in Sight
25 m   pased dead people."

The image of Fort Bridger apparently was strong. Quesenbury:

"July...9...Tuesday...25.[miles]   Another late start, but
our horses fared well by it. Came to a considerable stream, cut up by
islands, the waters of which were very cold.[1010] In one place it was a
little over belly deep. On the W. banks there were innumerable numbers
of blocks that the teamsters had used in raising the beds of their
wagons[1011] to prevent the water from running in them.
-----Forgot to mention that we passed Bridge's Fort yesterday morning.
It is a poor concern, and looked more like a picketed horse lot than a
human habitation.
    Nooned on a branch running to our right, probably a tributary of the
river we crossed to day, the waters of which also run to the right. We
saw fine grass near us which we could not get at on account of the
danger of miring, but found tolerably good lower down, by crossing
at a place where the way was made across.
    In the evening the country became more rolling, the soil and grass
better. Late we entered a valley, looking out all along for a camping

---

Willow *Salix amygdaloides* Anderss. "the only species native to the Rocky
Mountain region which is typically a tree." Ibid. p 133. There are many more
which grow more as bushes and "Identifying willows often is a difficult task
even for the professional botanist." Petrides... *Field Guide*... p 246.
[1010]Bear River, eight miles southeast of Evanston, Uinta County, Wyoming.
[1011]The blocks were placed between the axles and the wagon beds.

place. Found one close by the road and just on the bank of a branch. Wood scarce but we made out with dry willow."

The emigrants traveled down Echo Canyon, then south up the Weber River on the toll road. It seems strange that Quesenbury the artist did not sketch nor describe Echo Canyon. Both Quesenbury and Mitchell concentrated on hurrying to Salt Lake, ahead of as many emigrants as possible. <u>Mitchell</u>:

"10 [July] Wendsday   Started Soon   a man come to us Sayin his party had lost 10 horses & mules Stolen by indians   we continued down this valy between bluffs high   bad road   difficult crosing in places & bad geting by the trains beforre on the account of the narow pass between the high hills   we nooned late where this creek emtys into weber river   plenty of Snow to be Seen above & below us on the mountains   we took the left here a new road lately made by the mormans for tole by legislative act of mormanism taking up the Weber river South and the old one runing down the river South [sic]   we camped on the river in good grass and good water & grass between trains."

<u>Quesenbury</u>:

"July...10...Wednesday...20 [miles]   Earlier start this morning than usual. Before we left camp, a man came to us enquiring for lost horses. They are probably stolen.
    Passed several trains, and was told by men belonging to them, that an Indian fight had taken place yesterday morning,-that Indians had attacked a Mississippi Pack Company, and that four whites and two Indians were killed etc. I place no confidence in the reports.
    Till we nooned our way was down the valley we entered yesterday evening. Came to Weber river where we found a sign board on a mound, informing the Emigrants that a toll would be imposed on all those who took the left hand road, to the Salt Lake. The road had been opened by the Mormons,[1012] and the toll was made by Legislative authority.
    Nooned on Weber River.[1013] Grass bad. We have a shade to sit under to day. White hawthorn grows here. Started and got a mile when Mr. Mitchell found out he had left his gun where we nooned. He walked back and got it. Our route lay S. up Weber River, for eight or nine miles when we camped in good grass just above a party of Pennsylvanians. Several other trains were camped below.
    A mile or so back the grass was burning, and after we struck the river we saw several places that had been burned. This probably will cause suffering to the Emigrants behind."

Whether the fire was accidentally or deliberately set to delay emigrants behind, the result was the same; loss of grass for animals. In 1849, John Rankin Pyeatt, traveling through this same area in the Evans/Cherokee wagon company wrote: "the grass in this cuntry is much better then in Arkansas it contain so much seed

---

[1012]Pioneered by Parley Pratt.
[1013]The first two times Quesenbury wrote "Weaver" River, then overwrote it to make "Weber."

that it is all most equal to grain for cattle."[1014]

The Mitchell/Quesenbury group turned south at Echo, traveled through present Coalville, Hoytsville, and Wanship to Kimball Junction, and to Altus on their way to Salt Lake City. Wagon trains, individuals, and dead stock were scattered along the narrow, steep toll road. It took them two days. On this one occasion Mitchell recorded the two days as one. <u>Mitchell</u>:

"**11 [July] Thursday** very frosty and cold   we continued up the river 5 or 6 miles and turned Short up a little creek to the west   at the head of it we pased a vast number of emegrants and turned on to another creek runing towards the Salt Lake   we nooned on this creek fine water is on this creek & grass with great Snowbanks to our left near us   we crosed another great divide with large pine trees on it. to our disapointment when we were on this divide we expected to see the Salt Lake vale   a gorge[1015] the road pased for a long distance   dead [stock] lying all along Sometimes in the water and trains drinking the water below   we pased many...[1016] waggons on this Streem with great trouble the pass being So narow it run into a canion   So narow that a horsman could not travel along Side of a waggon   near the mouth of this canain is a toll bridge cept by the mormans   price for Single anamal 10 cents   for a waggon 75   here we were in eight miles of Salt lake citty   we intered the [?] of a high ridg and could See the morman Settlements as far as our eyes could let us See   it is the finest vally for farming that ever I Saw   wheat the princeple crop surounded by numerous ditches for wattering of the pures water So constructed that they can at any time water thousands of acres bountifuly   Some of their [wheat] they had lately harvested, Some they were cuting and others not even headed out   they can harvest from Soon in July till in august late   owing to the time they Sow and the maner of watering."

<u>Quesenbury</u> recorded the two days separately.

"**July...11...Thursday...1850**   This morning before the sun had been up more than twenty minutes we were off. Passed trains as usual. The road still continued up Weber River S. and occasionally S.E. After going about six miles we entered a valley running west. Kept up this valley, crossed over a ridge and came to a broad valley where several wagons were nooning. Thinking that a great many more would stop at the same place we kept on to another valley two miles and a half further on which we turned up, and found in it good grass and uncommonly clear, cold water. Nooned near some willows which by a little cutting gave us another good shade.

Mitchell and Crum cleaned up for a decent entry into the Mormon City. I will be more modest and pass through so quietly that I will be unnoticed.[1017]

[1014]Pyeatt letter, Salt Lake, August 12, 1849.

[1015]Parley's Canyon.

[1016]The following was inserted and written up the right side of the page in a very small margin. "12 friday camped on head of this inglishmen." Leaving that out makes the entry readable.

[1017]Having followed William Quesenbury from Arkansas along the trail, it seems out of character for him to use "modest" "quietly" and "unnoticed" to describe

There is a range of Snow mountains to our left. Our water comes from them.

Left my inkstand where we nooned and had to go back for it. Road rough through the mountains this evening. Grass scarce. A great many dead animals along the road. Some in the water.

An Englishman from Chicago Illinois camped with us. He had a poor old dun mare with sore withers, which he walked behind and drove.

July...12...Friday   Road at first as bad as ever but as we got nearer the toll ground we found that it had been worked on more than behind. Many dead animals were lying by the way so offensive that we dreaded to pass them.

Paid ten cents for each animal and went ahead into the city. Was disappointed in it. The Mormons farm on the Mexican plan. Lost my pistol in keeping my pony off a wheat field the road runs through."

Mitchell and Quesenbury were in Salt Lake City. Quesenbury commented at his first look at the city: "Was disappointed in it" Perhaps the appearance of adobe construction had prompted the remark. Reportedly the Mormons learned adobe construction while wintering 1846-47 at Pueblo, (Colorado). He also wrote: "The Mormons farm on the Mexican Plan." Quesenbury would have seen both adobe construction and Mexican farming most recently in the Greenhorn/Pueblo vicinity where he observed farming: "is of the Mexican style." Mitchell, on the other hand, wrote of Salt Lake: "it is the finest vally for farming that ever I Saw...surounded by numerous ditches for wattering of the pures[t] water."

THE REST OF THE 1850 COMPANIES TRAVEL TO SALT LAKE CITY

As the mostly Cherokee, Taylor pack company arrived at Fort Bridger, they were twenty-one days behind Mitchell and Quesenbury; the last of the four companies from the Southern Cherokee Trail. "113 miles from this place to the Salt Lake" Brown wrote.

"**[July] 28...30 miles**   Traveled 30 miles today   crossed Bear Creek [River] at noon. Camped 1/2 mile to Right of the Road. Good water & grass. **Camp 72**   we pass Graves, Dead cattle & horses almost every half mile.
[near The Needles, Utah/Wyoming border]

"**[July] 29...30 miles**   today we struck into a Narrow valley, with high Rockey Bluffs on the right of the Road and high hills on the left [Echo Canyon]. Plenty of grass along the valley. Many springs of very cold water. we Traveled along the bank of a creek which runs through the valley, crossing it a Great many times   at evening we came to Webbers River, quite a large stream, good water & timber, grass

himself. Perhaps he was writing tongue in cheek.

scarce. At this place the Road Forks. The left hand is a cutoff to Salt
Lake. We took the right hand which leads down the River, 2 miles &
camped having made 30 miles   **Camp 73--.**"
[SE of Henefer, Morgan Co., Utah]

In his margin: "the Mormons have a toll bridge on this road."

"July 30th...30 miles   This morning we traveled down the
River 1 mile & a half, when the Road crosses Turns to the left into a
narrow valley. at noon we came to a large creek along the up which we
Traveled crossing very often. Late in the evening we reached the very
steep top of a very high ridge we traveled a few miles fa[r]ther and
campe[d] 1/2 mile to the left of the Road in a hollow. Good water,
Timber & grass. Made today 30 miles   **Camp 74--.**"
[head of Emigration Canyon, east of Salt Lake City,
Salt Lake Co., Utah]

The company arrived and passed through Salt Lake City. <u>Brown</u>:

"[July] 31...11 miles   Traveled through deep winding hollow
at 12 oclock we reached the "Mormon City." 11 miles today to the City.
we passed through the city, crossed the River Jordon one mile from town
and camped on the Bank.   **Camp 75--.**"
[west bank of Jordan River, Salt Lake Co., Utah]

Captain Taylor's packing company arrived last of all the 1850
groups that started out from the Verdigris River. The Mitchell and
Quesenbury pack group of nine arrived first, on July 12. Between
these two groups there were, probably in this order: 1) the John
H. Wolfe pack company; 2) the Edmonson ox train; 3) the Holmes ox
train; 4) the Oliver ox train. There was now a nineteen-day spread
in the travel of these Cherokee Trail emigrants.

Captain Taylor's company entered Salt Lake city and passed
through, spending virtually no time at all. Crossing the "Jordon"
they camped. The next day they traveled 13 miles west on the
Hastings Cutoff.

INTERLUDE IN "SALT LAKE CITTY"

The Mitchell/Quesenbury pack group had business in Salt Lake
"citty," spending Friday and Saturday obtaining provisions and
supplies. The first order of business was to get flour.

<u>Mitchell</u>:

"12 [July] friday...we went to chaises Mill to get flour and could
get none   Streckler & crum went 6 miles South to another Mill
queshenbury & me went to town to get horses Shod and prepair for our
Journey onward   we got back at night to late to cook   eat our Supper
with Chais   fine peas for Supper   good light bread & a little butter

with milk   we bought wheat from Chase to feed in the Shief[1018] at
eight cents for Shief   had a charge about leting our horses get loose
and to Stay with them as it [is] at the risk of a heavy fine if horses
were found graising inside of their [Mormon] fencing."

    Quesenbury:

"**July...12...Friday**   Stopped at a mill to get flour. There was
none to be had. Crum and Strickler went to another mill five miles off.
Mr. Mitchell and myself went into town to get the horses shod. Left my
gun at a gunsmith's. Went round town and came back to the shop, Got four
Shoes put on, which cost me $4. At night Old Chase the miller permitted
Mr. Mitchell and myself to get into an old carry-all and write. We got a
candle from him. Set up till midnight and went to bed. Our horses were
hitched to some wagons in the mill yard."

In the previous publication of the Quesenbury diary, the miller's
name was transcribed as "Chan," which made the search for him
interesting but futile. When the Mitchell diary was compared with
Quesenbury's, it was evident that the name was "Chase." Isaac
Chase came to Utah September 20, 1847.[1019] Chase had 110 acres of
land "on which were numerous springs and Brother Chase built a
small gristmill."[1020] With Brigham Young, Chase built the mill
situated in Liberty Park. Named for him, it was the first mill and
ground the first flour in Utah.[1021] Chase married his second wife
Elizabeth Calvert on July 7, 1850, just five days before his
encounters with Quesenbury and Mitchell. He was 58 1/2 years old,
which is probably why 27-year-old Quesenbury called him "Old
Chase." Nevertheless, the impression from both diarists is that
Chase was kindly, with Christian virtues, and he aided them.
Quesenbury had already "Lost my pistol in keeping my pony off a
wheat field the road runs through." Chase had warned Quesenbury
and Mitchell about allowing their horses to wander untethered.

[1018]Sheaf--A bundle bound with straw or twine of cut stalks of grain, with
grain in the heads.

[1019]Brigham Young entered the Salt Lake Valley July 24, 1847.

[1020]"ca 1854-55 President Young and father Chase formed a partnership and two
new mills was erected, which were the first improved and up to date Gristmills
in the territory. Sometime in 1858 President Young bought Brother Chase out."
Bradshaw Journal, Ms 1560, LDS Church Archives.

[1021]Patricia N. Howard, "Index to Deceased Members' Batch Numbers" *Pioneers
and Prominent Men of Utah: Biography*. (Salt Lake City, UT: LDS Reference Unit,
1982) p 800. Chase was a High priest and captain of 50 in Jedediah M. Grant's
Company. Isaac Chase died May 2, 1861 in Salt Lake City. Another source notes
that Chase's Mill was built by Frederick Kesler and operated by Isaac Chase,
father-in-law of Brigham Young. Clarissa (Clara) Ross Chase was a stepdaughter
of Isaac. Everett L. Cooley, ed. *Diary of Brigham Young* (Salt Lake City: Univ.
of Utah Library Tanner Trust Fund 1980).

Events that followed were a direct result of company members Crum and Strickler not hearing that admonition. Mitchell:

"**14 [13] [July] Satterday.**[1022] Strickler and crum returned from the mill with flour   Some of us went of[f] to get baking done blackSmithing tin cans made and the others to mind our horses   it took all day to get our affairs ready to Start next day   Stricklers horses were taken by the marshal and given up to him   Chase fined for giving liberty to Strickler to graise his horses."

Quesenbury of course included the incident in his diary:

"**July...13...Saturday...1850** Crum and Strickler got back early. All except myself went up in town for various purposes. Mr. Mitchell took our flour up the gun smith's for the women to bake into crackers. But they required butter for the baking and none was to be had nearer than eight miles and that at 25 cents a pound. In the evening he went and brought the flour back declining the butter business--he also brought my gun. Crum got me a tin canteen at $1.50.

This evening the Sheriff came and attached Strickler's horses that were grazing two hundred and fifty yards down the creek from the mill. Strickler and myself had got special permission from Old Chase to graze our horses there.

The Sheriff seeing that Strickler was innocent though he hoped to have fined him, could not but hold "the good old father Chase" to account and so summoned him to attend at Squire Farr's office. About sun set Chase came back and said he had been fined twenty-nine dollars. We cooked our own meal in the millyard this evening--having eaten three with 'Good Old Father Chase'."

If all went to town except Quesenbury, he might have been primarily responsible for Strickler's horses being in the wrong place. Not surprisingly, Chase's hospitality wore thin. This however was not to be the last of the business of the stray horses. The next day, Sunday, there were further developments.

Mitchell:

"**15 [14] [July] Sunday** crum left us and was to wait for us   we had to Stay till 1 oclock to put letters in the mail   and then took the valy north by the Sulpher and hot Springs[1023]   we went 9 miles and camped near the mountain to our wright and the Salt lake to our left."

Contrast the the four lines of Mitchell's with the following statements of Quesenbury's. Forthright and explicit in his

---

[1022]Saturday was July 13, 1850. Mitchell picks up his error on July 25.
[1023]The Children's Museum of Utah is located 1.8 miles north of Pioneer Park, near the various springs "virtually every source account mentions the extraordinary mix of hot, warm, cold, and sulfur springs." Will Bagley, "Hensley's Salt Lake Cutoff" in Utah Crossroads Chapter, Oregon-California Trails Association field trip papers, taken from Peter DeLafosse, ed. *Trailing the Pioneers: A Guide to Utah's Emigrant Trails, 1829-1869* (Logan, Utah State Univ. Press 1994.)

descriptions of the day's events, <u>Quesenbury</u> wrote:

> **"July...14...Sunday.** 'Good Old Father Chase' intimated that he wanted us away, so we settled our bill with him, and after considerable packing, left. Went up in town to a store for some articles. Got a hatchet at another store, -also some saleratus, soda or something gathered from the plains.
>
> Then to the P.O. [postoffice] We were told the P.M.[Postmaster] was one of the preachers that day and that we could not get our letters mailed till twelve o'clock.
>
> In the mean time we went in the church. One chap, the P.M. I think was preaching which amounted to nothing but sickenng praise of the Mormon's and a recapitulation of their sufferings--He stated that he had lost two brothers who were martyrs to holy Mormonism, and that since that time he had learned to swear a little.
>
> He was followed by a very violent tall bald headed man, who explained the meaning of the brother's words -"since that time he had learned to swear a little." He said the brother had probably never taken God's name in vain in his life, but that "he had sworn by Elijah's God that he would have revenge for the death of his brothers"
>
> The tall bald gentleman was followed by Brigham Young the Prophet and Chief Cook etc, who was more violent still. He touched a variety of subjects--the Constitution of the U.S., which he praised and said the authors of it were inspired to make it--that Jo Smith was killed because he dared reprove wickedness in high places. He then spoke about flour, wheat, &c. giving orders that no more flour was to be sold under 25 cents a pound. He stated that he owned the mill[1024] near where our horses were staked and that he had to pay the $29. So the prophet or good old Father Chase told a lie."

This situation was probably further complicated by the fact that Chase was a father-in-law of Brigham Young; his stepdaughter Clarissa was a wife of Brigham. Quesenbury's original expressed disappointment was sustained by his experience in Salt Lake City. In the afternoon of July 14 they traveled north.

[1024]Many of the means of production were owned by Brigham Young, or the Mormon Church. Quesenbury may not have known there was a difference. In any event, it is interesting that the judge would fine either Young or the Mormon Church.

Chapter 8. SALT LAKE TO CALIFORNIA
Via The Hensley Cutoff 1850

**Took the Valy North by the Sulpher and Hot Springs...
Camped near the Mountain to our Wright and
the Salt Lake to our Left**

--James Mitchell

James Mitchell and William Quesenbury, along with seven other packers, arrived at Salt Lake on July 12 via Emigration Canyon. Quesenbury said Mitchell and Crum "cleaned up for a decent entry into the Mormon city." But of himself Quesenbury said "I will be more modest and pass through so quietly that I will be unnoticed." If any friend or even acquaintance had read this at the time, they would have smiled. Imagine William Quesenbury the artist, teacher, newspaper scribe, hunter, fisherman, adventurer, Mexican War veteran, commentator, and later newspaper editor and college art teacher doing anything unnoticed. Indeed, his conduct in Salt Lake City didn't go exactly unnoticed. The two diarists and Strickler went north out of the city on the Hensley or Salt Lake Cutoff, pioneered in 1848 by Samuel J. Hensley.[1025] By 1850 the Hensley was a well-used route north, west and northwest toward its junction with the California Trail near the City of Rocks in Idaho. No doubt others of the splintered parties from Arkansas, Cherokee Nation, and Missouri must have traveled over it in 1849 and 1850, but there is no known primary evidence. The Mitchell and Quesenbury diaries chronicle this route around the north end of the Salt Lake. Departing Salt Lake City on July 14, 1850, Quesenbury wrote:

"Then we started, passing salt springs hot springs took the right hand and found grass after a little hunting--wood scrub oak. Left the guide book[1026] this evening near a salt marsh where we grazed--went back for it--right at the spot where I left it, I met two Arkansas men, Alexander Sweeney and Wilson."[1027]

[near Bountiful, Davis Co., Utah]

[1025]Hensley, his nine men and their mule train had become mired in the salt flats on the Hastings Cutoff before retreating and pioneering the Hensley.
[1026]Evidently purchased along with other supplies in Salt Lake City.
[1027]Alexander Sweeney and Wilson remain unidentified.

<u>Mitchell</u>:

"16 [15 July][1028] **Monday...25 miles** we got to Webber river 25
miles [we are] above Brownsville[1029] pasing here & their good
Settlements."

<u>Quesenbury</u>:

"Monday...15...July Tolerable early start--passing wagons all
day. Nooned in a steep hollow of good grass--all three of us went to
sleep. Came on and camped on Weber river above the ford a mile. Fine
grass. Letters."
                    [near the Davis/Weber Cos. line, Utah]

For the next several days Mitchell comments on the landscape;
Quesenbury remains critical of what he sees. Both note the several
Mormon toll ventures. <u>Mitchell</u>:

"17 [16 July] Tuesday Pased the village [Brownsville] and
traveled near the mountain we nooned on a march [marsh] near hot Salt
Spring[1030] close to the mountain   the lake here Spreads out near the
high lands and [?] of acres covered white with pure Salt   Snow to our
right   we camped nere Boxelder."

<u>Quesenbury</u>:

"Tuesday...16...July Late start. Crossed Weber river-but little
larger than where we crossed above, coming on. Passed Brownsville-a
miserable attempt at civilization-also some branches, and one clear
beautiful stream [Willard Creek]. Camped on what we thought was Box
Elder. Was troubled some in finding a camping place, but found one to
the left of the road. Bad wood."
                    [near Brigham City, Box Elder Co., Utah]

<u>Mitchell</u>:

"18 [17 July] Wendsday very warm   we got to Bear river ferry &
crosed   paid $1 for each pack to the mormans and made our horses Swim.
it [is] 36 1/4 miles from Salt lake citty to Bear river an ugly Streem
there no timber in Sight   we camped a little below the fery."

<u>Quesenbury</u>:

"Wednesday...17...July...1850   Tolerably early getting off.
In two or three miles after we left camp crossed a stream which must
have been Box Elder. Nooned on a sluggish marsh pond[1031] which we
crossed to the left. At about 4 p.m. we got to Bear river. Found a
couple of skiffs planked over and a rope drawn across the river, which
constituted the ferry of the Mormons.

[1028]Mitchell's entries here are off by one day. Correct date is bracketed.
[1029]"Until 1850, the Mormon settlement was known as Brownsville or Brown's
Fort, after Captain James Brown of the Mormon Battalion, who used his men's
back pay to purchase Utah's first white settlement from Miles Goodyear in
November 1847." Bagley..."Field trip"...Now Fort Buenaventura State Park.
[1030]Near the Weber/Box Elder Counties' line.
[1031]Box Elder Lake, now drained. Bagley..."Field trip"...

Waited till an Iowa company crossed. Swam our horses and ferried our packs at $1 a pack. Camped below on the river. Horses on the flat below. Sage wood scarce."

[east of Tremonton, Box Elder Co., Utah]

Apprehension about indians they met led them to travel a long day. The search for good water and grass urged them on for a second long day. Mitchell:

"19 [18 July] Thursday [35 miles] in 2 miles we got to another tole concern mudy[1032] 25 cets for man & horse   we went a little north of west   the day very warm   we Stoped at 23 miles to camp. at the cold & warm Springs the water is all Salt & warm we left in consequence of the warm Salt water & indians and went 12 miles further in the night to good water and bad grass."

Quesenbury:

"Thursday...18...July Off about same time as yesterday. Began to find today that the Mormon guide book told lies about distances, and descriptions of places. The day has been almost insupportably warm-- perhaps warmer than yesterday. Passed the toll bridge on Mud Creek [Malad River]. 25 cents a man.

Came on under a burning sun to Cold and Warm springs which we found to be alike in temperature. Went up above and unpacked our things. Four or five mean looking Indians came to us. We concluded not to trust them near us without guard, so we packed up, went back to the springs, watered our horses and left about three quarters of an hour of sun.[1033] Travelled till about eleven at night when we came to water. Went on about a mile and laid down, turning our horses loose."

[near Hansel Spring, SE of Snowville, Box Elder Co., Utah]

Mitchell:

"20 [19 July] Fryday breakfast was Soon got mush and we Started with hungry horses   in 6 miles got to a Strange branch cold alkili water [Deep Creek] and [had] to go 6 miles further down to wher this Streem Spreads out and Sink to get grass   at grasin place we Stayed and let our horses fill their Selves   from here we to go 15 miles furthe[r] to Some Sinking Springs[1034] on the point of the mountain it was Some time in the night when we got to these Springs   people were camped all round and the grass eat out   we had water with us and went round the point of the mountain to grass   we had traveled 63 miles in 2 days and till late at night neerly without grass."

Quesenbury:

"Friday...19...July Very bad grass here; Left as soon as we got breakfast. Came to Deep creek[1035] crossed and hunted for grass, and

[1032]"Stansbury map...shows that the trail forded the Bear River directly east of present Tremonton, and then turned southwest for 1.5 miles to cross the narrow but steep-banked Malad River." Bagley..."Field trip"...
[1033]"three quarters of an hour of sun." = 45 minutes before sundown.
[1034]Cedar Spring or Emigrant Spring, 6 miles west of Pilot Spring.
[1035]Named by Samuel Hensley in 1848. "This ford was probably located at a big bend about one mile west of Snowville." Bagley..."Field trip"... This is in Box Elder County, about three miles south of the Utah/Idaho border.

found none till we came to the sink of same creek, though we halted a few minutes in the dryest poorest grass of the whole world.

Cooked and ate. Mr. Wells a tiresome talker dined with us praising our mush all the time.

Started and traveled till near eleven o'clock again, passing Pilot Springs,[1036] and some that were encamped there. Came to a wagon. I rode out and enquired for grass. We could see the lights of the campers far up on the mountain sides--We reached them at length--Turned to the left, and laid down again turning our horses loose."

[near Emigrant Spring or Cedar Spring, Box Elder Co., Utah]

From their campsite elevation, they could see not only Salt Lake, but also the snow-covered mountains near the city. That impressed Mitchell:

"21 [20 July] Saturday...22 miles we could See the Salt lake from here   the Snowa [snowy] mountain at the Salt lake citty could be Seen. men were round us Kilen the large rabbits[1037] with rocks & pistols we camped on cases [cassia] creek 22 miles."

Quesenbury:

"...Saturday...20...July. Remained for two or three hours this morning grazing our horses. We then set out at a brisk gate passing several clear branches of water, in one of which I got me a whetstone.[1038] Came to Casus creek;[1039] and kept up it for two miles. Encamped on it in a bend. Tolerable bottom grass. Measured coffee."

[Raft River, Cassia Co., Idaho]

Even though both diarists declared they camped on Cassia Creek, it seems more logical this was Raft River. "I...believe many travelers confused the...two....Raft River begins in Lynn, Utah, flows near Almo, through Malta and the Raft River area until it meets the Snake River between American Falls and Burley [Idaho]. Cassia Creek begins in Elba, Idaho and flows to Malta where it joins the Raft River."[1040]

The next day they met the road from Fort Hall. "The cutoff from Fort Hall...to the Humboldt River, extended southwest up the

---

[1036]Approximately 18 miles west of Snowville, state route 30, Box Elder County, Utah.

[1037]Probably the Black-tailed Jack Rabbit *Lepus californicus*; however the range of the White-tailed Rabbit *Lepus townsendii* overlaps, and is another possibility. Palmer...*Mammal*... pp 286-87. Once common throughout the western United States, most have been eradicated.

[1038]A hard, fine-grained stone for honing (sharpening) tools.

[1039]James Clyman, 1844, en route for Oregon: "this brook is called cassia." Marker set by Oregon-California Trails Association (OCTA). See "News from the Plains" Newsletter (April 1994).

[1040]"It depended on the route being traveled as to which body of water you followed. It was possible to follow each and pass through the City of Rocks." Personal communication February 14, 1996 with Kathleen Durfee at City of Rocks National Reserve.

Raft River...over Granite Pass to Goose Creek...up the east bank
to its head on the great divide that separated the Columbia river
basin from the Great Basin...into Thousand Springs Valley (Elko
County) down...valley to Cold Water Creek...up this creek...then
ascended the mountains...and descended gradually into valley five
miles farther to the headwaters of the Humboldt, near the site of
Wells, Nevada."[1041]

Mitchell:

"**22nd [21 July] Sunday** Started Soon and nooned on a bench
between the mountains in Juniper   Stade insight of the fort Hall road
and insight of Steeple rock   a vast of trains before   we got coffee
we crosed a mountain the very hilly and rocky 22 miles   camp on goos
creek."

Quesenbury:

"**Sunday...21...July.** Started very early and kept a brisk pace
till about eleven when we stopped and nooned about a mile from the
junction of the Ft. Hall and Salt Lake roads, and about the same
distance from the Steeple Rocks. Took a drawing of the rocks [Twin
Sisters].
    We have been constantly in among trains this evening, all pushing on;
one chap was carrying his outfit on his back.
    Came down a very steep hill, turned to the left after crossing a
small branch, [Birch Creek] and found grass in a hollow; where we
camped.
    Got some sugar and coffee from an emigrant this evening. A man named
Rogers gave me a wagon whip, just the thing I wanted."
    [near Utah/Idaho/Nevada border, Cassia Co., Idaho]

Quesenbury had previously sketched The Needles, east of Salt Lake.
For the next several days they traveled among the throng of
emigrants, occasionally finding and visiting with some they knew.
Mitchell:

"**23 [22 July] Monday** our horses I heard going of[f] at daylight
and we feared the indians had them   we persued them 2 miles and found
them standing   got coffee   the country here is very mountaneous with
patches of Juniper timber in places   we got to goos creek in a bout a
mile and as for a head as we could See the realty was lined with trains
of waggons   packers   foott men &c-   the road continued up this valy
for 18 miles   we nooned in about 14 miles   near this valey [we] pased
a vast [number] of thise tyered teams as we done every day   found
young george Crum and pased him an old acquaintance   it is astonishing
the dead animals we pased in this valey   camped in juniper on ridge."

[1041]Called the Fort Hall-Raft River-Goose Creek Cutoff to the Humboldt River,
it necessitated a long detour to the north so as to avoid the Great Salt Lake
and the Great Salt Desert west of it. Effie Mona Mack, *Nevada, A History of
the State from the Earliest Times through the Civil War.* (Glendale, Calif:
Arthur H. Clark Co. 1936) pp 110-11.

Quesenbury:

"Monday...22...July...1850. Got up before it was fairly light, and found our animals gone. They were heard far off up the hill in the rocks. Others were heard up the hollow to the right. I started after those that went up the hill and found their tracks which I followed for about a mile and a half and found the horses. Strickler came as soon as I found them and we took them back. He got his mare in the hollow he went up, down and almost choked to death with the lariat. Our start in consequence of the horses was not as early as yesterday's, but our gate[1042] faster. Overtook a nephew of George Crum[1043] with his family; passed wagons all the time till we nooned. This was to the right, on Goose Creek, which stream we struck two miles after we left camp this morning.

Left the spring where the road leaves Goose Creek, time enough to get about four miles. We turned to the right and camped by a large juniper[1044] tree on the side of a hill. Tolerable grass."
                [NE corner of Nevada near Goose Creek, 25 miles
                    SE of Jackpot, Elko Co., Nevada]

Mitchell:

"24 [23 July] Tuesday got into thousand Spring valy and then on cold water creek [Thousand Springs Creek]   here we pased boyling hot Springs and camped on cold water creek   we pased foot man an begger."

Quesenbury:

"July...23...Tuesday. Good start. Entered thousand spring valley in four or five miles. No appearance of grass.

Kept on over to Cold Water Creek, but it was dry where we struck it. Nooned on it without water. Kept up dry creek four or five miles and camped to the right of the road in the edge of the flat. We used water from a mud spring, there being so many dead animals in the branch. There are two fiddles going over among some Illinoians."
                [Thousand Springs Creek, about 30 miles NE of Wells,
                    Elko Co., Nevada]

Mitchell:

"25 [24 July] Wendsday nooned on cold water thence over to Kaynon creek and camped on the head."

Quesenbury:

"July...24...Wednesday. Got off at 6 o'clock. Continued up the valley. Passed some hot springs near the road. Nooned on the side of a hill to the left. Poor grass.

Found a spring at the head of the branch, where two men had mended their wagon and were waiting for mules. Passed over a rolling country, entered another valley in which we met a company of packmen returning from California.

[1042]It is unusual for Cush to use the wrong word. He obviously means "gait."
[1043]George Crum started on this journey with the McNair party and was with Mitchell and Quesenbury until they left Salt Lake City. His nephew is unknown.
[1044]Rocky Mountain Juniper *Juniperus scopulorum* Sarg. can grow as a tree 40-55 feet high and 15-30 inches in diameter. This species would be at the west edge of its range. Preston...*Rocky Mountain*...pp 78-79.

Camped to the right of the road on the bench of a mountain about a half a mile below a spring of tolerable water. Grass very good. Sage wood plenty."
[Bishop Creek, about 10 miles north of Wells, Elko Co., Nevada]

An uncountable number of snakes were seen the next day before they reached the waters of the Humboldt. Mitchell:

"25th [July] Thursday lost all confidence in our gide Book pased Snaks. we camped in the wide grasy valy of the humbolt river."[1045]

Quesenbury:

"Thursday...25...July. Strickler's gray horse gone this morning. He found him down towards the water.
Started early and passed on over much such a country as before. Came to a valley where some men were engaged in killing snakes.[1046] Vast numbers had been killed at the same place and were lying all along the road for a hundred yards. It seemed that the killing had been going on for some time. Nooned on the head waters of Humbolt river, to the left of the road, just above some men who were helping out a mired horse.
Camped early on account of the finest grass we have had on the trip-- on the left of the road. Sage wood a good distance off."
[Humboldt River, west of Wells and west of the mouth of Bishop Creek, Elko Co., Nevada.]

Customarily they took both nooning places and campsites away from the beaten wagon track. Quesenbury's hunting skills are complimented by Mitchell:

"26 [July] fryday Started Soon   before nooning pased 77 waggons and the finest grass that ever I have Seen & quesenbery Kille 3 curlues[1047]   we got down the river till the valy become narrow and the grass eaten out next to the road with Some hunting to cros Slows [sloughs] that were very Swampy   we found good grass and a Safe place to camp next to the river   the finest Supper we had of the 3 curlues ques[enbury] Kiled the best of Birds."

Quesenbury:

"Friday...26...July...1850. Earliest start yet. Down the Humbolt Valley. The grass appeared good all the way. We passed the grave

[1045]The first mention of the Humboldt River, to which they have been heading since turning southwest near Steeple Rocks (City of Rocks), Idaho.
[1046]"following is a list of snakes indigenous to the area: Great Basin Gopher Snake *Pituophis melanoleucus*; Rocky Mtn. Rubber Boa *Charina bottae utahensis*; Striped Whipsnake *Masticophis taeniatus*; Great Basin Rattlesnake *Crotalus viridis lutosus*; Western Yellow-Bellied Racer *Coluber constrictor mormon*; Wandering Garter Snake *Thamnophis elegans vagrans*; and Night Snake *Hypsiglena torquata*." Personal Communication with Kathleen Durfee at City of Rocks National Reserve February 14, 1996.
[1047]Mitchell and Quesenbury use "Curlue" and "Curlew" to describe large shorebirds. In this particular area, and because Quesenbury calls it a new kind of curlew, it is probably the Long-billed Curlew, largest of shorebirds. In migration, it frequents wetlands, such as marshes, mud flats, sandbars and shorelines. The Long-billed Curlew's range includes northern Nevada.

of a man who was killed a few nights ago whilst on guard, by an Indian.

Saw a new kind of curlew. Killed three of them, which we took to our nooning place and picked--on the left of the road near the river. We fished some to day. Caught nothing but the smallest size.

My pony undertook, after drinking, to play his old trick of going to the other bank, and the first step he took plunged him in swimming water.

Camped in a secure place over a slough--cooking our curlews and eating them."

[Humboldt River, near Halleck, Elko Co., Nevada]

Unfortunately, this is the final daily entry in the James Mitchell diary. Mitchell:

"27th [July] Satturday   continued down the vally it become narrow and grass Scarce   we even could not get a place worth Stoping to noon on   about 3 oclock we tried crosing Slews and Succeeded in geting good grass   here we remained till next morning."

Perhaps Mitchell just ran out of paper in his small book. Upside down on this page were some mileage notes he made before entering Salt Lake and one more item: "Father Chais at great Salt Lake citty...I left my eight[1048] shooting gun here."

Along the stretch of road which parallels the Humboldt River, Quesenbury did not sketch at all, but he was able to do something else at which he was very good--hunt birds. Quesenbury:

"Saturday...July...27.   Tolerable good start. The valley of the river became more cut up with sloughs than heretofore. Tried some time to get over into grass but could not succeed. Got over on a grass bridge but the grazing was poor. Found a dying horse and a packsaddle that had been abandoned. We also found some currants or gooseberries,-- three different kinds, of which we ate as long as we wished.

Camped about 2 P.M. to give our horses a resting spell, crossing a slough on another grass bridge. Strickler who crossed below had some trouble with his horses.

Took my gun and went below to see if I could find anything to kill-- nothing was stirring. Came back and parched[1049] coffee. Strickler has fished this evening and we are satisfied that the Humbolt is not a fish stream."

[Humboldt River SW of Elko, near the mouth of South Humboldt River and the Hastings Cutoff junction, Elko Co., Nevada]

Packing allowed them to take the several cutoffs, which were questionable for wagons. Quesenbury:

"Sunday...28...July...1850.   Started early. The road led over hills [Greenhorn Cutoff]. Took a near cut [Carlin Canyon] which took us to the river. The way was a bad one. Two Dutchmen were at the river grazing an old pony. They were packing a shovel to the mines.

[1048]Shotgun, 8 gauge. It is unclear why Mitchell left the gun at Salt Lake.
[1049]Parching means roasting green coffee beans in a heavy skillet.

Nooned on poor grass on the river. Took to the hills again. Turned to the left and camped in a hollow. Bunch grass tolerably dry..."

[near Emigrant Pass, west of Carlin, Eureka Co., Nevada]

Quesenbury:

Monday...29...July. Late start. Came to spring water near the road A footman wanted [illegible] Wouldn't let him have any Our way was still among the hills. Took another cut off which was a bad one; it brought us to the river near some Root Digger's [Paiute Indians] camps.

Grazed just above the road--

Occasionally in the valley of the river we perspire but never on the highlands. There is never any Dew scarcely except in the river flats, where the humid atmosphere is almost dew all the time.

After going about a mile from our nooning place I discovered that I had left my cup behind. Went back for it. Camped after crossing the river [at Gravelly Ford] and keeping down ten or twelve miles on the S. side. Two Illinoians came up and camped with us.

After we had gone to bed, we heard a gun and soon after a company of packmen came along. We asked them a question or so about the gun, and they seemed bent on camping with us. They enquired how many we were, and we told them two companies. They then went below a hundred yards or so and stopped."

[NW of Beowawe, Eureka Co., Nevada]

Quesenbury:

July...30...Tuesday...1850. About seven o'clock when we got off. Road dusty and disagreeable. Nooned near some packmen from whom we borrowed a couple of tin pans to water our horses with.

Found some currants which I got by wading the slough. The dust this evening has been more disagreeable and oppressive than at any time previous. Some saw a lake to our left late in the evening. Tried to get to it, but did not succeed. Came to a well from which we got water, and then took our course for the river, but were stopped by mire and water near a pond. Great quantities of curlews were flying about.

Camped near the pond. After supper I discovered that my pony and our mule were gone, and I remained during the night very uneasy about them.

We all hunted around but could hear nothing of them. A couple of Irishmen camped near us to night."

[near Battle Mountain, Lander Co., Nevada]

Quesenbury:

Wednesday...31...July...and last. Found my runaways just at day break. Took my gun after breakfast and went out after the curlews. Killed only one.

Nooned on a slough which we bridged with willows. A man came to us hunting stolen oxen and horses, and another one came asking for bread. He was a Dutchman walking with a heavy pack on his back which he said he had carried all the way from the frontier.[1050]

Camped at night on an island which we got to over a hay bridge some one had made. Presently, a pack company came and camped below us, and a wagon close to us--the latter seemed inclined to turn their horses on our grass to which Mr. Mitchell objected, and they put their animals over another slough."

[north of Valmy, Humboldt Co., Nevada]

[1050]The "frontier" of the time was generally a north-south line from western Iowa through western Arkansas.

"Our grass" was apparently determined by who got there first and what they decided was theirs. It is interesting that Mitchell should be the one to object rather than Quesenbury, who had demonstrated that he was not timid. Quesenbury:

> **"August...1...Thursday.** Our start was later than usual. The road has been very crooked to day and I am inclined to think we have travelled at times a little E.-of-N.[1051] Nooned to the right on a slough below a pack company. Took my gun, went down the slough and killed four young ducks.[1052] Had to wade for them. Laid them down to shoot at others and could not find them. Called for help to hunt them and just as Mr. Mitchell came I found them. Got bothered about the road, which branched out in all kinds of circles, crosses, forks, nigh cuts, &c. Found the right track. Came on over a ridge, struck the river, saw a man learned from him that we had to cross the river. Went to the ferry. It was half a wagon body.
>
> Concluded to wait till morning. Went out and took down the river at the foot of the hills. Found bad grass after hunting down and nearly back for a mile.
>
> Before we got to the ferry, Old Nell, Dog and Strickler's pony took a miring frolic."
>
> [near Golconda, Humboldt Co., Nevada]

Cherokee Captain Taylor's company, including diarist Brown, arrived at Salt Lake on August 1, while Mitchell, Strickler, and Quesenbury were traveling down the Humboldt River. Traveling fast, they continued passing other companies; more Arkansas friends were seen by the three packers. Quesenbury:

> **"Aug...2...Friday...1850.** Mr. Mitchell was up before day cooking. Got to the ferry before anyone else. Crossed over safe. Started--got a little bacon from a man at 37 1/2 cents lb. Kept down the river till we struck the road, which showed more sign of emigration than the one we had left.
>
> Searched along the sloughs for grass. Crossed one, found a willow bridge over another, and good grass. Nooned a long time, letting our animals fill up.
>
> Our road this evening kept down the river. It was unusually thronged with wagons. I notice a great many dead animals along. The water is bad, causing our horses to urinate continually. Took a near cut which led us among sloughs, and from which we got to the highland with difficulty. Camped without grass near the slough. Two Yankees were just above us and some packers and wagons below and to our right. Found they were Arkansas men[1053] and that Wm. Rutherford[1054] was with them.

[1051]Southeast of Red House, the Humboldt does flow a little east of north.
[1052]Duck species would have rather large young by August 1; the most probable are Mallard, Northern Pintail, Northern Shoveler, or Green-winged Teal.
[1053]Possibly this train was seen by Mrs. Frank on the south side of the Humboldt. "Friday, August.2...The Arkansas train camped near us. We traded pickles and acid with them for tea and sugar." Mrs. Margaret JA. Frink, *Journal of the Adventures of a Party of California Goldseekers* (Fairfield, Wash.: Ye Galleon Press 1987) p 78.

Tebbett's team was along. Wm. Rutherford came down to see us--he was up feeding horses--and talked till ten or eleven. He gave us some grass, which he had got by swimming the river.

Dog[1055] got mired again to day as we left our nooning place."

[SW of Winnemucca, Humboldt Co., Nevada]

Quesenbury:

"Saturday...3...August. Got breakfast and started. Bad prospect for grass. Kept on down for two or three miles. Strickler went over a slough and found grass which we cut with our butcher knives and fed our horses. Continued on without nooning. Looked all along for grass till we came to a bend of the river, that answered tolerably for a camping place by cutting grass with our knives.

Several footmen have been looking at our animals very anxiously as they went by.

Cooked the young ducks, I killed the other day. They were the most loathsome food ever cooked tasting precisely as the slime of the slough smells."[1056]

[near Mill City, Pershing Co., Nevada]

Traveling on August 4 they passed the turnoff to Oregon, the Applegate-Lassen Trail. Contrast the numbers of diary notations about the cutoff in 1849, with these in 1850, including Brown, which do not even mention passing the turnoff. Quesenbury:

"Sunday...4...August. Dog mired again this morning, but we got him out and started. As yesterday parts of the road were very sandy. After going till near eleven, the prospect for water and grass being very bad we turned to the left for the river which we reached after a long hot ride. Made coffee for nooning. Some packmen nooned below us, grazing their horses on the salt grass we had been careful to avoid.[1057] The river bends to the left, and we struck out across the bend. Our way was very sandy. Turned in to the left and camped under a sand bank on a slough, cutting grass for our horses with our knives."

[Lassen Meadows, Rye Patch Reservoir, Pershing Co., Nevada]

Large numbers of dead animals and abandoned goods seen were the result of long, wearisome wagon travel. Quesenbury:

"Monday...5...August. Cut grass again. Started and came to the road about three miles below. We counted 21 dead animals within a few hundred yards of each other. There has been more destruction of property along the road here than at any part we have seen. Hats, boots, shoes, tents, wagons, wagon covers, stoves, clothing, everything of the kind lie strewn thick along.

[1054]An Archibald Rutherford started with the Rector/Leeper party in 1850, taking the California Trail along the Platte. William is unknown.

[1055]Dog is the name of Quesenbury's pony.

[1056]Duck species which eat from the mud, or aquatic plants on the bottom include Green-winged Teal and Northern Shoveler.

[1057]Salt Grass *Distichlis stricta* grows in the interior of the western states. Another Salt-Marsh grass of the western interior is Alkali Cordgrass *Spartina gracilis*. Pohl...*Grasses*...pp 25, 136.

Saw the grave of a little child, aged 3 y. on the side of the road.
The rabbits or some animals had scratched most of the sand away and the
head board was all that told there was a grave there.

Turned in at noon. I swam the river for grass, cutting it with my
knife.[1058] It took six trips to get it over--Pulled it over with our
lariats. Saw Rutherford's company again this evening. They were packing.
Pushed on to get to the sink. Rode till ten o'clock and laid down,
hitching our animals to the small artemesia [sage] around."
                    [north of Lovelock, Pershing Co., Nevada]

The next two days they passed men returning home from
California. To find grass, they stay near the sloughs. Quesenbury:

"Tuesday...6...August...1850.   Disturbed all night by trains
that were passing. One chap enquired if we had seen anything of the sink
go by, and at daybreak another came up and told us it was day.

Went on a short distance and turned in to the river found a narrow
bottom with some bridges over sloughs. We took our animals over them.
Pulled up some grass. Nooned a long time, made coffee, baked bread.

People were passing continually on the other side. One chap told me
he had found a piece of gold. I washed a pan of sand, but found no gold.

Struck out for the road. Saw two packmen going back. They were from
California. Rode back a mile talking with one. Took me some time to
catch up. Turned in to the river again. Found a company of packmen
there, one of whom was an old friend of Col. Rector since they were
schoolmates together. He was asking me of Maj. Rector.[1059]

Got in the bend of the river behind sloughs again. Our N.Y. friends
have broke their gun off at the breech and offer it for a pound of
flour.: it cost $75. Our place is very miry, and the mosquitoes more
ravenous than ever were seen before."
                    [near Lovelock, Pershing Co., Nevada]

Quesenbury:

"Wednesday...7...August. Late start owing to the thinness of
grass, to the scarcity of wood, and to the biting of mosquitoes. We were
bit last night till after midnight. No sleep till then.

Made again for the grass above the sink. Came to a slouth with some
cold springs near it, and quantities of dead stock in it. Met a couple
of returning Californians. Rode back a couple of hundred yds. with them.

Came to the beef market under stretched wagon sheets. Good beef sold
at from .20 to .40 cents. Poor at from .15 to .25 cents. Got a mess of
the poor. Started to grass across the sloughs and found that the beef
man had told a lie. Cooked a snack returned to the beef market, and
bought a bundle of grass for each of our animals. Came on and camped on
the left of the r[iver]. in better grass than we have had for some time;

[1058]Robert Little journeyed from Arkansas in 1850: "We traveled down Humboldt
river two hundred miles and had always to swim in to get food for our starving
animals....We had to cut the grass...below the surface of the water and many
have been drrowned [sic] in trying to get food enough to keep their animals
from perishing." *Fort Smith Herald* 15 November 1850 vol 4, no 12, p 2.

[1059]Major Elias Rector, in an article in the *Arkansas Gazette* 22 November 1849
wrote of his plans for a California trip with Col. Matthew Leeper. They
gathered 90 men from Fort Smith and Fayetteville. Cherokees joining the
company included John Rollin Ridge and brother Aeneas. The 1850 company went
via Fort Scott to Council Grove, north to the Platte River, then along the
Platte on the main Oregon/California Trail.

but Strickler and myself went down into the slashes[1060] and cut a load for the little mule which we had to pack ourselves--it getting away and running back to camp."

[south of Lovelock, Pershing Co., Nevada]

They met a man from the Arkansas Rector/Leeper company who they knew. For the next few days, before arriving at the Humboldt Sink, they found and made use of some abandoned goods. Quesenbury:

Thursday...8...August. Moved lower down in the grass cutting region. Saw a Negro of Rollin Ridge's[1061] who told us Maj. Rector and his crowd had just left.

A man gave me a reap hook. Strickler reaped the grass. Parched coffee and ground it. Found a stove near by, which we used."

[south of Lovelock, Pershing Co., Nevada]

Quesenbury:

Friday...9...August. Recruiting our animals today. A great many teams have left--and have left a great many things: ovens, skillets, tents, wagon sheets, scythes, books, horse shoes, hobbles, stoves, ropes, clothes &c. &c. &c.

Got the bottom of a wagon body and made a shade for us. Got a skillet and baked bread on the stove."

[South of Lovelock, Pershing Co., Nevada]

Quesenbury:

Saturday...10...August. Started tolerably early. The road leads due N. about 4 m., then turns S. The road was freer from dust than usual. Came to a broad sheet of water that was coming[?] over the flat. It was not more than a foot or so deep as far as we rode into it some fifty yards.

Nooned a short time by the side of the lake. Came on to the lake that every body called the sink of the river [Humboldt Sink]. Went a mile or more down it and camped. Left my boots in this lake where I went out to get water. They stuck in the mud and pulled from my feet.

Wood was very scarce. We got an axle tree, a scythe snath[1062] and a few other abandoned things by hunting over the whole country around."

[Humboldt Sink, SW of Lovelock, Pershing/
Churchill Cos. lines, Nevada]

[1060]Wet or swampy ground overgrown with rushes and trees.

[1061]The slave named Wacooli accompanied Cherokee John Rollin Ridge and his brother Aeneas to the California goldfields in 1850. At this point in their journey, the Rector/Leeper company was splintered; Ridge's trio packed from Deer Creek (Glenrock, Wyoming). At Salt Lake they recruited themselves and their animals and cured 90 lbs. of beef themselves. They obtained flour at 25 cents lb. because the harvest was in. Ridge, his brother Aeneas, and Wacooli departed Salt Lake taking the Hensley Cutoff to the Humboldt River. Mark L. Evans of the original Rector/Leeper company wrote from Pacific Springs on June 26 that "Leeper, Ledford, Rector and Spring are behind...Rollin and Eneas Ridge, Auchey Smith, Jack Stricklin, Jim Yoes...also Moses Stout, are behind intending to pack....Many are going by Salt Lake, but we will take Sublett's cut off." *Fort Smith Herald* 21 September 1850 vol 4, no 4, p 3.

[1062]"Snath" is clearly written. The meaning is unknown.

Quesenbury, Mitchell and Strickler were packing through the Forty-Mile Desert south of the Humboldt Sink. It took them the entire day and much of the night, during which time he saw his first mirage, a common phenomenon in the dry west. Quesenbury:

"Sunday...11...August. Got up before day. Fed away the last blade of grass we packed yesterday and by fifteen minutes before Sunrise were on our way.

The road turned to the right around a water country, and after five or six miles we came to a slough too deep to ford with our packs. We stripped our animals and carried our things over on our shoulders. Then went ahead in the desert. Saw a vast bare plain before us which we took to be a lake,but as we came near found nothing but a dry desolate plain.

The destruction of property from wagons, down to every article of an outfit has been immense. Vast quantities of animals lie dead on the road. Some are dying, some standing.

We nooned for a few minutes about twelve o'clock, drinking the coffee we prepared last night. An unusual number of wagons have been abandoned at the first sand ridge, and for a few miles beyond, W. Came to a salt well from which we watered our animals. Many emigrants are lying in the desert, having sent their teams to the river.

About an hour by sun came to a water wagon. The price was a dollar a gallon. Went on and came to another; the price was .75 cents a gallon. Remained twenty minutes resting our animals. We were then just entering the sand. Asked nearly every man we met how far it was to the river, and no two agreed. The sand continued heavy and deep till we reached Carson's river which was just at moon down. Went above the trains and trading establishments ate a snack and lay down for the night after feeding and tieing our horses. Our grass was bought from a grass theif [sic] at .25 cents a bundle.

I counted to day since we left the sink, four hundred and fifty-four dead animals."

[Carson River at Ragtown,[1063] Churchill Co., Nevada]

Next day they sought feed for their own animals. Quesenbury:

"Monday...12...August. Got breakfast and went up the river about four miles. Bought seven lbs. beef on the way. (beef 37 1/2clb. Turned in to the river to rest and graze our animals.

After waiting three or four hours we packed up and went up the river two miles; crossed over safe by raising our packs, and found good grass. We camped under some large cottonwoods. A great many persons have their animals over here; a great many are cutting and drying grass for long, dry, stretches ahead. We are crowded with men, horses, and cattle.

I was told this evening that Maj. Rector took the Trucky Road[1064] at the sink a day or so ago."

[Six miles west of Ragtown, Churchill Co., Nevada]

[1063]Ragtown, from its appearance with laundered clothes draped on sagebrush.
[1064]Truckee Trail (North of Lake Tahoe) "passed west of the Humboldt Lake, extended across the Truckee Desert in a southwest direction to the Big Bend [following] to a point near the present town of Verdi, Nevada. In the short distance of forty miles...the river was forded thirteen times....up Dog Valley Grade...along the river to [present] Truckee, California...turned due west... along the north shore of Donner Lake, passed up and over the summit of Donner Pass." Mack...Nevada...p 117.

David Spring, a member of Major Rector's 1850 party, noted:

> We came the Truckey river route from the Sink, because no one
> scarcely had traveled it....we had generally good grass...Good pure
> water, and air uncontaminated by carion....it is a bold, rapid and
> dangerous stream...to [be] cross[ed] 27 times; but was so full that
> we only crossed it three times, taking to the mountains....any man
> is a fool who will bring a wagon over it.[1065]

Quesenbury, Mitchell and Strickler were traveling the Carson
route. One reason for taking the Carson was that they, as well as
other emigrants, knew about the 1846 Donner/Reed tragedy on the
Truckee route. Quesenbury:

> **"Tuesday...13...[August].** Packed up and crossed back: In two
> miles we left the river[1066] and struck over the hills, coming to the
> river again in about fifteen miles. Saw some packmen under some cotton-
> woods who told us the river was swimming. Went on a hundred yards and
> found other packmen who told us the river was not belly deep. Crossed
> over under their directions. The grass was not good, but a long stretch
> was ahead, and we concluded to stop for the night, making our camp under
> large cottonwoods again. Wood plenty, water handy."
> [NE of Dayton, Lyon Co., Nevada]

Quesenbury found an opportunity to replace the boots he left
in the mire of Humboldt Sink on August 10. Quesenbury:

> **"1850...Wednesday...14...August...26 m. Desert.**
> Commenced preparations before day and by sunrise we were on our way.
> Some packmen came to our camp as we were about leaving.
>   Bought some dried applies in the desert from four men who abandoned
> their wagons and were selling off their surplus, to pack. Got me a
> very good pair of boots at an abandoned wagon. Strickler got him a pair.
>   Came to the river at half past one, or two, forded over, went up
> half a mile and unpacked for nooning. My mules both wallowed[1067] after
> crossing the river. We then made two or three miles and commenced
> hunting grass. Found some which we thought would do, across a slough.
> Went round by the river, watered our animals, got camp water, and
> unpacked under a cottonwood.
>   Strickler found better grass on an island in the slough to which
> we took our horses. After supper I took my blankets and went over
> and slept by the horses."
> [near Dayton, Lyon Co., Nevada]

Quesenbury gets yet another opportunity to show his rather
extraordinary skill with a gun.

[1065]David Spring letter to brother Dr. N. Spring from Nevada City, California
August 23, 1850 *Fort Smith Herald* 13 December 1850 vol 4, no 16, p 2.
[1066]Near Desert Wells, present Silver Springs, Nevada.
[1067]For the first time Quesenbury told the number of his animals: two mules
and his pony, named Dog. Horses are fond of wallowing, i.e. rolling the body
about indolently or clumsily in mud and dirt.

Quesenbury:

"Thursday...15...August. My pony, Dog, was gone this morning. I found him down the slough. Soon after leaving camp we scared up two sage hens.[1068] Followed after them. Shot and missed. Followed again, and killed them both, at one shot, flying.

Crossed over to the road. The ford was rocky and the river appeared to have the appearance of a mountain stream.

Crossed the 12 mile desert and came to the river. Nooned above a trading thief's establishment on the flat. Grass very bad. The road then turned to the left and went 8 m. before coming to the river again. In about a mile after it did, we camped in good grass to the left. An Illinois packman camped with us. Water very handy; wood very unhandy."
[NE of Genoa, Douglas Co., Nevada]

While others were in the most dire straits, this pack party was in a rather comfortable state. Quesenbury:

"Friday...16...August. Left soon after sunrise. Came to a trader's. Pork still $1.25; flour $2.00. Strickler left his gun and had to go back for it. We grazed our animals whilst he was gone.

Passed the Mormon Station[1069] and turned to the left for nooning. Whilst lying on the grass, two men came by, one of whom was from Arks. [Arkansas]. They gave us a great deal of information about the mines; told us of some of our friends; showed us some gold dust, and remained chatting about an hour, then went on to meet their friends.

Continued up the river valley till camping time, when we turned towards the mountains on the right and camped on a moist slope among warm and cold springs. Grass and wood good."
[NE of Woodfords, Alpine Co., California, near the
Nevada/California state line]

It isn't clear whether the trader noted above was an independent or from Mormon Station. Quesenbury's prices are similar to that Abner Blackburn charged in 1850 at Mormon Station. According to Hampden S. Beatie, flour was worth $2 a pound, fresh beef $1 and bacon $2.[1070]

The three men continued to and through Carson Canyon, wreckage everywhere. Quesenbury:

"Saturday...17...[August]...1850. Early start in about seven miles we came to the cañon,[1071] and by half past one P.M. we got through it. The road was the most rugged we have passed over and from the wrecks

---

[1068]Sage Grouse, most abundant where sagebrush provides 15 to 50% of the ground cover, is the largest North American grouse, males weighing 5-7 pounds.
[1069]Genoa, Nevada was the first permanent settlement in Nevada. By 1851, the Mormon Station had passed through three owners: Abner Blackburn, summer of 1850, first builder; Moore in late 1850; John Reese in mid-1851, who built, fenced, and farmed getting ready for the heavy 1852 emigration.
[1070]Dale L. Morgan, *The Humboldt: Highroad of the West* (Lincoln and London: Univ. of Nebraska Press 1970) p 200.
[1071]Carson Canyon, seven miles long.

of wagons, it must be destructive on such property.

We have had good water today fresh from snows, and we have travelled through pine timber, and have seen some of the largest trees that we ever saw anywhere. Turned to the left, crossed the creek and nooned on the slope of the mountains. Gathered flower seeds while nooning.[1072]

The country is still as broken as ever, but the road led up the river valley, on to tolerable grass. Came to a trader's and bought some beef from him. Went on a mile and camped under pine trees to the left of the road. Our horses are grazing on the flat."

[north of Red Lake, east side of Carson Pass,
Alpine Co., California]

They crossed over the highest point of the route. Quesenbury:

"Sunday...18...August. Early start. Road rough. Met Magruder[1073] on the mountain and we got off our animals and sat down and talked like old friends would. He was on his way to examine the Carson river mines. Remained chatting half an hour with Magruder, and then went on. Came to another lake, larger than Red Lake which we passed this morning. Red Lake is a poor concern--not half what I expected to see. Turned down the lake last come to, for three qrs. of-a m.[mile] and went up on the mountain side and nooned.

Our road in the evening was still bad--none of it level. About 1/2 past 3. we came to the foot of the highest point we have to pass over. We ascended it. For near a mile our way was upon Snow, at the lower edge of a long large snow bank. Crossed over the ridge [West Pass] and hesitated awhile about a cut off which I had no idea of taking. Turned to the right down into a valley and after hunting for grass awhile found some that we thought would do, near a small lake [Silver Lake].

The wind blowed intensely cold before bed time, and we had to destroy some fire, that had caught too far along a log, with snow from a bank which lay within ten feet of us."

[near Silver Lake, Amador/El Dorado Cos. line, California]

Despite the rough terrain and cold weather, Quesenbury took time to sketch. It was the first since Twin Sisters, his "Steeple Rocks," at City of Rocks in Idaho. Several 1850 sketches remain unidentified. Quesenbury:

"Monday...19 [August]. Late start. Weather cold till sunrise. Took two sketches.

Started and went up to the road which has improved none since yesterday. Our way was winding, up hill, down hill and rocky. About nooning time found two bundles of grass that some person had lost. Gathered on them and fed them to our animals a mile further on. Passed many trading establishments to day. Flour has fallen to .62 1/2 cts lb.

We bought some at that price. Came to the Leek Springs--no grass there; passed them, turned to the left at the top of the mountain, and found good grass on a slope.

The flour we bought is from Chili; and makes the whitest bread perhaps I ever saw."

[near Leek Spring Valley, El Dorado Co., California]

The need for grass and concern for animal health urged

[1072]Gathering flower seeds was completely in character for Quesenbury.
[1073]Unidentified, but obviously a friend.

Mitchell and Strickler to travel on together. The same concern prompted Quesenbury to stay behind.

> **"Tuesday...20...August.** Late start again. The road is still up or down a hill all the time. Came to water at Deep Valley [Camp Creek] in about 8 m. Two trading posts there.
>
> Ascended the mountain again and turned to the left to noon. Kept down the valley, following Strickler who led us nearly back to where we left Deep Valley. Remained only a short time and took a trail that led us to the top of the mountain again. The road leads on a ridge [Iron Mountain Ridge] all the way we are told, to the mines. Turned to the right and camped cutting oak limbs for feed for our animals.
>
> Strickler concluded to go on and get nearer grass. I preferred remaining and letting mine rest, as the road had been bad, and I had no idea of going in the night on a rough ground. We divided our provisions and Mr. Mitchell and Strickler went on. After they had gone, I went over and talked with some Illinoisans about a hundred and fifty yards off; then came back and laid down beneath the pines, solitary and alone--the first night I have been so, since I left home."

[east of Pleasant Valley and SE of Placerville,
El Dorado Co., California]

Alone, Quesenbury records a milestone in his life:

> **"1850...August...21...Wednesday.** My birth day. I am now twenty eight years old. Got up at daylight, made a cup of coffee and left. Dog ran back to camp after I got into the road, and for a long time on the way he was unmanageable. Came about two o'clock P.M. to Johnson's ranch,--bought hay at .15 cents a lb. 20 pounds.
> Sold Dog--the last of Dog.
>
> Went down to the branch beyond the ranch and fed myself and mules."

So ends the William M. Quesenbury diary for his trip to California in 1850. Unlike 1849 and other 1850 travelers from home, he seems not to have suffered privation or illness of any kind. He lost no animals. Quesenbury was able to hunt, fish, and sketch at will, much as he would do at home. Fortunately, both his diaries and his trip sketches are extant. The diary, with those of James Mitchell and John Lowery Brown, clearly and descriptively recorded the use of the 1850 Edmonson/Cherokee Trail as far as Twin Groves, Wyoming. The sketchbook of the entire round trip accompanied him, but was lost until 1995. It was in the family collection of an 1851 traveling companion. He returned home in 1851. "We see that our old friend William Quesenbury, of Cane Hill, is now on his way home, by the overland route, in company with nine or ten persons."[1074] If Quesenbury kept a diary of his return trip, it is unknown.

[1074]*Fort Smith Herald* 26 September 1851 vol 5, no 6, p 2. Source not noted.

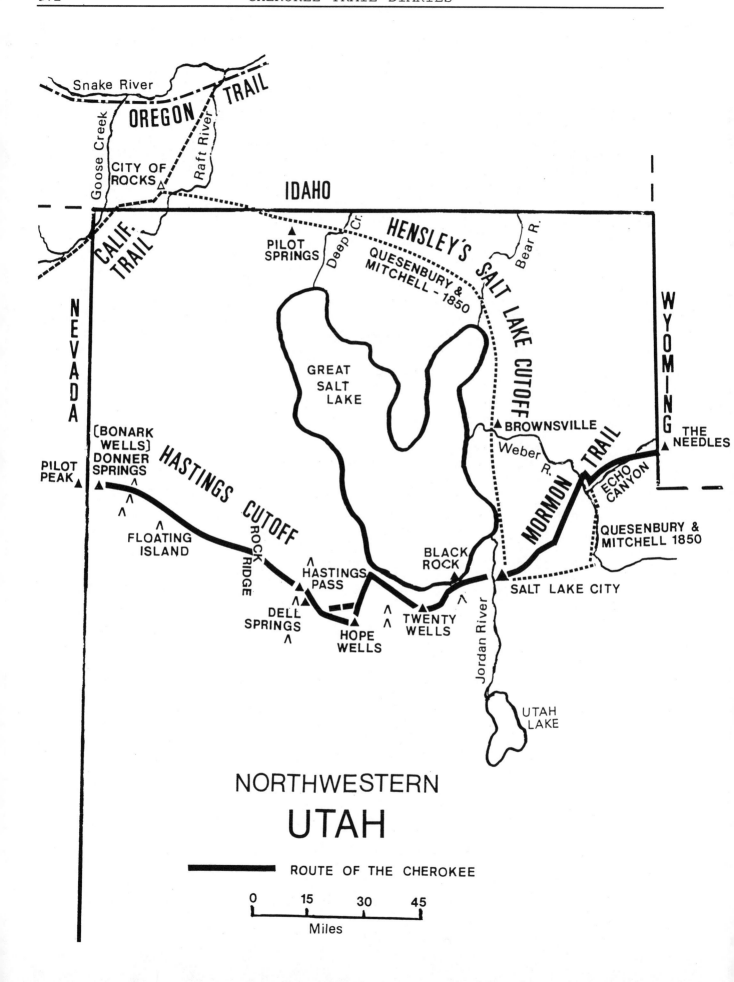

NORTHWESTERN
UTAH

———— ROUTE OF THE CHEROKEE

```
0      15      30      45
|———|———|———|———|———|———|
         Miles
```

Chapter 9. SALT LAKE TO CALIFORNIA
Via The Hastings Cutoff.

There are Two Routs...the Northern [and the] Cutoff
Heretofore Trveled only with Pack Animals....
We Took the Cutoff Rout
--John Lowery Brown

Thomas Fox Taylor had assumed the role of captain of the Cherokee company at the Cache la Poudre River. At the Green River many members of Captain Taylor's company decided to pack; others retained their wagons, proceeding with either the Holmes or the Oliver ox companies. References to them and their wagons surfaced later when diarist Brown, with the packing company, caught up to the ox trains on the Hastings Cutoff. Brown arrived in Salt Lake City at noon July 31, 1850. His was the last of the documented companies of ox trains, horse/mule wagons and packers who traveled over the southern Edmonson/ Cherokee Trail that year. Brown passed through the city, crossed the Jordan River and camped on the west bank. The company was ready to proceed the next morning.

Some members of the Taylor company reportedly stopped longer at Salt Lake. "They [Mayes'] tarried a week and helped the Mormons cut wheat with old-fashioned cradles."[1075] The Mayes' family arrival at Salt Lake coincided with harvest. Their efforts may have been an advantageous exchange--labor for wheat. Samuel Houston Mayes and oldest sons George Washington Mayes and John Thompson Mayes, cousin Richard Fields, and uncle Devereaux J. Bell would have been a more than adequate field crew.

Opposite the page dated August 1, Brown noted the information gathered by the company to help decide which route to take.

at this place there are two Routs to the diggins, one called the Northern Rout, down the Humbolt River, another called the "Cutoff heretofore traveled only with Pack animals but this Season, the Emegrants are going it with their waggons." about 80 miles from the city, there is said to be a Desert Destitute of water or grass 75 miles wide, and which is covered with hard crust of Saleratus, which a shower of ten min[u]tes duration will render it impassable, though it never rains.

[1075]Foreman...*Marcy*...p 111 from a reminiscent interview with son Samuel Houston Mayes, who was not on the 1850 trip.

Whoever gave the company this information about the Hastings
Cutoff made two errors. First, the 1849 Evans/Cherokee wagon
company from Arkansas and Cherokee Nation had traveled this route.
Captain Oliver, ahead on the Hastings in 1850, had Evans' 1849
journal of the traverse. Second, in 1849 it did rain. That rain
was ruinous to the Evans/Cherokee wagons, left with possessions in
the desert twenty-one miles east of Donner Spring.[1076]

Other emigrant companies preceded Taylor's 1850 company.
Reported to be approximately 300 people, one was guided by
Auguste Archambault, who had been with Stansbury in the just-
completed survey around the Salt Lake.[1077] William P. Bennett, an
emigrant with this mixed packer and wagon party wrote "We left
Salt Lake [July 22]."[1078] John Wolfe, captain of the Cherokee
packing company, reportedly wrote a letter from Salt Lake to the
Cherokee Advocate dated July 22.[1079] It is possible his entire pack
company was included in the group of 300 traversing the Hastings.
Grant Foreman mistakenly put both Wolfe and Taylor in the same
company, probably because they both left the Verdigris River
rendezvous in the same company. According to Foreman, "Wolf's
company left Salt Lake City August 2."[1080] Captain Taylor wrote a
letter to the Cherokee Advocate: "we left the Salt Lake the 2nd of
August."[1081] Taylor's wagon company, last in line in 1850, became a

---

[1076]See Vol I, Chapter 8 "Great Salt Lake to California."

[1077]"Thursday, June 27.--The survey of the lake was finished yesterday...camp
was broken up....discharged...the hands...no longer required." Stansbury...
Salt Lake...p 211 and "Thursday, July 16.--To-day we took a final leave of
this singular lake." Ibid. p 212.

[1078]Charles Kelly, "Gold Seekers on the Hastings Cutoff" William P. Bennett
Diary Utah Historical Quarterly vol 20, (1952) p 16.

[1079]Letter not found in the newspaper issues; only "We received a small
publication per last mail, from the Great Salt Lake City, California, containing a list of names of Emigrants, that had passed there on the 22d of July
last--and among others, were many of the names of our friends who left here
last spring. They probably sent us a copy for the purpose of letting us know
their whereabouts." Editor Carter didn't list the names. Cherokee Advocate 22
October 1850 p 2 Editor's column. Quesenbury and Mitchell left Salt Lake on
July 14; Holmes, Oliver and Taylor, with Brown as diarist, arrived July 31.
Therefore, this list probably contains the names of members of the Edmonson
and/or Wolfe companies, who would have arrived between the Quesenbury/
Mitchell, and Taylor companies.

[1080]Foreman...Marcy...p 106.

[1081]Cherokee Advocate 3 December 1850 p 2, col 1-2 "From California dated
Sacramento City, Cal. 27th Sept. 1850."

pack company only after crossing the Green River. Wolfe's company had packed from Pueblo, Colorado, and was far ahead.

Another 1850 emigrant, Robert Chalmers, already on the Hastings Cutoff, at Donner Spring noted the arrival of a company, probably that guided by Archambault: "July 28...The guide arrived with...two or three hundred....They had lost some... animals."[1082]

News of this large company ahead was surely available to the Taylor, Oliver, and Holmes companies. It was enough to instill confidence that they could make the desert crossing safely. In the diary margin Brown noted the company's decision: "From this place we took the cuttoff Rout." Captain Taylor moved west from Salt Lake City on the Hastings Cutoff one day, then rested. Brown:

> **"Aug 1st...13 miles** Traveled 13 miles to the first water which is a large spring of water, which tastes a little salty, but is very good. plenty good grass, no timber. **Camp 76--."**
> [east of Black Rock,[1083] Salt Lake Co., Utah]

"[August] 2   Lay Bye."

Diarist Brown made his first mention of the Holmes and Oliver ox trains, last seen at the Green River on July 22. Brown:

> **"[August]   3...27 miles** Traveled by the edge of the Lake. passed many salt Springs at noon, 12 miles. we passed a mill[1084] belonging to the Mormons. at 3 oclock A.M.[1085] we came to good water & grass where we camped   Olivers & Homes, ox Trains camped near Made today 27 miles **Camp 77--."**
> [Twenty Wells, Grantsville, Tooele Co.,[1086] Utah]

Brown's margin note called it: "Willow Spring." The first Hastings Cutoff death occurred here. Whether they stopped for a funeral or because it was Sunday is unknown. Brown:

> **"[August]   4** This morning a man died in Capt Olivers Train (Palmer)[1087] We **lay Bye** today."

[1082]Kelly..."Gold Seekers" Robert Chalmers diary...pp 48-49.
[1083]Brown did not mention the Black Rock; neither did 1849 diarist Crawford.
[1084]Mormon literature dates a gristmill from 1854 built for Ezra Taft Benson, later the property of Brigham Young. No mention was found of an earlier mill other than the Chase Mill located further east, close to the Jordan River.
[1085]The "A.M." was left out of the 1934 publication by editor Muriel Wright.
[1086]By September, 1850 newly-arriving Mormons were "counseled" to settle in Tooele. Kate B. Carter, comp. "Journal of Mary Ann Weston Maughan" *Our Pioneer Heritage* (Daughters of Utah Pioneers - Lessons for February, 1959) p 380.
[1087]This man is identified only as "Old Palmer." Palmer also mentioned in a letter from John Nevins in Foreman...*Marcy*...p 114.

That there were many other emigrants taking this Hastings route is indicated by Brown's entry:

> "[August] 5...35 miles Traveled today 35 miles to good water and grass. found a great many emegrants here resting their horses & cattle, before entering the desert, also cutting grass to carry to feed their stock with Camp 78--."

[Hope Wells, west side of Stansbury Mountains, Tooele Co., Utah]

Brown's margin note identified the place as: "Elbow Spring."

According to Grant Foreman:

> Wolf's company..."traveled 75 or 80 miles when we had to lay by for the purposes of recruiting our stock and cutting hay to take with us" across ninety miles of Salt Desert.[1088]

Foreman evidently used Captain Taylor's letter again as the source of information about Wolfe's pack Company. Taylor wrote:

> [we] traveled 75 or 80 miles, when we had to lay by for the purpose of recuiting our stock, and cutting hay to take with us across a desert of ninety miles.

Cholera struck a well-known Cherokee. Return Jonathan Meigs began his journey with the Cane Hill Company after crossing the Verdigris River. He moved to McNair's Cherokee company for a few days. Before reaching the Santa Fe Road he broke off to go with Wolfe's wagons. At Pueblo, when Wolfe's company changed to pack, Meigs kept his wagon rejoining McNair/Taylor from Pueblo to the Green River. There Taylor/McNair's company converted to pack, but Meigs kept his wagon, joining either the Holmes or Oliver ox trains to Salt Lake and out over the Hastings Cutoff. Brown:

> "Aug 6 Lay Bye. Resting stock   today about 2 oclock Mr. R.J. Meigs[1089] was taken sick with the colera, and about 9 oclock same evening he died--."
>   [Hope Wells, Tooele Co., Utah]

[1088]Foreman...Marcy...p 106.

[1089]Well known Cherokee agent from 1801 until his death in 1823 in Tennessee, Revolutionary War Col. Return Jonathan Meigs's son Timothy had a son Return Jonathan Meigs. Marrying Jennie Ross, daughter of long-time Principal Chief John Ross in Tennessee, Meigs went to Indian Territory with the Ross family during Cherokee Removal in 1838-39. When his home in Park Hill, Indian Territory was attacked in 1845, he and his family escaped, but the home was badly burned and plundered. In 1849 Meigs' ad in the Cherokee Advocate indicated he intended going to California via the Isthmus of Panama. He went in 1850. During the time when members of the Cane Hill California company were waiting for Meigs to catch up to them, Quesenbury and Mitchell both recorded several comments about the "venerable" Meigs, indicating a rather strong dislike of either the man himself; or having to wait so long for him.

Captain Taylor's letter home confirmed Meigs' death.[1090] On an opposite page Brown noted there was a doctor among some new arrivals, and a new total number in the company. Before the companies traveled again, there were more cholera deaths, and Brown began recording the company members who died along the way.

> **"Aug.6.**-Dr. Barker of Missouri with eight men Joined our company which now consists of 53 persons-
>   Dr. Barker attended Messrs. Meigs Russell and Tuff during their sickness."

> "Deaths   Charles McDaniel July 25
>   R.J. Meigs, August 6
>   Runaway Tuff & Russell, Aug 7
>   Henry Street & Davis, Aug 17
>   G.M. Martin Aug 17
>   Tolbert Bean Sept 6th."

> **"[August] 7 Lay Bye**   this morning we Buried Meigs, Runaway Tuff & Russell,[1091] the two last having died this morning. we moved two miles back among the hills. and Lay Bye, Meigses waggon & other effects were taken charge of by Mr. John Clark,[1092] which was the request of the (Deceased)   **Camp 79.**"
>   [two miles east of Hope Wells, Tooele Co., Utah]

Captain Taylor wrote:

> Russell and Tuff[1093] from Honey Creek were attacked the same night [as Meigs]; the former died during the night and the latter about day-light the next morning. We buried them the next morning and started on our journey about two o'clock P.M.

The fear of even more death triggered their resolve to secure the services of Dr. Barker. Cholera was with them, and they considered it essential to keep a doctor with them. <u>Brown</u>:

> **"Aug 8...15 miles**   the company started this morning. we cut grass and filled our canteens with good water, which is said to be all the good water we would get until we crossed the Desert. We traveled untill Noon 15 miles when we came to Sulphur Spring,[1094] where we stoped   we

---

[1090]*Cherokee Advocate* 3 December 1850. Taylor's letter was dated September 27 after arrival in California. The editor noted the death of "our neighbor and much respected citizen...Meigs."

[1091]These are the only mentions of these two in either the Quesenbury or Brown diaries. Fifteen slaves had begun the journey in the combined companies. Perhaps Runaway Tuff got his name because of participation in the 1842 Slave Uprising in the Cherokee Nation.

[1092]A John Clark was married to Mary Ann Nave, a cousin of Meigs' wife Jennie.

[1093]Foreman...*Marcy*...pp 106-07 called this man "Huss."

[1094]Located on the east side of Hastings Pass, it was also called Redlum Spring.

found no grass   here Jack Hilldebrand[1095]was taken very sick with the
cholera. The company were detained waiting on him, and in consequence
of the Sickness pervading in the company & apprehending more the Company
deemed it proper to engage the Medical services of Dr. Barker though it
was therefore agreed & stipulated that each member of the Company should
pay the said Doct. on their arrival in the diggins or as soon after as
possible the Sum of Five Dollars & he the said Doct. is to attend to
all cases of sickness that may occur in the Company   **Camp 80--.**"
[Dell Spring, east slope of Cedar Mountains, Tooele Co., Utah]

Captain Taylor's letter:

> Jack Hildebrand was attacked; we stopped for the night and the next
> morning put him in a wagon and pushed on as we could not stop no longer
> without wood or water. Hildebrand soon recovered.

The *Cherokee Advocate* editor wrote "Those who went the Evans
[route], arrived in [California]" during the first or second week
in August.[1096] "Those" were no doubt packers, possibly from the
Edmonson company. Taylor's company was struggling in the desert.

Another set of notes in Brown's diary outlines what they
anticipated in crossing the desert, how they planned to accomplish
it, and what might be the outcome. Brown:

> Aug. ~~Aug. 8 at this place we enter the desert~~ it is 70 miles across it
> [the Salt Desert] without Grass or water and persons crossing it will
> have to travel day and night to get across. Many persons have perished
> with their animals while crossing. perhaps we may find water sooner than
> we expect, as we have had several showers of rain for the last two or
> three days.

The Taylor pack company, having engaged the doctor, then made
arrangements to transport their sick, which allowed them to
continue traveling. Brown:

> **"Aug 9...40 miles.** This morning Hildebrand was better though
> unable to travel on horseback. we therefore made arrangements with J.M.
> Estell[1097] to haul him to California   also to haul B.F. Trott [1098](who

---

[1095]Jack Hildebrand's sister, Barbara Hildebrand Longknife, was pregnant and
traveling with her husband William Longknife. Jack Hildebrand was noted in the
Quesenbury diary as trading with the Indians near Fort Mann on the Arkansas
River with some others and "did well." Hildebrand died in California in 1852.

[1096]*Cherokee Advocate* 5 November 1850. Quesenbury and Mitchell arrived in
California on August 21.

[1097]James M. Estill leased the "United States Farm" at Fort Leavenworth for
three years beginning October 11, 1842, agreeing to supply 12,000 bushels of
corn and 8,000 bushels of oats; he was to receive $3.50 for every ton of hay.
A supplementary contract in January 1843 gave him privilege of crossing the
Missouri River on ferries with his wagons, teams, etc. at half the normal
rate. Barry...*West*... p 461. On August 20, 1847 Estill of Weston, Mo.
contracted to deliver fresh beef at Fort Laramie on September 1. Barry...
West...p 710. Missouri papers' 1850 advertisements indicated there were agents
to take letters for the emigrants (50 cents each-prepaid) at 18 towns from St.

was also sick) across the Desert. at this place the Desert commences
it is 85 miles from this S----[ulphur]Spring to where good water and
grass is to be found. after making Suitable arrangements for the Sick
of our Co--at four oclock A.M.[1099] we started   the Road passed over
hills & through winding hollows [Hastings Pass] for a few miles when it
entered the Desert   we traveled at the rate of four miles an hour.
Good Road firm and hard. at two oclock in the morning we stopped to
rest, & fed to the horses the grass which we had cut and packed since
the morning of the 8th   Slept, having made 40 miles. **Camp 81."**
     [about eight miles north of Knolls, Tooele Co., Utah]

In May 1850, James M. Estell and James W. Denver began
operations on their "Express Mail Line for the California
Emigration." They purchased three spring carriages and twenty-four
horses to go to Pacific Spring near South Pass. One carriage would
go through to California; the other two would bring mail back to
the States. Each of the wagons carried twenty-four mailbags, each
stamped with a letter of the alphabet. An express went in advance
of the carriages handing out printed alphabetical lists of the
letters as it passed the emigrants.

On July 10, Estill wrote to Brigham Young from Pacific Spring
notifying him of his coming to Salt Lake. On July 27 Estill was in
Salt Lake laying a proposal before Brigham Young for a stock
investment company for mail and passengers between Independence
and San Francisco.[1100] On August 9, proceeding from Salt Lake to

---

Louis to St. Joseph, Missouri; with stops at Fort Kearney and Fort Laramie. On
May 20, partner James W. Denver left Fort Leavenworth; meeting Estill west of
Big Blue four days later. Denver went ahead May 28, arriving the next day at
Fort Kearney; Fort Laramie June 8; reaching Pacific Springs June 20.
"California Express mail stops to take letters back to the States for the
emigrants" was noted near Pacific Springs on June 21 by diarist Ingalls...
Journal......1850-51 p 42. At Pacific Springs the partners headquartered until
mid-July. Mark Evans of the Arkansas Rector/Leeper party mailed a letter June
26 from Pacific Springs.(Estill postoffice?). On July 14 the westbound Denver
party left for California, catching up with Estill the next day. July 14
Estill's men left Pacific Springs for the east. August 15 they arrived at
Weston, Mo. with a reported 4,000 letters. Barry...*West*...pp 937-39. Estill
travels in proximity to the Cherokee company, mentioned by diarist Brown at
the head of Carson Canyon on September 18, when Estill is hauling Oliver
Hazard Perry Brewer, another of the company. The Cherokee company arrived at
"Ringgold & Weavervill" on September 24. James Estill wrote again to Brigham
Young from Mormon Tavern, California October 2.
[1098]Benjamin F. Trott was orphaned by the 1830s death of his mother Sallie
Adair, sister to George Washington Adair, member of Captain Taylor's company.
Ben's uncle Samuel Mayes was also on the trip. Ben, 21, was enumerated in El
Dorado County (California) with two Adairs, three Mayes, a Goss, and a Candy.
[1099]Muriel Wright added [P.M.] in the 1934 editing. Brown noted a rate of four
miles an hour; total mileage 40; stopping at two the next morning.
[1100]Barry..*West*...pp 936-37.

California, Estill met and contracted with Captain Taylor's Cherokee emigrants on the Hastings Cutoff.

Leaving camp in the middle of the desert, Captain Taylor's company endured one of their longest marches, to Donner Spring. After 20 miles they met the first of the enterprising water "agents." Brown:

> **"Aug 10...45 miles.** Started by sun rise having stopped about 3 hours to rest. We found (by daylight) the Desert to be covered with a hard crust resembling Salaratus, no grass or groath of any kind except wild sage now and then   we Traveled Steadily. within 25 miles of the spring we came to where some Emegrants had waggons loaded with water which they had brought from the spring to sell to folks, as they came up they sold it for one dollar per gallon   at four oclock this evening we reached the Springs having Traveled 45 miles since morning without stopping & without water for our horses. Good water & Grass. **Camp 82...** this evening a young man of Dr. Barkers mess died of the Diarear."
> [Donner Spring, Box Elder Co., Utah]

On July 29, an emigrant had written from nearby Pilot Peak: "no doubt a great many would not have got through, had it not been for the active part of those who got across early and hauled water back for those behind."[1101]

Captain Taylor's letter: "we traveled day and night till we got through the desert." In the margin, Brown wrote: "A great many Dead horses, Cattle & dogs which died for want of water. These springs are called Relief Springs."[1102] Here three more of the company breathed their last. The deceased were noted by Brown:

> **"Aug 11** today we **lay Bye** resting our horses. this morning G.M. Martin was taken very sick. about 12 oclock two men belonging to Capt Olivers train Died within a few minutes of each other and were both buried in one Grave   today about 2 oclock G.M. Martin[1103] died. After burying him the Co--removed up on to one of the Kanyons of the mountain about 3 miles distance. Good water & Grass. **Camp 83-- .**"
> [east slope of Pilot Peak, west of Donner Spring, near the Utah/Nevada border]

Brown named the Oliver company men who died at Donner Spring

[1101]Kelly..."Gold Seekers" John B. McGee diary...pp 16-17.

[1102]T. H. Jefferson's "Relief Springs" are further west, in Nevada.

[1103]Gabriel Martin was a brother of Susannah Martin, wife of Clement Vann McNair, first captain of the entire Cherokee/Cane Hill company. Gabriel's brother, Brice Martin, in the 1849 Jeter Lynch Thompson party, perished of cholera on the California Trail near North Platte, Nebraska. In the original editing of the Brown diary Wright identified Dennis W. Bushyhead with this 1850 group. However, Dennis made the trip in 1849 in Thompson's group. The 1850 Bushyhead is Edward (Ned) or Daniel, perhaps both.

and were buried in one grave: "Davis a white man & Henry Street a Seneca."[1104] Captain Taylor's letter gave more information:

> C.V. McNair, Gabriel Martin and a black man belonging to Peter May were also attacked. Martin lived but a short time; the other two recovered.

The *Cherokee Advocate* reported that Peter May died "on his way to California, near the Salt Lake." But Captain Taylor's letter printed two weeks earlier mentioned only that a black of Peter May's was ill. Later in the trip, both Peter and John May were reported to be "very sick...left behind...and...may have died."[1105]

Company members continued to get sick. Apparently Estill transported Ben Trott in his express carriage for three days, leaving him with the Taylor company at Pilot Peak. Brown:

> **"Aug 12**...B.F. Trott came to us last evening quite unwell   today we **lay Bye**, waiting on C.V. McNair, B.F. Trott & others who were too unwell to travel--."
> [East slope of Pilot Peak, near the Utah/Nevada border]

Some action was necessary for the good of the majority. More members of the company might die. The decision was to split the company. Those too ill to travel were left in the care of Dr. Barker; the rest traveled on.

The distance between Camp 83 and Camp 84, one day's pack travel in 1850, took the Evans/Cherokee forty-niners two days to travel with wagons. Brown:

> **"Aug 13**...**35 miles**. This morning several of our men being to weak to travel Dr. Barker and part of the Co--remained with them. and myself and the rest of the Co--traveled on about ten miles to a Spring[1106] of Good water. at this place another Desert commences, which we had to travel over During the night   we remained at this place untill late in the evening when we started and traveled on about 25 miles when we came to water where we stopped untill morning. No Grass   **Camp 84."**
> [Big Springs, south of Oasis, Elko Co., Nevada]

During the day, the Company had crossed Pilot Creek Valley, Silver Zone Pass, and the Goshute Valley.

Traveling south, the Taylor Company found a good place to rest, staying for an additional day.

[1104]This is the only diary mention of either Davis or Street.
[1105]*Cherokee Advocate* 17 December 1850.
[1106]Unnamed spring South of Pilot Peak (Roy Tea map).

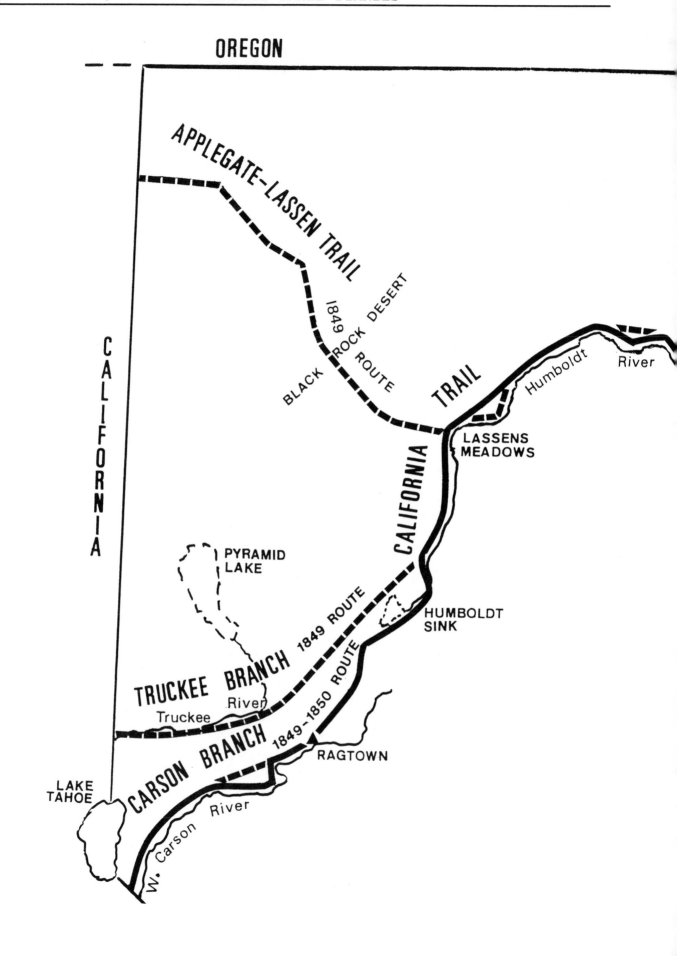

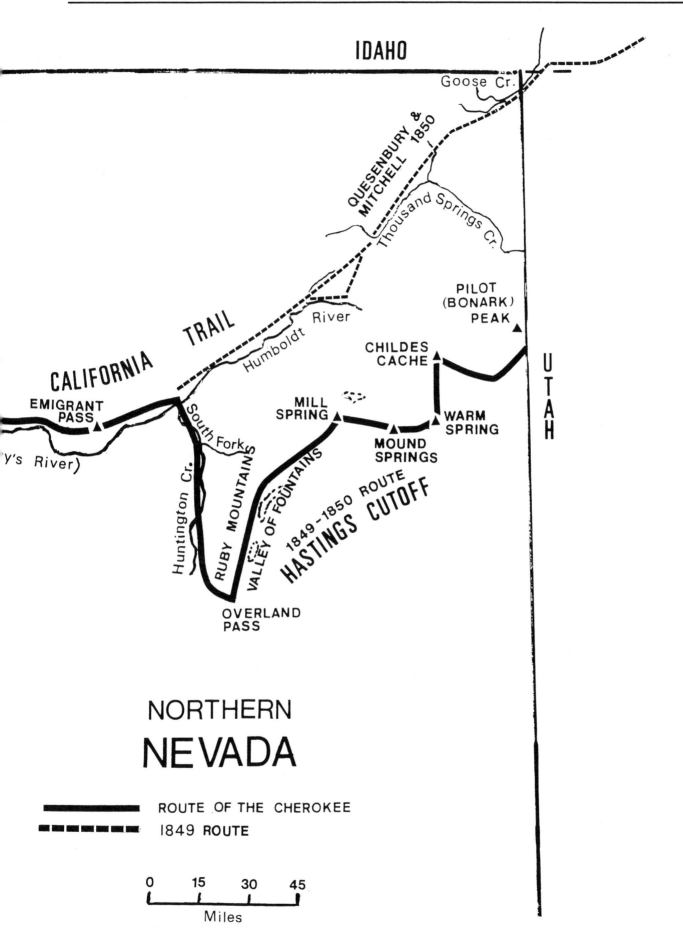

IDAHO

Goose Cr.

QUESENBURY & MITCHELL 1850

Thousand Springs Cr.

PILOT (BONARK) PEAK ▲

CHILDES CACHE ▲

CALIFORNIA   TRAIL

Humboldt   River

UTAH

EMIGRANT PASS ▲

y's River)

South Forks

Huntington Cr.

Ruby Mountains

MILL SPRING ▲

VALLEY OF FOUNTAINS

MOUND SPRINGS ▲

WARM SPRING ▲

1849–1850 ROUTE
HASTINGS CUTOFF

OVERLAND PASS

NORTHERN
NEVADA

━━━━━━━━ ROUTE OF THE CHEROKEE

▰▰▰▰▰▰▰▰ 1849 ROUTE

0   15   30   45
Miles

Brown:

"Aug 14...15 miles Early start this morning   Traveled about 15 miles and campe[d] on the side of the mountains   Good water, very good Grass. **Camp 85--.**"
[Flowery Lake Springs, Elko Co., Nevada]

"[August] 15   Lay Bye all day."
After one day of rest the company moved again. Turning west they crossed the Pequop Mountains and Independence Valley, Spruce Mountain Ridge, and Clover Valley to their next camp. Brown:

"[August] 16...38 miles.   Started this morning and Traveled down the valley.at noon we came to tolerable good water & grass 18 miles.[1107] we stopped two hours & then Traveled due west. after traveling about 20 miles we came to wells of water which had been dug in a wet marshy Spot of ground. Bunch Grass. 38 miles since morning   **Camp 86--.**"
[Warm Spring; Jefferson's Mill Spring; SW of Snow Water Lake, north of the jct. of U.S. 93/Nevada 229, Elko Co., Nevada]

Turning southwest the company entered Ruby Valley, camping at the foot of the Ruby Mountains. Brown:

"[August] 17...20 miles Early start. Traveled twenty miles due west   Camped on a large Spring of Good water at the foot of the Mountain. Good Grass on the Branch **Camp 87--** Since Leaving the Elbow Spring the country is a perfect Desert. Except the places where we camped where we found water & grass."
[Sulphur Springs, east side of Ruby Mountains, north end of Ruby Valley, Elko Co., Nevada]

They continued south along the Ruby Mountains. Brown:

"Aug 18...20 miles This morning our course was South for a few miles Then due west. at 2 oclock we came to good water and grass at the foot of the Mountains 20 miles. we stoped at this place for the night **Camp 88--.**"
[near Harrison Pass Road and Nevada 229 jct., Elko Co., Nevada]

The company traveled south through today's Ruby Lake National Wildlife Refuge to Overland Pass, and crossed it, camping on the west side of the Ruby Mountains in Huntington Valley. Brown:

"19 [August]...25 miles after Traveling about two miles we passed a great many springs of hot water. We traveled along the foot of the mountains the sides of which were covered with green grass & the top with snow. Crossed many Branches of good, cold water continually & the valey covered with green grass, which to us is quite a "God-Send." Camped on a bold Running Branch. Large Cottonwood trees. Made today 25 miles. **Camp 89--.**"
[west side of Overland Pass at Huntington Creek, White Pine Co., Nevada]

[1107]Mound Springs. Brown wrote in the margin: "branch running east"

Evidently there were some who were discontented with the pace, as evidenced by the several changes in the composition of companies which took place the next day. Brown:

> **"[August] 20...25 miles** This morning a Seperation took place in the company C.V. McNairs, May's & Martins'[1108] messes accompanied by Dr. Barker & his men seperated themselves from Capt Taylors Co-- Capt Taylors Co--was joined by Dr Palmer & Eleven men, 33 persons altogather we continued down the valley 25 miles. Many springs of good water and plenty good grass. **Camp 90--."**
> [west side of the Ruby Mountains, South of Jiggs,
> Elko Co., Nevada]

From the entry it seems likely that those who had been sick and placed in the care of Dr. Barker, plus Dr. Barker's mess, separated from Captain Taylor's group. This separation of the Cherokee company was apparently not along extended family lines.[1109] Dr. Barker had been given a contract with the entire company to take care of the sick until they reached California.

At this point, Brown did not say which company he was going to be traveling with. The next day Brown recapped the distance traveled from home. He mentioned Captain Oliver for the first time since August 11 at Donner Springs. The ox trains of Oliver and Holmes could not possibly have kept up the pace of these packers, but probably caught up because the packers had three "lay bye" days due to illness.

[1108]Gabriel Martin died August 11 at Donner Spring; his mess traveled on.
[1109]Clem Vann McNair married Gabriel Martin's sister Susannah. Another of Gabriel's sisters, Martha Martin, married George Washington Adair, who, with his son William Penn Adair was part of this group. George Washington Adair's sister Nannie married Samuel Houston Mayes Sr., who with sons George Washington Mayes [Sr.] and John Thompson Mayes was also with this group. Another sister of G.W. Adair was Sallie, son Benjamin Walter Trott was along; another of G.W. Adair's sisters, Mary, whose son Benjamin Franklin Goss was on this trip. G. W. Adair's first cousin Devereaux Jarrette Bell and wife Juliette Lewis Vann Bell were in this group, and George Washington Candy, who married D. J. Bell's sister Elizabeth. (Another of D.J.'s sisters, Sarah Caroline Bell was married to Stand Watie.) A first cousin of Gabriel Martin was Richard Fields, who married Rachel Elizabeth Goss, sister of Benjamin Franklin Goss, above. Tolbert and William Bean's mother Elizabeth was a sister of Clement Vann McNair. Oliver Hazard Perry Brewer, brother-in-law of Clement Vann McNair, and his "Brewer boys" John, Thomas, and Oliver were members. At least one Bushyhead started out with the Mayes party. Charlotte Bushyhead married George Washington Mayes Sr [above]. Her brothers, Daniel Colston Bushyhead and Edward Wilkerson Bushyhead may have both signed the agreement to Pack from Pueblo. George Nave was a nephew of Cherokee Chief John Ross; R. J. Meigs, who died at Hope Wells, was a son-in-law of Chief Ross; and John Clark was a nephew of Ross' by marriage.

Brown:

1,662 miles from this place to Grand River Cherokee Nation--Lay by today 21st of August[1110]   the Company being scarce of provisions, purchased 342 lbs of beef for which they had to pay 20 cts pr pound. Capt Oliver Camped near waiting on Arch Henry[1111] who is very unwell--

The next day Brown with Captain Taylor, starting again, encountered their first Indians. In 1849, the Evans/Cherokee Company was visited by Indians near Donner Spring on the Hastings Cutoff. Diarist Crawford identified them as Shoshone. As the wagon company progressed, the Shoshone had become more numerous, less friendly and more persistent in their contacts. Captain Taylor's 1850 company, on the west side of the Ruby Mountains came upon emigrants distressed by Indian encounters. Taylor and some Cherokee volunteered to help the emigrants. Brown:

"Aug 22   proceeded on & came to a creek about noon where there was some white Emigrants who had lost their horses the night before stolen by Indians. tho [the]...Company being informed of the fact six of our Company volunteered to go with the whites in pursuit of the Indians--The Company consisted of nineteen persons   the command was given to our Captain--, the ballance of our Company proceeded...& continued down this creek Northwest...**Camp 91**   to a fork of M[ary']s R[iver]."[1112]
               [Camp 91 was near Jiggs, Elko Co., Nevada]

Captain Taylor and his volunteers pursued the Indians. A battle ensued with no injuries to the volunteers. Meanwhile, the rest of the Company traveled down the valley. Brown:

"the volunteer Company to which I then belonged-took to the Mountains & after going some Eight miles found the Indians Encampment   we succeeded in driving off five horses--the Indians numbered about one hundred--but our Company Escaped unhurt--not withstanding the...Indians fired at us several times & shot at us with arrows as we made off with the horses   [August 23] the Company came on 11 miles & encamped on the same Creek   those of us that pursued the Indians overtook the Main Company today at noon & the whole Co. came on to this place 25 miles today on the same Creek--passed by dead body lying by the road side Emeg's killed by the Indians **Camp 92**--."
                [Huntington Creek, Elko Co., Nevada]

[1110]On August 21, 1850, diarists William Quesenbury and James Mitchell of the original Cane Hill California Company, with Strickler, were in California.
[1111]Archibald Henry is noted in Starr...*Cherokee*...p 320 as the first husband of Nancy Ann Rogers (Blythe). In *Cherokee Advocate* 20 January 1852 she was noted in Angel's Camp, California: "William E. Bean married Mrs. Henry, dau of Wm. Blythe...of the Neutral Land. Both of the Cherokee Nation." How and when Nancy got to California is uncertain, but she was a cousin of the Bushyhead travelers of this 1850 company.
[1112]Mary's River was often used to mean Humboldt River.

Brown noted in the margin: "30 miles." The foray to recover horses stolen by Indians lasted overnight, from noon of August 22 to noon on August 23. There is no separate entry dated August 23.

After the volunteers rejoined the rest of the company, they traveled to, and through, the narrow and deep canyon of the South Fork of the Humboldt River. Brown:

> "**Aug 24...35 miles...**Continued down the same creek   at noon we came to a large stream of water [South Fork of Humboldt River]. Good grass   this stream is a tributary of St. Marys River. we traveled down this stream to St. Marys River down which the Road from Ft Hall passes. The last ten miles of our road passes through a narrow pass high bluffs on each side of the way very Rough & rugged   35 miles since morning **Camp 93--.**"[1113]
>   [Junction of the California Trail and Hastings Cutoff, approximately eight miles SW of Elko, Elko Co., Nevada]

In 1849, diarist Crawford had recorded the difficult passage down the South Fork, sometimes in the river bed itself:

> [September 12, 1849] in this distance [about eight miles] we had to travil in the bed of the creek at least one fourth of the time; thier not being room for a road on neither side: The Bluffs in places being, perhaps 500 feet hig[h].

The 1849 Evans/Cherokee wagon company had spent twenty-six days, (August 17 to September 12) traveling the Hastings Cutoff from Salt Lake to the intersection of "the Main road." No deaths occurred. It took the 1850 packer and wagon companies twenty-three days (August 1 to August 24) to cover the same distance over the same route, with the incidence of eight deaths.

The 1850 packer and wagon companies turned west onto the main California Trail. Along the Humboldt River, they joined the flood of emigrants. Brown:

> "**[August] 25...20 miles** Traveled down the Valley of St. Marys R--This R. is about 30 yrds wide. No timber except willow, bold rugged & steep hills   grass scarce on account of the Great emegration which has passed on ahead of us   Camped on the River   Made 20 miles today **Camp 94--.**"
> [west of present Carlin, near the Eureka/Elko Cos. line, Nevada]

> "**[August] 26...25 miles** Continued down the River 25 miles. **Camp 95--.**"
>   [near Dunphy, Eureka Co., Nevada]

[1113]Brown's margin note:"continued down the fork of M's R."

The company supplies were dwindling fast. Brown:

> "[August] 27   Made **30 miles** today   Camped on the River
> Nothing but dry beef & coffee in camp **Camp 96--.**"
>   [east of Valmy near the Humboldt/Lander Cos. line, Nevada]

> "[August] 28   Camped on the River   Made **25 miles** today
> **Camp 97--.**"
>   [near Red House, Humboldt Co., Nevada]

The days were much the same as the company traveled along the Humboldt River. The entries were short: Date, Mileage, and Camp Number. Brown:

> "[August] 29   Camped on the River. Made today **25 miles**.
> **Camp 98--.**"
>   [near Bliss, Humboldt Co., Nevada]

> "[August] 30th...**20 miles** Lay Bye part of the day. Started at
> 11 oclock and made 20 miles. passed a dead Indian this evening killed,
> as we heard, by some emegrant while attempting to steal horses. Camped
> on the River. **Camp 99--.**"
>   [Winnemucca, Humboldt Co., Nevada]

> "[August] 31st   traveled **25 miles** & camp on the River. **Camp
> 100^d--.**"
>   [near Pershing/Humboldt Cos. line, Nevada]

> "Sept. 1st Traveled **6 miles**. Camped on the River. **Camp 101.**"
>   [near Cosgrave, Pershing Co., Nevada]

In 1849, diarist Crawford recorded in this same area: "crossing some verry Sandy Points which Put into the river. This part of the river is Poor and without grass."

During the next day, Brown's Cherokee company passed the turnoff to Oregon--the Applegate/Lassen Trail. Brown:

> "[September] 2   Traveled **30 miles** today   Camped on the River.
> **Camp 102--.**"
>   [in the vicinity of Lassen Meadows--present Rye Patch
>   Reservoir-- Pershing Co., Nevada]

In 1849, many diarists wrote of their approach to this "cutoff" debating and deciding whether to take it days ahead of actually getting to it. The 1849 Evans/Cherokee wagon party passed it on September 23, Crawford noting: "passing the Oregon road to day, which road Crosses the Siera Mountain to the North of our rout." It seems odd that this Oregon--Applegate/Lassen cutoff merited not even a mention in 1850 from either Quesenbury, ahead, or Brown.

In the margin, Brown wrote simply: "No Bread." <u>Brown</u>:

   "[September] 3   Traveled **30 miles** today Camped on the River.
   Camp 102..."
              [near present Oreana, Pershing Co., Nevada]
The monotony of the long days of the river traverse shows clearly
in most of Brown's entries along the Humboldt. The numbering of
this second "camp 102" is obviously an error on his part. A check
of the original diary confirmed he had written it twice. <u>Brown</u>:

   "[September] 4th   Traveled **20 miles** ~~to the Sink of the
   River~~ camped at a well. **Campe 103--."**
          [near present Lovelock, Pershing Co., Nevada]
    Shortly after leaving this camp, emigrants chose either the
Truckee route or the Carson route to cross the Sierra Nevada.
Captain Taylor's company, with no comment from Brown, chose to
take the Carson Route. Though provisions were critically short
most of the next day was spent cutting grass to sustain the stock.
Traveling at night, they arrived at the Humboldt Sink. <u>Brown</u>:

   "[September] 5...25 **miles** This morning we lay Bye grazing our
   horses as it is said to be 75 miles to the next grass. We have had no
   bread since Aug 28th. hardly any meat   provisions scarce among the
   Emegrants. No flour to be had for love or money   we cut grass &
   packed it on our horses to feed to them on the Desert   at four oclock
   this Evening we started. Continued down the waters of Marys River which
   at this place spreads out and resembles a large mill pond. we crossed
   the River and traveled untill midnight when we stopped untill morning
   where we fed the grass to our horses which we had been packing for them.
   25 miles--**Camp 104--."**
     [Humboldt Sink, east of Ocala, Churchill Co., Nevada]
In both 1849 and 1850, the route from Lovelock lay to the
southeast, following the south side of the Humboldt River, along
the West Humboldt Range to the ill-defined Humboldt Sink. There
the emigrants camped.
    Anguish and physical suffering plagued the emigrants, white
and Cherokee alike. Another company death was recorded before
reaching the Carson River. <u>Brown</u>:

   "[September] 6 Early start this morning   we found at daylight
   that we were near the last waters of the River fairly out on the Desert
   which is sandy plain for which reason traveling over it is very slow.
   We suffered more crossing this Desert, than we had since leaving home,
   and we saw more property destroyed on this plain, Waggons, horses,
   mules, and cattle, than we had yet seen in crossing over the same number

of miles   about noon we passed C.V. McNair and Co.[1114] Talbert
Bean[1115] was taken very sick early this morning and died this evening.
Men dying almost every hour of the cholera   about four oclock we
reached Carsons Creek, where we found a great many traders from
Sacramento City, with Flour Bacon &c &c to sell to emegrants   Great
many folks here. great many dying. **Camp 105--.**"
 ["Ragtown" eight miles west of Fallon, Churchill Co., Nevada]

Captain Taylor's letter confirmed their plight:

We...got along without sickness till we reached the sink of St. Mary's
River, where we had another desert of 43 miles to cross. In crossing the
desert, Talbot Bean was taken, and died the same day; and his remains
now lie on the desert. Nearly all of us took the diarrhoea; after
getting across the desert, we rested here, (Carson's river, 250 miles
from this city,) [1116] eight days

Though Taylor's letter indicated they rested eight days on Carson
River, some of the company, including diarist Brown, continued to
move, albeit slower. Brown:

 "Sept 7...12 miles today traveled up Carsons creek 12 miles and
camped. T.F. Taylor[1117] drunk and not come to camp **Camp 106-.**"
     [Lahontan Dam, near Lyon/Churchill Cos. line, Nevada]

Captain Taylor's reported "drunk" could perhaps be laid to his
relief at getting through in spite of illness and death that had
plagued them since their departure from Salt Lake. Brown:

 "[September] 8 Today Traveled **5** miles and camped on the creek
waiting for Taylor & others, who have not come in yet. **Camp 107--.**"
         [approximately three miles east of Silver Springs,
                    Lyon Co., Nevada]

Brown did not name the "& others" they were expecting in camp with
Captain Taylor. In the margin Brown described Carson River:

Carsons Creek is about 15 or 20 yds wide with good grass in the Bottoms.
Large cottonwood trees and small willow on the Banks.

Afflicted by illness, part of the Cherokee traveled on. Brown:

 "[September] 9 traveled **8 miles**, and camped on the creek
Several of our Co--sick. heard of Taylor and others being on ahead sick
Camp 108--."
 [east of Fort Churchill Historic State Park, Lyon Co., Nevada]

[1114]Brown had not seen Clement Vann McNair since August 20, date of separation
of the company on the west side of the Ruby Mountains. At that time, McNair
and several members of the company were ill and waiting until health improved
before traveling on.
[1115][Talbert] Tolbert Bean's Mother Elizabeth was a sister of Clem McNair.
[1116]"This city" is Sacramento.
[1117]Thomas Fox Taylor took over command of the entire company after the
crossing of the Cache la Poudre River in Colorado.

Bancroft and others mentioned that partaking of the waters of
the Humboldt Sink (and subsequent waters) was responsible for
sickness, emigrants carrying their water-borne illnesses all the
way to Sacramento.

The company members overtook Captain Taylor, previously
reported to be behind them. Brown:

"Sept 10 Traveled **10 miles** to where we found Taylor. our
sick all Better   Camped on the bank of the creek **Camp 109--**."
[SW side of Churchill Butte, Lyon Co., Nevada]

The next day, in this bleak environment, cholera came very
close to Brown. For the next four days the company delayed, caring
for Jonas and others. Brown:

"[September] 11...3 miles. Jonas (a black Boy)[1118] in my mess
very sick also several of the Co-- Traveled today 3 miles & camped on
the creek   **Camp 110**."
[near Table Mountain, Lyon Co., Nevada]

Again in the margin Brown recorded: "Rugged hills destitute of any
growth whatever." Brown:

"[September] 12   Lay Bye on account of Sickness. A Peak of
the Siera Nevada Mountains covered with Snow in view--."

"**[September] 13 Lay Bye**. Jonas not expected to live--."

"Sept 14...8 miles This morning about 10 oclock Jonas died & was
buried about 12 oclock   we started and traveled 8 miles up the creek.
Camp 111--."
[NE of Dayton, Lyon Co., Nevada]

Brown seems to have regarded Jonas as a regular company member
rather than a slave. The Cherokee were aware that California would
be admitted only as a free state. Their own newspaper had carried
the ongoing national debate. Crossing the border into California
with blacks would necessitate their immediate release, or a plan
for their freedom. Brown may have been more enlightened than
either his mother's cousin, Mrs. Pack, or Captain Taylor, whose

[1118]Jonas was sent with John Lowery Brown by Mrs. Elizabeth Pack, a first
cousin of Brown's mother Rachel Lowrey. Cherokees had held blacks as slaves
since the late 1700s. During the Removal of the 1830s, many slaves went west
to Indian Territory with their owners. In 1842 there was a slave revolt in the
Cherokee Nation. In 1849 and 1850 some Cherokee took slaves to California.
However, California stood fast in the resolve to be a free state. Brown, who
never mentioned any of the others of his mess, devoted four entries in as many
days to Jonas.

letter identified Jonas as property:

> all recovered, except the black Jonas, belonging to Mrs. Pack, who died.
> Only four of the company escaped sickness. We left several of the
> company behind sick, and others may have died. Peter and John May were
> both very sick.

After Jonas' burial, the company resumed travel up the Carson
River. Brown:

> **[September] 15...30 miles** Continued up the Creek 30 miles
> today   camped on a Spring branch, running from the mountains
> & emptying into the creek. **Camp 112--.**"
>   [near Stewart, Douglas/Carson City Cos. line, Nevada]

In the latter part of the next day, the Cherokee company
passed through Genoa, a trading establishment called Mormon
Station. Brown:

> **[September] 16...[20 miles]**...today we entered Carsons Valley.
> traveled along the foot of mountains on our right, the sides of which
> are covered with pine trees, & the tops spotted with snow   very many
> springs of good water running from the mountains into the creek, also
> basins of warm & hot water   the valley [is] covered with good grass.
> we camped at the foot of the mountain on a bold & swift running stream
> of water.[1119]   **Camp 113--.**"
>   [south of Genoa, Douglas Co., Nevada]

The Oliver ox train was about five days behind Brown. At "the
Foot of the Sierre Nevada Mountains," Barbara Hildebrand Longknife
delivered her first child, Mary Jane.[1120]

After camping near Genoa Brown added news of a shorter route,
which they did not take.

> At this place, & up this Stream, there is a "pack Rout"[1121] across the
> mountains which is said to be the nearest though the roughest way, than
> the waggon Road.

Brown:

> **"Sept 17th...10 miles**   continued along the foot of the
> Mountains 10 miles camped in bunch of timber to the left of the road
> **Camp 114--.**"
>   [Nevada Highway 206 near the Nevada/California
>   state line, Douglas Co., Nevada]

[1119]Daggett Creek.

[1120]Mary Jane's application for Cherokee enrollment identified her birthplace.
William and Barbara's second child, Anna, was born in 1859 in California. In
1865 Barbara took her two girls to Honolulu.

[1121]The route, south of Lake Tahoe, was used by the Pony Express in 1860.

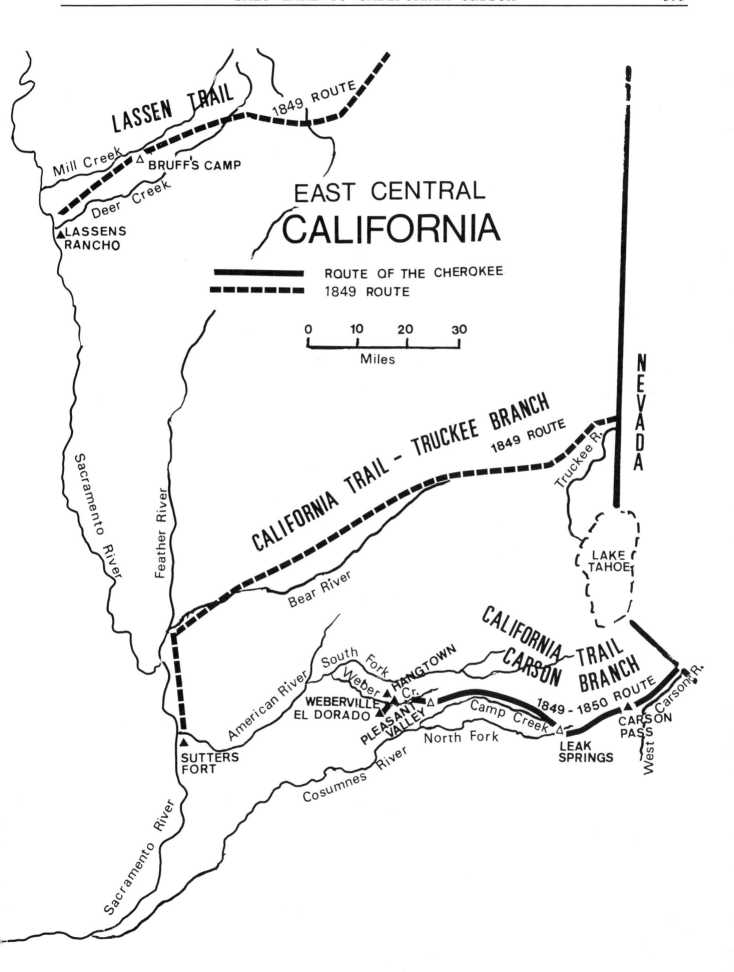

The relatively easy traverse south along the foothills of the Sierra Nevada was over. They were about to enter Carson Canyon. Brown described the day.

> **"[September] 18...15 miles.** This morning after Traveling eight miles we came to a large "Kanyon" very narrow rough, Rockey road. very rough for waggons. Steep rocky Mountains on each side. we traveled along up a clear, bold running Stream called "Kanyon creek." [west fork of Carson River] we passed through the Kanyon, seven miles and camped[1122] at the foot of the hills 1/2 mile to the right of the Road Grass very good. This evening T.F. Taylor & Mess, myself and Mess camped at this place waiting for Perry Brewer who is with J.M. Estill being too unwell to ride horseback. Estill not being expected to get through the kanyon untill tomorrow. Mays, Adair & Fields with their mess's traveled on. Made today 15 miles Large Pine trees all up this Kanyon. Snow Peaks near on ahead--...**115 Camp** the mountains are covered with large Pine trees."
> [about eight miles west of Woodfords, Alpine Co., California]

Perhaps eight persons, four to a mess, waited at the head of Carson Pass for James M. Estill to bring Oliver Hazard Perry Brewer in Estill's express carriage. Estill had been hauling the ill and infirm for this company since August 9 at Dell Spring, east of the Great Salt Desert. Brown started up and over Carson Pass, not disclosing whether they were joined by Estill, and with no mention of Brewer until September 23. Brown:

> **"[September] 19...25 miles.** after traveling Seven miles this morning we reached the Base of the mountain. we reached the Summit[1123] of the first Ridge over the worst Road that I ever traveled. Pack animals can hardly get up, much Less Loaded waggons. after reaching the Summit, we descended gradually, still over very rough road, a few miles when we reach into a valley with a Lake[1124] in it. Many streams of water running from the Snows of the mountains into the Lake. we crossed the valley which is 1/2 a mile across and then began the ascent of the last Ridge.[1125] this mountain is higher than the other, though not so steep, nor the Road so Rockey. we had to pass over Snow, near the Summit. on reaching the Summit[1126] we caught up with Mays, Adair, & others. immediately after reaching the Summit, we began to descend. we traveled a left hand Pack Rout, which here leaves the

---

[1122]"At the top of the canyon emigrants came into Hope Valley, where most camped overnight." Jeanne H. Watson, "The Carson Emigrant Road" *Overland Journal* vol 4, no 3 (Summer 1986).
[1123]Known as the "Three-Quarter Mountain" on Carson Pass. Ibid. p 7.
[1124]"Caples Lake, formerly called Twin Lakes." Ibid. p 8.
[1125]"known as 'Snow-Top Mountain'." Ibid. p 9.
[1126]"West Pass, the highest point in the United States crossed by wagons." Ibid. p 9.

waggon Road for ten miles, the Wagon Road[1127] running round fifteen miles,[1128] and very rough road. camped on the side of the Mt. a Lake below. Good grass   Made today 25 miles   **Camp 116--.**"
    [east of Plasse, Amador/El Dorado Cos. line, California]

"**[September] 20...10 miles.**   Passed down by and partley around the Lake [Silver Lake] and up a very steep hill, when we intersected the waggon road. passed on a few miles fa[r]ther an camped two miles to the left of the road,   Made today 10 miles   **Camp 117--.**"
    [SE end of Iron Mountain Ridge, near El Dorado/
        Amador Cos. line, California]

"**Sept 21st...15 miles**   this morning it began to rain, and rained all day and night. we traveled slowly. Passed the Leak Springs and came to "Camp Creek" where we camped, having made 15 miles today   **Camp 118--.**"
    [adjacent to Iron Mtn Ridge, El Dorado Co., California]

"**[September]   22...15 miles**   Cloudy & Rainy. we traveled down Camp creek half a mile, when we took to the hills again   came to the Fork of the road. Made today 15 miles   Camped 2 miles to the right of the road   **Camp 119--**"
    [SE of Pollock Pines, El Dorado Co., California]

"**[September]   23...10 miles.**   this morning we found that four of my horses & one of Brewers[1129] had been stolen during the night. My packs were carried on by Mays & Adair, and we all walked. Came to Pleasant Valley[1130]   Made today 10 miles   **Camp 120--.**"
    [Pleasant Valley, 4 miles south of Camino, about nine miles
        SE of Placerville, El Dorado Co., California]

Brown and his traveling companions, having lost all their horses, continued to walk. They arranged with the Mayes' and Adairs to take their packs. Captain Taylor wrote:

Nearly all our horses either gave out, died, or were stolen on the way. I did not get thro' with one of my own. The Brewers got through with one mule and two horses. After losing our horses, my company had to scatter, in order to get along.

Footsore and weary, they entered the gold region.

[1127]Upon examination of the original diary, the words "for ten miles, the Wagon Road" were found to have been omitted in the 1934 editing.
[1128]"[the] Road turns to the left to circle the Silver Lake Basin....In 1979-80 the U.S. Forest Service constructed a rock wall...to prevent four-wheel drive vehicles and trail bikes from using the trail between Caples Lake and West Pass." Ibid. p 10.
[1129]Oliver Hazard Perry Brewer, and/or perhaps his sons.
[1130]Muriel Wright wrote that the Huntington Library bibliographer told her Pleasant Valley was ten miles southeast of Placerville.

<u>Brown</u>:

"[September] 24...10 miles. we all walked to Ringgold &
Weavervill[1131] made today 10 miles **Camp 121--."**
     [south of Placerville, El Dorado Co., California]

Captain Taylor wrote that John Brown stopped at Weberville:

John Brown, Washington Adair, and Brewer's two sons came through with us
to a place called Weaverville, which is fifty miles east of this city
[Sacramento], and under the great Sierra Nevada Mountains, when they
stopped.

     The journey nearly over, there was apparently not much to
write about, but <u>Brown</u> kept faithful count of his camps:

"[September] 25 Lay Bye."

"[September] 26...10 miles. walked on to Lynches' Trading
house. Made today 10 miles **Camp 122--."**

"[September]27...2 miles. Walked on to "Leapers[1132] Trading
Post" 2 miles **Camp 123--."**

After the scattering of the company, Taylor went to Sacramento to
mail his letter dated September 27:

I came here alone, and intend returning to the company to-morrow; but
don't know what we will do.[1133]

On foot, with only his packs, a few friends, and seeking a place
to go, <u>Brown</u> wrote:

"[September] 28...5 miles. Moved up on to the head of
Dead Mans Hollow. 5 miles **Camp 124--."**
     [Near El Dorado,[1134] El Dorado Co., California]

[1131]Settlement south of Placerville on Weber Creek, founded by Charles M.
Weber in 1848.

[1132]There is an inclination to wonder if one of the 1850 emigrants, Matthew
Leeper, who left Fort Smith April 1 as co-leader of a party with Elias Rector,
was the person running "Leapers Trading Post" south of Placerville on
September 27. According to the William Quesenbury diary, Elias Rector was in
the vicinity of Ragtown on August 12 "I was told this evening that Maj. Rector
took the Trucky Road at the sink a day or so ago." That would have put Rector
well over the mountains by the end of August. Matthew Leeper had come to
Arkansas Territory in 1829 as Receiver of the Land Office in Fayetteville. He
and his father James had claimed land in everybody's name, including all of
their slaves, so their landholdings were considerable. Leeper was also a Mason
by 1826 in Tennessee, and Jr. Warden of Washington Lodge #1, Fayetteville,
Arkansas at the time of charter. By 1856 he was back in Arkansas, appointed
Indian Agent for all Indians north of the Rio Grande and south of Arkansas
River. In 1861, his superior was Elias Rector. Rector himself had a long and
illustrious career.

[1133]*Cherokee Advocate* 3 December 1850.

[1134]Location according to Muriel Wright, editor of the Brown diary in 1934.

Twelve days later, <u>Brown</u> made another diary entry:

> **"Oct. 10** My Mess moved to the Arkansas Log Cabbin
> the Cherokees here are G.W. Adair & Mays and their Mess's
> we commenced building Cabbins for the Winter."

William and Barbara Longknife, members of the Oliver ox train, arrived in California October 6. On October 18, they were enumerated in the Census of 1850 at "Placerville & vicinity."[1135]

In 1849, the portion of the Evans/Cherokee Company which included diarist Crawford and John Rankin Pyeatt terminated their California journey on the Cosumnes River, about ten miles south of El Dorado. In the Pyeatt/Crawford group were seventeen men who went all the way through from Cane Hill, Arkansas, to the Cosumnes River. Arriving October 22, 1849, (nearly a month later than the 1850 Cherokee travelers) the first order of business had been to build what they called the Arkansas Cabin, a double cabin with a dogtrot (or breezeway) in between, a style which might have attracted attention in California. Pyeatt wrote his wife of his intention to move out of the cabin in February 1850 but he said:

> most of us will leave it soon and go to the rive[r]...while som of the
> boys talk of staying hear and keeping intertainment for travelers
> we have mor or less of them evry night   sometime wear crowded and we
> make them pay 3 dollars a night.[1136]

The 1850 censustaker "On the Consumnes River" on September 12, identified "Arkansas Cabin" as Dwelling #5. Occupants were from the 1849 Evans/Cherokee company.[1137]

The "Arkansas Cabin" mentioned by diarist Brown in 1850 was probably the same location. Brown recorded G.W. Adair and Mayes and their messes were also there. On October 4, Cherokee Adairs and Mayes[1138] were enumerated in the 1850 El Dorado County census "On Mathenias Creek." Others were at "Town of Mud Springs" on October 15.[1139]

[1135]El Dorado County House #5, family #20. In the house were 24 "families," one of whom was John Rollin Ridge, later a noted newspaperman in California.
[1136]John R. Pyeatt letter to Elizabeth Pyeatt from "Cosumenes Califonia" February 17, 1850.
[1137]John T. and Andrew Edmiston, James and Mathew Diven (the youngest--17) William Goddard, John W. Newman, and John M. Wham, at 24 the oldest.
[1138]Samuel, George and Samuel Mayes, George and William Adair, Benjamin Trott, Benjamin Goss, and John Candy.
[1139]House #3--Thomas Fox Taylor, Oliver P., George and Anderson Brewer, David

After six months of outdoor living, they once again had a roof over their heads.

Brown:

"**Nov 2** I and my mess moved into our Cabbins which was the first time that I slept in a house since the night of the 27th of April--."

"**[November] 11** Adair & Mays & others commenced "throwing up" dirt so as to be ready for the rainy season."

"**[November] 14** My mess commenced throwing up dirt at the same place with Adair & Mays--John A. Huffaker[1140] was taken sick with the Diarier and died   Dec. 11."

A final date follows: "February 12, 1851." There is no further documentation of Brown's trip home.

The Cherokee/white companies suffered more deaths in 1850 than the Evans/Cherokee Company in 1849, which lost only two. Many 1850 deaths were reported home to the *Cherokee Advocate* including:

Late from California
Letters have been received during the last week, by several of our citizens, dated as late as the first week in December last. Some deaths are reported among our Cherokee friends, by diarrhea, with symptoms of cholera. Sam Dick from Caney, this District, is one who fell a victim to the disease--one or two others were mentioned, but their names not recollected; they were thought to be from the upper part of the Nation.[1141]

Members of another Cherokee/white party, reportedly ninety men led by Major Elias Rector and Matthew Leeper, had traveled the Northern Route in 1850.[1142]   Rector summarized the emigration:

"The trip was a long and unpleasant one...There was much suffering on the way, by the emigrants, and from the accounts daily received, the suffering has increased. The grass and water, on the road, especially on Humbolt river, was of the worst quality--in fact, on that river, for near three hundred miles, there was a greater destruction of property, than on any other part of the road. *There is not a man, who came the northern route that will return that way;* and it is the opinion of most persons, that THE ROUTE CANNOT SUPPORT ANOTHER EMIGRATION."[1143]

Taylor, M. Benge, and John R. Candy; House #8--James and Maria Cols(t)on; House #9--George Nave, Joseph Coody, John and Edmund Ross, Edward Bushyhead, and (Dr.?) Barker.
[1140]Unidentified. A Michael Hufaker who had two daughters and no sons is listed by Starr...*Cherokee*...pp 368, 371.
[1141]*Cherokee Advocate* 18 February 1851, editor's column, p 2.
[1142]Cherokee John Rollin and Aeneas Ridge and Capt. Lewis Evans' son Mark left home in the Rector/Leeper company.
[1143]Rector to Captain Rogers from Sacramento September 6, 1850. *Fort Smith Herald* 8 November 1850 vol 4, no 11. The use of italics and Capital letters is probably the work of editor Wheeler. This same edition of the *Herald* contained

Clement Vann McNair, Captain of the 1850 Cherokee
Emigrating California Company

the first of several parts of Captain Marcy's Report of his 1849 trip
accompanying emigrants to Santa Fe along the Canadian River; and his return
trip along a track from Dona Ana (New Mexico) to Fort Smith. In the same
edition was notification of the formation of a committee of citizens "for the
purpose of adopting such measures as might facilitate emigration from Arkansas
to California, by way of Marcy's route to Dona Ana." Editor Wheeler was, of
course, a member.

EPILOGUE

There is a natural curiousity about the emigrants on these 1849 and 1850 Cherokee Trails. What did they find in California? What did they do there? How many longed for home--and subsequently returned? While there is no comprehensive information about these questions, there are bits and pieces available from various sources. Some are included here.

As a group, forty-niner Cherokees are credited with the working of several kinds of claims, leaving the name Cherokee attached to camps and bars in various counties. One such, the town of Cherokee in Butte County, memorializes teacher S. O. Potter bringing the Cherokee to that place in 1849. The associated names are Cherokee Flat, Cherokee Camp, Cherokee Canal, Cherokee Creek, Cherokee Ravine.

Before the arrival of the 1850 emigration, Johnson Thompson, newly-arrived by sea, wrote that he found his folks with a majority of Cherokee emigrants on Thompson's Bar, Cherokee Bar, and Watt Smith's Bar of the Yuba River, citing others on the middle Fork. Jonathan Mulkey advised Cherokee to stay home, but also wrote: "The gold is now got in, or near the banks in spots or veins of small extent, yielding to the laborer from ten to twenty dollars per day."

Forty-niner commissary Martin Matthew Schrimsher reported the "mining business to be laborious, and the miners constantly exposed to the severest fatigue and hardships, having to work in the water most of the time, their clothing scarcely ever getting dry on them...none but the stoutest constitutions are able to stand it for any length of time." In September 1850 he went home.

A.M. Wilson, captain of the Cherokee and Mississippi Company via the southern route, was in latitude 38 in 1849, doing well, but said he "I consider [the extent of gold] as good as we heard...before we left home." Mining wasn't the only enterprise. Besides what they could mine Wilson said "I can make thirty or forty dollars per day with my waggon." Some Cherokee arrivals via the Southern Route reported from "Toowatleme" (Tuolumne) and Stanislaus Rivers noting "A man can make money here at any thing except doing nothing."

A few saw exactly what kind of business was possible. During the first two weeks in California, John Rankin Pyeatt wrote of his group: "we have dug gold bilt a cabin hunted deer mooved 4 miles in all made by diggin and selling venison to the Indians 35 ounces of gold we have killed 21 deer sold them from 5 to 23 collars apiec." Because they had what others did not--a roof over their heads, they rented out the floors to sleep on and sold meals, called "providing intertainment" in those days. In subsequent letters home Pyeatt wrote to wife Elizabeth of the many ways he could make a lot of money "a good saw mill would clear from five hundred to eight hundred a day...I would like to bild one in this cuntry if Elizabeth and the children was hear." Pyeatt wrote several more times pleading with Elizabeth to join him, knowing that they could make enough to do them comfortably for the rest of their lives. In the end she never came. John and son Andrew started home; Andrew died and was buried at sea. John returned to Arkansas to live out his life, dying in 1897 at 92.

Some forty-niners realized they couldn't keep a large group together unless provisions were available. Jeter Lynch Thompson, captain of the 1849 "cholera" company that traveled via the main Oregon/California road, wrote in November from the Feather River mines, claiming that no provision teams could get to Sacramento because of the winter weather. Thompson was building a boat to make the run. His plans for the coming year were to cultivate "a few acres of truck" on property he had "established a ranch for herding stock." Thompson took slaves with him to California; his plan was "give them a half of every Saturday's labor, in order that they may purchase their liberty...if they be industrious and faithful one year, they may then have their freedom."

Others realized the emigrants had to eat. In 1853, newly-arrived Matilda E. Rieff found relative forty-niner Mr. Stout growing "the finest vegetables in the world...during the week [early September] Mr. Stout has sold 12,000 melons and very many tomatoes [many kinds of vegetables] and about 12 or 13 thousand lbs of cabbage...all...very fine."

Devereaux Jarrett and wife Juliette Vann Bell were running a

store and restaurant in Drytown, California in 1855. They returned
to Cherokee Nation. He subsequently died in Rusk County, Texas as
a result of imprisonment during the Civil War.

Some turned to professional life. Cherokee Edward Bushyhead
"Ned," brother of forty-niner Dennis, mined for awhile in El
Dorado (1850 census) and Calaveras (1852 California census)
counties, and started a newspaper in Calaveras. By 1868 he had
taken his printing equipment to San Diego, starting the *San Diego
Union*. Ned became San Diego County Sheriff, and San Diego city
police chief. He never went back.

Much has been written about the editing and writing career of
John Rollin Ridge, forty-niner, who wrote under the pen name of
Yellow Bird, his Cherokee name. He was the first editor of the
Sacramento Bee. Besides newspaper work in northern California, he
wrote poetry and several books, including one about Joaquin
Murietta. In 1866 he went to Washington D.C. as a delegate
representing the southern sympathizers in the Cherokee Nation.
Unsuccessful, he returned to California. He and his family rest in
Grass Valley.

By the time the 1850 emigrants arrived, much of the gold
mining country was crowded. Capt. Thomas F. Taylor noted the
Cherokee had to spread out in order to survive. A letter from 1850
emigrant John Nevins is typical in recording the scattering "over
the country in every direction, all dissatisfied...all want to get
home again." Remembering that a Cherokee forty-niner had written
of their propensity to stick together "through weal or woe,"
scattering would have been difficult for most of them. Jeffrey
Beck, in the party that discovered gold in future Colorado,
advised: "remain at home, and be content with a little hog and
homminy."

Some, no doubt felt as did Lovely Rogers, Cherokee forty-
niner, who wrote in 1872 from California: "I should love to ramble
over my native hills again...a las! a las!"

Those who did return home did so immediately, or after a few
years of trying to make either enough money to make the trip, or
trying to strike it big. Judge Hiram Davis went back in February
1850. Isaac Murphy, member of the pack company, of whom Davis

wrote: "Poor Murphy I fear for him, his ponys are trifling and poor, but no persuasion can prevent him from going [with the pack company]." went back to Arkansas and became the first Governor after the Civil War. Judge Hiram Davis, Judge Hoge, and Elias Rector all returned to illustrious careers in Arkansas. Alexander D. Wilson arrived in March 1851. Squire Marrs mined for three years, returning home in 1852. Leonard Schular moved his family to Mt. Pleasant, Texas after returning from California.

Some came home better off than most: "they managed to get enough of the precious stuff to bring them home, and how much more is not said." *Cherokee Advocate* June 3, 1851. Peter Mankins, forty-niner, returned home with reportedly several thousand dollars, as did H.J. McRoy and Edward Freyschlag, James C. Devin and John Skelton. As testament to their success, many Arkansans and citizens of Cherokee Nation were able to purchase land or build substantial farms and homes after they came back.

James T. Craig, captain of the 1850 Cane Hill Emigrating Company stayed only nine months before returning to Cincinnati, Arkansas, resuming his old business. James Vann returned and resumed "his chair" as editor of the *Cherokee Advocate* December 1851. After returning to Arkansas Matthew Leeper was appointed Indian agent. Under the Confederates, he was government agent for the Indians north of the Rio Grande and South of the Arkansas River.

Some were determined that mining had a bright future and followed it, in other parts of California and beyond. "We leave in the morning for the 'Trinity' River, 250 miles up the river 'Sacramento.'" Cherokee forty-niner Senora Hicks came with Jeter Lynch Thompson's cholera company. He was with Major Rucker's rescue team on the Lassen Trail in 1849. Subsequently Senora went to Nevada to mine. There a mining district bears his name. His brother Charles Renatus Hicks went back to Cherokee Nation where he was later killed.

James Bailey, forty-niner, farmed in Shasta County for about eight years. In 1862 he and a partner filed a homestead and mining claim in Nevada. On a trip to Susanville for goods for his store in Nevada he was killed, and buried where he fell, on the

Applegate Trail between the Humboldt River and Rabbithole Springs.

Some died accidentally, or from disease, or from attack. H. Porter Pyeatt drowned in the American River in May 1850, while his son James was on the way to join him in California. Alfred Cunningham, 1850 wagonmaster, died in Sacramento February 1851 "leaving a wife and five children" at home. Forty-niner Nathan Lewis succumbed in April 1850 to Lung Fever; Jo and Andrew Colville were killed at the Feather River in early 1850 by Indians.

At least one traveled farther west. Barbara Hildebrand Longknife delivered her first child "at the foot of the Sierra Nevada" in October 1850, prior to getting to the mines. On October 18 she was enumerated in Placerville with husband William and unnamed child 1/12 years old (Mary Jane). In 1854 they were in Coloma, El Dorado County where she was a laundress. By 1857 her daughter Mary Jane became nearly blind from "billious fever." In 1859 her second daughter Anna Diane was born. Later Barbara wrote that her husband had become so cruel and dangerous "I was obliged to leave him and with my two children came to Honolulu, Hawaiian Islands where I have remained ever since." Barbara died in Hawaii in 1905 and is buried in Nuuanu Cemetery in Honolulu.

Some stayed in California. Christian Freyschlag and perhaps his sisters Barbara and Hermina did, even after brother Edward went back to Fayetteville.

Dennis Bushyhead, forty-niner, came to California to stay. "I left the Nation with the intention to make it my home no longer." He stayed in California for nearly twenty years, when he returned to Cherokee Nation, was elected Treasurer, and then Principal Chief for eight years.

The Company Captains

Forty-niner Capt. Lewis Evans obtained licenses to trade in Yuba County, California in 1850, 1851, and 1852. A letter from former schoolteacher S. O. Potter dated February 14, 1851 on the Feather River to the *Cherokee Advocate* included "I have just been informed that Capt. Evans, of Evansville, Arkansas, the popular conductor and pioneer, is mining about one mile from me--I shall give him a call." Based on his past Arkansas business and community activity, it would be in character for Evans to conduct two or more businesses at the same time. Evans, 51 years old in 1850, then disappeared from California and Arkansas records. However, in 1895, son Albert's obituary in St. Louis identified Albert as a wealthy stock dealer. The pursuit of the Lewis Evans journal and map goes on--primarily in Texas.

Clement Vann McNair was a Solicitor in Saline District, Cherokee Nation in 1841-42; Senator in 1845 and 1847. In 1846 he was a delegate to the Treaty negotiations in Washington D.C. McNair was the first captain of the 1850 Cherokee company. Though there are stories that McNair never returned to Indian Territory, he returned in 1851. McNair returned to California, however, settling in Calaveras County, where he, his family, and some of his relatives ranched and prospected. He lived until 1897.

Thomas Fox Taylor, 1850 Cherokee captain from the Cache la Poudre River to California, returned to Cherokee Nation in time to be noted as a member of the National Council--and be elected President October 7, 1851. He later fought outstandingly and bravely for the Confederacy in Cherokee Nation as Lt. Col. of a regiment under Stand Watie's command. Taylor was killed in 1862 at Bayou Menard, near the first meeting-place of 1850 Cherokee emigrants for California.

The Diarists

Forty-niner James Sawyer Crawford started the diary for his trip home from California by recapping his stay in California.

> Landed on the Cosumnes on the 22nd Octr 1849. On the 9 and tenth of Nov we moved 3 or 4 miles East of the river, and built Cabins to winter in, we remained there till he 25 of Feby, and moved towards the American river, and we Landed at Ilinois town on the 29th March 1850; and left on Thurs the 11 April 1850, and Stop on the N Fork of the American river on April 12th. Here we remained till the 19th of Octr 1850. and returned to the Cosumnes on the 22nd Octr 1850 here we remained till the 16th day of Nov and Started for home on that day we arrived in Sacra City on the 17th and took passage on the Mcssone[?] Same day, and next morning we Landed at San Francisco Here we took pasage the Ship South America and lef the Wharfe on the 22nd. and on the 24 we lost Sight of land."

Crawford traveled via Panama to Baton Rouge, Natchez, Vicksburg, Napoleon, Arkansas, to above the Arkansas Post where "we grounded." February 4, 1851, he entered his last: "on the 4th we got off in the morning 8 oclock." Crawford died on February 17 in

Fayetteville, Arkansas, without ever seeing his Cane Hill home
again. He left wife Harriet and seven children, the youngest born
December 1849. The "we" of his writings likely were other
Crawfords--brother William, and cousin Andrew Alexander. Andrew
reportedly brought each of his children a gold nugget upon his
return. He subsequently died after the Battle of Shiloh in 1862.

William Minor Quesenbury worked for a while as an editor at
the *Sacramento Union,* then returned to Arkansas in 1851 via the
main Oregon/California Trail. The sketches he made along both
routes merited preservation by the Nebraska State Historical
Society. In Arkansas he returned to teaching and newspaper work.

James Mitchell returned to Arkansas. Whether this James
Mitchell is the father or the son is unknown. In letters and other
available materials, no trip to California is mentioned. The
father was 57 years old in 1850. The son was 17. The son became a
teacher, a deputy surveyor; was elected to the legislature; was a
captain in the Confederate Army; professor at Cane Hill College
and Arkansas University; a newspaper editor in Little Rock; and
finally postmaster at Little Rock. Because of his attitude on the
trail, and that Quesenbury calls him "Mr. Mitchell," we are
inclined to believe it was the father who wrote the 1850 diary.

John Lowery Brown returned to Cherokee Nation and married Ann
Scrimsher. They made their home at Fort Gibson.

Back over the Trail

Even though the Cherokee Advocate editor wrote in 1851: "We
have none that left for the Golden region this Spring," diaries
and letters show that both Cherokee and whites continued to use
the Cherokee Trail, or middle route for years.

Some came back over the trail immediately. Alfred Oliver
returned in February 1850, in time to captain a company in April.

Some saw the opportunity in cattle raising, a long-term
business demanding they make more trips back over the trail.
Samuel H. Mayes Sr. was back in Cherokee Nation in 1851. By the
next spring he had gathered 1,000 cattle to take back to
California. Sons Frank and John T. went with Sam over the Cherokee
Trail. Frank stayed in California running the ranch near
Sacramento until 1862, when all was sold. Frank started home, but

never made it, falling to Indian attack near Soda Springs, Idaho.

Forty-niner John W. Carter returned home to Arkansas in March 1850. In 1853 he took 700 cattle, probably not his first, over the Cherokee and Lassen trails for his Trinity River ranch, and William Shores' Scott's Valley ranch.

Calvin Hall Holmes, forty-niner, made several subsequent trips over the trail with cattle--the first in 1852, and another in 1854. He is remembered as a pioneer of Knight's Valley.

In 1854 Wm. H. Engels went on a cattle drive to California, staying only for the year.

By 1856 thousands of cattle were being taken to California from Cherokee Nation and Arkansas.

Emigrants to Oregon started over the trail in 1852, many more in 1857.

Mormons came over the Cherokee Trail from Texas to Utah, beginning in 1853, and continuing for several years.

In 1854 Kansas became a territory. Business along the trail was brisk, encouraging development of settlements like El Dorado, Kansas, situated at the crossing of the Walnut River. Business was good until the strife of the Civil War. The last Cherokee over the trail were fleeing north in February 1862. Loyal to the Union, they were driven from their homes in the mid-winter by other Cherokee loyal to the Confederacy. They camped two miles north of El Dorado. The settlement took care to provide food and comfort, and several Cherokee families remained on the Walnut until the end of the war.

From Oklahoma, Missouri, Arkansas, and Texas they would emigrate to California, and later to Kansas, Utah, Colorado, Idaho, Montana, and Oregon. Through Kansas the route shut down in 1862, during the Civil War. But in Colorado and Wyoming the Cherokee Trail continued to be important for settlement until the early 1900s.

APPENDIX A

Route of the Cherokee

The following 29 maps trace the route of the Cherokee from Oklahoma to the goldfields of California: Lewis Evans in 1849 and John Lowery Brown in 1850.

Trails have been marked on United States Geological Survey state maps "with highways and contours." **Scale 1:500,000.** One inch is approximately eight miles.

Some rivers and creeks have been enhanced, they were so important to the early travelers. **All trail locations are approximate.** True accuracy is not possible with this scale map. In some places the exact location of the trail is not known.

Legend

1850 ROUTE	Route of **John Lowery Brown** in 1850
1849 ROUTE (dashed)	Route of **Lewis Evans** wagons in 1849
(solid line)	If not marked *1849 Route* or *1850 Route*, this is the **Combined 1849 - 1850 Route**
▲67	John Lowery Brown **campsite (& number)**
●	Lewis Evans **campsite**
▲	**Site** or **landmark**

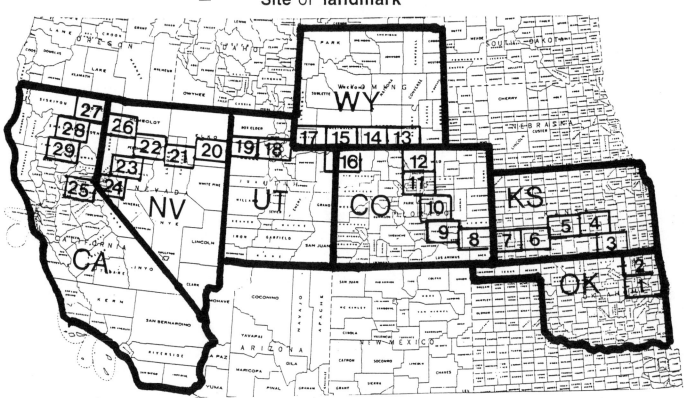

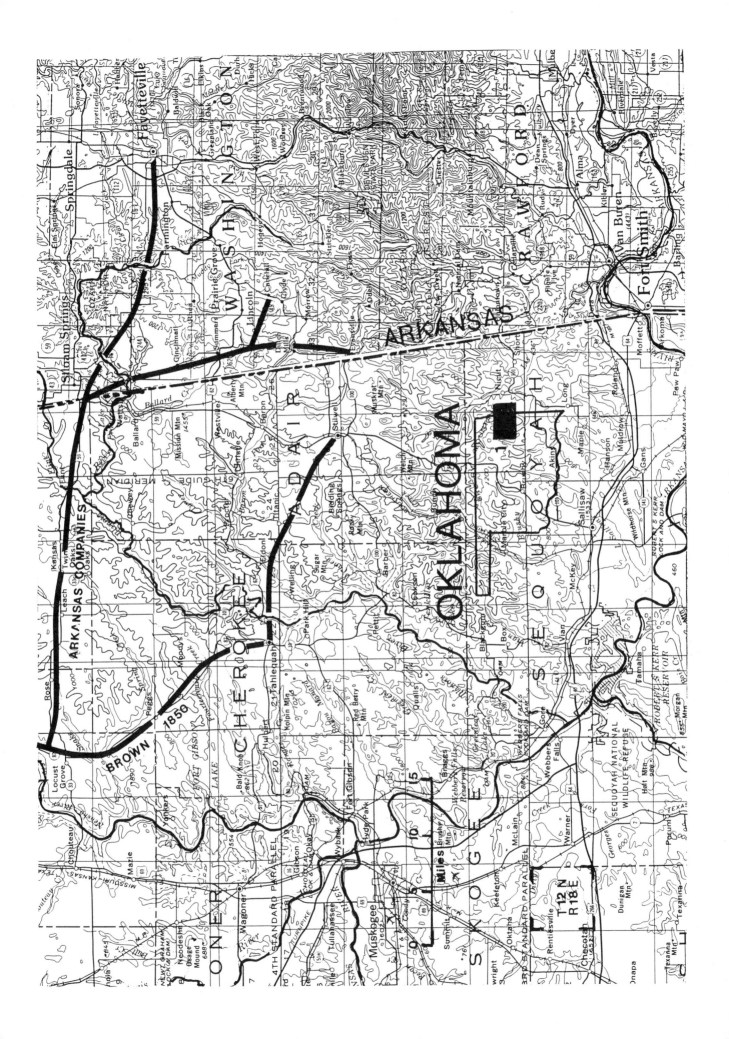

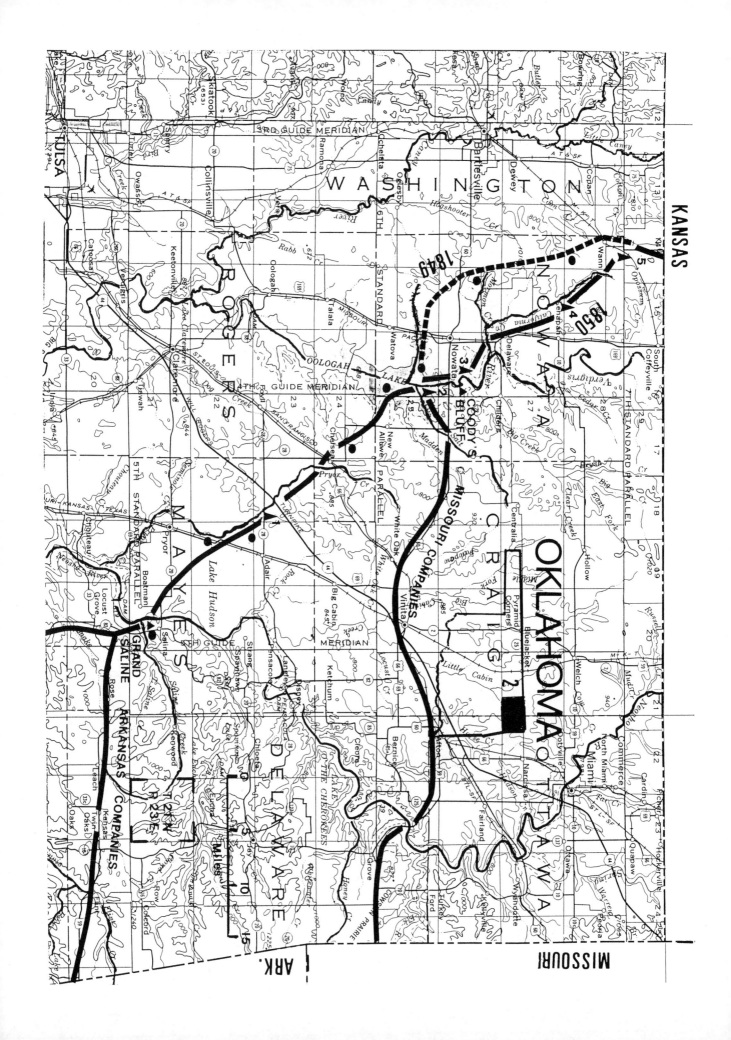

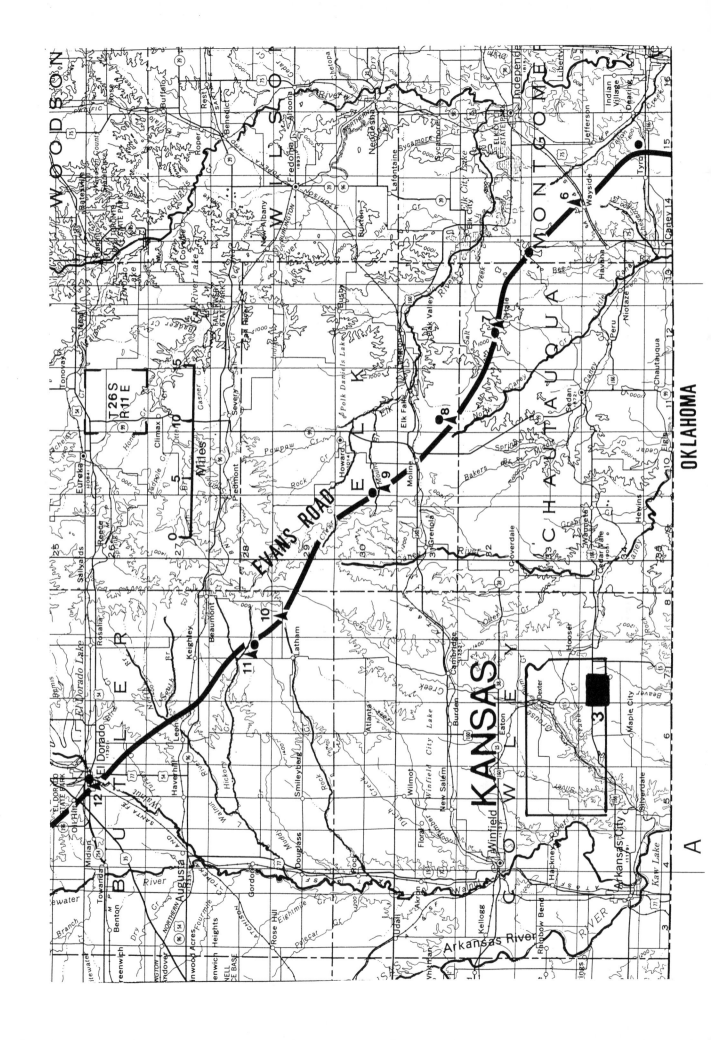

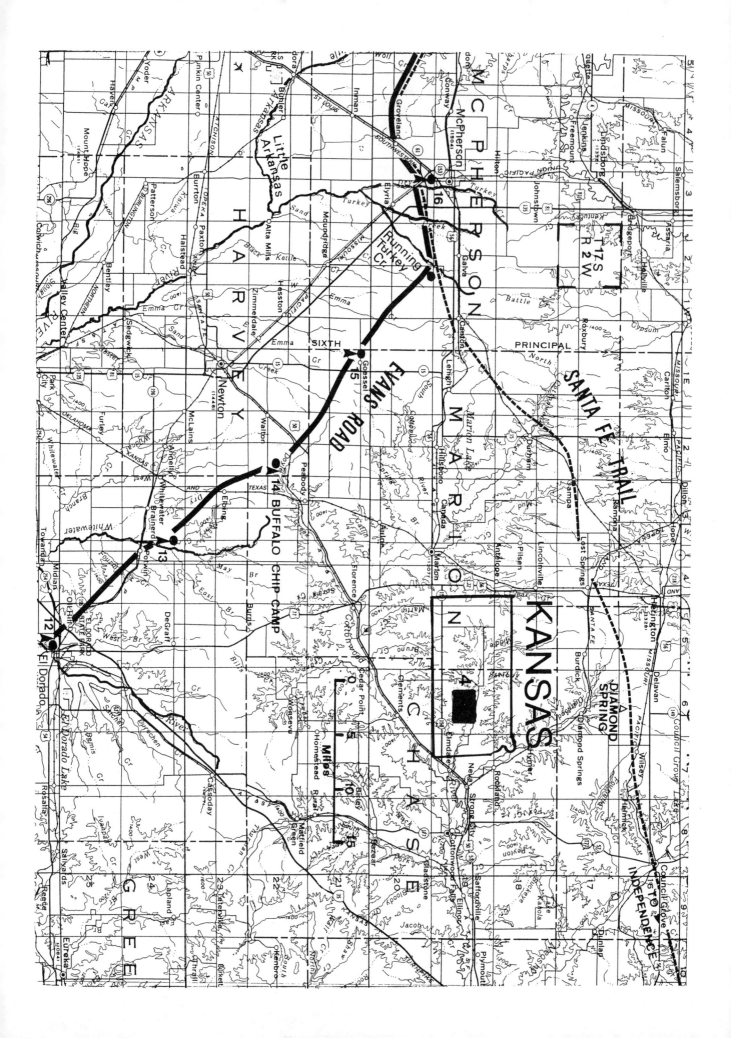

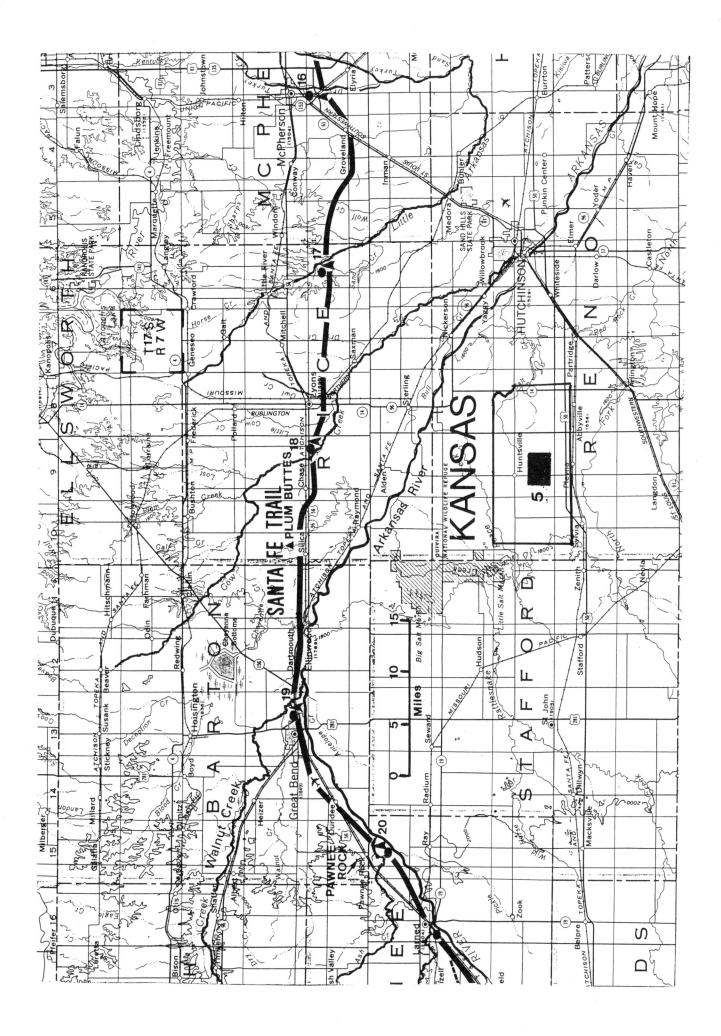

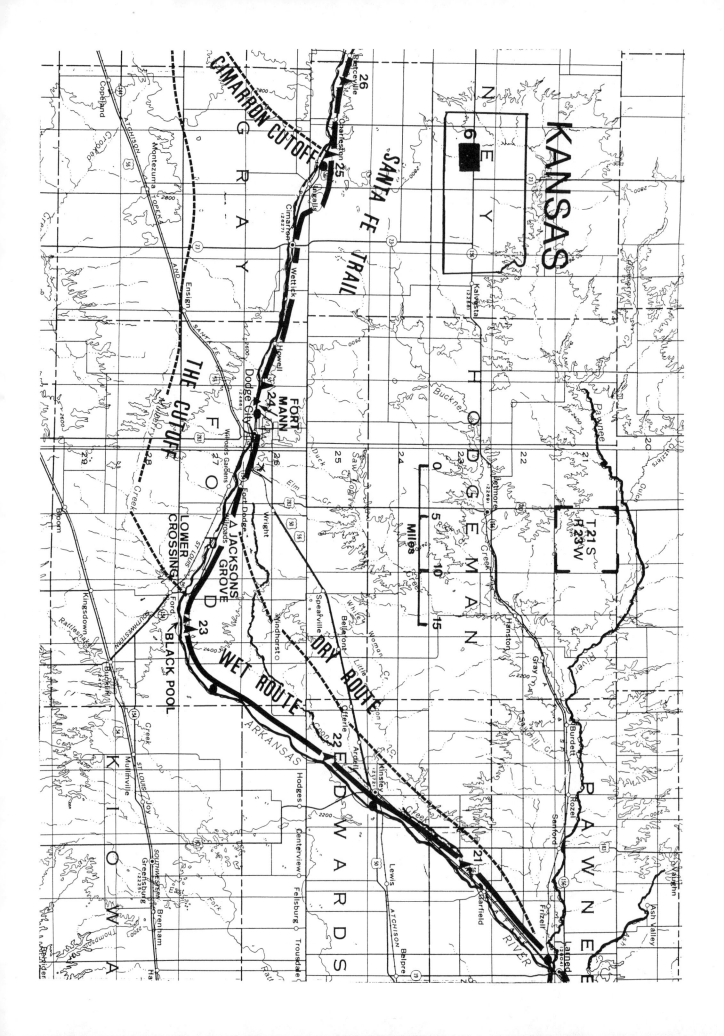

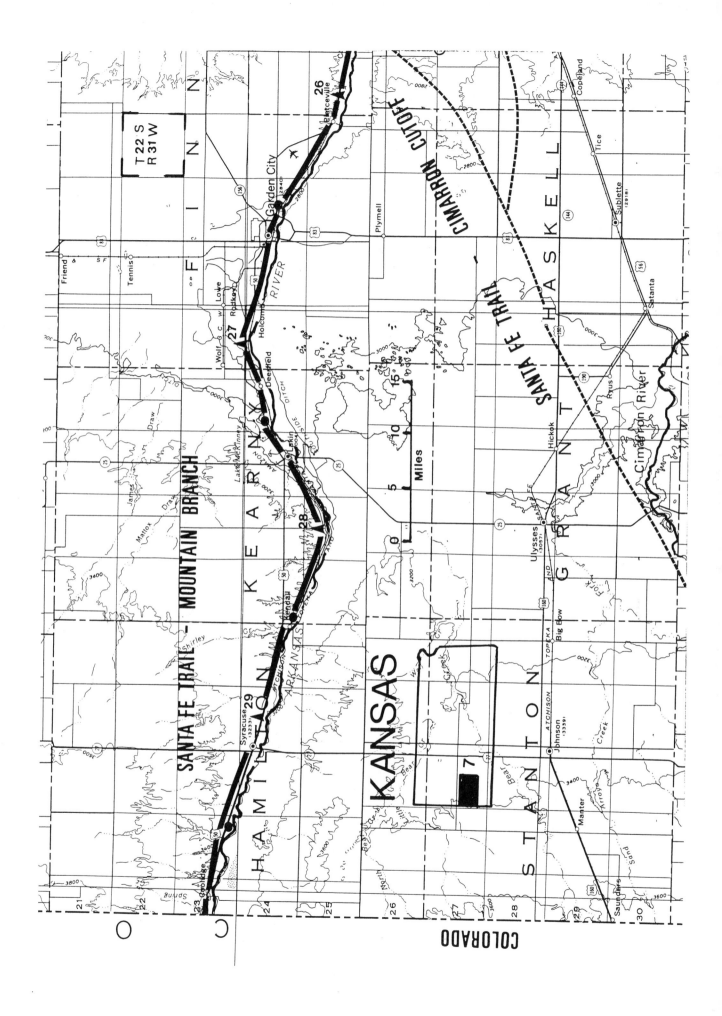

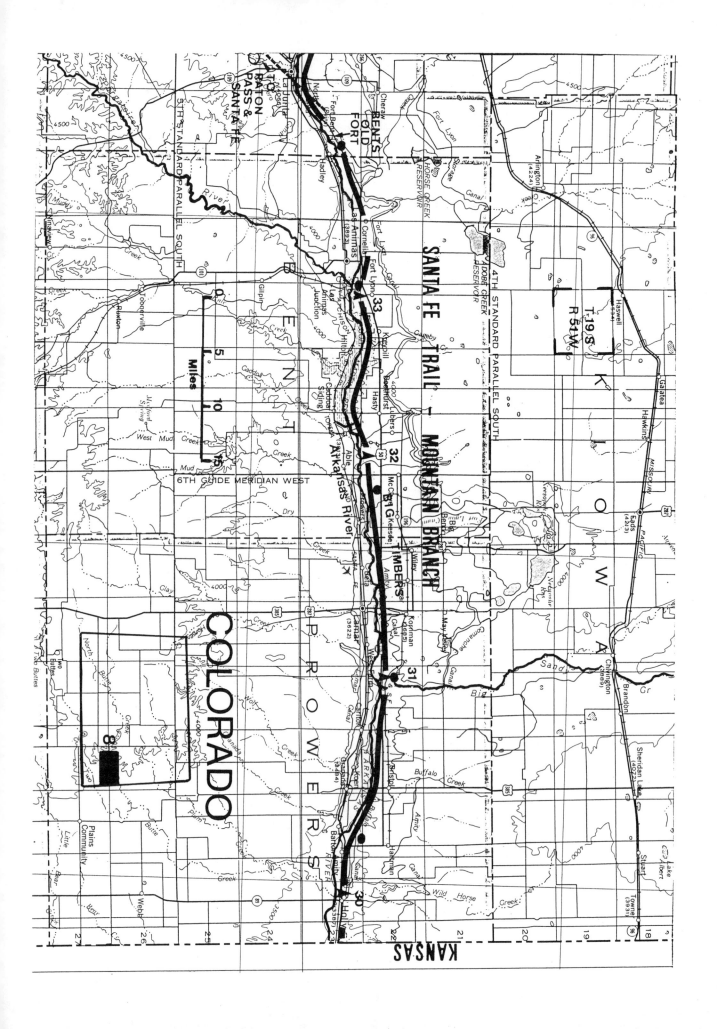

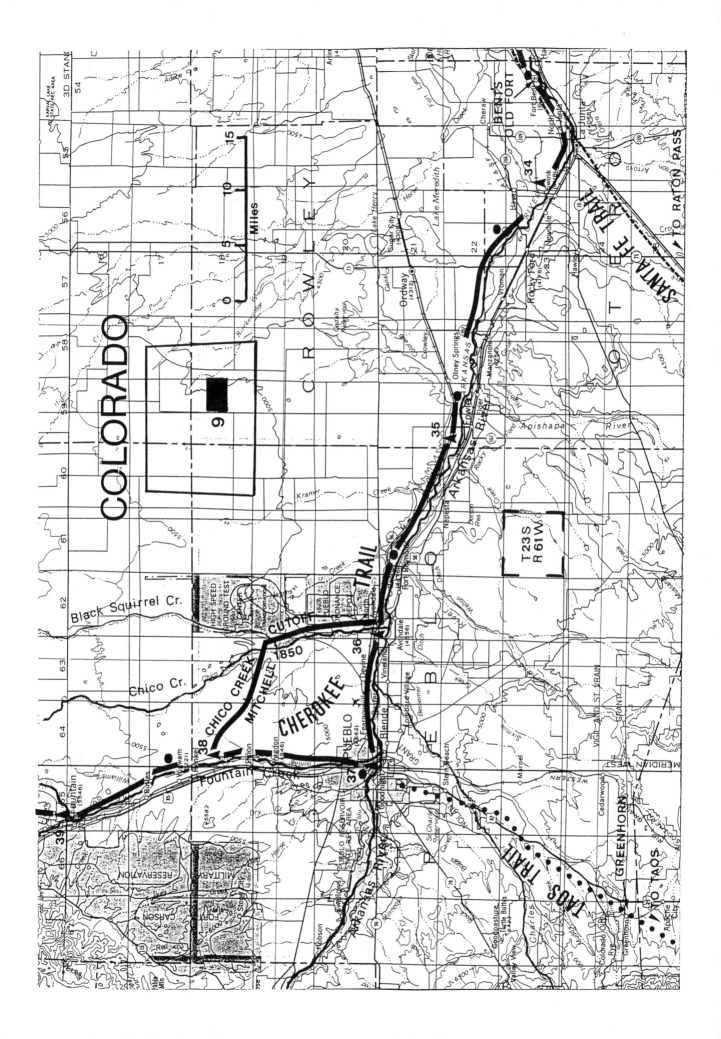

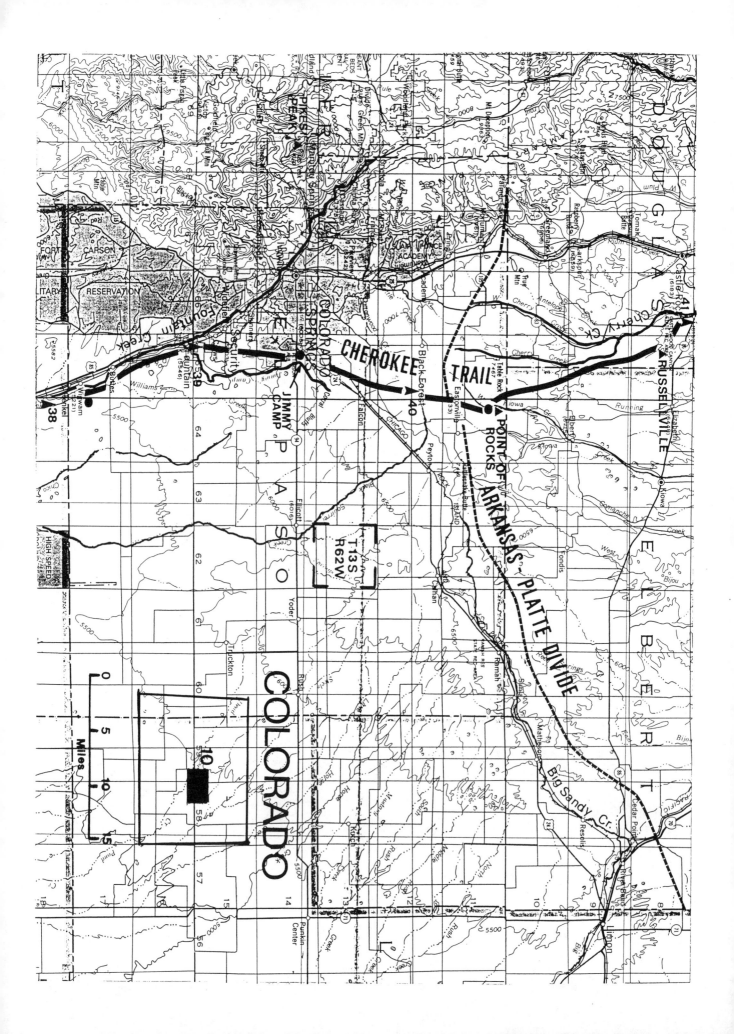

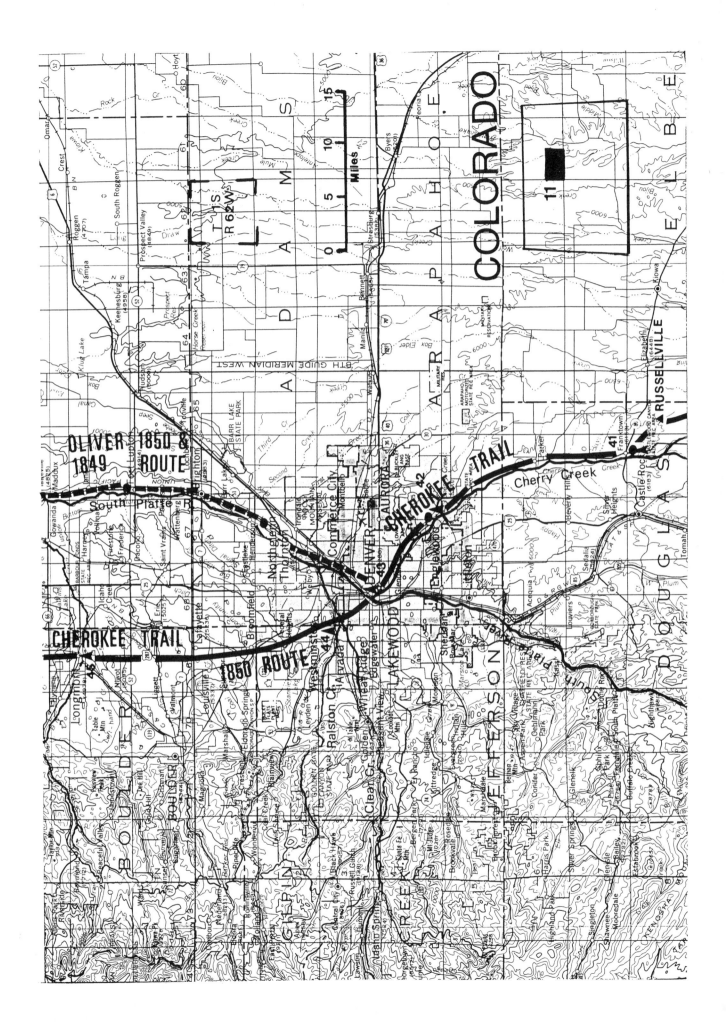

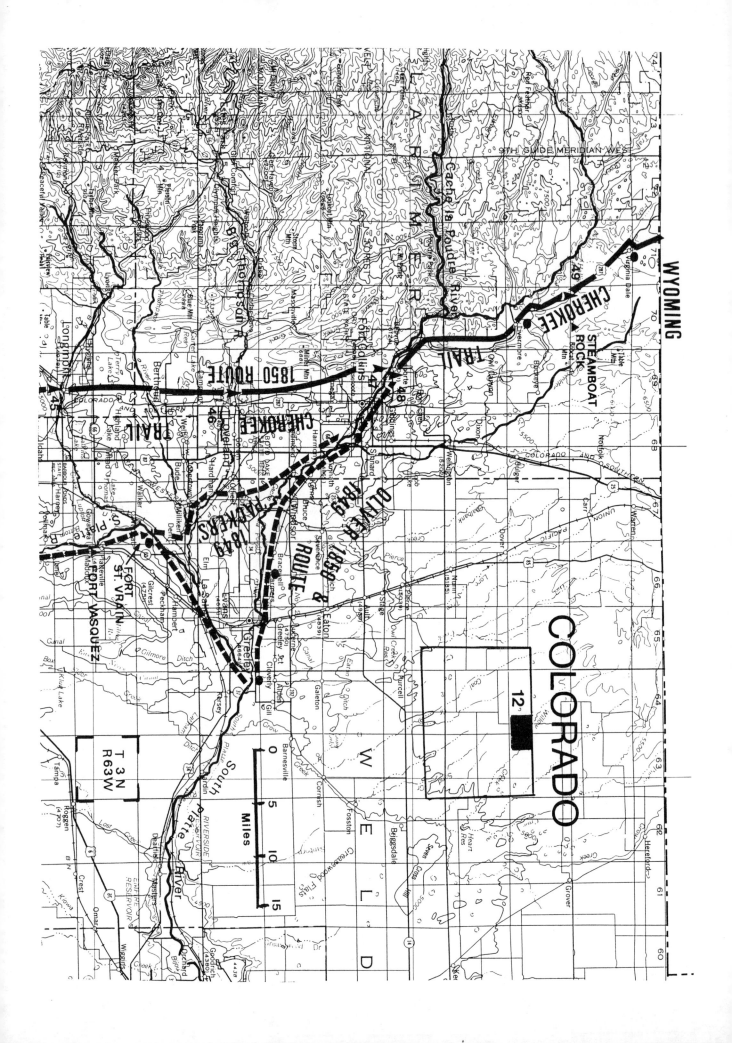

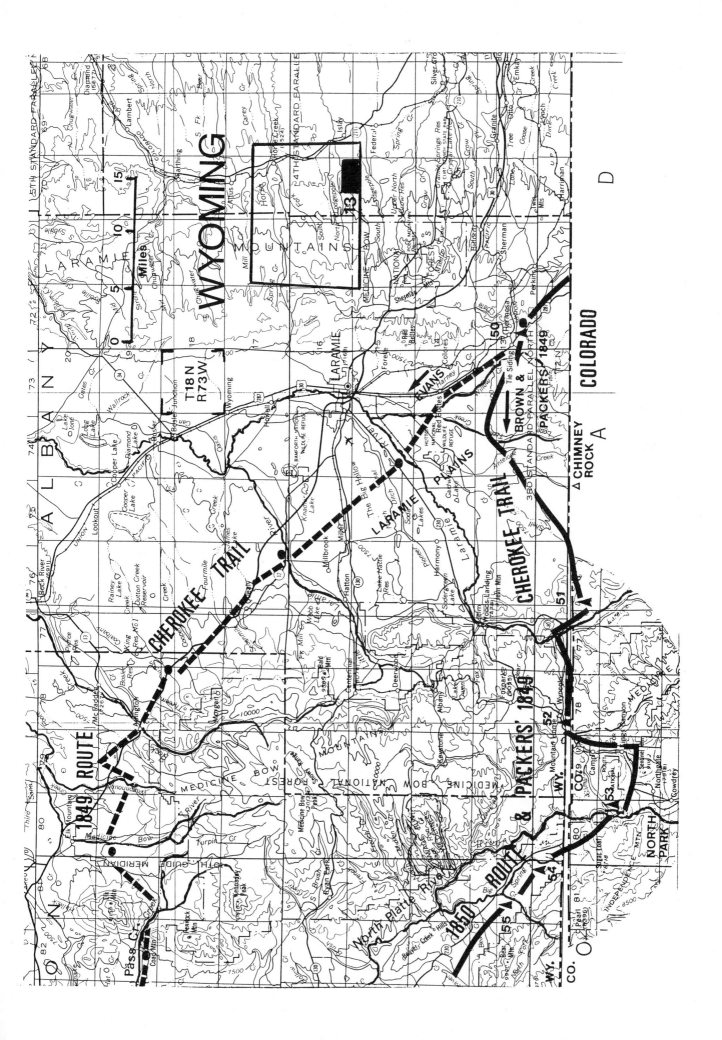

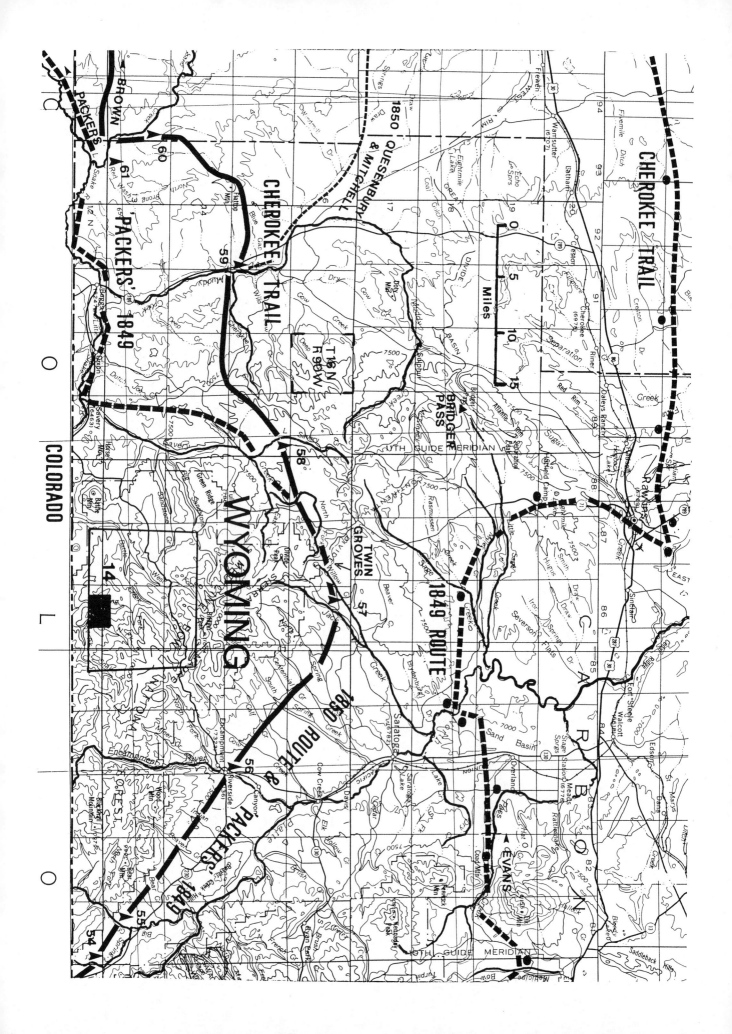

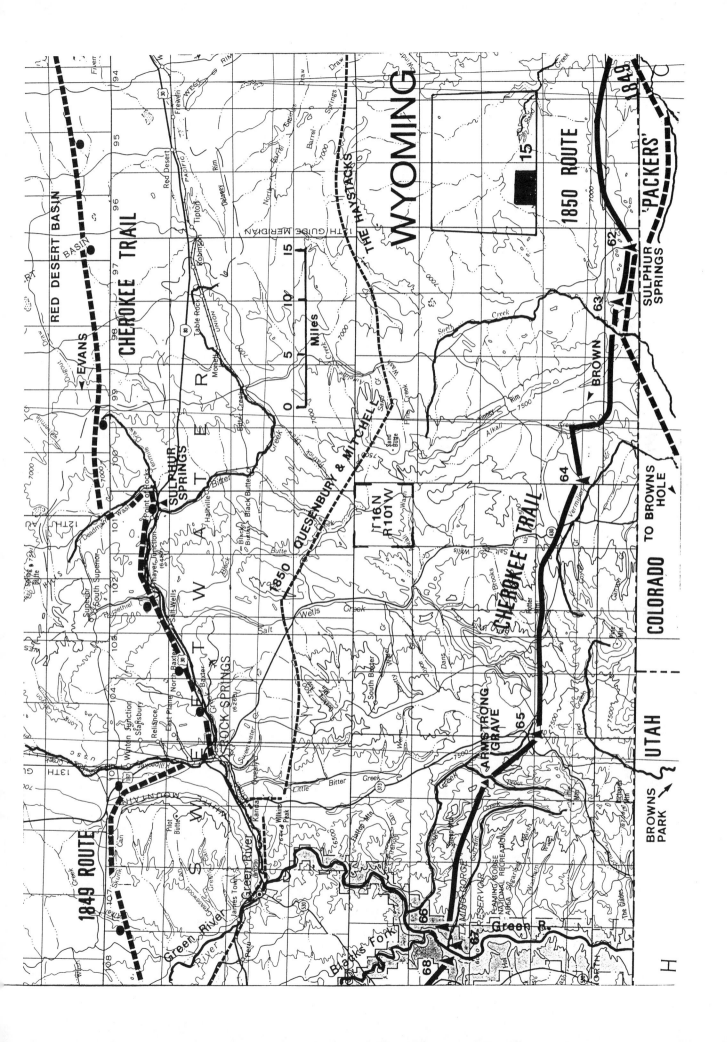

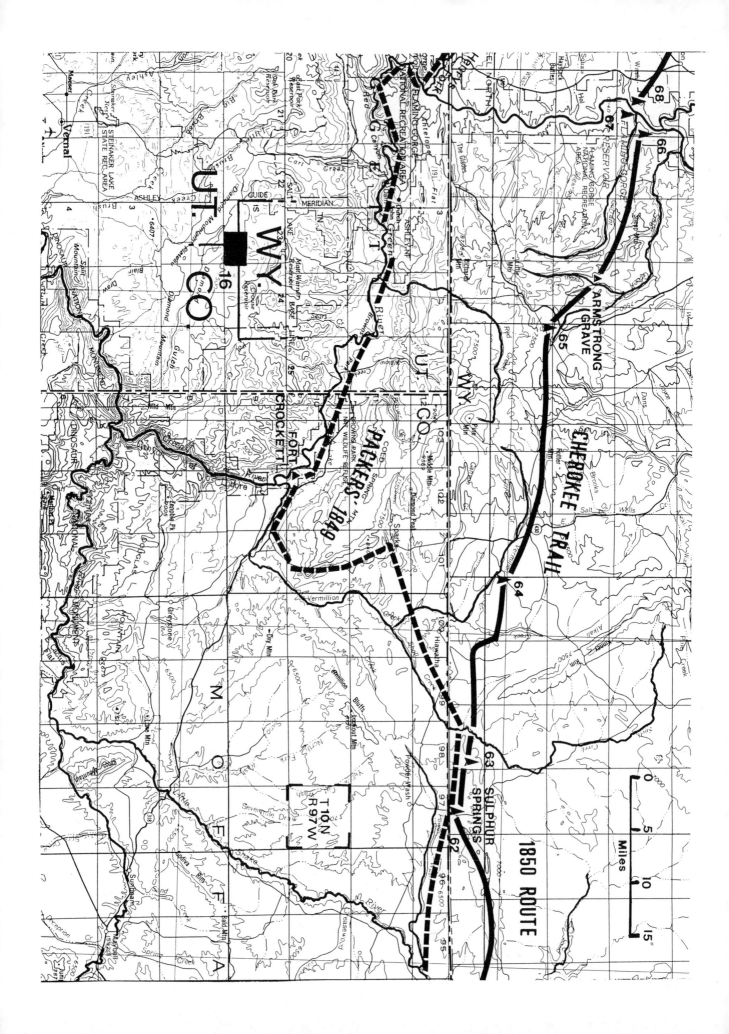

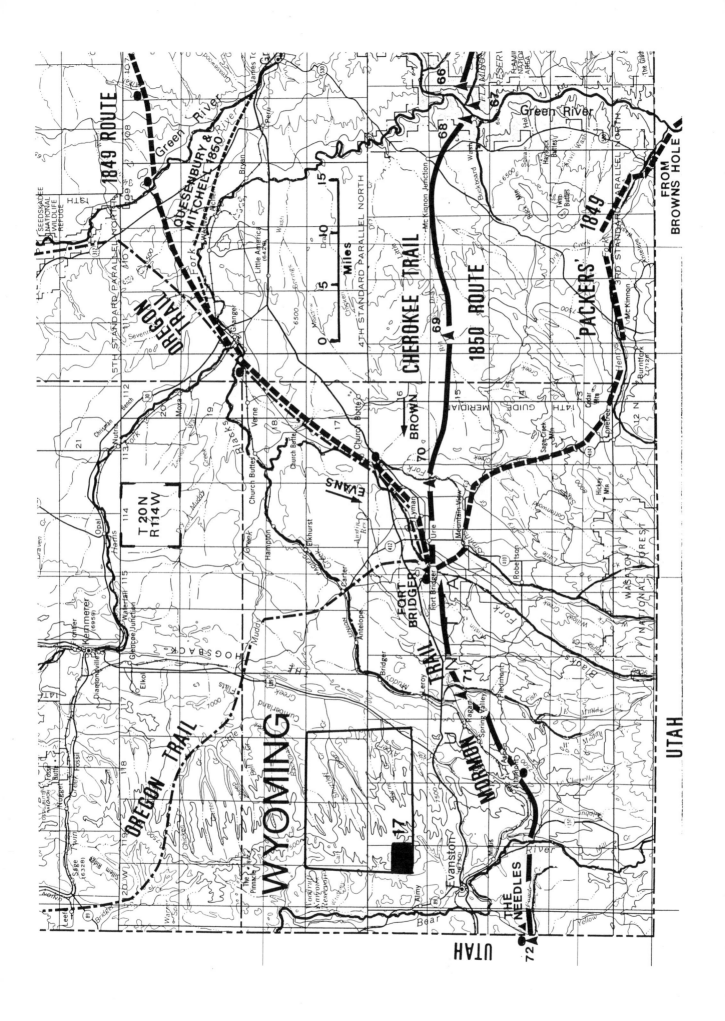

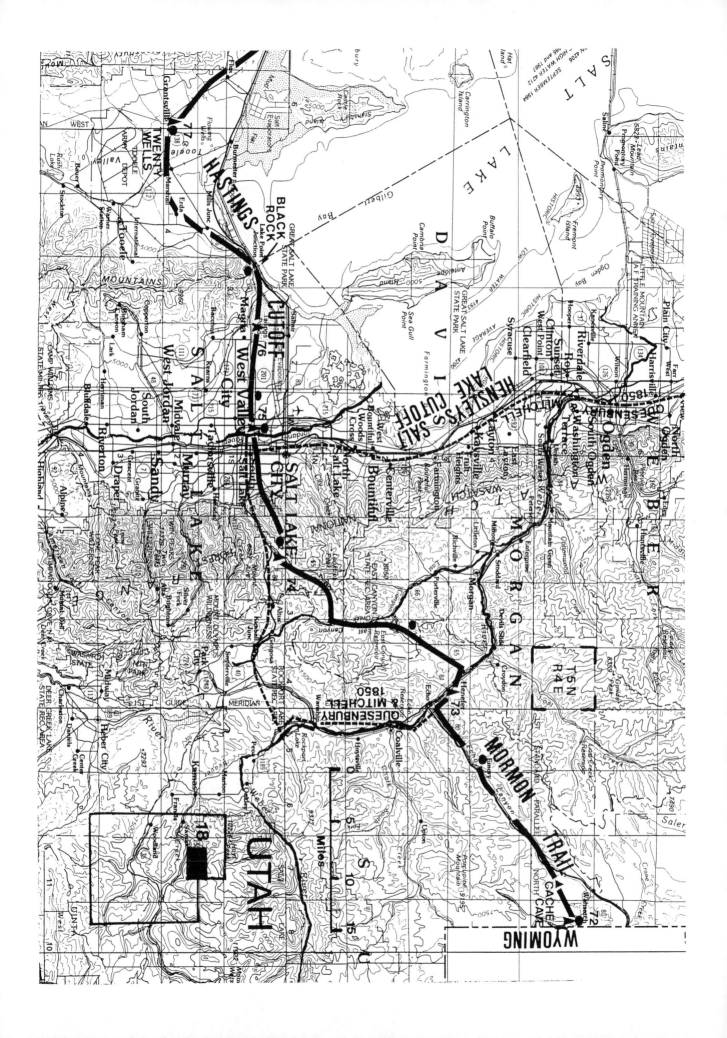

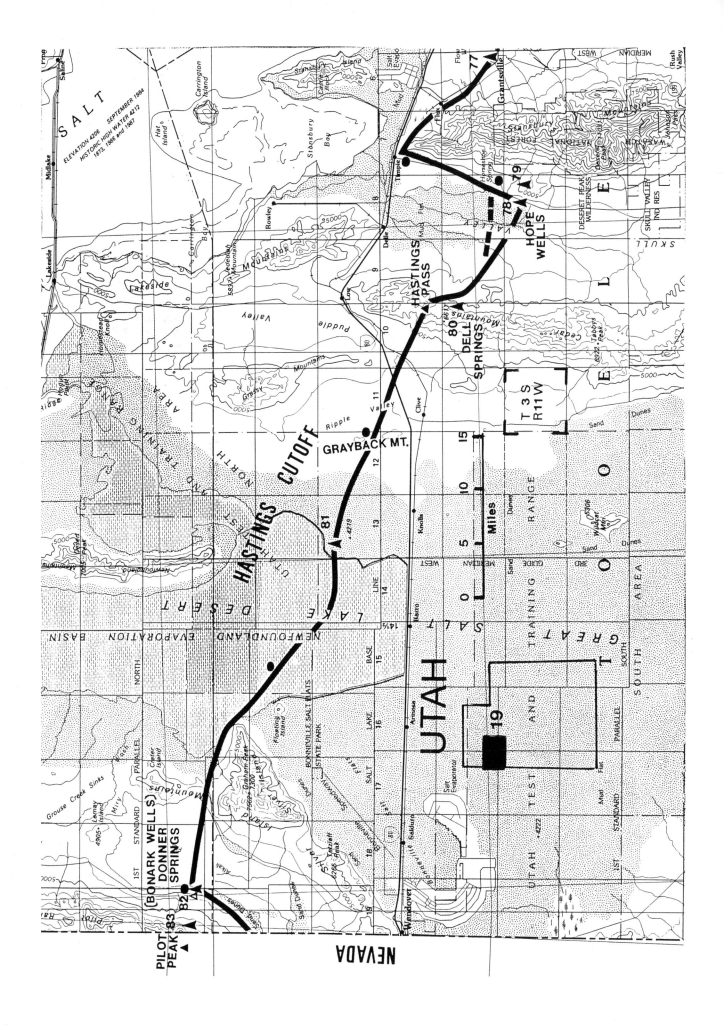

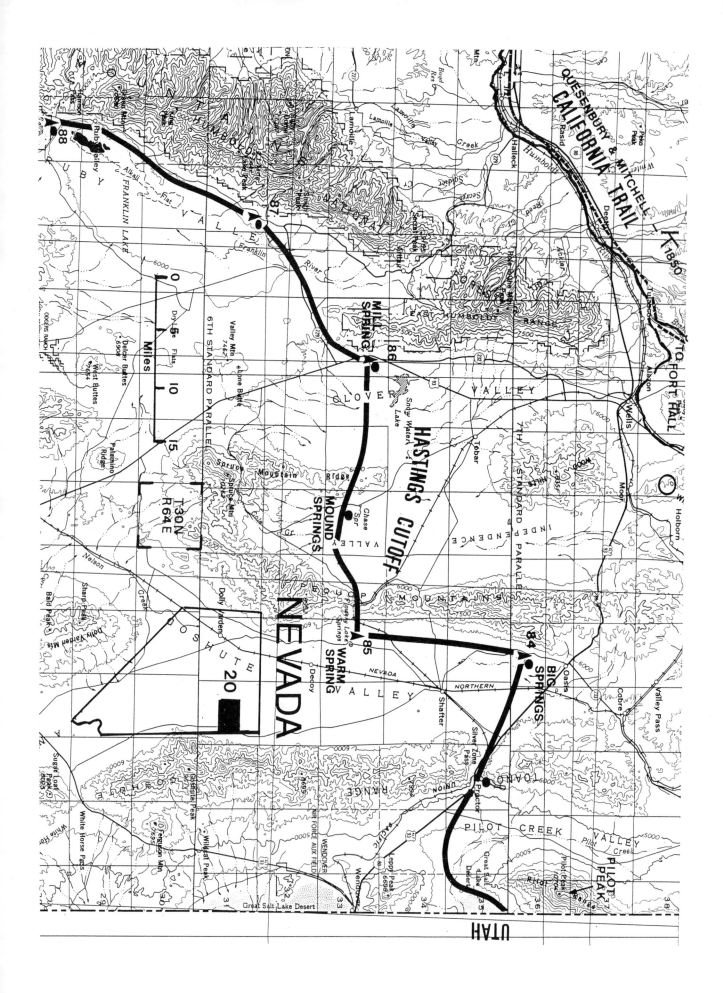

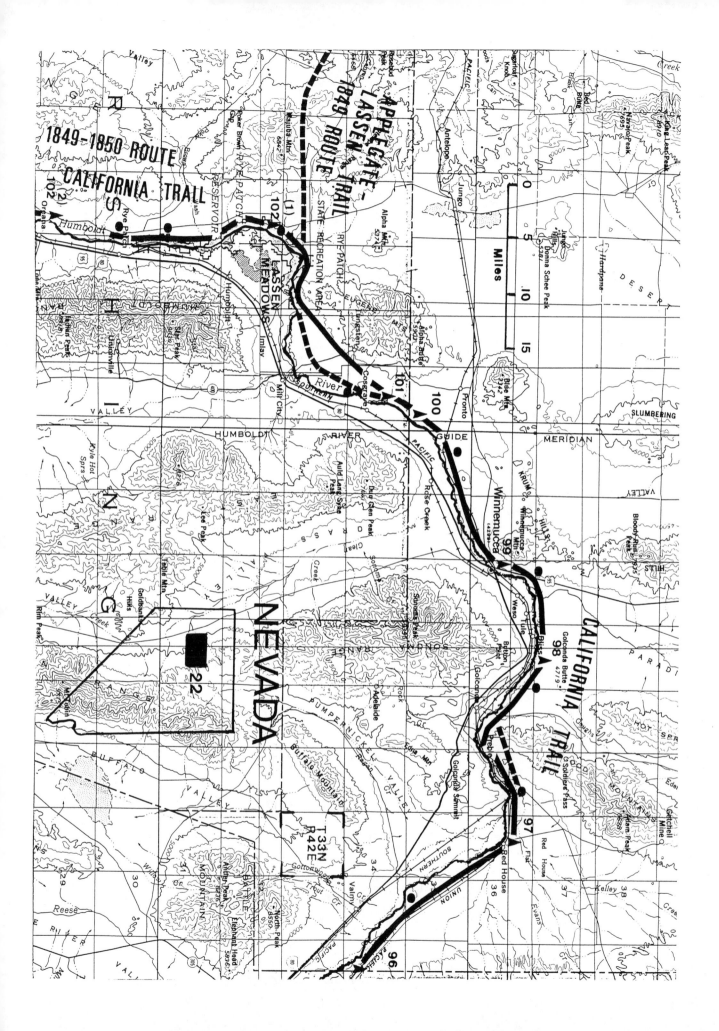

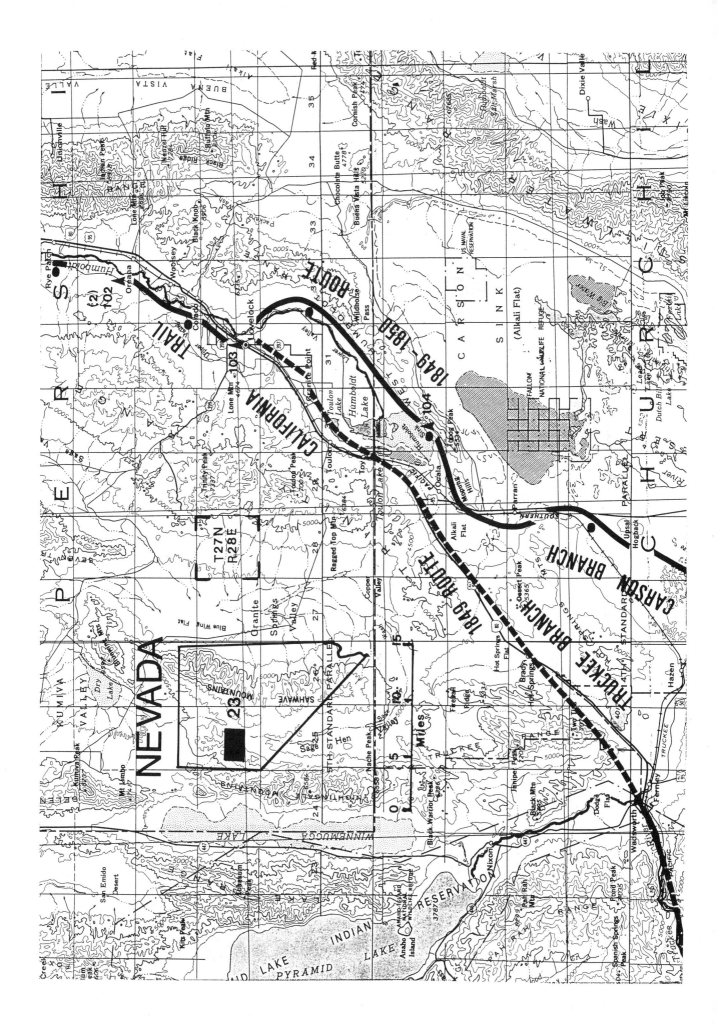

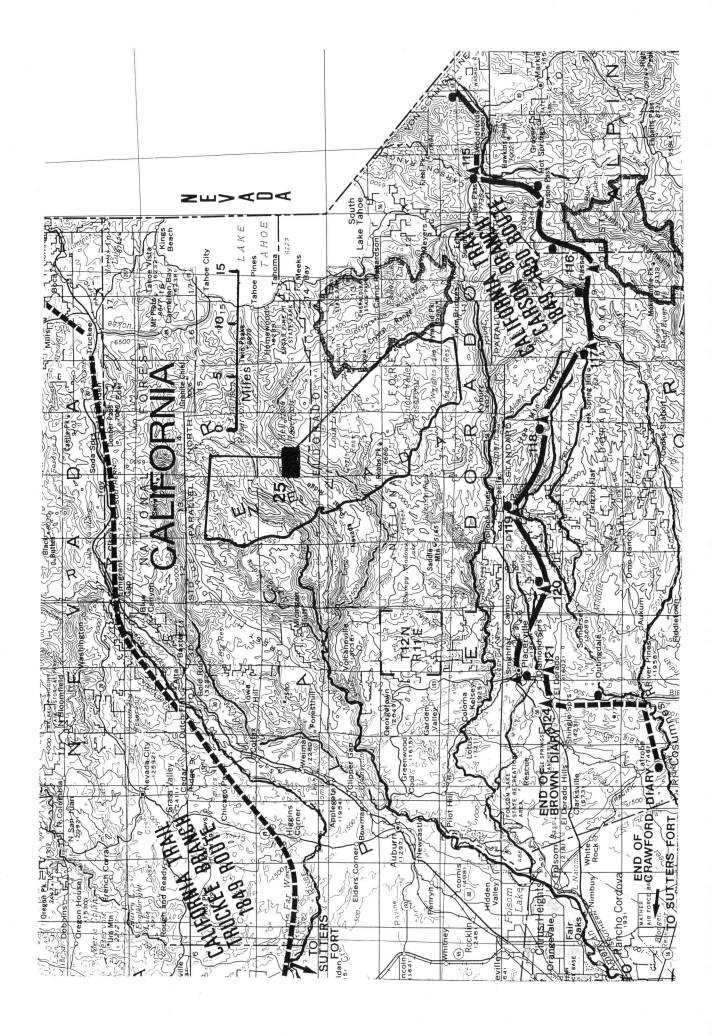

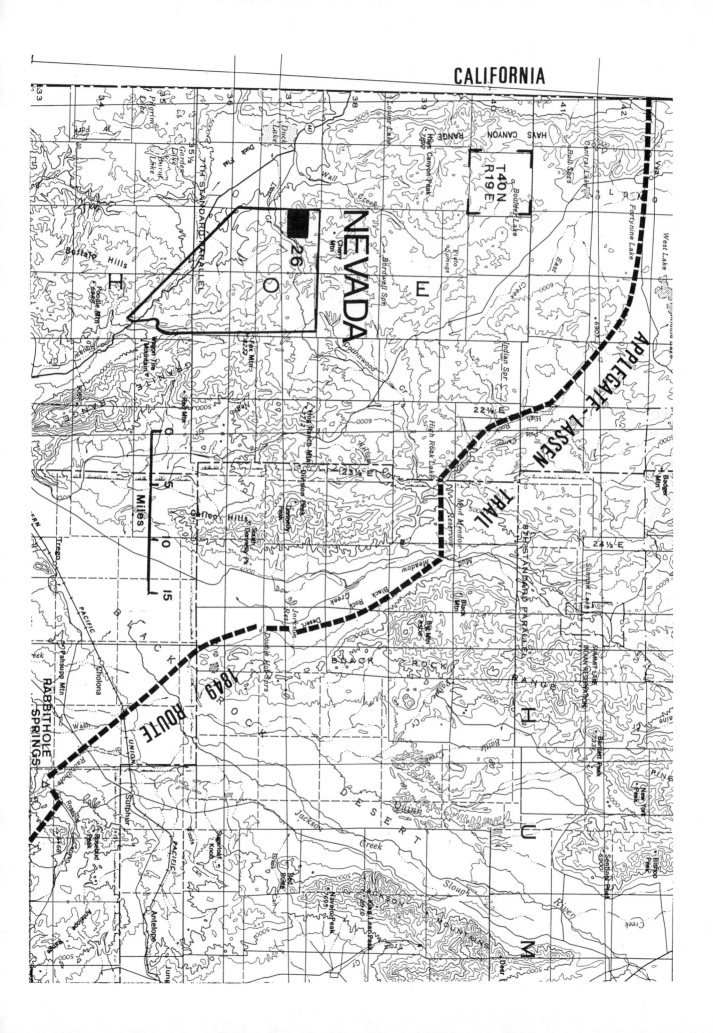

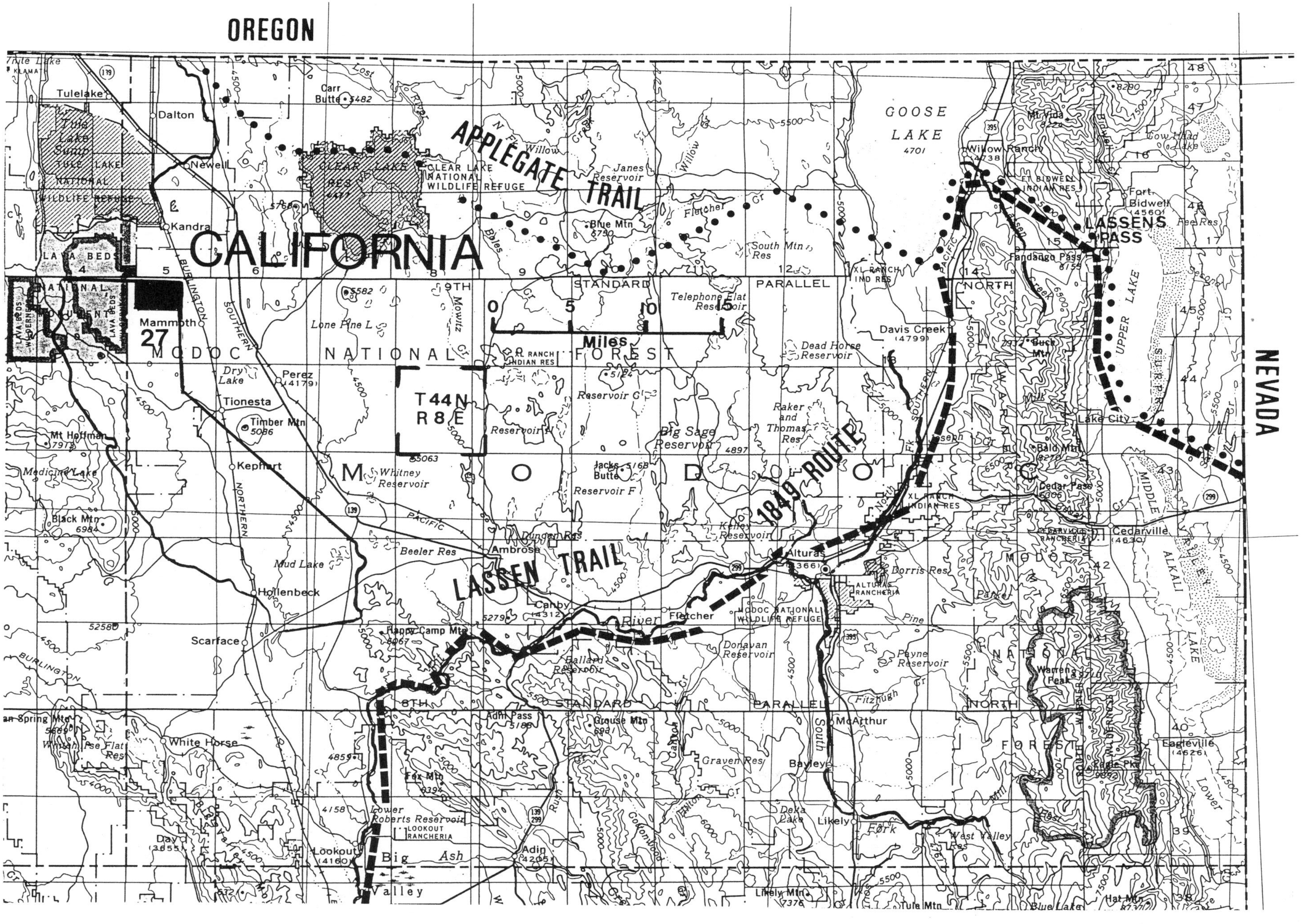
OREGON
NEVADA
CALIFORNIA
APPLEGATE TRAIL
LASSEN TRAIL
1849 ROUTE
LASSENS PASS
GOOSE LAKE
4701
UPPER LAKE
MIDDLE ALKALI LAKE
MODOC NATIONAL FOREST
M O D O C
T44N R8E
0 5 10 15
Miles
9TH STANDARD PARALLEL NORTH
8TH STANDARD PARALLEL NORTH
Tulelake
Dalton
Newell
Kandra
Mammoth
27
Tionesta
Perez (4179)
Dry Lake
Timber Mtn 5086
Kephart
Mt Hoffman 7913
Medicine Lake
Black Mtn 6984
Hollenbeck
Mud Lake
Scarface
White Horse
Day (3655)
Lookout (4160)
Big Valley
Adin 4205
Adin Pass 5188
Happy Camp Mtn
Canby (4312)
Ambrose
Beeler Res
Whitney Reservoir
Alturas (4366)
Fletcher
Dorris Res
Likely
Likely Mtn 7376
Tule Mtn
Bayley
McArthur
Davis Creek (4799)
Willow Ranch 4738
Fandango Pass 6155
Fort Bidwell (4560)
Lake City
Cedar Pass 6305
Cedarville (4630)
Eagleville (4626)
Bald Mtn
Buck Mtn
Mt Vida
Blue Mtn 5750
Carr Butte 5482
Lone Pine L
Big Sage Reservoir
Jacks Butte
Reservoir F
Reservoir C
Dead Horse Reservoir
Telephone Flat Reservoir
South Mtn Res
Janes Reservoir
Raker and Thomas Res
Donavan Reservoir
Payne Reservoir
Ballard Reservoir
Graven Res
Deka Lake
Lower Roberts Reservoir
LOOKOUT RANCHERIA
ALTURAS RANCHERIA
XL RANCH INDIAN RES
FT BIDWELL INDIAN RES
CLEAR LAKE NATIONAL WILDLIFE REFUGE
CLEAR LAKE RES 4477
TULE LAKE NATIONAL WILDLIFE REFUGE
Tule Lake Sump
MODOC NATIONAL WILDLIFE REFUGE
LAVA BEDS NATIONAL MONUMENT
LAVA BEDS WILDERNESS
SOUTH WARNER WILDERNESS
Warren Peak
Eagle Pk
Crouse Mtn
Fox Mtn
Fletcher Cr
Pit River
South Fork
BURLINGTON NORTHERN
SOUTHERN PACIFIC

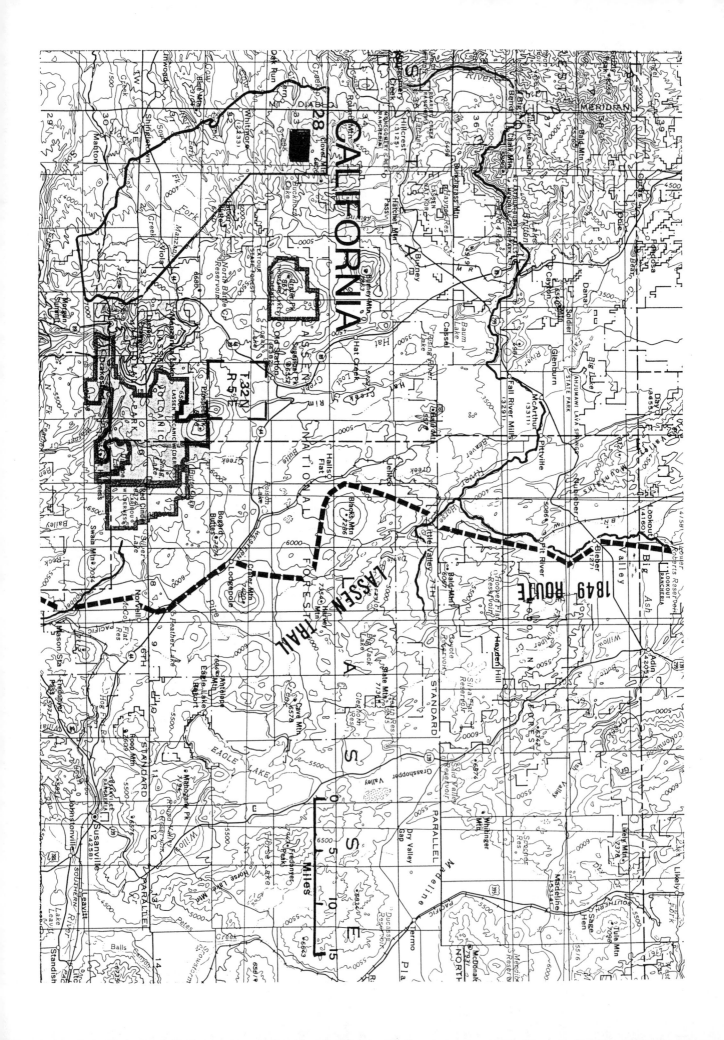

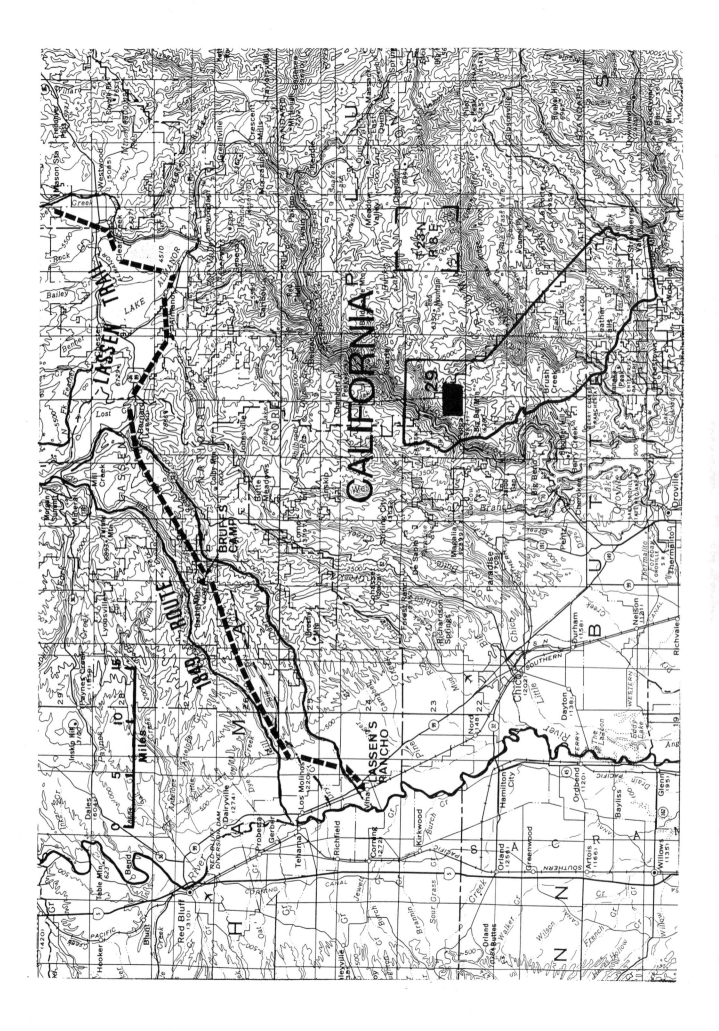